CONTENTS

YOUR GAP YEAR

CONTENTS

your gap year

The most comprehensive guide to an exciting and fulfilling gap year

Susan Griffith

DISCLAIMER

The opinions expressed in the case studies set in this style of box are entirely those of the featured organisation.

While every effort has been made to ensure that the information contained in this book was accurate at the time of going to press, some details are bound to change within the lifetime of this edition. If you do take a gap year or come across something which might be of interest to readers of the next edition, please write to Susan Griffith c/o Crimson Publishing, Westminster House, Kew Road, Richmond, Surrey TW9 2ND, or email her at info@crimsonpublishing.co.uk. Substantial contributions will be rewarded with a free copy of the next edition, or any other Crimson title (see inside back cover).

Your Gap Year
This seventh edition first published in Great Britain 2011 by
Crimson Publishing, a division of Crimson Business Ltd
Westminster House
Kew Road
Richmond
Surrey
TW9 2ND

First published in 1999 as *Taking a Gap Year*. Seventh edition 2011.

A catalogue record for this book is available from the British Library.

ISBN 978 1 85458 590 5

Typeset by RefineCatch Ltd, Bungay, Suffolk
Printed and bound by Ashford Colour Press, Gosport, Hants

PART III – GAP YEAR PLACEMENTS

YOUR GAP YEAR

CONTENTS

PREFACE

After a year of tsunamis, earthquakes, famines and brutal repressions of peaceful demonstrations, even the most adventurous students might be tempted to think that they had better stay at home. The main deterrent to taking a gap year in 2011–12 has been the shocking tripling (rhymes with crippling) of tuition fees, which has understandably forced as many as 10,000 students to scrap their idea of taking a gap year. I feel sorry for all those unlucky people born in about 1993 who happen to be hitting university just as the government decides to impose this prodigious and unfair fee increase. In on family I know, the eldest spent a glorious few months on her gap year in South America, her younger brother did a marine conservation project in Fiji, and now in the summer of 2011 the youngest treated herself to week's volunteering at a farm in France before embarking straight away on her university career.

Not surprisingly, sharp increase has been reported in the number of people booking shorter adventures, dubbed mini-gaps or even 'snap-gaps'; ie volunteering and travel adventures compressed into two or three months. So far there hasn't been a stampede to follow in the footsteps of Simon Calder, travel editor at the *Independent*, who a couple of years ago went round the world on a 'gap month'. The whole point of the gap year is that it isn't just a longer-than-usual holiday. Even government careers advice encourages the practice, claiming that 'taking a year out of studying to do something else can do wonders for your skills, confidence and CV? Filling a leisurely year out with a medley of experiences can bring so many once-in-a-lifetime benefits, at home and abroad, comprising work and play, earning and spending, challenge and self-indulgence.

After the tuition fee increase begins to bite from September 2012, students might as well take a gap year, either before or after university, since delaying loan repayments by a year won't make any odds. With heavy demand for fewer university places, many applicants on results day will find that they have missed out for the current academic year, and will be staring at a gap year by default. Similarly, in new graduates are facing one of the most difficult job markets ever. In these troubled times, the idea of flitting off to a distant corner of the world on a gap year might sound reckless. On the contrary, it could be exactly the right approach to the problem. Australia, New Zealand and Canada have strong appeal, since their economies (based on the export of natural resources) have been weathering the economic storm far better than the UK, USA and Europe. Furthermore, all have increasingly liberal visa arrangements to court young, energetic, job-seekers.

This seventh edition has uncovered scores of exciting new possibilities in obscure places. For example, fascinating programmes allow volunteers to work in Aboriginal communities in Australia, and aspiring journalists to join a scheme in La Paz to write for the English-language publication-*Bolivian Express*. For the first time, this book includes a volunteering opportunity in the Maldives for young, enthusiastic people to help out in schools, and 2011 saw the first ever marine conservation project for gappers taking place in the Cook Islands in the South Pacific.

The range of choices can be overwhelming: studying lemurs in Madagascar; learning Spanish and kitesurfing in coastal Ecuador; interning with an engineering firm in Britain; picking fruit in New Zealand; surveying coral reefs in the Philippines; spending a season at an American summer camp; teaching English in Thailand. The possibility of arranging a DIY gap year without the shelter of a fee-charging company is also covered. Sifting the responsible wheat from the profit-mongering chaff is no easy take when faced with the ever-increasing schemes vying for attention. This book offers you solid advice on how to avoid disappointment and rip-offs.

The 'gap-yah' has attracted a certain amount of mockery as the preserve of the ultra-privileged. The first-hand stories that pepper this book, told by gap year students from all backgrounds, prove what nonsense that is. This book is written to renew optimism and spark the imagination of all potential gappers.

Susan Griffith
Cambridge
August 2011

ACKNOWLEDGEMENTS

This seventh edition of *Your Gap Year* would not have been possible without the help of scores of gap year students, year out organisations and an army of travel informants who have generously shared their information and stories by email, telephone and, in quite a few cases, down the pub. My warmest thanks are owed to the following gap year travellers and volunteers who shared their stories so generously since the last edition:

Kellen Brandel – *El Salvador*
Jonny Christy – *Thailand*
Andrew Cummings – *Bolivia, Argentina, France*
Camilla Davies – *South America*
Risette de Haas – *South Africa*
Sue Fenton – *Nepal*
Anna Frayling Cork – *Argentina*
Lynn Munro – *South Africa, New Zealand*
Georgina Nightingall – *Italy, Ghana*

Robert Noessler – *Chile*
Helen Reid – *Bolivia, Ecuador, South Africa*
Rosanna Ruff – *China*
Kirsten Shaw – *South Africa*
Ali Steele – *Australia*
Pete Thompson – *Canada, New Zealand*
Adam Whale – *France*
Craig Young – *Adventure Sailing to Norway*
Laurence Young – *Switzerland*

Great fun was had in February 2011 visiting the happy household of post-university gap year Brits in the civilised suburb of Hawthorn in Melbourne, Australia. I would like to thank Hugh, Ali, Seb, and Alan for sharing their insights into the struggles and rewards of jetting off with working holiday visas to make their way in that buzzing antipodean city.

While every effort has been made to ensure that the information contained in this book was accurate at the time of going to press, some details are bound to change within the lifetime of this edition. Addresses, phone numbers and prices are particularly susceptible to fluctuations, so the ones quoted here are intended merely as a guide.

If in the course of your gap year travels you come across something which might be of interest to readers of the next edition, please contact Susan Griffith at s.griffith@ntlworld.com. Future editions will depend on up-to-date reports from gap travellers who have been inspired to take a year out before or after university. The best contributions will be rewarded with a free copy of the next edition or any other Vacation Work/Crimson title.

PART I

PLANNING
YOUR GAP YEAR

ONCE IN A LIFETIME
BEFORE YOU GO

ONCE IN A LIFETIME

As James Bond failed to notice, you only live once. Superlatives such as 'amazing', 'incredible' and even 'blissful' pepper the travel reminiscences of people who have had adventurous gap years, even the ones who have spent the first six months working behind the till at their local supermarket in order to save enough funds. A once-in-a-lifetime experience need not require any derring-do. Cycling through Patagonia or tracking the endangered black rhino is not for everyone. It could simply be breaking away from your friendship group to work in a ski resort in the Canadian Rockies or leaving home for the first time to go InterRailing or surviving the uncomfortable bus journey from Bangkok to Siem Reap.

Nothing can compare with the joy of the open road. Certainly not overdue assignments and a late student loan payment. The sense of possibility and adventure while travelling brings feelings of exhilaration, long submerged in the everyday routines of school and home. Cheap air travel has opened up parts of the globe once reserved for the sons and daughters of the seriously affluent. When travelling in far-flung corners of the world, you suddenly escape the deadlines, the chores, the clutter, the feeling of stagnation when you have been doing the same old thing for a long time. Even 18-year-olds can get into ruts.

Travelling spontaneously means you have the freedom to choose from an infinite spectrum of possibilities. Those who have experienced independent travel usually catch the bug and long to visit more places, see more wonders and spend a longer time abroad. Today, trekking in the hinterland of Rio de Janeiro or diving in the Philippines can be within the grasp of ordinary school leavers and college graduates. The longing might stem from a fascination left over from childhood with an exotic destination such as Madagascar or Spitsbergen. The motivation might come from a friend's reminiscences, a television travelogue, or a personal passion for a certain culture or natural habitat or sport. At some point in your schooling a vague idea begins to crystallise into an actual possibility.

That is the point at which the purple prose of brochure-speak must be interrupted by hard-headed planning. The first question is always: how can I afford such a trip? How can ordinary people possibly make their dreams reality? The conventional means to an exciting end is to work and save hard. A grim spell of working overtime and denying yourself a social life is one route to being able to join an overland expedition through East Africa, a windsurfing instructor's course on a Greek island or a bungee jump in New Zealand. Picking up bits and pieces of work and volunteering along the way can go some way to reducing the cost. Informal ways can be found of offsetting the cost of travel. Work-for-keep arrangements on a Canadian farm or Costa Rican eco-lodge will mean that you have to save far less than if you booked a long-haul package holiday to those destinations – in some cases little more than the cost of the flight and onward transport.

Volunteering or working abroad makes it possible to stay overseas for an extended period, to have a chance to get below the surface of another culture, to meet foreign people on their own terms and to gain a better perspective on your own culture and habits. Those who go down this route often relish being able to do something completely unfamiliar in an alien setting. The hundreds of pages that follow will help you to discover the means of doing just that.

TRAVEL TIP

The only essentials for having a great time on your gap year are motivation and money (and without the former you are unlikely to be able to save or fundraise the latter).

WHY TAKE A GAP YEAR?

For many young people approaching the end of school, the decision about whether or not to take a gap year can be a fraught one. The first question to ask yourself is: does the idea have a strong appeal? If you close your eyes and imagine yourself in the student union bar at university and then transport yourself in your imagination to an Amazonian rainforest or a Tanzanian village school or an Italian language class – what gives you more of a buzz? Think of the bad bits. Think of yourself sitting in a college library swotting for yet another exam and then picture yourself swatting mosquitoes while you're doing some manual job in the broiling sun of the tropics. If the idea of striking off to some remote corner of the world, far away from family and (most likely) friends, gives you the heebie-jeebies, then perhaps that kind of gap year is not for you. You can always come back to the idea after college (discussed below). What you want to avoid is spending a year hanging around passively waiting for something to turn up.

Deciding whether to take a year off and then how to spend it may not be as momentous as some other life decisions such as which university course to choose, but it is as individual. No parent or adviser or guidebook or even friend can make the decision for you. All that outsiders can do is set out the possibilities and see if any of them takes your fancy enough to pursue it. Do as much research as possible, let the ideas swill around in your head and see what floats to the top.

There is no doubt that it is easier to stay on the funicular that leads directly from the sixth form to higher education. After all, the majority of school leavers still do just that. Yet the number of people deferring is much higher than it used to be and an increasing number of students from a variety of backgrounds are at least giving the idea some serious thought. In many circles, taking a gap year is still considered something that only the rich and privileged do; but the explosion in the number of specialist organisations helping students to set up gap years is the result of a democratisation of the concept. Of course there are still plenty of people from top public schools and privileged backgrounds who take gap years (famously, both Princes William and Harry did) but anybody who is determined and enthusiastic enough can do it.

Try not to get too worried by all the emphasis on taking a 'constructive' and 'structured' gap year, if all you want to do is spread your wings, travel and see what turns up. Teachers, parents, and organisations sometimes go overboard in insisting that everything has to count for the future, and may fall prey to a near-obsession with what looks good on a CV. This is an aspect of culture in the highly developed west that might be usefully challenged on a backpacking trip in Cambodia and Laos or a volunteer school-building scheme in Madagascar. The much maligned phrase 'university of life' contains an important truth: that life experiences and getting to know yourself better may be hard to measure on any league table but are just as educationally valuable as writing waffling essays about the semiotics of film.

Many 17-year-olds are simply too young to make the choices expected of them regarding university and careers. If you are in this category, an extra year of exposing yourself to different experiences might provide some answers or at least whittle down some preferences. Otherwise there is a danger that you will drift along to university with the crowd and find that your heart just isn't in it. This is what happened to **Ross Fairgrieve**:

> *As I got towards the end of my A levels, I knew I wanted to get away for a bit. The degree I was hoping to study, however, was a four-year course with the third year being in Australasia so I didn't really want to take another whole year out beforehand. I therefore decided that I'd finish my exams, jet off somewhere nice for the summer, and then come straight back and go to university. While I'm sure this works for some people, it didn't really happen for me. I spent my summer on Koh Tao, a little island in the Gulf of Thailand that's almost singularly dedicated to scuba diving. After two and a half months I came back to England and headed straight off to a grey, autumnal East Anglia. Unfortunately my heart was still in*

Thailand and after a month I had thrown in the towel and was working full-time to get back out there. So much for my cunning time-saving plan! Anyway, I now had a gap year to fill. Leaving university was actually the best thing that could have happened. I then had a much clearer picture of what I wanted from university and applied for a slightly different course (I changed from Oceanography and Meteorology at UEA to Oceanography single honours at Southampton). Reapplication was no problem; I was just applying with the next year of school leavers. It's worth remembering, though, that applying for university during your gap year rather than deferring your entry does mean that you might have to go to interviews so you will lose some flexibility in the planning of your year.

For some, a gap year serves the same purpose as Dorothy's trip to the Land of Oz, which is to make them appreciate home. **Afton Blight**'s nine months in Peru persuaded her that T S Eliot hit the nail on the head when he wrote in *Four Quartets*, '*We shall not cease from exploration and the end of all our exploring will be to arrive where we started and know the place for the first time*':

Living in Peru allowed me time apart from everything I knew in my farming background in the Midwest. Although I enjoyed my time volunteering with SKIP (Supporting Kids in Peru), I realised I truly missed working in agriculture. I love being outside, the variation of tasks, and working with big machines. Upon my return I knew I wanted to attend Michigan State University to further my knowledge in animal and crop science. I wasn't choosing this career because it was convenient, I chose it because it is something I see myself doing and liking for many years. SKIP did not directly result in me discovering my passion for farming, but it allowed me to discover who I am and my interests. It also revealed to me things that I am not cut out for, like teaching English for more than a short time!

At the opposite end of the spectrum from those who don't have a clue what they want to do, **Marcus Starling** knew exactly what he wanted when he left school and used both a pre- and post-university gap year to impressive effect. Before uni he spent a month assisting an MEP in Brussels, six months as an ancillary teacher in a school in Leicester to earn money, two months on a study scholarship in Germany, and three months working on a kibbutz in Israel. After university he was not accepted on to the Civil Service Fast Stream, so he decided to gain some work experience abroad by joining the JET teaching programme in Japan (see *Asia* chapter) before reapplying. He got through the process second time round and went on to work for the Training and Development Agency for Schools.

PROS AND CONS

If major doubts remain about what the next step in your life should be, there is nothing better than taking a year out to do something completely different, to give yourself time and space to decide, away from all the pressures of home and school. Students repeatedly say that travelling or working/volunteering abroad helps to focus their minds on what they want to do next. But how might future employers view this time out? The majority of businesses have been shown to value gap years. Some company application forms even include a question about the gap year. A report commissioned by the national volunteering organisation CSV (Community Service Volunteers) showed that, of members questioned from the Association of Graduate Recruiters, 100% believed a constructive gap year helps young people to prepare for the workplace. In total, 88% thought that a well-structured gap year helped to furnish graduates with skills such as communication, decision-making and relationship building.

The culture is changing, however; education is no longer seen as a linear progression without interruption. Fifteen months is a miraculous period of time in which to pursue dreams and create memories. There will of course be opportunities later in life to take a break from routine – after university, between jobs, after having a child, sabbatical leave, after retirement, etc. But the combination of freedom from responsibility and leisure time is much harder to manage later on.

The standard objections raised by the doubting Thomases of the academic and parental world go as follows.

- You'll be a year behind your friends.
- You'll lose the impetus to study (though you may lose that over the four months between A levels and university anyway).
- You'll be seduced by travel and find it difficult to settle back into a comparatively boring routine on your return.
- You'll be seduced by the things that money can buy if you spend your year out earning enough money to save and spend, and then will find it difficult to contemplate reverting to the poverty of studenthood.
- You'll be seduced full stop and abandon everything for love.

Parents will be relieved to learn that the vast majority of gap year students do not lose their way. Some are changed enormously but very few bring grief to their families by cashing in their return ticket to settle in Koh Samui or Goa. The experience of working hard at a local job in order to fund a gap year experience is usually enough to persuade even those who are lukewarm about the benefits of higher education to stay on as a student for a few more years.

There is a general and growing perception that we live in dangerous times. To take just one illustration, a generation ago hitch-hiking was considered a perfectly normal activity, whereas now it has all but disappeared. With heightened alarm worldwide about personal security and some high-profile tragedies, some potential gappers and certainly their parents see gap years abroad as full of risk and danger. This anxiety probably afflicts young women more than young men, though the statistics show that this fear is irrational.

Another oft-touted objection is financial. The massive increase in university fees under the coalition government has made it more difficult to justify taking a year off before university. If your poor parents are contributing to your university education, it seems too much to expect them to contribute large wads of money for a gap year jolly, and you will not want to add to your own burden of debt. As is well known, university debts do not have to be paid back until graduates are earning more than £21,000 a year. The levels of debt with which students will now leave university are so horrendous that to delay the paying back for one more year may strike you as trivial in the scheme of things.

The tripling of tuition fees for most British universities from 2012 has discouraged many from deferring entry for 2011–12. Until now, the deferral rate has changed little since 2002, taken as a percentage of university acceptances overall, with more than 7% of university entrants taking up a university place a year late. It would be such a pity if young people coming up to the end of school, especially all the younger siblings of the hordes of students who enjoyed the freedom of the gap year, feel constrained to plough on to university, and miss out.

MY GAP YEAR: KATIE WHITE

Katie White, from New England, had the determination to take a year off. Since the practice is less common in the USA, young Americans have to be more determined than their British counterparts.

I knew I would have to deal with friends and family thinking something obviously must be wrong if I was not going straight to college. But on the positive side, my gap year would take pressure off my getting into the perfect college, knowing that I could reapply if I crashed and burned in my applications. Secondly, I wouldn't be going to college burnt out and unenthusiastic (as several of my friends ended up doing their freshman years). I hoped to return refreshed and inspired and with a clearer idea of what I wanted to study. This has proved true since I've returned. I recently opened the course catalogue for pre-registration and had a much more informed sense of what I wanted to pursue, such as Spanish, Latin American Studies, Art, and Environmental Studies, based on my gap year experiences in Costa Rica and Italy. I didn't feel any pressure to take certain courses for graduate school or to get ahead in my major; I just registered for classes I was passionate about or intrigued by.

After saving money over the summer by working at a summer camp, I spent from the end of August through mid-December volunteering at the Monteverde Friends School in Costa Rica where I worked with students in fifth to eighth grades, teaching English Literature and Language, and World History. I lived with a local host family whose children attended the school. After returning home for a few months to earn money, I left for Tuscany in March after being accepted as a Farm Intern at a medium-sized farm and agriturismo called Spannocchia. I worked with seven other interns that spring, with each of us specialising in a certain part of the farm, mine being the vegetable garden. Now I am home for the summer, working and getting ready for college this fall.

My gap year included so many exquisite moments that I really don't think I can pick one out. I remember lying on the roof of our hotel in Panama with my fellow teachers, looking up at the stars for hours, and feeling so relaxed and free and independent. I skied a lot this winter along trails in Massachusetts and Vermont, and I will hold forever in my memory one evening when I came out of the woods and the sun was shining on the snow, and smoke was wisping out from the chimney of the lodge, and everything was just so brilliant, I couldn't believe I was a part of it. In retrospect, these small wonders and moments of overwhelming gratitude for and pride in my decision to take a gap year are what stand out.

My low points revolved around learning to balance my own health and safety with my adventures. I was 18 when I left for Costa Rica and had no idea how little I knew about living on my own. Little by little, however, I learned to change my sheets, do my laundry, eat well-rounded meals, seek out advice, and thank people for their help. So my low points of feeling messy or sick or lonely shuffled me along to becoming more self-sufficient. I learned how to make tortillas and tamales, bake bread, start a vegetable garden from scratch, fix doors that had fallen off their hinges, use a power wrench, speak a bit of Spanish and Italian, and keep track of my own finances.

One of the greatest rewards of this gap year was the realisation that I didn't have to be funnelled through life; nothing should hold me back from doing what I love. I now feel that even if I get sucked into my workaholic mode again, I can sit myself down and say that there was a time when it wasn't like this and it doesn't have to be like this now. I know a simpler and more rewarding - albeit temporary - lifestyle that I can use to ground myself as I go through life. I know how to take a step back now.

SOLO OR IN COMPANY?

You have to be fairly lucky to have a friend who has the time, money, and motivation to join you on your chosen gap year travels or project. Probably the single most common deterrent for school leavers contemplating a gap year is that they lack the self-confidence to strike off on their own. Joining an organised gap year scheme should allay these fears because this will introduce you to a ready-made group of peers at a pre-departure orientation, through group travel, or on arrival. Similarly you can simply join a backpacking tour group (see Travel chapter below).

If you don't have a suitable companion and are convinced you need one, you can search on appropriate internet forums such as Lonely Planet's Thorn Tree – lonelyplanet.com/thorntree – www.travbuddy.com, www.companions2travel.co.uk (trial membership is free, membership £5 for one month) or gapyear.com's 'Find a Travel Mate' (www.gapyear.com/travelmates), any of which might turn up a like-minded companion. An application on Facebook called 'Backpacker' allows you to find out who is staying at hostels you're heading for, message them, and possibly fix up onward travel together.

But there is no guarantee you will connect instantly with strangers found this way. Many travellers emphasise the benefits of travelling alone, especially the chance to make friends with the locals more easily. Most are surprised that loneliness is hardly an issue, since there is always congenial company to be met in hostels, harbourside pubs, overnight trains, etc. Some people even team up with each other if they happen to be heading in the same direction. Of course, if you are working in a remote rural area and don't speak the language fluently, you will inevitably miss having a companion and may steer away from this kind of situation if it bothers you. If you are anxious about the trials and traumas of being on your own, try a short trip to see how you like it.

Women can travel solo just as enjoyably as men, though they may need some convincing of this. Travelling with friends is usually more fun but removes the perilous sense of possibility and adventure that some people love most about travelling. As one young solo woman traveller described it, '*the glorious moments, the stick-out-your-thumb-and-be-glad-for-whatever-is-going-to-happen-next moments, the feelings of triumph and absolute freedom, are uniquely yours*'.

Travelling can put a strain on the best of friendships. **Alice Stueck** comes from the small town of Abernethy (which has a population of 140) in the Canadian Prairies of Saskatchewan. Barely 18, she and a school friend hatched a plan to save money and see Europe. They arrived in England in the hostile month of November and stayed with some relations of Alice's travelling companion... and stayed and stayed. It seemed easier to remain in a comfortable house in the Home Counties than head off to who knows where. On a short trip to Paris, Alice began to suspect that she and her friend should have organised a trial trip together before committing themselves to the big adventure because their travelling styles were completely at odds. While the friend was keen to tick off the major tourist sites and spend a lot of money, Alice wanted to take things more slowly and give herself quiet periods to absorb what she was seeing. She also didn't want to blow her budget in the first few weeks. Things reached a crisis point back in England and she fled to the home of a friend of a friend of her mother's who happened to live not far away. She was tempted to go straight home but knew she would regret that later so decided to pause and catch her breath. Persuaded by her new hosts to leave 90% of her luggage behind and to join the Youth Hostel Association (YHA), she set off, albeit a little timidly, on her first solo trip, taking in Oxford, Bath, and London. Gaining confidence she booked a no-frills flight to Valencia, where she had a wonderful time.

A further layer of complication is added if you are in a relationship with someone who is not keen on joining you in your adventures. Frequent contact by telephone, email or (dare I suggest it?) letters will help keep things on course. Compromise is one answer, for example by organising a trip that might be shorter than otherwise or planning to rendezvous with your partner part way through the gap year. What most people hope is that their relationship will survive a serious separation, though at age 18 this is probably less likely than couples of more mature years. It would be a shame to have your decisions dictated by someone who might not be all that important to you once you get to university. **Camilla Burgess**'s story is typical: her boyfriend tried to dissuade her from going to volunteer for three months in Ghana during her gap year and then put pressure on her to cut her stay short, which she did (thereby incurring a financial penalty). They split up almost as soon as she got home. **Becky Warden-Brown**'s relationship also didn't survive her gap year:

> *My lowest point was flying out to Thailand to meet my boyfriend at the time and then discovering he was cheating on me. I felt so alone in a foreign country and just wanted to go home. But I'm so happy I stayed and I had the best time of my life. It forced me to be independent, which I had never been able to do before.*

When choosing a volunteer programme, one important consideration is whether you will be 'alone' in your placement or with other gappers. After **Laura Parker** spent three months of her gap year in a town in northern Cambodia through Outreach International, she was persuaded of the benefits of solo placements:

> *Living and working with volunteers of the same age from home could make the transition less frightening, and you'd probably build some lifelong friendships. But for others that may defeat the point*

of travelling to a foreign country and integrating with the people you are helping, or who live there. Equally, being based in a small rural town with few Western comforts and no other English speakers around could seem terrifying. But the likelihood is that you'd be taken in by the local community far more readily, you'd pick up more of the language, and could have a unique experience.

WILL A GAP YEAR CHANGE YOUR LIFE?

The short answer is probably not – but maybe. In the first place, six months of slogging at a local chain store or pizza restaurant usually works wonders to persuade you of the value of continuing your education. But six months spent overseas doing something completely different does have the potential for prompting a radical change of direction. For example **Joe Keely**'s six months in Tanzania steered him down a completely new route:

> *Not only did I achieve a fantastic feeling of well being, make great friends, and create great memories from this six months, but I have (excuse the cliché) found myself. Before I left for Tanzania I was going to follow the electronic and electrical engineering line. I have now changed course and wish to become a journalist and have looked into working for Oxfam on completion of university. I wouldn't have dreamt of such a change before I left, a change I am very grateful for now. This year gave me the break and the sense to choose what I really wanted to do in life and to see my life from a different angle. In fact, the only problem with the gap year is it makes life back here seem so much more dull.*

Parents worry that a gap year will derail plans for higher education. It is certainly not unknown for a young person to change their mind about university after a gap year. **Anja Ludgrove** expected to return to Britain to do a law conversion course after learning to snowboard but was so enamoured with the lifestyle that she stayed on for several seasons as an instructor. Parents have to ask themselves whether they should be concerned by this. In these enlightened times of flexibility in education, the possibility always exists of resuming studies at a later stage.

Faye Mold is yet another student whose gap year – doing a divemaster course in Thailand – helped to shape and clarify her priorities:

> *At school we were not really given that much advice. We did have talks from major gap year companies which made me very excited, but I already knew what I wanted to do (scuba diving) and the school never let us forget that it was all heading for university, which weighed me down somewhat. I didn't go to uni in the end (originally I was going to study Criminology) but saved up and went travelling again and I feel this was the best education I could get. I now realise I was only going to uni because the school pressurised me into thinking I would be a nobody if I didn't have a degree, which I now know is not true after meeting so many people abroad. My family are very supportive and have always said they just want their children to be happy so they were not disappointed about my decision not to go to uni (although for a while I could not help thinking they were). I have not regretted my decision at all. I am currently applying to join the Met Police and after my probationary period (if I pass) I want to specialise. So who knows – I may try to join the police underwater search and recovery team, so my diving would be put to good use.*

Simon Preddy's gap year had exactly the opposite effect: '*It was taking a gap year that made me realise that I needed to go to university if I wanted to realise my passions in life. That turned out to be teaching and also having a voice in the world (ie journalism), as seeing some shocking things in Uganda made me question why none of it would be reported in the UK.*'

One experienced observer of the effect that structured gap years have on school leavers is quoted as saying: '*These kids don't get lost in a gap year, they get found.*'

DECIDING WHEN TO TAKE YOUR GAP YEAR

There are good arguments for taking a gap year before university and after university – and a few lucky people take both. After A levels, many students are utterly sick of exams and books and timetables. They want to experience Life with a capital L, and freedom and independence. University can satisfy these cravings up to a point, but heading off to work in a New Zealand ski resort or study Spanish in Ecuador or backpack round India or pick apples in Tasmania or volunteer at a village school in Tanzania – all of these guarantee a complete break from anything that has gone before.

STRAIGHT OUT OF SCHOOL

It is not at all unusual for young people in their A level years to feel fairly unfocused about their future. A huge number follow the unexamined assumption of family and peers that they will go to university but they may not have a clear idea what to study or where to study it. At a basic level, many 18-year-olds simply do not feel ready for university, and when they do drift off to a place of higher learning, possibly having chosen according to the pin-in-a-map technique, they may not have the motivation to last the distance. The obvious answer to this quandary is to take some time out, to give yourself time to mature and a chance for preferences and interests to develop. Most wet-behind-the-ears school leavers have very limited horizons and a year of travel, volunteering, and work is sure to expand them. A wider acquaintance with the world can be academically beneficial and arguably almost essential for lots of courses such as politics, media and communications, modern languages, art history, and so on.

A specially targeted gap year project will always impress, such as living and doing a course in a country whose language you want to study, or touring the ancient sites of the eastern Mediterranean if you want to study classical civilisations. But even a 'bog standard' gap year of working and travelling can do wonders for enhancing self-confidence and independence of thought. Anyone who has managed to rub along with a group of strangers on an Arctic expedition or engaged in drinking games with some Slovenian students met while backpacking in Europe is bound to feel less timid about tackling their university's freshers' week. Entering the canteen at uni for the first time can hold few terrors for someone who has stepped out of Bangkok or Delhi Airport and found their way around an alien city. Anyone who has experienced a homestay with a Mexican or Thai family will have learned a great deal about tolerance and respect for difference. Those who have backpacked on a shoestring and stayed in a few dives will not be too shocked by the declining standards of hygiene in their hall of residence.

Just as an average 18-year-old may not have a well-worked-out pathway for their future, so they may not have much of a clue about what they want to do or where to go in their gap year. Their tastes are unformed. As a result many are attracted to the whirlwind kind of travel, to give them a snapshot of many different places so they can sort out where they would like to spend more time on a future trip. InterRailing is a classic gap year choice, and almost everybody wishes that they had spent longer in a few places rather than dashing from station to station, hostel to hostel. Generally speaking, no-one goes InterRailing twice, but it serves a valuable function in giving first-time travellers a taste of what the world holds.

STRAIGHT OUT OF UNIVERSITY

If the student who has just finished A levels feels in dire need of a major break, how much more has the university graduate deserved it? They may have partied in their first year, but the final year is usually an intense scramble to finish dissertations or complete scientific projects, and of course to sit final exams. Many feel that they have really earned a break from all this pressure and obligation, and the idea of subjecting themselves to a round of job interviews fills them with dismay.

Everyone knows that job prospects for graduates at home have become quite bleak. Last year graduate vacancies in the UK were down by an average of 15%, which is a devastating figure. Many candidates, who less than a decade ago would have waltzed into an entry-level job with career prospects, are now finding it impossible even to get an interview. Doing unpaid internships has become the norm rather than the exception, and even these are difficult to arrange without having strings to pull. Flitting off to a distant corner of the world on a gap year might seem irresponsible in these troubled times, but it could be exactly the right approach to the problem of job stasis and defeated morale. Joining a project or taking an unpaid internship abroad on a gap year can pep up a CV in lots of ways – perhaps in improving facility in a foreign language, and in providing opportunities to develop new practical skills in fields such as teaching, marketing, and conservation.

Rosanna Ruff vividly describes the employment vacuum into which she stepped after graduating from university and how she solved it with the help of the internship agency CRCC Asia (see entry in 'Directory of Work Experience Abroad'):

> On accepting my certificate of graduation and passing from undergrad to graduate, I found myself left with a lingering sense of unease. My three years spent at Exeter University had been among the most fulfilling and contented of my life. Dressed in my cap and gown and surrounded by proud parents and elated professors, stepping up to accept my certificate, I was also stepping into the unknown. Until this moment, my path had been neatly sketched out for me: school, sixth form, university. I had fulfilled the expectations of my parents, my schoolteachers, my professors, and yet all too suddenly this comforting canopy of guidance was retracting. I found myself, for the very first time, truly at my own crossroads.
>
> Time and time again, over a celebratory glass of champagne, that terrifying inquest would commandeer the conversation. 'So, what is next for you, then?' A fumbled attempt at an answer would follow, or a foolhardy bid to muffle the offensive cavity in my expected path. Whether they believed my hollow words or saw straight through my efforts, tilted their head, nodded empathetically and instantly branded me as yet another Credit Crunch casualty, the whole ordeal was exhausting.
>
> In truth, enveloped in essay submission, dissertation refinement and revision for finals, this day, this question had hurtled quite unexpectedly towards me. Employment had been a distant ideal, but a faraway notion amid paper after paper and revision card after revision class. At the age of five, being a farmer was my greatest ambition. At the age of 10 a fashion designer was all I set my heart on. By 15 I would settle for nothing less than British Prime Minister, and suddenly at the age of 21, graduate in History and Politics, I was drawing a blank.
>
> I set about finding something worthwhile to fill my summer before applying to graduate jobs and vacation schemes in the autumn. Recommended by a friend, I contacted CRCC Asia in search of an internship abroad. If there is one thing I have learnt from copious presentation evenings, employment fairs and meet-and-greets, it is that in order to be desirable you must set yourself apart from the rest. There must be something different, something distinct about your application. CRCC has provided me with the perfect opportunity to become that elusively unique candidate.
>
> The 'sleeping giant' has awoken. China is a progressive, innovative, youthful nation at the forefront of global advancement. Beijing is a vibrant city with boundless prospects. It exudes excellence – and as a young graduate there could be no better place to get acquainted with the working world. Sitting amongst the bustle of my hectic Chinese law firm offices, I could not be happier with my decision. Coached in Chinese business etiquette and armed with enough Mandarin to make my colleagues smile, I settled comfortably into my month-long placement. While unprecedented downturns in the international market meant doors were closing, CRCC helped me find an alternative path into the employment sector.

Because graduates are three years older and wiser, and have been exposed to many more ideas and possibilities, they may have a clearer idea of what aspects of the world they want to explore (see **Kirsten Shaw**'s story, below). Their choice of gap year destination and/or activity might grow organically out of subjects that have grabbed their attention at university. They have already learned the art of fending for themselves, and will not worry as much about suffering from homesickness as they might have done when they were 18. Solo travel may not hold the terrors it would have when they were younger; on the other hand they might be in a relationship that they are reluctant to jeopardise. All these contingencies are very personal and there is no right or wrong time to fly the coop. **Samantha Thornley** found that in her last year of college she became less interested in the business world and more interested in the *actual* world. She was aware of how much of the world she *hadn't* seen and how much she didn't know, and felt an urgency to remedy this: '*I knew that if I didn't take the chance now (after graduating from college) I never would*', so she went off to teach in Vietnam.

One of the disadvantages of the post-university gap year is that many new graduates are oppressed by escalating student debt, and find it difficult to justify to themselves jetting off to spend yet more money. Unlike the young gapper who has a deferred place at university already sorted, the graduate gapper has no such fixed structure and may feel uneasy at the prospect of returning to the job market following a long break after uni. With the recession biting, they may feel it is irresponsible to jet away from the troubled job market.

Partly against her will, **Kirsten Shaw** had been persuaded to go straight to university after school. She couldn't wait to get away after uni and spent most of 2010–11 in South Africa, doing an interesting (unpaid) job for the NGO Daktari, building marketing and fundraising campaigns using social media, writing grant proposals and newsletters and generally helping out at this private wildlife reserve. She has some interesting reflections on the benefits of this kind of experience.

Coming from French schooling, gap years are generally frowned upon. Although I went to the UK to do my degree, the French mindset remained and my parents urged me to take a year out only once I had completed my degree. In hindsight, I should have taken a year off before university, giving myself time to think of what I really wanted to do with my life.

I think taking a gap year is almost entirely beneficial – it throws you out into the world in one fell swoop, and the further afield you go, the harder you land on your backside, and the quicker you get up and plough forward. For those who lack social skills to start, you acquire them quickly, you learn to be self-reliant, to always make a plan. Whether you work in the bush or in a city, you always come across bridges that need to be crossed or, in some cases, walls that you will run straight into. Yet learning curves appear in all walks of life. I was lucky enough to cross bridges and run into walls in the sanctuary of the South African bush. You learn what you want and don't want out of people, out of life. I don't mean to say you learn it all on your gap year, but you definitely build a base. At the end of the day, the more you take yourself out of your comfort zone, the more beneficial the experience will be.

The only negative point in relation to taking a gap year after your degree is that in comparison to your classmates, your professional life might start a little later. While you are soaking up the beauty of South America and breeding alpacas in Peru, others might have started a career, achieving the status of 'full-time employment'. If you are a career-orientated person, then this might bother you. If like myself you think that life experience far outstrips full-time employment, then there is no reason to stay at home.

To pay for a gap year and aeroplane tickets, we all need to have money in the bank. I made mine the conventional way – I spent the summer waitressing (in France you are paid well in comparison to other countries such as the UK), rising above complaining clients and the heat, as I knew that South Africa awaited me at the end of the long, bleak tunnel. Living at home I was able to get by on a day-to-day basis with my tips, and put away most of the salary I earned. I knew how cheap life in the bush was in comparison to Europe, so three months' worth of wages would keep me going for my seven months at Daktari Wildlife Orphanage and Bush School. It was unbelievably worth it.

CLASSIC GAP YEAR CHOICES

Googling 'Planning a Gap Year' will give about two and a half million results. The book in your hand describes rather fewer, but still covers hundreds of specific gap year options as well as providing an enticing taste of travelling on the five continents of the world. The year has been freed up – now what? Many people feel overwhelmed by the welter of choices, knowing that as soon as they plump for one, all other options are closed down.

After the stress of A levels, most students want to cut loose with some mates, whether wild camping in Scotland or clubbing in Majorca. A large number kick off their gap year with an InterRail trip (see 'Getting Around' in the Europe section). Many plan to get back home in time for results day in mid-August in case the envelope contains any surprises that need follow-up action. Next comes the hard graft at a local pub or store or temping to save up for a more ambitious trip. A favourite departure time is in the new year, though some gappers work through until Easter to save enough for a long-haul flight or an expensive gap year programme. Of course there are an infinite number of variations on this basic outline. For example, participants in a gap year programme with a September start date might spend the summer earning money.

The first crucial decision to make is whether just to travel or to join a project, expedition or course. If pure travel is your choice, turn to the Travel and continent-by-continent chapters. Most gap years involve a combination of working locally to save money, travelling and possibly signing up with an organisation that makes placements overseas. The mainstream volunteering choices are conservation, community work (often teaching or working with children) and construction.

One advantage of joining a scheme is that it makes you stay put for an extended period instead of drifting from place to place in what can end up giving a superficial view of the countries visited. The great travel writer Dervla Murphy expressed her views on this subject in an essay in *The Traveller's Handbook*:

> *The past decade or so has seen the emergence of another, hybrid category: youngsters who spend a year or more wandering around the world in a holidaymaking spirit, occasionally taking temporary jobs. Some gain enormously from this experience but many seem to cover too much ground too quickly, sampling everywhere and becoming familiar with nowhere. They have been from Alaska to Adelaide, Berlin to Bali, Calcutta to Cuzco, Lhasa to London. They tend to wander in couples or small packs, swapping yarns about the benefits – or otherwise – of staying here, doing that, buying this. They make a considerable impact where they happen to perch for a week or so, often bringing with them standards (sometimes too low) and expectations (sometimes too high) which unsettle their local contemporaries.*
>
> *Of course one rejoices that the young are free to roam as never before, yet such rapid 'round-the-worlding' is, for many, more confusing than enlightening. It would be good if this fashion soon changed, if the young became more discriminating, allowing themselves time to travel seriously in a limited area that they had chosen because of its particular appeal to them, as individuals.*

The chapters that make up this book survey the range of possibilities and provide lots of concrete information to help you decide whether to earn a salary in a high-tech industry in Britain or join an expedition to Patagonia (or both). Details are provided on volunteering in residential situations in the UK and abroad, work experience, courses and homestays, seasonal jobs such as working in ski resorts, au pairing, English teaching, pure travelling: all are covered.

A traveller wrote in 1899: '*We took this trip around the world on bicycles because we are more or less conceited – like to be talked about and see our names in the newspapers.*' In some sixth forms a certain amount of oneupmanship prevails about who can do the most adventurous and exotic trip (though most end up going to Thailand or India or Australia where there are whole colonies of gap year students). Paraguay and Outer Mongolia are great if you have a particular interest in those regions but if you would be happier working on an American summer camp or a Scottish sailing school or attending a language school in Barcelona, so be it. It is possibly a mistake to think of the Himalayan gap year as vastly superior to the one spent closer to home. Trekking in northern Thailand does not necessarily trump working in a Swiss ski resort or volunteering to teach Gypsy children in Spain. Do not fall into the trap of making plans to impress. Find the route that suits you.

MY GAP YEAR: ELLA HICKSON

Ella Hickson was not as tempted as her peers by the attractions of Thai beaches and the Australian outback, having come to the conclusion that the more popular gap years have become, the less variety in the choices young people were making.

My gap year was a little different. Yesterday I was perched on a wall in Vienna. My co-percher was a Geordie lad by the name of Elliott. With the facade of St Peter's Church in front of us, I started talking about why keys were associated with St Peter's. All very interesting I'm sure to an art enthusiast or history buff, but neither are really Elliott's scene - his Great Masters come from the Champions League. In spite of that the questions kept coming: how can you tell it's a saint? Why was Da Vinci such a good guy? And so forth. It was bizarre, he was genuinely intrigued and an hour later all four lads had got involved. All my resources, gathered a year previously on an Art History Abroad (AHA) course, were being seriously stretched.

When I explained what I had done on my gap year I knew it was a million miles from anything those lads would ever think of doing, and yet here they were, now round a table with pints in hand, still plying me for information about columns and the Vatican. I was answering to 'Miss, why isn't England Catholic now?' and 'Why is the Pope so rich?' I pondered their enthusiasm a little cynically; they did already have my number, so what was this about? Suddenly the 'Miss...' jokes stopped and four football lads all agreed that they had learnt more in the past few hours than they had in the last year, and all agreed they wished they had done something similar. It was so good to get someone else excited about art. It's an unstoppable infectious buzz that defies my generation's outdated maxim that learning just isn't cool. It's that same buzz that AHA gives its students and that those students then go on to spread wherever they go. AHA provides gappers with an unimaginable wealth of knowledge, a grounding in art and architecture that exceeds simple facts; AHA teaches students how to look, to get the back story and most importantly it starts a passion for learning which is fundamental in all areas of post gap year life. I did my best to show my Geordie friend how to see stories, histories, people and passions - money and politics, I'm sure I went on a bit but I knew that if I could get him to be even half as interested as my tutors made me, I'd be doing a good thing.

AHA still gives students the chance to dance till dawn and sample local drinks but it also teaches you to wax lyrical on Titian. Not only can I tell someone where the best bars are in Naples but also where the best Caravaggios are. Personally, I gained a passion and enthusiasm about art that has helped me decide where to head in life. I have changed my university course to Art History, I've done work experience at the Tate and have set up my own small company dealing in non-professional artworks in my university city of Edinburgh.

As I waved goodbye to the lads at Vienna station, they had decided to go to Venice, Florence, Naples, and Rome. As I'm writing down where they have to go to find good limoncello and prosecco, where the best clubs are and where to stagger home to, I hear a voice from the back 'Where was that Tintoretto guy? Which one was the dome that they can't work out how it was built? How do you spell the name of the murderer who painted grubby people?' So if anyone sees a bunch of boys, pints in hand, looking for Caravaggio, could you show them the way?!

USING A GAP YEAR AGENCY

The ambition of many gap year students is simply to travel with a mate. However, if you have set your sights on volunteering or doing work experience or joining an expedition, it will be more difficult to fix this up independently. Although some 18-year-olds fresh from school have the confidence and maturity to set off without anything set up (perhaps with a working holiday visa for Australia or a return ticket to Lima), many will prefer to enlist the help of a mediating organisation or agency to set up a placement and provide a back-up service if things go wrong.

Assuming you want to do something other than just travel, you must decide whether to throw in your lot with a sending organisation or arrange something independently. Many of the advantages of going on an organised scheme are self-evident but it is worth noting a few here:

- It makes the choice available less overwhelming since placement agencies have a finite number of destinations and opportunities.
- It saves you the time spent contacting many organisations abroad and the anxiety of liaising with them, assuming they do express interest. Pre-departure orientation will be provided. Even just a briefing booklet can be helpful and reassuring. Agencies are usually in a position to give reliable advice on necessary health precautions, insurance and flights.
- Back-up is available if you have an accident, become ill, or the placement is unacceptable in some way.
- It offers reassurance for anxious parents. The agency often provides a conduit of communication between the gap year student and their family.
- Placement is usually in groups or pairs, so moral support is always available from gap year or volunteer partners.

Angela Clegg sums up why she was happy to use an agency for her trip to Africa, in her case Cross-Cultural Solutions:

After A levels I was looking for something that had variation and I discovered that a nursery project in Tanzania offered by Cross-Cultural Solutions (CCS) included formal lectures, Swahili lessons, free evenings and weekends and most importantly a compound to live in with fellow volunteers from all over the world. For my first big trip away I needed to feel safe. CCS matched up volunteers who would be in Amsterdam airport at the same time en route to Africa, which was brilliant because it meant we were less nervous about arriving in Africa without knowing anyone. My advice for anyone doing the same thing is that, if you have any reservations about doing it alone, use a company like CCS. Throughout all of my preparation they were right there with help from reassuring phone calls, to a participants' handbook, to putting you in touch with previous volunteers. They also gave me advice on fundraising, and sent me a letter to prove I was fundraising for my trip.

The majority of students coming home from a gap year are grateful for the help and back-up given to them by their agency, claiming that they considered the fee they paid well spent. On the other hand, some find that their agency's local representative is not easy to contact and therefore not of much use. Others who end up not needing to make use of the support network begrudge the fee. The fee paid to a sending agency can be viewed as an insurance policy which many students and their parents are more than happy to pay. However, problems can arise when clients are paying Western prices, because it leads them to expect a Western standard of service that may not be possible in remote parts of developing countries. You should try to research the company and the project as thoroughly as you can, to avoid the ones that put profit above everything else. For a list of searching questions to put to a provider, see the introduction to the chapter *Specialist Gap Year Programmes.* You should try to find out what the company offers to justify the expense, and whether they make any financial contribution to the worthy projects on which they send volunteers.

Only you know whether you have the stamina and initiative to create a constructive gap year without the umbrella of a placement organisation. Bear in mind that locally run non-governmental organisations (NGOs) may profess to need your help but may have little experience in dealing with the kinds of problem faced by homesick 18-year-olds. Without a like-minded person around, you might feel lonely and isolated. On the other hand, some gap year students do arrange their own job/placement, with or without contacts, and find the experience immensely gratifying. Arranging something independently shows great initiative (always something worth boasting about on future CVs), and of course saves the money that would otherwise go to a middle man.

GOING IT ALONE

Arranging your own placement can be hard work. **Rick Padfield** had seen his older sister Eleanor arrange her own volunteer placements in South America on her gap year, and was even more ferociously determined to do it on his own. He wanted to have 12 months in Africa, which he did, and ended up spending a total of £3,800 over the whole period, including travel. He sent off a blizzard of emails to family friends, schools, charities, and organisations in Africa and, impressively, arranged three-month placements in Kenya, Uganda, and Ghana. The school in Kenya asked him to arrange to come in a pair so he even persuaded a friend to join him. But after they had been in their Kenyan placement for a month, 24 trainee Kenyan teachers were suddenly assigned to the school, so he and his fellow volunteer were 'fired'. If something doesn't work out with an arrangement made privately, there is no-one in the background to put alternative arrangements into place. Rick and Tom were lucky though, as the farm on which they were staying then offered them a GPS mapping project which filled several weeks.

OVERCOMING ANXIETY

Often the hardest step is committing yourself to a decision, that is, fixing a departure date and destination. Once you have booked a place on a scheme or bought a ticket and explained to your friends and

MY GAP YEAR:
HELEN REID

Helen Reid devised one of the most varied and interesting gap years that has come to light for this new edition of the book. Before going to Oxford in October 2011 to study Politics, Philosophy and Economics, she took a gap year that was divided between three months in South Africa (September to December) and five months in South America, including a highlight as a journalism intern (see entry for *Bolivian Express* in the work experience directories).

In South Africa, I lived in a small rural Zulu village where my cousin and his wife live and, thanks to them, I got a placement as reporter for a local NGO which worked with AIDS relief. I went along with different workers - nurses, marriage counsellors, food deliverers - every day and wrote about the different work they did. At times, it was a very harrowing experience seeing the AIDS sufferers living in such isolation, miles away from roads and hospitals. But I also learned a lot and enjoyed the report writing at the end of it. This was for a month, and the rest of the time I lived with an aunt in Cape Town and did some waitressing work.

In South America I planned to do a different thing each month: February volunteering in the jungle in Ecuador, March travelling through Peru, April working with the **Bolivian Express** (journalism), May working at a conservation centre in Brazil and June working at a yoga centre in Argentina. My main source of information about volunteering programmes was www.volunteerlatinamerica.com, through which you can get a personalised brochure of volunteer opportunities in many countries. Also, I did lots of personal research on the internet. I think finding organisations this way ensures that they are legitimate, local and a more rewarding experience than going through a large gap year agency and ending up spending most of your time with people from back home.

The first stop on my trip in January was Colombia. Thanks to a Colombian friend there, I was placed in a children's home and did some work for a short while as an English and maths teacher. On to Ecuador, where I worked for a month with the foundation FUNDECOIPA in the rainforest (www.fundecoipa.com). It was a very rustic, very physically difficult but very rewarding time. I was living with a family of Shuar Indians who taught us their culture and stories, and made us work cutting trees, planting crops, building beds, water tanks, etc.) We were very isolated (three hours' walk through the jungle to the nearest tar road) but it was worth it, unforgettable, and I learnt a lot from their lifestyle; they live solely off what they harvest from the jungle.

The Bolivian Express is a monthly magazine containing articles about history, culture, and current issues in La Paz and Bolivia in general. The interns all live together in a beautiful 17th-floor apartment with great views over the city, full kitchen, access to the internet, even a piano and guitar. The minimum stay is a month and some interns stay for six months or a year. We didn't have fixed hours; we found a subject we were interested in writing about and then it was our job to organise interviews with relevant people, visit places, exhibitions, read the papers. We were given guidance by some of the founders of the magazine but mostly were very independent in our research and writing, which I enjoyed. We were treated like responsible adult journalists. I was an intern for a month and wrote two articles but only one appeared in the May 2011 issue, the other being used later. My choice for the May issue's theme of 'Top Tens' was to write about the top 10 Aymara names. For this article, I had to interview Bolivians who had decided to ignore the habit of naming children after Catholic saints and rather go back to their indigenous Aymara roots to affirm their unique cultural identity. As well as being a valuable cultural exchange for me, the magazine enables the largely American and European tourist and expatriate readership to see into Bolivian culture. The experience of interviewing Bolivians, recording the interviews and then transcribing and translating them was very valuable to me as I am thinking of going into journalism later. Seeing the finished magazine, the result of collaboration with skilled fellow interns, editors, and an incredible graphic designer/photographer, was a real treat which gave me a feeling of intellectual fulfilment which I think can sometimes be missing from a gap year!

family that you are off to see the world, the rest seems to fall into place. Inevitably, first-time travellers suffer pre-departure anxieties as they contemplate leaving behind the comfortable routines of home. But these are usually much worse in anticipation than in retrospect.

Prepare yourself for a horrid 48 hours after saying goodbye at the airport (tip: don't look back after going through passport control). **Jake Lee**, who went to Sri Lanka in his gap year, puts it rather brutally:

> Let me just state for the record: it doesn't matter who you are, but if you are travelling alone to a faraway place for a relatively long time, you will cack yourself on the plane. The excitement you previously had turns to fear, and you are desperate for the plane to turn around. I don't think there is anything you can do about this. Just ride it out. As a Buddhist monk at my school always said, 'There is never anything to worry about – nothing'. This is true.

BEFORE YOU GO

Every successful gap year combines periodic flights of fancy with methodical planning; any homework you do ahead of time will benefit you later, if only because it will give you more confidence. Your first task in the planning stages is to consider some of the programmes and organisations described in this book and to make contact with the ones that tempt you to find out more. If an organisation offers a project that appeals, the next step is to find out whether you are eligible. Usually the hardest part is not being accepted to join but raising enough money to fund your travel. But before you get to that stage, you must sort out what you are going to do about further or higher education.

UNIVERSITY APPLICATION

Applying to university is a stressful and complicated business, on which your school should offer detailed advice. The worst aspect of it is the uncertainty of outcome. Conditional offers are the bugbear of prospective students because they mean it is difficult to make definite plans until you know your A level results. Of course the specialist placement organisations are used to coping with the problem and can offer support throughout. Many school leavers feel forced to make up their minds about university courses too early. More mature students make better decisions about what they want to study and are statistically less likely to drop out.

It is important to ascertain what line the department or university you're applying to takes on gap years. Until recently, the vast majority were more than tolerant. However, increased competition for places – more than 200,000 applicants were left without a place in 2011 – has made some universities reluctant to offer deferred places. Some have started to cap the number of deferrals on offer, up to 10% in the case of Exeter University. As a result of this squeeze on deferrals, organisations involved in gap year travel are not as quick as they once were to urge students to sort out their university applications before taking off. A shortage of deferrals does not necessarily limit the number of gap years: it simply means that more gappers will have to apply to university during their gap year, which, for students with strong A levels, has its advantages, not least for admissions tutors sick of making offers on the basis of predicted grades. Candidates with a weaker academic profile can use a gap year, to improve their attractiveness to universities, eg by undertaking some relevant work experience.

TIMING

Wherever possible, students should begin preparations for a gap year well in advance. There are so many plans to make and problems to sort out that the best way to avoid panics and disappointments is not to leave things to the last minute. If you are applying before A levels, application forms have to be submitted to UCAS by 15 January of your A level year at the latest (earlier for Oxbridge and some courses such as medicine). This leaves just over five months until your exams are finished, which may seem plenty of time to decide how to spend your gap year until you realise that some of the schemes are already filling up or that you'll have to raise several thousand pounds in order to join your preferred programme. Similarly, many Year in Industry jobs require early application to ensure the chosen company and placement have places left.

PRE-A-LEVEL APPLICATION

Students need to crystallise their reasons for taking a gap year before writing their personal statement or before being interviewed. It may be beneficial to stress the fact that time spent in the 'real world' will encourage a more mature outlook. Tutors are fully aware of the fact that many students who defer for a year go on to do comparatively better at university. According to a survey carried out on behalf of the Year Out Group, nine out of 10 university vice-chancellors agreed that a structured year out benefits the personal development of the typical undergraduate.

Attitudes to the gap year vary from tutor to tutor, subject to subject. If you are aiming for a top university, it makes sense to speak personally to the admissions tutor of your course. For years, a high proportion of first-year students at the best universities arrived after a year out, dispelling the anxiety that there is vestigial distrust of people who take a year out. The received wisdom on gap years and medical studies, however, is that a year out will be tolerated only if it is spent in some way related to medicine. Many medical schools are reluctant to accept people straight out of school and prefer older students who will have more chance of sticking the course. Students need to impress on the university that they really want to have a place on that particular course and that come hell or high water they will return to take it. Having a coherent plan and focusing on the potential benefits will make the university realise that you are serious about spending the year in a responsible manner. Questions about gap years often form part of an interview and can potentially be impressive.

Once it has been decided that a gap year is the best plan, this needs to be indicated on the UCAS form. To offer deferred entry is then at the university's discretion and they will send their conditions to UCAS, who in turn send this to the student. It is certainly easier to apply to university while you are still at school and have the momentum and infrastructure in place all around you. On the other hand, the fact that the whole UCAS process must now be conducted online means that all you really need the school for is your tutor's accompanying letter, which you can still request after leaving.

POST-A-LEVEL APPLICATION

If you haven't applied for deferred entry in the upper sixth, then you can apply during your gap year. Applying for university during your gap year means that you might have to go to open days and/or interviews in the winter, so you will lose some flexibility in the planning of your year. For example, **Pascale Hunter** had to interrupt her six-month gap year trip to Australia and South East Asia, at great expense, to fly back to England for a few weeks in January and attend interviews for the midwifery courses she was applying to.

Come results day, some students inevitably find that they have not done as well as anticipated and have not met their conditional offer. Several options are now possible.

- Carry on with your gap year plans and apply again the following year with the same exam results, probably to different courses.
- Contact your first choice university to see whether they will take you despite missing your grades (unlikely these days with such a rise in applicants).
- Proceed to early entry in Clearing, bearing in mind that places gained through Clearing will be for that year and not for the year after. Courses with vacancies are published in the *Independent* and on the UCAS website (www.ucas.com) – and these have been decreasingly sharply. Speed of reaction and decisiveness are essential at this stage because lots of people are competing for remaining places. You must communicate directly with the institutions, which is easier said than done since the phone lines are often jammed in the days following results day.
- Plan to resit and reapply to your preferred university.

Even at this stage, a gap year might help your cause. An article about gap years in the *Guardian* quoted the admissions tutor for English and drama at Loughborough University who said that he might give a student who misses their grades another chance if they have taken a gap year: '*Students who have taken gap years have gone through the jolly japes of puberty when they start university. They understand that the world is different in different places and they appreciate things more because of that.*'

If your first choice university will not offer a place, you need to ask yourself some hard questions. Was the original choice of course suitable anyway? Would it be better to apply for something else? If your first choice course was vocational, it could be worthwhile having a serious chat with the careers service to reassess the situation, particularly if your grades fell a long way short. Reapplying post A level for the following year is straightforward; universities will either make an unconditional offer or reject your application. When A level results were published in August 2010, Mary Curnock Cook, Chief Executive of UCAS, voiced her opinion that a gap year should be seen as a 'bridging year' (her coinage), as a chance to upgrade your university application. (She would say that, wouldn't she?)

MY GAP YEAR: CAROLINE GOSNEY

Caroline Gosney felt compelled to take a gap year when she discovered in August that she had not met her university conditional offer. In other words, some people choose to have a gap year and some have one thrust upon them.

Last year on results day I was devastated. I hadn't done enough work during my final year at school and had missed my grades for my first choice university. Rather than take my insurance choice I decided to take a year out, retake the necessary modules to get my grades and reapply. The restaurant where I was working kept me on and I worked for five and a half months to afford to travel. That was a learning curve in itself, as it requires immense discipline to get up at 8am every day through horrid weather when travelling seems so far away. All my friends were either heading off to uni or had planned their gap years months in advance so I felt rather alone. The possibilities for gap year travel are endless and deciding where to go and who with is a nightmare if it's all done very last minute!

I had always wanted to go to Africa and decided Blue Ventures based in Madagascar looked perfect for me. Leaving your family and friends for two months to go somewhere that has no mobile phone reception and email access only once a week is terrifying but is a truly valuable experience as you learn pretty quickly to fend for yourself. The whole experience is something I will never forget. I have never felt as happy as when I was living in a leaky hut, infested with cockroaches and getting up at 5.30am to head out into the Indian Ocean and dive with species of flora and fauna seen nowhere else in the world.

The other part of my gap year was spending five weeks InterRailing around Europe with a close friend who had done the complete opposite and done far better in his A levels than he had expected to. We had a riot, visiting nine cities. Of course, Europe was a completely different experience from Madagascar but equally valuable.

My gap year has been fantastic. Ironically, I can't imagine not taking one now and if I had fulfilled my offer requirements last August I wouldn't have met the people I have, done the things I've done and grown so much. Part of me thinks that if you plan it too carefully you build your expectations up too high and it's never as good as you imagine it will be. Gap years are all about spontaneity and broadening your horizons, so if you do worse than you expected it isn't the end of the world and I really urge you to consider taking a year out. However, if you aced your A levels you have nothing to lose, except the experience of a lifetime.

TIMETABLE FOR UNIVERSITY APPLICATION
Plan A

Lower sixth	Autumn/spring	Begin to think about university courses and the possibility of taking a gap year
	Spring/summer	Visit university open days. Speak to admissions tutors about taking gap years. Students should try to visit as many universities as possible to get a feel for the place
Upper sixth	September to December	Fill in UCAS forms and clearly mark preference for deferred entry. Hand in no later than 15 January (or 15 October for medicine and Oxbridge applications)
	October to April	Make plans for gap year (apply to placement scheme/s, volunteer organisations, consider travel options, etc). Save as much money as possible to fund your gap year
	January to March	Receive conditional offers from universities
	Around April	Submit final decision for first and second (insurance) choice university courses
	May/June	Sit A2 Exams
	August (third Thursday)	Results Day
		• Sufficient grades: accept the place and enjoy the gap year
		• Insufficient grades: implement Plan B

Plan B

Upper sixth	Late August	Phone universities to see if they will still offer a place. Be prepared to stay on the phone for a week. Clearing has been going on since mid-July
		If yes, take the place offered and proceed with original gap year plans
		If no, reapply the next year for alternative courses and proceed with original plans
		Find a college to study for resits and proceed as below
	15 September	Closing date for Clearing
Gap year	September to May	Study for resits and spend spare time working, doing voluntary work, taking a skills course, etc
	September to December	Reapply to universities via UCAS (presumably no deferred entry this time)
	January to March	Receive offers
	May/June	Resit examinations
	June to September	Free time for travelling, work, etc
	August	Results day (again)
First year	September or October	Freshers' week at university

FUNDRAISING

For many gap year students, a shortage of money is the main obstacle. The most straightforward way of gathering together some cash for travels is to work locally and save like mad. Many gappers find that their parents are more willing to help them financially if they want to pursue a worthwhile ambition such as spending a month in Spain to learn the language or joining a voluntary scheme in the developing world. Of course many 18-year-olds baulk at the idea of accepting hand-outs from parents. **Becky Warden-Brown** made a deal with her parents that they would match whatever she earned. Another possible compromise is the one arrived at by **Alice Mundy**, whose ski instructor course in Canada cost a cool £6,000 before insurance or spending money. To finance her gap year she worked for around seven months over the year but the majority was covered by a loan from her parents which she will pay back once she is earning enough (possibly as a snowboard instructor in her vacations). Funding a trip or a project yourself will impress future employers more than taking a hand-out, and will also cause less envy if you happen to be travelling with a friend who has not been given money by his or her parents.

As we have seen, many of the most attractive gap year schemes are expensive (£3,000+), so fundraising becomes a major issue for those sixth-formers and others who have decided on this kind of gap year. Others who simply want to travel will also have to save a substantial sum that should include a contingency fund as well as the minimum for airfares and living expenses.

Jo Beker found it rewarding to raise the funds herself for her BSES expedition to Amazonia:

The fact that you have to fundraise for this expedition yourself makes the whole experience way more exciting! You know that you're going on this brilliant adventure because you found the money and you paid for it yourself and somehow that makes it feel more worthwhile! Having said that, the fundraising is not easy. We each had to raise just over £3,000 which is pretty daunting. I organised a range of events at school in order to help me fundraise including a second-hand book sale and stalls at a Christmas bazaar. On top of that I was sponsored to run the Brussels half-marathon, which not only was a great way to raise money but it also helped me to make sure that I was physically fit for the expedition. I also found that because BSES is very highly regarded, many organisations were willing to donate and be supportive. As BSES aims to promote equal opportunities for all, there is a mentoring and bursary scheme that Young Explorers can apply for.

Anyone undertaking a marathon, cycle ride or any sponsored event for a charitable purpose might want to register with JustGiving.com, one of the easiest ways for your supporters to donate money online. Also consider setting up a Facebook group and urging your 542 Facebook friends to support you.

Sometimes there isn't enough lead-up time for this, in which case you might follow a few tips from **Jonny Stephens**. Although the Chair of Governors at his school had warned him that it was going to be very difficult to raise £2,000+ in three months for a medical project in Ghana, Jonny and his friend **Rachael** were undaunted. They enlisted the readers of their local newspaper *The Cornish & Devon Post* and set about carrying out fundraising activities, culminating in a memorable wine and wisdom evening and auction at Bude Rugby Club just before they set off, which raised over £1,600, thanks to support from friends, families and local businesses.

Once you have resolved to meet a particular target, it is surprising how single-mindedly you can pursue it. Most sending agencies provide extensive advice and support on fundraising, and a lot of useful tips and tricks can be found on the web: www.gapyear.com/fundraising carries plenty of information and links to real-life examples. For example, **Tori Oram** from Kent, who was 'binge-saving' to join a wildlife project in South Africa, got sponsored to sit in a bath of (donated) cat food for an hour on the forecourt of a petrol station and raised £1,200 in an hour. Other non-squeamish fundraisers have undertaken to eat maggots and slugs in exchange for sponsorship money. A surprising number have made a sizeable profit by selling unwanted items on eBay.

If you have signed up for an organised placement, you will probably have been sent a timetable for paying the placement fee in instalments. Estimate how long it will take you to reach your target and stick to the deadline come what may. It might help to break the saving down into smaller amounts, so that you aim to save £X per week. Dedicated savers consider a 70-hour week at a local job quite tolerable (which will have the additional advantage of leaving you too tired to conduct an expensive social life). Bear in mind that saving over a long period, especially from a job which doesn't pay well, can be depressing since you will have to deny yourself all those expensive little treats. **Kitty Hill** is just one of the many gap year students who spent six months working 60-hour weeks, and the valuable thing she learned from that experience was that '*it is a million times nicer to be in a job you enjoy than a job you hate but pays a bit better*'.

LETTER WRITING

Some year out organisations provide a template for a letter seeking sponsorship and a list of suggested trusts to try. It helps to include a photo and make the letter succinct. Although time-consuming, handwritten letters are thought to attract more attention than slick computer-generated ones. The more obvious care you have taken, the better your chances of success so, for example, you should try to find out the name and job title of the person to whom your request will be referred, and enclose a letter of endorsement from your head teacher. Be aware, however, that a great many businesses and charities have a policy of not funding individuals.

MY GAP YEAR:
CLARE COOPER

In writing a report about her very successful post-university gap year in Ghana, Clare Cooper describes the trepidation she felt at the prospect of raising the necessary funds to join an AfricaTrust Networks team.

I accepted the offer (against the better judgement of some friends and family) and, armed with positivity, I began the mammoth task of raising £2,500. Already working as a care assistant to cover living costs, I took on two extra jobs in a bar and cinema to begin saving. I wrote literally hundreds of letters to local shops, businesses, schools, charities, and churches explaining what I was doing and appealing for sponsorship. To raise awareness of my fundraising, the local newspaper ran a story on me explaining that I would be working with orphans in West Africa and any help with my fundraising would be much appreciated. I followed up this article by visiting local businesses in person asking them if they had received my letter and if not could I leave them another one. I found that using the local paper and visiting people in person was really effective.

Still a fair distance from my financial target, I had exactly six weeks left to raise the money or I couldn't go. As I worked in a cinema in a thriving local arts centre I decided to organise a fundraising art exhibition. After a couple of weeks of manic organisation and with the invaluable help of friends, family, and local artists, we held an exhibition of local arts, craft, and textiles. The day was a real success, with lots of visitors and many of the artists selling work. With less than a month to go, I was closer to my financial target, but still not there, and running out of time and ideas. With the priceless help and support from the managers, staff and locals in the bar I worked in, we organised an African-themed fundraising day. We had a barbecue, bring-and-buy stall, face painting, children's games, arts and crafts, and a traditional story telling, followed by an evening of music from a number of local bands, a raffle with great prizes provided by local shops, restaurants, and businesses, and a fantastic African fire sculpture and fireworks display. As well as raising the rest of the money, the night was a great way of saying thank you and goodbye to all my friends and people who had been fundamental to my fundraising.

Target organisations, companies, schools and clubs with which you or your family have links, or which might have some connection with your project. The skills you gain in fundraising are themselves impressive when they appear on a CV. Local businesses are usually inundated with requests for donations and raffle prizes and are unlikely to give cash but some might donate some useful items of equipment. Keep track of all the individuals and businesses that have contributed and be sure to send them a thank you note mentioning your fundraising target and progress and then another letter describing the success of your gap year venture.

If you want to go down the route of applying to trusts and charitable bodies, consult a library copy of the *Directory of Grant Making Trusts* (new edition published each April) or contact the Association of Charitable Foundations (www.acf.org.uk), which can offer advice on how to approach grant-giving trusts. Also check the National Charities Database on www.charitiesdirect.com. Local service clubs such as Rotary, Lions Club and Round Table, comprising business people, might be willing to consider a well-presented application for support, especially if you offer to give a presentation on your return.

If your gap year is being organised by a registered charity, always include the charity reference number in your letter of request since this may be needed by the organisation's accounts department. In fact, the policy of a great many grant bodies is not to support individuals and so you may meet mostly with rejections. (One enterprising fundraiser, though, got his friends and family to sponsor him for every rejection.) A potential alternative source of benefactors can be found not in the library or on the internet but in your parents' address book. **Kitty Hill** hit upon a more painless way to raise money than her 60-hour-a-week job:

For sponsorship I wrote to everyone on my parents' Christmas card list asking them to sponsor me for a day of my trip, at about £30 a day. Then I promised to send them a postcard on that day. I raised about £2,500 with this method.

Impressive world traveller **Tom Grundy** has one further recommendation; he suggests writing to millionaires, particularly recent lottery winners.

FUNDRAISING IDEAS

The ingenuity which sixth-formers have demonstrated in organising money-making events is impressive. If you happen to recall ideas that worked for Comic Relief, think of ways of adapting these. For example, one fundraiser got everybody he knew to sponsor him to stay up a tree for a week. You may choose to shave your head, jump out of an aeroplane, organise a fancy dress pub crawl or a thousand other ways to raise money. Try to organise events that will be fun as well as expensive for your well-wishers. For example if you organise a fundraising quiz in your local pub, give away a few prizes such as glitter nail polish. If you have been sponsored to do a bungee jump or swim a mile, hand out sweets when you go round to collect the pledges. If you are seeking sponsorship from businesses, think of ways in which they might benefit – you could, for instance, promise to wear the company T-shirt in a publicity photo on the top of Kilimanjaro or down the Amazon. Other ideas include holding a sweepstake on a big sporting event, hosting a garden fête with stalls and raffles, charging admission to a ceilidh or a salsa evening. One gap-year student who went to Mexico organised a huge fashion show which cost £5,000 to put on but raised a massive £11,000.

Publicise your plans and your need for funds wherever you can. Local papers and radio stations may be willing to carry details of your planned expedition, which may prompt a few local readers or listeners to support you. Try to make a specific request such as the following, which **Ollie Perkins** had published in the free *Cambridge Weekly News* with his email and street addresses included:

Ollie is off to South Africa to work with orphans and young offenders. He is asking for donations of old recorders and piano music because he wants to teach music when he goes off with the Africa Inland Mission for six months (City Mission in Cape Town). He is a keen jazz pianist and ex-King's chorister, and wants to help with the church choir.

Ask family and friends to give cash to your fundraising effort instead of birthday and Christmas presents. Consider possibilities for organising a fundraising event such as a concert or a barn dance, a quiz night, wine tasting, or an auction of promises. (If your mum or dad was ever on the PTA, ask them for advice but don't expect them to run your campaign for you.)

SOURCES OF FUNDING

Very few programmes can be joined free of charge. European Voluntary Service (see entry in the 'Directory of Specialist Gap Year Programmes') provides full funding for a six- to 12-month stint as a volunteer on socially beneficial projects in Europe and beyond. In 2011, the British government introduced a new funded programme called International Citizen Service (see directory entry) whereby up to 1,250 Britons aged 18–22 will be given the chance to spend up to three months working in the developing world; a financial contribution will be expected of volunteers on a means-tested basis (£0 to £2,000). The government-funded companion scheme, National Citizen Service, is open only to Year 11 students. The aim here is for young people from different social backgrounds to mix with each other in outdoor activities and volunteering in the UK.

Otherwise you will have to earn, scrounge or fundraise. Most gap year companies are commercial and charge accordingly. A few agencies and organisations offer bursaries or scholarships such as Lattitude Global Volunteering, a registered charity, and the Royal Geographical Society which offers a £4,000 scholarship to geography students who would not otherwise be able to have a gap year (details in the sections on Expeditions).

Some schools (not exclusively fee-paying schools) have odd bursaries and travel scholarships which the careers teachers will be able to tell you about: various scholarships and grants are available to those who fulfil the necessary requirements. To take just a couple of examples: the Caley Gap Scholarship of up to £1,000 is offered by the Royal Caledonian Schools Trust (http://rcst.org.uk) to the children of past or current Scottish servicemen and women, or people with a Scottish parent living in Greater London on a low income. Applicants must submit a proposal for a worthwhile project abroad which will be of at least six months' duration.

The Peter Kirk Memorial Scholarship (www.kirkfund.org.uk) funds 10–12 young people aged 18–26 to investigate and write about some aspect of modern Europe. Awards of up to £1,500 are made to those carrying out research over 6–12 weeks. The deadline for applications is early in November, with interviews in London in December. Among the school and university leavers awarded £1,500 for 2011, one 18-year-old from Richmond planned to investigate the meaning of being French in Sarkozy's France.

The Winston Churchill Memorial Trust (www.wcmt.org.uk) awards about 100 four- to 12-week travelling fellowships to UK citizens of any age or background who wish to undertake a specific project or study related to their personal interests, job, or community. The deadline for applications falls in October. Past winners are listed on the website with their topic of study; most are older than school/college leaving age.

Sixth-formers at one of the 240 independent boys' and co-ed schools that belong to the Headmasters' and Headmistresses' Conference (HMC) may apply for one of the 30 annual Bulkeley-Evans gap year scholarships worth between £300 and £500, with a couple worth up to £1,000, for those with financial need. Full details of eligibility can be found on the website www.gapyear-bulkeley-evans-hmc.co.uk or can be requested from the Administrator (tonybeadles@me.com). Applications should be in by the beginning of May.

The London livery companies can be worth investigating. For example the Worshipful Company of Cutlers offers at least three Captain F G Boot scholarships per year, valued at £500–£1,000 depending on the financial need of the successful students. Applicants must be aged 17–25 and planning to spend at least six consecutive months in a foreign country to increase their understanding of the language and culture of that country. The closing date for applications is 12 June; details from the Clerk to the Cutlers' Company (www.cutlerslondon.co.uk/bootinfo.pdf).

The Royal Society for Asian Affairs (www.rsaa.org.uk) invites potential gappers (aged 18–25) planning to go to Asia to apply for a Peter Holmes Memorial Award towards a project of purposeful travel. Applications for the £1,000 award should be made by 31 October; email sec@rsaa.org.uk for more information.

The Allan and Nesta Ferguson Charitable Trust dispenses as many as 165 gap year grants of £300 to gap year students planning a structured and worthwhile placement (www.fergusontrust.co.uk).

Members of the Globetrotters Club could be eligible for one of their Independent Travel Awards (http://globetrotters.co.uk/independent-travel-award.html). These go to club members of any age planning 'the most adventurous, unusual or enterprising foreign, solo, strictly independent trip'.

INSURANCE

Any student heading abroad should have travel insurance. Within Europe, private insurance is not absolutely essential because European nationals are eligible for reciprocal emergency healthcare in the European Economic Area (EEA). The European Health Insurance Card (EHIC) entitles EU nationals to emergency healthcare in any member state.

Outside Europe, a solid travel insurance policy is essential. Research carried out by the Foreign and Commonwealth Office (FCO) revealed that more than a quarter of young travellers aged 16–34 do not purchase travel insurance, which means that about three million people are taking a serious risk. Most students and backpackers shop around to find the cheapest policy. But if you are going outside the developed world or considering doing any kind of adventure sport, give some thought to what the policy covers; for example, look closely at whether the policy will repatriate you or fly one of your parents out to you in an emergency. Check the exclusions carefully and the amount of excess you'll have to pay if you claim.

In situations where you might be two days from civilisation, it is imperative that you (or your sending agency) have watertight insurance. During **Tom Watkins**' expedition with BSES, one of the members of the expedition had a fit. He was picked up by helicopter in less than half an hour (and was subsequently fine). At that point, Tom was very glad that his expedition organisers had the best policy that money could buy, even though he had earlier felt disappointed that he had not been allowed to go rock-climbing for insurance reasons.

Most insurance companies offer a standard rate that covers medical emergencies and a premium rate that in addition covers personal baggage, cancellation, etc. Always read the fine print. Sometimes activities like bungee jumping or scuba diving (now quite commonplace in parts of the world) are excluded. Some travel policies list as one of their exclusions 'any claims which arise while the Insured is engaged in any manual employment'. If you are not planning to visit North America, the premiums will be significantly less expensive. Most insurance companies operate 24-hour helplines in the UK, which can be dialled from anywhere in the world. Quite a few of the gap year expedition and volunteer agencies offer bespoke policies drawn up by the long-established brokers Campbell Irvine (www.campbellirvine.com), which are not the cheapest but provide automatic cover for many extras.

Some basic companies to consider are listed here with an estimate of their premiums for 12 months of worldwide cover (including the USA). Expect to pay roughly £25 per month for basic cover and £30–£40 for more extensive cover.

MIND THE GAP YEAR

Not the most fun part of planning a long trip away, but one of the most necessary nonetheless. Insurance is something you purchase 'just in case', and some see this as a reason not to bother; 'I am invincible', 'nothing will happen to me, I am very careful', 'I have always been lucky'! The problem is you can be the most careful of travellers but accidents still happen. And if these accidents happen in a distant country, with insufficient medical resources, costs can rise quickly. There was a case recently where a traveller was in a coma and due to his lack of correct travel insurance, his family and friends had to raise £20,000 to repatriate him back to the UK.

Sorry for the grim beginning to this article, but the point must be made: insurance is very important. Now on to what to look out for when purchasing your insurance.

Emergency Medical Expenses – Most gap year travel insurance covers emergency medical expenses, getting home (repatriation) and ambulance costs. The Foreign and Commonwealth Office (FCO) cannot help you with the costs of medical repatriation.

Pre-existing Medical Conditions – Don't be frightened to tell the insurance company. Most of the time they will agree to cover the condition, sometimes they may ask for extra premium, but at least you know you're covered. If you don't tell them, any claim relating to that condition may not be paid, or in some cases even an unrelated claim may not be paid and the policy voided.

Cancellation – If you can't go on your trip at the last minute because you are sick or injured, insurance will pay for your flight and any other costs that you may not get back from the tour organiser etc. If your trip costs more than the insurance provides, ask the insurer if the sum insured can be extended. If not, look around.

Travel Provider Failure and FCO Warning – If your airline goes bust or the FCO has recommended not to travel to the destination you have booked, some travel insurance policies will cover these cancellations, but many won't. Check that the policy you buy does – this is very important in the current climate.

Personal Liability – What happens if you swing round and accidentally knock someone into the road, they are hit by a passing car and badly injured? You can be sued. Travel insurance will pay for the amount they sue for (if successful) and legal costs. Get a policy that does not exclude you accidentally injuring a travelling companion (it can happen, and many policies exclude this), and which also covers trip accommodation and volunteering.

Working or Volunteering on Your Travels – If you're injured at work, people seem to think the employer will pay. They won't, unless it was their fault. You will have to prove this, which can take years. Make sure the policy covers working/volunteering, and watch the small print, as some policies will cover working but not if being paid and some will only cover certain types of work.

Sports and Activities – Most gap year and backpacker insurance policies have a lengthy list of sports and activities; the problem is second guessing what you're going to do. Many insurers group activities, and if that is the case pick the highest grouping that you think you might do, or choose a gap year policy that covers all unplanned (not booked before leaving home) sports and activities.

Kit: All Your Stuff – Some of the cheaper policies do not cover your personal belongings/effects, which is fine if that's what you choose. If you're not taking much with you and the value is low that's probably a good choice. Take a look at everything you're taking with you and check that the policy you buy covers them (if you want them covered). Be aware that many policies won't cover iPods, cameras, laptops, etc.

When to Buy – You can buy travel insurance any time before you leave, but it is more beneficial to buy insurance when you book your travels, so that you're covered if you have to cancel.

If travelling in the EEA, make sure you have an EHIC (as well as travel insurance), as this could provide limited free medical treatment if hospitalised, but it will not provide repatriation or other areas of cover that travel insurance offers.

Ace Travel Insurance (www.acetravellerinsurance.com). Strapline on website: 'For backpackers, gap years, work and study abroad'. Gap year policy for people up to age 44. Budget cover for 12 months £169; standard cover £208.

Austravel (0870 166 2020; www.austravel.com/travel-info/insurance). Specialist in travel to Australia and New Zealand sells a range of competitively priced insurance policies for budget travellers, eg £130 for three months' cover per adult. Cover for adventure sports is available too.

Club Direct, West Sussex (0800 083 2466; www.clubdirect.com). Work abroad is included, provided it does not involve using heavy machinery.

Columbus Direct (0870 033 9988; www.columbusdirect.com). One of the giants in the field of travel insurance. From £220 for 12 months' worldwide cover.

Direct Travel Insurance (0845 605 2700; www.direct-travel.co.uk). Consistently among the cheapest, eg 12 months' worldwide minimal cover starting at £144.

Downunder Worldwide Travel Insurance, London W2 (0800 393 908; www.duinsure.com). Can be extended while you're on the road. 12 months' cover costs £193, £234, or £279.

Endsleigh Insurance (0800 028 3571; www.endsleigh.co.uk). 12 months of gap year insurance covering work abroad, volunteering and adventure activities costs £284 (essential cover only), and £312 for comprehensive cover.

FYI (+353 1 874 8458; www.fyi.ie). Irish backpacker specialist insurer which sells policies in sterling as well to clients under 35. Price for 12 months is £218, plus £8 for excess waiver.

gosure.com (0845 222 0020; www.gosure.com).

Mind the Gap Year (0845 180 0060; www.mindthegapyear.com). Specialists in gap year and travel insurance. Providing great cover for working and volunteering and including free online planning services. Worldwide (excl. USA, Canada & Caribbean) standard cover starts at £55.95 for one month through to £329.00 for 12 months – longer periods available.

MRL Insurance, Surrey (0845 676 0691; www.mrlinsurance.co.uk).

Navigator Travel Insurance Services, Manchester (0161 973 6435; www.navigatortravel. co.uk).

HEALTH AND SAFETY

RISKS

Anyone with a vivid imagination will be able to think of many things that might go wrong with a gap year. Several young women and men who have been on gap year projects have had fatal accidents or, worst of all, as in the 2011 case of the British tennis coach and his friend from university, have been murdered. A much less remote possibility is being mugged, losing your passport, or having your backpack stolen. You may get sick or lonely or fed up. You may make a fool of yourself by allowing yourself to be tricked by a con artist who sells you some fake gems or rips you off in a currency transaction. You may feel desperately homesick and long for a situation in which you do not have to behave like an adult when you have only had an adolescent's experiences.

While some identify the initial decision to go abroad as the hardest part, others find the inevitable troughs more difficult to cope with, such as finding yourself alone in a cheap hotel room on your birthday, running out of money faster than anticipated, or getting travellers' diarrhoea. But if travelling requires a much greater investment of energy than staying at home, it will reward the effort many times over.

Friends and family are seldom reluctant to offer advice, and normally the perceived risks are far greater than the actual ones. When **Cathleen Graham** from Canada announced that she was bound for rural South Africa with a sports-coaching charity, many came forward to express grave concerns for her safety as a young woman:

> *People's reactions to my choice of destination were determined by what they saw portrayed about South Africa in the media. Of course, people who knew me best knew this was an opportunity that suited me. You really need to develop a strong filter for listening to people's opinions before you go: are they sound and balanced, or more reflecting the person's own fears and anxieties if they were the one going?*

Some gap year travellers undergo a process of disillusionment, which is not a bad thing in itself since no-one wants to live in a world of illusions. You harbour a desire to see some famous monument and find it surrounded by touts or chintzy boutiques. The reality of seeing the Taj Mahal or walking down the Gorge of Samaria in Crete or meeting an Amazonian Indian may be less romantic than you had imagined. (See Alain de Botton's elegant *The Art of Travel* for an in-depth study of the conflict between dreams of travel and the reality.)

In rare cases, gappers can be traumatised by what they experience in a year out. According to the senior tutor of a Cambridge college who regularly meets students before and after their gap year, most come back having changed a great deal since they accepted a university place, compared with the students who have not deferred for a year. Some benefit enormously, but not all. He recalls one in particular who had gone to work in a Romanian orphanage with young children with AIDS. She came back so traumatised that she suffered from nightmares for a long time afterwards. But usually the changes are not so dire.

Several short courses specialise in preparing young people for potential danger and unpredictable situations abroad; see entries in the 'Gap Year Safety and Preparation'.

DOs AND DON'Ts FOR YOUR GAP YEAR

According to Anthony Lunch, Chief Executive at MondoChallenge Foundation, the following practical considerations will help to ensure a smooth and rewarding gap year.

Plan early

■ *Look at the advice concerning personal safety given by the FCO (www.fco.gov.uk).*

■ *Be aware of the laws, customs and dress code for the country. Guidebooks should provide all this information.*

■ *Online banking is a great way to manage your finances while you are away. But many internet cafés are slow and access may not always be easy or secure, so don't leave important transactions until the last minute.*

■ *Calculate how much money you will need for your trip and make sure you have some extra. Find out if you can use a credit or debit card to withdraw money at your destination.*

■ *Visit your doctor for advice on vaccinations and medication needed.*

■ *Contact the relevant embassy or consulate for advice on obtaining a visa. Many have online forms and often visas can be obtained on arrival although having one in your passport ahead of time can be comforting. Make sure your passport has enough blank pages, or get a new one well before you leave.*

■ *Shop around for travel insurance and make sure you are covered for everything you intend to do, eg trekking.*

■ *Make sure your family or friends at home are aware of your travel itinerary.*

■ *If you are volunteering through an organisation, ask for the contact details of the most recent volunteers on your project. They will be able to give you advice about the project.*

On arrival

■ *Register your details and itinerary on the FCO's LOCATE service (www.fco.gov.uk/locate) in countries where embassy officials may need to track you down in the event of an emergency.*

■ *Keep photocopies of important documents (passport, insurance info, plane tickets) in separate bags from the original copies or send scanned images to your email account for ready access.*

■ *Take advice from your local manager about your personal safety and your belongings.*

■ *If you are staying in one country for more than several weeks, consider getting a cheap local mobile phone or a local sim card for your UK mobile. Local texts and calls tend to be cheaper and incoming calls from abroad are free, which avoids the massive charges when using your UK mobile.*

TRAVEL WARNINGS

Travel inevitably involves balancing risks and navigating through hazards real or imagined. The FCO runs a regular and updated service; you can ring the Travel Advice Unit on 0845 850 2829 (£0.04 per minute via BT) or check their website (www.fco.gov.uk/travel), which gives frequently updated and detailed risk assessments about any trouble spots, including civil unrest, terrorism, and crime.

Some believe that the FCO's travel warnings err on the side of caution to the detriment of NGOs struggling to attract volunteers, so try to balance the official warnings with a first-hand account from someone who lives in the place you are considering. The director of the charity Sudan Volunteers Programme describes what he sees as the FCO's bias:

We continue to be dogged by the negative and, I believe, misleadingly indiscriminate travel advice issued by the FCO, which puts off potential volunteers, or more particularly their families. It stems, it seems to me, from the alarming experiences of embassy staff which induces them to put up ever higher fences to guard their premises and of course this siege mentality brings about an ever greater ignorance of the actual conditions. There was one threat to embassy security about two years ago and an American official was murdered in Khartoum in January 2008. There were otherwise no attacks on foreigners in recent years in Khartoum or smaller northern towns. I do not belittle these outrages, but they cannot be described as 'indiscriminate' as they were in the FCO warning.

Several years ago, the FCO launched a 'Know Before You Go' campaign to raise awareness among backpackers and independent travellers of potential risks and dangers and how to guard against them, principally by taking out a watertight insurance policy. The same emphasis can be detected on the FCO website www.gogapyear.com. However, no insurance policy can help you if you are caught breaking the law, as happened to two British law graduates in 2009 who were arrested in Brazil for attempting insurance fraud, admitted their guilt, and were sentenced to 16 months' community service. It might seem an easy wheeze to pretend that you've been robbed in order to claim on your insurance policy, but it is risky as well as immoral.

BRITISH CONSUL HELP

A British Consul can:

■ *issue an emergency passport; contact relatives and friends to ask them for help with money or tickets; tell you how to transfer money; cash a sterling cheque worth up to £100 if supported by a valid banker's card; as a last resort, give you a loan to return to the UK; put you in touch with local lawyers, interpreters, or doctors; arrange for next of kin to be told of an accident or death; visit you in case of arrest or imprisonment, and arrange for a message to be sent to relatives or friends; give guidance on organisations that can help trace missing persons; speak to the local authorities for you.*

A British Consul cannot:

■ *intervene in court cases; get you out of prison; give legal advice or start court proceedings for you; obtain better treatment in hospital or prison than is given to local nationals; investigate a crime; pay your hotel, legal, medical, or any other bills; pay your travel costs, except in rare circumstances; perform work normally done by travel agents, airlines, banks, or motoring organisations; find you somewhere to live, a job, or a work permit; formally help you if you are a dual national in the country of your second nationality.*

The hard truth is that nothing can guarantee immunity from random accidents, whether tsunamis, landslides, or motor accidents. Almost every year, at least one gap year traveller dies, filling the hearts of parents everywhere with dread. In a couple of cases, the parents involved in tragedies have been prompted to become involved with promoting gap year safety. For example, the parents of Caroline Stuttle, the British backpacker who was pushed off a bridge to her death in Queensland by a drug addict, have set up Caroline's Rainbow Foundation. This charity works to raise awareness of the importance of safe travel to young people, by means of its website (www.carolinesrainbowfoundation. org), podcasts, and travel stories with travel tips. Similarly, Ian French, whose daughter Georgia died in a bus crash just two weeks into her gap year adventure in Peru, founded GapAid (www.gapaid. com), a charity to promote safer travel for young people. They endorse Mind the Gap Year Insurance (listed above).

MY GAP YEAR: EMILY LOGIE

When writing at the end of a very successful gap year, which took her to an animal project in South Africa and travelling in South America, Emily Logie reflected on how a family tragedy had affected her time out.

Walking my dog this morning, I passed the spot by the roadside where I stood when my parents told me that my sister had been killed in a bus crash on her own gap year travels in Ecuador back in April 2008. Having spent much of the last year travelling myself, this was the first time I had visited this spot again and I found myself welling up with emotion. No-one can ever know how they will react to such news but all I remember was doubling over with searing pain in my stomach and fighting the urge to run away.

Just over a year later, I have returned from my own gap year, visiting Southern Africa (South Africa and Botswana), South America (Ecuador and Galápagos Islands), and Northern Africa. I had always planned to take a gap year as both my parents had enjoyed travelling and working abroad during years out before and after university. Going on to study a degree in veterinary medicine I have always been keen to gain work experience and work with animals. I have to admit that some people were more than shocked that I was going ahead with my gap year plans after my sister's accident, but my parents had made numerous statements to the press stating that others shouldn't be put off, and I only wanted to strengthen that by going ahead. I was more than happy to do this publicly and was interviewed for various newspapers as well as appearing on radio and television. I felt that keeping a low profile wasn't going to help anyone, especially myself, and I had huge amounts of support from friends and family.

At Easter, I was in Ecuador with my parents and the families of the other four girls killed in the same bus accident. Again, we had a lot of media attention and made it clear that other young people shouldn't let this put them off travelling. I have just enjoyed the best six months of my life and couldn't talk more enthusiastically about my travels. My gap year has been a rollercoaster of emotions and experiences. I have loved and hated it, cried, laughed, and enjoyed some of the most memorable days of my life!

The father of Becci Logie has bravely said in public that he hopes the tragedy would not stop other young people travelling and following their dreams, which is exactly what his other daughter has done.

REASSURANCE FOR PARENTS

The departure of a child from the family home is traumatic enough when they're merely going to university, but is much more frightening if he or she is travelling to the ends of the earth on a year out adventure. When you were 18, you probably hadn't even heard of, let alone considered visiting, some of the destinations that gap travellers now visit, from Vientiane to Antananarivo, Patagonia to Sulawesi. The relative cheapness of long-distance flights, the range of gap year providers offering remote destinations, and the raised expectations of the new generation account for these heightened travel ambitions. How you as a parent react will have a lot to do with what you did when you were 18. The parents who motorcycled through Afghanistan to India or hitch-hiked round Greece with no money may be more sympathetic than the ones who carried straight through from school to university or a job.

The parental imagination is bound to dwell on the possible disasters (and the actual ones such as the Queensland hostel fire a few years ago). Feelings of helplessness when a child is far away fuel these anxieties. But a calm assessment of the risks will result in a startling realisation – that staying at home is just as risky. Clubbing in a city centre or driving on a British road pose risks, too, though parents don't tend to focus on those. According to an article in The Times *headed 'Gap year away safer than rock festival at home', research published in the* Journal of the Royal Society of Medicine *showed that taking part in a structured expedition brought with it a lower risk of death or injury than attending a music festival in Britain or going to a scout camp.*

As the number of young people taking gap years abroad increases, it is inevitable that more accidents will occur. The raised profile of young people travelling abroad on their gap year means that these accidents tend to be widely reported. So if a young man slips down a waterfall in Costa Rica or a bus veers off the road on an Ecuadorian mountain pass, the world hears about it. By the same token, some reported tragedies take place in Britain, as in the case of a young woman working at a Plymouth supermarket in her gap year who was murdered by the store manager. But mostly, if an 18-year-old dies of a drug overdose or is killed on his bicycle in his home town, this is not reported nationally.

It is arguable that children nowadays are over-protected, and should be given more not less freedom so that from an early age they learn to be streetwise and how to negotiate dangers outside the home. Some say that adventures are now too easy. Young people are lulled into a false sense of security by the number of people doing likewise. A trek round Annapurna can be arranged in an instant, but that does not mean that a blizzard won't reduce visibility to zero inside 20 minutes.

A parent will want to take every reasonable precaution on his or her child's behalf, knowing that all 18-year-olds believe themselves immortal. They should check with the Foreign and Commonwealth Office on world trouble spots (www.www.fco.gov.uk/travel). They should consider giving their son or daughter a gold-plated travel insurance policy as a birthday present, or urge their child not to skimp on insurance. Investigate global roaming sim cards and think about treating your child to one. Try not to be too prescriptive about how often your son or daughter contacts you because if they are out of contact for some reason you will worry unnecessarily. A few causes of tragedy are avoidable, such as in the case of a girl who died of heat stroke and dehydration on an expedition in Borneo. Urging your child to take sensible precautions such as dressing modestly in countries where it is expected, not flaunting valuables, or not falling prey to smooth-tongued con artists, may have some beneficial effect. Those who can't rein in their anxiety might investigate enrolling their progeny on a gap year preparation course (see entries for Objective Gap Safety, Safetrek and Ultimate Gap Year in the Directory of Courses), although any parents considering investing in one of these courses might wonder how useful they are. Most of what they try to impart is basic common

> *sense, which is something that can be in short supply at 18. One of the companies describes a case in which their training came in handy: 'One of our ex-students was on a bus in Ecuador that was held up. Although he had everything he owned taken, he was fine – having been taught that nothing is worth risking your life for. Thanks to the fact that he had taken scans of his passport and all other relevant documentation, which he had emailed to himself, he got a new passport in a record-breaking 2 days.'*
>
> *Really, the hard truth is that it is time to let go. Try to give your child lots of credit for their initiative, enterprise, and courage, and remind yourself daily that they are now grown up. It is amazing how anxieties vanish once your child has actually left home. As the mother of a son who went to Togo for part of his gap year put it: 'It's curious how my high anxiety lasted for about 24 hours after I waved him off. Since then it's been pretty much uninterrupted envy and bile.'*

An innovative company, Tripbod (www.tripbod.com), formerly called Your Safe Planet, provides intro-ductions to trusted locals in your destination who will share their inside travel knowledge and who may also have links to local community-run volunteering projects that are free to join, if that is what you or your child are after. The costs will rise the longer the trip, eg from £50 for a week to £350 for six months.

Supporting your offspring can be hard work, especially for the 'helicopter parent' who likes to hover.

A Canadian mother describes the key role she played when her daughter (aged 17 and a half) was in the planning stages of a gap year placement at a school for the deaf in south India:

> *One of the recent low points was when I was waiting for my daughter and her friend to show up at the travel agent and they came in (late) asking whether they should put money in the parking meter! I tried to remain calm while I suggested they read the instructions and then make an executive decision. I try not to think about all the practical skills they will have to acquire very quickly when they are off on their own. I have got her a fantastic (cheap and very flexible) flight from Halifax to India at the end of August and back from Kuala Lumpur to Toronto at the end of April. I have confirmed all her insurance coverage. I have acquired signing authority on her bank account, I have photocopied all the relevant documents, and I have supplied her with an extra card on my Visa account. She has managed to do much less, although she is spending a fair bit of time making CDs for her friends and dreaming about what she will do next summer.*

HEALTH PRECAUTIONS

No matter what country you are heading for, you should obtain the Department of Health leaflet T7.1 *Health Advice for Travellers*. This leaflet should be available from major post offices or any doctor's surgery. Alternatively, you can request a free copy on the Health Literature Line 0300 123 1002 or read it online at www.dh.gov.uk, which also has country-by-country details. Increasingly, people are carrying out their own health research on the internet; check for example at www.fitfortravel.scot.nhs.uk and www.travelhealth.co.uk. The website of the World Health Organization (www.who.int/ith) has some information including a listing of the very few countries in which certain vaccinations are a requirement of entry. The BBC's travel healthcare website (www.bbc.co.uk/health/travel) is a solid source of information ranging from tummy trouble to water quality and snake bites.

Be prepared to pay for the necessary inoculations which are not normally covered by the NHS. Your own GP surgery should be able to give you good advice and the injections may be considerably cheaper than at a private specialist clinic. To give an example of how high the costs can be, check the price list on the MASTA website (see next paragraph), where immunisations against hepatitis A with typhoid cost £84, Japanese encephalitis £52, cholera £60, and so on.

A company that has become one of the most authoritative sources of travellers' health information in Britain is MASTA (www.masta-travel-health.com). It maintains a database of the latest information on the disease situation for all countries and the latest recommendations on the prevention of tropical and other diseases. This advice is provided via a personalised health brief based on your destinations and the nature of your trip, which is emailed to you from their website for a charge of £3.99. Along with vaccination recommendations, it also provides practical advice such as protection against malaria, information on disease outbreaks, and other non-vaccine-preventable health risks for travellers. MASTA's network of travel clinics administers inoculations and sells medical kits and other specialist equipment such as water purifiers, mosquito nets, and repellents. Note that arguably the advice errs on the side of caution (which means they also make more profit). Private specialist clinics abound in London, but are thin on the ground elsewhere. A worldwide searchable listing of specialist travel clinics is maintained by the International Society of Travel Medicine (www.istm.org), although many countries are not included.

The Hospital for Tropical Diseases in central London (Mortimer Market Building, Capper Street, Tottenham Court Road, WC1E 6AU) offers appointments at its Travel Clinic (020 7388 9600) and operates an automated Travellers Healthline Advisory Service (020 7950 7799; www.thehtd.org) which charges 50p a minute (average phone call lasts about seven minutes). Other travel clinics include Nomad Travel Clinics, which have several branches in London including in Victoria (020 7823 5823; www.nomadtravel.co.uk), and also in Bristol, Manchester, and Southampton. They offer walk-in appointments, though you may have to wait at busy times. The Royal Free Travel Health Centre at the Royal Free Hospital (Pond Street, London; 020 7830 2885; www. travelclinicroyalfree.com) is a well-regarded private clinic, and the Trailfinders Travel Clinic (194 Kensington High Street; 020 7983 3999; www.trailfinders.com) is long-established. Several online shops compete for travellers' custom, among them Travelpharm (0115 951 2092; www.travelpharm.com), which carries an extensive range of mosquito nets, anti-malaria drugs, water purification equipment, and travel accessories. The website carries lots of health information. Note that if you want to buy medications online you will have to send a prescription with your order; GPs normally make a charge for this service, eg £15. For advice on protecting your sexual health, Marie Stopes International (0845 300 8090; www.mariestopes.org.uk) is helpful. The government's publication (www.dh.gov.uk, search for 'drugs abroad') and the National Drugs Helpline (0800 776 600) can give information on drug laws abroad. For routine travellers' complaints, it is worth looking at a general guide to travel medicine such as *The Essential Guide to Travel Health: Don't Let Bugs, Bites and Bowels Spoil Your Trip* by Dr Jane Wilson-Howarth (Cadogan, 2009). Americans seeking general travel health advice should ring the Center for Disease Control & Prevention (CDC) Hotline in Atlanta (+1 877 394 8747; www.cdc.gov). CDC issues travel announcements for international travellers rated from mild to extreme, ie minimal risk to a recommendation that non-essential travel not take place.

Travel health books all emphasise the necessity of avoiding tap water in developing countries and can recommend ways to purify your drinking water by filtering, boiling or chemical additives: tablets of chlorine dioxide are now generally preferred to tincture of iodine, readily available from Boots or other chemists. Remember that ice cubes, however tempting, should be avoided. Drinking water can also be purified by filtering. MASTA and Nomad market various water purifiers; among the best are the 'Aquapure Traveller' (from £35) and the 'MSR Sweetwater Microfilter' for £70. Tap water throughout Western Europe is safe to drink.

MALARIA

Malaria is undoubtedly the greatest danger posed by visits to many tropical areas. The disease has been making a comeback in many parts of the world, due to the resistance of certain strains of mosquito to the pesticides and the preventive medications which have been extensively relied on in the past. Last year, 1,761 people returned to the UK with malaria, mainly from Nigeria and Ghana. Because of increasing resistance, it is important to consult a specialist service as mentioned above. Specialist websites such as www.malariahotspots.co.uk or www.hpa.org.uk/infections/topics_az/malaria/default.htm offer more details. You need to obtain the best information available to help you devise the most appropriate strategy for protection in the areas you intend to visit. Research indicates for example that the statistical chance of being bitten by a malarial mosquito in Thailand is once a year, but in Sierra Leone it rises to once a night. Start your research early since some courses of malaria prophylaxis need to be started up to three weeks before departure. It is always a good idea to find out in advance if there are any side effects you may suffer as well.

Falciparum malaria is potentially fatal. The two main prophylactic drugs are Doxycycline and Malarone (atovaquone), though Lariam is also in use. Doxycycline is a cheap antibiotic and antimalarial but some people suffer from side effects such as nausea on an empty stomach and increased skin-sensitivity to sunlight. One tablet must be taken daily from a week before entering a malarial zone until four weeks after leaving; tablets purchased online cost about 14 pence each. Malarone by contrast costs £2.25 per tablet so some people buy only a week's supply before arriving in their destination and then buy the drug at a local pharmacy where it will generally be much cheaper than in the UK. **Lisa Bass** spent a complete gap year in Madagascar and shared her thinking about how to protect yourself when malaria is so prevalent. She recommends Coartem (trade name for artemether lumefantrine).

Unfortunately, these prophylactic medications are not foolproof, and even those who have scrupulously swallowed their pills before and after their trip as well as during it have been known to contract the disease. For example, **Tom Grundy** habitually took his Lariam on a gap year placement in Uganda – enduring the discomfort of taking this powerful drug on an empty stomach and anxiety about possible side effects such as brain damage and depression – and also used repellent coil burners, impregnated mosquito nets, Doom room spray and repellent gel. And yet he still succumbed to the disease 10 months after getting back to Britain.

It is essential to take mechanical precautions against mosquitoes. If possible, screen the windows and sleep under a permethrin-impregnated mosquito net since the offending mosquitoes feed between dusk and dawn. (Practise putting your mosquito net up before leaving home since some are tricky to assemble.) Some travellers have improvised with netting intended for prams, which takes up virtually no luggage space. If you don't have a net, cover your limbs at nightfall with light-coloured garments, apply insect repellent with the active ingredient DEET and sleep with a fan on to keep the air moving. Try to keep your room free of the insects too by using mosquito coils, vaporisers, etc.

DEET is strong (not to say toxic) enough to last many hours. Wrist and ankle bands impregnated with the chemical are available and easy to use. Cover your limbs as night falls (6pm on the Equator). Wearing fine silk clothes discourages bites – and keep the repellent topped up.

Prevention is vastly preferable to cure. It is a difficult disease to treat, particularly in its advanced stages. If you suffer a fever up to 12 months after returning home from a malarial zone, visit your doctor and mention your travels, even if you suspect it might just be flu.

RED TAPE

PASSPORTS

A 10-year UK passport costs £77.50 for 32 pages and £90.50 for 48 pages, and should be processed by the Identity and Passport Service within three weeks. The one-week fast-track application procedure costs £30–£35 extra and an existing passport can be renewed within one day if it is done in person at a passport office, but only if you have made a prior appointment by ringing 0300 222 0000 and will pay the premium fee of £129.50. Passport office addresses are listed on passport application forms available from main post offices. All relevant information can be found on the website (www.ips.gov.uk).

Most countries will want to see that your passport has at least 90 days to run beyond your proposed stay. If your passport is lost or stolen while travelling, first contact the police, then your nearest consulate. Obtaining replacement travel documents is easier if you have a record of the passport number and its date and place of issue, so keep these in a separate place, preferably as a photocopy of the title page, which can be scanned and emailed to yourself.

TRAVEL VISAS

Outside the Schengen Area of Europe in which border controls have been largely abolished, you can't continue in one direction for very long before you are impeded by border guards demanding to see your papers. After 9/11, immigration and security checks are tighter than ever before and many countries have imposed visa restrictions, particularly on North Americans. Embassy websites are the best source of information, or you can check online information posted by visa agencies. For example, CIBT (www.uk.cibt.com) allows you to search visa requirements and costs for any nationality visiting any country.

Getting visas is a headache anywhere, and most travellers feel happier obtaining them in their home country. Set aside a chunk of your travel budget to cover the costs: to give just a few examples of charges for tourist visas for UK citizens applying in London, it is £40 for India, £60 for China, £39 for Jordan, and £44 for Vietnam. Last-minute applications often incur a higher fee: for example a Russian visa costs £75 if applied for a week in advance, but £133 for short notice processing. If you do not want to pin yourself down to entry dates, you may decide to apply for visas as you travel, for example from a neighbouring country, which in many cases is cheaper, though may cause delays and hassle. If you are short of time or live a long way from the embassies in London, private visa agencies will undertake the footwork for you, but at a price, in the region of £40–£45 per visa.

If you intend to cross a great many borders, especially on an overland trip through Africa, ensure that you have all the relevant documentation and that your passport contains as many blank pages as frontiers which you intend to cross.

Always reply simply and politely to any questions asked by immigration or customs officials. **Roger Blake** has a word of warning: '*Arriving in New Zealand was not really a problem other than a strange encounter with a customs officer: "Are you bringing drugs into the country?" "No!" "Do you take drugs?" "NO!" I reply. She asks "Why not?" This is the kind of carefully planned (and corrupt) trap for would-be drug users that you occasionally come across. Anyway, no worries on my part.*'

STUDENT CARDS

With an International Student Identity Card (ISIC; www.isic.org), it is often possible to obtain reduced fares on trains, planes, and buses, and discounts on hostels, museums, theatres, and so on. The ISIC is available to all students in full-time education and those who can show a letter of acceptance from UCAS. There is no age limit, although some flight carriers do not apply discounts for students over 31. To obtain a card (which is valid for 15 months from September), you will need to complete the ISIC application form, provide a passport photo, proof of full-time student status (NUS card or official letter), and the fee of £9. Details are available from any branch of STA Travel. The card entitles you to get in touch with the ISIC helpline, a special service for travelling students who need advice in an emergency. However, this does not in any way replace the need for insurance.

MONEY

The average budget of a travelling student is at least £25 a day, although many survive on less in cheap countries. Whatever the size of your travelling fund, you should give some thought to how and in what form to carry your money. Travellers' cheques are safer than cash, though they cost an extra 1% and banks able to cash them are not always near to hand, even in Europe. It is advisable also to carry cash and a debit or credit card. Sterling is fine for most countries but US dollars are preferred in much of the world such as Latin America. The easiest way to look up the exchange rate of any world currency is to check on the internet (eg www.oanda.com or www.xe.com/ucc) or to look at the Monday edition of the *Financial Times*. The travel chapters include some snapshots of exchange rates for countries of most interest to gappers.

The most straightforward way to access money abroad is by using your bank debit card in hole-in-the-wall ATMs. There is usually a minimum fee for a withdrawal so you should get larger amounts out at one time than you would at home. Read the fine print on those boring leaflets that come with your debit card because it may be that your bank will encumber you with various loading fees, withdrawal fees, and transaction fees. For example, the transaction fee for withdrawing foreign currency abroad or paying at point of sale with a standard Maestro card is 2.65% in addition to the ordinary exchange rate disadvantage, plus cash machine withdrawals cost 2.25% of the sterling transaction. In everyday language, this means that every withdrawal from a hole in the wall is costing upwards of £5. The point-of-sale charge is more reasonable (£1.25). If you are going to be abroad for a considerable period drawing on funds in your home account, it would be worth shopping around for the best deal, which is at present offered in the UK by the Norwich and Peterborough Building Society. In 2011, it abolished fees on its newly launched Visa debit card (although conditions apply). Research can be carried out on www.moneysavingexpert.com.

Remember that hole-in-the-wall cash dispensers abroad will not show your bank balance, so be sure to set up online banking before you go so that you can track your balance wherever you have internet access.

Travel Money Cards sold by a number of companies including the Post Office are prepaid, reloadable cards that can be used like debit cards at ATMs and most shops but are not linked to your bank account. You can purchase one online and load it with sterling, euros or US dollars. Be aware that the exchange rate and transaction fees may not be better than the rival methods. A survey of the benefits can be seen at www.moneysavingexpert.com/travel/cheap-travel-money/ with a comparative list of commission charged by the main providers such as Cashplus.

GAPPERS' TIP

Regardless of how short the stop, ALWAYS have emergency money hidden behind a zipper, unless you enjoy the feeling of helplessness and unnecessary stress.

The tip above comes from **Kirsten Shaw**, who found herself stranded (February 2011) in the Middle East en route home from seven glorious months in South Africa:

> *The only disaster that happened during my gap year was on the way home to France, passing through Dubai. I sat by the gate waiting for my flight to board, listening to music, eyes slightly closed, unaware that my watch was an hour late and that the entirety of my aeroplane had checked in and left without me. I flew to the check-in desk hoping to get on the next plane, only to be told that I had to pay a €50 surcharge to get a new ticket. My only credit card was overdrawn to the hilt, and I had €5 spare change in case I fancied an overpriced airport coffee. I had no phone and no way of getting on the plane. All the tears, sniffling and mournful looks in the world could not get me on that flight. I was eventually allowed to use a phone by a kind ground steward who permitted me to call my grandmother, who called my parents at 4am French time. After many hours of waiting to see if my long-suffering parents were able to move money across to Dubai on a Sunday, I boarded the plane with a weary smile and a business-class ticket tucked in my passport – a present from Emirates on account of my public outburst of emotion.*

Theft takes many forms, from highly trained gangs of children who artfully pick pockets in European railway stations to violent attacks on the streets of American cities to spiked drinks in Russia. Risks can be reduced by carrying your wealth in several places, including a comfortable money belt worn inside your clothing, steering clear of seedy or crowded areas and moderating your intake of alcohol. If you are robbed, you must obtain a police report to stand any chance of recouping part of your loss from your insurer (assuming the loss of cash is covered in your policy) or from your travellers' cheque company. Usually, insurance policies impose an excess of £50 or £100 so it is often not worth claiming for stolen cash.

Haggling is a topic of endless fascination among world travellers. Try to avoid boasting about how hard a bargain you are able to drive. Remember that in some countries, the rickshaw driver or temple guide could feed his family that day with the 50p you saved. But spreading largesse randomly is not advisable either. It is not uncommon for children to skip school in order to frequent tourist haunts where they stand a chance of being given a few coins.

TRANSFERRING MONEY

Assuming your account at home remains in credit and you don't lose your cash/debit card, it shouldn't be necessary to have money wired to you urgently. If you run out of money abroad, whether through mismanagement, loss, or theft, you will probably contact your parents who may be willing to top up your account (probably as a loan). If you cannot use a hole-in-the-wall money machine for some reason and need to contact your bank, it is much easier if you have set up a telephone or internet bank account before leaving home since they will then have the correct security checks in place to authorise a transfer without having to receive something from you in writing with your signature. You can request that the necessary sum be transferred from your bank to a named bank in the town you are in – something you have to arrange with your own bank, so you know where to pick the money up.

Western Union offers an international money transfer service whereby cash deposited at one branch can be withdrawn by you from any other branch or agency, which your benefactor need not specify. Western Union agents – there are 90,000 of them in 200 countries – come in all shapes and sizes, eg travel agencies, stationers, chemists. Unfortunately it is not well represented outside the developed world. The person sending money to you simply turns up at a Western Union counter, pays in the desired sum plus the fee, which is £14 for up to £100 transferred, £21 for £101–£200, £37 for £500 and so on. For an extra £7 your benefactor can do this over the phone with a credit card. In the UK, ring 0800 833 833 for further details, a list of outlets, and a complete rate schedule. The website www.westernunion.com allows you to search for the nearest outlet.

Thomas Cook and the UK Post Office offer a similar service called Moneygram (www.moneygram.com). Cash deposited at one of their foreign exchange counters is available within 10 minutes at the named destination or can be collected up to 45 days later at one of 176,000 co-operating agents in 190 countries. The fees are very slightly lower than Western Union's. The Post Office website (www.postoffice.co.uk) explains how it works.

ACCOMMODATION

Bookings at hostels worldwide can be made on www.hostelbookers.com, www.hostels.com, www.hostels.net and www.hostelworld.com. The original Youth Hostels Federation is called Hostelling International (www.hihostels.com), and consists of 4,000 hostels in 80 countries. Membership costs only £9.95 for those under 26 (01629 592 700 in the UK; www.yha.org.uk).

St Christopher's Inns operates a friendly chain of hostels, found across the UK and also in Paris, Berlin, Bruges, Amsterdam, and Prague. They publish extensive online travel resources and reward part-time travel writers with free nights for work done; contact editor@st-christophers.co.uk.

MAKING CONTACTS

The importance of knowing people, not necessarily in high places but on the spot, is stressed by many gap year travellers. Some people are lucky enough to have family and friends scattered around the world in positions to offer advice or even accommodation and employment. Others must create their own contacts by exploiting less obvious connections.

Dick Bird, who spent over a year travelling around South America, light-heartedly explains how this works:

> *In Bolivia we are practising another survival technique known as 'having some addresses'. The procedure is quite simple. Before leaving one's country of origin, inform everyone you know from your immediate family to the most casual acquaintance that you are about to leave for South America. With only a little cajoling, they might volunteer the address of somebody they once met on the platform of Clapham Junction or some other tenuous connection who went out to South America to seek their fortunes. You then present your worthy self on the unsuspecting émigré's doorstep and announce that you have been in close and recent communication with their nearest and dearest. Although you won't necessarily be welcomed with open arms, the chances are they will be eager for your company and conversation. Furthermore these contacts are often useful for finding work: doing odd jobs, farming, tutoring people they know, etc.*

If you or your travel companion has a relative or family friend willing to offer accommodation, think carefully about whether it is worth accepting. If you are looking forward to joining the 'travelling scene' but are stuck in a remote suburb struggling to be a good guest, you may regret saving a few nights' hostel expenses. On the other hand, living with the locals might prove a highlight. Being a good guest becomes easier with practice. If a family friend, well-known or otherwise, offers hospitality, avoid arriving empty-handed (the Irish use the expression for this, 'coming with one arm as long as the other'). A token box of choccies or small food item from wherever you are coming from is a symbolic gesture that goes a long way. Don't overstay your welcome and be sure to send a thank you note (or email) after you have left.

After doing a six-week building project in Chiang Rai in early 2011, **Jonny Christy** and two friends planned to stay with an old friend of his parents who lived in Singapore with his Japanese wife. Although Jonny's family had been only on Christmas card terms for several decades, his parents urged him to make contact, so he did. Due to operational difficulties, the gapping trio had to change their time of arrival at short notice and ended up giving their hosts three hours' rather than three days' warning, but that was fine. They couldn't believe the luxury into which they had stepped, with each of the three assigned their own double bedroom. They had to be sensitive, since this was at the time of the Japanese tsunami, and his hostess had family and friends in Japan. A day or two after they arrived, the hosts were scheduled to go away on holiday and left the lads in the care of the home help who ensured that they were well fed, washed and had clean handkerchiefs! Apparently she also stoked them up on comfort food like bangers and mash before they proceeded to Malaysia (to attend the Grand Prix in Kuala Lumpur).

Even if you aren't lucky enough to have ready-made contacts like this, it is possible to stay with locals. Hospitality exchange organisations can make travel both interesting and cheap (and induce a panic attack in parents). When you register with the Hospitality Club, Global Freeloaders, place2stay. net, or the Couchsurfing Project, all of which are completely free, you agree to host the occasional visitor in your home in order to earn the right to stay with other members worldwide. The online community with the highest profile is www.couchsurfing.com. Like so many internet-based projects, the system depends on users' feedback, which means that you can check on a potential host's profile in advance and be fairly sure that dodgy hosts will be outed straightaway.

WHAT TO TAKE ...

PACSAFE

Jonathan Dorn, *Backpacker* Executive Editor, introduces Outpac Designs' Pacsafe, which was launched in 1997. Shortly after, this product won the coveted *Backpacker*'s Editor's Choice Award.

As I approached the ticket counter for my flight to Montana, the agent gave me the same skeptical look my mother used to when I'd ask for an advance on my allowance. After poking at the steel mesh encircling my backpack, the ticket lady said, 'You'll have to put your pack in a plastic bag so that thing doesn't damage our conveyor belts.' Such sweet irony – a pack that might damage the airline's property instead of the other way around. My pack was safely ensconced in the Pacsafe, a protective cover that thwarts not only airport goblins but also knife-wielding thieves.

The Pacsafe has travelled with me across three continents, delivering my gear unscathed to a dozen distant trailheads. Using the security cable and padlock, I've chained my load to trees and lampposts and ducked into stores for supplies. I've even used it to bear-bag my food.

The Pacsafe fits like a standard rain cover and either wraps around your pack's hip-belt and harness so they don't catch on conveyor belts or lets them hang free so you can shoulder the pack. It cinches closed with a tug on a steel cable and locks with a small brass padlock. When not in use, the Pacsafe folds into a grapefruit-sized pouch. But best of all, it's nearly indestructible. Despite my best efforts with hammer and hacksaw, I couldn't dent the stainless steel mesh or plastic components.

The consensus: the Pacsafe... a wise pound of prevention.

Packing for travelling as a backpacker will always entail compromises because you will be limited in the amount of clothes and equipment you can take with you. When you're buying a backpack or rucksack, try to place a significant weight in it in the shop so you can feel how comfortable it might be to carry on your back, otherwise you might be misled by lifting something usually filled with foam.

Any number of specialist stores and websites peddling travel gear are fun to browse but try to be discerning about what is really necessary. The Gap Year Travel Store (0845 652 5508; www.gapyeartravelstore.com) specialises in selling backpacking equipment to gappers and independent travellers. Another long-established supplier with a huge range is Nomad's online store (www.nomadtravel.co.uk). These ranges are tailored to budget travellers and offer travel products and accessories of all descriptions at keen prices.

If you plan to camp in a hot country, you might think about taking a tropical quilt rather than a sleeping bag. You can either spread out the quilt as a bed to sleep on or it can be folded to create a lightweight sleeping bag. The other advantage is that it is much lighter to carry and takes up less room in your luggage. Alternatively, it can be wrapped around your shoulders for warmth in an air-conditioned space or on a chilly evening in the mountains. However, it will not provide enough warmth if you're planning to travel at high altitude; a down vest might be a solution and can also double as a comfortable pillow. Another consideration for those going to high altitudes, such as Cusco Peru at nearly 10,000ft, is altitude sickness; the prescription drug Diamox has been recommended to alleviate the symptoms. (The on-site alternative is coca tea.)

Now a seasoned traveller, **Tom Grundy** reminisces about his preparations for going to Uganda in his gap year: '*Two days of packing later, I was set to go. My nervous inexperience was reflected in the 40kg suitcase I packed containing "just the essentials" (including eight bottles of shower gel, 30 packs of Polo mints, six tubes of toothpaste, washing-up gloves, thesaurus, and washing line).*' While aiming to travel as lightly as possible, you should consider the advantage of taking certain extra pieces of equipment such as comfortable walking boots or a tent if you will have the chance to travel independently. If you are travelling in a part of the world where theft is rife, invest a few pennies in a padlock, which will act as a deterrent if nothing else. One travelling tip is to carry dental floss, useful not only for your teeth but as strong twine for mending backpacks, hanging up laundry, etc.

In the tropics you must carry water, in order to prevent dehydration. Belts with zips worn under a shirt are very handy for carrying money unobtrusively. A bandana is also advisable in the tropics to mop up sweat or to put round your face in windy desert conditions. Some even have backgammon and chess sets printed on them to provide portable entertainment.

With wi-fi becoming more available in accommodation and cafés worldwide, some travellers now consider a laptop or smartphone an essential piece of equipment. Gaptrac (www.gaptrac.co.uk) provides a range of state-of-the-art functions and uses GPS to record your route for friends and family to follow in real time. After joining for £10 plus VAT per month, you are assigned a username and password to pass on to followers who can then access your blog, photos, and even audio files.

If you have plumped for a placement scheme where you'll stay put for a while, you might allow yourself the odd (lightweight) luxury, such as iPod speakers, short-wave radio, or a jar of peanut butter. **Camilla Burgess**, who spent three months in Ghana, recommends taking a bar of Vanish laundry soap; hers was in huge demand, since clothes become very dirty in big cities in the tropics.

HANDY TRAVEL TIPS FOR BACKPACKERS, FROM VENTURE Co.

■ *Keep a record of travel documents such as passport number, driving licence, travellers' cheque serial numbers, insurance policy, tickets, emergency number for cancelling credit cards, etc. Make two copies: stow one away in luggage and give the other to a friend or relative at home. Email this information to yourself so that you can access it at any time from an internet café.*

■ *Make sure your passport will remain valid for at least six months beyond the expected duration of your trip.*

■ *Carry valuable items (such as passport, essential medicines, and of course money) on your person rather than relegating them to a piece of luggage which might be lost or stolen.*

■ *Only pack items you are prepared to lose or have stolen.*

■ *Remember to ask permission before taking photographs of individuals or groups. In some cultures it can be insulting.*

■ *Take advantage of loos in expensive hotels and fast food chains.*

■ *Learn a few key words and phrases in the local language, so as not to seem arrogant in assuming everyone communicates in English.*

- Read up on a country before you arrive or during your travels to help avoid problems and enhance understanding.
- Make sure your equipment and clothes don't look brand new so that you will be less likely to attract attention to yourself.
- Most importantly, make sure you get that perfect balance between travelling safely and enjoying yourself. Any problems during your trip could ruin it, but equally if you are over-cautious you might miss out on something amazing.

Good maps and guides always enhance one's enjoyment of a trip. Most people you will meet on the road will probably be carrying a Rough Guide or a Lonely Planet. These are both excellent series, though try not to become too slavish about their advice and preferences. Rough Guides has a series of 'First Time' titles which could be of interest to gappers, including *Around the World, Europe, Africa, Asia*, and *Latin America*. Even though so much advance information is available over the internet (web recommendations are given at the end of this book's Travel chapters), nothing can compete with a proper guidebook to pore over and take away with you. If you are going to be based in a major city, buy a map ahead of time. Visit the famous travel book shop Edward Stanford, with branches in Bristol and Manchester, as well as the parent store in Covent Garden, London; their searchable catalogue is online at www.stanfords.co.uk.

The Map Shop in Worcestershire (0800 085 4080/01684 593 146; www.themapshop.co.uk) and Maps Worldwide in Wiltshire (0845 122 0559; www.mapsworldwide.co.uk) both do an extensive mail order business in specialised maps and guide books.

If you are going to a country to learn or improve a language, you might take a good dictionary and a language course at a suitable level, for example the *Take Off In...* series from Oxford University Press (www.askoxford.com/languages) for £25 including mp3 downloads, the BBC (bbc.co.uk/languages), Linguaphone (0800 136 973; linguaphone.co.uk) and Audioforum (audioforum.com). For more information about language learning, see the *Courses* chapter.

Preparation is half the fun, but choose like-minded company before discussing your intended anti-malarial regimen and your water sterilising equipment since you don't want to turn into a pub bore.

On top of all these practical preparations, you will want to prepare yourself mentally, to try to imagine what it will be like in some distant corner of the world, doing things completely outside your past experience. **Angela Clegg** concentrated her efforts on researching Africa:

> Before you go you spend so long trying to prepare yourself mentally, but when you get there you just adjust instantly. I think the hardest thing for me was not preparing for living with 15 other volunteers. I researched culture shock in preparation for African culture but neglected to think about the different people I would be living with day in day out. I found myself in a kind of Big Brother/Real World scenario. Again, once I had adjusted to it, I wouldn't have changed a thing, as I feel as though those people will be friends for life after what we went through, experienced and saw together.

Give yourself time to get excited about your plans, so try to avoid a last-minute scramble, and not be working and partying flat out up until the moment of departure.

... AND WHAT TO LEAVE BEHIND

Make sure you leave a record of all-important documents with your parents plus at least four signed passport photos, which may be needed for university loan applications and by some university admissions departments. Whereas forms can be emailed, faxed, or posted to you abroad for your attention, it is difficult to arrange for photos to be sent and impossible if you are on a placement teaching at a village school in Tanzania or Nepal.

Depending on your destination, don't take your designer shirts and trainers. For tropical countries, leave behind anything that isn't made of natural fibres. Some travellers can't live without their iPhone or iPad, though gadgetry of this kind marks you out in many parts of the world as extremely affluent.

STAYING IN TOUCH

The revolution in communication technology means that you are never far from home. Internet cafés can be found in almost every corner of the world where, for a small fee, you can access your email, keep in touch with your friends via Facebook, check relevant information on the web or upload and distribute digital photos. Sending photos home electronically has become a piece of cake, as is setting up your own website, blog (ie web log) or even vlog (video log) to share travel tales with family, friends, and interested strangers. Lots of companies will help you create your own blog free of charge, for example Wordpress (www.wordpress.com) is free and easy to use. Other main contenders for free blog hosting are blogspot.com (go to www.blogger.com/start); www.travelpod.com, http://blogs.bootsnall.com, and the well-named www.getjealous.com. If you do decide to keep a blog, remember that less is more: the folks back home probably don't have the time to read all the ins and outs of your long bus journeys and negotiations with hoteliers. Try to record the most interesting highlights for public consumption.

Travellers Connected (www.travellersconnected.com) is an online community site for travellers that is free to use. You can register your profile and contact travellers around the world to seek insider tips. It also allows you to set up a free travel blog with photos.

MOBILE PHONES

Roaming charges for mobiles can cost an arm and a leg. Contact your mobile phone company to check on coverage; if not you may need to take it into a shop to have the phone unlocked. Also check what deals your provider offers, which can be spectacularly complex. Vodafone's 'Passport' is a free tariff option available with any handset (abroad.vodafone.co.uk), which allows you to make calls at your home tariff after paying a 75p connection fee. It is available in most of Europe, Australia, New Zealand, and Japan, but not North America.

If you are going to be on the move a lot, you might want to investigate a gadget that can charge your mobile and iPod using solar power: the Solio charger (www.solio.com) retails from about £50.

A plethora of companies in the UK and US sell pre-paid calling cards intended to simplify international phoning. You credit your card account with an amount of your choice (normally starting at £10 or £20), or buy a card for $10 or $20. You are given an access code that can be used from any phone. Lonely Planet, the travel publisher, has an easy-to-use communications card called eKit (lonelyplanet. ekit.com), which offers low-cost calls, voice mail, and email. A company called 0044 (0044.co.uk) sells foreign sim cards, which allow you to take your mobile with you and call at local rates while you're away. Its global sim card costs £20 compared with £30 from GO-SIM (www.gosim.com).

Warn friends not to call your UK mobile while you are away; you will be paying for all incoming calls when overseas. If you are staying in one country for more than a few weeks and use your phone a lot, consider getting either a cheap local mobile phone or a local sim card for your UK mobile. Even better, ensure your UK contacts have the special access codes available for low-cost dialling from landlines to your destination. One of the most often recommended discount companies (for people phoning abroad from the UK) is www.telediscount.co.uk, which offers unbeatable prices: in many cases you can make international calls at local rates.

For very anxious gappers and/or parents, there is a back-up system on the market called SafetyText (www.safetytext.com), which was launched by the father of the British woman Lucie Blackman who was murdered when she was working as a hostess in Japan. SafetyText is a delayed text messaging system, which depends on the user remembering to cancel the text once he or she has arrived safely.

VISITS FROM PARENTS

Many gappers are lucky (or unlucky) enough to have parents who want to visit (and can afford to do so). After months of teaching in a Tanzanian village or backpacking in Laos or assisting at a New Zealand adventure sports centre, suddenly there are the dear old things from home. Whereas flying the coop might have been a major attraction at the outset, most students welcome the chance to turn temporarily back into being somebody's child. Often parental visits coincide with time off, and may mean a sudden rise in your standard of living. Whereas some luxury-starved students will embrace this brief change of fortune with glee, others may find that it jars with their growing sense of what is appropriate in certain countries. You are bound to take pleasure in having the boot on the other foot: this is your chance to guide your parents round and allay their anxieties, it is now you who is expert in the best cafés in Granada or the *tro-tro* timetable in Ghana. No doubt you will catch beaming smiles of pride on their faces as you navigate with confidence. Enthusiastic fledglings might be tempted to rave about all the things that are superior in the place they are living (which could be a little hurtful to visitors from home), whereas others take the opportunity to share their catalogue of moans. Try to avoid both.

Parents' plans can sometimes come unstuck when overtaken by events. Eighteen-year-old **Dan Hanfling** baked a creditable cake when he had an interview in the autumn for a job in a ski chalet in a French ski resort. But on arriving in the Alps, he learned that he was expected to service a number of chalets by carrying supplies, cleaning toilets, etc. This job was a lot less glamorous than he had imagined, and he returned to England after just a few weeks. Unfortunately, his parents (avid skiers) had already booked a holiday in the same resort so that they could all be together at Christmas.

It has even been known for more than one set of parents to travel together to visit their darlings, in which case the collective noun should surely be a 'smothering' of mothers.

MY GAP YEAR: CHRIS MILNER

After graduation, Chris Milner spent eight months in the Sudan through the Sudan Volunteer Programme and he describes how his parents' visit made him realise how far he had travelled.

My parents were arriving in Sudan for a visit. For me, this was to be a fantastic personal experience but it was also an opportunity to discover how much I had learned since walking up the jetty towards Wadi Halfa three months earlier. Their visit represented a chance to sit in the markets, drink the gingered coffee, suffer the insufferable heat, and queue for buses with a beginner's mind. I had now lived in Omdurman for three months and had become somewhat accustomed to life in Sudan. The rush of colours, faces, smells, and sounds that had at first merged into a single overwhelming sensory experience had each disassociated into their constituent parts, and were now reaching the appropriate senses. At first, seemingly random events led me to Uud concerts, Sufi ritual, and river boat trips. Certainly large amounts of cake were consumed ... and other activities such as evenings watching Celine Dion videos could be avoided without causing too much offence.

My parents arrived late and we took a taxi back to Shuhadda from the airport. Immediately and for the first time, I realised how familiar the city had become, how easy it was to predict the conversation with the driver, and how comfortable I felt … In short, Sudan was not what it once was. It had become for me a real place in which people lived, including me, and this gave me the freedom to both praise and criticise it. I took them along to meet my group of students at the Abdel Karim Centre. The 'AK' is a community-led organisation that believes in creating an environment in which young people can learn, take control of their lives, and use the skills they develop to move Sudan forward. I liked it there very much.

The parents were an instant hit and the lesson plan went out the window (actually we always studied on the roof) and for two hours we all took part in conversations on many topics, from love to taxation. I really can't describe how proud these young people should be of themselves - not because of the hardship in which some of them live (although that is another story). Their generosity of spirit, willingness to give, willingness to accept, willingness to welcome, and enthusiasm for life was quite inspiring.

My parents and I were lucky enough to visit Juba together. However, for me, the highlight of their stay in Sudan was the party organised by the students at Abdel Karim to celebrate their visit. The amazing and sometimes tiring fact about being a volunteer is that in Sudan, everything is Sudan. Through my students and friends, I could learn about it. Through my parents I realised I was a part of it.

Some parents don't just visit, they join in, as Scottish mother **Sue Wrenn Fenton** describes:

My daughter, Mairi, was on a traditional gap year before going to Glasgow University. I asked her if she would mind if I muscled in on her plans and she very kindly agreed to share the last part of her year out with me. I had found a locally-run charity in Nepal, Hope and Home, on the internet, which didn't fleece foreign volunteers like some of the other organisations I had researched (and Mairi had experienced!) The small charge covered a week's orientation (Nepali language lessons, sightseeing, and local cultural events) while staying in a guesthouse with other volunteers. Mairi and I were then placed in a girls' orphanage in Kathmandu and lived with a Hindu family close by, who provided all meals. We tried to help the girls, aged three to twenty, in all aspects of their daily life and education. We also trekked in the Annapurna area, flew to Everest in a light plane, and saw elephants in Chitwan. It was magic to spend time with Mairi, out of our comfort zones and away from home, not as mother and daughter with all those inherent parental trappings but as colleagues. This has formed the basis of a solid, new, grown-up relationship. She taught me a great deal, as did the girls in the home.

COMING HOME

Coming home and experiencing reverse culture shock is a problem for some. Settling back in will take time, especially if you have not been able to set aside some money for 'The Return'. It can be a wretched feeling after some glorious adventures to find yourself with nothing new to start on. Life at home may seem dull and routine at first, while the outlook of your friends and family can strike you as narrow and limited. If you have been round the world between school and further study, you may find it difficult to bridge the gulf between you and your stay-at-home peers who may feel a little threatened or belittled by your experiences. After a brilliant gap year divided between volunteer teaching at an international school in Costa Rica, skiing in the Appalachians, and working on a farm in Tuscany, **Katie White** observed:

> *My high school friends have not been very supportive of my decision to take a year off. I still can't tell if it was/is jealousy or resentment at my opportunity, or that I seemed arrogant because I was stepping out of the box. High school social dynamics are dicey at best, and for some reason I generated some not-so-warm-and-fuzzy feelings with my decisions.*

Kirsten Shaw came home after a brilliant gap year in South Africa with a classic case of reverse culture shock:

> *Coming back to live at home in my small town in France after seven mind-blowing months in the African bush felt like coming back to square one. I feel like a party balloon that has been blown up nice and strong, and on my return, someone has slowly been letting the air out, making the farty noise that kids make to drive adults insane. All travellers acquire their own travelling preferences along the way, and coming back to what one might call 'home' is done with mixed feelings, depending on the individual. After returning from three months of manic jumping from one country to another in Central America, I crossed the threshold of my family house and burst into floods of tears in relief. Coming back from seven months in South Africa left me howling in grief at what I had left behind.*

The restlessness passes, the reverse culture shock wears off soon enough and you will begin to feel reintegrated. **Andrew Cummings** has an interesting perspective on coming home from his gap year in 2011, which consisted of interning on a magazine in Bolivia, working as a waiter in Buenos Aires, travelling around South America, and finally another magazine internship in Paris:

> *It seems strange, but I'd say that in a way a high point of the year out was coming back and missing it all. I think it's really difficult to gauge just how valuable a year out can be until you're finally back home. Realising that I'd been to places, met people, and done things that (I think) have had a positive effect on my life, so much so that I missed them, helped me to understand that, faced with the decision to take a year out, I'd definitely made the right choice.*

Gap year experiences are great conversation openers when you're meeting new people at university or the workplace. As has been noted, what you did in your gap year provides an easy topic of conversation for future interviews, so in official contexts you should be prepared to put as positive a spin on it as possible. Any evidence of initiative and organisational abilities will help. If you travelled alone you can boast of your independence; if you travelled with friends you can claim to have learned about co-operation and teamwork.

PART II

GAP YEAR TRAVEL

TRAVEL TO THE FOUR CORNERS
EUROPE
AFRICA
ASIA
AUSTRALIA AND NEW ZEALAND
LATIN AMERICA
NORTH AMERICA

TRAVEL TO THE FOUR CORNERS

It would be a pretty sad gap year that didn't include at least some pure and unadulterated travel. If you have one or more friends who want to go with you, many happy sessions can be spent in the pub poring over maps and planning the itinerary. If your friends are all disappearing in different directions, do not be put off the idea of going on your own or finding a travel companion elsewhere (see earlier section on travelling 'Solo or in company'). Cost is usually the crucial factor for gap students wondering where to go or how to get there. Those who go through a sending agency will either have their travel arranged for them or be offered plenty of guidance. But for those students who want to organise their trip independently, here is some general advice.

The purest form of travelling is on public transport, cheek by jowl with the local people. By creating your own route and using your wits to find your way, you'll find yourself obliged to interact with local people rather than being cocooned in a foreign-run tour. When engaging with local people, always follow the golden rule of trusting your instincts. It may be stating the obvious, but you should never accept an invitation to go somewhere or participate in an activity that makes you feel uncomfortable or threatened. Even if you run the risk of offending a 'host', you need to keep your internal compass functioning. Bear in mind that foreigners may be viewed as easy targets for some form of exploitation, principally financial. If you feel that an offer sounds too good to be true then it almost certainly is.

While juggling bus or train timetables and the need to find suitable accommodation, try not to rush. The slow pace of life as a traveller, especially in the developing world, is something to be savoured not bemoaned. Even with an entire year at your disposal, you cannot possibly 'do' all of a country let alone a continent. Little can be gained from racing through an area, ticking off sights, which is both exhausting and unrewarding and will leave you with very superficial impressions of a culture and its people. Taking your time and getting to know a smaller number of places more deeply cannot fail to reward. It is by doing this that you will meet more local people and really come to appreciate the essence of a country, soaking up the atmosphere beneath the tourist façade.

Once you have been carrying your pack for a couple of weeks, caught the right buses, met a few other travellers, you will probably laugh at your pre-travelling misconceptions of danger and risk. In the developing world you will have encountered the warm welcome and endless curiosity with which ordinary people greet travellers from a far land. Remember to carry photos of your family or postcards of your home country, as these can spark off much discussion.

For practical tips on what to pack and how to stay safe, see the chapter *Before You Go*.

THE BEATEN TRACK

A report by an academic was published a few years ago lambasting the negative impact that backpackers have on places where they congregate (the Red Sea, Kathmandu, Goa, Kho Pha-Ngan, Machu Picchu, etc). The organisation for responsible tourism, Tourism Concern (www.tourismconcern.org.uk), is also worried by the number of young people who travel to places they are not really interested in just to meet up with other travellers, to eat, drink, and socialise in exactly the way they would at home but without as many inhibitions. There is even a novel about it: for a satirical account of the wrong way to go about being a gap year traveller, read William Sutcliffe's *Are You Experienced?*, based on his own gap year experiences. In this extract, the anti-hero Dave is being lectured by an old-hand traveller in India:

Hippies coming for spiritual enlightenment have been replaced by morons on a poverty-tourism ad-venture holiday. Going to India is no longer an act of rebellion but an act of conformity for ambitious middle-class kids who believe that a trip to the Third World shows the kind of initiative which com-panies are looking for. You come here and cling to each other as if you're on some kind of extended management-bonding exercise in Epping Forest ... It's a modern circumcision ritual, a badge of suf-fering you have to wear to be welcomed into the tribe of Britain's future elite. Your kind of travel is all about low horizons dressed up as open-mindedness. You have no interest in India and no sensitivity for the problems this country is trying to face up to. You treat Indians with a mixture of contempt and suspicion reminiscent of the Victorian colonials. Your presence here in my opinion is offensive and you should all go home to Surrey.

Hard-hitting stuff – but worth pondering. It has to be acknowledged that it is the rare gapper who goes primarily for the museums and temples and all the other cultural high points described in guide -books. However, it is to be hoped that young travellers are genuinely interested in meeting local people, in noticing different cultural assumptions, and generally coming away with a bit more understanding of the way the world works in different corners of it.

SPECIALIST TOUR OPERATORS

If none of your friends is free to team up with you, it might be worth thinking about joining a group of like-minded people on an overland expedition or adventure tour. There are distinct advantages to having your travel arrangements organised for you en route. For a start, you can hand over most concerns about personal security to someone else. Travelling with an overland company saves time and stress usually expended on things such as the bureaucratic snags of border crossings and pro-vides help with food, accommodation, activities, and excursions. Taking advantage of such insider knowledge removes all the hassle of solitary independent travel. For example, Oasis Overland (www.oasisoverland.co.uk) specialises in adventure travel for young travellers with truck-based overland expeditions in South America, Africa, the Silk Road, and the Middle East lasting from 15 days to 40 weeks. Some trips attract more mature travellers while others (such as the 'Egypt Encompassed' trip) run on local transport, stay at simple hostels, and are suited to partying young people.

Most overland companies cater for the backpacking market and keep prices down by providing ba-sic accommodation, often camping, and expecting participants to share the cooking and other chores. Overland trips include optional adventurous excursions, such as mountain trekking, white-water rafting or adrenaline sports. At the lowest end of the spectrum, a trip might cost between £100 and £150 a week, plus $125 a week (payable locally in US dollars) for the food kitty. The longer the trip the lower the weekly cost: for example, Oasis Overland trips start at £95 per week plus £37 a week local pay-ment (for food and camping fees) on 40-week trans-Africa trips, and go up to around £140 a week plus £70 kitty for shorter South American trips (see 'Directory of Expeditions'). Many other companies charge far more, eg $100 a day. One of the most exciting trips on the market is available on the Oz-Bus which travels between London and Sydney, visiting 18 countries en route. The cost of the 85-day trip is £5,299 (0800 731 9427; www.oz-bus.com), or the trip can be halved: London to Kathmandu or Bangkok to Sydney.

Agencies that specialise in trips for backpackers can be just what a solo gap year traveller needs to overcome a reluctance to strike off into the unknown, though most small-group tours comprise a slightly older clientele (partly because they aren't cheap). If that doesn't worry you, operators such as Intrepid Travel (www.intrepidtravel.com) can allow you to experience a country at closer range off the beaten path of larger groups. Intrepid runs hundreds of trips in dozens of countries. Their 'Basix' trips are meant to be no-frills small-group trips suitable for first-time backpackers, lasting from a couple of days in northern Vietnam to seven weeks from Bangkok to Beijing; the latter trip costs from £2,835.

OASIS OVERLAND

Karen Jones joined Oasis Overland's 23-week Trans Africa Expedition to Cape Town:

The Trans Africa has been one of the most fantastic, awesome experiences of my life. I didn't really know what to expect and was a little apprehensive about travelling across Africa in the back of a truck with 23 strangers for 23 weeks!

We all met at Luton airport on a cold November evening, weighed down with massive backpacks and all wondering what the coming months would bring. On arrival in Gibraltar, we were met by our Oasis crew, Andi and Grant and a huge yellow truck – our new home! The truck was great, fitted with coach seats, lockers for our gear, and a stereo, as well as carrying food, water, and cooking equipment. Andi and Grant were organised and friendly and really made the trip.

Our journey took us from Morocco across the Sahara to the Dogon tribe of Mali and the beaches of the West African coast. We travelled through the rainforests of Nigeria and Cameroon as well as Gabon, Congo, and Angola where we saw no other travellers and in Namibia we walked up Africa's highest sand dunes and watched amazing wildlife. We arrived into the city of Cape Town after 23 weeks of camping in the bush, sandmatting through the desert, pushing the truck out of enormous, muddy potholes, getting bitten by mosquitoes, cooking over the camp fire and drinking warm beer as well as seeing incredible wildlife, experiencing new cultures, meeting amazing people, travelling through stunning landscapes and making friends for life. I still think I had good reason to be a little apprehensive, it was hard going at times, but these occasions turned out to be the best memories and what made the trip such an adventure!

Here is a selected list of overland operators whose websites provide detailed information about their trips. The average age on most of these would be 20–40 with a higher ratio of women to men. For more companies, see the directory of tour operators maintained by Overland Expedition Resources (www.go-overland.com). Specialist companies that operate only in one region (eg Africa) are mentioned later in this book.

The Adventure Company, www.adventurecompany.co.uk.

Dragoman, www.dragoman.co.uk.

Exodus, www.exodus.co.uk.

GAP Adventures, www.gapadventures.com. Originally a Canadian company; the acronym stands for 'Great Adventure People', so not specifically for gap years.

Gecko's Adventures, www.geckosadventures.com (billed as 'grassroots adventures').

Imaginative Traveller, www.imaginative-traveller.com.

Intrepid Travel, www.intrepidtravel.com. Now incorporates the long-established Africa specialist Guerba.

Kumuka Expeditions, www.kumuka.co.uk.

Oasis Overland, www.oasisoverland.co.uk. Covers Africa, Middle East, Egypt, and Latin America.

AIR TRAVEL

Air travel has changed beyond recognition, with no-frills airlines forcing national carriers to drop their fares in order to be competitive. A few low-cost airlines have tried to break into the long-haul market but it is a lion's den. The Canadian Zoom Airlines failed in 2008, as did the Hong Kong airline Oasis which had been flying passengers between London and Hong Kong for £150. Meanwhile, there has been a surge in regional discount carriers on the Ryanair model, including Kingfisher Red and SpiceJet in India, AirAsia in Malaysia and South East Asia, Jetstar which links many Australian cities plus South and East Asia, Tiger Airways in Australia (grounded at the time of writing due to safety concerns), WestJet in Canada, Mango in South Africa, GOL in Brazil, and so on. All these airlines have their own websites and many allow online bookings, some at remarkably low prices.

For long-haul flights, especially to Asia, Australasia, and more recently Latin America, discounted tickets are available in plenty. The major student travel agency STA Travel is one of the best starting places. STA Travel specialises in student and youth travel offering low-cost flights, accommodation, insurance, car hire, round-the-world (RTW) tickets, overland travel, adventure tours, ski, and gap year travel. STA Travel has about 40 branches in the UK and hundreds more worldwide staffed by experienced travellers. 'Gap Year' is one of the icons on the STA homepage and the company estimates that it deals with about 14,000 enquiries per year about gap year travel. For bookings and enquiries, call STA Travel on 0871 230 0040 or log on at www.statravel.co.uk to find fares and check availability. You can also request a quote by email or make an appointment at your nearest branch.

Other reliable agencies specialising in long-haul travel including for student and budget travellers are:

Austravel (0844 050 2816; www.austravel.com). Part of the giant tour operator TUI.

Flight Centre (0844 800 8660; www.flightcentre.co.uk). Branches around the UK.

Marco Polo Travel, Bristol (0117 929 4123; www.marcopolotravel.co.uk). Discounted airfares worldwide.

Student Flights (0844 800 8610; www.studentflight.co.uk).

Trailfinders, London W8 and other branches (0845 054 1010 worldwide; 0845 050 5940 Europe; www.trailfinders.com). 22 branches in UK cities plus Ireland and Australia.

Travelbag, Alton, Hampshire (0871 703 4701; www.travelbag.co.uk). Originally Australia and New Zealand specialist, owned by ebookers.

Travel Nation, Hove (01273 320580; www.travel-nation.co.uk). Staffed by real experts who specialise in finding the best deals on RTW flights, discounted long-haul flights and multi-stop tickets.

Western Air, Totnes, Devon (0845 680 1358; www.westernair.co.uk). Good on rail and coach passes as well as RTW itineraries and long-haul flights.

> ### THINKING ABOUT YOUR CARBON FOOTPRINT?
>
> *Anyone who cares about the future of our planet or has seen, Al Gore's film An Inconvenient Truth will want to give some thought to minimising their carbon footprint. Of course it is best for the planet if you don't fly at all, but if you do, consider offsetting your emissions with a donation to fund tree-planting or other mechanisms to reduce the impact of air travel on the environment, offered by many companies such as NativeEnergy (www.nativeenergy.com) and Climate Friendly (https://climatefriendly.com).*

Other discount agents advertise in the travel pages of newspapers such as the *Independent*. Phone a few outfits and pick the best price. General websites such as www.cheapflights.co.uk, www.travelocity.com, www.expedia.com, and www.opodo.com are good starting points, though comparison shopping this way can be time-consuming and frustrating. Even after long hours of surfing, the lowest internet fares can often be undercut by a good agent, particularly if your proposed route is complicated. For example, an agent is more likely than the internet to come up with an offbeat route down under using Etihad and Sri Lankan Airways to travel via Abu Dhabi to Mumbai, overland to Trivandrum in Kerala, on to Colombo, Singapore, Sydney (or Melbourne or Perth) then back to London for less than £1,200.

When purchasing a discounted fare, you should be aware of whether or not the ticket is refundable, whether the date can be changed and if so at what cost, whether taxes are included, and so on. **Roger Blake** was pleased with the RTW ticket he bought from STA Travel that took in Johannesburg, Australia, and South America. But once he embarked he wanted to stay in Africa longer than he had anticipated and tried to alter the onward flight dates:

> *That is the biggest problem of having an air ticket. I had planned for six months in Africa but I've already spent five months in only three countries. I have been into the British Airways office here in Kampala to try my verbal skills but have been told the 12-month maximum period of validity is non-negotiable. How stupid I was to presume I would get a refund when it states clearly on the back of the ticket that they 'may' be able to offer refunds/credit. A lesson for me, and a warning to future world travellers, to check before they buy whether or not the ticket is refundable or extendable.*

ROUND-THE-WORLD FLIGHTS

The idea of going all the way around the world holds more than a touch of romance. From the early heroic navigators such as Ferdinand Magellan to the fictional traveller Phileas Fogg, circumnavigators of our planet have always captured the imagination of adventurous souls. The first question is always: how can I keep the cost of such a trip down to a manageable level? Magellan had the backing of the King and Queen of Spain; Phileas Fogg was a gentleman of independent means. The first step to achieving this goal is to understand how RTW fares are calculated.

The price of RTW tickets has remained fairly consistent over the past few years, though taxes and fuel surcharges have leapt up. You shouldn't count on getting much change from £1,000 even for the most limited route. Check www.roundtheworldflights.com (020 7704 5700) or Travel Nation in Hove, Sussex (www.travel-nation.co.uk) for ideas. RTW fares start at about £865 including tax for three stops, departing London between April and June (New York, Auckland, Fiji). The cheapest fares involve one or more gaps called 'surface sectors' which you must cover overland. For example, prices on a ticket to New Zealand via Australia with stopovers in Bangkok, Singapore, or Tokyo start at less than £1,000.

The most common RTW itineraries are ones that have been specially marketed by groups of airlines that co-operate and have formed various alliances. A good travel agent will quickly tell you which alliance of airlines (if any) is best suited to your needs. Fare levels change according to how many stops and what distances you want to cover, so you will need to make some careful calculations about your route, and whether you want to travel 26,000, 29,000, 34,000, or 39,000 miles. Note that if you don't particularly want to include North America on your itinerary, you may not really need a RTW ticket.

Generally speaking, RTW itineraries must continue in one direction with no backtracking and invariably must be completed within 12 months with no possibility of extending. Fares that differ between low, shoulder, and peak season depend on your date of departure from home. If possible, try to start your RTW trip between September and November or April and June. The standard RTW stopovers are Singapore/Bangkok, Sydney/Auckland, and Los Angeles/New York, with a free stopover in the Pacific such as Fiji or the Cook Islands thrown in. Many fares are quoted without tax so keep reminding yourself to add on at least £200 and for a complicated routing as much as £500. The main alliances are:

One World (www.oneworld.com). Member airlines includes British Airways, Qantas, Cathay Pacific, American, Finnair, Iberia, JAL (Japan), Lan Chile, Malev, Mexicana, S7 (Russia), and Royal Jordanian. The OneWorld Explorer RTW fares are calculated according to season of travel and number of continents included. A five-continent trip will start at £2,000.

Star Alliance (www.staralliance.com). 27 international airlines including Air New Zealand, Singapore Airlines, Air Canada, Lufthansa, United, Lot (Polish), TAP Portugal, SAS, and South African Airways. The special RTW fare allows five stops and up to 26,000 miles. The website has a downloadable RTW mileage calculator tool.

Skyteam (www.skyteam.com). Member airlines are Aeroflot, AeroMexico, Air France, Alitalia, Czech Airlines, Delta, KLM, Korean, and others. Choices range from the basic 26,000-mile maximum with up to five stops to 39,000 miles with 15 stops.

Other options to consider include the World Walkabout pass available from British Airways (BA), Qantas, and Cathay Pacific. The restriction here is 25,000 or 29,000 miles and seven stopovers, including multiple stops in Australia. Departures in the low season (mid-April to mid-June) are good value at about £1,550 including tax, but are a third more expensive in the peak summer or Christmas season. Western Air in Devon (www.westernair.co.uk/roundtheworld.html) provides some sample mileages on its website: London–Santiago–Sydney–Perth–Tokyo–London comes in at 28,033 miles.

The Great Escapade (www.thegreatescapade.com) can be booked using Virgin Atlantic, Singapore Airlines, and Air New Zealand. It is possible to stay inside the 29,000-mile limit and still visit eight or more countries, for a fare starting at £946 before tax.

Travel agents such as the ones listed above can piece together various sector flights to create a bespoke route that can incorporate as few or as many stops as you like. Before contacting them, spend some time poring over an atlas and deciding where you are sure you want to go and on what approximate dates. A specialist agent will quickly be able to tell you whether one of the alliance promotions is better than a DIY itinerary. It is possible to include almost anywhere on a RTW itinerary – at a price. For example it is usually disproportionately expensive to zigzag between hemispheres, so flying London–Johannesburg–Bombay–Sydney–Tokyo–Santiago could end up being astronomically expensive. Be prepared to compromise on your wish list of destinations. Console yourself that this might be just your first gap year over your lifetime and there will be other occasions in which to fit in the highlands of Papua New Guinea or the Galápagos.

SAMPLE BUDGETS

With next to nothing:

- A couple of EU-backed programmes provide full funding. For example, participants pay nothing to join the European Voluntary Service (EVS) scheme in which they will spend 6–12 months as a volunteer on socially beneficial projects in Europe.

- Summer camp counselling programmes in the USA run by BUNAC, Camp America, and CCUSA advance you your transatlantic fare and later deduct this from your wages. The placement agencies charge varying fees but your end-of-summer wages will cover this.

- The Leonardo programme is a fully funded nine-week vocational training programme that operates throughout the EU (see leonardo.org.uk).

- Although the kibbutz movement in Israel is in steep decline, it is still possible to spend three to six months for a modest fee of $260 that includes registration, visa and insurance (www.kibbutz.org.il/ volunteers).

- Exchanging your labour for free accommodation and food works very well with the international exchange WWOOF (World Wide Opportunities on Organic Farms – www.wwoofinternational.org).

With £1,000:

- A month-long InterRail trip around Europe will cost £384 for the pass plus £25–£30 a day for living costs. If you stick mainly to the eastern countries (Turkey, Bosnia Herzegovina, Bulgaria, Romania, Slovakia) and cook for yourself in hostels some of the time, your budget will stretch much further than if you spend your time in Switzerland, France, and Scandinavia.

- Backpack in the developing world and concentrate on countries where your savings will stretch for many months. Assume you will have to spend at least half your budget on a return airfare. Ideas for the cheapest destinations are Nepal (especially trekking), India, Laos, Nicaragua, Bolivia, and Syria (when it re-opens its borders). (Tim Leffel's little book The World's Cheapest Destinations *is full of useful suggestions.)*

- Buy the cheapest return to New Zealand you can find in early February, hitch-hike from Auckland and get a job picking apples in the Hawkes Bay area where there is a perennial shortage of harvest workers (hawkesbay@picknz.co.nz) who earn at least the hourly minimum wage of NZ$12.75. Afterwards, blow your savings in Queenstown, adventure capital of the South Island.

- £1,000 won't last long travelling conventionally in North America, though with a J-1 visa from BUNAC (020 7251 3472; www.bunac.org) you can look for a seasonal job to cover your travel and leisure expenses.

With £2,000:

- Basic round-the-world fares start at £850 via Asia, though most end up costing on average £1,300 with extra stopovers and taxes for Australia and New Zealand. With your leftover budget you could backpack for months around South East Asia and/or have a shorter time in the more expensive Antipodes.

- An open-jaw ticket to Latin America allows you plenty of latitude to explore on the ground. For example, fares from London to Mexico City and out of Buenos Aires start at £750. If average daily spends are about US$10 in Bolivia, US$15 in Chile, and US$20 in Honduras and Guatemala, you could easily spend your whole gap year roaming the southern Americas.

- Book a language course in a romantic European location like Sorrento on the Bay of Naples or Granada in Spain. A sample four-week course through CESA in southern Italy would cost £785 plus £658 for homestay accommodation with breakfast. By booking a cheap Easyjet flight to Naples, plenty of money would be left over for exploring the Mediterranean.

- Various sending agencies such as *The Leap* and *Madventurer* offer five- or six-week travel/volunteer programmes in Africa which cost less than £2,000.

With £3,000:

- The majority of conservation specialists run exciting gap year trips and projects in far-flung corners of the world for on average £1,000 a month, so you can choose from helping to protect orang-utans in Borneo, study lemurs in Madagascar, or carry out a reef survey in the Bahamas.
- Incorporate an Everest Expedition (£2,000 for 35 days with Real Gap) into a volunteer and adventure trip to Nepal.
- Obtain a catering certificate in four weeks from the famous Leiths School of Food and Wine (£2,720) and then enlist its help to find you a job on a luxury yacht or in a ski chalet.
- Learn to dive or even qualify as a PADI Divemaster on a Thai island with, for example, Personal Overseas Development (www.podvolunteer.org).

With £4,000+:

- Join an expedition to the Norwegian Arctic with BSES.
- Work with big game on a South African game reserve.
- Train to become a snowboard instructor in New Zealand, Patagonia, the Canadian Rockies, or the Alps.
- Spend a year living it up in a beachside house in the South Pacific or the Caribbean.

EUROPE

Europe has always punched above its weight in terms of global influence. Although relatively modest in size, it boasts more than 30 national cultures, vastly different climates and landscapes, and one of the most ambitious peacetime organisations in history, the European Union. Added to all this, it has a quite amazing past. Greek ruins, Roman forts, and Gothic cathedrals all trace the story of Western civilisation, providing a kind of living history through which the interested gapper can wander and wonder, one foot in the past, the other in the present. And hot on the heels of the EU expansion into Eastern Europe have galloped budget airlines and youth hostel entrepreneurs; so budget-conscious gappers can balance more expensive western destinations such as Sweden and Switzerland with cheaper chill-out periods in Estonia and Slovenia.

Europe's sheer variety can seem to border on the unmanageable, but it can easily be broken down into bite-size chunks that share certain borders or traditions (eg Northern Europe, Scandinavia, Central Europe, the Mediterranean, Alpine, Balkans, and finally Russia, the Baltic Countries, and the Ukraine). So with trains, planes and boats willing to whisk you away and few problems with border controls, why not develop a taste for the continent on our doorstep?

THE LURE OF EUROPE

A gap year in Europe offers unrivalled access to some of the world's most famous cities, scenery, cultures, and languages. After all, it is pretty darn good to sit in Rome, the Eternal City, sipping an espresso while eavesdropping on the world's most sensual language. Or leave the well-trodden track to meander down a country lane in Romania, shadowed by a dramatic castle far above. Europe has a seemingly endless capacity to surprise, to flaunt its fashionable modernity, while clinging to slow-paced traditions. Its people can be intimidatingly chic, reassuringly generous, or depressingly impoverished; even its most famous monuments have a way of differing from their postcard images. Somehow they are larger or smaller than expected, their surfaces surprising or their air of authority humbling.

You can follow tried and tested touring routes through the continent, or branch off and create your own. It is easy to follow the crowd to the Mediterranean for some indolent sun worshipping, then grab a cheap flight to party-capital Barcelona, before continuing the fun in Eastern Europe, where cities such as Riga have developed reputations as party meccas. Should you wish to learn a language, then you will be spoilt for choice by the variety of courses on offer (see 'Directories of Courses' later in this book). But if you're no linguist, don't worry too much – many Europeans, particularly the younger generation, have a fair grasp of English. It is, however, polite to make at least some effort with the local language. Learning to order a beer is a good start, but a premature conclusion.

Then there is cost – gappers and their money are soon parted in Europe, but there is a chance you can pick up casual work, thanks to the blessed absence of red tape within the EU. The ability to play a musical instrument soulfully on a street corner might replace some of your funds, although you will need to check the busking conventions for each place you visit.

Overall, Europe does benefit from some planning as a gap year destination, but a canny gapper can save enough by tight budgeting to allow for the occasional splurge – perhaps an adrenaline-charged white-water rafting trip in Austria, a music festival, or that exhilarating dog-sled ride in snowy Lapland.

GETTING THERE

Most gap year travellers these days turn to the internet for travel advice and information. Low-cost airlines have exploded over the last decade, opening up all corners of Europe to adventurous gappers as well as to less adventurous stag and hen parties. The rules have changed, so that it is no longer permitted to advertise £10 flights which end up being £85 after taxes, fuel surcharges, and a fee for

UNMISSABLE HIGHLIGHTS

- Sample the delights of Paris, the city of romance, full of twisting streets, chic cafés, and cheap wine and cheese.
- Find that Lapland, the land of the Midnight Sun, is warmer than expected in summer.
- Explore the Greek island of Santorini, with its famous volcanic caldera and gravity-defying villages.
- Join pilgrims from all over Europe as they gather in the dazzling medieval city of Santiago de Compostela in Galicia.
- Chill out in Berlin, a place both exquisitely trendy and reassuringly relaxed.
- Visit the world's smallest state, the Vatican City in Rome.
- Walk around Dubrovnik's city walls.
- Ski in the lofty Alps in summer or winter or, for an alternative range, try the Carpathian Mountains, curving through Eastern Europe.

checking baggage have been added. With unavoidable extras, the cheapest flights start at about £70 return and usually, the earlier you book on off-peak no-frills flights out of Stansted, Luton, or regional airports, the cheaper the fare (though not invariably). Bookings should be made online because telephone bookings are more expensive; if you don't have your own debit or credit card, borrow one from a co-operative parent.

Make sure that you factor in the cost, and time, of getting from the airport to your city of choice. Cheap airlines often use small airfields some way from the city (or indeed from anywhere). If France or Belgium is your first destination, it can be easier to take Eurostar, costing from as little as £69 return (London St Pancras to Paris; cheapest fare must be bought in advance). Check out the cheap airlines' websites: www.ryanair.com, www.easyjet.com, www.bmibaby.com, www.flybe.com, www.jet2.com (Leeds-based) and www.thomsonfly.com (Coventry-based).

This style of flying has spread to the continent and discount airlines have proliferated including vueling.com (Spanish), airberlin.com, germanwings.com (both German), transavia.com (Dutch), wizzair .com (Hungarian), smartwings.com (Czech), norwegian.no and so on. Central sources of information include flycheapo.com and whichbudget.com. Scheduled airlines like BA and Aer Lingus have had to drop fares to compete and are always worth comparing. After saying all this, you may wish to consider the environmental impact of flying. Gappers heading for Europe (unlike their counterparts going to New York or Thailand) can choose to avoid those nasty polluting flights: visit ferries.co.uk as a starting point for your maritime ambitions.

Before the era of cheap flights, budget travellers' transport of choice was the long-distance coach. Eurolines is the group name for 32 independent coach operators serving 500 destinations in all European countries from Ireland to Romania. Return fares start at £39 for London–Amsterdam if booked at least a week in advance. Bookings can be made online at nationalexpress.com or by phoning 08717 818 181. So called 'funfares' mean that some off-season fares from the UK are even lower. For smaller independent coach operators, check advertisements in London-based magazines such as *TNT*. For example, Poltours (020 3411 4833) links the UK with many cities in Poland; one-way fares start at around £50, return £75, but discount coach trips to the country have been made almost redundant by cheap airlines such as Wizz Air.

GETTING AROUND

InterRail is still one of the most popular ways to enjoy a variety of experiences and sights within a short time span and tight budget. The Global pass, covering the whole of Europe for one calendar month, costs approximately £385 for those under 26 and £582 for those 26 and over. Shorter durations of 22 and 15 days are also available for £300/£450 and £272/£384. If you plan to make a few long journeys in a certain number of days, investigate Flexipasses; they permit five days of travel within 10 days, or 10 days of travel within 22 days. Also you can buy one-country passes that will cover three, four, six, or eight days of travel within one month. A number of specialised agencies sell InterRail products and add different mark-ups, with variation as much as £25. Passes can be bought online (in which case you will probably have to pay an extra £5 or £10 or so for Special Delivery), or in person at branches of STA Travel and similar outlets. Websites to check include www.raileurope.co.uk, www.trainseurope. co.uk (0871 700 7722), www.interrailnet.com, www.railpassshop.com or the marvellous site for train travellers everywhere, www.seat61.com.

Even in the furthest corner of Eastern Europe, clean, efficient, well-staffed trains run on time. Inter-Rail gives you the freedom to travel at a reduced rate, it usually represents a saving compared to the cost of paying for the individual journeys and it means that you can go somewhere 'just because you like the sound of it'. Every experience will be different. Before you buy InterRail tickets, you need to know what you're getting for your money.

Alongside the usual travel books such as a Lonely Planet or Rough Guide, you're likely to need your own train information: the *Thomas Cook Rail Map* (£9.99) can prove invaluable for all the routes where direct trains are unavailable and alongside this is Thomas Cook's *European Rail Timetable* (£13.99).

Very often in high season (June, July, August), you will find the trains you need are booked up for days in advance. This can mean either losing the spontaneity and booking a week in advance, staying in one place a few more days than planned, or taking shorter regional journeys. If you are travelling outside high season, bear in mind that some train services will be unavailable and some attractions will be shut, although this means you can avoid crowds at the most popular destinations. Whatever happens, leave in the direction of home a good couple of days before your pass runs out.

Night trains are particularly useful, because you don't lose a day travelling. It isn't always easy to work out costs in advance as seat reservations are almost always compulsory and can cost anywhere between €3 and €30, requiring a budget of a potential extra £150 per person.

Couchettes and sleepers are not included in the InterRail pass and must be paid for at the normal supplement of up to €25 (less in Eastern Europe). Sleepers on the 'Trenhotels' can add as much as €40 each. If you're travelling as a couple, couchettes (at least in the Catholic countries) mean you will be in separate carriages altogether as they don't allow mixed sleeping accommodation and for two it can be far more economical to sleep in the seating carriages. This is also a great way to meet fellow backpackers and to pick up tips on what to see and where to avoid.

It pays to know about the discounts available on InterRail – for example the P&O ferry from Dover to Calais, the Hellenic Mediterranean ferries between Italy and Greece (25%), or the Eurostar discount. Some of these are listed in the back of the ticket book, but a little research goes a long way.

Stations are very often the hub of a small town and families frequently wait on the platform to offer rooms in their homes to tourists in order to supplement their income. This can be much cheaper than the hostels and the families are prepared to help you with timetables and translations. As well as making you feel at home, this offers the chance to see how real people live rather than just the inside of another chain hostel.

MY GAP YEAR: JENNY HARDIE

Jenny Hardie went InterRailing and wrote about her voyage of discovery.

After a month of train travel with InterRail I am bronzed, toned, and still in one piece. I had a fantastic time, following a route that defied all logic and convention, and involved endless laughter, confusion, and foreign officials. Even if things don't always go perfectly - well, that's a story to tell when you get back.

My boyfriend and I made the rather dangerous assumption that once we had our InterRail tickets, we'd have our travel expenses covered, apart from a few negligible charges for seat reservations on long-distance trains. Not quite! We found that reservations are almost always compulsory and we ended up spending at least £150 each on seat reservations alone. Nothing fancy, just the standard second-class seats that the InterRail ticket covers. I wouldn't try and get away without paying these either. There are endless ticket inspections and some trains where they won't even let you on without checking your tickets and passports.

Waking up in a new country is a magical experience and I wouldn't hesitate to recommend the night trains, with the added advantage that you don't lose a day travelling. Normally we just booked seats when we slept on trains and made ourselves comfortable. If you make an effort to get on, people don't mind waking up with your foot in their face.

We had no planned route, and when Western Europe started to diminish our rather small savings, we headed east. Eastern Europe is one of those places that cause backpackers to cling together for safety. The frequent searches, passport checks, and questioning are a bonding experience and we made some great friends. One piece of advice is never tell them you've just come from Amsterdam. One night, on the Czech border, seven young men burst into our carriage. They were dressed in hooded jumpers and rucksacks and were demanding our passports. They turned out to be German customs officials but naturally we all thought we were being robbed. If you question their authority, they empty your bag. Another time, on the train from Budapest, we were evicted from our seats by the police and had to stand for 17 hours. In both cases, there was a real sense of community and a party atmosphere as we helped people out and were in turn helped by fellow travellers.

The majority of countries have no problem with InterRail tickets, but in Spain they don't cover first-class travel and there is no second-class option. Eventually, we found that you could pay €15 for an upgrade. In Romania, InterRail marks you out as foreign and we met a few unscrupulous ticket inspectors. On the train out of Bucharest, one such inspector chased us along the train to levy his imaginary fine of around £50 (it varied as he tried to bargain the bribe, but it had to be cash). He told us if we wouldn't pay the fine (and we wouldn't - we had legitimate tickets and no money) then we would have to get off the train at a remote station at 3am. We hid from him in the toilet and as soon as we made it over the border, the Hungarian ticket inspector had no problem with our tickets. But set against that bad Romanian experience, we were really lucky in Transylvania and found a kind lady who couldn't do enough for us - she even did all our washing. Her concern when we drunkenly wanted to use the gas cooker at 1am was more for our safety than that of her house.

Seeing the sunset in Madrid and exploring Roman ruins under palm trees in Croatia were fantastic experiences, which I hope to repeat some day. The advice we were given and the help we received in so many places have given me a renewed faith in human nature. Lastly, I hope you have a loving family to come back to - you can't use InterRail in your home country and the only time we were genuinely stranded was when no-one would pick us up from the ferry port at Dover.

Train travel throughout continental Europe is subsidised and therefore reasonably cheap in many countries, especially Italy, so buying point-to-point tickets is a good idea for those not covering too much distance. Often there is a huge differential in price between the elite high-speed services and the slower local trains. The coach equivalent of InterRail is the Eurolines Pass (www.eurolines-pass.com) which is available for 15 or 30 days. A 30-day youth pass in high season will set you back about €375. An attractive alternative is a hop-on, hop-off backpacker bus. The main contender is Busabout (www.busabout.com), which offers a Flexitrip pass to students for £319 that allows six stops within the whole operating season between May and October; many other permutations are available.

For fixed coach itineraries designed for gap year travellers, investigate the 18-, 27- or 32-day tours offered by London-based Topdeck Travel (www.topdeck.travel). These all-inclusive packages covering between nine and 14 countries cost from £1,320 to £2,315.The European landmass is one of the most expensive areas of the world to traverse. One of the cheapest ways is to pre-arrange a shared lift. Ride-sharing can be fixed up via websites such as Allostop in France (www.allostop.net), Taxistop/Eurostop in Belgium (www.taxistop.be), and Citynetz-Mitzfahrzentrale in Germany (www.citynetz-mitfahrzentrale.de). The normal practice is that passengers pay a small registration fee and then make a contribution to the driver's expenses, according to distance. There are dozens of lift-sharing outlets across Europe, especially in Germany, where there are Citynetz offices in Berlin, Freiburg, Hamburg, Munich, etc. In most cases you will have to pay roughly five eurocents per kilometre that you want to travel. Matches can seldom be made straightaway, though, so this system is of interest to those who can plan ahead.

BUDGETING

Although parents will concern themselves unduly with this aspect of your trip (are you *sure* you have enough money? or, are you *sure* you want to blow that much?), it is very wise to give it at least more than a passing thought. After all, your meals, accommodation, beer rations and transport options depend wholly on you possessing the requisite amount of hard cash – at the right time. Carrying some cash in euros is a good idea, but try not to have more than €100–€150 on your person in case you are robbed. Easily spent, easily lost – such is the life cycle of cash. If it is hard to get to an ATM (say in rural Estonia), then at least the cost of living will be cheaper. A budget starting at €40 a day should suffice in Western Europe, transport excluded. Eastern Europe is much cheaper, although Russia is more expensive.

When you arrive in a city it is a good idea to think what paying attractions you really want to see and to intersperse these with general ambling around. These meanderings, away from tourist hot spots, can often be the most rewarding, leading you to hidden architectural gems or kooky local hang-outs. European café culture gives you licence to while away afternoon hours while nursing a small coffee or beer. Look for cheap supermarkets, of which Europe has plenty, and buy picnic essentials. Eating bread and cheese and drinking wine on the banks of the Seine is an excellent and very cheap way to pass a Parisian evening. Also, look out for food stalls, which will save you the expense of a sit-down meal. Falafel, for example, is a good bet – it has nutritional value, the good places let you pile your plate high with salad, and chickpeas are pretty filling. If you're keen to eat out, then lunch menus can offer unexpectedly good deals. It is often a good plan to ask locals or the expat community for advice on the best deals in terms of accommodation, food, free museum entry, free concerts, etc. Good places to ask are English language bookshops and youth hostels.

ACCOMMODATION

Hostels offer the cheapest beds in Europe, ranging from about £7 in Bucharest to £35 in Venice. In cities such as Berlin, Barcelona, and Milan, you will probably spend £20 even for a hostel bed away from the centre, and more for a centrally located place. Hostels are a great way to meet people and find out about the area, but you will not have much privacy.

Hostels fall into two categories: 'official' and independent. Hostelling International (www.hihostels.com), formerly the Youth Hostels Federation, consists of 4,000 hostels in 90 countries. Membership costs only £9.95 for those under 26 (01629 592 700 in the UK; www.yha.org.uk). Rules and guidelines apply, often including curfews (good if you don't want to be woken up in the early hours by drunken party animals, bad if you want to *be* a drunken party animal) and dorms are usually single sex. You know what you'll get, but they can be a teeny bit boring. Technically you need to be a member, but you can pay a supplement of £3 if you aren't. If you buy an International Guest Card and get it stamped every night (for a few euros extra), you can become a member after six nights. Private hostels are unpredictable, but often have fewer rules and more colour. Good hostel websites include www.hostelbookers.com, www.hostelworld.com and www.hostels.com, all of which allow online bookings; www.famoushostels.com lists a select few.

Hostels come in all shapes and sizes, including a sailing ship in Stockholm called Af Chapman (chapman@stfturist.se) and a former prison in Ljubljana (www.hostelcelica.com). These speciality hostels can get booked up very early, although in high season it is probably best to book ahead for any hostel, particularly if you plan to arrive in the evening. Some hostels charge extra for bedding and it is worth considering making or taking a sleep sack. Key deposits might also set you back €15, to be refunded when you check out. On the plus side, breakfast is often included in the price and some hostels offer other free services such as internet and railway or bus station pick-up.

Although hostels are popular with young people, they are often open to all ages so not always party centrals. Similarly, they can be packed to the rafters with school parties. Practise tolerance, buy ear plugs, or pay out a bit more for a single or double room. Keep your valuables on you as far as possible because theft can be an issue. If all the hostels are booked out, then ask for advice. Staff might know of another place or local families with vacancies. Alternatively, head back to the station and ask at the tourist information office or, in extremis, hop on a bus or train to a less well-known town where a bed will be easier to find. Sleeping in public places (ie train stations and parks) is a last resort and usually tolerated rather than encouraged. If you're stuck, sharing a hotel room may not be prohibitive. Visit www.hotels.com or www.laterooms.com.

In some cities it is almost as cheap to book an apartment if you are travelling in a group of at least four. Tourist offices and the internet can be helpful, but the real steals are achieved by asking around when you arrive. This will allow you to tap into the 'informal' letting market. For example, it is possible to rent a small house on a Greek island for under €70 a night in high season. The trick is to ask locals, starting with the manager of the café. It probably also helps if you are a group of girls, and you will need to head out to the less touristy areas.

Also, think how much you could save by camping. The latter does not need to remind you of soggy holidays in Cornwall. Try wild camping on the Swedish archipelago where there are no cars, pure water, and the spicy smell of cinnamon buns wafting over the pine trees from the local bakery. The down side, of course, is that you have to lug your stuff around and camping grounds are usually some way from the centre of town. Cycling and camping make a good combination. Most campsites will keep your passport from the time you check in until you leave. Some countries are fine about wild camping, others much less so. Sweden is probably best of all since it has the law of *Allemansrätten* which gives everyone the right of public access to private land for recreational purposes. It is best to check and if you are in rural areas then ask the landowner's permission. You'll be surprised how chilled most of them will be – they might even offer you breakfast!

CULTURE SHOCK

Although you won't feel it quite as strongly as you would in developing countries, culture shock is still an issue, particularly in areas of Eastern Europe. Traditional gender roles tend to be preserved in countries such as Romania, where many women work out of economic necessity rather than because there is any serious commitment to equality. Subsequently, western women may be a little perturbed

EXCITING WAYS TO GET INVOLVED

- Teach English, crafts or sport at a children's summer camp on the Dalmatian coast of Croatia (www.ccusa.co.uk).
- Do a three-month internship at a company in Berlin (www.gls-berlin.de).
- Get paid work at a club in Ibiza (www.balearic-jobs.com).
- Pick strawberries on a Danish island (www.samsobaer.dk/summerjob.html).
- Study art history in Florence or Spanish in Salamanca (www.arthistoryabroad.com and www.mester.com).
- Volunteer at a museum on the Greek island of Kefalonia through the Hellenic Foundation for Youth and Volunteering (www.fnec.gr).
- Learn to surf on the Basque coast of France (www.gap.surf.france.free.fr).
- Live and volunteer with orphans at a children's village in Russia (www.ecologia.org.uk).
- Work a season at a Swiss ski resort (www.jobs-in-the-alps.co.uk).
- Stay for free at a hostel in Amsterdam in exchange for doing some duties (www.flyingpig.nl).

by flagrant examples of male chauvinism. Being hassled, however, can happen in any big western city, particularly those with substantial immigrant populations and in southern Italy, rural Spain, and parts of Turkey. The best way to tackle unwanted attention is not to break step if you are walking, and to learn a few choice phrases if you are reading in a park. One young female traveller found that speaking Welsh was an effective deterrent. On the whole, this attention is never a real problem – just annoying. If you don't want to talk to anyone/go for a drink with them, simply tell them that you are not interested. Or buy a ring and tell them you're married.

Gay travellers should probably act discreetly in Central and Eastern Europe – Poland is staunchly Catholic, with a distinctly intolerant right-wing government, while Belarus is known to treat homosexuality with contempt. The Czech Republic, however, was the first former communist country to grant legal recognition to same-sex partnerships.

Sunbathing topless is best reserved for liberal Western European destinations. Depending on your background you might at first be taken aback by the readiness with which Germans and Scandinavians strip off. Being rowdy in public will probably not be noticed in most big European cities, especially in lively Spain and Italy, but east European cities such as Prague and Riga are attracting more than their fair share of stag and hen parties, and as a result are getting a little sour about drunken British 'savages' (to quote a Latvian MP). At one point. the mayor of Tallinn was reported to be racking his brains to find ways of discouraging unruly Britons from relieving themselves on the national Monument of Freedom.

For details of these and many other ideas for jobs, volunteering, and courses, see the country-by-country chapters.

WHAT TO EXPECT

What should you expect as you tour Europe? Decent transport, accessible culture and plenty of other travellers to exchange stories with. On the whole, it is very easy moving between countries, the obvious exception being Russia, for which you must organise a visa well before you go. On the whole, Europe is pretty safe and violent crime is thankfully rare. Common sense will get you through most minor annoyances. Beware of pickpockets, eg jostling gangs of children around stations or on crowded metros. Thieves can also target hostels and overnight trains, but camping sites tend to be fairly safe. Also, watch out for dodgy taxis that charge astronomical rates: make sure taxis are licensed and the meter is switched on, and ask how much the journey will cost before you get in. There are also certain scams running in Eastern Europe involving a fake policeman: if anyone asks to see your passport/money make sure that they are legitimate (ie have identification) before handing anything over. If they become difficult, insist that they take you to the local police station. Also, make sure that you get the right amount of money when you get your currency converted – some blackboards advertising cut-price rates may muddily suggest 0 when they mean 9. Again, check the rate before agreeing to the transaction, or better still, use a local ATM.

SCANDINAVIA

Sweden, Iceland, Finland, Norway, Denmark

CURRENCY

Finland uses the euro (£1 = €1.13)

£1 = 8.5 Danish krone	US$1 = 5 Danish krone
£1 = 9 Norwegian kroner	US$1 = 5.4 Norwegian kroner
£1 = 10 Swedish krona	US$1 = 6 Swedish krona
£1 = 185 Icelandic krona	US$1 = 113 Icelandic krona

BUDGET

€50–€75 per day excluding transport. Iceland is more expensive, although Scandinavia's big cities, such as Stockholm, will also knock your budget.

HIGHLIGHTS

Blonde women, glistening blankets of snow and the intoxicating glory of the Northern Lights and the Midnight Sun – this is the picture envisaged by most gap year travellers considering a trip to Scandinavia. You might also like to add Santa Claus, marauding Vikings, and ABBA. Many gappers are unfairly put off by high prices, but there are plenty of ways to save money in Scandinavia while enjoying some of the most stylish cities and spectacular wilderness areas in Europe.

Scandinavians have style – lots of it. After all, they came up with Ikea, which is practically a small nation in its own right. Stockholm, Helsinki, and Oslo are fast-paced and trendy, while Copenhagen and Reykjavik have well-deserved reputations as weekend party centrals. Urban centres such as Gothenburg, in southern Sweden, Aarhus in Denmark and Tromsø in Norway have a more edgy, youthful vibe. Alcohol can be ruinously expensive (£6 for a beer in Norway, £4.75 in Denmark), so hitting the town is definitely a 'splurge' activity.

For a cheaper cheerful holiday, head for the hills, islands, or beaches. The key to keeping costs down is to camp, preferably in the wilderness. Yes, there can be the odd (shy) bear and wolf, but on the whole it is very safe, and Scandinavians have elevated camping into an art form, erecting fabric palaces with minimum fuss. Popular places include the island of Gotland, off the coast of Sweden, and the Stockholm and Åland archipelagos. These places offer crystal-clear water (let's call it 'refreshing'), sandy beaches and a relaxed pace of life – although Gotland's ancient capital, Visby, is packed with partying Swedes in summer.

Head north on a sleeper train, and wake up in the Arctic Circle. Other northerly highlights are the Ice Hotel in Kiruna in Sweden and the Santa Claus Village, near Rovaniemi, Finland. Norway is justly famous for its fjords, the longest and deepest of which is Sognefjorden. Another highlight is the Lofoten Wall, comprising spectacular glacier-carved mountains soaring straight out of the sea. It is worth taking a couple of ferry rides to really appreciate their spectacular height and shapes. The Hurtigruten's fleet of ships pulls into every sizeable port and passes some of the best coastal scenes in Scandinavia (though prices are high, eg £675+ for the voyage south from the Arctic Circle to Bergen).

Iceland's scenery is out of this world – almost literally: US astronauts rehearsed their moon walking in its inhospitable interior. The 'land of fire and ice' seems to change and re-form before your eyes. Huge rivers, geysers, and geothermal springs are often accessible by public transport or tours and some have been harnessed for the public good – the world-famous Blue Lagoon is a weird blue spa in the middle of a lava field. Scandinavia is also unusually good at producing talented musicians and then throwing large music festivals to show them off. Look out for the Iceland Airwaves festival (www.icelandairwaves.com), held in Reykjavik in October, the Roskilde Festival at the end of June, the Copenhagen Jazz Festival held in early July and, 'Yran', which also takes place in July in Östersund (look out for the lake monster). For a quirky non-music festival you couldn't do better than Finland's Wife Carrying Championships, held in Sonkajärvi.

USEFUL SOURCES OF INFORMATION

Use It Oslo (Ungdomsinformasjonen), Møllergata 3, 0179 Oslo (+47 24 14 98 20; use-it@unginfo.oslo.no). Streetwise, its English language online budget guide to Norway, can be found at http://use-it.unginfo. oslo.no.

NORTHERN EUROPE
Germany, France, Benelux

CURRENCY
Euro (£1 = €1.13)

BUDGET
€35–€60 per day excluding transport. Germany can be at the cheaper end, particularly outside the major cities, and Amsterdam is at the higher end, depending on how many coffee shops you frequent.

HIGHLIGHTS

Northern Europe is the continent's powerhouse, a place of confident and prosperous countries with rich cultures, mediocre weather and a rather trying habit of throwing their weight around. Over the centuries they have begun world wars, laid the foundations of the EU, legalised prostitution, and grown some of the most powerful business empires in the world. Northern Europe's past will continue to draw visitors, whether it's the beer drinking traditions of Bavaria or the fairytale castles of Luxembourg, and its natural spectacles, from snow-capped mountains to luxurious beaches, will long continue to be enjoyed.

France has always been a place where you can enjoy the finer things in life, whether you prefer world-class museums, haute cuisine, or meandering around elegant streets, admiring chic people. The French are fiercely proud of their country, prioritising national identity above, say, monarchy (beheaded) or religion. Local cheese, bread, and wine is lovingly made, exhibited, and consumed. The French people have attracted more stereotypes than any other country: stubborn, rude, unbearably chic. Most of these are really aimed at Parisians, quite often by French 'provincials' who talk about their city cousins in less than respectful tones. Paris is the 'must visit' city of romance with wide boulevards, stylish cafés, ornate parks, and wonderful shops. For more than 1,000 years it has been a trend-setter, creating the can-can and the cinematograph, and publishing James Joyce's *Ulysses* when no other city dared. But if you really want to find out about the French people, then leave Paris.

If you prefer hot weather and beaches, head to the south. The Côte d'Azur is still the most popular beach spot, but seaside resorts along the Atlantic such as Biarritz are fast catching up. For a city that combines beaches and a chilled vibe, you couldn't do better than the stylish southern city of Montpellier. The Dordogne offers quintessentially French countryside, sparkling rivers and quaint châteaux, while the more industrial north is the place for Second World War buffs, Camembert devotees, and fans of Joan of Arc. In winter, do as the French do, and head for the French Alps. You can either blow your budget at resorts such as Chamonix or base yourself in attractive Grenoble, and catch the ski buses at slightly painful hours in the morning.

Germany is the most populous country in Europe, after Russia, and has always been a driving force in Europe – for worse when it came to Nazism and the Holocaust, and for better when it comes to diverting money to the less wealthy (to East Germany for a start, and more recently to struggling Greece) and taking their past on the chin. They have a slightly scary reputation as polite, formal, and efficient, but although this might be true on the institutional level, Germans you meet are often warm, relaxed, and fun. They can also be generous, especially when it comes to the size of the sausage/lump of cheese/cake on offer.

Just over two decades ago, Berlin was a divided city, split between the communist East and the capitalist West. Today, it is cosmopolitan and relaxed, with a buzzing nightlife, a great modern art scene, and an ambitious approach to modern architecture. Amazingly, it is still reasonably cheap compared with other major European capitals, so sampling its legendary nightlife won't break the bank. If you have only time for one part of Germany outside Berlin, try Bavaria. It has a definite national character, which includes a strong affiliation to lederhosen and beer. Go to Munich in the latter half of September for Oktoberfest, when vast beer tents fill to capacity with bacchanalian crowds. If you have time for a little more exploration, try the former GDR (East Germany).

Until at least the 16th century, Belgium, the Netherlands and Luxembourg were called the Low Countries. Amsterdam is justly famous for its liberal attitudes, beautiful canals, and excellent art galleries. Or so you may tell yourself – most people still come to Amsterdam for dope and the red light district, and only later discover its multiple charms. For real edge head to Rotterdam, Europe's largest port. Belgium, by comparison, can seem a trifle dull, but it offers excellent beer, chocolate, and mussels and chips, and can soon grow on you. Luxembourg is Europe's third smallest country, and a lovely little place, by all accounts, if you don't simply blink and miss it.

TRAVEL TIP

The Wochenendticket ('Happy Weekend ticket') in Germany is valid for the whole country on Saturdays and Sundays but only on regional trains. It costs €39 if bought online, valid for up to five people, which means that in theory you can get from the Austrian to the Danish border for less than €8 each. For people working or studying in Germany over a long period, it would be worth investing €115 in a Bahncard 50, which gives a 50% discount off all second-class rail fares. Singles to other European countries can also be bought for €29.

CENTRAL EUROPE
Romania, Hungary, Slovakia, Czech Republic, Poland

CURRENCY
Slovakia uses the euro (£1 = €1.13)

£1 = 28 Czech koruna	US$1 = 17 Czech koruna
£1 = 4.6 Romanian new lei	US$1 = 2.9 Romanian lei
£1 = 4.5 Polish zloty	US$1 = 2.75 Polish zloty
£1 = 300 Hungarian forint	US$1 = 184 Hungarian forint

BUDGET
€20–€40 per day excluding transport.

HIGHLIGHTS
Less than 25 years ago, these countries were cut off from Western Europe by the Cold War and Soviet-sponsored communism. Now they are paid-up EU members, busy embracing their European identity while hanging on to their traditions, history, and beliefs. As Brussels' bureaucrats have turned their attention eastward, so too have travellers, spurred on by cheap airfares and the promise of something a little different. Meanwhile, young Poles, Romanians, Hungarians, Czechs, and Slovaks have turned their attention west, coming to Britain in their thousands. Central Europe headily mixes the old and the

new, the cosmopolitan and the nationalistic. Its big cities have rapidly become lively must-see destinations, while rural areas tend to maintain their folk traditions and in some cases their primitive and picturesque ways of life as well. Although there are a number of overweening and ugly concrete buildings on show, they are often eclipsed by the grandeur of Roman ruins, Gothic cathedrals and Art Nouveau galleries, which have managed to escape destruction. Budapest is one of Europe's most exciting capitals, nicknamed 'The Paris of Central Europe', with a rich and varied cultural heritage. Summer sees a surge in visitors keen on the café culture, nightlife, or just strolling down broad avenues while the sun shines. Prague is another unmissable destination with a stunning and ancient cityscape, cheap beer, and an intoxicating mixture of traditional eateries and gourmet restaurants. Both cities suffer armies of tourists. Bucharest, Warsaw, and Bratislava are not nearly as inundated, although still engaging.

Prices are still reasonably low in terms of accommodation, particularly outside the major cities. You can still find a dorm bed in central Prague for £7–£10 a night. To say goodbye to the city crowds, head to Brasov in Romania, a beautiful base for appreciating some quite spectacular royal castles, some with scary associations with Dracula, or head to the university town of Timisoara, nicknamed the 'city of students'.

Although the Czech Republic comprises the ancient lands of Bohemia and Moravia, it has only been around as a country since 1993 when Czechoslovakia split. History lovers will find plenty to amaze in the Czech Republic, but it is probably more famous among younger travellers for its beer. If you would like to raise a glass to the creators of lager, head to Plzen, where the golden nectar was invented in 1842. Neighbouring Slovakia has a thriving outdoors scene, including a number of very good ski resorts, while Hungary boasts Europe's most incomprehensible language (related to Finnish), some excellent open-air thermal spas, and a love of paprika. Grappling with war, invasion, and occupation for centuries, Poland has a strong national identity as well as much cause for sorrow. While lively towns such as Gdansk and Wroclaw are forward-looking, places such as Auschwitz remain a horrific reminder of Poland's – and Europe's – tragic past. Krakow is arguably the most beautiful city in Poland.

Nature enthusiasts or adrenaline junkies should also make the most of Central Europe's beautiful countryside, particularly the Carpathian mountain chain, which offers excellent hiking and skiing opportunities. Slovakia has the highest peaks, called the High Tatras, which dwarf most of Central Europe. The Slovak Paradise mountain range is famous for its huge system of caves and cascading waterfalls. Romania and Poland also boast magnificent peaks. For the opposite experience, namely endless flat plains, visit Hungary's mysterious Alföld ('Great Plain'), where cowboys still ride.

MEDITERRANEAN
Spain, Italy, Portugal, Malta

CURRENCY
All use the euro (£1 = €1.13)

BUDGET
€40–€70 a day excluding transport. Italy and Spain tend to be at the higher end, Portugal and Malta at the lower end.

It's hard to plan any European trip without factoring in at least a couple of lazy days on the Mediterranean, glass of local wine in one hand, fork in the other, plate piled high with one of the region's delicious specialities. Meals are carefully prepared, enthusiastically eaten, and calmly digested.

Italy leads the field at *la dolce vita* (the good life), based on good food, wine, and company. Fashionable clothes are also popular, particularly in Milan, and young people often gather in the central square at night to preen, drink (usually very moderately), and generally show off. They are often typecast as volatile and sexy, which is true to a point, but many have a streak of old-fashioned conventionality, thanks to family loyalty, religion, or a plain old attachment to their roots.

Italy has a lot to live up to with its great legacy of painters, popes, and past democratic greatness, but its sheer vibrancy, which in Naples borders on chaos, means that it never feels like a museum. This is certainly true of Rome's Forum, where hordes of tourists can't dim the excitement of exploring a site that is literally on top of centuries of history, while Fiats and mopeds rush past barely missing each other. Just let your senses soak up the magnificent sites and the furious sounds – and then head to the stately Vatican, regal Pantheon or iconic Coliseum. Art lovers tend to make a beeline for popular Florence, whose cultural and artistic richness under the powerful Medici family culminated in the Renaissance. Romantics might prefer Venice, a surreal and beautiful city where you should get lost and thereby escape the tourist hordes admiring the Grand Canal and Piazza San Marco. Only in relative isolation can you really appreciate the city's mysterious fading grandeur. It's not cheap though, so base yourself in neighbouring Mestre, Treviso, or Padua, buy picnic food from their excellent markets, and then make a day trip (or two) into Venice by train. In winter, follow the Italians north to the Dolomites for some excellent skiing. The south feels like a very different country. Naples is the birthplace of pizza, rough and ready, while the Amalfi Coast is dramatically beautiful. The south is a great jumping off point for Malta, which has absorbed North African, Arabic, and Italian influences but has a national character quite its own.

Spain is equally committed to the good life, perfecting tapas as both a style of food and a distinct way of dining. Often lively and sociable, the Spanish are a complex people and Spain's landscape is equally diverse. Even if you are a nighthawk, it will take a while to adjust to Spanish time. No Spaniard goes out to a restaurant for dinner before 10pm and often much later. Keep yourself going with a tapas and a caña (a half pint in a long, thin glass) in the early evening. In backpacker meccas like Barcelona and certain resorts, expect to be swarmed by touts enticing you into their drinking establishments with offers of free vodka for the first hour or similar. The obvious places to visit are cosmopolitan Madrid or hip Barcelona. Madrid is the buzzing, energetic capital, Barcelona the stylish ex-Olympic city that attracts young people from all over the world. For that morning after, take a recuperating walk around Madrid's oldest quarter, the Madrid de los Austrias, or laze around on Barcelona's beaches. For a different atmosphere entirely head to the south, which has a magnificent Moorish heritage. Córdoba boasts a magnificent mosque (Mezquita), free if you visit between 8.30am and 9.30am (otherwise €8). The Alhambra in Granada is another breathtaking example of Islamic art and architecture. For the more stereotypical attractions, namely bulls and beaches, head to Pamplona for the *Sanfermines*, the famous Running of the Bulls festival in early July; Mallorca for great beaches; and Cabo de Gata near Cadiz for an uncluttered and more remote beach experience (accessible only by foot).

Galicia is the province on the undiscovered Atlantic coast of Spain. Because its climate is so much rainier than elsewhere in Spain, it is green and lush, and has some excellent walking tracks and wonderful seafood. The lovely city of St James (Sant Iago) is the end point for the famous pilgrimage from the Pyrenees to Santiago de Compostela which thousands of Christians, mystics, and keen walkers still follow every year. But beach bums won't be disappointed: a beach expert from the *Guardian* has declared that Las Islas Cies in Galicia is the best beach in continental Europe.

The strongest difference between Spain and Portugal lies in the people: the Portuguese are more reserved and discreet than Spaniards and the food is more varied, with fish and seafood understandably popular. Porto is the place to start if you like port (which isn't just a drink for your granddad). Visit the cellars and learn more, or just wander around the riverfront Ribeira district. Lisbon has a great nightlife, although dress can be glam, so haul out your best glad rags. Or move off the beaten track and sample the delights of Coimbra, a student city where tradition and parties walk hand in hand. Relaxation and/or surfing are best found on the beaches of the Alentejo – the Algarve can get a tad busy, attracting millions of tourists every year.

ALPINE
Switzerland, Austria, Slovenia

CURRENCY
Austria and Slovenia use the euro (£1 = €1.13)

£1 = 1.46 Swiss francs   US$1 = 0.90 Swiss francs

BUDGET
€40–€65 per day excluding transport for Switzerland and Austria, €25–€45 per day excluding transport for Slovenia.

HIGHLIGHTS
Gargantuan snow-capped mountains, shimmering melt-water lakes, and air so pure that breathing feels like a special treat – if this all sounds appealing then the Alpine countries of Switzerland, Austria, and Slovenia are for you. If on the other hand it sounds a bit poetic, then how about hurtling down precipitous slopes, chucking yourself out of a plane or crawling around canyons like Spiderman? Although Alpine countries, specifically Switzerland and Austria, tend to have a reputation for being a little stuffy, all formal manners and crisp bank notes, the scenery itself is anything but – a massive playground, perfect for all kinds of winter and summer activities.

Mountains make up 70% of Switzerland's landmass, with the Matterhorn being its most famous peak. Dozens of ski resorts beckon, but for high-adrenaline sports try the Interlaken area: although backpacker-friendly, the lure of bungee jumping, paragliding, etc may soon part you from a large wad of cash. If you're in Slovenia head to Bovec in the Julian Alps, where paragliding and canyoning are enthusiastically catered for. In terms of affordability, Austria is middle of the road, and offers some of the world's best snowboarding and skiing. Tirol is a picture-perfect example of Alpine scenery – base yourself in medieval Innsbruck and be sure to see the famous Golden Roof in the old town.

In summer, hiking is the vertiginous activity of choice. In Switzerland, there are 50,000km of designated hiking paths and it is hard to get lost – this being Switzerland the signs are plentiful. Austria is also well organised and the Austrian Alpine Club maintains a network of alpine huts for overnight stays. Hiking is extremely popular in Slovenia, with around 7,000km of waymarked trails, certain 'themed trails' and 165 mountain huts. Outdoor enthusiasts might also like to try watersports in Salzkammergut, Austria's answer to the Lake District, and cooling off in one of Switzerland's great lakes – even suited and booted Zurich has an enviable number of open-air bathing spots.

When the great outdoors palls, there are the urban delights of Vienna, Salzburg, Geneva, and Ljubljana to appreciate. Wealthy Vienna is stuffed to the gills with history, and you can take a stroll through the inner city and into the past. If the low-brow beckons, just nip into a café, or ride the *Riesenrad*, the Ferris wheel which stars in the film *The Third Man*. Salzburg is famous as the birthplace of Mozart and the location for the ever-popular kitsch that is *The Sound of Music*, while Geneva is the pied à terre for major European organisations such as the International Red Cross and the UN. Tiny Ljubljana boasts, with some justification, that it is a 'mini Prague'.

BALKANS

Greece, Turkey, Albania, Bosnia and Herzegovina, Bulgaria, Croatia, Macedonia, Montenegro, and Serbia

CURRENCY

Greece and Montenegro use the euro (£1 = €1.13)

£1 = 2.50 new Turkish lira	US$1 = 1.52 new Turkish lira
£1 = 163 Albanian leke	US$1 = 100 Albanian leke
£1 = 2.22 Bosnia and Herzegovina marka	US$1 = 1.35 marka
£1 = 2.22 Bulgarian lev	US$1 = 1.35 Bulgarian lev
£1 = 8.35 Croatian kuna	US$1 = 5.10 Croatian kuna
£1 = 70.8 Macedonian denar	US$1 = 43 Macedonian denar
£1 = 115 Serbian dinar	US$1 = 70 Serbian dinar

BUDGET

€25–€50 per day excluding transport, although Greece is at the higher end and can easily cost up to €60 a day. Macedonia and Albania are both at the lower end, and Turkey can be a real bargain if you don't go anywhere that is swamped with tourists.

HIGHLIGHTS

Light reflects off cubist white buildings, sand crinkles between your toes, archaeological sites trace the story of ancient civilisations and you have to pinch yourself to check that you're not dreaming. Yes, Greece can be this good. A favoured backpacker destination for decades, it offers, to put it crudely, those four useful ingredients for a good time: sun, sand, sea, and sex. Some islands such as Kos are well known for the latter, others such as Patmos still avoid the party image. Many do both, inviting package holiday tourists into certain tourist ghettos, leaving the rest of the island free for the more determined traveller to explore at leisure. Santorini, with its stunning caldera, is a good example – if you get out of the main town of Fira and avoid the south-east beaches, then the island is refreshingly uncluttered. An excellent way to get around is to hire a moped (you usually need to show a driving licence and pretend knowledge). Island bus drivers are well known for their imitation of grand prix drivers, but apart from that 'experience' the pace of life is reassuringly relaxed.

Greater Athens is a law unto itself, home to about a third of the population. The locals are convinced that their city is the new Barcelona for city-breakers, after vast improvements were carried out for the 2004 Olympics, and they are bewildered by the hostile press that portrays their country as a basket case. No signs of civil war will greet you, nor of boarded-up shops or deserted café terraces, but rather a vivacious and sophisticated urban centre. Athens is up there with Rome as a superb place to explore classical architecture and ancient history. The Acropolis is probably the most important monument of the ancient world. Mainland Greece, particularly the north, often gets rather brushed under the tourist carpet, but it is here that you can find the 'real' Greece, a place where the Orthodox church shapes people's lives and old men and women gossip endlessly. Northern Greece also has the country's highest mountain, Mount Olympus, ancient home of the gods, and snow-capped well into spring. The main route to the top takes two days, with a stay overnight in a shelter. The Peloponnesian peninsula in southern Greece is home to Olympia, birthplace of the Olympic Games, the ruined Byzantine city of

Mystras, and ancient Sparta. Greeks can be conventional, but they temper this with a relaxed approach to the beliefs and behaviour of visitors. What more can you ask?

If Greece were one side of a coin then Turkey would be the other. They are both made up of similar materials (sandy beaches, mesmeric water, civilisation-shaping history) and share a mutual love of family, food, and music. But Istanbul (once called Constantinople) was first the capital of the Christian Byzantine Empire and then later the epicentre of the Ottoman Empire. It is the Islamic influence that predominates today. Admire Aya Sofya and the Blue Mosque in Old Istanbul, before losing yourself in the Grand Bazaar, also known as the Covered Market, which has 4,500 shops, selling all kinds of trinkets that you never knew you needed.

For the sun 'n' fun aspect, most visitors head to the Mediterranean coast, famed for its incredible scenery and ancient ruins (including the city of Troy). The coast gets less busy east of Antalya. Republican Turkey has mainly adopted a western lifestyle, at least on the surface, and western Turkey can be very lively. For a hippie vibe, try Olympos, an abandoned port city, which is now famous for its air of dilapidation and ever-expanding treehouse camp. For something rather more crazy than cool, take the long journey east to Cappadocia. The fantastic landscape of strangely eroded rock cones has been inhabited for centuries, first by Byzantine hermits and others escaping persecution, and now by modern Turks who have erected television aerials on their rock towers and converted the caves into backpackers' hostels.

Croatia, Albania, Macedonia, Montenegro, Bulgaria, Serbia, and Bosnia and Herzegovina: what do they have in common? Well, for a start they were all at one time part of the Yugoslav Federation, which fell apart in recent history. Today they are fairly settled so that tourists – and developers – have been returning in droves. Croatia has always been popular, with 6,000km of coastline and almost 1,100 islands. You could call it 'the new Greece', but that is hardly fair because Croatia has its own Slavic soul. Most travellers head to the stunning Dalmatian coast crowned by Dubrovnik, 'the pearl of the Adriatic' according to no less a personage than the 'mad, bad and dangerous to know' poet, Lord Byron. For something less familiar, take the plunge and visit some of the other countries on the Balkan peninsula. They all have their beauties and the people can be very welcoming.

RUSSIA, BALTIC COUNTRIES, AND UKRAINE

CURRENCY

Estonia uses the euro (£1 = €1.13)

£1 = 46 Russian rubles	US$1 = 28 Russian rubles
£1 = 13.3 Ukrainian hryvnia	US$1 = 8 Ukrainian hryvnia
£1 = 0.8 Latvian lats	US$1 = 0.48 Latvian lats
£1 = 3.9 Lithuanian litas	US$1 = 2.37 Lithuanian litas

BUDGET

€20–€30 in the Baltic Countries, with Estonia the cheapest, and €50+ in Russia and the Ukraine.

HIGHLIGHTS

Russia occupies a special place in the western imagination: it seems to breed football club-owning billionaires, export internet brides, and became involved in a James Bond-style thriller involving rare poison and the KGB. The gregarious spirit of its people is coupled with a hideous and silted-up bureaucracy. Yet the relics of old-style communism fail to dim the glory of its imperial heritage. European Russia is familiar, whereas the rest of the country crosses 10 time zones and reaches almost to Alaska. In short, you could spend years trying and failing to understand Russia.

The two great European cities are St Petersburg and Moscow. The former is considered to be Russia's 'Imperial Crown', the second its 'familial heart'. The haunting magnificence of St Petersburg, its calm canals and brooding Winter Palace, cast a spell from which most visitors don't want to wake (although going out to the suburbs is a surefire way of doing this). The Winter Palace was home to the tsars and the backdrop to the 1905 and 1917 revolutions, but is best known today as the home of the Hermitage Museum, up there with the Louvre when it comes to being awe-inspiringly enormous. At the last count, the Russians reckoned that about three million artworks were on show. On the Petrograd side of the city, visit the Peter and Paul Fortress, which may sound like a nursery rhyme, but was actually mainly used as a political prison. Its most famous residents included Dostoevsky, Gorky, and Trotsky. If you can manage a mini-splurge, treat yourself to the ballet at Mariinsky Theatre.

Moscow, by contrast, is an enormous city, changing, tense, and powerful, mixing a reckless approach to western capitalism with the relics of the stolid communist lifestyle. Begin your visit at Red Square, where Lenin's Mausoleum, complete with reverential fans, is located opposite a trendy western-inspired department store and shopping mall called GUM. The other must-see monolith is the Kremlin, almost a city in its own right. If Moscow still feels a bit close to home, then simply take the Trans-Siberian Express and slowly chug your way to Mongolia.

Thanks to the Orange Revolution and the election in 2005 of pro-Western reformist Victor Yushchenko, things have changed in the Ukraine. Its capital, Kyiv, has wakened up to flash cars, chic clothes, hot clubs, and chilled-out bars, but peel off the flash veneer, and you'll find an old city, whose religious heart is the Caves Monastery. Its underground labyrinths are lined with mummified monks. If that atmosphere (by which I mean old rather than dead) is more to your taste, take a train to Lviv, whose beautiful buildings showcase most of the architectural movements of the last five centuries.

The Baltic countries of Lithuania, Latvia, and Estonia have rapidly become a phenomenon, combining old towns that are World Heritage Sites with a riotous party culture. Stag and hen parties have been quick to descend, but these countries have a lot more to offer than cheap beer. Try bobsledding in Sigulda or canoeing in Gauja National Park, both in Latvia, or admire the world's first Frank Zappa statue in Vilnius. Unexpectedly, one of the best beaches in the world is the 100km-long Curonian Spit in Lithuania, backed by fragrant pines and graced with untouched sand dunes lining the Baltic Sea.

GETTING A VISA FOR RUSSIA

An officially stamped Russia Tourist Voucher showing exact dates of entry and exit is a requirement of getting a tourist visa. It is straightforward to use an agent (for a fee of $20–$30) who will file some paperwork in Russia and send you an email with a hotel reference (no obligation to stay there). With this document and a further fee of £95 six working days in advance (or a whacking £128 at short notice), the Russian consulate will grant a single-entry visa for a maximum stay of one month.

TRAVEL RESOURCES

USEFUL WEBSITES
www.bugeurope.com, 'the backpackers' ultimate guide'.
www.flycheapo.com, links to all the no-frills routes and carriers in Europe.

USEFUL GUIDEBOOKS

Europe on a Shoestring (7th edition, Lonely Planet, October 2011), £17.99. Note that it is possible to buy digital pdf chapters country by country for £2.99 (http://shop.lonelyplanet.com/europe).

Rough Guide to First-Time Europe (Rough Guides, 2010), £19.99.

Thomas Cook European Rail Timetable, £13.99.

Rick Steves' Europe Through the Back Door (Avalon Travel Publishing, 2012), £14.99.

TRAVEL READING

Classic fiction

Ernest Hemingway, *A Moveable Feast* (Arrow Books). Absorbing memoirs about the author's years in Paris during the 1920s.

Mikhail Bulgakov, *The Master and Margarita* (Penguin Classics). An inspiring satire on Russia and the Ukraine written during the 1930s.

Günter Grass, *The Tin Drum* (Vintage Classics, first published in 1959). Written as a memoir and set in the war years in Germany.

Graham Greene, *The Third Man*. A novella set in post-wartime Austria and turned into a brilliantly atmospheric film starring Orson Welles.

Miguel de Cervantes, *Don Quixote*. A literary classic bringing to life the world of ordinary Spanish people in the 17th century.

Homer, *The Odyssey*. This is one of the two seminal ancient Greek epic poems.

Diary of Anne Frank (Penguin). A young Jewish girl's diary about living in hiding in Amsterdam during the Second World War.

Lighter/modern travel writers

Patricia Storace, *Dinner with Persephone* (Granta Books, 1998). A great account of life in Greece as seen through the eyes of an outsider.

Henning Mankell, *The Wallander Mysteries* (Random House). Set of eight crime novels set in Scandinavia.

Tim Parks, *A Season with Verona* or *Italian Neighbours* (Vintage Books, 2003). The author is an English expat living in Italy.

Alan Furst, *The Polish Officer* (Random House, 2001). A gripping tale of espionage revolving around a Polish intelligence officer and set during the Second World War.

William Blacker, *Along the Enchanted Way*. A remarkable account of remote valleys in Romania in the 1990s and early 2000s, where the way of life had barely changed since the Middle Ages. The author falls in love with a gypsy with whom he has a son.

Milan Kundera, *The Joke*. A satirical novel about communist Europe.

Patrick Leigh Fermor, *A Time of Gifts* (John Murray, first published in 1977) and *Between the Woods and the Water* (John Murray, 2004). The author describes a 1,200-mile walk from Holland to Constantinople undertaken in 1934 when he was 18.

Jan Morris, *Europe*. A personal appreciation of the continent by the doyenne of travel writing.

AFRICA

AFRICAN CONSERVATION EXPERIENCE

Sigrid Johnston, African Conservation Experience volunteer at Tuli Conservation Project (www.ConservationAfrica.net), writes about a land of dust and magic.

Tuli is a word meaning dust, depicting the conditions in the Tuli Block in Botswana during the dry season. I was fortunate enough to visit Tuli Conservation Project as the season changed in November and December 2010, experiencing the blossoming native flowers and thriving mopane trees. Few words truly describe Tuli and its unique rhythm. It is a destination off the main tourist track where volunteers can become in tune with nature by actively living and working alongside the wildlife.

The project collects crucial data to be utilised by researchers on a wide range of African wildlife. More interesting is the fact that as a volunteer you are privileged enough to actually feel Tuli with its native inhabitants. And what makes it a mesmerising experience is that your exposure to the wild is truly diverse; ranging from watching a majestic herd of elephants on the marsh plains to observing a dung beetle robustly roll elephant spoor up a hill. It really is the small things that captivate you, such as taking a shower under the stars and being awoken by the sun and bird chorus right outside your hut. By giving part of yourself to the Tuli project, it returns the favour even more than can be imagined. It changed me as a person and that is a testament to the power of Tuli.

Africa is the birthplace of humanity, home to many natural wonders of the world, and full of a pulsing vibrancy that blows away ideas about it being the dark or hopeless continent. Twenty-first century Africa is a remarkable collection of extremes, often right next to each other. The wealth of skyscrapers sits beside slums. The scorching heat of the dry season gives way to torrential downpours. Before going, many people think of Africa in terms of the animals and stunning scenery, but what most visitors remember is the people: hustling and fighting their way through life, often challenging, but generally welcoming and demonstrating insight born of the knowledge that the past and their ancestors are never far away.

DISCOVERING AFRICA

After Asia, Africa is the world's second largest continent (30 million km²) and second most populous (having just passed one billion). These statistics are a good starting point for talking about Africa because despite its significant size and population it remains marginalised, often forgotten by the wider world, at least until tragedy befalls as it did in 2011 with the famine in the Horn of Africa. A gap year in Africa provides the chance to discover a diverse place that is often misunderstood and misrepresented. Though you must go on a safari, by stepping off their beaten track and avoiding beach hotels, you can look into a place that faces many challenges but that offers so much more as well. A good example is Ethiopia, tainted for so long by images from the 1980s of starving refugees that ignore the lush, green landscapes and the ancient civilisations that through thousands of years built breathtaking monuments such as obelisks, castles, and huge rock-hewn churches down into the earth.

The outside world tends to view Africa in terms of poverty, corruption, and war, but Africans are more likely to be positive, and proud to be African. Ideas and roles are always changing but people are still deeply religious, with a spiritual understanding of the world that can be confusing, but potentially exciting for someone who is used to a more dry, scientific approach. African hospitality warms the hearts of those who encounter it – although some people can find it smothering at times. Family and kin are very important, but so are national pride and African identity. It's all a bit more complex than the 'ancient tribal hatreds' that the western press talks about.

The majority of Africa's population still lives in rural areas – about 60% across the continent, although much higher in some countries – and getting to know Africa means heading out into the bush. In the countryside you can still find people farming or raising livestock the same way they have for centuries. However, they are also equally likely today to be talking on a mobile phone while they do so. Rural life can demonstrate remarkable knowledge and understanding of the earth and its preservation. It can also be a place to see tremendous problems with land distribution leading to overcrowding, deforestation, and erosion.

Pole pole ndiyo mwendo ('slowly is the way') is a Swahili proverb repeated in different ways across the continent. Time can be understood in a cyclical manner that westerners may find infuriating. The main point to remember is that things happen for a reason and will happen in good time. On the Mombasa to Nairobi train, for example, look out for the Europeans who demand that they get more soup immediately, only to realise their mistake as the extra soup pours over them as the train goes round a corner. The happiest travellers in Africa are those who use the chance to move at a different pace and take the time to look around and enjoy the journey.

The two most common choices for gappers are probably:

■ the full travelling option going overland, for example from Cairo to the Cape or vice versa. This will give you the chance to see the diversity of experiences that the continent has to offer;
■ an equally exciting option that gives a more in-depth look at a smaller area, which is to work in a voluntary programme in one country, explore the area intensively, and also take the chance to pass through surrounding countries.

GETTING THERE

As a gap year traveller, you may like to book your flight through a student travel agent such as STA Travel or the Flight Centre. This is especially useful if your route is complicated. Key Travel (www.keytravel.co.uk) is also knowledgeable and often has some great prices, as well as being the agent of choice for lots of non-profit organisations. For a straightforward return, it's often hard to beat Opodo (www.opodo.co.uk) or similar. A specialist agency is the Africa Travel Centre (London WC1; 0845 450 1520; www.africatravel.co.uk). A return flight to Johannesburg or Cape Town in the low season (April–June) can be found for approximately £400.

As an early introduction to colonial heritage, BA flies direct to most places in Anglophone Africa from the UK, while for most of Francophone Africa, Air France may be your best option with a transfer in Paris, or even direct. KLM Royal Dutch Airlines, transferring at Schiphol, have many options to the continent, often in co-operation with Kenya Airways. Cheaper options can often be found through Gulf Air and Emirates – but these will require a longer route through the Middle East. **Kirsten Shaw** shopped around before her gap year as a volunteer in the South African bush:

Using www.skyscanner.net, I found the cheapest tickets to South Africa possible, stopping in Cairo at 4am. Cairo airport is probably the dullest airport I have ever had the misfortune to stop at, unless you like heavy gold jewellery and fashionable headscarves. Michelle and Ian [directors of Daktari, where Kirsten worked] tested this method of air travel too. They flew to France on 11 September on Afriqiyah Airways, the Libyan airline, and got their tickets for a third of what you pay for on any other airline. Why not?

However, this was before the recent conflict in Libya, so it's probably not a good choice at the time of writing.

Often cheapest, and cheerful, but leaving at strange times and frequently with lengthy transfers through Addis Ababa, Ethiopian Airlines have one of the most extensive networks of any airline serving Africa. In fact, the Addis transfer sometimes includes a night in a hotel and a chance to see a little bit of that fascinating place.

GETTING AROUND

Getting around the continent by air is very variable. Links are better than they were, but it's still surprisingly common that the cheapest flight to a neighbouring country will mean travelling via Europe. Internal flights within a given country are often reasonable, but you should first have a look at a company's reputation with a quick internet search. Quite a number of African airlines are banned from European airspace but these tend to be the pirate operations found in places that you don't want to be anyway (for example, all 50 airlines of the Democratic Republic of Congo are banned). On the more positive side, Kulula (www.kulula.com) is fairly priced, reliable and flies within Southern Africa. Precision Air (www.precisionairtz.com) is a good option for getting around East Africa. You can comparison-shop for flights on www.travelsupermarket.co.za.

Back on the ground, buses of highly diverse quality can get you to most places you want to reach. A very simple rule to be aware of is that generally the more you pay, the more careful the driving and the higher the level of comfort. On a strict budget and looking for adventure, the cheapest bus will get you to your destination eventually, after you've had to contend with burst tyres, sharing a seat with several other people and their animals, and definitely no air conditioning. Even paying a little more should be considered because this increases the chances that the tyres are not bald, that there is a spare tyre and that the brakes function. Sometimes the clue is in the name; for example, the reassuringly named intercity bus company in Tanzania, Scandinavia Express Services, has a better safety record than cheaper rivals. With long-distance buses it is usually possible to book by going to the ticket office in person, and you should report on time for departure, but don't expect the bus to leave at the time the ticket says. Over shorter distances you can normally just turn up and buses leave once they are full.

Trains can be a fabulous, and staggeringly slow, option. Journeys can last for days, rather than hours, so do find out when you expect to arrive. Third class may look appealingly cheap, but will be less attractive in the middle of the night when pickpockets go to work – although at least with no bed it's easier to stay awake. Second or first class may be the option you take the next time.

On top of these standard ways of moving around you may also like to hop into a horse-drawn *gari* in Ethiopia or a whizzy little auto-rickshaw in many different places. Rules have generally been tightened up in recent years, but you will at some point be able to marvel at the quantity of human cargo that can be crammed into a bush taxi (Nigeria), *matatu* (Kenya) or *daladala* (Tanzania). Wear a seatbelt when available and avoid the seat next to the driver (sometimes known as the 'death seat' due to its unfortunate position in a head-on collision). Overcrowding and discomfort are reduced in Northern Africa, and travelling by *louage* (shared minibus-taxi) in Tunisia is cheap and efficient.

You are unlikely to find a taxi with a meter, but make sure it's switched on if you do. Otherwise, negotiation will be required. Ensure that you carry this out before setting off. It can be useful to check with local people what they consider reasonable and drivers will often go at least close to this figure.

UNMISSABLE HIGHLIGHTS

- See the Serengeti migration, with 1.4 million wildebeest and 200,000 zebra and gazelle making their way across the plains.
- Victoria Falls is where you'll find 'the smoke that thunders', by some measure the largest waterfall on the planet.
- Soweto has the only street in the world where two Nobel Peace Prize winners lived (Nelson Mandela and Desmond Tutu), and you can ponder South Africa's painful but inspiring struggle there.
- Zanzibar is the spice island with narrow Arabic-style streets and laid-back golden beaches.
- The holy city in northern Ethiopia, Lalibela, has monolithic churches hewn down into solid rock some 800 years ago.
- Vibrant, colourful Fes is one of the most demanding but rewarding of Northern Africa's cities.
- Sossusvlei is an ecosystem in Namibia that seems to work without water, shaped into giant red sand dunes.
- An exciting present that defies the brutal history of slavery can be found in Cape Coast — a colonial fort on the coast of Ghana.
- The Great Pyramid of Giza in Egypt is the only surviving wonder of the ancient world.
- Visit the Atlas Mountains for some amazing trekking or the chance to say you went skiing in Africa.

Resign yourself to paying over the odds until you become more skilled or know what the local price is for a given journey (for example 20p for a quarter hour's drive in Ghana). Africa's roads are the most dangerous in the world. A lot of driving, including on small, pothole-ridden tracks, is conducted at break-neck speed. Drunk driving is rarely viewed as anything other than necessary. Commercial drivers (passenger and freight) may often drive for days, staying awake only through the use of stimulants such as cola nut, or *quat*. Paying a bit more, and assessing the sobriety of a driver (intoxication can also include glue sniffing and drugs) will help, but moving by road is always a risk.

BUDGETING

An idea of how much you will end up spending is given in the country sections below. Prices vary wildly, but generally cities are much more expensive than rural areas. You need to be flexible in your tastes because what might be a cheap snack at home may be imported and so surprisingly pricey. Street food can certainly be an option to keep costs down, but its risks include diarrhoea and even typhoid. Taking organised trips, such as those available in overland trucks, will increase your costs, but may get you to places you wouldn't otherwise reach, and show you things you might not have noticed.

MY GAP YEAR: DANIEL BRACKSTONE

Daniel Brackstone's route gave him the chance to work in and wonder at Africa, getting to know people and places that he'll never forget.

When I decided to take a gap year, I wanted something that would challenge me. I wanted to push my limits and make friends at the same time. It was important to really get to know a place, but to keep moving around and seeing new things. I started off taking a Kiswahili language course at the University Institute on Zanzibar ($7 an hour). I wrote to them, but you can really just turn up and arrange something. I was also able to set up a homestay with a family. That was expensive but allowed me to really feel I was more than just a tourist.

After enjoying the mysterious nature of Stone Town, and spending delicious time at the beach, I took my new language skills to a volunteer programme at a home for HIV-positive children in Kenya (www.nyumbani.org/volunteer.htm). Working with children anywhere is intense, but this was nothing like I'd come across before. Nairobi is also crazy. You have to watch yourself, but all the bars and discos can be great fun, and allow you to escape from the emotion of work once in a while. The local staff and the other international volunteers taught me so much, it felt like having 50 mentors who all knew so many things, and looked at the world in so many different ways.

I'd decided to save my safaris for Tanzania, but in Kenya I took the bus up to Fisherman's Camp on Lake Naivasha, and then a bus the next day to Hell's Gate National Park. You can just hike through and camp, walking past herds of giraffe on massive plains, and then into the breathtaking gorge. It feels like stepping into some kind of prehistoric landscape, especially with the sound of the geothermal power station at night sounding like a monster. Tanzania was then all about the Ngorongoro Crater for a beautiful trip, seeing most of the big five game animals. I took the train as well, just to enjoy two days watching the landscape, towns, and hanging out in the bar talking to the other people – not only Tanzanians but also a Congolese guy who was embarrassed that my Swahili was better than his! That got me through to Malawi where I went to the lake. I'd met a man who told me that if he could be promised that heaven was like the shores of Lake Malawi, he'd be good for the rest of his life. I would too.

Those are just a few of the things I did. I went wine tasting in South Africa near Cape Town, and in Jo'burg I went to the Hector Pieterson Museum where you learn about how even children were willing to die for a better life. I also went to Ponto D'Ouro in Mozambique, which is really weird because it's full of South Africans playing with their big adventure toys. It was the first time I've seen people who take their own plane on holiday! I focused on Eastern and Southern Africa, and I loved the bustle of the towns, the quiet of the countryside, the majesty of the animals and the pride of the people. There was so much to be done that I didn't even get to start on the west and the north – but I've been bitten by the Africa bug that everyone told me about. I didn't think it could be true, but it does feel like going home, being where your ancestors came from, and it changed my heart and soul in ways I couldn't have imagined.

EXPECT A CHALLENGE

In Africa you will not just be a stranger, you will be a rich stranger. Any idea of explaining that you are going on to be a student and about to incur massive debts, or that you don't yet have a job, can be quickly dismissed. If your iPod cost £180 then it is worth more than the amount of money that half of Africa's population survives on in a year. Of course, this doesn't mean that hassle for money and scams are any less irritating. It also doesn't mean that throwing money around will make any dramatic difference to people's lives. But at the same time, not everybody in Africa is poor. Some very wealthy people are to be found in some of the most inequitable societies in the world. There is no simple solution to the money issue. Some people find it very hard to make friends either because of their guilt, or because they feel they are being befriended for ulterior motives. It helps if you can relax and just accept that you will be subsidising others if you want to go to certain places.

On the subject of money, it should also be mentioned that Africa can sometimes be surprisingly expensive. Often there can be a lack of mid-range budget accommodation and food. The budgets below are only indicators; be prepared to negotiate prices almost everywhere.

Colonialism and to some extent slavery also need a mention. Power relations between Africa and the West have been distorted for a long time. It can be strange to hear someone talk of things being better under colonial rule, or terrifying to hear unfriendly attitudes to white people. It is equally unpleasant to listen to travellers who regard Africans as fools and themselves as wonderfully superior. This is an assumption that is found all too often, and your experience will be better if you identify it and address it. An anecdote may illustrate this well. While sitting on a beach on Zanzibar, a group of travellers saw a fisherman come down to his boat. The tide had gone out and the boat was left dry, out of the water. The travellers were laughing that the silly fisherman had come down too late to go out fishing – he'd misunderstood the tides or overslept, clearly. After looking at his boat for a long time, the fisherman brought down his tools and began fixing his craft, having waited for the tide to be out and having carefully considered what needed doing and then expertly fixing it.

A mention of HIV/AIDS is necessary when talking about Africa. As well as a simple warning to be careful and carry condoms (this applies to both sexes), be aware of the social effects of the ongoing pandemic, not least AIDS orphans (estimated to number 14.8 million in Sub-Saharan Africa). It's actually quite difficult to talk about HIV because, unless you are working in a project concerned with 'the scourge', you may barely notice it. HIV is one of Africa's greatest problems, but remains largely invisible. Deaths can still be registered simply as being, for example, from tuberculosis. Knowledge levels are high, but so is stigma, and it can appear that HIV and AIDS are things that only happen to 'other people'.

Before going to Africa, you might want to consider following a football team if you don't have one already. The English Premiership is huge in Anglophone Africa and Ligue 1 is big in Francophone Africa. As a way to start conversations, befriend taxi drivers, and so on, football is hard to beat. Local grounds may be practically deserted, but the FA Cup final, watched crammed into a bar with a television run from a car battery, is something not to be missed – particularly if the teams have African players. The team you pick will need to be a big one, so you can choose from the Premier League – Man U, Chelsea, Arsenal, or Liverpool.

CORRUPTION

Former Nigerian president Olesegun Obasanjo estimated that corruption costs Africa 25% of its collective national income every year. It is certainly prevalent, from the looting of national coffers by political leaders, to the payments made by western countries to secure contracts and bribes to policemen to have charges dropped. It is possible that you will be asked to pay a bribe, although this is less common than it is made out to be, and occurs most often where someone has been arrested, often for possession of drugs. Indeed, a common scam is to sell drugs to an unsuspecting traveller and then tip off the police, who will take a cut of the bribe they extort from the traveller. Generally, corruption is likely to be something that occurs around you, for example a driver being required to pay a policeman, and it tends to be done in ways so subtle that you are unlikely to notice.

EXCITING WAYS TO GET INVOLVED

- Learn to dive in the Red Sea (www.gapyeardiver.com).
- Take a walk with lions in Zimbabwe (www.amanzitravel. co.uk).
- Coach football in a South African township (www.score. org.za).
- Put on HIV-awareness workshops in schools in Uganda (www.volunteeruganda.org).
- Carry out underwater surveys in Madagascar (www. blueventures.org).
- Repair a school or build an orphanage in rural Tanzania (www.abroaderview.org/volunteer-tanzania/construction.php).
- Do work experience for Radio Fréquence Teranga in north-west Senegal (www.projects-abroad.co.uk).
- Work on a safari camp in the Okavango Delta (www. theleap.co.uk).
- Teach in a primary school in the Kilimanjaro district (www.village-to-village.org.uk).
- Learn Arabic in Rabat Morocco (www.cesalanguages.com) or take Swahili lessons while volunteering in Tanzania (www.globalvolunteerprojects.org).

EAST AFRICA

Kenya

VISA
£20 (single entry, valid for six months).

CURRENCY
£1 = 140 Kenya shillings (KShs)   US$1 = 85 KShs

BUDGET
£12–£18 a day in Nairobi, less in rural areas; £60–£75+ per day on safari.

Kenya is the home of the African safari. The name itself is Swahili for journey and Eu[...]
here conducted the first safaris. You can still see an outstanding variety of animal[...]
famed big five (lion, elephant, buffalo, leopard, and black rhino). This can be done i[...]
from luxury motor tours staying in grand lodges, to walking safaris with a Maasai guide, sleep[...]
the stars. The country straddles the Equator and offers remarkable scenery and a variety of cultures.
At its centre Mount Kenya presides over grasslands and thorn scrub. To the west the imposing Great
Rift Valley is full of lakes teeming with an amazing array of birdlife. The east coast offers white,
palm-fringed beaches and coral reefs, as well as the remains of ancient Swahili city-states and
Arab-influenced cultures and festivals. Kenya is also very much the gateway to or hub of East Africa.
Connections by road, rail, and air are good to Tanzania, Uganda, and Ethiopia. This is useful for a traveller or means that someone working in a project can use their holidays to explore the region, including
getting down to Zanzibar.

Staying in rural areas can still involve getting used to a lot of attention, especially from local children.
More unwelcome attention, such as aggressive taxi drivers or scams – especially fake safaris and
investment opportunities – are also to be found, especially in Nairobi. The capital is a great place to
party, meet other travellers and visit some decent monuments and museums. However, it is still often
referred to as 'Nairobbery', and moving around at night should be done with care, or avoided entirely.
A female traveller should take particular care. Regular marriage proposals are a nuisance, but a
real risk of violence also exists in some places. In terms of attention from the opposite sex, men
will find some amusement in the direct approach adopted by some bar girls, especially at the coast,
which has a reputation for sex tourism. A reminder is probably necessary of the economic circumstances that lead bar girls to look for foreign 'boyfriends', and also the very high rates of HIV to be
found.

Usual routes for travellers would involve arrival into Nairobi. Accommodation is fairly pricey (Nairobi
is also known as 'London 2'), but it is accustomed to backpackers, and decent, clean dorm beds can
be found starting at £5 per night. Travellers then tend to head out to the Rift Valley for hiking, safaris
through the Serengeti, and finish up with beach time at the coast. Many of these trips can be arranged
through agencies, but for the Rift Valley a great option for those with a tent is to take a *matatu* up to
Fisherman's Camp in Nakuru, then after a night there another bus to Hell's Gate and to trek through.
A great number of voluntary projects, from environmental care to looking after AIDS orphans, are available for gappers looking for placements.

Tanzania

VISA

£38 (or £43 for faster service, valid for three months).

CURRENCY

£1 = 2524 Tanzanian shillings (TZS)   US$1 = 1530 TZS

BUDGET

£18–£22 per day; £90–£110 a day for a safari in the north.

Dar es Salaam, Tanzania's commercial capital (its official capital is Dodoma, chosen for its central location), is taking off economically. Outside the big city, Tanzania offers the gap year traveller a real taste of
rural Africa and is one of the most popular gap year destinations. The country has been stable and safe
since the economically flawed but socially laudable stewardship of *Mwalimu* (teacher) Julius Nyerere

ended in 1985. Try to get out of the towns, which tend to be slow, and throw yourself into rural life. Tanzania also has the East African perks of stunning wildlife in game parks that are more expensive than those of Kenya, but the prices have been raised in the name of responsible tourism, and they tend to be more remote and less busy. Particularly recommended is the Serengeti and Ngorongoro Crater. Many companies compete in the town of Arusha, and it can be difficult to avoid the 'production line'-style operators.

Time in Tanzania also gives the chance for a visit to Zanzibar. Having bought a ticket at the port (never from touts, who offer residents' prices – and then follow it up with extortion on the boat), the ferry to Stone Town from Dar es Salaam only takes a couple of hours. You then find yourself in the most intriguing town, with narrow Arabic-style streets and bazaars. In fact, the Swahili culture and language of Zanzibar is a fusion of Arabic and African culture, which emerged from its placement on the trade routes using the monsoon winds, meaning that it was once the headquarters for the Sultan of Oman. Out of town (about an hour in a shared minibus that can be picked up in the morning from Forodhani Gardens near the House of Wonders) you can head to the north coast, but be prepared for the unsettling contrast between the full moon backpacker parties, discos and the huge Italian hotel, and the desperately poor villages behind. Much more pleasant is the laid-back east coast. The sea is not quite as perfect, but the welcome is much more personal.

Ethiopia

VISA
£14 (valid for one month).

CURRENCY
£1 = 28 birr	US$1 = 17 birr

BUDGET
£10–£15 per day (more in Addis).

At the time of writing, the dominant image of Ethiopia is of starving babies dying in camps. Drought has ravaged parts of the country, yet other parts are lush and intriguing with such a huge diversity of intricate cultures and histories to make you gasp. It is the only African country never to have been successfully colonised. A few years of military occupation has left a bit of Italian influence, but if you identify this in the coffee, then remember that coffee culture has been a part of the area for thousands of years – and many a myth and legend refers to it.

Ethiopia is a land of contrasts and extremes. In fact, it represents a small empire dominated by the north, once Abyssinia, and incorporates many different peoples. You can explore the ancient Axumite dynasty, whose empire extended into the Middle East, the remnants of the Jewish culture that was dominant before the coming of mystical Orthodox Christianity in 400AD, and Islamic practice that has evolved since its arrival 300 years later – still over a thousand years ago.

Ethiopia's highlands have mountains that soar to around 4,300m, while the sweltering lowlands plunge to the depths of the Danakil Depression below sea level. It is home to the oldest human remains in the world, well presented in one of the capital's fascinating museums. The 'New Flower' (in Amharic) that is Addis Ababa faces many challenges of urbanisation. However, it remains largely a pleasant and open city and offers a good starting point before heading off to explore the cultures of the south or the history and splendour of the north. On the Northern Historic Route can be seen the medieval city of Gondar, with its castles and churches, and also Axum, where the original Ark of the Covenant containing the Ten Commandments is said to be found. These jewels are perhaps even outdone by Lalibela, with its 11th- and 12th-century rock-hewn churches, carved down into the ground. These churches are surrounded by mystery and legend, and are said to have been built by angels. Remember also to visit the Simien Mountains, and Bahar Dar to explore the myriad monasteries on Lake Tana's islands.

After a long time as a closed country under a vicious communist regime (the *Dergue* or Council, which ruled until 1987), Ethiopia is now much more open. Its tourist industry is being privatised (although the state-owned Ghion Hotel chain has hotels in places such as Gondar that are sometimes beautiful, eg in old Italian palaces, though lacking in plumbing). Due to its history and reputation, Ethiopia is still frequently overlooked. Be sure to consider it as an opportunity to find somewhere truly off the beaten track.

SOUTHERN AFRICA

South Africa

VISA
Not required.

CURRENCY
£1 = 11 rand   US$1 = 6.75 rand

BUDGET
£15–£25 a day.

The billing of South Africa as a 'world in one journey' actually stands up pretty well to experience. Following the end of apartheid, it has become a destination of choice for backpackers and more well-heeled travellers alike, who can take in demanding visits to the dusty Transkei, high finance in Johannesburg, or stunning scenery and cuisine in the Winelands and Garden Routes of the Cape. It is also the top African destination for gap year volunteers working on particular projects. It remains an unequal and rather divided society, which is reflected in its levels of crime and political dissatisfaction – especially in Jo'burg. However, it is also a place of fascinating political awareness, with some of the best historical tours and museums in Africa.

To the wealthy, South Africa offers the option of sticking solely to five-star hotels and resorts, wine tastings, expensive cars, and professional game drives. However, cheaper travel, animals, and scenery are accessible for the budget traveller and even more readily for the volunteer (see *Africa* chapter). It is fascinating to see how South Africa engages with its history, including the political struggle against the racist apartheid regime (check out Soweto and the Robben Island Museum), colonial warfare (take a visit to the battlefields of the Zulu wars), and the intriguing mentality of Afrikaner nationalism (including the Voortrekker and Afrikaans monuments). Soweto tours can be arranged with most tour companies, which drive you around the main sites, including the Hector Pieterson Museum and the houses of Nelson Mandela and Desmond Tutu, and arrange a proper (staggeringly heavy) African lunch. Trips to Robben Island – departing from Victoria Waterfront in Cape Town – need to be booked well in advance. Even then, bad weather often leads to cancellations, so unless you have time to keep trying, you may be disappointed. After visiting these, you will have some insight into the struggle to create Nelson Mandela's vision of a 'rainbow nation'.

Crime is a huge problem in South Africa. Things are improving, including the upgrading of the central business district in Jo'burg, but violent crime – break-ins, muggings, car-jackings – remain prevalent, and many white South Africans live their lives as if under siege. Nonetheless, people are generally friendly and welcoming. As with anywhere, a bit of organisation and awareness will take an informed gapper a long way and make for a better experience. South Africa also has the best infrastructure in Africa, with some no-frills domestic airlines such as Mango (wwww.flymango.com), high-quality roads, and decent trains that are often under-rated but can make for a great trip. Buses can take you most places but a great way to explore is to take a road trip in a car – some backpackers take advantage of cheap second-hand prices to buy a vehicle, and hope to get a bit of money back at the end of their trip.

Botswana

VISA
Not required.

CURRENCY
£1 = 10.8 pula   US$1 = 6.5 pula

BUDGET
£20–£25 a day with hire car.

Botswana is included here to demonstrate the diversity of experiences that can be found in Africa. It's also added so as to talk about one of the continent's success stories. However, as you will spot in the budget suggestion above, Botswana is not a cheap option for the budget traveller. Seventy per cent of the country is dominated by the Kalahari Desert, meaning that travel needs assistance and is tough going. As part of its development plan and frugal fiscal policies, Botswana has gone for quality not quantity in its tourism, and it is expensive. Still, it's an interesting example and worth bearing in mind – but for the average gapper it will have to be regarded as a special treat, rather than taking up a big part of any itinerary.

If you can afford it, though, Botswana is something special. It is about the size of France, but with a population of under two million people, the majority of whom live in the east of the country, leaving the rest free for some of the most well-preserved and dramatic scenery and wildlife in Africa. The people are friendly and interesting and, if you get the chance, you may want to spend a bit of time in Gabarone playing 'Mma Ramotswe spotting' if you've read Alexander McCall Smith's charming books about the Number One Ladies' Detective Agency (and if you haven't, it's recommended that you do).

But the main reason people go to Botswana is the scenery and the wildlife. The Okavango River drains inland from Angola into Botswana's north-western corner and forms the Okavango Delta, the largest inland delta in the world. The water from this provides for a profusion of wildlife under huge skies, spreading out across grassy plains and stunning lagoons. The Moremi Wildlife Reserve, which covers 700 square miles (1,812 km^2) in the north-eastern corner of the delta, is considered by many to be the ultimate African safari destination.

The story of Botswana as a nation is rather heartwarming, with a more recent sting. At independence in 1966, Botswana was one of the 10 poorest nations on earth. A few years later copious diamond deposits were discovered which were managed with well-disciplined fiscal policy that saw the economy grow by an average of 9% per year for many years. Sensible planning continues to draw the benefits from mining and tourism but the economy has been restricted by incredibly high HIV prevalence rates – an estimated one in four citizens aged 15–49 has the virus, the second highest rate in the world after Swaziland. This has led to draining levels of health spending.

Zimbabwe

VISA
£40 (valid for three months).

CURRENCY
Most people bring US dollars as cash because of the ludicrous inflation that has afflicted the Zimbabwean dollar.

BUDGET
£12+ per day.

Up until about 2000, Zimbabwe was one of the most popular destinations for gap years in Africa, when the country was known as the breadbasket of Africa. A burgeoning middle class saw Harare become one of Africa's most vibrant and cosmopolitan cities. However, inequalities were unresolved and most land and commercial farming remained in the hands of white farmers. Resentment festered, especially on the issue of land distribution. This presented a massive threat to President Robert Mugabe's legitimacy so he began acquiescing to demands, which led to the violent grabbing of farms. Try to see the splendid documentary film *Mugabe and the White African* made in 2009, which movingly shows a Zimbabwean farmer and his family trying to defend their property from Mugabe's militia.

International isolation and corruption saw the Zimbabwean economy collapse. When inflation hit 7000% in 2008, the Zimbabwean dollar was officially suspended and transactions now take place in US dollars or another hard currency. The situation has improved somewhat since that low point: food and fuel shortages as well as power cuts are much less common, and travellers are finding hostels welcoming and friendly.

Victoria Falls is still one of the most magnificent natural wonders on the continent. There are still enough tourists to attract lots of touts and hustlers and a handful of voluntary schemes still operate in the beleaguered country, but travel to Zimbabwe is not recommended.

WEST AFRICA

Ghana

VISA
£40 (valid for three months).

CURRENCY
£1 = 2.50 cedi   US$1 = 1.50 cedi

BUDGET
£12 per day for basic standard, £20 allows a comfortable level of travel.

There is no bad time to head to Ghana. The weather is always hot, the political climate is stable, and crime is much lower than in other places. Widely regarded as the friendliest place in West Africa, if not the whole continent – if not the world – Ghana could be the ideal choice to ease you into Africa, or perhaps restore your faith later on. Ghana has an intriguing political history – its first president, Kwame Nkrumah, was instrumental in establishing the Commonwealth and a prominent exponent of pan-Africanism. Visitors, including gap year workers and travellers, now talk of one of the fastest-growing and most inspiring of African countries that still retains an exotic vitality. The country still struggles, however, with chronic water shortages.

Highlights to visit include Mole National Park, famous for its elephants, and the rainforests of Kakum National Park, with an aerial walkway through the canopy, not to forget beautiful beaches, waterfalls and rolling hills. Buses and *tro-tros* – jampacked minibuses where you might have to share a seat with a bucket of slopping fish – are a good way to get around but, as with most forms of shared taxi across the continent, they only leave when full and this can mean sitting in the heat for some time. Local people often wait in the shade or by the drinks stall until the time they know it will depart. Keep your eyes and ears open and ask discreetly where you can. Accommodation in Accra is varied, but can cater to the budget traveller in hostels for around £6 per night and hotels for more.

Ghana has one of the richest cultural environments in Africa, with masses of festivals, dance, music, colourful outfits, and traditional arts and crafts. Culture is dominated by the Ashanti region, but exciting events can be found all over. The Ghanaian government is making a concerted effort to encourage and celebrate its cultural heritage. Its troubled history is reflected in the slave forts and museums along the beautiful Cape Coast. Further west along the coast is Takoradi, where at certain times of year turtles come ashore to lay their eggs. You can also paddle out to a stilt village.

West Africa is also where football fever is at its most intense. Ghana's Black Stars are a respectable outfit, and local and international fixtures are well attended.

Senegal

VISA
Not required.

CURRENCY
£1 = 757 West African CFA   US$1 = 459 CFA

BUDGET
£22–£35 a day.

Coming from the UK, it can be easy to forget about Francophone Africa. The Francophone countries such as Cameroon, Togo, and Senegal offer different experiences and the chance to make use of your A level French, if you have it. Indeed, if you think you would like to improve your French but listening to tapes asking 'Where is the train station?' puts you off, then what better opportunity than to learn it in a colourful, musical situation where finding the train station will take you past markets, performers, and traditional healers? (And if you are hoping to travel by train, note this recent extract from the rail site www.seat61.com: '*the Dakar–Bamako train is definitely NOT RUNNING at the moment, and all passenger service has now stopped completely, except for Kayes-Bamako. A thrice-weekly Kayes-Bamako train is currently running.*')

People are drawn to Senegal by a vision of people wearing white *jallabiyas* (hooded cloaks) and making beautiful music. Small, friendly, and pretty successful, Senegal sits at Africa's most westerly point, with the Gambia almost entirely enclosed within it. Though vibrant and modern, Senegalese society remains rooted in the concepts of honour (*Diom*), hospitality (*Teranga*), and respect for older people.

The name Senegal is said to be derived from the Wolof name for dug-out canoes that many fishermen (fishing is Senegal's biggest industry) still use today, and are also used in the favourite Senegalese pastime of canoe racing. This takes place along the coast and is quite a sight. Senegal is also renowned for its moving, soulful music. Festivals between November/December and April/May/June are definite highlights. The only down side is you are likely to have to dance at some point, and you may pick up quite a crowd. Football is huge in Senegal and they haven't forgotten the glory of their victory over France in the 2002 World Cup. The national squad has a few Premiership players, but in your language class you might need to brush up your knowledge of French teams as well as your past tense.

UP-AND-COMING DESTINATION

Mauritania is one of those unexplored gems that travellers have been discovering as part of a popular overland route from Morocco to Senegal (and points beyond), now that the western Sahara region is relatively stable and a paved road connects Nouadhibou with the colourful capital Nouakchott. From the coastal road, you can see how the red sands of the Sahara change dramatically into the white beach sands of the North Atlantic.

NORTH AFRICA

Morocco

VISA
Not required.

CURRENCY
£1 = 12.9 dirham   US$1 = 7.8 dirham

BUDGET
£12–£18 a day.

Just a short hop from Europe is Morocco. Its position at the crossroads of East and West, as well as the Mediterranean and the Atlantic, makes for a unique experience and some fascinating history and culture. Parts of Morocco have become a little overloaded with backpackers and tourists over the past few years. However, if you take the time to find your way to lesser-known places then Morocco's mysteries are still there to be enjoyed. Chefchaon in north-west Morocco is a great place to hang out when you first arrive, get acclimatised, adjust yourself to street sellers and meet other backpackers. Small villages and eccentric markets will provide quality crafts and interesting conversation (often in French). Even in the cities, especially Fes (or Fez) and Marrakech, wandering though the souks takes the visitor to a different world of spice merchants and snake charmers. The smell of tanning mingles with mint tea, while the call to prayer from the myriad mosques makes its timeless, haunting demand. For the more adventurous adrenaline junkie, the Rif and Atlas Mountains offer stunning trekking and even skiing. The Saharan sands can be explored on camelback, horseback, or by four-wheel drive. Nomadic Morocco (www.nomadicmorocco.com) specialise in guided treks in the High Atlas mountains.

Finding your way out of the tourist traps and into Morocco's more interesting sites will take some effort. You also need to be aware that where tourists are commonplace, thieves and con artists tend to follow. However, if you keep your wits about you, and consider what you want and what you'll pay for a given item, you should find yourself some interesting things at reasonable prices. But remember: successful haggling requires courtesy (and practice).

Egypt

VISA
£15 (valid for six months).

CURRENCY
£1 = 9.8 Egyptian pounds   US$1 = 6 Egyptian pounds

BUDGET
From £12 a day.

Egypt, with its pyramid and feluccas, might seem a bit of a clichéd choice here. However, the popular uprising of early 2011 centring on Cairo's Tahrir Square, which resulted in the removal of President Mubarak, has made the country a more appealing destination. Most backpackers go for the Red Sea Riviera, diving, and sunbathing. If you visit the pyramids or the tombs, expect to be surrounded by coachloads of tourists. Taking a gap year in Africa is all about challenging perceptions, though, and having the time to look beyond common ideas. Amid the tatty souvenirs and the camel rides, remember the importance of Egyptian civilisation in developing so much – for instance architecture, medicine, and religion. While a little run down, the pyramids remain truly remarkable, and represent the only remaining wonder of the ancient world. Entrance charges are not prohibitive, usually between £2 and £8.

It is a good idea to get out of Cairo to Egypt's six oases, for picturesque towns and all the dates you can eat. You could even venture into the harsh Sinai region and find the burning bush that spoke to Moses in St Catherine's Monastery. Cairo is definitely an intense experience, with quite a lot of hassle from those with some kind of sale to make. In June and July, a heady soup of dust, heat, pollution, noise, and rather too many people around makes walking feel more like a test than a pleasure. But there is lots to see, do, buy, and experience. One of the world's largest bazaars (Khan el Khalili) allows you to keep your bargaining skills up to scratch. To see experts at work, though probably not make your own purchase, you can also head out to the Camel Market at Birqash, around 35km from Cairo. Most of the hundreds of camels that are sold daily come from Sudan. In fact, just people-watching with some sweet tea and a hookah pipe can take you out of the hustle and bustle and allow you to experience Egypt's more laid-back, social side. By making your leisurely way down the Nile, you can really bathe in the history and majesty of Egypt. If you're still feeling adventurous you can even rent a felucca (wooden sailing boat) to cruise down the river yourself.

TRAVEL RESOURCES

USEFUL WEBSITES
www.atta.co.uk, African Travel and Tourism Association.
www.bbc.co.uk/news/world/africa, BBC News Africa.
www.travelblog.org/Africa, Africa travel blogs.

www.africaguide.com, guide to Africa.
www.avert.org, HIV/AIDS information and work.

USEFUL BOOKS

Africa (Lonely Planet, 12th edition, 2010), £22.99. Over 1,000 pages. Lonely Planet also provides useful regional guides, if you are just visiting one part of Africa.

Africa Overland (Bradt Travel Guides, 5th edition, 2009), £16.99. Bradt publishes good guides to a large number of individual African countries (www.bradt-travelguides.com).

Chris Scott, *Sahara Overland* (Trailblazer, 2004), £19.99.

Don Pinnock, *African Journeys* (Double Storey Books, 2004), £15.99. A collection of travel essays by a South African travel writer. It would be irresponsible to suggest reading some stories and winging it; but showing some imagination is a good thing for African travel.

Paul Theroux, *Dark Star Safari: Overland from Cairo to Cape Town* (Penguin, 2003), £9.99.

WIDER READING

J M Coetzee, *Disgrace* (Secker & Warburg, 1999), £7.99. This and other novels by the Nobel Prize-winning novelist shed light on South Africa both during and after apartheid.

Meja Mwangi, *Striving for the Wind* (Heinemann, 1992), £9.99. A hilarious farce set in post-colonial Kenya.

Thomas Pakenham, *The Scramble for Africa* (Abacus, 1992), £14.99. How to divide up a continent in one easy conference, and all manner of confused marching about.

Martin Meredith, *The State of Africa: A History of Fifty Years of Independence* (Free Press, 2006), £10.99. Does what it says on the tin.

Chinua Achebe, *Things Fall Apart* (Penguin Classics). One of Nigeria's most famous novelists addresses the problem of European colonialism in Africa.

Adam Hochschild, *King Leopold's Ghost: A Story of Greed, Terror and Heroism* (Pan, 2006), £8.99. Very readable, but horrific, history of the Belgian Congo.

Nigel Barley, *The Innocent Anthropologist* (1983, re-issued by Waveland Press Inc, 2000). A laugh-out-loud account by an academic anthropologist of his research with the Dowayo people of Northern Cameroon.

William Boyd, *A Good Man in Africa* and *Brazzaville Beach* (Penguin, both 1999), both £8.99. Boyd grew up in Africa.

Chimamanda Ngozi Adichie, *Half of a Yellow Sun* (Harper, 2006), £7.99. Powerful novel about the chaos that engulfed ordinary people in the Biafran War.

Chimamanda Ngozi Adichie, *The Thing Around Your Neck* (Fourth Estate, 2009), £7.99. A collection of a dozen stories set in Nigeria.

ASIA

Asia is the largest and most diverse continent in the world, stretching from the Pacific Ocean to the Mediterranean Sea (assuming you consider the Middle East as part of Asia). It bundles together Tibetan refugee settlements in the Himalayas and Japanese temple gardens, elegant suburbs in Colombo, the jungles of Borneo, and the slums of Kolkata. The 'East' covers such a vast range of geography and culture that it is difficult to know where to begin when planning a route.

THE LURE OF THE EAST

Asia offers an astonishing range of attitudes and ways of life, which can seem very alien to anything you are used to. A great many gappers feel a little overwhelmed by the unfamiliarity of it all, the noise, colour, and craziness, the touts, and transport. Many prefer to stick to the beaten track where western tastes and expectations are catered for. After acclimatising a little, however, it is worth considering stepping off the well-trodden path, at least for a while. The most popular backpacker haunts, such as the famous Khao San Road in Bangkok and Pattaya, do not in any way reflect the local culture. Most young travellers will not want to miss out on the imagined pleasures of full-moon parties and banana pancakes, but this kind of commercial tourism often lapses into tackiness.

The hustle and bustle of urban commerce tends to absorb the unique characteristics of small communities. Although this is less true in the cities of Asia, it is true that a more faithful image of any country should be sought in small towns and villages, and by using local transport rather than air-conditioned tourist coaches. The best way of course is to settle in one place for an extended period as part of a volunteer project, such as teaching in a village school in Nepal or working at an elephant park in Thailand; for a multitude of suggestions, see the *Asia* chapter in Part V of this book.

In some places, the unhurried pace of life may cause frustration, especially when dealing with officialdom. But this is one of the glories of the continent. After slogging through A levels or finals, it is easy to luxuriate in the nonchalance and be amused by the absurd amount of paperwork. There is something to be learned from experiencing attitudes and customs so unfamiliar to our ultra-efficient western ways. No matter how much you read and talk to fellow travellers, you will be thrilled and surprised, and sometimes shocked and appalled, by the sights and culture that await exploration.

With the explosion of affordable air travel and the opening up of once-closed and mysterious countries such as Laos, not to mention China, young travellers have been swarming to the continent of Asia. Most choose between the Indian subcontinent (India, Nepal, and Sri Lanka), South East Asia (Thailand, Malaysia, Indonesia, Vietnam, Cambodia, and Laos) and the Far East (China, Japan, Korea, and Taiwan). Generalisations are dangerous, but certain issues crop up in various corners of the continent that deserve a little thought beforehand. Obviously Japan and Taiwan have a more westernised standard of living, but there are profound differences that can cause problems there too.

GETTING THERE

Most gap year travellers will book their flights through a student travel agent such as STA Travel or the Flight Centre, especially if their routes are at all complicated. If you are looking for a straight return, the cheapest flights are not direct and probably available from airlines which may be considered dodgy by overprotective mothers. Middle Eastern carriers (eg Qatar Airways and Emirates) and Asian carriers (eg the Taiwanese airline Eva Airways) are often worth investigating for low fares. Flying with them is guaranteed to be more interesting than flying on BA or Cathay Pacific. When **Sarah Spiller** fell in love with Sri Lanka after joining a turtle conservation project, she made several subsequent trips on Sri Lankan Airlines and felt that she was already on holiday the minute she stepped aboard.

UNMISSABLE HIGHLIGHTS

- Visit Angkor Wat temple complex in Cambodia, which is one of the wonders of the modern world.
- Join the pilgrims climbing Adam's Peak, Sri Lanka's holiest, to see the Buddha's footprint and the sunrise.
- Marvel at the dusk departure of thousands of bats from Niah caves in Sarawak, Borneo.
- Track rhinos on elephant back in Chitwan, Nepal's foremost national park.
- Admire the patience of fishermen at Fort Cochin in South India, who use an ancient kind of shore-mounted cantilevered fishing net.
- Contemplate China's recent history while standing in Tiananmen Square in Beijing.
- Find your way to Hunza, a hidden Himalayan valley in Pakistan where people are said to live to a great age because of their diet of apricots.
- Travel by Shinkansen (bullet train) in Japan; a seven-day rail pass costs little more than the Tokyo–Kyoto return.
- Visit Luang Prabang on the Mekong River in Laos, voted top city by readers of Wanderlust magazine.
- Sea kayak under the cliffs at Krabi in Thailand.

The famous overland route to Nepal has been problematic for a very long time now, though the re-launched Oz-bus (www.oz-bus.com) travels from London to Sydney via Iran and India. Assuming you can get a transit visa for Iran, it is not impossible to make the overland trip by public transport, which would be very rigorous and very cheap. Most travellers simply take advantage of the competitive discount flight market from London to Asian destinations. For example the cheapest quoted return price London to Mumbai is less than £370 including taxes, provided you're prepared to put up with a stopover in Muscat or similar. The cheapest advertised fare to Bangkok at the time of writing was £399 return on Royal Jordanian. The price of flights to Japan has dropped in the past few years, especially if you are willing to fly on Aeroflot with a change in Moscow. In London a wide range of travel agents advertise cheap fares to Asia.

MY GAP YEAR: PASCALE HUNTER

Pascale Hunter's route started by flying into Bangkok from Sydney. She was excited about rendezvousing with some friends from home and travelling around Thailand and Cambodia.

Fantastic white-water rafting near Chiang Mai, sea kayaking off Krabi in the Gulf of Thailand, sunrise after the full-moon party on Ko Pha Ngan and a quite different sunrise later with the magnificent temples of Angkor Wat in the foreground, a rescue centre for abandoned pets near Phnom Penh – these were some of the highlights of Pascale's seven-week trip.

To avoid hassles, Pascale and her friends mapped out their trip ahead of time through a travel agent in Bangkok to which their first tuk-tuk driver introduced them. The four girls excitedly boarded the sleeper train to Chiang Mai and, since this was their first foray into Asian travel, they were happy to be met at the airport by someone with a placard bearing their names who took them to their pre-booked hostel. They were amused rather than irritated by the many retail opportunities thrust upon them; while taking a tuk-tuk in Chiang Mai, they made unscheduled stops at no fewer than four factories (umbrellas, lacquer, jade, and silver).

During their five days in the north, they hiked, white-water rafted, joined an elephant trek, and did a half-day Thai cookery course. One day the girls decided to hire motorbikes (for about £4 minus petrol), undaunted that they had no licence or driving experience. Pascale lost track of her friends, one of whom it turned out had fallen off in a busy street and got quite a fright, though was unhurt.

The next destination in Thailand was the island of Ko Pha Ngan where they arrived in time for one of the famous full-moon parties. Their beach lodge arranged a minibus which picked up a number of other passengers whom they gradually realised were all 'ladyboys' going down to work the beach. When later Pascale noticed a backpacker dancing with one of these beauties, she didn't know whether she should alert him or not. Pascale enjoyed celebrating her 19th birthday by visiting a waterfall on Ko Samui and later proceeded to the coast of Krabi, a southern province of Thailand, with striking cliffs rising out of the sea.

Pascale's travel agent had fixed up bus transport from Bangkok to Siem Reap, jumping-off point for Angkor Wat, plus four nights in the Hil Ton hostel and Cambodian visa, all for 6,000-7,000 baht (approximately £120). The journey by road from the Thai border to Siem Reap was acutely uncomfortable, which persuaded them to opt for flying back at the end of their Cambodian trip.

Having spent a day roaming round the main temples at Angkor Wat, their attention was caught by a notice posted up at their hostel asking for volunteer teachers. They went along to Savong's School (www.savong.com) for two days, to help in the classrooms, first with secondary school-aged children and then with younger ones. Pascale felt that so many Westerners had participated in the scheme that it had become quite commercialised, which had taught the kids to clamour for western goodies.

Because of flight timings, they spent a whole week in Phnom Penh which was exceedingly hot. They visited the Killing Fields Museum and chilled in the backpacker enclave at Lakeside. They booked on a tour to a wildlife centre where unwanted pets were housed. Another must-do tourist activity in the capital is visiting one of the many orphanages that vie for foreign visitors by advertising on the sides of tuk-tuks. A donation of $30 was required, though at this stage Pascale and friends were within days of flying home and were down to almost nothing so they could not afford this, but were still taken.

This was right at the end of their trip, and they had not factored in the Cambodian and Thai departure taxes, which left them completely skint for their last weekend in Bangkok (and they had been looking forward to a final shopping spree). A café was showing their favourite film (the Holiday) and they managed to nurse a single Coke for the entire duration. When they got to Bangkok airport with their carefully saved 500 baht each for the departure tax, they were horrified to learn that the tax had just gone up to 700 baht. They had no alternative but to beg the remaining 200 baht from more well-heeled tourists in the check-in queue, a debt which Pascale's parents repaid the minute she got home. Ironically this, her scariest moment, came right at the end of what had been an amazing trip.

GETTING AROUND

If you intend to do a lot of flying around the region, it is worth considering the Visit Asia air pass marketed by the Oneworld group, available only to people who book their intercontinental flight on a member airline, ie British Airways, Cathay Pacific, Qantas, JAL, and a few others. Flights are available to 50 cities in China, Hong Kong, India, Indonesia, Japan, Malaysia, Pakistan, the Philippines, Singapore, South Korea, Sri Lanka, Taiwan, Thailand, Vietnam, and a few others, at various prices according to sector; see the website for details (www.oneworld.com).

Once you're installed in Asia, travel is highly affordable. The railways of the Indian subcontinent are a fascinating social phenomenon and also extraordinarily cheap. Throughout Asia, airfares are not expensive, particularly around the discount triangle of Bangkok, Hong Kong, and Singapore. The no-frills discount carrier Air Asia advertises some amazingly low fares, for example between Bangkok and Phnom Penh, and now flies from Stansted to Kuala Lumpur. The notable exception to the generalisation about cheap public transport in Asia is Japan.

In addition to ordinary buses and trains, Asian countries employ an impressive and ingenious range of vehicles to transport people cheaply. The shared taxi takes many forms, from the *dolmus* of Turkey, to the Suzuki of northern Pakistan, to the *bemo* of Indonesia. On your extended travels in Asia, you might find yourself travelling in a bullock-drawn cart or a horse-drawn *tonga* as well as the more commonplace modes of transport.

If a vehicle has a meter, make sure it is switched on and, if not, always fix the sum you are willing to pay before stepping in. When it comes to buses, you are usually safe if you hop on one that locals are taking. If you get in on your own you may find that you have 'contracted' the vehicle for your private use, which will increase the price by an order of magnitude.

Depending on how steady your nerves are, the style of driving may leave you aghast. Also some roads are atrocious, with massive potholes or unprotected hairpin bends. Keep this in mind if you are signing up for a 12-hour bus journey. Imagine yourself occupying a narrow seat for all those hours with your head hitting the ceiling every time you run over a pothole. The word 'luxury' is sometimes used rather loosely when describing coach travel in Asia.

TWO-WHEELING ADVICE

Gappers are often tempted to hire motorcycles in South East Asia, principally because of the very low prices (just a couple of pounds for a day). Companies require no licence and do not automatically provide helmets. According to the Foreign and Commonwealth Office, an average of 38 people die every day in motorcycle accidents in Thailand alone. Many travel insurance policies do not cover the kind of vehicles routinely hired out, so if you are involved in even a minor accident, you may end up having to pay a hefty fee.

BUDGETING

An idea of how much you will end up spending is given in the country sections below. On the whole, you will find that travel throughout South Asia is a fantastic bargain and very addictive. However, many gappers get caught out by steep visa costs and departure taxes, some of which must be paid in US dollars, and should you be misinformed, you run the risk of being caught short on your way out of a country if you happen to have run your funds down to zero. In the case of Thailand, and (as of April 2011) Cambodia, the departure tax is now included in the price of the air ticket.

CULTURE SHOCK

In all Asian countries, particularly India and Cambodia, you will be confronted with poverty such as is not known in the western world. Beggars are the most obvious outward sign of this poverty, and it is impossible to pass by without feeling pity. They are often disabled, blind, or limbless and, as a result, have no other way of making a living. Even if you are not the flashiest dresser, you will look down at your sandals and camera and for the first time realise how privileged you are. Whether you give them money is obviously a personal choice. Your decision will depend on your own financial position, the degree of pity you feel, your conscience, and how worried you are at the possibility of abetting professional begging. Be aware that if you give your spare coins to begging children, it rewards them for skipping school in order to harass foreigners. Many people think that if you are moved to help a community, it is better to fund some pens or books for the local school, or give to an orphanage rather than give money to clamouring individuals.

Once you move out of Europe, you are entering a world that is based on different religious, social, moral, and cultural values. Many young travellers are heedless of these differences and gravitate to beach resorts and party places which do a good job of masking local norms. But if you want to get a little deeper into the culture and visit local temples, be aware that modesty of dress and behaviour is required. The most famous sites such as Wat Pho in Bangkok post signs specifying 'no shorts' and you should remove footwear and headgear before entering any Buddhist temple (and also avoid taking photos of someone standing in front of a statue of the Buddha). Women should not wear clothing that is in any way revealing, particularly in Muslim countries. Outside the westernised resorts, it is advisable for women to wear loose-fitting tops with sleeves and light trousers; crop tops, singlets, and shorts give out a message that you may not intend. Anyone with light skin is bound to be stared at in any case, which can be discomfiting until you get used to it.

One of the most noticeable differences in attitude between the west and east is the attitude to privacy. For example, within 60 seconds of sitting down in a Delhi park, you are likely to be surrounded by a peanut salesman, a snake charmer, an ear cleaner, and umpteen children clamouring to see the cover of your book. It will sometimes seem as though you have been asked a hundred times a day 'Where are you coming from? How long in my country? What is your good name?' The first few times, you may be delighted to engage in conversation, but will eventually grow weary.

WHAT TO EXPECT

From the minute you arrive, you will be assailed by people touting for your custom. Who can blame them when there is so much competition for the western dollar? If you really do not want to be offered a service, try not to break step, while providing a polite yet dismissive response. If you are getting really fed up, pull your brimmed hat down, don sunglasses and pretend to be a deaf-mute.

All of this is quite harmless compared to the confidence tricksters you may come across. It would be impossible to list all the ploys and ruses that have been successful in the past, but they range from light deception (beggars pretending to be blind) to blatant blackmail (planting drugs on you then threatening to call the police). Between these two extremes there is a lot of scope for ingenuity. Even the most obvious methods (phoney tales of relatives' illnesses, promises to repay money, trading in fake gems) are made so convincing that cautious travellers have been caught out by them. Of course, there is no need to mistrust everyone you meet. For every thief and swindler, you will meet dozens of friendly, concerned locals who will warn you of lurking evil, keep an eye on your luggage in your absence, and so on.

EXCITING WAYS TO GET INVOLVED

- Build look-out posts in the jungle of Indonesian Borneo to help protect orang-utans (www.orangutan.org.uk).
- Teach at an English-immersion summer camp in Taiwan (www.kidscamp.com.tw).
- Coach sports in the Maldives (www.volunteermaldives.com).
- Help on an organic farm in Korea (www.koreanwoof.com).
- Work for a book publisher in Delhi (www.gapguru.com).
- Take a Vietnamese cookery course in Hanoi (www.hanoicookingcentre.com).
- Learn to dive in the Philippines in order to help survey a reef (www.coralcay.org).
- Volunteer at an orphanage in Cambodia (www.outreachinternational.co.uk).
- Teach English to Burmese tribal people in the refugee camps of northern Thailand (www.burma volunteers.org).
- Live in a Himalayan village as part of a community development programme (www.insightnepal.org.np).

TRAVEL TIP

The key for successful travelling in Asia is to remain sceptical of everything you are told. If you are told the buses and trains are not running because it is a national holiday, be sceptical. If you tell them politely that you do not want to step into their taxi or book up their recommended tour, be prepared to be followed and badgered for the next 20 minutes. Many touts open their pitches not with a hard sell but with an expression of interest in your country of origin or your recent travels. At first this will seem intrusive and unwelcome, but with time you will learn to deal with it with humour and nonchalance.

DRUGS

Sooner or later when travelling in Asia, someone will approach you and offer you one substance or another. Drugs offences in all countries carry heavy penalties. Occasionally, drug sales are also deals between informers and police, either for financial gain or to boost arrest statistics. Carrying any kind of drugs over a border is plain dumb. Anybody tempted should just Google 'drug smuggling' and their destination country to come up with tragic cases. The 1999 film *Brokedown Palace* is about two school friends who straight after high school head to Thailand for a cheap holiday where they meet a charming Australian. He persuades them to join him on a trip to Hong Kong and before they know it they are stopped at Bangkok airport carrying heroin and find themselves condemned to serve 33 years in a Thai women's prison. Never consent to carry a bag for someone else through customs; you may be acting as an unwitting courier, and ignorance is impossible to prove in court.

SOUTH EAST ASIA

Thailand

VISA
Free on arrival, valid 30 days; can be renewed by leaving the country and crossing back on a visa run, but this only extends visa by 15 days.

CURRENCY
£1 = 50 Thai baht   US$1 = 30 Thai baht

BUDGET
$30–$50 a day on the tourist trail; cheaper in rural Thailand.

Beaches of powdery sand and swaying coconut palms set against a glistening turquoise sea – this is the picture conjured by most long-haul gap year travellers considering a trip to Thailand. Bangkok is pre-eminent as a destination itself or as a stopover for gappers heading to or from Australia, and has become a favourite jumping-off point for the whole of South East Asia. Enticing images of rainforests and temples, night markets and beach parties draw many in an easterly direction.

The indigenous Thai urban vehicle is the motorised three-wheeler or *tuk-tuk* which Simon Calder of the *Independent* describes as '*a cross between a Reliant Robin and a bus shelter*'. Be sure to settle on a price before you step in, which is easier after you have been there for a while and know what the price range should be. The atrocious traffic of Bangkok can be avoided by taking the elevated Sky Train or the Chao Phraya River ferry. *Tuk-tuk* drivers target tourists and will often offer private tours or try to persuade them to book their travels through an agent. If you succumb to their blandishments, an agent may well simplify your travel arrangements, but you will have to be prepared to pay a premium. Some people will choose to avoid the middle-man altogether.

New arrivals should be prepared to be swept off by the first *tuk-tuk* driver to a travel agent who will purport to be working for the official Tourism Authority of Thailand (TAT) and who will fix up transport, accommodation, tours, and visas for an all-in fee. Some gappers are happy to pay over the odds to avoid the hassle and possible rip-offs along the way, although more experienced travellers can generally make similar arrangements more cheaply.

The usual route for travellers spending a few weeks in Thailand is to head north to Chiang Mai – often on the sleeper train that departs Bangkok at 7.30pm and arrives 14 hours later – to do some trekking or adventure activities (the second-class fare is currently less than 800 baht, or about £16).

Visits to elephant sanctuaries are very popular, though sometimes newly arrived gappers are not very impressed at the way the animals are treated, so it is better to do your research properly.

Travellers then head south to one or more of the party islands, possibly taking in the jungle at Kanchanaburi, where you can ride an elephant along the banks of the River Kwai, or the ancient city of Ayutthaya. The island of Ko Pha Ngan is famous for its full-moon parties, attended by between 10,000 and 20,000 people, all dancing to the pumping beats of more than a dozen sound systems. Most revellers stay up to watch the sunrise. The litter left by partygoers is appalling and may eventually prompt the local council to ban parties on this scale. Also be aware that undercover policemen attend looking for drugs.

Thailand caters to extremes, from the unsavoury Speedo-wearing older European men looking for a Thai girlfriend to those in search of a spiritual break. Although not as cheap as it used to be, the cost of living is still gratifyingly low, except in highly developed resorts that have priced backpackers out. You can eat a good meal for only 40 baht and a beer is 50–60 baht (though this is half the price of a cheap hotel room).

Cambodia

VISA
Buy on arrival by air or in advance in Bangkok (£15); valid for 30 days.

CURRENCY
£1 = 6,640 riels (KHR)   US$1 = 4,020 riels

BUDGET
$20–$30 a day (excluding temple entry fees).

From Thailand, backpackers can proceed to Malaysia, Cambodia, or Laos, and then on to Vietnam, depending on time constraints. The journey by road from Bangkok to Siem Reap is a gruelling one, because the six hours of travel in Cambodia between the Thai border and the jumping-off place for Angkor Wat are along unmade roads – although at least the danger of landmines along this stretch has subsided.

The temple complex at Angkor Wat is one of the wonders of the world. The archaeological park located just outside the city of Siem Reap in northern Cambodia comprises ruined 12th-century temples built by the ancient Khmer regime. The site covers hundreds of kilometres and would take days to see properly; a three-day ticket costs $40, whereas a longer one is $60. Few can resist an impulse to see the temples at sunrise or sunset – a ravishing sight, as long as you don't mind sharing it with 5,000 other people. Your guidebook can recommend some lesser visited places such as the sacred mountain of Phnom Kulen topped with a reclining sandstone Buddha and the River of a Thousand Lingas (Kbal Spean), a riverbed full of carvings of gods and phalluses (some of which will be submerged in the rainy season).

Travel on to the capital Phnom Penh can be by road or by boat, a wonderful six-hour sea trip. Many stay in the backpackers' ghetto Lakeside, which inevitably has more than its fair share of hassles, including dodgy motorbike ('moto') drivers and scammers. Tuk-tuks are cheaper than in Thailand; you can often hire one for a whole day for not much more than $10. Many backpacker lodges include free tuk-tuk travel as part of the deal.

Highlights include a trip to the Killing Fields Museum at $21, a notorious Pol Pot prison located in a former school on the outskirts of the city. Many NGOs, wildlife centres, and orphanages welcome visiting tourists. For destinations far removed from the tourist hordes in Phnom Penh and Siem Reap, try the relaxed coastal province of Kampot where you can swim in the phosphorescence at night, visit NGOs, and enjoy the nearby attractions of Kep, a crumbling colonial beach resort with amazing seafood and untouched islands. Elsewhere, try not to miss the spooky deserted town in the middle of the jungle up Bokkor mountain, and the wild north-eastern provinces of Mondulkiri and Rattanakiri, where you can go on elephant treks to remote minority hill tribes, swim in spectacular waterfalls, and escape from the sweltering heat of the lowlands.

Laos

VISA
Buy on arrival at the airport or Friendship Bridge (US$35); valid for 30 days only.

CURRENCY
£1 = 13,330 kip (LAK)   US$1 = 8,000 kip

BUDGET
US$20–$25 a day, with no trouble, one of the cheapest destinations in Asia.

In the years after it opened its borders in 1989, Laos was considered the most exotic, the most untravelled country in Asia. It is now a well-established part of the backpackers' trail. Highlights include the former royal city of the north, Luang Prabang, which sits on the Mekong River and is a good starting point for a slow boat trip. The northern hill tribes of Laos are less affected by tourism than those of northern Thailand and Vietnam.

Vietnam

VISA
Buy in advance in London (£44); if booking through an established operator it is possible to arrange the paperwork and pay US$25 for a visa on arrival.

CURRENCY
£1 = 34,500 dong   US$1 = 20,850 dong

BUDGET
$25–$40 a day.

Travelling round the region is very affordable, even if you take a flight, because Jetstar is a low-cost airline serving Hanoi and Ho Chi Minh City (HCMC). It is possible to get a bus from HCMC to Phnom Penh for less than $15, though you will pay a premium for a more comfortable ride. Ironically 'Open Tour' tickets with tour bus companies, which allow you to complete a long distance in stages, can be cheaper than buying point-to-point tickets on public transport. For example, Sinh Café charges $45 to cover the 1,000-mile-plus distance between Ho Chi Minh City and Hanoi, using some sleeper buses (www.sinhcafe.com/english_info/info_opentour.htm).

The Reunification Express is a train that runs the full length of the country (taking more than 30 hours) and stops at all the towns you might want to visit between Saigon and Hanoi, including Nha Trang (where you can join a trip on a party boat), Da Nang, and Hue. There are many natural and architectural sights to see in Vietnam, such as the spectacular Halong Bay or the Citadel and ancient imperial capital of Hue.

Although Vietnam is still a one-party state, it bears all the trappings of a capitalist society, complete with garish advertising hoardings and American pop music. There is a two-tier system for utilities and travel in Vietnam, which means foreigners pay substantially more than locals for almost everything. Hanoi in the north is smaller and more beautiful yet bustling and noisy, whereas HCMC is a Bangkok in the making with a slightly higher cost of living. This sophisticated, sprawling commercial centre boasts a skyline already dotted with skyscrapers.

The cities are wonderfully packed with good, cheap restaurants serving excellent healthy food, and it is quite easy to get by on $5 a day eating at Com Binh Dan or Bia Hoi, the Vietnamese street-side restaurants. Some of the very best food can be found at the smallest street stalls at ridiculously cheap prices.

The Vietnamese people are often very friendly. However, what you see is not always what you get. Behind that charming Vietnamese smile is more often than not the intent to extract money. Of particular note are the numerous women in search of a foreign husband, a foreign passport, and an airline ticket. Single men should beware. Internet access is widely available and improving, although it is still unreliable, slow, and censored.

Indonesia

VISA
Buy on arrival: $25 for 30 days. No extensions.

CURRENCY
£1 = 14,300 rupiah   U$1 = 8,650 rupiah

BUDGET
$15–$25 a day.

Three-fifths of the Indonesian population live on the main island of Java, where the hot, dusty, over-crowded, polluted, and poverty-stricken capital, Jakarta, is situated. Many young travellers prefer to head for the adjacent island of Sumatra, still largely covered by jungle and wilderness. The tourist industry on Bali suffered terribly after the terrorist bombings in 2002 and 2005, even though the lovely hinterland was largely unaffected, and as of 2011 there are renewed terrorist threats deterring travellers. The resort of Kuta, where several of the bombs went off, has long been spoiled by mass tourism and it is impossible to avoid persistent hawkers, tacky souvenir shops and nightclubs. Head instead to the popular tourist centre of Ubud, famous for its puppet theatre and *gamelan* music as well as its monkey temple and tropical ambience. Further inland, you will come to the tranquil inland lake of Bratan near the temple at Bedugal (one of 20,000 on the island) and the flower market at Candikuning. Sarong-clad women throughout the island gracefully make bamboo and flower offerings to the gods with a backdrop of volcanic hills and lush forests. The majority religion in Bali is Hinduism, whereas 87% of the Indonesian population is Muslim.

Indonesia is a fascinating country, and most visitors agree that the Indonesian people are fantastic. There are over 17,000 islands, fewer than half of them inhabited, with many different tribes and cultures, which make it difficult to keep the country unified. In fact, there has been quite a lot of unrest in the past few years, which is currently ongoing in central Sulawesi, Ambon, and Aceh. The Indonesian half of Borneo is called Kalimantan and is off the radar of most gappers; it can involve some very challenging travel conditions.

Travel by public transport is cheap but can be time-consuming, though internal flights are within the range of many. You can rent a motorbike for a day on Bali for about $6 or $7, but go carefully and watch for cows wandering on the back roads.

Malaysia (including North Borneo)

VISA
No visa is required for stays of less than three months.

CURRENCY

£1 = 5 ringgits	US$1 = 3 ringgits

BUDGET
$30–$40 a day.

The modern state of Malaysia comprises the southern part of the Malay Peninsula between Singapore at the tip and Thailand to the north, plus the two distant provinces of Sabah and Sarawak, which occupy the northern third of the island of Borneo. A mountain range with peaks of up to 3,000m forms a central spine and provides some hill resorts where you can escape the heat. The rainy season on the peninsula falls between November and February, so this is not a good time to plan a beach holiday. Vast stretches of the country are still covered by tropical forest. Compared with Indonesia and Cambodia, Malaysia is a relatively progressive country with a well-developed infrastructure, which (for some) makes it less appealing as a destination. It is also more expensive, so it is wise to budget at least $30 a day. As a result, the average age of travellers tends to be older than in Thailand. Cheap backpacker accommodation can be found in most places, though beach resorts tend to be more upmarket and therefore a lot pricier than the equivalent in Thailand.

The great attraction of Malaysia is its varied tropical scenery, from the coral islands and beaches on the east coast of the peninsula to the jungles of Sabah and Sawarak in East Malaysia. Malaysia also has its hill stations, which can make ideal centres for hill and jungle walking – especially Tanah Rata, the travellers' centre in the Cameron Highlands. Only 100km from Kuala Lumpur, Fraser's Hill is less frequented and very pleasant. The town of Malacca (or Melaka) is a picturesque colonial settlement on the coast. The wonderful Taman Negara National Park promotes eco-tourism.

Many beaches are magnificent, especially along the less developed east coast. Although Penang in the north west is the most famous, it can be spoilt by hordes of tourists, hawkers, and litter.

Burma

VISA
Buy in advance for £14 in London, valid for 28 days.

CURRENCY	
£1 = 10.8 kyat	US$1 = 6.5 kyat

BUDGET
$25–$35 a day (if you take taxis).

After being ideologically off-limits for 15 years, Burma is now back in the tourist fold, since Aung San Suu Kyi's National League for Democracy announced at the end of 2010 that the boycott on tourism should be lifted. The country is still in the grip of a totalitarian regime that oppresses its citizens even though at the beginning of 2011, democratically elected leader Suu Kyi was released from house arrest. But it is now agreed by most that discouraging visits from the outside world only punishes the ordinary people. Ideally, backpackers should spend as much money in local communities and with private enterprises rather than on the junta-controlled cruises, at its resorts, or in its big hotels. Fortunately the requirement to change money at government-run exchange desks at the airport has been dropped.

A typical itinerary would include the capital Rangoon, Mandalay (now less romantic than its name), Hsipaw, the beautiful Inle Lake, Kalaw, Bagan (an ancient temple complex on the banks of the Irrawaddy River), and back to Rangoon.

INDIAN SUBCONTINENT

India

VISA
Buy in advance for £40; valid for up to six months from date of issue.

CURRENCY	
£1 = 74 rupees	US$1 = 45 rupees

BUDGET
$15–$20 a day.

India's old associations of poverty, famine, squalor, and disease are being challenged by the country's booming urban economy and strengthening currency, partly based on hi-tech outsourced business. Lumbering night trains and hip nightclubs, the vast all-encompassing Mother India offers everything in between. All preconceptions give way before the vitality, colour, and cheerfulness displayed on the streets. Sights to shock, amaze, and amuse are everywhere; you cannot be bored in India. You may think you are prepared for culture shock but not for the sensory overload, for the visceral reaction to the noise and chaos and hassle, the heat and pollution, the astonishing energy. Many feel that a visit to India should be a requirement for all gap year travellers, to make them aware of how much we all take for granted. But it can be overwhelming for some and a certain level of maturity is needed to process so many contradictory sensations of disgust and exhilaration and every emotion in between. The way to enjoy it is to go with it rather than kick against it.

In contrast to the frenetic activity on the streets, the wheels of bureaucracy can grind exceedingly slowly. A relatively simple operation such as buying a rail ticket or cashing a travellers' cheque can take the better part of a day. You can almost hear yourself wind down and eventually will learn to be as patient as Buddha.

Young westerners can often be heard exclaiming with outrage at the discrepancy between the rich and poor in India (as if inequality didn't exist in Europe or North America). Certainly the sight of lepers outside the luxury hotels of Kolkata (formerly Calcutta) or pavement dwellers near the banking complexes of Mumbai is a shocking experience. A fear of exposure to extreme poverty and suffering discourages some gappers, which is a pity because there is so much more to this vast land. Stretching 2,000 miles from the Himalayas to the beaches of the Arabian Sea, India is capable of allowing any visitor to construct a thrilling itinerary. A civilisation as ancient and as complex as this is in many ways incorruptible, and infinitely rewarding.

India has three main seasons: the hot season, lasting from April to June, followed by the monsoon, which continues until September, and winter, which lasts from November until March. South of Mumbai, light clothing can be worn year round, but in the more hilly regions warmer clothes will be needed. The best time of year is between October and March, when midday temperatures on the plains range from 21 to 32 degrees Celsius. The south is always so hot that you will feel sweat trickling down your legs when you are sitting still. Keep up your liquid and salt intake to prevent heat exhaustion.

Spend time with your guidebook and talking to experienced travellers before deciding where to go. Concentrating on one region will reduce the travel hassles, so that many choose Goa (once a hippie enclave, now a package resort), Rajasthan (including a camel trek from Jodhpur), or the state of Kerala in the south, instead of the so-called Gold Triangle of the Taj Mahal and the Pink City of Jaipur. Others concentrate on mountainous regions such as the state of Himachal Pradesh (which includes Dharam-sala, where the Dalai Lama resides) or Sikkim to the east (for which you will need to obtain a special permit). Visiting a holiday destination favoured by Indian tourists or pilgrims is usually delightful and interesting. Try not to think of your first visit as a one-and-only because it is impossible to see more than a fraction of India at a time.

Whereas in most countries you get on a bus or train in order to be transported somewhere, in India you can view these modes of transport primarily as entertainment. Although buses are not necessarily cheaper than trains, they enable access to more remote regions and are often faster than rail travel. Windows on ordinary buses often lack glass and so you may be afflicted by swirling dust in the dry season. The railways of India are a wonderful institution. After choosing where on the spectrum of comfort you wish to travel (from air-conditioned with sleeping accommodation, down to second-class unreserved), you must patiently join all the requisite queues to purchase a ticket.

TRAVEL TIP

Try to sit on an aisle seat towards the middle of a bus, since the suspension favoured in Indian buses means that if you are near the back you have to find a fixed object with which to steady yourself. The front seat is most dangerous in the event of a road accident.

Food and accommodation are always easy to locate. India is predominantly vegetarian. Although meat is available, especially in the Mughal-influenced north, it is relatively expensive and more likely than vegetables to lead to digestive problems. Chilli-wise, food is much hotter in the south.

Sri Lanka

VISA
None required for stays of up to 30 days; local extensions available (but are expensive). However, the government may cancel the current visa-on-arrival system, so check with the embassy.

CURRENCY
£1 = 182 rupees   US$1 = 110 rupees

BUDGET
$30 a day, but easy to spend more on lavish meals and entrance tickets.

Once thought of simply as a tropical paradise, this teardrop-shaped island nation off the east coast of southern India seems to be recovering from years of conflict. The war with the Tamil Tiger rebels was declared over in 2009 and their stronghold in the north is now open to visitors for the first time in decades (apart from a few high-security zones). It is necessary to obtain a permit from the Sri Lankan Ministry of Defence before travelling to the northern districts of Jaffna, Kilinochchi, Mullaittivu, Mannar, and Vavuniya.

As was evident from the number of Britons killed and affected by the tsunami of Boxing Day 2004, Sri Lanka has become a very popular package tourist destination, partly because its scale and transport are more manageable than in India. Tourist hot spots such as Sigiriya, site of a ruined palace on top of a striking flat rock, Kandy, the city in the interior where the Temple of the Tooth can be visited, and Hikkaduwa, home of many exiled surfers, can all become impossibly crowded in the high season (especially Christmas). But there are hundreds of less-trammelled beaches and plenty of lush scenery, wildlife, and smiling people to discover for yourself.

TRAVEL TIP
In many ways, Sri Lanka is an easy country in which to travel and a good introduction to Asia for the apprehensive traveller. You should be able to get round comfortably on $30 a day.

One highlight that should not be missed is climbing the holy mountain Sri Pada, known as Adam's Peak. Thousands of pilgrims gather in the village of Dalhousie, where the ascent to see Buddha's footprint at the summit begins. Most foreigners choose to set off at 2am to avoid the daytime heat and to enjoy the surpassing beauty of the sunrise, together with the otherworldly shadow which the peak casts on the cloud to the west just after sunrise. The climb takes about three hours, and many find the descent down all those 5,200 steps tougher on the muscles.

Meals are almost always vegetarian and rice is the staple accompaniment. Coconut plays a large part in the diet and is mixed with chillies to make a delicious *sambal* or side dish. Sri Lankans think that a meal (including breakfast) without chillies is like a day without sunshine – vendors even sprinkle chilli powder on slices of fresh pineapple.

Nepal

VISA

£20 (valid for six months). Visas bought on arrival are more expensive, eg $25 for 15 days, $40 for one month, $100 for three months.

CURRENCY

£1 = 118 rupees   US$1 = 74 rupees

BUDGET

Less than $10 a day if trekking, $15 otherwise.

Nepal is like another world after the heat, hustle, and bustle of the Indian plains. For one thing, a quarter of the land surface is under ice and snow, and steeply terraced fields and villages can be found up to an altitude of nearly 4,500m. Trekking is one of the chief attractions. The scenery is as spectacular as everyone says and though the walking can be hard, the rewards are worth it. Many gap year travellers spend an extended period on a volunteer programme in Nepal, many of which include an element of cultural immersion and adventure activities (see section on Nepal in the last part of this book).

About half the people are of Mongolian (Tibetan) descent. On the whole, the people are friendly though more reserved than on the lowlands. There are only five towns with a population exceeding 100,000, and three of those are in the Kathmandu Valley. The year 2011 has been declared Nepal's Year of Tourism, though problems with Maoist-dominated unions declaring a general strike put a damper on moves to boost tourism. Since the Maoist rebels secured the abolition of the monarchy and turned King Gyanendra's palace into a museum, Nepal's political problems have not completely disappeared. But once again Nepal is a promising destination for a gap year. The Foreign and Commonwealth Office (FCO) continues to urge trekkers to join group tours operated by reputable companies, although many of the standard treks (eg Pokhara to Jomson) can be done independently. The most popular trekking season is October/November. Trekking during the summer monsoon is possible, although you may encounter flooded river paths, leeches, and obscured views. Winter is fine for trekking, provided you are carrying a good-quality sleeping bag for the very cold nights, and you don't plan to cross any high passes.

If you don't have the time or stamina for trekking, the huge Royal Chitwan National Park, southwest of Kathmandu, presents a remarkable contrast with the mountainous north. It is the home of many jungle animals, including the rarely seen Bengal tiger and a decent population of rhinos, which can be seen more easily from the back of an elephant. Unfortunately, ongoing poaching is a problem. Lodges inside the park are pricey, but you can stay in budget places in the village of Sauraha on the Rapti River.

Pakistan

VISA

Buy in advance: £104 (since March 2011).

CURRENCY

£1 = 140 rupees   US$1 = 84 rupees

BUDGET

$15 a day (even cheaper than India).

As a tourist destination, Pakistan has suffered some grievous blows in the form of the 2010 floods that devastated so much of the country, and in the rise of terrorist attacks. Only the more experienced traveller is likely to be tempted by this destination, although its fascinating ethnic diversity and wonderful mountain scenery in the Karakorams are accessible to gap year travellers too. Unfortunately, a number of terrorist bombs have gone off and the FCO is advising against all travel to Peshawar, the Swat Valley, northern and western Balochistan, and many other tribal regions. Large tracts of the country remain underdeveloped for tourists, which makes it attractive to those who are fed up with the backpacking crowds. One place that remains as peaceable as it has always been is the gem of northern Pakistan, the Hunza Valley along the Karakoram Highway, which links the capital Islamabad with Kashgar in China. Unfortunately, a giant landslide in 2010 replaced part of the highway with a giant lake, which locals have been traversing by boat. It is estimated that the road won't be passable until at least 2012.

Bangladesh

VISA

Buy in advance: £40 in London, cheaper in Kolkata (valid for two months).

CURRENCY

£1 = 122 taka	US$1 = 74 taka

BUDGET

$10–$15 (or even less) a day.

Relatively few travellers venture into Bangladesh, partly because of its uninviting reputation and also because of its inconvenient location. Bangladesh is something of a cul-de-sac because the border with Burma is firmly closed and so there is no route on into South East Asia. With an annual rainfall of over 200cm in many places, Bangladesh is one of the wettest countries in the world and is notoriously prone to flooding because the land is so low-lying. It is wise to avoid travel in the hot season (March to May), when the average daily temperature in Dhaka is about 32 degrees Celsius.

Bangladesh is a liberal Muslim state and local customs should be respected, especially during the holy month of Ramadan. English is less widely spoken than in India. The country is sited on two enormous river deltas, the Ganges and the Brahmaputra, and transport by boat is often preferable to travel by land. The old passenger paddle steamer known as the Rocket, which plies the 350km distance between Dhaka and Khulna, has survived cuts by the Bangladesh Inland Water Transport Corporation. Fares are remarkably cheap if you are prepared to use a sleeping bag on the deck, ie $2, but even a first-class bunk is affordable at $15.

FAR EAST

China

VISA
Buy in advance: £60 for four-day service, £100 for same-day.

CURRENCY
£1 = 10.8 yuan   US$1 = 6.5 yuan

BUDGET
From $35 a day, but more in big cities, especially Beijing, Hong Kong, and Shanghai.

Generalisations made about China in one year are bound to be obsolete the next, since the pace of change in that country is astonishing. To take just one example, city roads that were clogged with bicycles just a few years ago are now jammed with cars, evidence of the sudden new affluence of so many Chinese people. Prices have risen astronomically, especially in Shanghai and Beijing.

You are unlikely to feel as warmly welcomed as you do in either the Indian subcontinent or South East Asia. Whereas in India you can always find someone who knows some English, this is not the case in China, and it can be a frustrating challenge trying to communicate to a taxi driver that you want to be taken to the bus station. Outside Beijing, Shanghai, and the popular tourist spots such as Xi'an, home of the Terracotta Warriors (be prepared to feel exploited and disappointed here), and popular stretches of the Great Wall, you may not come across many western backpackers.

Travel within the People's Republic of China can initially be exasperating as you struggle with the inscrutable bureaucracy and the utterly incomprehensible nature of stations and airports (where little allowance is made for those who do not understand Chinese characters). Trains and buses go everywhere, though it can sometimes be tricky reserving a seat or a sleeper (hard- or soft-class), especially at holiday times when locals book up everything in advance. (It is estimated that in the Golden Weeks, around Chinese New Year and in October, up to 350,000,000 people are on the move.) Some long-distance buses offer sleeping couchettes.

It isn't always easy to spot a good restaurant in China, though you can usually find a dim sum establishment where trolleys of steamed dumplings and hard-to-identify dishes are wheeled round to the tables and you can take what you like the look of. The squeamish should probably avoid markets such as the one in Guangzhou in southern China, where you will see civets and domestic cats in cages, and market traders skinning frogs and selling live scorpions. You might prefer to stick to the staple foods of glutinous rice, soy beans and cabbage. The kind of food you may have learned to like in your local Chinese restaurant is not at all easy to track down.

Hong Kong is the exception, and many travellers to Asia find themselves having a stopover in this great city at some point. The fabulous skyscrapers illuminated at night, the view from Victoria Peak (achieved by taking the very steep tram up the mountain), and ferry rides to other islands in Hong Kong harbour can all be enjoyed between shopping trips.

Japan

VISA
None for stays of up to 90 days.

CURRENCY
£1 = 135 yen   US$1 = 82 yen

BUDGET
$90–$100 a day – Japan is notoriously expensive.

The tragedy visited upon Japan in 2011 was unimaginable. Visitor numbers have plummeted, and many are staying away for irrational reasons, since most of the country was unaffected (except psychologically) by the earthquake and subsequent tsunami and nuclear disaster. Remarkably, the train network that included Sendai and the afflicted region was fully restored in little more than six weeks, though timetables were still affected.

Knowing a foreigner (*gaijin*) is a considerable status symbol for many Japanese, so if you do brave a trip, you may find yourself befriended and spending time speaking very, very slowly in order to be understood. A glut of westerners in Tokyo, however, means that your welcome may be less than enthusiastic in that huge city, where there is such a shortage of personal space. In fact, non-Japanese are refused entrance to some Tokyo bars and restaurants. Many people head straight out of Tokyo for the ancient traditional cities of Kyoto and Nara with their temples and historic sites, which will seem like villages after the capital, and where you can actually see trees.

The cost of living, especially in Japanese cities, is notoriously high. Any entertainment which smacks of the west, such as going out to a fashionable coffee house or a nightclub, will be absurdly expensive. However, if you are content with more modest indigenous food and pastimes, you can get by on $60 a day. A filling bowl of noodles and broth costs about $10, though you may never take to the standard breakfast of boiled rice and a raw egg.

Accommodation will also be a significant expense. Private rooms can be rented at a *ryokan*, which means Japanese-style guest house, or in the countryside you can stay in *minshukus* (bed and breakfasts). Gaijin houses offer dormitory accommodation to foreigners for about half the price of a private room, and there is a network of youth hostels too.

Finding your way around is nothing if not a challenge in a country where almost all road and public transport signs are incomprehensible. What use is an A–Z if you can't read the alphabet? Fortunately some signs are transliterated into *romaji* in the familiar Latin alphabet. Japanese people will sometimes go to embarrassing lengths to help foreigners. This desire to help, wedded to a reluctance to lose face, means that passers-by may offer advice and instructions based on very little information, so keep checking. Young people in jeans are the best bets. Outside the big cities, the people are even more cordial. Wherever you go, you don't have to worry about crime.

Travel can be ruinously expensive. For example, the high-tech *shinkansen* (bullet train) from Tokyo to Sendai, a couple of hundred miles north, costs about $180 return. Tour operators do sometimes have special deals on train fares. For example, JR East (www.jreast.co.jp/e), which operates in Kanto in northern Japan, sells rail passes, for example a three-day pass, usable within 10 days, for 13,000 yen (about £100) which includes bullet trains. Even better value is the Japan Rail Pass available only to foreign tourists, which can be used on buses and ferries as well as trains. Prices start at about £210 for seven days (www.japanrailpass.net).

Shopping around for package tours is another good way to get to see Japan at the lowest possible price. Another option is the Willer Bus Pass, valid for three, four or five days within two months on long-distance buses, with prices starting at £75 (www.willerexpress.com).

South Korea

VISA
None for up to 90 days.

CURRENCY
£1 = 1,800 won   US$1 = 1,080 won

BUDGET
$40–$50 a day.

Korean backpackers show up all over the world, but there isn't much return traffic. The foreigners in Korea tend to be in the country for an extended period as English teachers. Visitors are often surprised to discover the richness and complexity of Korean history and culture, which is much less well known in the west than Japan's. Despite being a bustling metropolis of more than 10 million, Seoul has preserved some of its cultural treasures. The country's area is small and the public transport good, though traffic congestion at weekends can be a problem. Expect to spend as much as $50 a day if you are travelling around and staying in *yogwans* (traditional inns) or *minbaks* (homestay).

The people are friendly, although relationships between western men and Korean women are sometimes disapproved of. Anyone missing home will gravitate to the area of Seoul called Itaewon, where fast food restaurants and discos are concentrated, not to mention pickpockets and souvenir rip-offs.

Most people do not associate Korea with mountain ranges, but hill-walking is one of the main attractions, often in conjunction with visiting a Buddhist temple. You can climb Hallasan, an extinct volcano and the highest mountain in the country, on Jeju Island in the south, and many scenic peaks in Sorak National Park. Gyeongju is one of the oldest cities in Asia and is best visited in the spring when the cherry trees are in blossom.

For the curious, it is possible to join one of the many tours to the demilitarized zone (DMZ) between South and North Korea; however it is not possible to enter the reclusive Democratic Republic from the south.

Not many people (including taxi drivers) speak much English, so if you are trying to reach an obscure destination, ask someone in your hotel to write the name in Korean.

Taiwan

VISA
Not needed for stays of up to 90 days.

CURRENCY
£1 = 48 Taiwanese new dollars   US$1 = NT$29

BUDGET
$35+ a day.

Taipei has a rapid transit system which is far more enjoyable (not to mention safer and cheaper) than running a motorbike. Many hostels are located near the central station. In the old days, not a single visitor to Taipei, which is one of the most densely populated cities in the world, failed to complain of the pollution. But since the opening up of China, much of the industry has moved to the mainland and so the air quality has improved, though the million motorised vehicles haven't migrated.

The typhoon season lasts from July to October, bringing stormy hot humid weather and mouldy clothes. It is advisable therefore to head elsewhere, such as to the historic city of Tainan with its many old temples. Kaohsiung on the south-west coast is a large industrial city but one that has the advantage of being near the popular resort of Kenting Beach and within reach of mountain campsites such as Maolin. The geographical advantage of Taichung further north is proximity to the mountains, as well as a good climate and cultural activities. The tranquil East Coast National Scenic Area extends for nearly 200km along the Pacific coast. Volcanic mountains rise inland, creating a wide range of eroded landscapes. If you have time, catch a ferry to the tiny tropical island of Lanyu where the indigenous people are Yami rather than Chinese and where you can visit interesting caves.

Wherever you go, one of the highlights is the hospitality of the locals. Many Taiwanese will not accept a refusal of any food or drink offered, and even paying for meals or drinks can be a struggle. Shopping is a national pastime. Street markets are lively and colourful and can be found along alleys off main roads in the capital.

Taiwan is virtually crime-free. For the truly homesick, there are some English-style pubs with pool tables and dartboards. Eating out is just as much a pastime in Taiwan as it is in Hong Kong. There are countless little family-run restaurants which offer delicious and inexpensive food. Taiwan is also a fruit-lover's paradise.

TRAVEL RESOURCES

USEFUL WEBSITES
http://travelindependent.info, really useful snapshots of individual countries and a superb links page.

www.thailandguru.com, intended for expats living and working in Thailand but plenty of useful tips.

www.travelfish.org, '100% original Asia travel intelligence authored by dedicated travellers who know what they're talking about'. Covers Cambodia, Laos, Malaysia, Singapore, Vietnam, and Thailand.

www.pmgeiser.ch, Pongu's travel guide to many countries in Asia including China and Japan.

www.into-asia.com, Thailand and Indonesia.

www.indiamike.com, info, active forums, and blogs.

www.myanmar-travelnet.com, maintained by a Berlin-based individual who loves Burma.

USEFUL BOOKS

Lesley Reader and Lucy Ridout, *First Time Asia* (Rough Guides, 2010), £12.99.

David Stott and Vanessa Betts, *India Footprint Handbook* (Footprint Guides, 2011), £19.99. Good alternative to the usual Lonely Planet and Rough Guide offerings.

TRAVEL READING

William Sutcliffe, *Are You Experienced?* (Penguin, 1998), £8.99. Satirical account of the wrong way to go about being a gap year traveller. The anti-hero Dave's travels in India are based on the author's own gap year.

Emily Barr, *Backpack* (Headline, 2001), £7.99. Novel about an obnoxious young Londoner who gradually comes to appreciate the joys of extended travel in Asia (while narrowly escaping murder by a serial killer).

Haing Ngor, *Survival in the Killing Fields* (2003), £9.99. Moving memoir of life under the Khmer Rouge. The author won an Oscar for his role as Dith Pran in the 1984 film *The Killing Fields*.

Denise Chong, *The Girl in the Picture* (2001), £8.99. The biography of Kim Phuc, the girl burned by napalm in the famous photo from the Vietnam War.

Daniel Mason, *The Piano Tuner* (Picador, 2004), £7.99. Beautifully evokes the atmosphere of Burma. Written by a young American medical student who spent a year on the Thai–Burmese border region researching malaria.

Peter Hessler, *River Town: Two Years on the Yangtze* (John Murray, 2002), £9.99. Author was a young American EFL teacher in a remote town in China called Fuling.

AUSTRALIA AND NEW ZEALAND

The catchy, unmistakeably Australian, slogan, '*So Where the Bloody Hell Are You?*' adopted by Tourism Australia in one of its advertising campaigns, seems to be working. Australia and New Zealand have been hugely popular destinations for gap year travellers for many years, and yet don't seem to have become stale. Iconic images of the Sydney Opera House and Ayers Rock at sunset retain their power to attract.

Australia

VISAS

European nationals can participate in the eVisitor scheme by applying online in advance of arrival; there is no charge for this. The paperless visa, the ETA (Electronic Travel Authority), must be obtained by other nationals, including Americans and Canadians, again via the Australian Immigration Department's website (www.immi.gov.au/e_visa/visitors.htm), which will incur a fee of A$20.

CURRENCY

£1 = A$1.54   US$1 = A$0.93

BUDGET

Minimum US$50 a day excluding travel.

THE LURE OF DOWN UNDER

Australia is like nowhere else on earth. If the beach–beer axis were just a tourism authority myth, people would soon desert the country. But it isn't a myth. Australia really can seem like one perpetual party held by sun-bronzed surfers in an endless summer. The frisson of the bizarre and dangerous wildlife just adds to the thrill (though, fortunately, stories are far more common than actual encounters).

In response to its phenomenal popularity as a destination for so many young Europeans, Australia has developed a massive industry to cater specifically for backpackers. Hostels, both official and private, are full of gap year travellers and working holidaymakers who will advise newcomers on the best travel deals and adventures, and the places to go to find jobs (see *Australia* chapter later in this book for information about working and the working holiday visa). Specialist travel offices specifically target the backpacking community, which in Australia includes everybody from people fresh from school to professionals in their 30s who choose to stay in 'backpackers' (the Australian word for hostels). Alluring possibilities present themselves at every turn – learn-to-surf trips, cave tours with Aboriginal guides, sailing adventures, winery visits, reef snorkelling, and so on.

TRAVEL TIP

Some gappers are seduced into pre-booking too many activities before leaving home, but when they arrive they see how many other choices there are.

UNMISSABLE HIGHLIGHTS

- Snorkel at Magnetic Island on the Great Barrier Reef.
- Sample some McLaren Vale Shiraz wines at the cellar door.
- Wander round the ancient domes and gorges of the eerie Olga Rocks (Kata Tjuta) in the Red Centre.
- Join the Neighbours tour of Ramsay Street in Melbourne.
- Cycle round the car-free Rottnest Island near Perth, spotting quokkas (marsupials peculiar to the island).
- Hike the Cradle Mountain track in Tasmania.
- Catch a film at the open-air Moonlight Cinema in Perth.
- Buy provisions at the Vic Market in Melbourne for a picnic at Hanging Rock an hour north of the city.
- Feed the wild dolphins at remote Monkey Mia on the coast of Western Australia.
- Join the glamorous Sydney set, who descend on Bronte Beach for Sunday brunch.
- Take a boat tour at night on Djarradjin billabong in Kakadu National Park to search for 'eyeshine', the reflection of torchlight from pairs of crocodile eyes.

GETTING THERE

Australia is within reach of many gap year travellers simply because of the falling price of international airfares. Per mile, the flight to the Antipodes is cheaper than most destinations, though recent tax hikes have increased the outlay required. Malaysia Airlines, Emirates, Qatar, Royal Brunei, and JAL often turn out to be the cheapest, although Qantas has been competing strongly with promotional fares of less than £700 return available through specialists like Austravel (0800 988 4676; www.austravel.com).

The cheapest time of year to depart for Australia or New Zealand is between April and June, while mid-season prices are charged between July and November and again in February/March. Normally the cheapest fares go early, so as soon as you decide, start to shop around. Whatever you do, avoid flying in the weeks before and after Christmas.

Australia is almost always included in RTW tickets, which might add only £100–£200 to the cost of a straight return. So even if your main destination is only Australia it is worth thinking about a possible stopover in Asia en route. Spending time in South East Asia will guarantee that your travel fund will last longer, since the cost of living is much lower in Phnom Penh than in Perth (see *Asia* chapter).

GETTING AROUND

Distances in Australia are unimaginably greater than Britons are accustomed to and so you will have to give a lot of thought to how you can pare down your itinerary. Richard Branson's Virgin Blue (www.virginblue.com.au) has some good deals, and his Pacific Blue flies across the Tasman to New Zealand. Sample Blue fares in 2011 started at A$140 Sydney to Cairns and A$149 Melbourne to Christchurch (via Brisbane). Compare also the no-frills domestic airline Jetstar (www.jetstar.com), a subsidiary of Qantas.

If you plan a major tour of Australia, you might consider purchasing a Greyhound coach pass although they are expensive. The all-Australia pass valid for 12 months costs an astronomical A$2,510. If you just want to get from one coast to another as quickly as possible, point-to-point tickets, eg Sydney–Adelaide (24 hours for A$200 or A$155 via Melbourne) are the best idea. Students and backpackers are eligible for the Rail Explorer Pass which gives six months of unlimited travel on the *Ghan*, the *Indian Pacific* and the *Overland* for A$590 plus fuel surcharges (+61 8 8213 4592; www.gsr.com.au/backpackers).

A multiplicity of private operators has sprung up to serve the backpacking market, such as Oz Experience (which has a reputation as a party bus) and Adventure Tours. Firefly Express operates daily services between Melbourne, Sydney and Adelaide; a sample one-way Sydney–Melbourne fare is A$60.

Having your own transport is a possibility for groups of friends travelling together. Some places have second-hand cars and camper vans for sale which they will buy back at the end of your stay, for example Travellers Auto Barn in Sydney, Melbourne, Brisbane, Cairns, Perth, and Darwin (www.travellers-autobarn.com). Expect to pay A$2,000+ for an old car (such as a gas-guzzling Ford Falcon) and more for a camper van; the more you spend, the better your chance of its lasting the distance and being saleable at the end of your stay.

Car hire is expensive, but occasionally 'relocations' are available, ie hire cars that need to be returned to their depots. Just pick up the *Yellow Pages* and phone through the rental companies asking about relocation deals, which is exactly what **Roger Blake** did when he wanted to travel from Adelaide to Melbourne:

> *The Great Ocean Road is renowned as one of the most scenic drives in the world and I was determined not to see it from a tour bus window. I phoned a hundred and one rental companies looking for a relocation (taking a vehicle back to its state depot due to one-way rental demands). I got lucky because they desperately needed one to leave the next day. Only A$1 per day rental, and they were so desperate that they even gave me A$100 for fuel. So I spent the following three days on my own in a flash four/five-berth Mercedes-Benz motorhome on the spectacular Great Ocean Road along the coast of Victoria. The whole drive is dangerously scenic. And the cost to me? A whopping A$63!*

Apollo Motorhomes lists the dollar-a-day camper van relocations it sometimes has available on its website (www.apollocamper.com.au/reloc.aspx). The best places to start are Cairns, Darwin, Adelaide, and Broome, where drivers are sometimes even given several hundred dollars for fuel.

If you can't afford the luxury of organised transport or buying your own vehicle, you might be drawn to the idea of hitching a lift, though this has become an endangered pastime (though not as dangerous as people assume) in Australia, as almost everywhere else. The Queensland coastal road has a notorious reputation. Violence is rare, but if you are unlucky you might be evicted from the truck unless you comply with the driver's wishes. Backpackers' hostels are a good bet for finding drivers going your way, provided you are able to wait for a suitable ride. Try also the lift-sharing forum on www.backpackingaround.com.au or www.shareyourride.net.

BUDGETING

There are so many temptations for a gap year traveller that money seems to soak away like water poured on the Nullarbor desert.

With the current unfavourable exchange rate for Britons, Australia is considerably more expensive than it used to be. Living a relatively spartan existence will still cost A$50 a day. Because the tourism infrastructure for backpackers is so extensive, you have to pay out significant sums to access the Barrier Reef, take surfing lessons, and so on. The effectively marketed Sydney Bridge Climb – 'for the climb of your life' – illustrates this perfectly. A dawn climb in peak season costs a whopping A$300 for three hours. If you are on a budget you will have to resist all these packaged adventures; for example you can walk or cycle across the bridge for nothing or pay A$9.50 to climb the 200 steps up the pylon at the southern end of the bridge, which gives a superb view.

> **TRAVEL TIP**
>
> *Significant discounts on travel, accommodation, etc are offered to people with a card that identifies them as backpackers including an international student card, YHA membership card, or other backpackers' hostel group card such as VIP or Nomad (see next section).*

ACCOMMODATION

Australia is incredibly well provided with congenial hostel accommodation. The average cost of a dorm bed in a backpackers is A$22–$28. Often a double room costs only a little more per head, but these are often booked up in advance. Backpackers' accommodation provides more than just a place to sleep; they become the centre of your social life, and the bar or garden often fizzes with conversation about the next unmissable destination or activity. Many hostels hire out bicycles, put on local tours to places difficult to access otherwise, and organise barbecues, picnics, and adventure sports.

A free booklet listing all 107 YHA hostels is widely available (www.yha.com.au). One of the most successful groups of non-YHA backpackers' hostels is VIP Backpackers Resorts of Australia, which is especially strong in New South Wales and Queensland (www.vipbackpackers.com). A booklet listing its Australian hostels is distributed far and wide or can be obtained from overseas by purchasing the VIP card for A$43, which gives discounts and benefits. Many VIP hostels have noticeboards advertising jobs, flats, car shares, etc.

The Nomads Backpacker chain has about 22 hostels in Australia, many of them renovated pubs. Nomads (www.nomadsworld.com) sell a discount card called the MAD Card for A$37.

WHAT TO EXPECT

The seasons in the southern hemisphere are opposite to those north of the Equator and it can be difficult getting used to university terms down under, finishing for the summer holidays in December and the ski season beginning in June. With luck, you will bask in sunshine and swim in balmy seas. But Australia's vastness means that there are tremendous variations from zone to zone, encompassing alpine zones such as Tasmania and sub-Equatorial monsoonal regions such as Darwin. July in Melbourne can be chilly and wet, and the annual rainfall in sunny Perth is higher than in London.

All Australians have been endlessly drilled to 'slip, slop, slap' – slip on a shirt, slop on some high-factor sun protection, and slap on a hat – and fair-skinned new arrivals should do likewise to avoid sun damage. Darwin and Cairns are true tropical cities and are therefore subject to rainy and dry seasons, invariably referred to in Australia as the Wet and the Dry. These areas are probably best avoided in the wet season, which lasts from about December to April. If you are there long enough to follow the seasons, you would ideally spend June to September in Queensland and the Red Centre, and then enjoy the long balmy evenings and sunny days of summer in the south east.

Australia is an overwhelmingly urban culture that treasures its bush lore. While the people cling to the edges of their vast island continent (80% live within 20 miles of the sea) they glorify their untamed interior. Another endearing characteristic is their preference for leisure over work. At weekends everyone is at the beach, a barbecue, or a sporting event. At their best, Australians can be gifted and colourful raconteurs. Be prepared to take some good-natured joshing, especially on the subject of cricket. Their quirky and ironic sense of humour, aversion to pomposity, and prevailing geniality make for some lively conversations.

Eight million Britons have relations living in Australia. If you do set off with a list of addresses to look up and feel inhibited about making contact with strangers, give it a chance. Always make it clear you are a traveller on the move, rather than a freeloader (known locally as a 'bludger').

If the local people are friendly and benign, the wildlife is less cuddly. One of the more staggering facts about Australia is the number of aquatic nasties that will not hesitate to deliver a fatal sting, bite or snap. The chief menaces are sharks (though popular beaches are usually protected by sea nets), crocodiles, and an unpleasant little creature known as a marine stinger. These potentially lethal creatures are also known as sea wasps and box jellyfish, and are common on the coast of Queensland and the Northern Territory from December to March. The only sensible way to escape the threat is to follow the advice of signs posted on beaches and stay out of the water during the season.

There are just as many dangers awaiting on land, though of course very few backpackers actually come across any redback or trapdoor spiders, or deadly western taipan and brown snakes. They are far more likely to encounter maddening midges and sandflies; take plenty of strong mosquito repellent or use local concoctions such as tea-tree oil, or mixing a third of Dettol with two-thirds baby oil (repulsive but effective).

Sydney and New South Wales

Partying in Sydney is the sole ambition of many first-time world travellers. With one of the most magnificent settings of any city in the world (apart perhaps from Rio), a vibrant youth culture and a taste for hedonism, it is hard to imagine anyone not liking Sydney. Wherever you look there are hip little cafés, fantastic ethnic restaurants (many allowing you to bring your own wine), great bookshops and plenty of ambience. Sydneysiders share with New Yorkers the easy confidence that their city is the Big Smoke. But unlike New York, a great deal of Sydney's life is lived outdoors, whether swimming at Bondi Beach, listening to free entertainment in Martin Place downtown, or supping a beer at a pavement café.

Most gap year travellers gravitate to one of the backpacker ghettos and make it their base. Once-sleazy King's Cross has been somewhat rehabilitated, though many prefer one of the beach suburbs like Coogee or Manly (try the iconic Shark Bar in the New Brighton Hotel on the Corso, refurbished for 2011), or leafy arty Glebe not far from Sydney University. Newtown has some hostels, though is best known for its amazing range of eateries.

Many of the city's pre-eminent pleasures are free or very cheap – a ferry from Circular Quay to Manly Beach ('Seven Miles from Sydney and a Thousand Miles from Care'), a stroll through the Royal Botanic Gardens downtown (looking up to admire the resident colony of flying fox bats), poking around

EXCITING WAYS TO GET INVOLVED

- Take a jackaroo or jillaroo course before getting a paid job on a Queensland country property (www. leconfieldjackaroo.com).
- Stand up on your surfboard on the first day of a course at Byron Bay, New South Wales (www. mojosurf.com.au).
- Earn money by picking apples in the Huon Valley of Tasmania (www.huonvalleybackpackers.com).
- Get a few days' well-paid casual work before and after major horse race fixtures in Melbourne (www. melbourneracingclub.net.au).
- Work a season in a ski resort in the Australian Alps (www.thredbo.com.au/about-thredbo/snow-jobs).
- Intern with an Australian PR firm or volunteer in a remote indigenous community (www.internships.com.au).
- Volunteer in the rainforest at a tropical research centre in far north Queensland (www.austrop.org.au).

the colourful Saturday markets such as Paddington Market and Glebe Market or the amazing Fish Market (which sells all kinds of food) or nursing a drink at a Sunday afternoon session in a pub that features free jazz.

The sooner you leave Sydney, the better chance you have of not blowing all your money in a few weeks. Most head north along 'the Route' to the favourite backpackers' resort of Byron Bay and on to Queensland. Those who are heading south of Sydney have the chance to explore the wonderful south coast, often overlooked by foreign travellers. Heading south, the so-called Sapphire Coast between Eden and Bateman's Bay is a favourite vacation destination for Australians.

The state boasts 58 national parks, which come in all shapes and sizes. The Blue Mountains, accessible on an hourly rail service from Sydney to Katoomba, are criss-crossed with walking tracks of varying degrees of difficulty. Even nearer the city, Ku-ring-gai Chase National Park features the Basin Track which leads you to some atmospheric Aboriginal rock carvings of hunters and kangaroos.

All manner of adventure tours can be booked in New South Wales. Among the most popular are a surf tour to Byron Bay and Crescent Head (for example with Mojo Surf; www.mojosurf.com.au).

Queensland

Queensland's reputation as a tropical paradise has taken a serious hit with the devastating floods that turned three-quarters of the state into a disaster zone in January 2011. Urgent rebuilding got under way as soon as the waters receded, though the losses to the Australian economy have been massive. The hardest-hit area was Toowoomba and the Lockyer Valley inland from Brisbane, leaving the majority of the popular tourist regions relatively unscathed.

That means that great expanses of the Queensland coast continue to meet most people's expectation of paradise. Variations on the theme include the many offshore islands turned holiday playgrounds, the sleepy sugar plantation towns, the travellers' haven of Cairns and the outback wilderness beyond. What makes the coastline exceptional is the immense and fascinating Great Barrier Reef lying off most of the eastern shoreline, usually at least a 45-minute (expensive) boat ride away. Less paradisal – except in name – but still extremely popular are the unabashedly commercialised resorts around Surfers' Paradise on the Gold Coast.

Once just a sleepy state capital, Brisbane has been shedding its redneck image. The city is now a curious mix of the crumblingly tropical, the handsomely colonial and the gleamingly modern, embroidered by pleasant parks and the slow, murky Brisbane River which turned so dangerous during the floods. But the condition of the capital is of little concern to the wide spectrum of visitors to Queensland. Most gappers head straight past and up the coast.

One essential reason for the popularity of Queensland is the glorious climate. Places such as Townsville plaster over all their promotional literature '300 days of sunshine a year'. Queensland's weather is sub-tropical in the south of the state and becomes more tropical the further north you go, with a summer wet season (October or November to March).

A huge number of travellers trek through Airlie Beach en route to the Whitsunday Islands, often for a pre-booked inter-island sailing trip with a company such as Awesome Adventures Oz. Expect to pay A$100+ a day for a six-day package. Another highly recommended island destination is Fraser Island, which is a gigantic sand island with lots of wildlife.

Most gappers end up signing up for a diving course, yacht cruise or four-wheel-drive expedition which they end up enjoying so much that they do not begrudge the drain on their travel coffer. Depending on your tastes, the sheer number of foreign backpackers on the Route can become oppressive. In Cairns, for instance, visitors entirely swamp locals, and competition for the tourist dollar is unceasing and sometimes bitter. But do not be deterred: Queensland is a vast state where it is the simplest thing to camp in a gregarious unspoiled little town or hike in a national park. Try for example Hinchinbrook Island, accessible by launch from Cardwell, with wild mountain scenery and plenty of wildlife. If you don't want to stay at the low key eco-resort where the boat lands, walk about 45 minutes to a simple campsite on the coast, where the pleasure of eating oysters prised from the coastal rocks goes some way to compensating for the belligerent sandflies.

The Northern Territory and the Outback

To foreigners and Australians alike, the Northern Territory has traditionally been equated with Ayers Rock, or Uluru – the red rock rising from the red centre of Australia, symbolising the uniqueness of this country. Uluru is the world's largest monolith and its appearance, rising suddenly from the stark desert, is magical. Only when you get close to it does its massive scale become overwhelming. The most spectacular aspect is the change of colour that sometimes takes place at sunset and sunrise. When this happens, it lasts for only a few minutes but is captured by a thousand cameras. The scenes on the 'sunset strip' west of the rock can be almost comical, with visitors clamouring for the best photographic vantage point, as if waiting for the arrival of a celebrity. You can either climb the rock very early in the morning before the heat of the day makes it impossible, or walk round the base (9.5km), pausing to look at paintings by the Anangu Aboriginal people for whom it is sacred.

Close to Uluru are the Olgas, a range emerging from the stark desert that many find even more intriguing. Nearby – always a relative term in the Territory – is the town of Alice Springs. Australia's Red Centre is semi-desert, with hot, dry summers and cold winters. At its heart is Alice Springs, which once epitomised the pioneering spirit of a nation, where visitors plan their assault on the Rock 450km away. One of the best tours is a three-day camping-under-the-stars trip with Mulga's Tours (www.mulgas.com.au); it includes Ayers Rock, the Olgas and Kings Canyon for A\$250, plus A\$25 entrance fee for Uluru National Park.

'The Track' or Stuart Highway is the central spine that covers the 1,500km distance between Alice Springs and Darwin. Darwin, capital of the territory, is surrounded by swamps, gorges, and more than a few crocodiles. The north is tropical – hot throughout the year with a pronounced wet season, always referred to as 'the Wet', from November to April. You could easily blow A\$1,000 visiting the places of interest around Darwin. Pre-eminent among them is Kakadu National Park, which is the state's other must-see destination. The supply of accommodation inside Kakadu is decidedly finite and should be booked ahead, especially during the high season. One of the most interesting places to stay is Kakadu Culture Camp (www.kakaduculturecamp.com), which is owned and run by an Aboriginal family, whose members are also qualified park rangers. Night billabong boat tours cost A\$80. You can also pitch a tent next door for A\$10 per person.

Local tour companies typically offer two-, three- or five-day four-wheel-drive trips to Kakadu, featuring visits to waterholes to see wildlife, information about Aboriginal culture, bush barbecues, and adventure activities such as canoeing and climbing. Although Kakadu is the most popular destination, you might consider the less visited Litchfield Park (Wangi), which is nearer Darwin; it has the scenic Tabletop Range as a backdrop, huge termite mounds, hot springs, and waterfalls, to compensate for a shortage of crocodiles. This is a feasible destination for people without a four-wheel-drive vehicle.

TRAVEL TIP
Remember that programmes run by local tour companies can be quite different depending on whether it is the Wet or the Dry.

Victoria and Tasmania

Although the smallest state in Australia (apart from Tasmania), Victoria contains as great a variety of terrain as any other state, encapsulating almost the entire range of Australian landscapes and climates in microcosm: from the Little Desert to the Snowy Mountains, rich pastures to rainforest, and tumbling vineyards to dramatic coastline. Victoria has a wealth of little-known natural attractions.

From the urban point of view, Victoria comprises both big-city style and small-town country life, laced with a fascinating colonial history. The sophisticated city of Melbourne seems to be luring many young backpackers who at one time had eyes only for Sydney. In recent years, Melbourne's cityscape has shot skywards, old buildings have been renovated and the Yarra River foreshores cleaned up. The glitzy Federation Square piazza provides a focus for Melbourne culture with galleries, art cinemas, and restaurants. As well as being a cultural mecca, Melbourne boasts the best sporting venues and arguably the finest food in the country.

Picturesque cosmopolitan neighbourhoods are dotted around the heart of Melbourne: St Kilda, once a seaside resort for the wealthy, now a trendified bohemian beachside suburb; Port Melbourne, a refurbished waterfront area; Carlton, Fitzroy, and Richmond, paradises for cut-price gourmets. 'Ramsay Street' can be visited in a distant suburb on the official *Neighbours* tour for A\$50, or you can make your own way to Pinoak Grove (train to Glen Waverly, bus 888 to Nunawading).

Outside Melbourne, the highest concentration of backpacker facilities is along the scenic Great Ocean Road mentioned above. The 200km stretch of road hugs the coastline through picturesque seaside resorts, many with superb surf beaches, then cuts inland through the lush forested hills of Otway National Park.

Tasmania is distinctly dissimilar to the rest of Australia, softer and damper than the dry environment of the mainland and with spectacular wilderness scenery which has turned it into an eco-destination, especially worth seeing if you are not going to make it to the South Island of New Zealand. Its reputation for wet weather, backwardness, and the expense of getting to the island deter many would-be backpackers, thus indirectly preserving the unspoiled character of the island. The discount airline Jetstar advertises one-way fares Melbourne to Hobart for A$49, so the expense is not prohibitive.

The south east is the site of the historic capital of Hobart and some fascinating remnants of the island's past as a colony of penal servitude. Hobart's setting – overlooking the broad Derwent River estuary and surrounded by rugged hills – is more beautiful than that of any other state capital except Sydney. Salamanca Place, with an excellent food market and free weekend concerts, contains some splendid sandstone warehouses converted into a pleasant mixture of antique shops, galleries, and restaurants, all within easy walking distance.

If your time in Tasmania is limited, get a flavour of the island by sailing or flying to Devonport and heading north-west. The top left-hand corner of Tasmania has the same ingredients of dramatic coastline, rugged mountains, towering forests, and undulating pasture that the island possesses in such abundance.

The major hiking trail is the 80km Overland Track which takes on average six days and passes Tasmania's highest peak, the 1,617m high Mount Ossa. It is so popular that it is necessary to book between November and April (www.parks.tas.gov.au) at a cost of A$160.

Western Australia

Western Australia (or 'WA' as it is invariably known) is a vast and vibrant state with immense variety: the clean and cosmopolitan city of Perth and its pretty port of Fremantle, the fertile south west and the wild northern regions with their rugged mountains and deserts. More than any other state, WA brings home the immense scale of the Australian continent. Because of the vast distance (and expense) involved in getting there, many gappers neglect it, missing out on a fantastic climate, a young and lively population dedicated to enjoying themselves, and encounters with wildlife.

Perth's clubbing scene is centred on Northbridge. For a casual night out, watch for the special backpacker nights advertised widely, which may involve three-hour 'happy hours' and free or heavily discounted bar food. Two of the favourites are the Hip-e Club in Leederville, which hosts backpacker party nights on Tuesdays. Obviously, in a limited time it is not possible to see much of this vast state. From Perth, you can travel down the lovely south-west coast to great surf beaches or far to the north to Monkey Mia, where dolphins happily frolic with swimmers, and laid-back tropical Broome, a backpackers' mecca. You can choose to get around by bus, by backpacker tour or something in between, the jump-on jump-off bus run by Easy Rider (www.easyridertours.com.au). Many other tour companies compete to take you to the famous Pinnacles, 230km north of Perth, weird calcified humps and pillars of eroded limestone, and to the gorges at Kalbarri.

South Australia

Adelaide has a grace and charm lacking in bigger, brasher cities. A beautifully planned and sited city, with suburbs on the seashore and the Adelaide Hills rising up to the east, it is a pleasant place to spend time on your trans-Australian travels. South Australia has a rich blend of varied coastline, fertile farmland (producing three-fifths of Australia's wine), rugged mountain ranges, and seemingly endless stark desert.

In keeping with the relaxed lifestyle which they enjoy, natives of Adelaide and its environs are casual and friendly. Try the pubs and clubs around Hindley Street or clean-cut King William Street, or mix with the student fraternity at the University of Adelaide.

Adelaide is favoured with a continuous stretch of accessible sandy beaches, safe from sharks and overeager developers. From anywhere in the city, you need only head west to find somewhere to lay your towel on the 32km of wide gently sloping beach. Don't expect the massive breakers of the Indian and Pacific oceans; the placid waters of Gulf St Vincent are protected from the high seas by the Yorke Peninsula and Kangaroo Island.

Nearly 10 hours' driving time from Adelaide, Coober Pedy in the South Australian outback is a bizarre place which is mostly below ground. The name is Aboriginal for 'White Man's Burrow', which accurately describes the dwellings of the opal hunters who live here. The inhabitants escape from the unremitting summer heat by residing underground in homes hewn out of the rock. Several backpackers hostels are underground, including the Radeka Underground Backpackers on Hutchison Street (beds for A$32).

New Zealand

VISA
Tourists from the UK need no visa to stay for up to six months. Information about the working holiday visa is given in the chapter on New Zealand near the end of this book.

CURRENCY
£1 = NZ$2.06   US$1 = NZ$1.25

BUDGET
US$40–$50 a day.

THE LURE OF NEW ZEALAND
New Zealanders sometimes refer to their country as 'Godzone' (God's Own) and assume that foreigners will agree with them that New Zealand combines most of the attributes of an ideal country (other nationalities are guilty of this too, but with less justification). Yet the tragic earthquake has left many New Zealanders reeling, and Christchurch is not the carefree and beautiful city that it was before 22 February 2011, especially since aftershocks have continued to occur at intervals.

Travelling gappers will find themselves warmly welcomed and the object of much friendly interest and curiosity, which makes New Zealand uniquely attractive. Even people involved in the tourist industry often seem to take a more personal than commercial interest in visitors' welfare. It is hard to imagine a country where travellers will feel as safe and pampered as New Zealand.

New Zealand's spectacular topography is its real trump card. The natural wonders – volcanoes, glaciers, fjords – do not disappoint. This tiny country encompasses alpine ranges and mangrove swamps, glaciers and rainforests. The climate may come as a shock if you have been travelling in the hot, dry areas of Australia. Rainfall is terrifically high on the west coast of the South Island, where some of the country's foremost attractions are located. An entry in the visitor's book of a mountain hut on the Routeburn Track reads, '*In New Zealand you don't tan – you rust*'. But it's often balmy and beautiful.

Almost everybody seems passionate about sport. Not only do they avidly follow the fortunes of their national teams, they pursue outdoor activities themselves like tramping (ie hiking), sailing, skiing, and diving. They are also amazingly innovative when it comes to exploring their remarkable country and have invented a host of sports and vehicles. The most famous is bungee jumping, but there is also zorbing, surf-rafting, dune-surfing, rap-jumping (abseiling head-first), and river sledging.

UNMISSABLE HIGHLIGHTS

- Go tramping (hiking) in Tongariro National Park, familiar as the Land of Mordor in the *Lord of the Rings* movies.
- Visit the albatross colony on the Otago Peninsula near Dunedin.
- Bodyboard down the sand dunes at Ninety Mile Beach in the far north.
- Go on the hi-tech High Ride in New Zealand's National Museum Te Papa.
- Jump off a 102m platform above the Shotover River with an elastic band around your ankles.
- Eat sophisticated seafood at one of the trendy eateries on Auckland's Ponsonby Road.
- Go punting on the River Avon in Christchurch.
- Admire the stunning alpine views from the windows of the TranzAlpine train that crosses the South Island coast to coast.
- Explore the huge Polynesian flea market at Otara, a suburb of Auckland.
- Escape the crowds at thermal Rotorua by pedalling a hire bike around the lake.

GETTING THERE AND AROUND

Air New Zealand has been offering some very competitive return fares and also RTW fares lately, and a stopover in Sydney can be added at little extra cost. If you are combining Australia with New Zealand without a RTW ticket, you should investigate the trans-Tasman airfares available from Pacific Blue or Jetstar as mentioned above. Hope that your visit will coincide with a price war on domestic flights. Recently, Jetstar was advertising a one-way Auckland to Wellington fare of NZ$69 (though allowing carry-on bags only).

Once in New Zealand, distances are so much more manageable and the scenery more varied than in Oz that road travel is a delight. Backpackers often decide to buy a vehicle (from about NZ$2,000) or rent a car, though this is available only to those over 21. Backpackers buy and sell used cars and vans in Auckland and Christchurch (www.backpackerscarmarket.co.nz) or check adverts in www.auto trader.co.nz. Look for a vehicle with a couple of months of WOF (equivalent to MOT in the UK) remaining.

The integrated coach network is operated by scheduled coach companies Intercity and Newmans. Investigate the coach passes including the innovative Flexipass (http://flexipass.intercity.co.nz) in which you buy a certain number of hours of travel, starting at 15 hours for NZ$115. The New Zealand Travelpass (www.travelpass.co.nz) permits unlimited coach travel plus the trans-Tasman ferry, for a specified number of days of travel within one year; seven days of travel costs NZ$570 at the back-packer rate, while 14 days costs NZ$1,124. You can also get cheaper passes limited to one island. But before booking any of these, investigate Naked Bus (www.nakedbus.com), which operates like Megabus in the UK and USA. If you book well in advance, you can get some NZ$1 fares. They have also introduced bus passes to undercut their rivals; an unlimited one-year pass costs NZ$597.

In addition, there are private shuttle services between fixed points. Try, for example, Atomic Travel (www.atomictravel.co.nz) between Christchurch and Queenstown, Wanaka, and Dunedin, or the West Coast Shuttle operating between Christchurch and Greymouth (mainly for skiers). The main back-packer companies with hop-on hop-off services in New Zealand are Stray Travel (www.straytravel.com), the Magic Travellers Network (www.magicbus.co.nz), which picks up from hostels around New Zealand, and Kiwi Experience (www.kiwiexperience.com), which has the reputation for being one giant pub crawl for 18–21-year-olds.

New Zealand is famously welcoming to hitch-hikers. A combination of friendly trusting locals and like-minded travellers with transport means that you don't usually have to wait long. To minimise anxiety, try arranging a lift ahead via www.jayride.co.nz.

BUDGETING

If you stick to all the free activities at your disposal such as swimming, tramping, and admiring the scenery, the daily cost might be NZ$50. But once you decide to try bungee jumping or glacier walking or go out to eat at foodie restaurants, the daily spend will be three times as much.

Lynn Munro was lucky enough to be granted a gap year scholarship by the Royal Geographical Society (open to geography students), and used part of it to travel round New Zealand from January to May:

The majority of my time was spent walking through New Zealand, from glaciers to rainforest. It really was a trip of a lifetime. Travelling independently allowed me to meet fellow travellers and to complete some of New Zealand's most famous walks. The highlight was a four-day walk along the Kepler Track through dense rainforest, alpine vegetation, alongside rivers, up incredible mountains, before walking alongside a mirrored lake. This walk truly summed up the time I had in New Zealand. It was on the Kepler Track that I decided to accept the university offer of a place to study Environmental Science and Outdoor Education.

ACCOMMODATION

New Zealand has a marvellous network of cheap and cheerful hostels and mountain huts for 'trampers'. Many hostels (also called 'backpackers', as in Australia) belong to the YHA, the VIP network, and Budget Backpackers Hostels group (see www.bbh.co.nz, which has 300+ member hostels and links to travel info). If you buy a membership card in any of these groups, you get a discount every time you stay in one of their hostels.

Camping on beaches, in fields, and in woodlands is generally allowed if you ask the permission of the landlord. Some Department of Conservation sites with no facilities are free of charge, or you might be allowed to camp in the grounds of a hostel and use their facilities for a modest rate.

North Island

The North Island is far more densely populated than the South, and Auckland is the biggest city, though Wellington is the capital. Whereas the most sensational geographical phenomena of the South Island are due to glaciation, the remarkable feature of the North is its volcanic history.

Auckland's harbourside location, complete with overcrowded bridge and rising number of excellent informal eateries, justifies a comparison with Sydney. But most backpackers head out of the city fairly promptly, often north to the Bay of Islands resort area. Paihia and Russell are jumping-off points for experiencing the glorious ocean scenery of the Bay of Islands and also have many places of historical interest, such as New Zealand's oldest church and the hotel with the oldest licence. A half-day walk from Opua to Paihia takes you through mangrove forest, populated by strange clicking crabs and snapping shrimp. From Auckland, others set out in a southerly direction, perhaps to the rugged and mountainous Coromandel Peninsula with its lovely unspoiled wilderness and empty beaches – even in summer – or to sulphurous (and touristy) Rotorua.

Tongariro National Park, roughly halfway between Auckland and Wellington, incorporates the highest peaks of the North Island, which are all active volcanoes, so the ground is hot to the touch. Many gappers choose to walk the Tongariro Crossing, a long one-day traverse between Mount Tongariro and Mount Ngauruhoe, which Peter Jackson (New Zealand director of *Lord of the Rings*) chose to stand in for Mount Doom.

Wellington is another Antipodean city with a magnificent setting, steep hills descending to its spacious harbour. For such a small city, Wellington is surprisingly cosmopolitan, with a fantastic range of restaurants representing every imaginable cuisine. Don't miss visiting Te Papa and Courtenay Place, a centre for eating out. The splendid National Museum of New Zealand, Te Papa (www.tepapa.govt.nz), is free to enter. It features excellent exhibits on Maori and Polynesian culture, and an interactive display called Awesome Forces in which an earthquake and volcanic eruption are simulated, although this might not be treated as light-heartedly as it was before the recent earthquake.

From Wellington, you can catch the scenic Interislander ferry to Picton on the South Island. The one-way fare for a foot passenger starts at NZ$60 with a student discount.

South Island

Some say that the further south you travel from Auckland, the further you travel into the past, ending at a fisherman's house on Stewart Island with no electricity, motor car or telephone. Travelling south along the east coast you will pass through laid-back Kaikoura, famous for whale-watching and on to the third city of New Zealand. Christchurch has been too busy repairing all its crumpled roads, buildings, and sewerage system to have time to promote itself as the most English city outside England, with its punts on the River Avon and a red double-decker tour bus. At the time of writing there was limited traveller accommodation in Christchurch, since buildings deemed to be safe were in use as emergency accommodation for displaced locals.

The many lovely beaches within easy reach of Christchurch have been mainly deserted since the earthquake, partly because of a fear that the waters are polluted after the damage to the city's drainage system. A little further away is the Banks Peninsula, which has a feeling of remoteness. Try the fish and chips in the main resort on the peninsula, Akaroa.

Over on the west coast, the spectacularly pristine Franz Josef and Fox Glaciers are worth examining up close. Fox Glacier Guiding (www.foxguides.co.nz) is one of several companies offering hiking tours and ice adventures to suit all fitness levels. An alternative independent walk is to Robert's Point, which is situated beside Franz Josef Glacier, affording good views of its blue and deeply crevassed surface. The three-hour walk through dripping temperate rainforest is not overly strenuous, though the slippery stream crossings can become a little tricky and, as throughout New Zealand, people who suffer from vertigo might not enjoy the swing bridges and rockface ladders.

EXCITING WAYS TO GET INVOLVED

- Become a volunteer hut warden for the NZ Department of Conservation (www.doc.govt.nz).
- Earn money by picking kiwi fruit in the Bay of Plenty, New Zealand (www.seasonalwork.co.nz).
- Exchange your help for free room and board at a horse trekking centre in New Zealand (www.wwoof.co.nz).
- Spend 10 weeks learning to become a snowboard instructor in Queenstown (www.snowtrainers.com)
- Assist teachers at a boarding school with the outdoor education programme, sports coaching, music or art (www.lattitude.org.uk).

If you have seen just one glossy New Zealand calendar, chances are that the photos of mountains, lakes, and fjords were taken in the south-west corner of the South Island, an area of sublime landscapes. Even more attractive to many gap travellers is the social scene and possibilities for adventure in Queenstown, capital of Fiordland. Not many backpackers can withstand the pressure to participate in at least one of Queenstown's attractions; in fact, there's not much point in coming unless you do. You will be subjected to a barrage of enticing offers: not to miss happy hour, to dabble in a dangerous sport, or plan an excursion further afield to Milford or Wanaka. Despite the huge number of beds in Queenstown, it is a good idea to book ahead in the summer and also during the ski season if you want a central location. The busiest time of all is the Winter Festival at the end of June.

TRAVEL RESOURCES

USEFUL WEBSITES

www.australia.com, official site of the Australian Tourist Commission.
www.citysearch.com.au, links to eating out, gigs, etc.
www.australianexplorer.com.
www.backpackerboard.co.nz, lots of useful job info and tips on budget travel for backpackers in New Zealand.

USEFUL BOOKS

Bug Australia: The Backpacker's Ultimate Guide and *Bug New Zealand* (published by Explore Australia, both 2010), £12.99. A change from the usual guidebook series, but not as good.

TRAVEL READING

Peter Carey, *True History of the Kelly Gang* (Faber and Faber, 2004), £8.99. A journal-style book that brings to life the harsh realities of life in 19th-century Australia.

Thomas Keneally, *The Commonwealth of Thieves: Story of the Founding of Australia* (Vintage, 2006), £9.99. A lively depiction of the Sydney experiment of founding a penal colony.

Clive James, *Unreliable Memoirs* (Picador, 2008), £7.99. Television presenter and author's engaging memoirs.

Nevil Shute, *A Town Like Alice* (House of Stratus, 2000), £7.99. Alice Springs is the setting for this endearing tale about an English woman who is a prisoner of war in Malaya, but then finds love and settles in the Australian outback.

Patrick White, *Voss* (Vintage, 1994), £8.99. Novel with detailed descriptions of colonial life in Australia.

Murray Bail, *Eucalyptus* (Harvill Press, 2000), £7.99. A romantic tale set in the countryside of New South Wales.

Kate Grenville, *The Secret River* (Canongate, 2006) and *The Lieutenant* (2010). Beautifully written novels vividly evoking the colonial past and with great sympathy for the plight of the Aboriginal inhabitants.

Keri Hulme, *The Bone People* (Picador, 1986), £8.99. Booker Prize-winner about a reclusive artist, a Maori factory worker, and his mute young son, with poetic evocations of South Island landscapes.

Janet Frame, *An Angel at my Table* (Virago Press, 2008), £12.99. Autobiographical account of the author's mental breakdown and years spent in a NZ mental hospital.

DOWNUNDER FILMS

Many excellent films have come from Australia, such as Ten Canoes, *filmed in remote Arnhem Land with characters speaking in an indigenous Aboriginal language and* Jindabyne; *it's by the same director as the excellent* Lantana, *and confronts tensions between white and Aboriginal communities. Also recommended is* Rabbit-Proof Fence. *Classic films such as* Picnic at Hanging Rock, Breaker Morant, Gallipoli, *and* My Brilliant Career *are good not just as movies but also as commentary on aspects of the Australian character and situation.* Priscilla Queen of the Desert, Muriel's Wedding, *and* Strictly Ballroom *are all wonderfully quirky Australian films. You probably won't want to see* Wolf Creek *before setting off on a trip to the outback, but Baz Luhrmann's over-the-top* Australia *is thoroughly enjoyable.*

LATIN AMERICA

The Latin American continent is inconceivably vast, stretching from the Caribbean tropics, round the Equator, and down to the icy Antarctic glaciers of Patagonia. It is a land of superlatives, home to the world's tallest waterfall, driest desert, largest rainforest, longest river, southernmost city, biggest carnival, and most remote tribes. With many places well geared up for tourism, and its wealth of cultures and landscapes, it is an exciting place to explore, whatever your interests. Its mixture of opposites is fascinating, with the Virgin Mary and *Pachamama* (Mother Earth) worshipped at the same altar, and ancient ruins, colonial architecture, and modern cities all vying for attention. Most journeys will take in the monumental (like the Inca fortress Machu Picchu in Peru and the Mayan temple city Chichén Itzá in Mexico), natural wonders such as Iguazu Falls, or the Costa Rican cloud forests. Yet even the everyday sights and experiences in markets and bus stations rarely fail to charm visitors.

The gringo trail may be a well-trodden one, but there are still plenty of things left to discover, and those willing to explore further afield, on local 'chicken buses', and visit the smaller indigenous towns and villages are likely to be taken aback by the warmth of the people they meet. The Latin passion for life can be infectious, which isn't hard to understand given that fiestas, impassioned football matches, and delicious food are all features of daily life. This exoticism leaves many young travellers captivated, but of course it isn't all parties and *playas* (beaches). Some of the world's poorest citizens live in the *favelas* (slums) of Brazil or the *barrios jóvenes* (squatters' settlements, literally 'young districts') of Lima and Mexico City. The rise of urban poverty is alarming, and is partly why so many Latin Americans are so highly politicised. The region is experiencing a shift leftwards, and you are likely to bump into *manifestaciones* (protests) or *huelgas* (strikes) at least once. Less romantic than the ubiquitous face of Che Guevara would have you believe, these can often affect bus routes and travel plans, although thankfully this is probably the most serious it'll get – the days of guerrilla forces and civil war are long gone in all but a very few regions on this map. Should this stir your social conscience, opportunities for volunteering in the Americas abound, as detailed later on in this book. This, as well as allowing you to stay put for a while to learn the language, is by far the best way of experiencing the continent, offering an intimacy with people and places that seems distant along the standard gringo trail.

CLASSIC ROUTES

Latin America provides thousands of diversions, and it is relatively simple to put together an itinerary that combines a variety of natural settings, from mountain ranges to jungles and rainforests laden with wildlife, and the mysterious ruins of ancient empires, to chill-out beaches, sleepy colonial towns, and modern metropolises with their lively nightlife. You will have to rein in your ambitions to see too much because if you just rush around ticking off sights, you will come away exhausted and with very superficial impressions.

Central America

Making a zig-zag up or down the long thin region of Central America will allow you to visit sights on the Caribbean and Pacific coasts as well as cooler inland hill towns and volcanoes. Mexico City is one of the cheapest places to reach from the UK, so is a sensible place to start. Head south to the Yucatán peninsula via Palenque, where you can take in the Mayan ruins at Chichén Itzá. Continue down to the temples at Tikal over the border in Guatemala, rising up from the jungle canopy – breathtaking at dawn. Have a break from ruins at the picturesque Lake Atitlán, surrounded by Mayan villages, perhaps followed by a Spanish course in Antigua, or an aside to the famous market town of Chichicastenango. Head east to Copán in Honduras, and then onwards to the Caribbean island of Utila – one of the cheapest places in the world to pick up a Professional Association of Diving Instructors (PADI) qualification. If time and budget still allow, travel through Nicaragua's colonial cities of León and Granada down

UNMISSABLE HIGHLIGHTS

- Hike to the awe-inspiring lost Inca citadel of Machu Picchu.
- Soak up Carnaval in Rio: music and dance are Latin America's lifeblood, and this party tops them all.
- Dive in the Bay Islands, Honduras (world-class scuba-diving at rock-bottom prices), where, if you time it right, you can swim alongside the world's most majestic fish, the whale shark.
- Lose yourself in the Amazon by taking a slow boat trip from Peru to Brazil.
- If your budget doesn't stretch to the Galápagos, head to Tortuguero, Costa Rica, to watch giant sea turtles lay their eggs on the sand by night.
- Live it up like an Argentine in Buenos Aires: sample the you've-got-to-taste-it-to-believe-it steaks, washed down with fine yet affordable vino, then catch a match at La Boca football stadium or party at a *milonga* (tango club) till dawn.
- Take a salar trip in Bolivia: surreal multicoloured lakes and geysers next to the endless white of the world's largest salt flats.
- Time travel in Cuba: an island with a revolutionary past and a rebellious present — it looks like it's stuck in the 1950s yet, with the recent resignation of Fidel Castro, feels on the brink of massive change.
- Marvel at indigenous medical knowledge and take a leaf, literally, out of the locals' book: chew coca or drink coca tea for altitude sickness in the Andes.
- Go down Potosí's co-operative mines in Bolivia, and get to grips with the extreme conditions the miners put up with in the hope of striking gold.

to Costa Rica. Here you have endless eco-tourism opportunities, from the turtle nesting beaches of Tortuguero to zip wiring in the Monteverde cloud forest. The Arenal volcano spouts fire by night, and you can get off the beaten track in the southern Corcovado National Park. Fewer gap travellers venture further south to Panama, but the ones who do are rewarded with a spot of island hopping in the idyllic Bocas del Toro region. Flying home from San José, the capital of Costa Rica, will set you back at least £400; flights entering Mexico City and leaving San José can be found for less than £600.

Patagonia and the Southern Cone
If you're into the outdoors, Patagonia offers some of the most impressive hiking and scenery in the world. Fly into the Big Apple (Buenos Aires), and head for the Península Valdés for whale watching. Bus or fly to the world's southernmost city, Ushuaia, and spend time checking out the remote Tierra del Fuego ('land of fire') National Park. Not far north are the glaciers at Calafate and the beautiful lakes and volcanoes of the Torres del Paine on the Chilean side of the border. Continue to the Lake District, and perhaps stop in Bariloche for the skiing between June and September. Rediscover urban pursuits in the many fine eateries and watering holes of the Chilean capital Santiago or Mendoza, before heading north into Bolivia on the train to pick up the next route.

The West
Start with a trip to the surreal Salar de Uyuni, a desert of salt in south-western Bolivia with geysers and multicoloured lakes (easily accessible from Chile or Argentina). Proceed by bus to Potosí and descend into the silver mines before appreciating the colonial charm of Sucre or the hectic Cochabamba market en route to La Paz. Explore the nearby mountains and valleys, bike down the world's most dangerous road and perhaps divert to Rurrenabaque for a jungle or pampas trip. The stunning Lake Titicaca and the Isla del Sol are worth a few days, and are far less commercialised than the floating islands on the Peruvian side. From here, head to Cusco and hike the Inca trail to Machu Picchu (though be aware you have to book this in advance and be accompanied by a guide). Explore the Sacred Valley before setting out on a rainforest trip in the Manu National Park. Continue up the coast, try sandboarding and surfing, with a possible detour to the mysterious Nazca Lines, before crossing into Ecuador. From here, an aside to the Galápagos and its unique wildlife would be pricey but unforgettable. Quito and Cuenca are perfect for Spanish courses (especially if you are doing this trip in reverse), and you could wind up relaxing on any one of Ecuador's Pacific beaches. You will have to give serious thought as to whether or not you want to include Colombia in your travels since it is one of those countries that everyone warns you about, mentioning foreigners who have been kidnapped there. On the other hand, many who have braved it have told tales of safe, easy, enjoyable travel in this beautiful, little-visited country, especially in the lovely old town of Cartagena, and you may decide the risks are minimal as long as you avoid dodgy areas.

The East: Brazil and the Amazon
Fly into Rio and enjoy the beaches and nightlife before nipping across to the spectacular Iguaçu Falls (just as accessible from Argentina). From here, head for the Pantanal for outstanding wildlife viewing and back to the coast, taking in the musical Salvador before arriving in Belém, gateway to the Amazon. Take a boat to Manaus, the jumping-off point for trips into the wild interior. From Manaus, go northwards to Guyana for the impressive Kaieteur falls, and a unique mix of Caribbean, African and European cultures, and continue on to Venezuela (more waterfalls here … including the record-breaking Angel Falls).

MY GAP YEAR:
TIM TAYLOR

Tim Taylor designed an ideal route from Cancún, Mexico, down, around and across to Rio de Janeiro, Brazil, but then had an even better time when he missed his first flight.

With a backpack full of clothes, a bloodstream full of inoculations, and a passport full of potential, I was all set. When I was delayed by US Immigration in New York and forced to miss my flight, I took the first flight to Central America, which was to San José, and all of a sudden I was just going to have to wing it, which would prove to be the more fulfilling way to travel.

As a tourist destination, Costa Rica is more commercially advanced than its near neighbours. Thus it was a perfect place to comfortably spend the first days of a year travelling alone. The fact that Costa Rica has become a popular travel destination, especially for the US tourist, means the dollar has flooded the market and pushed up the prices. However, I found with great surprise that the other countries that make up the vertebrae of Central America offer the same experiences only at lower costs. I whiled away many days at the rainforests of Panama, the volcanic lakes of Nicaragua, the diving resorts of Honduras, the surf zones of El Salvador, the remarkable Mayan ruins of Guatemala, and the crystal waters of Belize, most notably diving the Blue Hole beside the Barrier Reef. From Belize, I ventured up Mexico's Yucatán Peninsula, skipping among Mayan ruins, until I reached the urban metropolis of Cancún for a bargain-price flight to Cuba.

Cuba is a country unlike any other I have visited. It requires far more than the two weeks I had to do it justice. It takes almost that long just to comprehend the dual-currency system. At the moment, Cuba is not set up for wandering backpackers, especially not a solitary one. There are no hostels as such. As a budget traveller, I stayed in casas particulares - government-controlled homestays. Havana is a lively, cultured, buzzing city, and the Museum of the Revolution gives a fascinating (if not altogether balanced) account of Fidel Castro's rise and reign. I had enough time to ride the tourist-only buses around the western half of the island, dropping in on the colonial city of Trinidad, the Che Guevara Memorial at Santa Clara, and numerous beautiful beaches. But before I blew my budget, it was time to move on to the South American mainland.

I travelled along the north coast from Colombia - highly under-rated and exceptionally friendly and safe for tourists - and into Venezuela, crossing over into Guyana and gradually working my way along the Amazon River and into Peru. The slow passenger boat from Manaus is one of those experiences I appreciate far more now it's over (secondary enjoyment): five days of cramped and smelly conditions, continuously watching your belongings, eating cold rice and beans, while tiptoeing along mile after mile of vast river. Yet, it was the most awe-inspiring journey of my entire trip.

In contrast to my Amazonian adventure, I stuck with the highlights programme for Peru, Ecuador, and Bolivia. The ancient and mysterious Nazca Lines, the strange reed islands on Lake Titicaca, and amazing Andean hikes in Peru, the pièce de résistance being the spectacular Inca Trail to Machu Picchu.

In Ecuador, straddling the eponymous Equator, a quick jaunt to evolution's gift of the Galápagos Islands, and more amazing Andean hikes. In Bolivia, a tour of the unimaginably inhumane working conditions of the Potosi mines, the blinding white splendour of the salt deserts at Salar de Uyuni.

My next campaign was supposed to be a journey to Patagonia, zig-zagging southwards between Chile and Argentina. However, the southern hemispherical seasons, and more accurately my inept knowledge of them, conspired against me. So in mid-June I cut the journey short, and began working my way slowly towards Rio de Janeiro instead.

With the final days of an incredible year rapidly disappearing, I am acutely aware that I have but scratched the surface of a remarkable and varied continent. For every 'thing to do' I tick off one list, another two are added to the 'what I mustn't miss next time' list.

Luckily, British nationals can travel to all the countries of South and Central America without a visa, though they will need one for Cuba and one or two other Caribbean nations. North Americans should check beforehand since they do require visas for Brazil (for a whacking $160) and a few other countries.

GETTING THERE

For students the cheapest deals can often be found with STA Travel, although their discounts will really come into their own when booking open-ended and multi-destination flights. The biggest hubs and therefore cheapest destinations from Europe are Buenos Aires, Rio de Janeiro, Mexico City, and San José. It is also worth keeping an eye on special promotional fares offered by British Airways and Iberia.

Expect to pay about £500 for return fares from London to San José, Rio, Quito, and Buenos Aires. If you want to split your trip between two cities, it can make sense to buy an open-jaw ticket, flying into one and out from another. In that case, you will need to save £700–£750+, for instance, to fly into Mexico City and out of Buenos Aires, or into Buenos Aires or Rio and out from Lima. Flight prices go up around *Carnaval* in Rio (40 days before Easter) and Inti Raymi in Cusco (the all-important Inca festival of the sun around the winter solstice in June), so you must weigh up the desire to experience such events against your budget.

Two fully bonded London-based agencies that specialise in travel to and around this area of the world are Journey Latin America (www.journeylatinamerica.co.uk) and South American Experience (www.southamericanexperience.co.uk), which along with STA consistently offer the lowest fares and the most expertise.

GETTING AROUND

Travel around the region can involve many twists and turns, and these are not just on the roads themselves. Following in the tracks of the young Che Guevara, as seen in the film *The Motorcycle Diaries* is, unfortunately, the exception rather than the rule, and most travellers will find bus travel the most affordable and convenient. Every country has an extensive bus network, with varying levels of comfort on offer. In Argentina, paying a few extra pesos will get you fully reclining seats, waitress service, and complimentary champagne, while at the other end of the scale, in most of central America the fabled 'chicken buses' ply the long route between cities, stopping at every single village on the way, to pick up seemingly impossible numbers of people and sacks of produce, including the chickens that give the vehicles their name. Most travellers on a pan-South American journey end up feeling as though they have spent a third of their entire travelling time on buses, often 16 hours at a stretch.

Slicker, direct tourist buses of course exist alongside these (at about 10 times the speed, and price), although there is certainly much to be gained from travelling alongside local people. You'll come away with far more authentic impressions of a place, and getting to know your fellow passengers – especially the two or three with whom you are sharing a seat – will make the time race by (even if the vehicle doesn't). Night-time bus travel is also a good way forwards: you save on accommodation and can knock off some of the hours sleeping (bring a blanket along Andean routes – temperatures plummet after sundown). Think carefully, however, about arrival times, and whether you want to turn up in a bus station in the small hours of the morning bearing in mind that sleepy, disorientated gringos with bulging backpacks are prime targets for thieves. Many hostels offer pick-ups from bus stations; it's worth booking ahead to secure this if the bus terminal area has a dodgy reputation, as is not infrequently the case. Booking in advance for popular routes and at festival times is a good idea, although tickets bought on the day tend to cost less than those booked beforehand; and getting to the bus terminal at the specified hour – 90% of the time the bus will leave late, but naturally the one time you count on this and turn up late, it will doubtlessly have left you behind.

> **TRAVEL TIP**
>
> *Keep your wits about you at all times on buses; it's not uncommon for people to wake up and find their wallet missing from their hand luggage, even if they fell asleep with it in their lap.*

The other option for inter-regional travel is by air, the only answer if you are short of time, or can't face another 24-hour rollercoaster bus journey along winding unpaved roads. Short internal flights with national carriers, such as Bolivia's Amaszonas or Honduras' Sosa Airlines can cost less than $50, and bargains are usually available at the last minute as well as in advance. Like buses, flights are subject to inexplicable delays or changes in schedule – the Taca airlines being a notorious culprit – so try to remain as flexible as possible, and embrace the exasperation!

Certain airlines such as LAN or Brazil's TAM offer flight passes in the region, which represent good value only if you want to cover a lot of ground. The prices of the individual flight sectors depend on the distance and how mainstream the routes are. For example, the LAN Visit South America Airpass mainly covers flights within Chile, Argentina, and Peru. TAM's South America air pass operates in Argentina, Bolivia, Brazil, Chile, Paraguay, Peru, Uruguay, and Venezuela, and is calculated according to mileage, starting at US$339 for up to 1,900 miles and up to $1,236 for 8,200 miles. The cost of air pass sectors is reduced significantly if you have arrived on an international flight with the relevant airline.

Rail and river travel are also feasible in some areas, yet these are usually the attraction in themselves rather than a means of getting somewhere. Notable exceptions are in the Amazon basin, where roads are scarce. It is also worth noting that in many developing countries, heavy rains can render certain routes impassable, so plan your itinerary carefully in the rainy season (mainly January–March), and ask around before setting out.

As far as local travel goes, taxis and minibuses are the most widespread way of getting around. Taxis can be licensed or unlicensed, and while the former are clearly safer, it is almost impossible to avoid the latter, since many car owners keep a taxi sign in the window, simply to earn a little pocket money. As a rule, these aren't dangerous; however, be more vigilant when sharing a taxi with others (known as a *colectivo*), and a young woman travelling alone might feel uncomfortable getting into a *colectivo* with only male passengers. The cheapest way of getting around urban areas and their immediate environs (rarely more than a dollar) is by minibus. Known as *combis*, *flotas*, *micros*, and myriad other names, these abound in most cities and towns, and are manned by a sort of conductor figure – this is usually a 10-year-old boy, hanging out the door and shouting the destinations at top volume. Just listen for your stop and hop on.

For information on travel in Latin America, it might be worth joining South America Explorers, which maintains clubhouses in Lima, Cusco, Quito, and Buenos Aires (www.saexplorers.org); membership costs $60 or $90 for a couple.

WHAT TO EXPECT

The real reason travel in Latin America is rewarding is the attitudes and customs of the people you meet. Latinos are incredibly open and talkative by nature, and visitors who learn some Spanish or Portuguese before or during their trip will find casual conversations with local people one of the most enriching aspects of their trip. No visitor can fail to notice the vast inequalities in today's Latin America, with cities such as Rio showcasing the flashy lifestyles of the wealthy just around the corner from the unimaginable poverty of the slums. Begging is not as widespread as in, say, Asia, but in large cities you will certainly come across entire families living on the streets. It is impossible to ignore the fact that these are almost always indigenous people, whose rights and identities have been trampled on since the first European conquistadors set foot on the continent. Always use the word *indígena* as opposed to *indio* (feminine *india*) when referring to indigenous people, to show respect.

Another aspect westerners may find frustrating is the *mañana* attitude prevalent, well, everywhere. For instance, '9am sharp' means sometime before noon; bureaucracy moves at a snail's pace, and buses will leave when they feel like it. Female travellers may resent the Latin *machista* attitude: cat-calls will follow most fair-skinned females (particularly blondes), and while these are generally of a harmless, appreciative nature, it can be trying at times.

Latin America is a safe enough place to travel in, providing you are sensible and take the necessary precautions. Pickpockets and bag snatching are the most common forms of crime, and in some places are almost an art form, especially at festivals, in stations, and on buses. Keep a good grip on your possessions, or better still, carry only what you need, and girls – keep your money in your bra.

EXCITING WAYS TO GET INVOLVED

- Learn to speak Spanish at an eco-hotel in rural Nicaragua (www.mariposaspanishschool.com).
- Fix up a work experience placement in accounting, marketing or journalism in Ecuador (www.elep.org).
- Help out on a horse ranch in Argentina (www.wwoofargentina.com).
- Be part of a small team that shoots a documentary film for a good cause in Colombia (www.actualitymedia.com).
- Help special needs children in Urubamba, Peru (www.kiyasurvivors.org) or street children in Quito (www.cenitecuador.org).
- Join a diving course on the Caribbean coast of Venezuela (www.gapyeardiver.com) or train as a ski instructor in Patagonia (www.peakleaders.co.uk).
- Subsidise a stay on the Galápagos Islands by becoming a student volunteer at the Charles Darwin Research Station (www.darwinfoundation.org).
- Teach English in Amazonian Ecuador (www.youvolunteer.org).
- Protect turtles in Mexico (www.experiencemexeco.com) or maintain forest trails in Costa Rican national parks (www.asvocr.org).
- Arrange a working holiday in Chile's tourist industry (www.chileinside.cl).
- Intern at a dive shop in Honduras while acquiring a PADI scuba diving certificate (www.subwaywatersports.com).
- Join a gap year expedition that includes adventure travel, language learning, and volunteering (www.ventureco-worldwide.com).

MY GAP YEAR: CAMILLA DAVIES

Camilla Davies enthusiastically describes her four-month adventure in four countries of South America.

I write this nearly a year to the day after arriving in Ecuador on VentureCo's Inca and Amazon trip, anticipating new experiences, culture, and excitement. My time in Bolivia, Chile, Ecuador, and Peru absolutely exceeded those expectations. From the blistering cold beauty of a 6000ft Mount Cotopaxi sunrise, to the glorious, otherworldly heights of Machu Picchu, my 15 weeks were packed with highs, made all the better for the warm, accommodating locals met along the way. Starting in Quito, Ecuador, I soon became fast friends with my fellow venturers; sharing dorms, food, and most importantly toilets! Travelling with 19 others creates a special bond and I left Heathrow those months later eager for their company again.

VentureCo issues each travelling group with a local guide - for us it was the unbeatable Wilson Garcia, who is not simply a leader, but a friend, a confidante, and a very wise man. Local leaders know all the haunts and will undoubtedly have a friend in every village, town, and city. This proves a great asset along the way; whether warning me against the old man's Bolivian bar, or guiding us towards the best alpaca meat in town, Wilson really added to my VentureCo experience.

But VentureCo is not all about nature. Far from it! Interaction with locals is essential for understanding a country and its people; lessons in Spanish helped us communicate with locals and this makes so much difference, whether in chatting up the Ecuadorian barmaid or sharing with host families in home stays.

So ... favourite moments of the trip? Getting spat at and having fire breathed on me by a witch doctor/shaman on my third day. Served as a nice introduction to Ecuador! A night-time monkey infestation of our Bolivian jungle lodge (note: don't leave Mars bars near hungry monkeys). Trekking for four days in the same set of clothes then the joys of a warm shower. All-nighters in LaPaz, Bolivia. Llamas. Waking up after a few too many mohitos/pina coladas/pisco sours laughing at the night's antics. Horse-riding in the Atacama Desert, which looks like an alien landscape. The infinite whiteness of the Bolivian Salt Flats. House parties in the VentureCo house in Puerto Lopez ... you've gotta love the reggaeon [Latin urban music]. Meat with two carbs every night. Dancing with the locals. Salsa! Inca Kola. Construction work - digging those foundations in the baking sun. Rafting in Tena, Ecuador; the cause of severe sunburn and blisters, but what a laugh. Being unashamedly clad in Gringo attire. Market towns and enthusiastic locals, who love to share their culture with you (for instance, in Ecuador you get whipped on your birthday ... apparently!). The unavoidable 'when I was in South America ...' moments that seem irresistible for months after your return. Friends met along the way. Swimming near the dolphins in brown water. I could go on ... South America has left a big impression on my life and I would encourage anyone to take a visit.

The advice to keep your money in your bra would have been no help to **Barry Irvine**, who tells the sad story of what happened to him on a bus to Quito in May 2010:

One of the guys (who I thought was from the bus company) was trying to be 'helpful' and offered to put our bags in the overhead bins. There was no way I was letting my bag out of my sight so I put it under the seat in front of me and then under my feet. I kept dozing in and out of sleep, and at various points thought I felt my bag moving, but I assumed it was the movement of the bus. Just before we arrived at Quito I moved my bag back in front of me and suddenly noticed that it didn't seem as full as normal. That's when I discovered that my beloved MacBook Air, the charger, and my sunglasses were missing. After looking under my seat (obviously a futile effort) and searching around the bus for the man and his potential accomplice, I sat back down again feeling stupid and upset. The situation could have been a lot worse. In the same compartment of my bag, my money belt (usefully not around my waist: I think I've learned another lesson here!) with hundreds of dollars and all my bank cards in it, still remained. And my passport in the front compartment was still there too. I told some Americans my story and they said that just before we got on the bus the driver had mentioned that there were thieves operating on this bus route and to keep your bags in your lap and not put them in the overhead lockers. It's a shame we missed that message!

Another thing to watch out for are dodgy tour operators who take a deposit one day and are gone the next. As mentioned, protests and strikes are commonplace. Occasionally these turn nasty, and tear gas is sprayed as if it were water: observe such gatherings, if you must, from a distance.

As a rule, travel here is fantastically affordable, with places such as Bolivia and Guatemala requiring little more than $15 a day. Watch out for unexpected departure taxes (Peru's ever-increasing rate is currently at $31 but in a growing number of cases it is included in your air ticket, as with Ecuador since February 2011), as well as 'airport use' and 'bus terminal use' fees. Consider paying more to support eco-friendly tour organisations, and always tip porters and guides. You can often opt to pay for tours in dollars, as well as the local currency – sometimes this is cheaper, other times it is not, so always check exchange rates.

SOUTH AMERICA

Argentina

CURRENCY	
£1 = 6.7 pesos	US$1 = 4 pesos

BUDGET
From $30 per day.

Since the devaluation of the peso, tourism in Argentina has boomed, and this should be taken advantage of while it lasts! Buenos Aires is a European city with a Latin flavour, a prime party place, bristling with history and culture. It is best explored district by district, each one distinctive in character and appearance. There's the artsy San Telmo with its antiques markets and legendary steak houses; chichi Palermo for boutiques and nightlife; and colourful La Boca – a pilgrimage for those who call themselves football fans. Whichever *barrio* (district) you're in, take a look at the omnipresent graffiti – not gormless UK-style tags, but witty political quips and pictures. On Thursdays, walk around the Plaza de Mayo (pronounced 'masho', in a thick Argentine accent) with the mothers still protesting over the 'disappearance' of their sons during the 1976–1983 dictatorship.

GAPPER'S TIP

If you go out to party and feel let down by the lack of choice, it might be because you're too early. After a hefty steak dinner, the norm is to sleep it off until about 1am and then go dancing until daybreak.

The mighty Iguazu Falls (*Iguaçu* is the Portuguese spelling, used in Brazil) are an easy detour from the capital, before getting lost in the vast outdoor playground that is Patagonia. Whale watching at the Península Valdés is awe-inspiring, June to December being the best season, although sea lions and seals are permanent residents and penguins come to chill out between October and March. Giant glaciers at El Calafate, unparalleled and highly accessible hikes past blue waters in the southern hemisphere's own Lake District, and skiing in Bariloche are all highlights. Bariloche is meant to be the Switzerland of Argentina, but it definitely has its own (superior?) charm, and offers riding, paragliding, mountain biking, etc. A quirkier attraction is the Chubut valley with its Welsh-speaking villages, settled back in the 1860s, where those missing home cooking can order scones and afternoon tea. To the north, Mendoza is a deservedly popular region, famed for its highly affordable and good-quality wines, offering even the grubbiest of backpackers the chance to feel slightly civilised again. Cycle tours between vineyards, stopping to sample the produce, are highly recommended. Trips to Aconcagua, the highest peak in the Andes, can be arranged from Mendoza. Barren northern Argentina is 'off the beaten track', although punctuated by the buzzing university city of Córdoba, pretty, colonial Salta, and several natural hot springs.

Bolivia

CURRENCY

£1 = 11.8 bolivianos   US$1 = 7 bolivianos

BUDGET

$20 per day.

Bolivia deserves its billing as the most 'authentic' country in South America. The poorest Latin American nation, Bolivia is currently led by Evo Morales, the first indigenous president of the country, whose popularity is partly due to his legalisation of coca growing. 'Different' things to visit in La Paz include the Museo de la Coca and the San Pedro prison, effectively a walled city within a city, where the more – ahem – successful inmates have luxury pads on site.

Only outside hectic La Paz ('the Peace') are you likely to find any actual *paz*, on one of the many scaleable mountains or scenic Inca treks in the immediate environs. A thrilling day out is mountain biking the 'world's most dangerous road', which involves an exhilarating drop from snow-capped peaks to subtropical climes in a few hours.

Most of Bolivia's population is clustered up on the *altiplano*, through which the gringo trail weaves its route. Sucre has beautiful colonial plazas and a pleasingly high concentration of chocolate shops. If you brave the sweltering tunnels with bad smells and low oxygen down in Potosí's silver mines, you will meet the miners (and their young sons) who do this daily, chewing coca to cope with the hunger and solitude, for very little financial reward.

The salt flats of Salar de Uyuni are a perspective-free white desert in the dry season, and a glassy mirror during the rains. Tours also take in the geysers, at the (literally) dizzying heights of 5,000m above sea level, and the flamingo-festooned red and green lagoons – your photos just won't do it justice. Cochabamba's sprawling market is interesting, particularly the 100% genuine witchcraft section, where locals really do buy dried llama foetuses for good fortune, unlike in La Paz's touristy version. Another unmissable *altiplano* destination is sacred Lake Titicaca on the Peruvian border. Locals say that Bolivia has the 'titi', and Peru only got the 'caca' – perhaps a little unfair since the sparkling blue waters and intriguing ruins put in an appearance on both sides. The Bolivian side is less touristy than the floating reed islands off Puno, Peru. The more adventurous might head off to the northern pampas for a wildlife boat trip – expect to get close and personal with pink dolphins, parrots, piranhas, monkeys, and caymans. The hyper-adventurous can make for the remote and wild Noel Kempff Mercado National Park, one of the most pristine areas of the Amazon jungle, with stunning waterfalls.

Peru

CURRENCY

£1 = 4.61 new soles   US$1 = 2.81 new soles

BUDGET

$40 per day.

Machu Picchu is the primary destination for many people who travel to the continent. Although some visitors have exceedingly high expectations of the Lost Citadel, it rarely disappoints. However, one word of caution: even at dawn, it's still crawling with tourists. It is at its most crowded from late morning on, when the tour buses begin to arrive. Yet its grandeur and beauty remain intact. Walking up the super steep Huayna Picchu in the early morning is a novel way of seeing the site, although those who have hiked the Inca trail may pale at the sight of so many steps.

The four-day Inca trail proper must be booked months in advance for the high season (mid-April to September). Fees associated with the famous trek routinely make the total investment in the experience $300–$500. Bear in mind that there are beautiful alternatives in the same area.

If taking the train, consider starting from Ollantaytambo in the Sacred Valley, as this is the cheapest option (from $31 one way). Ollanta is a lovely town in itself; stop off at the Hearts Café on the plaza and think of something you could donate to a women's shelter like your windproof jacket or other obsolete Inca trail gear.

Cusco is bristling with Inca ruins, great cafés and bars, and souvenir shops, set among well-kept colonial buildings. Undiscovered it is not, especially during the festival in late June when *Inti* the sun god is honoured. To escape the SAGA busloads, head for one of the many pristine jungle lodges in the south west, or make for the coast (via the bright white city of Arequipa), where you too can worship the sun, sandboard on the dunes at Huacachina, surf, or sail to 'the poor man's Galápagos' – the fauna-filled Ballestas Islands – to watch frolicking penguins, sea lions, and flamingos. Not to be outdone, the Colca Canyon is home to the giant Andean condor which might just want to share the walking tracks. More superb walking and climbing is to be had around Huaraz in the Cordillera Blanca (white mountains), but true off-the-beaten-track adventures are found in Peru's lightly inhabited Amazonian north. Iquitos is its main settlement: purchase a *hamaca* (hammock), and barter passage on a slow boat down the Amazon to Brazil. Coastal towns like Huanchaco are also popular for their laid-back vibe, cheap living, and decent surf waves.

Brazil

CURRENCY
£1 = 2.6 reais   US$1 = 1.56 reais

BUDGET
$30– $55 per day.

Brazil is a country of epic proportions, beauty, and style. It has its fair share of icons such as Sugarloaf Mountain and Copacabana Beach in Rio, but it's the locals that leave the strongest impressions: passionate about dancing, football, beaches, and food, life is unavoidably fun here. However, crime, drugs, and poverty are prevalent: never wander alone after dark, don't stray into *favelas* (slums) and watch the film *City of God* before your trip.

Rio de Janeiro's legendary beaches are made for people-watching, and by night the city swings to the beat of a thousand samba drums, especially during February *Carnaval*, which involves manic revelry in all its forms. The serious could even join a samba school beforehand and take part in the processions.

Culturally rich Salvador da Bahia on the north-east coast is distinctive because of the many descendants of African slaves whose culture survives in interesting ways. The *Carnaval* here in the heart of African Brazil beats to the distinctive *axé* and *pagoda* rhythms and is just as flamboyant, and marginally less of a crush. In the north, you may be fortunate enough to attend a *Candomblé* ritual – a potent blend of African magic, spiritualism, and fortune telling (by reading shells). In Salvador, you are bound to come across a performance of capoeira in the street, a mesmerising martial art-cum-dance. Brazilian cuisine is as sensual as its people, that is to say, *muito* (very). *Feijoada*, the national dish – a sort of meaty, beany stew – is addictive.

The obvious top natural attraction is the mighty Amazon: Manaus offers jungle trips and treks of every variety, and anyone headed to the region is bound to travel by boat at some point – evocative at best, and tedious at worst. In the southern part of the interior, the Pantanal is a vast area, offering some of South America's best wildlife watching, especially in the rainy season when the animals are confined on higher patches of land (capybara, armadillos, alligators, anteaters, and, for the lucky, jaguars). The culture of Portuguese-speaking Brazil is as diverse as its landscape, with quirks not found elsewhere in Hispanic Latin America.

Chile

CURRENCY
£1 = 770 pesos   US$1 = 467 pesos

BUDGET
$50 per day.

Long, skinny Chile is a travellers' playground, where the buzzword is 'outdoors'. Head south to discover the real meaning of chilly – exploring the Torres del Paine National Park, where it is possible to climb inside ice caves on spectacular glaciers in the lee of gigantic peaks. Another thrill in Chilean Patagonia is the world-renowned Futaleufú river, where the waters are as white as the rafters' knuckles. Also aim for the many hikeable volcanoes, such as Pucón. The more temperate Lake District is another perfect setting for rafting and climbing, or perhaps just chilling out on the black sand lakeside beaches (it's not dirty – it's volcanic). If that sounds too taxing, you can hot-foot it to some of the region's many hot springs.

In the warmer north there are many South Pacific beaches, notably at La Serena, or for some added surfing action, head to Arica or Iquique. Although pricey, paragliding at Iquique and skiing June to October shouldn't be left off the outdoors enthusiast's itinerary. Moving north past (or via) the wineries, *altiplano* Chile offers geysers and more lakes (with flamingos), as well as the world's driest desert, the Atacama. Here, duneboarding ticks the thrill-seeking boxes, and the small *salares* (salt lakes) give a taster of the mighty Salar de Uyuni a short train ride over the border in Bolivia.

Urban Chile also has its attractions: the skyscraper-filled, Andes-backed capital, Santiago de Chile, is an entertaining place to hang up your hiking boots for a while, and indulge yourself at some of South America's finest eateries and drinking spots. Most museums are free on Sundays, and one well worth a visit is La Cascona, to learn about one of Latin America's most famous writers, the poet and communist Pablo Neruda.

Ecuador

CURRENCY
Ecuador uses the US dollar.

BUDGET
$25–$30 per day.

Ecuador is another South American country combining the best of the Andes, Amazon, and Pacific, but with the unique addition of the Galápagos Islands. The emphasis on eco-tourism and local indigenous traditions distinguishes Ecuador from its neighbours. The capital, Quito, is recognised as one of the best places to study *español* – or *castellano*, as Latin Americans prefer to call it, anxious to shed colonial ties. There are very many highly rated schools, which can also offer homestays, salsa lessons, volunteer placements, and so on.

Quito itself is schizophrenically split into the Old Town and New Town, both full of bustling street markets and buses, but only the Old Town has a backdrop of pretty colonial buildings, while the New Town is a silver urban jungle. Street performers and pretty plazas abound in the invitingly wanderable old town. More strenuous pursuits lie just outside the city, such as climbing the Volcán Pichincha or energetically hopping from one hemisphere to the other at the Mitad del Mundo (meaning 'half of the world'), a popular Sunday hangout 20km north of the city for *quiteños* (people from Quito), with live music groups adding to the atmosphere.

Guayaquil is Ecuador's largest city and, due to recent gentrification, is no longer a seedy port. All the same, few travellers warm to it, as life is hot, sticky, and stressful. Up in the highlands, the town of Otavalo is worth a detour, especially on market days, when animals, crafts, foods, and other unidentifiable objects are traded at a frenetic pace (and volume) by local indigenous groups in traditional dress. There are also accessible lagoons in the area, and weekly cock fights (not to everyone's taste). The high peaks of Volcán Chimborazo and Cotopaxi provide opportunities to hike, bike, and climb, as well as purchase a panama hat (they originated here).

Cuenca is a charming picture-postcard colonial town on a river, with a healthy student nightlife. The Amazon *Oriente* (east) is perfect for kayaking and paddling, from Coca to Iquitos, Peru, or simply for watching wildlife. Mating whales can often be seen from Machalilla National Park between June and October. But it is the Galápagos that really steal the show. Costing about $1,000 a week they don't come cheap, but live-aboard vessels show you the highlights, and can bring you face to face with sea lions, white-tipped reef sharks, spotted rays, penguins, land and marine iguanas, giant tortoises, frigate birds, blue-footed boobies, and all the creatures, mostly unafraid of humans, that thrive on this ecological marvel. Another possibility is to stay on land, for example at a hotel in the main town of Puerto Ayora, from which you can join all-day excursions to different islands.

Colombia

CURRENCY
£1 = 2,950 pesos   US$1 = 1,783 pesos

BUDGET
$35 per day.

Colombia is one of the most rewarding and interesting travel destinations in South America, far less visited than its neighbours, mainly due to its dangerous reputation. Paramilitary and guerrilla groups are still active and kidnappings of foreigners do take place, but only in rebel areas, which can be avoided. Keep abreast of the political situation and safety updates via the local news and through reports from fellow travellers. The Colombians, not yet jaded by mass tourism, are exceedingly friendly and welcoming to travellers, though petty theft is rampant.

Cartagena, a strikingly attractive colonial port city dripping with history, is deservedly top of many Colombian itineraries; few are left uncharmed by its walled old town, beautiful old buildings and nearby fishing villages, beaches, snorkelling, and scuba diving. Take a fun day trip from here to the El Totumo mud volcano, where you can wallow in warm 'therapeutic' mud.

The other imperative dip to take in this country is into a García Márquez book. The Colombian Nobel Prize-winning author has created an incredible world of fiction in his short stories and novels, which intoxicate and delight as much as Colombia itself. His 'magical realist' style blends historical fact and indigenous beliefs, seen through hazy tropical eyes, and simultaneously helps comprehend the Latin American way of life while further mystifying it.

Scuba and snorkelling are to be indulged in all along the Caribbean coast, especially off the Islas de Rosario, a national park with unspoilt coral reefs; the San Andres and Providencia archipelago, and at Tanganga. Near Santa Marta, also on the coast, you can make an ambitious side trip to see the famous overgrown Ciudad Perdida ('lost city'), one of the largest pre-Columbian settlements found in the Americas. Built between the 11th and 14th centuries, and 'found' again by tomb raiders less than 40 years ago, it can now be reached on a six-day return trek through the rainforest (cost $200).

Cali and Medellín are both vibrant and cultured, while Bogotá is a heaving city where anything is possible for those with the cash. Head to the *salsatecas* (like a *discoteca*, but for salsa) for some dancing, a national obsession. Near Bogotá is a unique cathedral carved from rock salt inside the salt mines at Zipaquirá, as well as the sacred Guatavita Lake.

Venezuela

CURRENCY	
£1 = 7.1 bolivar fuerte	US$1 = 4.3 bolivar fuerte

BUDGET
$30 per day.

Venezuela is a country synonymous with oil, economic crises, and the burly face of anti-USA rhetoric from president Hugo Chavez, now suffering from cancer. Yet the actual meaning of the country's name is Little Venice, after the houses on stilts the Spanish first set eyes on here, centuries back. The capital, Caracas, has little to recommend it – get straight out. Mérida is much more pleasant and offers paragliding, rafting, climbing, and so on. It is also home of the world record-holding Heladería Coromoto, with over 800 ice cream flavours.

The great outdoors really does do amazing things at the Salto Ángel (Angel Falls), in the south – the world's tallest waterfall, cascading down from one of Venezuela's many *tepuis*, distinctive table mountains home to loads of unique plants and animals. Roraima is the biggest of these, and a five-day trek up, over, and past its waterfalls is reasonably easy to co-ordinate. Many travellers to Little Venice don't leave without a few days on (or just off) the coast, to follow watery pursuits: the scuba and snorkelling in the Los Roques archipelago are *excelente*.

Guyana, Suriname, and French Guiana

CURRENCY	
French Guiana uses the euro (£1 = €1.13)	
£1 = 340 Guyana dollars	US$1 = 205 Guyana dollars
£1 = 5.45 Suriname dollars	US$1 = 3.30 Suriname dollars

BUDGET
Guyana $40 per day; Suriname $30 per day; French Guiana $60 per day.

A region frequently overlooked by the majority of *mochileros* (backpackers) – mostly because of the higher prices and weaker infrastructure – this trio of countries still has its share of attractions and offers a culturescape very different from the rest of the continent. Guyana in the east is a former British colony, Suriname was Dutch, and French Guiana is still part of France, a *département d'outre-mer* or overseas territory. The Europeans never properly got their teeth into the Amazon interiors of these countries, where indigenous tribes carry on as they have done for centuries. Geographically, the three countries follow a similar pattern: attractive port towns and beaches along the vaguely industrialised northern coast, and dense, pristine rainforest inland. French Guiana's highlights include the Îles du Salut (former penal colony islands) and the rocket launches at the Space Centre; Suriname offers a host of canoeing and trekking opportunities, especially up Mount Kasikasima; while Guyana's top trip is to the towering Kaieteur Falls. Ethnically, this region is nothing short of surprising, with European influences, Amerindian natives, and Asian immigrants – those on RTW tickets pining for Asia can even visit a Hmong refugee crafts market in Cacao, French Guiana.

Paraguay and Uruguay

CURRENCY

£1 = 6,780 guaraní (Paraguay)	US$1 = 4,100 guaraní
£1 = 32 pesos (Uruguay)	US$1 = 19.4 pesos

BUDGET
$35 per day.

Less superlative than its neighbours, chilled-out Paraguay still has enough to entertain its visitors. Wildlife is plentiful and the Chaco and north-eastern wetlands all afford prime animal spotting. Ruins of Jesuit missions and colonial architecture fill in the gaps, with the German-speaking Mennonite colonies offering a cultural contrast to the rest of the country. Uruguay's petite dimensions and relative prosperity make it a manageable destination. Party hard with vacationing *porteños* (from Buenos Aires) in Punta del Este; wander the diminutive cobbled Colonia and ponder its many quirky museums. Not to be outdone in the steak stakes, Uruguayan cuisine is very good – enjoy a slap-up *churrasco* (grilled steak) in a Montevideo restaurant.

CENTRAL AMERICA
Costa Rica

CURRENCY

£1 = 810 colones	US$1 = 500 colones

BUDGET
$35-$40 per day.

Having missed out on the dictatorships and civil wars suffered by many of its neighbours, Costa Rica is an anomaly in the region. This peaceful, democratic state with no army has famously supported conservation, so that there are now more than 70 national parks. Animals to be ogled include monkeys, manatees, sloths, snakes, iguanas, armadillos, dolphins, whales, four species of giant turtle, and countless butterflies, birds, and bats. The heart of Costa Rica lies in the natural world, evident in the national buzzword, *pura vida*, which you will hear about 5,000 times a day. This is an all-encompassing phrase, meaning variously 'Hey', 'What's up?', 'Peace', and 'Cool', among other things, although it literally translates as 'pure life'.

Costa Rica's Caribbean and Pacific coasts both boast great beaches, yet have a different atmosphere from one another. The northern coast is home to a Caribbean rasta culture, and is more relaxed and easygoing than the south, where the Pacific breakers are ideal for surfing. The Cahuita National Park on the Caribbean side has some good snorkelling on the coral reefs, as well as hiking in the park itself. The Tortuguero National Park in the north, whose name refers to the sea turtles which nest on its beaches, is among the most popular. The best seasons to observe the turtles with a guide at night are April/May and July to October. It is nothing short of miraculous to see these enormous creatures slowly heave themselves on to the beach, dig a hole, and proceed to lay hundreds of tiny eggs in the sand, before disappearing as silently as they came. Poaching, once a problem here, is now being brought under control – note that the park is run on tourist revenue. Canoeing trips are popular here, and you stand a good chance of seeing crocodiles or the elusive manatee.

Another worthy contender for best park is in the Monteverde cloud forest in the central highlands, with its rare unspoilt ecosystem. Zip wiring is a fun way to enjoy the forest: this involves 'flying' through the canopy, suspended from a cable in a harness, theoretically observing the animals, but realistically whooping and squealing with adrenaline, scaring them all away. A short bus ride from here is the Arenal volcano – one of many in the country, but the most likely to delight pyromaniacs with its fire-breathing, lava-spitting, night-time antics. Worth a trip are the geothermal hot springs nearby.

Many sections of the Pacific coast are built up. The unashamedly Americanised Tamarindo and Montezuma on the Nicoya peninsula are surf havens, and diving and turtles can be found here too. Untouched wilderness is to be found on hikes in the southern Corcovado National Park.

In the centre of the country, San José is a cosmopolitan city, with many *museos*, bars, and a stimulating arts scene to recommend it.

Guatemala

CURRENCY

£1 = 12.2 quetzales   US$1 = 7.5 quetzales

BUDGET

$20– $25 per day.

Guatemala is one of the richest destinations in Central America, culturally speaking. Mayan traditions are alive and kicking, many Catholic saints correspond to Mayan deities, and sacrifices still take place at religious ceremonies. Guatemalans are among the poorest Central American citizens, yet are unbelievably generous to those they meet. Show an interest in learning the Mayan language (most still speak Spanish as a second tongue), and people will certainly be willing to help. Despite a few pleasant parks and plazas and a lively music scene, Guatemala City is smelly, congested, and crime-ridden. Most travellers prefer to spend their time in Antigua or Xela (the local name for the city of Quetzaltenango). Guatemala's token postcard colonial town, Antigua, is now a veritable gringoville, with all the requisite bars and clubs. There are many language schools here, where the emphasis is less on picking up Spanish than on partying.

If you still have the energy, try climbing the many volcanoes near Antigua, particularly still-active Pacaya (and don't forget to buy marshmallows to roast on the lava). Xela, Guatemala's second largest city, also has a dazzling array of language schools, where students actually seem interested in learning Spanish. Xela also has volcanoes within reach: Quetzaltrekkers is a non-profit company held in high local regard, which funnels trekkers' fees into a free school and shelter for local street children (see entry in 'Directory of Volunteering Abroad'). You can find similar ventures elsewhere in Guatemala; for example, if you go hiking in Nebaj, go with the Trekking Ixil project.

Around Xela, the natural hot springs ('spa') at Fuentes Georgina are definitely worth an afternoon. A centre in Momostenango runs courses in Mayan ceremonies, beliefs, and horoscopes for the inquisitive traveller, while Chichicastenango is a famous and colourful market town, best visited on Thursdays and Sundays. Some of the most enjoyable Mayan villages are the scenic settlements on the shores of Lake Atitlán. Skip Panajachel ('gringotenango') unless you want to hire a bike, then visit the lakeside towns of bohemian San Pedro, San Marcos, popular for its retreats, and Santa Cruz, known for its lake diving. The small villages around the lake are all interconnected by launch boats, and the variety in atmosphere among these villages means that you can choose one that suits. Well-known party town San Pedro attracts many foreigners who come to attend one of the many Spanish schools. Rooms are available for 15–35 quetzales (around £1–£3). Street dinners of tacos and a wonderful warm sweet rice milk drink cost around 10Q, while 30Q allows you to eat in a restaurant. Most hostels have kitchens of some description, and at the beautiful market up at the top of the hill in San Pedro you can find fresh vegetables and fruit, spices, and rice. Around eight backpacker bars offer live music, all advertised around the town, as are free film nights at Dinoz, Buddha Bar, etc. Musicians passing through will find many venues happy to swap free drinks for music.

San Marcos is not only at the end of the lake, it is at the other end of the spectrum, containing as many holistic and therapy centres as San Pedro has bars. San Marcos' niche crowd veers towards

MY GAP YEAR:
ANNA LING

Anna Ling's chosen place to settle for a few months was Santa Cruz on Lake Atitlán.

At Santa Cruz, my current abode, I have found a wonderful in-between place, with yoga lessons and a sauna, balanced with weekly parties and poker nights. I am based at the Iguana Perdida hostel (www.laiguanaperdida.com), the first building near the launch stop. With the daily dinner shared on a long table, guests and workers together, it feels very much like a family. The hostel runs on the basis of voluntary work. I exchange five hours of work a day, six days a week, for my bed and three meals a day, on top of various perks like free internet and half-price drinks. Work generally consists of sitting behind the bar, taking orders and chatting to guests. One of my responsibilities is to organise the dressing-up clothes for the Saturday night Cross Dressing parties. The hostel almost always has positions opening and the owners ask only that you stay at least two weeks. I personally recommend this relaxed work-for-keep system above getting a paid bar job, as wages barely cover living costs. (The cost of staying here for non-working guests is between 25Q and 35Q, plus food is about 75Q a day for cheaper meals.) My shifts start at 7.30am or 1pm, leaving the afternoon or evening free for joyous activities.

the spiritual, taking advantage of an incredible range of sessions and/or training in alternative healing. San Marcos is almost completely silent, and if you're looking to pamper yourself or to calm your mind after some debauchery in San Pedro, it's a tranquil heaven. But it is not a place to live on a budget or make money unless you are a trained therapist of some kind.

The jungle at Petén is home to Tikal, an eerily beautiful complex of Mayan temples, whose tall stone pyramids peek out over the canopy. At dawn, this sight is breathtaking, and accompanied by the tune of thousands of monkeys and birds. Other Mayan ruins lie deeper in the jungle, but are difficult to reach. On the Pacific coast, black sand beaches, mangrove swamps and turtle nesting sites of Monterrico (and a turtle hatchery or two looking for volunteers), and deep-sea fishing at Iztapa can all be enjoyed. The Caribbean coast is characterised by its *Garífuna* (descendants of black slaves) culture.

Guatemala is a wonderfully cheap place to travel or stay in – language courses with homestays and food rarely cost more than $100 a week. Language institute staff can often put you in touch with volunteer organisations if you want to get more involved in the country.

El Salvador

CURRENCY
The US dollar is in almost universal use.

BUDGET
$20+ per day.

Long the domain of bullets and guerrillas, El Salvador is better known for its bloody civil war than for its tourist industry. Now however, peace prevails, and those jaded by the *ruta gringa* (gringo trail) find this a refreshing haven – locals are curious towards foreigners, and the landscapes are as dramatic as elsewhere on the continent. Whether it's the typical dish of *pupusa* or the people, the famous surfer beaches in the south or the towering volcanoes scattered throughout the country, El Salvador proves that good things come in small packages. A typical itinerary might blend trekking in the mountainous interior, for instance at El Imposible National Park, or along the Ruta de las Flores, taking in the volcanoes and crater lakes of the Sierra Apaneca Ilamatepec, followed by some down time on the Pacific *playas*. Perquín in the north east offers some insight into a not-so-distant conflict; while Suchitoto in the north west provides a glimpse into colonial El Salvador, with cobbled street and a local *mercado* (market). El Pital and La Palma in the north are also good destinations for those who want to experience the local culture. San Salvador, the capital, offers many modern amenities and commodities.

Belize

CURRENCY
£1 = 3.16 Belize dollars   US$1 = 1.9 Belize dollars

BUDGET
$50 per day.

English-speaking Belize is very easy to travel in … provided you have the money. Island hopping and watersports reign supreme, and these are more pricey. The legendary Blue Hole (an underwater sinkhole teeming with fish and friendly sharks) and the surrounding reefs offer some of the region's best diving and snorkelling, and Caye Caulker is the ultimate backpacker hideaway. If you find the Latino *mañana* pace a little slow, then brace yourself for Belize's Caribbean outlook – you'll be hard pushed to find a more chilled-out lifestyle. The buses, however, are as efficient as clockwork, and the energetic will find plenty of hiking and white-water rafting.

Honduras

CURRENCY
£1 = 30 lempiras   US$1 = 18.5 lempiras

BUDGET
$20–$35 per day; more expensive on the Bay Islands.

Long a backpacker favourite, Honduras' long, lazy Caribbean coast, cool interior and Mayan ruins are the main draws, although those with more time to spare should make for one of the last remaining wilderness areas in the region, the Mosquitia jungle. Not to be missed are the Bay Islands, off the northern coast, with Roatan and Utila being best suited to backpackers with budgets. These English-speaking islands, once a refuge for pirates, have a colourful history. Diving on Utila is spectacular, with pristine coral reefs, vast shoals of tropical fish and, if you go between May and September, the elusive whale shark. Totally harmless, these huge fish play in the shallows so even snorkellers have a chance of meeting one. A PADI open water course costs about $250, and a learn-to-dive package with bed and breakfast plus transfers would be about $600.

The Mayan ruins at Copán (also accessible from Guatemala) are impressive, and can be visited in a day. National parks and cloud forests – Pico Bonito and La Tigre have been receiving rave reviews – grace the interior, but the adventurous should head to the Mosquito Coast where travel is by dug-out canoe and tourists are rarer than jaguars, so accommodation and food are sparse. Bring insect repellent (even though the name comes from the Miskito natives rather than the pesky insects).

Nicaragua

CURRENCY
£1 = 35.5 cordoba oro   US$1 = 21.8 cordoba oro

BUDGET
$20–$30 per day.

Nicaragua is safe, affordable, and back on the backpackers' list of desirable destinations. Roads are still in their infancy, and travel can be tough, but attractions abound, and the people are talkative and opinionated – all good practice for your Spanish. Granada and León are Nicaragua's rival colonial cities, which more than make up for the big bad Managua. León, the former capital twinned with Oxford, has a pretty cathedral, cobbled streets, and shady parks, and is steeped in colonial and revolutionary history. It is near the south coast and has a couple of large climbable volcanoes nearby. Granada is on the shores of the fascinating Lago de Nicaragua, and is just as aesthetically pleasing, with some excellent cafés and restaurants. Nearby Masaya, flattened in 2000 by an earthquake, is now the *artesanía* (handicrafts) epicentre of Nicaragua, with many tempting markets. Explore the Lago's fishing villages, ruins, beaches, and wildlife on the Isla de Ometepe, as well as the artistic communities of the Solentiname archipelago in the south. The turtle nesting beaches of the Pacific coast also feature on many itineraries, although many travellers fresh from Costa Rica will be distressed by the different attitudes to conservation.

Panama

CURRENCY	
£1 = 1.60 balboa	US$1 = 1 balboa

BUDGET
$25 per day.

There is more to Panama than hats and a canal, but many travellers don't make it this far. It's the cul-de-sac of central America, because travel further south is impossible due to the dense, bandit-ridden jungle of the Darién Gap. Panama City is a delight as far as capitals go, with clubs and bars nestling behind colonial façades, and the obligatory trip to the canal, a waterway first proposed by the Spanish as long ago as the 16th century. Whereas the area east of the canal is wild Darién jungle, the Bocas del Toro archipelago to the west is another isn't-life-tough Caribbean watersports paradise, where you take water taxis between bar, beach, and turtle sanctuary.

Mexico

CURRENCY	
£1 = 19 pesos	US$1 = 12 pesos

BUDGET
$20–$35 per day.

The largest of the Central American countries, Mexico can be pricey or cheap depending on how far off the tourist trail you have strayed. Its beaches, festivals, and ruins are an inevitable draw. Stick to the south rather than the industrialised north, where it tends to be more Tex than Mex. Mexico City is a sprawling metropolis, known for its chronic pollution and crime, and most travellers fly in and straight out. The south's most interesting regions are the Yucatán peninsula and the state of Chiapas. Mayan temples and pyramids are dotted around these areas and Mayan traditions are still upheld. The most impressive Mayan sites are at Chichén Itzá, Palenque (both World Heritage Sites), and the ruins of the walled city at Tulum, overlooking the Caribbean. Chichén Itzá has been called the Disneyland of the Mayan world, so expect to jostle for space with the fannypack-wearing crowds. The nightly light show is spectacular or cheesy depending on your sensibilities. These sites are still amazing, however – but you must get there as early in the day as you can.

The Caribbean coast offers some unparalleled snorkelling and diving, particularly on the Isla Mujeres (check out the turtle farm) and off the island of Cozumel. Swimming is the best way to escape the year-round heat, and visiting the *cenotes* of the Yucatán is a refreshingly novel experience. These are sinkholes of fresh water, some underground, surrounded by stalactites and crazy rock formations.

Cancún, the largest city of the 'Mayan Riviera', is very Costa del Sol, favoured by US frat groups on Spring Break. The smaller Playa del Carmen has a more stayable feel to it, but many recommend staying at Tulum, where you can sleep in rustic cabins on the beach. Mérida is also a pleasant Yucatán destination, one of the cleanest and prettiest cities in Mexico, with a thriving theatre scene and many galleries.

The state of Chiapas, the country's poorest, is home to the Zapatista movement – a left-wing group supporting indigenous rights. Mexico's second city, Guadalajara, is the arts capital, with innumerable music, film, and book festivals all year round. Moving west, Puerto Vallarta on the Pacific coast is less touristy than its Caribbean cousins, and offers the possibility of humpback whale watching between November and March. If possible, time your visit to Mexico to coincide with the *Día de los Muertos* (Day of the Dead) on 1 November, which roughly corresponds to the Anglophone world's Hallowe'en. Families make technicolour shrines to deceased relatives and sit up all night drinking and feasting in graveyards, keeping the dead company.

When budgeting for travel within Mexico, calculate up to $8 per hour of travel on comfortable de luxe buses.

Cuba

VISA
Required: £15 in London, valid for up to six months.

CURRENCY
£1 = 1.59 convertible pesos   US$1 = 1 convertible peso

BUDGET
$50 per day.

Bridging the link between the Caribbean and Latin worlds, Cuba is a fascinating island brimming with things to be seen, learned, and confused by. New arrivals will have their own romantic images of the country, from Che Guevara and old pastel-coloured American cars to dressed-up old ladies smoking fat cigars, and palm-fringed beaches. Unfortunately, the state-regulated tourist industry makes travel costs pretty steep, in a country where the average monthly wage is $18. Under Fidel Castro, tourist activities and movements were limited: foreigners had to stay in state-run hotels (think Soviet architecture) or in tourist enclaves from which Cubans were excluded, or in *casas particulares* – family-run homestays. It was almost a case of apartheid, with foreigners kept at a distance from locals as much as possible and required to pay far higher prices for services. However, the policy of restricting certain hotels and services to tourists was ended by new president Raul Castro, and it is possible that very soon the long-time embargo on US citizens visiting Cuba will be lifted. A Freedom to Travel to Cuba bill is under consideration by a Congressional committee at the time of writing. Until the bill is passed, however, most travellers will continue to arrive in Havana on cheap flights from Canada or Cancún.

Mosquitoes are not the only things buzzing in *La Habana*, which is cultured, hip, and edgy – art and music thrive, and this is the cultural and political focus of the island. The old town is a beautiful colonial zone, with plenty of bars and museums to visit. before heading out to the outlying beaches. Avoid the all-inclusive resorts of Varadero, and try to get to Trinidad – another pretty colonial city, with excursions to waterfalls and beaches, and nearby hiking opportunities, as well as some very vibrant nightlife; the eternal flame and Che Guevara memorial can be found in Santa Clara, and you can explore the beautiful countryside of the Pinar del Río province in the west by bike or by horse.

TRAVEL RESOURCES

USEFUL WEBSITES
www.bootsnall.com/South-America, updated monthly, listings, travellers' forums, and tips about
    travel, also covers other regions of the world.
http://baexpats.org, community forum for people living in Buenos Aires.

www.brazilmax.com, well-laid out information about this continent within a continent.
www.andeantravelweb.com/peru – comprehensive resource for trekking, affordable accommodation, etc for Peru.

USEFUL BOOKS

Footprint South American Handbook (Footprint, 2011), £22.50. Updated yearly, the most consistently recommended guide for accuracy and background information. Footprint Guides also publishes the *Central America Handbook* (2011, £16.99).
South America on a Shoestring (Lonely Planet, 2010), £21.99.
The Rough Guide to South America on a Budget (Rough Guides, 2009), £19.99.

TRAVEL READING

Gabriel García Márquez, *100 Years of Solitude* (Penguin, 2007), £9.99. Or read one of his quirky short stories, such as *I Only Came to Use the Phone*.
Laura Esquivel, *Like Water for Chocolate* (Black Swan, 1993), £7.99. Amusing tale of love and food in revolutionary Mexico.
Rigoberta Menchú, *I, Rigoberta Menchú: An Indian Woman in Guatemala* (Verso, 1984). The author is a Nobel Peace Prize winner.
Stephen Benz, *Green Dreams: Travels in Central America* (Lonely Planet, 1998). A witty account of fellow travellers and locals, with an emphasis on eco-tourism.
Hugh Thomson, *Tequila Oil: Getting Lost in Mexico* (Phoenix, 2010). A swashbuckling tale of a journey by an alcohol-fuelled 18-year-old, who in 1979 drove a gas-guzzler the length of Mexico, without insurance or even a driving licence.
Peter Robb, *A Death in Brazil* (Bloomsbury, 2005), £9.99. Acutely observed account of both the violence and beauty of Brazil.
Louis de Bernières, *The War of Don Emmanuel's Nether Parts* (Vintage, 1991), £7.99. About mysticism and traditions. Other hilarious accounts of Latin life by the same author include *The Troublesome Offspring of Cardinal Guzman* (fiery women and passions) and *Señor Uno and the Cocalord* (about drugs wars blighting the continent).

SOUTH AMERICA ON FILM

City of God *(2002) is a fast-paced, hard-hitting yet uplifting film about life in Rio's most dangerous slum. Also check out films by Walter Salles such as* Central Station, *and of course* The Motorcycle Diaries. *Mexico has produced some excellent films in the past decade, including* Amores Perros, Y tu mamá también *and* Pan's Labyrinth.

CURRENCY
£1 = US$1.65 £1 = C$1.56

BUDGET
US$50–$100 per day in USA; US$40–$60 per day in Canada.

TREKAMERICA

Sian Barrow took on the 64-day Trailblazer road trip.

The Trailblazer was the most amazing experience of my life! I can't even begin to put into words just how fantastic it was. I'd never been to the USA before, so after contemplating doing a three-week trek, I decided to go all out and book the monster nine-weeker.

The things that I saw and experienced over that time were just outstanding. Quad biking and jet skiing, a helicopter over the Grand Canyon, Independence Day in Key West, sand dune buggying and nearly getting married in Vegas – the list is endless! Moraine Lake in Canada is the most beautiful place in the world. Chicago, Seattle, Colorado – I'd move to these places tomorrow, and the 4 July celebrations in Florida were absolutely wicked!

The friendships that I made will last for ever. Spending 24/7 together brings you so close so quickly and within a day of the start of the tour we felt like we'd known each other a lifetime.

If you have any doubts about whether or not to do TrekAmerica's ultimate road trip, the 64-day Trailblazer, you absolutely, 100% have to! It will change your life, I guarantee. It's the best way to see America, and having an American tour leader who knows the country just makes the experience so much better.

However much of the world I travel around, I still don't think anything could beat my trek. The people that I was lucky enough to travel with made it a million times better than I could have ever imagined, and I just want to thank you all for giving me the best experience of my life.

Visit www.trekamerica.com.

THE LURE OF NORTH AMERICA

This vast and wealthy continent is crammed with all sorts of wonders, natural and man-made, and is peopled by a fascinating ethnic mix. Even though the shine has come off President Barack Obama, the USA is a more attractive proposition than it was in its previous incarnation. But even if you do have reservations about the stance of the 'moral majority' of Americans, the friendly, culture-loving folk of Minneapolis or the liberal-minded students of California should not be tarred with the same brush.

Politics aside, many travellers will derive immense pleasure from visiting some of the great American icons – Walt Disney World, the Statue of Liberty, the Grand Canyon, the Golden Gate Bridge. But on the doorstep of all these fabled landmarks are many less well-known wonders. The Grand Canyon is undoubtedly stupendous, but nearby Monument Valley is also breathtaking and much less crowded. While Manhattan offers the archetypal urban experience, the sleepy artists' colonies and beach resorts on Long Island make a fascinating destination. The bars along New Orleans' Bourbon Street are once again thriving after the disaster of Hurricane Katrina. But also in the French Quarter (which was barely touched by the hurricane), you can visit a voodoo temple.

America is not the known quantity many gappers expect it to be, based on a steady diet of US sit-coms and rock lyrics. At times it can be the futuristic, wild, and dangerous place depicted in the media, and at other times as homespun as apple pie. Places such as Las Vegas, Orlando, and Hollywood are in many ways as over-the-top and vulgar as anyone could wish, while others, such as Seattle, or Georgetown in Washington DC, are more sophisticated and thoroughly congenial.

The world's second largest country (after Russia), Canada is a thinly populated geo-political eccentricity. It also has a staggering diversity of landscape and people, and is often a welcome antidote to the excesses of the USA. Most gappers confine themselves to the cities of the southern belt; Vancouver, Toronto, and Montréal are all within a few degrees of latitude almost straddling the US border. They are all clean, safe, full of character, and within reach of natural wonders. But to see the best of Canada, the visitor should try to reach the fringes, such as the national parks, the maritime provinces on the Atlantic coast, or remote parts of British Columbia in the west.

Travel round North America can be by turns wonderfully rewarding and deeply confusing, practically as well as culturally. Can such a high degree of gregariousness be genuine or might this friendly American be trying to con or convert you? In all cases, exploring this mighty powerhouse will be a huge and memorable adventure.

GETTING THERE

The price of flying across the Atlantic has barely risen in real terms for decades, though with increased taxes and fuel surcharges, it is difficult to find a flight for less than £350 return. Fares in 2011 are considerably higher than they were two or three years ago, especially in the summer season. To take a random example, the base price of an Air Canada low-season return London–Toronto might be £159, but the taxes amount to an additional £200+. The low-cost Canadian charter operator Canadian Affair (www.canadianaffair.com) sells the cheapest flights to Canada from regional airports.

For the USA, competition is fiercest and therefore prices lowest on the main routes between London and New York and Los Angeles/San Francisco, though reasonable deals on mainstream carriers to cities such as Denver and Detroit are sometimes available outside peak season. In many cases, summer fares will be twice as high as winter ones. One-way fares are also available to eastern seaboard cities such as Washington and Boston; however, passengers arriving on the Visa Waiver Program (see below) must show a return or onward ticket as proof that they do not intend to stay in the USA. Outside summer and the Christmas period you should have no problems getting a seat across the Atlantic; at peak times, a reliable alternative is to buy a discounted ticket on one of the less fashionable carriers which fly to New York, such as Air India or El Al.

UNMISSABLE HIGHLIGHTS

- Hike the Appalachian Trail (but ignore Bill Bryson on the danger of bear attacks).
- Shop in famous department stores such as Macy's on Broadway or Neiman-Marcus in Dallas.
- Watch a baseball game in Boston, Detroit, Toronto, or anywhere where the fans are passionate.
- Rent a wreck for US$30 a day and drive the beautiful coastal Highway 1 from LA to SanFran.
- Lose some money at the roulette tables of Las Vegas.
- Sample maple syrup at a sugar bush in Québec or boiled lobster in the Canadian Maritimes.
- Ride the Empire Builder train from Chicago to Seattle through magisterial mountain scenery.
- Swill bourbon in Kentucky's Blue Grass Country (but only if you're over 21).
- Hire a canoe to explore 7,725km² Algonquin Park in Ontario.
- Be spooked at the sight of the Bates Motel from Hitchcock's Psycho at Universal Studios Hollywood.

GETTING AROUND

The USA and Canada share the longest common frontier in the world, which gives some idea of the potential problems and expense of getting around. Bus, train, and air travel generally work out to be cheaper per mile than in Europe. In the USA, consult any branch of STA (+1 800 781 4040), and in Canada look for an office of Travel Cuts, the youth and student travel specialist (www.travelcuts. com).

In both the USA and Canada, the car is king. A driving licence is regarded almost as a birthright and many young men spend a lot of time talking about their wheels. Eighteen-year-olds are permitted to rent by some companies like Rentawreck (www.rentawreck.com), but may be expected to leave a credit card number as a deposit. In states where young drivers are permitted to rent, there may be a surcharge, for example the minimum renting age in Michigan is 18, but Alamo imposes an extra daily fee of US$28 to drivers aged 20 and under, and US$14 for 21–24-year-olds. Clubbing together to buy an old banger can be affordable, though insurance costs for young drivers will bump up the cost (but it will still be much less than the UK equivalent).

The term 'drive-away' applies to the widespread practice of delivering private cars within North America. Prosperous Americans and Canadians and also companies are prepared to pay several hundred dollars to delivery firms who agree to arrange delivery of private vehicles to a different city, usually because the car owner wants his or her car available at their holiday destination but doesn't want to drive it personally. The companies find drivers, arrange insurance, and arbitrate in the event of mishaps. You get free use of a car (subject to mileage and time restrictions) and pay for all gas after the first tankful and tolls on the interstates. Usually a time deadline and mileage limit are fixed, though these are often flexible and checks lax. A good time to be travelling east to west or north to south (eg Chicago to Phoenix) is September/October, when a lot of older people head to a warmer climate. On the other hand, when there is a shortage of vehicles (eg leaving New York in the summer), you will be lucky to get a car on any terms.

Unfortunately, most companies are looking for drivers over the age of 23 or even 25, so students aren't likely to be eligible. If you or an older friend are interested in pursuing this idea, check the Yellow Pages under 'Auto Transporters' for a local provider, though the company with national coverage is Auto Driveaway (+1 800 346 2277; www.autodriveaway.com), which has dozens of franchised operators across the USA, from Salt Lake City to Syracuse, Saint Louis to Seattle. Go to www.autodrive awaydc.com/carlist.html for a current list of available cars. From Toronto, an established company is Toronto Drive-Away Service (+1 800 561 2658; www.torontodriveaway.com), whose website contains driver recruitment information; the minimum age is 25. The busiest season is mid-March to May when many Canadian cars need to be driven back from Florida, Arizona, and California. Depending on supply and demand, gas is sometimes paid for plus an expense allowance of up to $400. An alternative to the specialist agencies is to ask at a travel information centre for car rental firms that arrange delivery of rental cars to the places where there is a seasonal demand, for example to Florida or to ski resorts in the winter.

The deregulation of US domestic airlines some years ago resulted in some amazing discounted fares. Southwest Airlines based in Dallas (www.southwest.com) is one of the better-known discount airlines offering cheap fares and no-frills service (though its reputation has suffered after one of its Boeing 737s developed a six-foot hole in the fuselage in 2011). Southwest was advertising a one-way fare of US$119 plus a few extras between Newark and Denver (summer 2011). Small airlines keep springing up, serving lesser-known cities; check out for example Allegiant Air (www.allegiantair.com).

Normally, the cheapest advance purchase coast-to-coast fares are about US$175. Other low-cost airlines include Spirit Airlines (whose hub is Fort Lauderdale and has many connecting flights to the Caribbean and Central America), JetBlue (whose home is New York), and US Airways (with hubs in Philadelphia, Charlotte, and Phoenix). The best advice within the USA is to ask locals and study local newspapers, as fare wars are usually fought using full-page advertisements. In Canada, check out the routes and fares available on low-cost Air Canada Jazz and WestJet.

Attempts to revive long-distance train travel in the USA have not been terribly successful, and several grand old routes come under threat from time to time. Amtrak (+1 800 USA RAIL/872 7245; www. amtrak.com) offers limited rail passes such as '7 days in 21' around California for US$159 or the whole network starting at US$389 for eight journeys within 15 days. The basic three-and-a-half day train trip from Toronto to Vancouver costs C$530 or C$468 for those aged 25 or under. With fares at those levels, it is worth considering the Canrail pass; the low-season youth fare of C$545 permits seven one-way trips in economy class throughout the VIA Rail network during a 21-day period. Between June and October, the price climbs to C$872. The Via Rail infoline in Canada is +1 888 842 7245 (www.viarail.ca).

South of the Canadian border, bus passes are a travel bargain for people who want to cover a lot of ground. Greyhound still markets bus passes lasting seven, 15, 30, or 60 days, and fares have been holding fairly steady, currently US$246, $356, $456, and $556, respectively (www.discovery pass.com). Promotional advance purchase fares of US$122 to cross the continent (New York to San Francisco) are good value. Megabus (www.megabus.com) is expanding its network in North America and now operates in Canada on the Montréal to Toronto route as well as between New York and Toronto, Chicago, and Detroit and so on. The earlier you book online, the better the bargain. It offers a handful of $1 fares and many long-distance trips available for $10, eg Washington to Boston.

Other forms of transport in the USA are probably more expensive but may have their own attractions, such as the adventure trips run by Green Tortoise (494 Broadway, San Francisco, California 94133; +1 800 867 8647; www.greentortoise.com) which use vehicles converted to sleep about 35 people and which make interesting detours and stopovers along their routes in the south west and throughout the USA. One of the most popular youth tour companies is TrekAmerica (0844 346 3020; www.trekamerica.co.uk/ygr). Their biggie is the 64-day Trailblazer tour which crosses 33 states and costs £3,779, plus a food kitty of US$10 a day.

TRAVEL TIP

Hitch-hikers are a rare breed throughout the continent, except in mountain resorts or wilderness where people need lifts into remote areas, though ride-sharing possibilities exist; try www.erideshare.com. The system of Allo-Stop is well developed in the province of Québec, but has been ruled illegal in Ontario after complaints were received from coach operators; join www.allostop.com for C$6 to access available rides (website is in French only).

BUDGETING AND ACCOMMODATION

Between the high cost of covering the vast distances, whether by air or land, and the relatively expensive accommodation costs, the USA and Canada are not countries where your average gapper spends months on the road. Of course, many cover their costs by working at a summer camp or at a seasonal job (see *USA* and *Canada* chapters near the end of this book), and then spend the final few weeks of their J-I visa's validity seeing some of the country. Most people estimate a daily spend of US$50–$100.

Travellers should calculate on spending at least US$20 on a dorm bed in American hostels and more than twice that for a private room, less if camping with one or more friends. Of interest to travellers with their own transport, budget motels line the approach roads to every town. They can be affordable if you are travelling with a few friends and are prepared to squash up. Cheap national chains include Motel 6 and the more upmarket Super 8. Motel 6 prices are usually in the range of US$45–$70 for a room with two double beds.

Official YHA hostels are listed at www.hiusa.org, while the promising sounding www.usahostels. com lists international travellers' hostels only in San Francisco, Los Angeles, San Diego, and Las Vegas. RTW backpackers are sometimes shocked by the contrast between your average city hostel in the USA and in Australia/New Zealand or Europe, as gap year student **David Hardie** reported:

> *In LA, the hostel was a dive. This seems to be the case with most hostels in the US. One of the people staying at our LA hostel was a black dwarf named Jacky whose job it was to impersonate Chucky, the evil doll from those films. Another hostel resident wanted us to join him to go and trash his ex-girlfriend's car. There isn't really a backpacking scene in USA. Unlike Australia many people staying in US hostels are older and in between jobs, usually low lives.*

Therefore, it might be wise to choose your accommodation with more care than elsewhere. For hostel accommodation in Canada, see the hostel links at www.backpackers.ca. To keep costs down, a brave

EXCITING WAYS TO GET INVOLVED

- Study the behaviour of whales and dolphins in Hawaii as a research intern (www.oceanmammalinst.com).
- Look after the children of a Texan executive (www.aupairamerica.co.uk).
- Construct trails in the Grand Canyon or other national parks (www.usaconservation.org).
- Improve your French in the chic yet friendly city of Montréal (www.visavis.org).
- Volunteer to work with First Nations children in the Canadian Arctic (www.frontiersfoundation.ca).
- Work in the British pavilion at Disney World's Epcot World Showcase in Florida (www.yummyjobs.com).
- Learn to snowboard or pick up a winter job at the buzzing resort of Whistler, two hours north of Vancouver (www.whistlerblackcomb.com).
- Take up a one-year internship for graduates in an East Coast company (www.istplus.com).
- Coach soccer at a summer camp in New England (www.ukelite.com) or sports at Canadian camps (www.go-nyquest.com).

gapper might wish to join one of the free hospitality networks such as www.couchsurfing.com with a large number of North American adherents willing to give travellers a free bed for a night or two, mentioned in the section about accommodation in 'Before You Go' p41.

VISAS

Under the Visa Waiver Program, citizens of the UK and 35 other countries who have a machine-readable passport do not need to apply for a tourist visa in advance for stays of less than 90 days. However, since 2009, visitors have to obtain prior authorisation via ESTA, the Electronic System for Travel Authorization, which can be easily done online for a fee of $14 (make sure you use an official website and not a commercial scam site that charges an unnecessary extra fee). Individuals entering visa-free or with a visitor visa for business or tourism are prohibited from engaging in paid or unpaid employment in the USA. Those planning trips of more than 90 days, including those who wish to work or study, must obtain a visa in advance from the Embassy. This requires a pre-arranged face-to-face interview and the payment of a fee that varies, eg US$200 for a J-1 visa (even if the visa is denied) as well as completing a long and detailed form.

British travellers and tourists arriving in the USA on the Visa Waiver Program face increasingly rigorous restrictions. Upon arrival you will have a digital photograph and an inkless fingerprint taken. Check the embassy website (http://london.usembassy.gov).The non-immigrant visa of most interest to gap year students is the J-1, which is available to participants of government-authorised exchange programmes primarily for registered students. For details, see the *USA* chapter at the end of this book (p481). British and Commonwealth citizens do not require visas for entry to Canada as tourists for up to six months. To work or study in Canada, you must obtain the appropriate visa before you leave your home country.

WHAT TO EXPECT

Like every nationality, the people of the USA can be egocentric. They take great pride in living in the richest country in the world with its much-vaunted belief in freedom, democracy, and justice. This sometimes blinds them to the poverty in which so many of their fellow citizens live, as was so poignantly revealed after Hurricane Katrina devastated New Orleans in 2005. There can be a certain narrow focus to their view of the world, partly because relatively few Americans have travelled abroad, and many have a shaky grasp of the geography of the rest of the world. Don't be unduly surprised if you are asked 'What is the capital of London?'

The multi-ethnic character of America is well known. The number of Hispanics and Chicanos (naturalised Americans from Mexico) represents 14.8% of the total US population of 305 million, and has overtaken the number of African Americans, who make up 13.4% of the total. Racial sensitivity frequently surfaces. Even among people who appear to be tolerant, you need to tread warily (eg in mentioning problems in the Middle East) to avoid inflaming concealed prejudices.

Glamour and squalor vie for supremacy in the great cities of the USA. You should keep your wits about you since a busy shopping street that seems perfectly safe in the day can turn empty and spooky at night. Be careful wandering at random after dark since it is very easy to turn off a safe street into a deprived area which you might find threatening. Muggings are far more common in Washington and Chicago than they are in London, so never count your travel funds in public or display expensive items. If you find yourself being mugged, do not resist. Ideally, you will be carrying US$50–$100 in cash that you can quickly hand over.

Canadians are less volatile, almost universally friendly, and just plain 'nice'. The fastest way to antagonise a Canadian is to mistake him or her for an American, and then to say 'Well there isn't much difference anyway.' Yet Canada is so heavily dependent on the USA both culturally and economically that it isn't always easy to spot the difference, and certainly the accents can often be mistaken. Attune your ear to the sound 'ou' as in the word 'about' which Canadians pronounce in a short clipped way, almost like 'abote'.

Those newly turned 18 who have relished the chance to go to pubs and clubs legally will be disappointed in most of North America. The minimum legal age for the purchase of alcohol is 21 across the USA and 19 in most Canadian provinces except Alberta, Manitoba, and Québec where it is 18 (and not so strictly enforced in the latter, because of the French influence). Elsewhere, do not expect to get away with showing some home-forged ID, since age limits are strictly enforced.

WHICH TRAIL TO FOLLOW?

The greatest hits of North America are well known to just about everyone, and it will simply be a matter of choosing from among the wealth of options – the great cities of New York, Chicago, San Francisco, and Vancouver might form the series of dots to be joined up by an On the Road-style trip via Niagara Falls, the Grand Canyon, and the Rocky Mountains. Or your lodestar cities might be Atlanta, Nashville, Albuquerque, Los Angeles, and Seattle, via the wide open spaces of Texas, Death Valley, and the glaciers of Oregon. Most gappers, however, will concentrate on one particular region. Typically, travellers go north from New York to Boston or south to Washington, possibly taking in the hip city of Philadelphia or Salem, Massachusetts, home of 17th-century witchcraft trials in America. Manhattan is of course unmissable, though you should venture into New York's other boroughs, perhaps to visit the Bronx Zoo or to take the ferry to Staten Island. Ellis Island, a short ferry ride from Lower Manhattan, commemorates a staggering 12 million immigrants who were processed here on arrival in the new world, many with tragic histories. One top pick for New York is Central Park – take a good walk round and spend the rest of your life recognising it in films.

Other favoured trails include the Old South beaches and plantations of the Carolinas and Georgia; the Gulf Coast between Florida and New Orleans; and southern California, with side trips to Yosemite National Park and Las Vegas. Arizona is home to the be-all and end-all of natural wonders, the Grand Canyon, whose immensity and beauty are sufficient to compensate for the crowds and commercialism. It is also next to the fascinating state of New Mexico whose capital, Santa Fe, is a town for lotus eaters. For the really ambitious (and well-heeled), Alaska and Hawaii are possibilities.

In Canada you will probably have to choose between exploring the centre (the Toronto–Montréal corridor) and the west between the Rocky Mountain resort of Banff and the great coastal city of Vancouver.

TRAVEL RESOURCES

USEFUL BOOKS

Rough Guide to the USA (Rough Guides, 2011), £16.99.
Rough Guide to Canada (Rough Guides, 2010), £15.99.
USA Travel Guide (Lonely Planet, 2010), £17.99.
Time Out City Guides. Available for New York, Boston, Chicago, Las Vegas, San Francisco, Los Angeles, and Washington in the USA, plus Vancouver and Toronto in Canada.
Both Lonely Planet and Rough Guides also publish regional and city guides.

PART III

GAP YEAR PLACEMENTS

SPECIALIST GAP YEAR PROGRAMMES
EXPEDITIONS
WORK EXPERIENCE
VOLUNTEERING
A YEAR OFF FOR NORTH AMERICANS
PAID SEASONAL JOBS
AU PAIRING
COURSES
DIRECTORIES OF COURSES

GAPGURU

At GapGuru, we believe that a gap year abroad is an opportunity to learn more about yourself and the world around you. Travelling, living, and working overseas exposes you to new cultures, communities, and challenges, giving you endless opportunities for personal development. But above all else, it can be a lot of fun!

GapGuru volunteer projects give you the chance to share your energy and enthusiasm with communities in need and make a difference on your gap year, which is exactly what Lucy Fisher did when she volunteered in India:

'I spent six weeks in New Delhi teaching music and other subjects in a school and vocational centre for children and adults. I wanted to experience something completely different, broaden my horizons and, most of all, set myself a new personal challenge. I can assure you that it was the best decision I've ever made!

'My time in India exceeded all my expectations. I had seen pictures of India so I had some idea of what to expect, but seeing it for yourself is something quite different! At first it was chaotic and quite unnerving, but it's amazing how quickly you adapt.'

Lucy settled into her teaching role quickly and found that 'the children were very keen to learn, and the amount of faith the staff had in my ability to teach was very reassuring. Every day I would walk into classes of children who were stood to attention, with bright eyes and smiling faces.'

While slightly unnerved by the prospect of teaching her first solo lesson, the experience exceeded her expectations: 'My adrenaline was pumping because something I had done seemed to make a small but significant difference to these children.'

Volunteering on your gap year can help you gain new skills, confidence and understanding, and with competition for university places and graduate jobs greater than ever, this can really help you stand out from the crowd.

This is also true for gap year internships, which can bolster your CV with unique life experience that is testament to your own independence and confidence. This can be particularly valuable in competitive disciplines such as journalism and medicine.

Laurence Sharifi took a medical internship in India with GapGuru: 'I came to India for medical work experience, so that I could have the opportunity to immerse myself completely in the life of a doctor and see whether this was really the career for me. The hospital and its staff were amazing and I learnt more about medicine and life as a physician than I could have ever hoped.'

Get in touch with GapGuru to find out how you could make your gap year worthwhile!

SPECIALIST GAP YEAR PROGRAMMES

Specialist gap year placement organisations and companies can arrange the logistics and save you (and your parents) a great deal of anxiety. They find voluntary and occasionally paid placements, provide orientation and sometimes group travel, and, crucially, provide back-up, usually in the form of an in-country representative who can sort out problems. Mediating agencies come in all shapes and sizes. Some are charities with stable programmes in a range of countries and links forged over many years with certain schools and NGOs. Others are more entrepreneurial and are always seeking new projects in developing countries to which they can send paying volunteers. Gappers on the cusp of choosing should be aware that not all providers are the same, and that they should not just choose the first one that pops up on Google or put on a slick presentation for their sixth form.

A plethora of companies and some, but fewer, charities offer a wide range of packaged possibilities, from work experience placements in French businesses to teaching in Himalayan schools. This section provides a general description of the programmes run by companies that specifically market to those on a gap year. Younger school leavers should be aware that 18 is often quoted as a minimum age. Further details of programmes mentioned here are included in the country-by-country chapters, with stories of people who have done placements.

Mediating agencies charge high fees and all participants must pay or fundraise substantial sums. In recent years, the expectation that parents will finance the year off has declined and most companies provide much more detailed advice on how to obtain sponsorship and raise money. Fees and services differ enormously, so research is essential, preferably well in advance. Generally speaking, the high-profile organisations that invest a lot in publicity are considerably more expensive than the more obscure small charities active in just one country. Before committing yourself and your backers to a large financial outlay, you must be sure that your choice of organisation is sound and that its programme matches your requirements. Researching all the possibilities is time-consuming and sometimes confusing, since it can be difficult to compare programmes simply on the basis of their publicity.

The word 'voluntourism' has been coined for the more superficial kind of volunteer experiences, and in some cases is what is being offered by the profit-driven companies that commercialise and commodify the experience of helping in developing countries. Not long ago, the director of VSO (Voluntary Service Overseas) expressed her concern at the rise of this phenomenon, and feared that many year out programmes represented a new form of colonialism. This in turn prompted some of the gap year companies committed to their development work to respond in the editorial pages of newspapers with the following:

> *Your prominent coverage of the views of Judith Brodie, director of VSO UK, puts into relief a critical need for greater transparency and accountability amongst organisations operating within the UK's largely unregulated gap year and volunteer travel industry. The proliferation of poorly planned, spurious and increasingly profit-oriented gap year schemes poses a growing threat to the legitimacy of reputable UK-based volunteer organisations, large and small, working throughout the sustainable development sector.*

The non-profit trade association, the Year Out Group, aims to promote and advise on structured years out. Its website (www.yearoutgroup.org) has links to its 38 member organisations and contains guidelines and questions to ask when comparing year out programme providers, most of which are common sense, eg find out whether it is a charity or a profit-making company, look at safety procedures and in-placement support, ask for a breakdown of costs, and so on. The Year Out Group is primarily a trade association, and Tourism Concern has expressed its fear that the organisation is not as selective in its membership is it might be, since it has no external auditing procedure and no funds to investigate claims made by members. Note that the Year Out Group cannot intervene in any dispute between member companies and disgruntled clients.

GLOBAL MEDIA PROJECTS

Lindsay Hall went on a media placement in Mexico.

I came to the cosmopolitan city of Guadalajara on a radio journalism placement with Global Media Projects. However, the trip proved to have a lot more in store for me. Not once did it ever occur to me that I would be working the red carpet at Guadalajara fashion night, part of the MTV awards, or that I would be setting turtles free into the Pacific Ocean. It's all these stories that made my trip to Mexico a truly memorable experience.

Sitting at my desk on the 12th floor, with panoramic views of the city, I was no doubt the envy of many friends back home in Gibraltar. Being a reporter is a hectic and unpredictable job. You don't have the pleasure of knowing that you can walk out the office at half-five, go home and relax ... In fact it's the complete opposite. My day started at 5.30am when my wretched alarm went off and I robotically jumped out of bed. At 6.30 I was in the office gathering the latest news from Europe. At this point, Sky News and the BBC became my most reliable and trusted friends. At 8.30am I was live in the studio with my headphones on waiting to be introduced by Pepe Diaz, head of news here at the radio station. Nothing could have prepared me for the nerves and anticipation I experienced seconds before going on air live.

All I can say to future volunteers on the journalism placement is to really throw yourself into your work and learn from others around you ... Most importantly, enjoy it, and don't waste an opportunity like this. It is thanks to my journalism placement in Mexico that I got my job as a reporter for the Gibraltar Broadcasting Corporation.

Thank you Global Media Projects, but most of all thank you Mexico ... Until next time!

To follow in Lindsay's footsteps visit www.globalmediaprojects.co.uk

GLOBAL MEDICAL PROJECTS

Jonny Stephens and Rachael Brown went on a medical placement in Ghana.

We are both in the sixth form at Budehaven, and are hoping to make a career of medicine. We decided that gaining some practical experience of healthcare in a developing country would stand us in good stead when we started to apply for university places and medical schools. So we started researching on the internet and found Global Medical Projects, who place volunteers in hospitals and clinics all over the world. We elected to join their project in Ghana and were based at a poorly equipped, and seriously understaffed, hospital in Cape Coast.

We were allowed to participate very fully – the doctors and surgeons were very happy for us to observe operations and to participate in hospital life as fully as was sensible. So we talked to patients, prepped them for operations by shaving them, taking them to theatre, staying with them during their operation, and taking them back to the ward afterwards. On our first day alone, literally within hours of going into the hospital, we were allowed to observe a birth by caesarean section, which was a fantastic experience. The two of us were always allowed to follow the doctors on their ward round, and we were encouraged to ask questions and to make comments, so that often we felt that we were being treated as medical students, which was strange in some ways but also very gratifying. There was never a time when we were excluded from anything, which gave us a great feeling of being wanted and trusted.

If anyone is thinking of doing volunteer work overseas, we would both say 'Go for it!' But plan well in advance, book flights as soon as you can. It was worth every penny of it!

To follow in Jonny and Rachael's footsteps and join the medical project in Ghana, visit www.globalmedicalprojects.co.uk

GOOD PRACTICE STANDARDS

A new national standard of good practice and risk management among gap year and adventure travel providers was introduced by the British Standards Institution in 2007 and is endorsed by the Royal Geographical Society (RGS-IBG). The BS 8848 kitemark is granted to companies and organisations that maintain high standards of safety and procedures. **Shane Winser** *at the RGS feels strongly that gappers and their parents should be encouraged to ask companies whether they are BS 8848 compliant and if not why not:*

> *I am getting increasingly concerned about the number of British-based companies who are acting as re-sellers of gap year experiences and yet taking little or no responsibility for carrying out checks on those who are providing the experiences. Worse still, some will not even divulge details of the project provider until the deposit is paid.*

A good organisation should be able to tell an applicant exactly what work they will be doing and precise contact details for the overseas project. Assuming you care about such things (and even if you don't beforehand, you probably will after spending some time in a developing country), ask the company what financial contribution they make to the voluntary project and about their ethical tourism policy. Some gap year companies wait until a paying customer has signed up before finding a placement abroad and these are often less satisfactory. Sustainable development means 'development which meets the needs of the present without compromising the ability of future generations to meet their own needs'.

Everybody will tell you that you have to set the wheels in motion about a year before you are ready to go. But in fact lots of people start their gap year with nothing fixed up. It turns out that all those organisations whose literature contains dire warnings of the consequences of procrastination often have last-minute vacancies, so it is worth ringing around whenever you decide you want to go for it. With the recent explosion in gap year provision, there is often an over-supply of places, and in many cases they need you more than you need them.

This chapter sets out the programmes of more than 100 leading organisations which are equipped to organise all or part of your gap year for you. The majority are based in the UK, though some American organisations welcome all nationalities on to their programmes. The organisations listed below specifically target those on gap years. Many other organisations listed in the other directories in the *Volunteering*, *Work Experience*, *Au Pairing*, and *Courses* chapters, and also in the country-by-country chapters, welcome gap year students with open arms but do not specialise in catering for them.

Another consideration is the financial soundness of the company. Not all gap year companies have financial protection for the consumer in the form of a licence under the Air Travel Operators' Licensing scheme (ATOL) and personalised insurance certificates. The 1992 Package Travel Regulations state that any company that arranges a package (and this is simply two or more elements of travel such as flights, accommodation, and transport) should have coverage in place, whether it be a bond, an insurance policy, or being licensed by ATOL.

SOURCES OF INFORMATION

The internet is awash with sites that claim to be definitive sources of information for people planning a gap year and yet link to just a handful of advertisers, usually the most commercial companies operating in the field. The main sites and services are:

Careerscope Gap Year Magazine (www.careerscope.co.uk). Can be read online. Updated annually (www.careerscope.co.uk/gap/index.html).

Gapadvice.org. Independent advisory service that provides unbiased up-to-date information, research, and advice on gap years for individuals (of all ages) and organisations. The director is Phil Murray. Fees for individual advice are: £50 for basic service; £125 or £200 for more personalised consultation.

Gap Daemon (www.gapdaemon.com). Community website for gap travellers.

Gap Enterprise Consultants (Oxfordshire OX27 8DG; 01869 278346; johnvessey@gapenterprise. co.uk; www.gapenterprise.co.uk). Pre-university gap year consultancy that offers private consultations to help structure, plan, and prepare for a year out. Gap Enterprise advises on skills courses, work experience, paid employment, travel, projects, expeditions and volunteer placements worldwide. The fully inclusive fee of £650 covers confidential questionnaire, four-hour interview, comprehensive written report (including client-specific contacts list), and follow-up. The director is John Vessey.

Gapwork.com. Publisher and provider of gap year and working holiday information. It provides a range of information on gap years, including listings of accommodation providers, employment opportunities, and gap year organisations, and some first-hand content.

Gapyear.com. Largest gap year community in the UK, dedicated to helping people plan and prepare for their year out. The massive website www.gapyear.com claims to have more than 100,000 pages of information about 100 countries and a section to help plan an RTW trip (www.gapyear.com/rtw) in association with STA. Users can find travelmates, access a database with thousands of opportunities, pose questions on the message boards, and buy kit.

iGapYear.com. Has a growing database of gap year options.

Mapthegap.co.uk. Dedicated to news and travel features for those planning a gap year.

WorldWide Volunteering (WWV) (www.wwv.org.uk). Non-profit-making organisation designed to help people of all ages get involved with volunteering and find a placement that suits them. WWV's online database of 1,700 organisations offers a potential total of 1.5 million placements and is free for all to use. The site also carries volunteers' stories.

When trying to decide among competing options, check feedback sites online for candid reviews, for example www.abroadreviews.com offers 'unbiased reviews of international programmes'. The site www.go-volunteerabroad.com gives each of its listed programmes a star rating based on users' feedback. It is worth paying attention to companies that win acclaim in the Volunteering category of the annual Virgin Responsible Tourism Awards announced each November at the World Travel Market. The winner in 2010 was Blue Ventures (see entry in 'Directory of Specialist Gap Year Programmes'), while honourable mentions went to Biosphere Expeditions, BTCV, and the Great Projects, all mentioned elsewhere in this book.

Of course, Facebook and other networking sites have become another port of call for students looking for feedback on particular programmes. A couple of years ago the mainstream agency Frontier attracted some negative publicity after an article was published in the *Guardian* (www.guardian.co.uk/travel/2008/sep/06/gapyeartravel.workingholidays), describing the experiences of some disappointed participants. One of them, **Hannah Lemkov**, aged 19, volunteered through Frontier to work with Peace Child as an English teacher in Bangalore, and afterwards set up a Facebook group called 'Volunteers Against Frontier', which is still active. Everyone has to weigh up complaints and rebuttals and decide whether or not the evidence justifies eliminating them from your list of possibilities.

Wherever you look, services and niche websites target gap year students, from Gap Year NZ (www.gapyear-newzealand.co.uk) to Traveltree.co.uk, a website directory that enlightens visitors with opportunities for gap year ideas as well as adventure and educational travel, internships, and volunteering opportunities. Many of these are referred to in the appropriate context throughout this book.

The *Jobs Abroad Bulletin* is a useful one-man and one-woman site (www.jobsabroadbulletin.co.uk), which delivers actual job vacancy details each month. Its strapline is 'Find paid jobs, volunteer work and gap years around the world'. Also look at www.overseasjobcentre.co.uk from the same people.

Gap year fairs are held around the country through the spring and early summer, and are generally free and open to anyone. One series is organised by Futurewise. which oversees a dozen or so fairs held at various schools between April and September (http://ehcourses.inspiringfutures.org.uk). Visiting one of these fairs gives you a chance to meet representatives of various companies in person as well as real live former gappers. Many sixth-form careers departments organise gap year information evenings, though these are often partisan events at which a few gap year company representatives are pushing their schemes. Remember that there are always more options out there than are in front of you at one of these events. **Ed Fry** went along to one of these at his school but wanted more independent advice:

> *I was given some advice at school as to how I might wish to structure my gap year in terms of travel, work and so on, but many of the people that came to speak at school had a commercial slant to their talks which made me slightly dubious of their advice. Teachers were very helpful in terms of advising on countries to visit and things to do. A short course was also offered on how to stay safe in your gap year, but it was at an extra cost and basically all common sense.*

DIRECTORY OF SPECIALIST GAP YEAR PROGRAMMES

ADVENTURE ALTERNATIVE
PO Box 14, Portstewart, Northern Ireland
BT55 7WS
☎ (0)2870 831 258
✎ office@adventurealternative.com
🖥 www.adventurealternative.com

PROGRAMME DESCRIPTION: Gap year volunteering programmes, primarily for those on gap years plus medical students, career breakers, and others, in Kenya, Nepal, and Borneo. Combined teaching/community/ medical or environmental work, group activities (eg climbing, trekking, rafting, safaris), and independent travel. In Kenya, participants teach and work in clinics and primary education in rural and slum schools or in orphanage or rescue centre for street children. In Nepal, participants help to build a village school or work in a Kathmandu primary school. Medical electives are also available for doctors and student doctors in Kenya and Nepal. In Borneo, community and tree planting projects take place deep in the jungle of Sarawak. 1-month summer expeditions in Kenya called Africamps for young people 16–25 combine working on a community project eg with street children, climbing Mount Kenya and going on a safari to the Indian Ocean.

DESTINATIONS: Rural and inner city slums in Kenya, Himalayan Nepal, and the jungles of Borneo.

NUMBER OF PLACEMENTS PER YEAR: 50 for Kenya, 30 for Nepal, 20 for Borneo.

PREREQUISITES: Hard-working, committed, enthusiastic volunteers who are not fazed by the hardships of living in a developing country. All nationalities and ages welcome.

DURATION AND TIME OF PLACEMENTS: 2–12 weeks, but can be flexible.

COST: From £650 for short expeditions; sample price is £1,250 for 2 months in Kenya, £1,850 for 3 months (includes food and accommodation), plus an estimated £800 for flights, inoculations, insurance, and other necessities. Africamps cost £1,695, excluding airfares.

CONTACT: Gavin Bate, Director; Chris Little or Andy MacDonald, Expedition Co-ordinators.

AFRICA, ASIA & AMERICAS VENTURE
10 Market Place, Devizes, Wiltshire SN10 1HT
☎ (0)1380 729 009
✎ av@aventure.co.uk or info@aventure.co.uk
🖥 www.aventure.co.uk

Founding member of the Year Out Group. Africa, Asia & Americas Venture is an organisation that enables students to gain teaching, sports coaching, community, and conservation work experience (unpaid). Participants work in small groups/pairs, but are part of a larger group of up to 30 18–24-year-old volunteers.

PROGRAMME DESCRIPTION: Students are placed in selected rural secondary and primary schools for approximately 3 months, teaching a variety of subjects and helping with extracurricular activities, especially sports. This is followed by 2–3 weeks of backpacking before going on safari to areas of interest and outstanding beauty in the chosen country.

DESTINATIONS: Africa (Uganda, Kenya, Tanzania, Malawi, South Africa); Asia (India, Nepal, Sri Lanka, Thailand, China); Americas (Costa Rica, Ecuador, and Mexico).

NUMBER OF PLACEMENTS PER YEAR: 380–420.

PREREQUISITES: Students going on to further education or undergraduates considering taking time out can apply. Participants are generally aged 18–24 when they join the scheme, although any age may apply. Volunteers should enjoy working with young people.

DURATION AND TIME OF PLACEMENTS: 3 weeks to 4 or 5 months, with departures all year round.

SELECTION PROCEDURES AND ORIENTATION: On application, a company representative will ring to answer questions and to get to know the potential participant. A face-to-face interview will then take place in UK (telephone call if applying from outside UK) so that a satisfactory placement and partner can be found.

COST: The basic cost (2011) is £1,995 for 3 weeks (Kenya only), £2,165 for 5 weeks (2012), £3,500 for

3–5 months, which covers orientation course, living/food allowance, accommodation, a 6–8-day group safari, and in-country back-up. Prices do not include airfares, entry visas, or insurance. Special price for 6-week summer trip to Uganda is £1,565 (2011).

AFRICAN CONSERVATION EXPERIENCE
Unit 1, Manor Farm, Churchend Lane, Charfield, Wotton-Under-Edge, Gloucester GL12 8LJ
☎ (0)1454 269 182
✆ info@ConservationAfrica.net
🖥 www.ConservationAfrica.net

Member of the Year Out Group.

PROGRAMME DESCRIPTION: Conservation placements on game reserves in Southern Africa. Tasks may include tracking elephants, hand rearing a rhino, studying dolphin behaviour and restoring and maintaining the bushveld habitat.

DESTINATIONS: South Africa, Botswana, and Mauritius.

PREREQUISITES: Open to people of all ages who have reasonable physical fitness and ability to cope mentally. Enthusiasm for conservation is essential. Programme may be of special interest to students of environmental, zoological, and marine sciences, veterinary science and animal care.

DURATION AND TIME OF PLACEMENTS: 2–12 weeks throughout the year.

SELECTION PROCEDURES AND ORIENTATION: Candidates are matched to a suitable project based on the information provided on their application form but do have final say. Prospective participants can meet company representatives at various talks and events in the UK and elsewhere.

COST: Students can expect an average total cost of about £2,200 for 2 weeks up to £5,200 for 12 weeks, which includes international flights (from London), transfers, accommodation, and all meals. Support and advice given on fundraising.

CONTACT: Alexia Massey and Katrina Steele.

AFRICATRUST NETWORKS
Africatrust Chambers, PO Box 551, Portsmouth, Hampshire PO5 1ZN
☎ (0)23 9273 0987
✆ info@africatrust.org.uk
🖥 www.africatrust.org.uk

PROGRAMME DESCRIPTION: UK NGO that makes residential placements for pre-university and mainly post-university students, to teach young children, help with disabled, homeless, blind, and orphaned children, etc.

DESTINATIONS: Ghana (Cape Coast and Kumasi), Cameroon, and Morocco working with the UK Registered Charity, Moroccan Children's Trust (www.moroccan childrenstrust.org).

PREREQUISITES: Volunteers must be at least 18 (most are 21+), in good health, and preferably non-smokers. A level French is needed for Morocco.

DURATION AND TIME OF PLACEMENTS: 3 and 6 months.

SELECTION PROCEDURES AND ORIENTATION: Application form available on website. References will be taken up and interviews scheduled in London. Briefing information on health, fundraising, and projects is sent. There is a compulsory pre-departure briefing in London for volunteers and their families, plus induction course.

COST: Cameroon project is subsidised: £850 for 3 months, £1,700 for 6 months. Other prices on application.

AIL MADRID SPANISH LANGUAGE IMMERSION SCHOOL IN SPAIN
C/Nuñez de Balboa 17, 2°D, 28001 Madrid, Spain
☎ +34 91 72 56 350
✆ info@ailmadrid.com
🖥 www.ailmadrid.com/gapyear/home

PROGRAMME DESCRIPTION: 12-week Spanish language course in Madrid and other cities in Spain, with work placement options.

PREREQUISITES: Minimum age 17, average age 22.

DURATION AND TIME OF PLACEMENTS: 12–48 weeks with flexible start dates.

COST: 12-week programme from €3,500.

CONTACT: Maya Bychova.

AMANZI TRAVEL
4 College Road, Westbury on Trym, Bristol BS9 3EJ
☎ (0)117 904 2638
✆ info@amanzitravel.co.uk
🖥 www.amanzitravel.co.uk

PROGRAMME DESCRIPTION: Worthwhile volunteer placements throughout Africa providing opportunities to help conserve endangered wildlife; work on teaching and community development projects, and help at medical clinics and hospitals. Projects include working with big cats at the leading Lion Breeding/Release Project at Victoria Falls; helping at the Bushman Medical Clinic in Namibia; looking after AIDS orphans in Cape Town; teaching disadvantaged children in schools in Zambia or Tanzania; coaching the local children's football team in Mwanza, Tanzania; and helping at wildlife sanctuaries throughout Africa. A range of adventure activities and safari trips (3–56 days) are also offered, plus courses in photography and in how to become a Field Guide or Game Ranger.

DESTINATIONS: Botswana, Kenya, Mozambique, Namibia, South Africa, Tanzania, Uganda, Zambia, and Zimbabwe.

NUMBER OF PLACEMENTS PER YEAR: 500.

DURATION AND TIME OF PLACEMENTS: 2 weeks to 1 year, with flexible start dates.

PREREQUISITES: All ages, including gap year students.

SELECTION PROCEDURES AND ORIENTATION: Comprehensive pre-departure pack and full orientation on arrival.

OTHER SERVICES: Tailor-made trip itineraries including flight arrangements and advice on insurance.

COST: From £300 for short placements. Sample cost £1,295 for 4 weeks in Namibia.

CONTACT: Gemma Whitehouse, Managing Director.

ART HISTORY ABROAD
The Red House, 1 Lambseth Street, Eye, Suffolk IP23 7AG
☎ (0)1379 871 800
✎ info@arthistoryabroad.com
🖳 www.arthistoryabroad.com

Year Out Group founding member.

PROGRAMME DESCRIPTION: Programme based around the great art, architecture, and sculpture of Italy, this course is about European civilisation in the broadest sense. Participants spend 6 weeks travelling throughout Italy including Venice, Verona, Florence, Siena, Naples, and Rome. No classroom work is involved and all tuition is on-site and in groups of no more than 10; 2-week summer holiday courses in Italy also available. A new course in Contemporary Art and Architecture based in London has just been introduced.

NUMBER OF PLACEMENTS PER YEAR: 27 per course, 4 times per year.

DURATION AND TIME OF PLACEMENT: 6-week course offered 4 times a year (autumn, spring, early summer, and late summer) and 2-week courses offered in July/August.

COST: £6,990 for the autumn, spring, and early summer courses including travel to, from, and within Italy, hotel accommodation, and breakfast throughout, all museum entry, expert tuition in small groups, as well as drawing and Italian conversation classes and a private visit to San Marco in Venice. Fees do not include lunch or supper. Price for 2-week summer courses in Italy is £2,750. London-based courses from £1,090.

ACCOMMODATION: Shared rooms in hotels in the centre of each city visited.

AU PAIR IN AMERICA
37 Queen's Gate, London SW7 5HR
☎ (0)20 7581 7322
✎ info@aupairamerica.co.uk
🖳 www.aupairamerica.co.uk

Parent organisation (American Institute for Foreign Study) founded in 1967, and the au pair programme authorised in 1986.

PROGRAMME DESCRIPTION: Au Pair in America operates the largest and longest-established legal childcare programme to the United States. Au pairs are placed with a screened American family for a minimum of 12 months and maximum of 24. Other programmes that run alongside are the EduCare in America (for students who work shorter hours to allow more time for studies and receive less pocket money), and Au Pair Extraordinaire (for qualified and experienced carers).

NUMBER OF PLACEMENTS PER YEAR: 3,000–4,000 from around the world.

DURATION AND TIME OF PLACEMENTS: 12–24 months. Au pairs provide 45 hours of childcare per week.

PREREQUISITES: All nationalities are eligible, provided there is an established interviewer network in their country. Ages 18–26. Must have at least 200 hours of recent non-family practical childcare experience gained within the past 3 years. Must hold a full driving licence and be available for 12 months.

SELECTION PROCEDURES AND ORIENTATION: Applicants must submit a complete application and attend a personal interview with an appointed Au Pair in America interviewer. Au Pair in America has representatives in 45 countries and agent/interviewers throughout the UK.

COST: Around $500 programme fee (may vary). Au pairs who successfully complete their 12-month minimum stay will receive a $200 completion payment.

BENEFITS: Free return airfare London to New York, 4-day orientation programme held near New York, legal

J-1 visa, weekly payment of $195.75, up to $500 study tuition allowance, medical insurance, 2 weeks paid holidays, optional 13th month travel, year-long support from US community counsellor, placement in an established au pair 'cluster group'.

AUSTRALIAN INTERNSHIPS
Suite 1, Savoir Faire, 20 Park Road, Milton, Brisbane, Queensland 4064, Australia
☎ +61 7 3305 8408
🖰 info@internships.com.au
🖳 www.internships.com.au

PROGRAMME DESCRIPTION: Two programme options for candidates interested in seeking hands-on experience in Australia: Professional Internship Programme and Hospitality Internship Programme (see entry in 'Directory of Work Experience'). The company has recently developed a programme whereby volunteers join projects arranged in co-operation with Aboriginal and Torres Strait Islander communities in Australia (see entry for Volunteers Australia in the 'Directory of Volunteering Abroad').

AZAFADY
Studio 7, 1A Beethoven St, London W10 4LG
☎ (0)20 8960 6629
🖰 info@azafady.org
🖳 www.madagascar.co.uk

PROGRAMME DESCRIPTION: Azafady is a UK-registered charity and Malagasy NGO providing opportunities to work with a grassroots organisations tackling conservation issues and extreme poverty in Madagascar. Working closely with local communities, volunteers can choose to join the award-winning 10-week Pioneer Programme and work on projects as diverse as well construction, school-building, tree planting, and environmental or health education, to help on the Lemur Research and Conservation Programme, or to join the Short-term Programmes for 2 or 3 weeks to assist with school-building or English teaching. Programmes are particularly suited to those interested in development and ecology (who may be looking for experience as an entry point into an ethical career), or who simply want to make a difference and have a meaningful career break experience.

DESTINATIONS: South-east Madagascar.

NUMBER OF PLACEMENTS PER YEAR: 14–20 per group, 8 groups per year approximately.

PREREQUISITES: Enthusiasm and cultural sensitivity. All ages welcome; past age range 18–70. Training given.

Volunteers learn basic Malagasy so that they may work together with members of rural communities and gain a unique insight into the culture.

DURATION AND TIME OF PLACEMENTS: 2–10 weeks with main start dates in January, April, July, and October.

COST: Successful applicants pay personal pre-project costs such as flight, vaccinations, and visa, and are required to raise a minimum charitable donation of between £595 and £2,650, depending on project and duration. Volunteers are provided with extensive fundraising resources and advice.

CONTACT: Sarah Lamb, Volunteer Co-ordinator.

BASE CAMP GROUP
30 Baseline Business Studios, Whitchurch Road, London W11 4AT
☎ (0)20 7243 6222
🖰 contact@basecampgroup.com
🖳 www.basecampgroup.com

PROGRAMME DESCRIPTION: Adventure training company founded in 2002, offering ski and snowboard instructor courses in the French and Swiss Alps, Canadian Rockies, and Argentina, and watersports programmes in Egypt and Morocco, plus mountain biking in Whistler, Canada. See separate entries in 'Directory of Sport and Activity Courses'.

BLUE VENTURES
309 a/b Aberdeen Centre, 22–24 Highbury Grove, Islington, London N5 2EA
🖰 enquiries@blueventures.org
🖳 www.blueventures.org

PROGRAMME DESCRIPTION: Volunteers needed for award-winning marine conservation project. Blue Ventures conducts marine research, and works with local communities to sustainably manage marine resources in south-west Madagascar, northern Belize, and eastern Malaysia. Volunteers participate in all research programmes, community projects, and alternative livelihood schemes. Non-diving conservation work might involve cetacean surveys, accompanying local fishermen or beach clean-up operations. The Blue Ventures volunteer programme has been awarded a number of international responsible tourism awards and has pioneered successful conservation efforts.

NUMBER OF PLACEMENTS PER YEAR: Up to 18 at one time, with expeditions throughout the year.

DESTINATIONS: The village of Andavadoaka in south-west Madagascar has been the Blue Ventures expedition site since 2003. Blue Ventures now also operates in the fishing community of Sarteneja in northern Belize and on the beautiful island of Tioman in the Malaysian South China Sea.

PREREQUISITES: No diving or scientific background required as all necessary training is provided on-site. The Blue Ventures international team of volunteers comprises all ages and walks of life from age 18.

DURATION AND TIME OF PLACEMENTS: Typical stay of 6 weeks, although shorter and longer stays are available.

COST: £2,200 for 6 weeks for volunteers requiring dive training; £2,000 for PADI Advanced divers or equivalent. Short stays of a fortnight are available from £900 at Tioman project. Volunteers will be expected to provide personal diving kit (ie mask, snorkel, wetsuit, fins), torch, sleeping bag, malaria prophylactics, inoculations, and flights.

CONTACT: Kathleen Edie, Expedition & Volunteer Co-ordinator.

BRITISH COUNCIL ASSISTANTS PROGRAMME
10 Spring Gardens, London SW1A 2BN
☎ (0)20 7389 4596
✆ assistants@britishcouncil.org
🖳 www.britishcouncil.org/languageassistants

PROGRAMME DESCRIPTION: English Language Assistants Programme for modern language students and recent graduates. Applicants should be aged 20–30 with at least 2 years of university-level education. For most countries A/AS level in the language of the destination country is the minimum foreign language requirement. There is no language requirement for China.

NUMBER OF PLACEMENTS PER YEAR: 2,500 (in 2010–11).

DESTINATIONS: Country-by-country details are available on the website. Most posts are in Austria, France, Germany, Spain, China (graduates only), and Latin America. Posts also exist in Italy, Belgium, Switzerland, and Québec (Canada).

DURATION AND TIME OF PLACEMENTS: One academic year, ie September or October to May or June, depending on country. One-semester posts available in Austria.

SELECTION PROCEDURES AND ORIENTATION:
Application forms are downloadable from the website from October for a deadline of 1 December. Interviews necessary for posts outside Europe and in Switzerland.

COST: Travel costs, visas and vaccinations where necessary. Monthly stipend paid to assistants varies from country to country, eg €950 gross in France.

THE BRITISH INSTITUTE OF FLORENCE
Piazza Strozzi 2, 50123 Florence, Italy
☎ +39 055 2677 81
✆ info@britishinstitute.it
🖳 www.britishinstitute.it

Housed in two magnificent buildings on either side of the River Arno in the historic centre of Florence, and minutes from all the city's museums, galleries, and churches, the British Institute of Florence has a long tradition of excellence in its teaching and is recognised as a centre for learning by the Tuscan Region.

PROGRAMME DESCRIPTION: The Institute offers students the opportunity to experience the life and culture of Florence within the framework of a structured programme of study. Courses are offered in Italian language, history of art, and life drawing. A regular programme of events including lectures, concerts, and films, is held in the Institute's Harold Acton Library overlooking the River Arno.

DURATION AND TIME OF COURSES: 1–12 weeks throughout the year.

COST: Fees vary according to the course chosen, eg a 4-week Italian language course costs €630 and a 4-week History of Art course €615. 4-week combined Italian and History of Art course is €1150.

ACCOMMODATION: Can be arranged in local homes, *pensione* and hotels. Price for homestay accommodation starts at approximately €30 per night. There is a fee of €25 for arranging accommodation.

BSES EXPEDITIONS
Royal Geographical Society, 1 Kensington Gore, London SW7 2AR
☎ (0)20 7591 3141
✆ info@bses.org.uk
🖳 www.bses.org.uk

BSES Expeditions organises overseas expeditions worldwide for 16–23-year-olds. See entry in 'Directory of Expeditions'.

BUNAC
16 Bowling Green Lane, London EC1R 0QH
☎ (0)20 7251 3472
✆ enquiries@bunac.org.uk
🖳 www.bunac.org

Founding member of the Year Out Group. BUNAC is a non-profit national student club offering work and travel programmes worldwide. It helps before and after arrival in the country of travel, and acts as a 'security blanket' if situations go wrong while the student is abroad.

PROGRAMME DESCRIPTION: Various work programmes in North America and elsewhere. A large number of students and non-students are placed on summer camps (see *USA* chapter). BUNAC makes it possible for candidates to obtain the necessary visas and publishes its own job directories which help members to fix up short-term jobs before or after arrival.

DESTINATIONS: Main destination is the USA. Other work programmes in Canada, New Zealand, Australia, and South Africa; volunteer programmes in South Africa, Ghana, Costa Rica, Peru, Cambodia, India, and China.

PREREQUISITES: Work America students must have documentary evidence that they are enrolled in a higher education degree course (gap year students not eligible). Work Australia, Work New Zealand and Work Canada are open to all 18–30-year-olds (see country chapters).

DURATION AND TIME OF PLACEMENTS: 9 weeks on summer camps in the USA. Participants on the Work America programme may work up to 4 months but must return to a full-time course in the UK in September/October. Other programmes in other countries can last up to 2 years.

SELECTION PROCEDURES AND ORIENTATION: BUNAC holds information evenings at venues around the country.

COST: Applicants need to pay a registration fee (includes £5 BUNAC membership fee), plus programme fees from £295 for up to 12 weeks of conservation volunteering in the USA to £2,095 for five months of paid teaching in China. Flights, insurance and spending money are extra.

OTHER SERVICES: BUNAC has an in-house travel agency GS World Travel (020 7250 0222; www.gsworld-travel.co.uk) which arranges flights. BUNAC also offers an online TEFL training course (partnered with i-to-i).

CALEDONIA – LANGUAGES, CULTURE, ADVENTURE
33 Sandport Street, Leith, Edinburgh EH6 6AP
☎ (0)131 621 7721/2
✉ info@caledonialanguages.co.uk
🖥 www.caledonialanguages.com

Established in 1994, Caledonia's main focus is arranging language, culture and adventure travel abroad.

PROGRAMME DESCRIPTION: Caledonia offers short- and long-term language courses with accommodation (usually homestay, but other options are available) throughout Europe and Latin America. It also arranges volunteer work placements in Latin America, work experience programmes, language and activity courses (eg Spanish and dance in Spain, Cuba, Argentina, and the Dominican Republic; Spanish and trekking in Cuba; Portuguese and trekking in Brazil; French and sailing in Nice), and language and learning courses (eg Italian and History of Art in San Giovanni; Spanish and cooking in Malaga, or French and cooking in Aix-en-Provence). Volunteer community projects in Latin America for language clients include working with children in Lencois, Brazil, conservation in the cloud forests of Costa Rica, kindergarten in Peru, or teaching English in Ecuador. Work experience programmes are sometimes available working with partner language schools, companies and organisations according to the client's skills and experience.

DESTINATIONS: Caledonia's partner language schools are in France, Spain, Portugal, Italy, Germany, Austria, Russia, Argentina, Peru, Chile, Bolivia, Ecuador, Costa Rica, Brazil, Mexico, Dominican Republic, and Cuba. Cuba is one of Caledonia's main destinations; tailor-made programmes can last year-round to include dance, percussion, music, touring, and trekking, with or without a language course.

PREREQUISITES: All levels are offered, from complete beginner to advanced. A higher level of Spanish or Portuguese is needed to work on volunteer and work experience programmes.

DURATION OF COURSES: Minimum 1 week (or 3–4 weeks if combined with volunteer placement) up to 12 months. Classes start all year round.

SELECTION PROCEDURES AND ORIENTATION: For volunteer and work experience programmes, a short language course is taken in the country for cultural and linguistic familiarisation before work can begin. Briefing meetings on the proposed work and occasional pre-placement site visits are arranged. Full back-up support is given by the language school in-country.

COST: Volunteers and work experience applicants must pay an arrangement fee of £250 plus VAT, fees for the pre-placement language course in the overseas country (eg £1,355 for four weeks Brazil, 20 lessons per week, with half-board single room accommodation). Accommodation is with local families.

CONTACT: Kath Bateman, Director.

CAMP COUNSELORS USA (CCUSA)
London office: Unit 6.04, 6 Morie Street, Wandsworth Town, London SW18 1SL
☎ (0)20 8874 6325
✉ info@ccusa.co.uk
🖥 www.ccusa.co.uk
🖥 www.ccusa.com

PROGRAMME DESCRIPTION: Camp Counsellor placement plus work experience in the USA. Placements on summer camps in Russia, Croatia, and Canada. Teaching in China. Volunteering in South Africa and many South American countries.

DESTINATIONS: USA, Canada, South Africa, China, Russia, and Croatia.

PREREQUISITES: Ages 18–30 for most programmes.

DURATION AND TIME OF PLACEMENTS: 9 weeks for camp counsellors, 3–4 months working in the USA (between late May and October), 4–12 weeks in South Africa, 12–18-month business training programme in America, 6 months in Canada (ski resort jobs November-April).

COST: Camp Counselors USA fee from £399, Work Experience USA Placement £478, Independent £313; Practical Training USA $995 (£600 for 12 months) or $1,495 (£910 for 18 months). First-year counsellors aged 18 earn US$800 in pocket money. Prices based on 2011 season and may be subject to change.

PROGRAMME DESCRIPTION: Gap year placements and expeditions in Africa, South East Asia, and Latin America for 18–25-year-olds (and community volunteering for adults 25 years upwards and for families). Co-located with rural communities, participants undertake a range of community and wildlife projects, and also have the opportunity to go jungle trekking, mountain climbing, or do a PADI scuba diving course.

DESTINATIONS: Kenya, Tanzania, Cambodia, Borneo, and Ecuador.

DURATION AND TIME OF PLACEMENTS: 1, 2, or 3 months.

SELECTION PROCEDURES AND ORIENTATION: Must be motivated and enthusiastic.

COST: Sample price: £1,450 for one month in Cambodia, £2,895 for 3 months combining Borneo and Cambodia. £1,630 for one month and £2,995 for 3 months on Camp Kenya.

Founding member of the Year Out Group (yearoutgroup. org).

PROGRAMME DESCRIPTION: Major provider of language courses in France, Guadeloupe, Spain, Ecuador, Argentina, Chile, Costa Rica, Mexico, Peru, Germany, Austria, Italy, Portugal, Greece, Russia, Morocco, and China. See entry in 'Directories of Courses'.

ATOL-licensed and member of the Year Out Group. Aims to provide full cultural immersion through challenging and worthwhile work placements with a safety net if required.

PROGRAMME DESCRIPTION: Gap year options ranging from voluntary teaching placements in developing countries to paid placements in prestigious hotels.

DESTINATIONS: Argentina, Australia, Brazil, China, Dubai, Ghana, Germany Honduras, Kenya, Madagascar, New Zealand, Romania, Serbia, South Africa, Thailand, and Uganda.

NUMBER OF PLACEMENTS PER YEAR: 120.

PREREQUISITES: A level or equivalent in native language, plus initiative, determination, adaptability, and social skills.

DURATION AND TIME OF PLACEMENTS: 1–6 months. Placements begin throughout the year.

SELECTION PROCEDURES AND ORIENTATION: Interview days held in Surrey every 6–8 weeks. All participants attend a pre-departure briefing; for those going to a developing country, this is a 2-day residential course. Participants are met on arrival in the country of destination and attend orientation with the local representative before proceeding to placement. Local representatives act as support during placement.

Changing Worlds is a member of Interhealth, which can provide health screening to all participants and act as travel health advisers.

COST: From £1,665 (for Romania); prices include return flights.

CONTACT: David Gill, Director.

CITY YEAR LONDON
58–62 White Lion Street, London N1 9PP
☎ (0)20 7014 2680
info@cityyear.org.uk
www.cityyear.org.uk

Volunteering scheme for young Londoners imported from America, launched by Mayor Boris Johnson in September 2010.

PROGRAMME DESCRIPTION: A year of full-time volunteering in schools as tutors, mentors and role models. Involvement also in after-school programmes and community projects to tackle inner city poverty and crime.

DESTINATIONS: Primary schools in deprived areas of Islington, Hackney, and Tower Hamlets, London.

NUMBER OF PLACEMENTS PER YEAR: 8–10 in pilot year (2011–12).

DURATION AND TIME OF PLACEMENTS: 11 months from September.

PREREQUISITES: Young people of all backgrounds, especially those who can share experiences wth the pupils they will be working with.

SELECTION PROCEDURES AND ORIENTATION: One day per week training, including personal and professional development.

COST: Free to participants. Up to £100 per week paid in expenses and subsistence costs. Timberland boots and uniform given.

CORAL CAY CONSERVATION
Elizabeth House, 39 York Road, London SE1 7NJ
☎ (0)20 7620 1411
info@coralcay.org
www.coralcay.org

Founding member of the Year Out Group. Hundreds of volunteers participate in Coral Cay expeditions every year to assist in conserving fragile tropical marine and terrestrial environments, building local capacity to protect these ecosystems in the long term.

PROGRAMME DESCRIPTION: The overall aim of CCC is to use good science to support the preservation of coral reefs and to support the dependent communities. Volun-

teers undertake dives to understand biodiversity and to gather scientific data which is used to compile reports for journals to establish new marine protected areas (MPAs).

DESTINATIONS: Currently 3 expedition sites: Southern Leyte in the Philippines, Tobago, and Cambodia. Possibility of setting up new onshore project in Kenya (see website for updates).

NUMBER OF PLACEMENTS PER YEAR: 200–500.

PREREQUISITES: No previous experience is required. Volunteers come from a diverse range of backgrounds, ages, and cultures. Scuba dive training is available up to PADI Divemaster level.

DURATION AND TIME OF PLACEMENTS: Expeditions depart monthly throughout the year. Volunteers stay for 2–16+ weeks or longer.

SELECTION PROCEDURES AND ORIENTATION: A free information pack is available on request, and free presentations are held on the second Wednesday and final Saturday of every month; places on these should be pre-booked.

COST: Sample prices: £1,550 for 4 weeks as a dive trainee, and £2,750 for 12 weeks if a qualified diver. Prices vary according to length of stay, type of project, and level of training required. Prices exclude flights and insurance; fundraising advice is given. Occasional special offers such as free PADI rescue diver, Reef Check International Ecodiver and PADI Emergency First Response.

COSMIC VOLUNTEERS
PO Box 11895, Philadelphia, Pennsylvania 19128, USA
☎ +1 215 609 4196
info@cosmicvolunteers.org
www.cosmicvolunteers.org

Tax-exempt charity (33-0998120), sending volunteers abroad since 2001.

PROGRAMME DESCRIPTION: Volunteering, internships and specialist travel programmes in developing countries. Volunteer programme includes teaching, medicine, orphanages, journalism, social work, HIV/AIDS care, Buddhist monks, environment, sports, organic farming, and turtle conservation.

DESTINATIONS: Bolivia, Cambodia, China, Ecuador, Ghana, Guatemala, India, Kenya, Nepal, Peru, Philippines, South Africa, Thailand, Uganda, and Vietnam.

NUMBER OF PLACEMENTS PER YEAR: 250+.

PREREQUISITES: Open to all ages (16–70+), with average age about 23. Must have open mind and be fluent in English. Most medical placements available only to health professionals and trainees.

DURATION AND TIME OF PLACEMENTS: 1 week to 12 months.

SELECTION PROCEDURES AND ORIENTATION: Applicants accepted year-round. Must sign up at least 30 days before programme start date.

OTHER SERVICES: Spanish language classes are available in Bolivia, Ecuador, Guatemala. and Peru.

COSTS: Varies with programme, from $795 one-time fee for Vietnam, to $1,995 for 12 weeks in Ghana.

CONTACT: Scott Burke, Founder and Director.

CROSS-CULTURAL SOLUTIONS
UK Office: Tower Point, 44 North Road, Brighton BN1 1YR
☎ (0)845 458 2781/2
✆ infouk@crossculturalsolutions.org
💻 www.crossculturalsolutions.org

See entry in 'Directory of Volunteering Abroad'.

CSV
Community Service Volunteers, Fifth Floor, Scala House, 36 Holloway Circus, Queensway, Birmingham B1 1EQ
☎ (0)800 374991
☎ (0)121 643 7690
✆ volunteer@csv.org.uk
💻 www.csv.org.uk/fulltimevolunteering

CSV is the UK's leading volunteering and training organisation. CSV's gap year volunteering opportunities are open to those aged 18–35 who commit to volunteer full-time and away from home for 6–12 months. See entry in 'Directory of Volunteering in the UK'. Other international volunteers can participate, provided they apply through one of CSV's international partners (details from www.csv.org.uk/ftvol).

DEUTSCH-INSTITUT TIROL
Staudach 23, 6370 Kitzbühel, Austria
☎ +53 56 712 74
✆ deutschinstitut@aon.at
💻 www.gap-year.at

PROGRAMME DESCRIPTION: Gap Year Winter Sports (September to December) in conjunction with German language course, specially designed for gap year students. Language instruction combined with ski and snowboard instruction, with possibility of training for ski/snowboard instructor's exams.

DESTINATIONS: Gap Year Winter Sports skiing/snowboarding in October and November takes place Thursday to Sunday at Kaprun at the foot of a glacier (45-minute drive from Kitzbühel). German lessons Monday to Wednesday take place in Kitzbühel. Programme includes 1-week trip to Salzburg, Vienna, Budapest, Prague, and Budweis.

PREREQUISITES: Any level of German can be catered for, including no previous study. Course designed for people who are already good skiers/snowboarders.

DURATION AND TIME OF PLACEMENT: 12-week programme (mid-September to mid-December).

COST: €8,200.

CONTACT: Louise Ebenhöh.

DEVELOPMENT IN ACTION
78 York Street, London W1H 1DP
☎ (0)7813 395 957
✆ info@developmentinaction.org
💻 www.developmentinaction.org

PROGRAMME DESCRIPTION: Arranges voluntary attachments to various locally based development NGOs in India for 2 months in summer or 5 months from September. See entry in 'Directory of Volunteering Abroad'.

ECOLOGIA YOUTH TRUST
The Park, Forres, Moray, Scotland IV36 3TD
☎ (0)1309 690 995
✆ volunteer@ecologia.org.uk
💻 www.ecologia.org.uk
💻 www.kitezh.org

PROGRAMME DESCRIPTION: Volunteer programme open to gap year students at the Kitezh Community of foster families in western Russia. Russian language is not essential, although students of Russian will quickly become fluent. (See entry in 'Directory of Volunteering Abroad' and further details in *Russia* chapter.)

EIL UK
Elphick House, 287 Worcester Road, Malvern, Worcestershire WR14 1AB
☎ (0)1684 562 577
✆ info@eiluk.org
💻 www.eiluk.org

EIL (Experiment in International Living) is a registered charity that specialises in increasing understanding between cultures. Educational and cultural programmes for young people in their gap year or long vacations. Partner offices in 30 countries.

PROGRAMME DESCRIPTION: Various programmes include European Voluntary Service (EVS) described below, volunteer programmes, homestays worldwide, language tuition, teaching English, environmental projects, and helping with specialist projects, all in line with the UN Millennium development goals (eg halting the spread of HIV/AIDS).

DESTINATIONS: Africa, Asia, Australasia, Europe, South America, and USA.

DURATION AND TIME OF PLACEMENTS: 4 weeks to 1 year.

COST: Costs vary depending upon the type of stay chosen.

EL CASAL BARCELONA
Balmes 163, 3–1, 08008 Barcelona, Spain
☎ +34 93 217 9038
info@elcasalbarcelona.com
www.elcasalbarcelona.com

PROGRAMME DESCRIPTION: El Casal is a gap year programme for well-motivated high school graduates who want to experience Spanish culture and who are looking for a rewarding and stimulating experience before they begin college.

NUMBER OF PLACEMENTS: 16.

PREREQUISITES: Minimum age 17, average age 18. All nationalities (though majority are North American). Participants should have at least 2 years of Spanish and a good academic record.

DURATION AND TIME OF PLACEMENTS: 100 days after September 2012 (programme is not operating 2011–12).

SELECTION PROCEDURES AND ORIENTATION: Normally, participants have been accepted to a selective 4-year college in the USA and have chosen to postpone their enrolment. Week-long orientation programme encompasses 'survival' and practical skills in Barcelona, host family adjustment workshops, and intensive Spanish workshops.

COST: €8,400 inclusive covers academic programme (spring or fall), room and board with a host family, excursions, day trips, all local transport, all expenses on the 6-day Camino de Santiago hiking portion of the programme, etc. Not included: transportation to and from Barcelona at the beginning/end of the programme, lunches, miscellaneous and personal expenses.

CONTACT: John Rosen, Director.

EUROPEAN VOLUNTARY SERVICE (EVS)
Youth in Action, British Council, 10 Spring Gardens, London SW1A 2BN
☎ (0)7389 4030
action2.enquiries@britishcouncil.org
connectyouth.enquiries@britishcouncil.org
www.britishcouncil.org/youthinaction

PROGRAMME DESCRIPTION: EVS forms part of the Youth in Action programme, managed by the British Council and funded by the European Union. It gives opportunities for young people (aged 18–30) to carry out a period of full-time voluntary service in European countries, engaging in cultural, educational, and training opportunities. The benefits of the programme are that it allows participants to learn new skills and gain confidence and independence, to enhance their employability, and to contribute to the local host community.

DESTINATIONS: Europe.

NUMBER OF PLACEMENTS: EVS provides several thousand volunteers with free travel, food, accommodation, insurance, and an allowance.

PREREQUISITES: EVS is an inclusive programme, open to all young people aged 18–30 and a legal resident in one of the EU member states (also including Turkey, Norway, Iceland, and Liechtenstein). No specific qualifications are needed and language training may be provided.

DURATION AND TIME OF PLACEMENTS: Standard voluntary service is for 6–12 months. Shorter-term placements are on offer (2 weeks to 2 months) to young people with fewer opportunities.

SELECTION PROCEDURES AND ORIENTATION: Applicants need to apply through an approved sending organisation (see www.britishcouncil.org/youthinaction) or contact the Youth in Action team.

COST: No cost to volunteers, as funding is provided through the Youth in Action programme. A personal allowance is also provided.

CONTACT: Youth Action Team contact in England: National Youth Agency ((0)116 242 7400; yia@nya. org.uk); in Scotland: Young Scot (contact Ben Peggie, Information Services Officer, (0)131 313 2488, benp@ youngscot.org); in Wales: Welsh Assembly Government (contact Karen Ann Williams, Youth Work Strategy Branch, (0)300 062 5604; karen-ann.williams@wales. gsi.gov.uk); and in Northern Ireland: Youth Council Northern Ireland (contact Bernice Sweeney or Mandy Cunningham, (0)2890 643 882; bsweeney@ycni.org or mcunningham@ycni.org).

Member of the Year Out Group. Flying Fish trains water and snow sports staff and arranges employment for sailors, divers, surfers and windsurfers, skiers, and snowboarders. Founded in 1993, it can help young people to fix up a year of travel, training and adventure, or to start a career in the action sports industry.

PROGRAMME DESCRIPTION: A gap year with Flying Fish starts with a course leading to qualification as a surfing, sailing, or windsurfing instructor, yacht skipper, divemaster or dive instructor, ski or snowboard instructor (see entry in 'Directory of Sport and Activity Courses'). After qualifying you can choose a period of work experience or go into a paid job in many locations worldwide, with advice from a Flying Fish careers adviser.

DESTINATIONS: Training courses are run at Cowes in the UK, at Sydney and the Whitsunday Islands in Australia, the Bay of Islands in New Zealand, Vassiliki in Greece, and Whistler Mountain in Canada. Jobs are worldwide with main employers located in Australia, the South Pacific, the Caribbean, and the Mediterranean.

NUMBER OF PLACEMENTS PER YEAR: 600.

DURATION AND TIME OF PLACEMENTS: 1 week to 12 months, with start dates year-round.

SELECTION PROCEDURES AND ORIENTATION: Applicants submit an application before training and will be asked to attend job interviews.

COST: Fees range from £800 to £11,000, but most gap year students choose a programme costing about £3,500. Accommodation and airfares are provided, with normal wages during employment.

Member of the Year Out Group. Merger of brands Trekforce and Greenforce.

PROGRAMME DESCRIPTION: Participants work as Fieldwork Assistants on various marine and onshore projects, carrying out tasks such as tracking animal movements and studying coral reef species. Training including diver training for the marine expeditions and language training for the land-based expeditions is provided. Internships, sport volunteering, teaching, community work, and many other projects also arranged worldwide. Participants on Trekforce expeditions to Belize, Borneo, and Amazon live with remote tribes, learn about their culture and customs, explore jungles, deserts and mountains, help build sustainable communities, assist with rainforest conservation and scientific projects. Programmes can incorporate a combination of expedition jungle training, project work, a Spanish language course, teaching in rural communities, trekking, adventure, and dive phases. 16-week expedition leader course also available.

DESTINATIONS: Fiji, the Bahamas, Tanzania, Ecuador, Nepal, India, China, South Africa, and Australia (for working holidaymakers; www.ozforce.org).

NUMBER OF PLACEMENTS PER YEAR: 1,000.

PREREQUISITES: No previous experience necessary; no qualifications required, as training will be provided in the field. Minimum age 17.

DURATION AND TIME OF PLACEMENTS: 8 or 10 weeks in Fiji (conserving coral reef), 1–6 months in many countries; up to 12 months in China, Ecuador, Australia, and Africa.

SELECTION PROCEDURES AND ORIENTATION: Applicants may attend one of the regular informal open days in central London. A briefing pack is provided on application, giving information about fundraising and relevant medical advice, etc. Participants can attend a training day prior to joining the project (cost included in contribution). The first week of the expedition is spent undertaking further training and familiarisation with the project and host country.

COST: Sample prices £2,300 for 6 weeks and £2,600 for 10 weeks of dive training and project in Fiji; £4,200 for a 5-month Belize expedition. Fees cover training and instruction, food, accommodation, and in-country transport, but not insurance or international flights. Fundraising advice is given to all participants.

Leading ethical gap year provider now allied to Mondo-Challenge (see entry below, p 192).

PROGRAMME DESCRIPTION: Specialist in India with recently added opportunities in other countries. Large range of volunteer placements and internships in teaching, medical, conservation, sport, business, etc. Additional travel possibilities include trekking in the mountains, and exploring beaches, cities, deserts, and temples.

DESTINATIONS: Throughout India. Also Tanzania, Chile, Sri Lanka, Nepal, Romania, and Ecuador.

PREREQUISITES: Minimum age 18 (at time of travel). No qualifications needed for many projects. Training programmes (eg Hotel Management) and openings in some fields such as business and medicine are possible for those studying or qualified in the relevant field.

DURATION AND TIME OF PLACEMENTS: 4 weeks to 12 months.

SELECTION PROCEDURES AND ORIENTATION: Applicants discuss possible projects before choosing. Pre-departure briefings are held and workplace orientations take place in India.

COST: Programmes start at £795 for 4 weeks, with a typical programme of 3 months costing around £1,850 including accommodation and most meals, but excluding flights and insurance.

ACCOMMODATION: A shared twin-bedded room with a local family or other suitable accommodation. All accommodation is checked and vetted.

GAP YEAR CANADA INCORPORATED
Box 4955, Banff, Alberta, Canada T1L 1G2
☎ (0)20 7096 1632 (UK)
☎ +1 403 762 3625 (Canada)
✍ info@GapYearCanada.com
🖳 www.GapYearCanada.com

PROGRAMME DESCRIPTION: Specialist gap year agency for people aged 18–30 who want to work for a season in Banff, Canada. Chalet accommodation and jobs are pre-arranged for the season, and assistance is given with visas, flights, and transfers. Sample jobs include guest services, ski rental and repair shop, retail stores, gondola operations, lift services, various food and beverage positions, trail crew, ski and snowboard instructors, valet parking, and hotel staff.

DESTINATIONS: Banff, Canada.

NUMBER OF PLACEMENTS: 100 (restricted by the number of chalets available for the season).

PREREQUISITES: Minimum age 18. Any nationality that is eligible for a Canadian student work visa (www.international.gc.ca/iyp-pij/country_menu%20_in-menu_pays_entrant.aspx). Must be adventurous, outgoing,

enthusiastic, and should be interested in learning to ski or snowboard, or improving skills.

DURATION AND TIME OF PLACEMENTS: Winter season (October till the end of May) at the resorts around Banff. Most winter employers prefer 6-month contracts. Minimum 3-month summer programme lasts from May/June to September/October.

SELECTION PROCEDURES AND ORIENTATION: Applications accepted on an ongoing basis though early application is recommended for the October start date. Agency helps with CV preparation, job placement, social insurance number processing, orientation in town on arrival, as well as setting up bank accounts for the season. Gap Year Canada organises activities and events throughout the season.

COST: C$5,500 for full 8-month winter season or C$5,000 for 6-month season, which includes accommodation in furnished chalets and all services. 3-week early season instructor training with full season accommodation and employment as ski or snowboarding instructor costs C$9,000.

CONTACT: Nancy Myles, Programme Director.

GAP YEAR DIVER
Tyte Court, Farbury End, Great Rollright, Oxfordshire OX7 5RS
☎ (0)845 257 3292
✍ sales@gapyeardiver.com
🖳 www.gapyeardiver.com

PROGRAMME DESCRIPTION: Scuba diving courses for all types of gappers in Egypt, Indonesia (Gili Islands), Venezuela, Costa Rica, Thailand, Bahamas, Fiji, and Belize. See entry in 'Directory of Sport and Activity Courses', and further details in chapter on Latin America.

GAP YEAR SOUTH AFRICA
PO Box 592, Cambridge CB1 0ES
☎ (0)20 8144 2423
✍ info@gapyearsouthafrica.com
🖳 www.GapYearSouthAfrica.com

PROGRAMME DESCRIPTION: Range of gap year projects arranged by on-the-ground organisation in South Africa, including sports coaching, teaching, HIV/AIDS and health awareness, environmental awareness, and medical projects, as well as surfing, scuba diving, and ocean adventure projects.

DESTINATIONS: In and around Cape Town, South Africa.

PREREQUISITES: Minimum age 17, average age 20. All nationalities accepted. No specific qualifications or skills needed, but rather general knowledge and an enthusiasm to teach or coach under-privileged children.

DURATION AND TIME OF PLACEMENTS: 3 months or 5 weeks, with weekly extensions if desired.

SELECTION PROCEDURES AND ORIENTATION: Applications accepted on ongoing basis until places are filled. Volunteers receive an induction on arrival in South Africa.

COST: For a 3-month trip the project fee is £2,495, for 5 weeks £1,395, and extensions are £180 per week. The project fee includes all accommodation in volunteer house, food during the week, transport including airport transfers, a selection of excursions as well as a donation in the form of resources to partner community schools.

CONTACT: Jonathan Rademeyer, Marketing.

GAP YEAR THAILAND
1 Vernon Avenue, Rugby CV22 5HL
☎ (0)1788 552 617
☎ (0)7899 887 276 (mobile)
✆ david@gapyearthailand.org.uk
🖥 www.gapyearthailand.org.uk

Professional education organisation whose key team members have a background in teacher education in universities in UK or in the Rajabhat Universities (teacher training universities) in Thailand. The programme is approved and endorsed by the South East Asian Ministers of Education Organisation.

PROGRAMME DESCRIPTION: Gap Year Thailand specialises only in Thailand, providing placements for volunteers as assistant teachers, teaching English (particularly conversational English) in schools or universities.

NUMBER OF PLACEMENTS PER YEAR: 20+.

DESTINATIONS: Thailand.

PREREQUISITES: Minimum age 18, average age early 20s. Must speak English as a first language. Teaching qualification not needed.

DURATION AND TIME OF PLACEMENTS: Minimum 2 months, up to 6+ months.

SELECTION PROCEDURES AND ORIENTATION: Applications accepted throughout the year. Telephone interviews. Pre-departure briefing weekend with some TEFL training, and further training in the orientation programme on arrival.

COST: £980 including accommodation, which can be homestay with family or in a teacher's house.

CONTACT: Dr David Lancaster, Chief Executive.

GLOBAL NOMADIC
84 Finchley Lane, Hendon, London NW4 1DH
☎ (0)20 7193 2652
✆ jeremy@globalnomadic.com
✆ info@globalnomadic.com
🖥 www.globalnomadic.com

Global Nomadic is a company and website which promotes volunteer placements and internships from around the world.

PROGRAMME DESCRIPTION: Global Nomadic works with reputable and proven project providers and its representatives have personally visited the vast majority of the projects. Placements available in many fields, including environmental conservation, media and journalism, human rights and law, economic development, and NGO management; veterinary and medical internships are also available, as well as paid teaching jobs in China and Thailand.

DESTINATIONS: Worldwide – from media internships in Mongolia to marketing on an organic farm in Mexico.

DURATION AND TIME OF PLACEMENTS: Rolling admissions, with summer as the busiest time. Placements last 2 weeks to 6 months.

PREREQUISITES: Ages 18–70. Internships are ideally suited to graduates at the beginning of their careers, though there are some possibilities for school leavers. All nationalities accepted, provided they can obtain the relevant visa. All placements require strong enthusiasm and initiative; some ask that you be studying the relevant subject, or already have a strong interest in the field.

SELECTION PROCEDURES AND ORIENTATION: Applications should be sent 3 months in advance, especially for summer placements. Some placements require a Skype or telephone interview (arranged by email). Clients are put directly in touch with the project co-ordinator. Full pre-departure support, ongoing email assistance, and a range of discounts on flights and insurance with partner agencies. Some placements offer a full orientation programme on arrival; others will simply throw you in at the deep end.

COST: No commission is added to the placement cost, only a flat placement fee of £195 ($325) to cover promotional and service costs. Fees paid directly to the project vary, ranging from subsistence costs to £750 per month inclusive.

CONTACT: Jeremy Freedman, Director.

GLOBAL VISION INTERNATIONAL (GVI)
UK Office: Third Floor, The Senate, Exeter
EX1 1UG
☎ (0)1727 250 250
✆ info@gvi.co.uk
🖥 www.gvi.co.uk
North American office: 66 Long Wharf, Suite
562 S, Boston, MA 02110
☎ +1 888 653 6028
🖥 www.gviusa.com
Australian office: Suite 206, 530 Little Collins
Street, Melbourne, VIC 3000
☎ +61 1300 795013
🖥 www.gviaustralia.com

See website for GVI's choice of top 10 gap year programmes.

PROGRAMME DESCRIPTION: GVI offer 150+ projects in over 40 countries worldwide on conservation and community expeditions, volunteer projects and internships (see entry in 'Directory of Work Experience') throughout Africa, Latin America, Europe, and Asia.

DESTINATIONS: Mexico, Costa Rica, Guatemala, Honduras, Nicaragua, Panama, Belize, Ecuador, Brazil, Peru, Nepal, India, Sri Lanka, Thailand, South Africa, Kenya, Namibia, Ghana, Uganda, Seychelles, Tanzania, Madagascar, Indonesia, Borneo, and Vanuatu.

NUMBER OF PLACEMENTS PER YEAR: 1,000.

PREREQUISITES: Minimum age 18. All nationalities welcome. No special training or qualifications are required as all training will be provided in the field.

DURATION AND TIME OF PLACEMENTS: 1 week to 2 years.

SELECTION PROCEDURES AND ORIENTATION: Online application plus application assessment.

COST: From £475 for some short-term projects in Latin America to £3,995 for a year-long internship in South Africa. Price for marine conservation expedition in the Seychelles starts at £1,745 for 5 weeks, including scuba diving equipment, training, and accommodation.

GLOBAL VOLUNTEER PROJECTS
7–15 Pink Lane, Newcastle upon Tyne NE1 5DW
☎ (0)191 222 0404
✆ info@globalvolunteerprojects.org
🖥 www.globalvolunteerprojects.org

PROGRAMME DESCRIPTION: Global Medical Projects (www.globalmedicalprojects.org) specialises in work experience projects for people hoping to go into medicine, or allied subjects such as physiotherapy, dentistry, and nursing. Global Medical Projects (www.globalmediaprojects.org) is for people looking for work experience in journalism. Opportunities also available to help with teaching, conservation, and orphanage work for those keen to get involved with local communities. Most programmes include basic language courses as well as 'culture' courses, such as drumming in Ghana, yoga in India, or learning Swahili in Tanzania.

DESTINATIONS: Ghana, Tanzania, China, India, Cambodia, Mexico, and Romania.

NUMBER OF PLACEMENTS: 100–200.

PREREQUISITES: Minimum age 17 (with parental consent), but most are 18/19 or older.

DURATION AND TIME OF PLACEMENTS: 2 weeks to 1 year. Most join for 1 month (summer) or 3 months. Projects available throughout the year.

SELECTION PROCEDURES AND ORIENTATION: Applications must be submitted at least 4 weeks prior to departure. References must be provided and CRB checks are compulsory for projects involving work with children. Journalism projects include time on a media course (unless you have a background in media or a media-related degree), and some of the medical projects include time in lectures at a medical college. Participants require visas for nearly all programmes; visa support given.

COST: £995–£1,795 for 1-month projects.

CONTACT: Kevin Dynan, Founder and Director.

GO GAP SPORT
Cabarete, Dominican Republic
☎ +1 809 571 0562
✆ info@gogapsport.com
🖥 http://gogapsport.com

PROGRAMME DESCRIPTION: Spanish language course combined with surfing, kitesurfing, and other activities.

NUMBER OF PLACEMENTS PER YEAR: 20–50.

DESTINATIONS: Dominican Republic.

PREREQUISITES: Minimum age 17, average age 17–20. No experience needed.

DURATION AND TIME OF PLACEMENTS: 2 to 6+ weeks.

COST: From £920 for 2 weeks to £2,617 for 6 weeks. Accommodation is in purpose-built camp offering single, double, or dorm beds in secure environment. Camp has pool, air-conditioning on request and pool table. All meals are included.

CONTACT: Clare Barnaby-Smith, Co-owner.

THE GREAT PROJECTS
Studio Six, 8 High St, Harpenden, Hertfordshire AL5 2TB
☎ (0)845 3713070 (UK)
☎ (0)1582 469 950
✆ volunteer@w-o-x.com
💻 www.thegreatprojects.com

Trading name of Way Out Experiences Ltd. Formerly the Great Orangutan Project, but now expanded to other species. Highly commended in the 2010 Virgin Responsible Tourism Awards in category Best Volunteer Organisations.

PROGRAMME DESCRIPTION: Company aims to provide privileged access to wildlife (orang-utans, baboons, dolphins, etc) on hand-picked conservation projects in selected countries.

DESTINATIONS: Borneo, Uganda, Peru, and India.

DURATION AND TIME OF PLACEMENTS: 2 or 4 weeks.

PREREQUISITES: All welcome.

SELECTION PROCEDURES AND ORIENTATION: Trips are escorted by at least one tour leader or facilitator, so orientation and training in handling and rehabilitating the species takes place on-site.

COST: £995–£1,250 for 2 weeks, £1,850–£2,000 for 4 weeks, including everything except flights. 25%–40% of this fee goes as a contribution to the project.

CONTACT: Afzaal Mauthoor, Managing Director.

HIMALAYAN GAP
1103 Radiant Lane, San Ramon, CA 94583, USA
☎ +1 925 230 2070
✆ info@himalayangap.com
💻 www.himalayangap.com

PROGRAMME DESCRIPTION: 5- or 10-week programmes that combine classes in yoga, Indian classical music, pottery and art, alongside a Hindi language course and community service opportunities with local NGOs. See entry in 'Directory of Miscellaneous Courses'.

ICS (INTERNATIONAL CITIZEN SERVICE)
27a Carlton Drive, London SW15 2BS
☎ (0)20 8780 7400
✆ enquiry@ics-uk.org.uk
💻 www.dfid.gov.uk/ics

ICS is a UK government-funded global volunteering experience which gives young participants the opportunity to make a real difference to some of the world's poorest people. ICS volunteers live and work with other youth volunteers in a developing country for up to three months. Placements are available through 6 specialist volunteering development agencies: International Service, Progressio, Restless Development, Skillshare International, Tropical Health & Education Trust (THET), and VSO.

PROGRAMME DESCRIPTION: ICS volunteers work in groups on community projects run by local organisations, in some placements working alongside other local volunteers. Accommodation is in rented premises or in a homestay with local families.

NUMBER OF PLACEMENTS PER YEAR: ICS is aiming to send 1,250 volunteers during its pilot year (2011–12).

DURATION AND TIME OF PLACEMENTS: Minimum 10 weeks; most placements last 12 weeks. Dates vary according to project and agency.

PREREQUISITES: Ages 18–22. Applicants must be either a UK citizen with a current UK address, an EEA citizen currently residing in the UK, or have indefinite leave to remain in the UK. They must also at minimum have a good grasp of conversational English. Volunteers will be selected against broad competencies and aptitudes such as the ability to work with others, flexibility and adaptability, and demonstration of positive, realistic commitment to the programme. They should be prepared for basic living conditions in a developing country.

SELECTION PROCEDURES AND ORIENTATION: The first step is to choose the programme/agency that best suits. The application and selection process is the same for each agency to ensure everyone gets an equal opportunity to participate. Once the application form is submitted, a decision will be made within about 10 days. If you are successful at this stage, you'll be invited to an assessment day after which you'll receive confirmation of whether you've been selected for the programme. Interviews along with other activities are essential elements of the assessment day format. All volunteers will be provided with pre-departure training and in-country orientation. When you return to the UK, you'll look at what you have learnt from your time overseas and have further training to help you make the most of your experiences.

COST: All ICS placements are funded by the government, but volunteers will be asked to make a contribution to the costs of participation based on their household income. It is hoped that these contributions can be met through fundraising activities before departure, with guidance from the volunteering agency. Candidates from a household earning less than £25,000 per year pay nothing. Otherwise the contribution is £1,000 if household income is £25,000–£40,000, or £2,000 from households earning over £40,000.

CONTACT: International Service – www.international service.org.uk; (0)1904 647 799; Progressio – www.progressio.org.uk/empower; (0)20 7354 0883; Restless Development – www.restlessdevelopment.org/volunteer; (0)20 7976 8070; Skillshare International – www.skillshare.org; (0)116 254 1862; THET – www.thet.org/ICS; (0)20 7290 3892; VSO – www.globalxchange.org.uk; (0)20 8780 7500.

ICYE-UK: INTER-CULTURAL YOUTH EXCHANGE UK
Latin American House, Kingsgate Place,
London NW6 4TA
☎ (0)20 7681 0983
✆ info@icye.org.uk
🖳 www.icye.org.uk

Non-profit-making charity offering both long-term (6 or 12 months) and short-term (3–16 weeks) volunteering opportunities in many countries (see 'Directory of Volunteering Abroad').

IMPACT TRAVEL
The Beeches, Grammar School Lane, Kirkham,
Preston PR4 2DJ
☎ (0)1772 672 098
✆ info@impacttravel.co.uk
🖳 www.impacttravel.co.uk

Impact Travel believes in socially responsible travel, and that communities where a meaningful relationship has been developed with local schools should be given ongoing support.

PROGRAMME DESCRIPTION: A selected few gap year-style volunteer projects in India and Nepal, such as working in needy schools and orphanages. Also offer short escorted trips including participation for a week in a community volunteer project.

DESTINATIONS: India and Nepal.

DURATION AND TIME OF PLACEMENTS: 1 week to 1 year for volunteering, but most are no more than 1 month.

PREREQUISITES: No age or nationality restrictions.

SELECTION PROCEDURES AND ORIENTATION: Discussions arranged to suit the volunteers. Cultural awareness training and specific advice on teaching preparation is available so that volunteer teachers are ready to face their classrooms.

COST: From £200 for one week (project only) to £800 for one-month placements with accommodation. Escorted flagship tours costing £2,000 include extensive travel itinerary, quality accommodation (with homestay options), transport, and an insight into the communities visited.

CONTACT: Jeremy Mannino, Company Partner.

INSPIRE VOLUNTEERING
Futuresense Ltd, Town Hall, Market Place,
Newbury RG14 5AA
☎ (0)800 323 350
✆ info@inspirevolunteer.co.uk
🖳 www.inspirevolunteer.co.uk

Inspire provides ethical and sustainable volunteer opportunities overseas. Volunteers' skills and aspirations are matched to projects in genuine need, ensuring that volunteers maximise their impact and experience.

PROGRAMME DESCRIPTION: Inspire volunteer programmes support underprivileged communities by deploying volunteer resources where the need is greatest. Volunteers are profiled and matched to specific projects, where they support teaching, childcare, healthcare, livelihood support, community work, and conservation. Volunteers work closely with local communities, NGOs, and charities to achieve the long-term development goals of UK registered charity, the FutureSense Foundation.

DESTINATIONS: India, Tanzania, Nepal, Sri Lanka, Romania, South Africa, Ecuador, Chile, and the Gambia.

NUMBER OF PLACEMENTS PER YEAR: Approximately 200.

PREREQUISITES: Volunteers must be aged 18 or over. All nationalities accepted. Business experience necessary for business development programmes. Relevant experience useful for other programmes but not essential. Volunteers must have enthusiasm, flexibility and good communication skills.

DURATION AND TIME OF PLACEMENTS: Programmes last from 2 weeks to 6 months with flexible start dates all year round.

SELECTION PROCEDURES AND ORIENTATION: Application can be made online or by phone, with acceptance subject to an informal interview and receipt of references. Volunteers are provided with pre-departure briefing and given local orientation by our in-country teams on arrival.

OTHER SERVICES: Inspire offers specialised travel programmes in India, Nepal, and Tanzania. Trips include treks, safaris, and cultural tours, and are fully guided.

COST: Costs vary depending on location but start from £795 for a 1-month placement. All accommodation and some meals are included.

CONTACT: Katie Guy, Volunteer Co-ordinator.

INTERNATIONAL ACADEMY
Sophia House, 28 Cathedral Road, Cardiff
CF11 9LJ
☎ (0)29 2066 0200
✉ info@international-academy.com
🖥 www.international-academy.com

Member of the Year Out Group. Instructor training in skiing and snowboarding to help people on a gap year or career break, or others, become qualified as instructors. See 'Directory of Sport and Activity Courses'.

INTERN OPTIONS
159–161 Temple Chambers, 3–7 Temple
Avenue, London EC4Y 0DA
☎ (0)20 7353 7699
✉ info@internoptions.com
🖥 www.internoptions.com

PROGRAMME DESCRIPTION: Unpaid internships in many industries, especially hospitality, horticulture, and travel, in Australia and New Zealand (see entry in 'Directory of Work Experience').

IST PLUS LTD
Churchlam House, 1 Bridgeman Road,
Teddington, Middlesex TW 11 9AJ
☎ (0)20 7788 7877
✉ info@istplus.com
🖥 www.istplus.com

PROGRAMME DESCRIPTION: Work and teaching abroad programmes for UK students, graduates, and young professionals. Programmes include Work & Travel USA, Internship USA, Summer Camps USA, Work & Travel Australia, Work & Travel New Zealand, Teach in China, and Teach in Thailand. IST Plus also offers a Volunteer Programme, helping disadvantaged children in Thailand.

DESTINATIONS: China, Thailand, USA, Australia, and New Zealand.

NUMBER OF PLACEMENTS PER YEAR: Unlimited.

COST: Australia £320; New Zealand £195; Asian teaching programmes £995–£1,095; Professional Career Training (PCT) in the USA starts at £740, excluding travel. Volunteer Thailand programme from £325.

i-TO-i VOLUNTEER & ADVENTURE TRAVEL
Woodside House, 261 Low Lane, Horsforth,
Leeds LS18 5NY
☎ (0)113 205 0076
✉ info@i-to-i.com
🖥 www.i-to-i.com

Founding member of the Year Out Group, i-to-i is a commercial company now owned by giant tour operator TUI Travel PLC.

PROGRAMME DESCRIPTION: i-to-i is partnered with 500 volunteer projects in 23 countries, involving teaching, conservation, community work, building, sports, and humanitarian tours. Online and classroom TEFL training and paid jobs abroad as well.

DESTINATIONS: Argentina, Brazil, Cambodia, China, Costa Rica, Ecuador, Honduras, India, Indonesia, Kenya, Malaysia, Nepal, Peru, Philippines, South Africa, Sri Lanka, Tanzania, Thailand, Uganda, Vietnam, and Zambia. Community teaching and conservation projects take place in most countries, while more career-focused programmes including marketing, media, and tourism are available in selected countries.

NUMBER OF PLACEMENTS PER YEAR: 5,000.

PREREQUISITES: Most projects require no experience or qualifications, although some skills development placements (eg media) require a CV. Teaching programmes include an i-to-i TEFL training course prior to arrival in-country.

DURATION AND TIME OF PLACEMENTS: Volunteer placements are from 1 week to a full year, starting year-round.

SELECTION PROCEDURES AND ORIENTATION: Volunteer placements include full pre-departure support but there is no formal selection process. i-to-i provides full project information packs and in-country orientation plus accommodation and meals. All teaching placements include a free i-to-i online TEFL course. (www.onlinetefl. com); price from £129.

COST: Sample costs £799 for 4 weeks working with underprivileged families in Goa, India, and £1,799 for 12 weeks working with disadvantaged children in South Africa (excluding airfares).

IVHQ (INTERNATIONAL VOLUNTEER HQ)
PO Box 8273, New Plymouth, New Zealand
☎ +64 6 758 7949
✉ volunteer@volunteerhq.org
🖥 www.volunteerhq.org

PROGRAMME DESCRIPTION: Affordable volunteering placements in developing countries all over the world. Volunteers work in a variety of jobs such as teaching, medical work, HIV/AIDS awareness, women empowerment, sports education, construction work, conservation work, and orphanage assistance.

NUMBER OF PLACEMENTS PER YEAR: 5,000+.

DESTINATIONS: Volunteer travel opportunities in Kenya (including Maasai district), Tanzania, Ghana, Uganda, and

South Africa; India, Nepal, Vietnam, China, Thailand, and Cambodia; Ecuador, Costa Rica, Peru (Lima and Cusco), Colombia, and Guatemala.

PREREQUISITES: Minimum age 18. All nationalities welcome, provided they can obtain the relevant tourist visa. No specific skills needed apart from medical programmes.

DURATION AND TIME OF PLACEMENTS: 1 week to 6 months. Average stay is 3–4 weeks.

SELECTION PROCEDURES AND ORIENTATION: Applications due at least 1 month before start date, but preferably 2–3 months. Pre-departure information booklet and on-site training and orientation on arrival in host country. Pre-departure programme co-ordinator assigned to each volunteer.

COST: US$220 registration fee, plus programme costs that vary according to duration and destination; eg US$500 for a month in Delhi and US$1,130 for 10 weeks in Ecuador. Accommodation included, mainly homestays or in volunteer dorms.

CONTACT: Daniel Radcliffe, Executive Director.

JAKERA
Playa Colorada & Merida, Venezuela
☎ (0)7803 043 475
✍ info@jakera.com
🖥 www.jakera.com
🖥 www.learn-spanish-in-latin-america.com

PROGRAMME DESCRIPTION: Adventure Travelling Classroom programme in Venezuela for 3 or 6 months that blends learning Spanish with travel and many outdoor activities such as scuba diving, hiking, and sea kayaking. Programmes include choice of community volunteering or work experience in combination with intensive Spanish (see entry in 'Directories of Courses').

JAPAN EXCHANGE & TEACHING(JET) PROGRAMME
JET Desk, c/o Embassy of Japan, 101–104 Piccadilly, London W1J 7JT
☎ (0)20 7465 6668
✍ info@jet-uk.org
🖥 www.jet-uk.org

PROGRAMME DESCRIPTION: The JET Programme is a Japanese government-run scheme to promote international understanding and improve foreign language tuition. UK graduates have the opportunity of working in Japan for a minimum of 1 year.

DESTINATIONS: Throughout Japan.

NUMBER OF PLACEMENTS PER YEAR: Around 200 places are offered to UK candidates; however, the number varies each year.

PREREQUISITES: Must have a first degree in any subject. Neither teaching qualifications nor Japanese language ability is needed for the Assistant Language Teacher (ALT) positions; however the Co-ordinator for International Relations (CIR) role does require Japanese language ability sufficient for everyday working situations. Detailed eligibility criteria can be found at www.jet-uk.org/eligibility/eligcri.html.

DURATION AND TIME OF PLACEMENTS: 1-year contracts begin in late July.

SELECTION PROCEDURES AND ORIENTATION: The application deadline is usually the last Friday in November. Orientations are given at the start of July in London, and in Tokyo upon arrival in Japan.

COST: None. There is no application fee and return airfares are provided to those who complete their contract. Salary of 3,600,000 yen is paid.

JOHN HALL VENICE COURSE
9 Smeaton Road, London SW18 5JJ
✍ info@johnhallvenice.com
🖥 www.johnhallvenice.co.uk

Annual pre-university course (late January to March) mainly held in Venice, which covers art, art history, architecture, music, opera, literature, global ecological and political issues, history, and world cinema. Cost for initial week in London plus 6 weeks in Venice is £8,970, with optional extensions in Florence and Rome. See 'Directory of Courses'.

THE KAREN HILLTRIBES TRUST
88A Main Street, Fulford, York YO10 4PS
☎ (0)1904 612 829
✍ admin@karenhilltribes.org.uk
🖥 www.karenhilltribes.org.uk

PROGRAMME DESCRIPTION: Volunteer placements for teaching at primary and secondary level (all year round). Also installing water systems (in summer) in northern Thailand. Volunteers live with host families, often the village headman.

DESTINATIONS: Upland and hill communities of north-west Thailand.

NUMBER OF PLACEMENTS PER YEAR: About 20, but only a few at any one time. Volunteers are usually placed in pairs in different villages.

PREREQUISITES: Gap year students welcome. Candidates should be team players, with maturity, and a genuine interest in helping the Karen hill tribe people. No TEFL qualification required. Village life can be primitive, with most families living in wooden houses on stilts. Volunteers are encouraged to get involved at all levels.

DURATION AND TIME OF PLACEMENTS: 2 or 5 months, or longer for teaching, starting October or January. Water system programme requires volunteers for 3 weeks in July or August.

SELECTION PROCEDURES AND ORIENTATION: Interviews held in York or London or by phone if necessary. Pre-departure briefings, meetings with past volunteers, training weekend, and continuing support given. Paid manager in Thailand.

COST: £1,000 (3 months), £1,750 (6 months) for teaching, £500 for water systems. Part of these costs is set against the cost of the project. Advice given on fundraising and sponsorship (also on website).

CONTACT: Penelope Worsley, Director.

KAYA RESPONSIBLE TRAVEL
Technology House, Lissadel Street, Salford, Manchester M6 6AP
☎ (0)161 870 6212
✆ info@kayavolunteer.com
🖥 www.kayavolunteer.com

Responsible travel organisation supporting grassroots voluntary projects worldwide, and giving volunteers an opportunity to contribute to positive action and enjoy travelling the world more responsibly.

PROGRAMME DESCRIPTION: Volunteers are placed in local projects in the fields of environmental conservation and community development, in Asia, Africa, and Latin America. Work experience can be combined with travel, and chance to live and work alongside the community.

DESTINATIONS: Belize, Bolivia, Costa Rica, Brazil, Ecuador, Peru, Mexico; Ghana, Tanzania, Zambia, Kenya, Zimbabwe, South Africa, Mozambique, Botswana; India, Nepal, Thailand, Vietnam, and the Philippines.

NUMBER OF PLACEMENTS PER YEAR: 500 in 2011.

DURATION AND TIME OF PLACEMENTS: 2 weeks to 6 or 12 months.

PREREQUISITES: Volunteers are aged 18–80; average age around 33. All level of skills accepted. Anyone with enthusiasm, passion, openness, and a willingness to work hard can contribute to some of the world's neediest communities. Volunteers with specific skills such

as medical, teaching, business, and construction are matched with appropriate placements.

SELECTION PROCEDURES AND ORIENTATION: Rolling applications throughout the year. Bookings preferred 3 months in advance, though last-minute placements are also possible. Business visas needed for some projects, with which Kaya assists. CRB check is required in some cases. Pre-departure training packs are given and all volunteers are picked up at the destination airport and taken to their homestay or volunteer accommodation.

COST: Fees vary from project to project and country to country, but start from £625 for 2 weeks, with an additional fee of £175 per week after that. Discounts can be negotiated for stays of longer than 13 weeks, and for multiple projects and/or locations.

CONTACT: Nicci Hawkins, Placement Adviser.

LANGUAGE COURSES ABROAD LTD
67–71 Ashby Road, Loughborough, Leicestershire LE11 3AA
☎ (0)1509 211 612
✆ info@languagesabroad.co.uk
🖥 www.languagesabroad.co.uk

Language Courses Abroad Ltd is a UK-based language travel agency, offering in-country full immersion language courses at more than 100 schools. Trading name is Apple Languages (www.applelanguages.com).

PROGRAMME DESCRIPTION: In-country language courses in Spanish, French, German, Italian, Portuguese, Russian, Chinese, Japanese, Greek, and others (see entry in 'Directory of Language Courses'), often in conjunction with work experience placements; available in Spain, Latin America, France, Germany, and Italy (see entry in 'Directory of Work Experience Abroad').

CONTACT: Scott Cather, Language Travel Adviser.

LATTITUDE GLOBAL VOLUNTEERING
42 Queen's Road, Reading, RG1 4BB. *Offices also in Canada, New Zealand and Australia*
☎ (0)118 959 4914
✆ volunteer@lattitude.org.uk
🖥 www.lattitude.org.uk

Registered charity specialising in international volunteering, with nearly 40 years' experience. Previously named GAP Activity Projects, it was a founding member of the Year Out Group.

PROGRAMME DESCRIPTION: Voluntary work placements in teaching, caring, environmental, outdoor activity, medical, and community projects. All placements are designed to make a difference in the world and to stretch the capabilities of volunteers.

DESTINATIONS: 17 countries worldwide from Canada to Malawi.

NUMBER OF PLACEMENTS PER YEAR: 2,000+.

PREREQUISITES: Age between 17 and 25.

DURATION AND TIME OF PLACEMENTS: 4–12 months (average 6 months).

SELECTION PROCEDURES AND ORIENTATION: Volunteers can apply at any time online. After an application is received, an interview will be held, after which the applicant will hear if they have been offered a place. There is a group briefing which all volunteers are encouraged to attend and a full orientation programme in-country on arrival. Any necessary courses such as teaching skills or language training must be attended before beginning the placement, either before departure or in-country.

COST: Volunteers pay a fee ranging from £1,750 to £2,300, depending on the programme. The fee includes pre-departure administrative support, briefing, orientation in-country, and 24-hour emergency helpline.

THE LEAP OVERSEAS LTD
121 High Street, Marlborough, Wiltshire
SN8 1LZ
☎ (0)1672 519 922
☎ (0)870 240 4187
info@theleap.co.uk
www.theleap.co.uk

Member of the Year Out Group.

PROGRAMME DESCRIPTION: Volunteering program-mes that combine projects in safari/eco-tourism, com-munity, and conservation, located off the tourist trail. For example, in Kenya volunteers can escort guests on safari, track elephants in the bush, and teach football or English to local kids.

DESTINATIONS: Placements are based in game parks, jungle, and coastal locations in Africa (Kenya, South Africa, Mozambique, Tanzania, and Zambia), South America (Guyana, Costa Rica, Argentina, and Ecuador), Asia (Cambodia, and India), and Australia.

PREREQUISITES: Minimum age 18 (majority are school leavers aged 18–20). Must be committed, enthusiastic, and motivated, able to work well in a team and prepared to get stuck in.

NUMBER OF PLACEMENTS PER YEAR: Around 300.

DURATION AND TIME OF PLACEMENTS: Departures in January, April, July, and September for 6 or 10 weeks.

SELECTION PROCEDURES AND ORIENTATION: Volunteers attend briefing/training course in the UK and receive an induction course on arrival in the country.

OTHER SERVICES: Flights can be arranged through ATOL partner agency STA Travel. Time given for adventure travel, eg white-water rafting, kitesurfing, and scuba diving.

COST: From £1,700 for 6 weeks; solo placements lasting up to 3 months cost £2,400 including accom-modation, food, transport, and back-up, excluding travel, visas, and insurance.

CONTACT: Guy Whitehead, Director.

LEARN OVERSEAS
47 Greenheys Centre, Pencroft Way, Manchester
Science Park, Manchester M15 6JJ
☎ (0)161 226 5300
☎ (0)790 304 0567
office@learnoverseas.co.uk
www.learnoverseas.co.uk

PROGRAMME DESCRIPTION: Gap year and career break work experience placements in India. Specialists in placements for students applying for medicine and related fields, or wanting to complete research projects. Mixture of hands-on, observation, and work-shadowing experience in Delhi.

DESTINATIONS: Delhi, India.

PREREQUISITES: Age 17+.

DURATION AND TIME OF PLACEMENTS: From 2 weeks to 4 months throughout the year.

COST: Typical 2-week placement costs £995, 16 weeks costs £2,995, including transport within the country, full board and lodging and weekend breaks, but excluding airfares and insurance.

MADVENTURER
The Old Smithy, Corbridge, Northumberland
NE45 5QD
☎ (0)845 121 1996
team@madventurer.com
www.madventurer.com

Member of the Year Out Group. Madventurer combines development projects and adventurous overland travel for all ages.

PROGRAMME DESCRIPTION: Expeditions that give gap year students and others the opportunity to undertake a range of voluntary work for a grassroots community or environmental project (building, teaching, sports instruction, healthcare, or orphanage) with the option then to travel on an overland adventure (trekking, rafting, touring). Placements can sometimes be arranged to complement area of academic study.

DESTINATIONS: Ghana, Tanzania, Uganda, Kenya, South Africa, Peru, India, Vietnam, Thailand, and Fiji.

PREREQUISITES: Minimum age 17. No experience is necessary to make a difference.

DURATION AND TIME OF PLACEMENTS: 2, 4, 6, 8, 10, 12, or 14 weeks, or longer.

SELECTION PROCEDURES AND ORIENTATION: Full-time crew supports venturers both before departure and overseas on project sites. Thorough pre-departure information, advice, support, and fundraising pack provided.

COST: Sample prices for 6-week trips: £1,245 in Asia, £1,345 in Africa and Peru, £1,445 for Fiji (not including flights).

CONTACT: Elaine Lawler, Office Manager (elainel@madventurer.com) or John Lawler, Chief of Operations (chief@madventurer.com).

MONDOCHALLENGE
Town Hall, Market Place, Newbury, Berkshire RG14 5AA
☎ (0)1635 45556
✎ info@mondochallenge.co.uk
🖥 www.mondochallenge.co.uk

PROGRAMME DESCRIPTION: MondoChallenge works closely with overseas NGOs and charities to provide career break volunteer opportunities in some of the poorest regions of the world. Volunteer programmes are community-based, and include teaching, livelihood support, childcare, healthcare, and development work. Volunteers live and work within local communities, giving them the chance to immerse themselves in a new culture, while using their skills to help others.

DESTINATIONS: India, Tanzania, Nepal, Sri Lanka, Romania, South Africa, Ecuador, Chile, and the Gambia.

NUMBER OF PLACEMENTS PER YEAR: Around 200.

PREREQUISITES: Volunteers must be aged 18 or over. All nationalities accepted. Business experience is required for business development projects. Other experience useful but optional. Volunteers must have enthusiasm, flexibility and good communication skills.

DURATION AND TIME OF PLACEMENTS: Programmes last from 2 weeks to 6 months, with flexible start dates all year round.

SELECTION PROCEDURES AND ORIENTATION: Application can be made online or by phone, with acceptance subject to an informal interview and receipt of references. Volunteers are provided with pre-departure briefing and given local orientation by our in-country teams on arrival.

OTHER SERVICES: MondoChallenge offers specialised travel programmes in India, Nepal, and Tanzania. Trips include treks, safaris, and cultural tours, and are fully guided.

COST: Costs vary depending on location and project type, but start from £545 for a 2-week placement. All accommodation and some meals are included.

CONTACT: Prakriti Malhotra.

NEXT STEP CONNECTIONS
Suite 17A, King World, Hi-Teach West Tower, 668 Beijing East Road, Huang Pu District 2000001 Shanghai, China
☎ +86 21 6322 5990
✎ contact@nextstepconnections.com
🖥 www.nextstepconnections.com

PROGRAMME DESCRIPTION: Professional internship programme offering year-round work placements in Shanghai, Beijing, Hong Kong and Mumbai. Placements may be found in many fields such as architecture, art, design, finance, IT, engineering, journalism, law, medicine, pharmaceuticals, advertising, marketing, and public relations. Links with big companies such as McCann Group, Publicis, CIBA, *China Daily*, *Shanghai Business Review*, Wieden & Kennedy, and more.

NUMBER OF PLACEMENTS PER YEAR: 100.

DESTINATIONS: China, Hong Kong, and India.

PREREQUISITES: Ages 18–35. Must be fluent in English, have motivation, good-quality CV, and interest in professional, career-geared programme.

DURATION AND TIME OF PLACEMENTS: 1–6 months. Participants choose their start date, length of stay, and field of placement.

SELECTION PROCEDURES AND ORIENTATION: Online application at least 2 months (preferably 3) before proposed arrival. 3 hours per week of Chinese lessons are part of programme. Monthly career and professional meeting with an executive recruiter at Next Step Connections office to carry out programme monitoring and overview. Each meeting tackles a different topic, and provides a better insight into the Asian job market and how to improve a CV.

REMUNERATION: None.

COST: £1,750 for 1 month, £5,650 for 6 months, including internship placement, housing, insurance, airport transfers, and back-up.

CONTACT: Jerome Le Carrou. Director.

NONSTOP ADVENTURE, NONSTOP SKI & SNOWBOARD
Unit 3B, The Plough Brewery, 516 Wandsworth Road, London SW8 3JX
☎ (0)845 365 1525
info@nonstopadventure.com
www.nonstopadventure.com
www.nonstopski.com
www.nonstopsnowboard.com

Member of the Year Out Group.

PROGRAMME DESCRIPTION: Ski and snowboard improvement and instructor courses in the Canadian Rockies, New Zealand, and French Alps. Also Surf Instructor course in Morocco, and mountain bike courses in British Columbia (Canada). (See entries in 'Directory of Sport and Activity Courses'.)

CONTACT: Adam Hillier, Course Adviser.

OPERATION WALLACEA
Wallace House, Old Bolingbroke, Near Spilsby, Lincolnshire PE23 4EX
☎ (0)1790 763 194
info@opwall.com
www.opwall.com

PROGRAMME DESCRIPTION: Marine and rainforest scientific research projects in Indonesia (South-east Sulawesi), Honduras, Guyana, Mexico, and Madagascar; desert and marine projects in Egypt; conservation in Peruvian Amazon; bush and marine projects in South Africa and Mozambique; and turtle and manatee monitoring and marine projects in Cuba. Projects aim to carry out large scale biodiversity monitoring in all areas to build a picture of threats both human and environmental to then create a management plan for area protection. Operation Wallacea projects lead to sustainable conservation and enable local people to protect their own environment from destructive practices.

DESTINATIONS: Honduras, Indonesia, Egypt, Cuba, South Africa, Peru, Mozambique, Madagascar, and Guyana.

PREREQUISITES: Minimum age 18. Enthusiasm needed. Volunteers from all walks of life and ages assist with surveys of marine, desert, bush, and rainforest habitats.

DURATION AND TIME OF PLACEMENTS: 2, 4, 6, or 8 weeks between June and September.

SELECTION PROCEDURES AND ORIENTATION: No deadlines. Dive training to PADI OW training given on-site (reef ecology, jungle training, bushcraft, etc) are included in the cost of the expedition.

COST: £975 for 2 weeks, £1,850 for 4 weeks, £2,500 for 6 weeks, and £2,950 for 8 weeks, excluding flights.

CONTACT: Pippa Disney.

ORANGUTAN FOUNDATION
7 Kent Terrace, London NW1 4RP
☎ (0)20 7724 2912
info@orangutan.org.uk
www.orangutan.org.uk

PROGRAMME DESCRIPTION: Volunteers are based in Central or West Kalimantan, Indonesian Borneo – the Foundation's current release site for ex-captive and rehabilitated orang-utans. Volunteers will get to spend time at Camp Leakey, the historical research site of Dr Biruté Galdikas, and may also work in other areas of the national park. Previous projects have included: general infrastructure repairs, trail cutting, constructing guard posts, and orang-utan release sites. Volunteers should note that there is no direct work or contact with orang-utans.

DESTINATIONS: Most likely destinations are the Lamandau Reserve near Tanjung Puting National Park in Kalimantan, or the Belantikan Arut region in the north west of Central Kalimantan.

NUMBER OF PLACEMENTS PER YEAR: 36.

DURATION AND TIME OF PLACEMENTS: 6 weeks, with 3 teams of no more than 12 departing April, June, and September.

PREREQUISITES: Participants must be at least 18 and become members of the Orangutan Foundation (£20 per year). They must work well in a team, be fit and healthy, and adaptable to difficult and demanding conditions.

SELECTION PROCEDURES AND ORIENTATION: All potential UK volunteers are expected to attend an interview at the Foundation's office in London or be interviewed by phone.

COST: Approximately £775; includes accommodation, food, equipment, materials, and transport for the duration of the programme, but does not include international and internal travel to the project site. Prices are confirmed before places are offered, and will depend on inflation and exchange rates.

CONTACT: Cat Gibbons, Development & Volunteer Co-ordinator (cat@orangutan.org.uk).

OUTREACH INTERNATIONAL
Bartletts Farm, Hayes Road, Compton Dundon, Somerset TA11 6PF
☎ (0)1458 274 957
gap@outreachinternational.co.uk
www.outreachinternational.co.uk

Member of the Year Out Group. Outreach International is a specialist organisation with carefully selected projects. There is enough variety to ensure that the interests and skills of individual volunteers can be put to good use.

PROGRAMME DESCRIPTION: Committed volunteers work on many varied projects, including with street children, in orphanages, teaching English, art or sport, doing medical work, conservation, marine biology, or participating in humanitarian aid. The needs of these hand-picked projects are constantly assessed, so volunteers are placed only where genuinely needed and where their skills can be utilised. Placements are ideal for anyone wanting a gap experience, and many are suitable for those considering a career in medicine, humanitarian, social, or environmental work.

DESTINATIONS: Mexico, Costa Rica, Ecuador, Galápagos, Cambodia, and Sri Lanka.

NUMBER OF PLACEMENTS PER YEAR: 100; Outreach International places each volunteer in the most appropriate project.

PREREQUISITES: Most of the projects are ideal for gap year volunteers aged 18–21 and some are ideal for people with some work experience. Ideal for confident young people with a desire to travel, learn a language and offer their help to a worthwhile cause. The projects focus on the most needy sections of the community.

DURATION AND TIME OF PLACEMENTS: 3–6 months. Departure times are January, April, June, and September.

SELECTION PROCEDURES AND ORIENTATION: Applicants will be invited to a meeting within 3 weeks of applying, in which projects can be discussed and an informed choice made about whether to proceed. The director visits each project at regular intervals and is familiar with their specific requirements. Volunteers are given a comprehensive briefing and language training, and are offered a good teacher training course and support with fundraising. Outreach International employs a full-time co-ordinator in all countries, who attends to the welfare of individuals. While the level of support is high, volunteers are encouraged to be autonomous and make their own decisions on their placements.

COST: £2,800 for 3 months, which includes unlimited insurance, visas, local transport, language course, in-country support, airport pick-up, food, accommodation, and all project costs. Additional months are around £500 each. Outreach International rents spacious houses close to the projects and offers volunteers the opportunity of living with a local family. Volunteers can also live together in an Outreach International house but work in pairs on their project.

CONTACT: James Chapman, UK Director.

OYSTER WORLDWIDE
Hodore Farm, Hartfield, East Sussex TN7 4AR
☎ (0)1892 770 771
✆ emailus@oysterworldwide.com
🖥 www.oysterworldwide.com

Member of the Year Out Group. A number of Oyster's projects are now entering their 10th year of receiving participants.

PROGRAMME DESCRIPTION: Volunteering with children and teaching English, helping in orphanages and coaching sports in a range of developing countries, or working at bear sanctuary in Romania. Paid work is available on a farm in the Australian outback, or hospitality work in Sydney, and hotels in the Canadian Rockies and Québec. In each location, Oyster has a representative to provide back-up throughout.

DESTINATIONS: Australia, Brazil, Canada, Chile, India, Nepal, Kenya, Romania, Tanzania, and Zambia.

DURATION AND TIME OF PLACEMENTS: 1 month minimum. Most participants stay at least 3 months, up to 6 months. Group departures are usually in September, January, and May. Other departure times are possible.

SELECTION PROCEDURES AND ORIENTATION: Interview and pre-departure training included, as well as language training and orientation on arrival. Full support throughout. French language classes provided in Mont Tremblant, Canada.

COST: Varies from £1,770 for 1 month in Romania to £3,725 for 4-month Chile placement. Sample prices for Canadian programme: £2,200. All prices include airfares.

CONTACT: Roger Salwey, Director (roger@oysterworldwide.com).

PEAK LEADERS UK
Mansfield, Strathmiglo, Fife KY14 7QE
☎ (0)1337 860 079
✆ info@peakleaders.com
🖥 www.peakleaders.com

Gap year ski and snowboard instructor courses in Canada, Switzerland, Argentina, and New Zealand. Mountain bike instructor courses and performance camps in Canada and Surf Camp in France (see 'Directory of Ski Training Courses' and 'Sport and Activity Courses').

PERSONAL OVERSEAS DEVELOPMENT (POD)
Formal House, 60 St George's Place, Cheltenham, Gloucestershire GL50 3PN
☎ (0)1242 250 901
✆ info@podvolunteer.org
🖥 www.podvolunteer.org

POD is a non-profit organisation arranging ethical and supported volunteering opportunities around the world. POD works with long-term projects known personally and where there is genuine benefit to local communities.

PROGRAMME DESCRIPTION: Volunteers are needed to help work with disadvantaged children, communities, animals, and conservation projects, including: caring for elephants and wild animals; joining an Amazon jungle conservation project; marine conservation; community-building projects; volunteering at orphanages and care homes; teaching English; and running summer English camps.

DESTINATIONS: Belize, Cambodia, Nepal, Peru, South Africa, Tanzania, Thailand and Vietnam.

DURATION AND TIME OF PLACEMENTS: 1 week to 6 months, with flexible start dates throughout the year. Summer mini-gaps are also available for school leavers going straight to university.

PREREQUISITES: No specific requirements for most placements, just a positive attitude.

SELECTION PROCEDURES AND ORIENTATION: Online application. Reference and phone interview may be required. A CRB check may also be conducted. A detailed information pack is sent to volunteers. Pre-departure and local training and introductions are undertaken on arrival in-country.

OTHER SERVICES: These working holidays can be incorporated into existing travel plans.

COST: Volunteer fees start at £375. Sample fees: 2 weeks at an orphanage in Cambodia or elephant care in South Africa for £449–£499. Placements include training, support and accommodation. Sample price for longer placements: one-off fee of £375 for dog and cat care in Thailand, plus from £50 per week living costs, 12 weeks' village teaching in Tanzania for £1,595.

CONTACT: The POD Team, led by Mike Beecham and Alex Tarrant.

PROJECT TRUST
Hebridean Centre, Ballyhough, Isle of Coll, Argyll PA78 6TE
☎ (0)1879 230 444
🖱 info@projecttrust.org.uk
🖥 www.projecttrust.org.uk

Established in 1967. Founding member of the Year Out Group.

PROGRAMME DESCRIPTION: Voluntary placements specifically for gap year travellers throughout the developing world. Volunteers can choose to take part in care work, community development and wildlife projects, educational projects, or outdoor activity projects, or they can act as English language assistants at schools.

DESTINATIONS: Africa (Uganda, Botswana, South Africa, Namibia, Senegal, and Swaziland), South and Central America (Honduras, Chile, Bolivia, Peru, Guyana, and the Dominican Republic), Asia (Thailand, China, India, Japan, Malaysia, Hong Kong, and Cambodia).

NUMBER OF PLACEMENTS PER YEAR: Around 200.

PREREQUISITES: Applicants should be aged between 17 and 19 and be aiming for university.

DURATION AND TIME OF PLACEMENTS: 12 months from August. Limited number of 8-month placements departing in January, for those needing to attend a university interview in the autumn.

SELECTION PROCEDURES AND ORIENTATION: In the period between August and March, candidates attend a 4-day course on the Hebridean Isle of Coll where their skills and interests are assessed. About 80% of those who take the selection course are offered a place within a week of leaving Coll. Training courses are held, also on Coll, during July, to teach skills relevant to the volunteers' work placements as well as country-specific briefings and how to live safely and healthily overseas. Once in the destination country, there is always at least one local representative on hand to help volunteers settle in, and a full-time desk officer based on the Isle of Coll for each country.

COST: Volunteers are required to raise £5,100 (2012/13 cost) for the 12-month programme, which includes the costs of selection, training, supervision, debriefing, airfares, medical insurance, board and lodging, and a living allowance.

PROJECTS ABROAD
Aldsworth Parade, Goring, West Sussex BN12 4TX
☎ (0)1903 708 300
🖱 info@projects-abroad.co.uk
🖥 www.projects-abroad.co.uk

Founding member of the Year Out Group. Company arranges volunteering placements overseas in a range of countries. Also arranges work experience placements in medicine, media, and other fields in selected destinations (see 'Directory of Work Experience Abroad').

DESTINATIONS: Argentina, Bolivia, Cambodia, China, Costa Rica, Ethiopia, Ghana, India, Jamaica, Mexico, Moldova, Mongolia, Morocco, Nepal, Peru, Romania, Russia, Senegal, South Africa, Sri Lanka, Tanzania, and Thailand.

NUMBER OF PLACEMENTS PER YEAR: 4,000.

PREREQUISITES: Minimum age 16. Optional UK briefing and TEFL weekend courses before departure.

DURATION AND TIME OF PLACEMENTS: Very flexible, with departures year-round. Placements last 2 weeks to 12 months.

SELECTION PROCEDURES AND ORIENTATION: Paid staff in all destinations arrange and vet placements, accommodation, and work supervisors. They meet volunteers on arrival and provide a final briefing before the placements.

COST: Placements are self-funded and the fee charged includes insurance, food, accommodation, and overseas support. 3-month placements cost between £1,395 and £2,595, depending on placement, excluding travel costs.

QUEST OVERSEAS
15A Cambridge Grove, Hove, East Sussex
BN3 3ED
☎ (0)1273 777 206
info@questoverseas.com
www.questoverseas.com

A founding member of the Year Out Group, Quest Overseas specialises in combining worthwhile voluntary work projects and challenging expeditions to Africa and South America for volunteers aged 17–24. Since 1996, Quest Overseas participants have raised £1.2 million for their charity and NGO partners.

PROGRAMME DESCRIPTION: 3-month Gap Year programmes in South America and Africa, plus range of shorter projects. Choice of South America programmes includes Spanish or Portuguese language course in Ecuador, Bolivia, or Brazil; 4-week voluntary work projects such as conservation work in the rainforests of Peru, looking after children in shanty towns in Peru or Brazil, or working in Ambue Ari animal rehabilitation project in Bolivia. Final phase is a 6-week expedition covering over 1,000km of Peru, Chile, and Bolivia, including Amazon jungle and Machu Picchu, or throughout Brazil, including surfing, diving, and hang-gliding over Rio. The Gap Year Africa programme is either a voluntary conservation project or a community development project in Tanzania, Kenya, Rwanda, or Malawi, followed by expedition through southern Africa, scuba diving course in Mozambique, etc. Summer trips lasting 4–6 weeks also available in most countries.

DESTINATIONS: Ecuador, Peru, Chile, Bolivia, and Brazil; or Kenya, Tanzania, Mozambique, and Rwanda.

NUMBER OF PLACEMENTS PER YEAR: 10–16 students in each team, and 12 expeditions per year.

PREREQUISITES: Volunteers are typically aged 17–24 and are on gap years or breaks from university.

DURATION AND TIME OF PLACEMENTS: 13-week programmes depart throughout January to April, with summer projects and expeditions departing in July. Flights can be open returns, so stays may be extended.

SELECTION PROCEDURES AND ORIENTATION:
Selection is by phone or personal interview. Preparation and expedition skills weekends are organised prior to departure.

COST: Gap Year South America costs £4,400 (£3,550 without Spanish language course), plus project donation of £700–£850 (2012). Gap Year Africa from £4,150, plus donation of £650–£850. Prices are inclusive of all activities, internal transfers, accommodation, food, and insurance, but do not include flights and personal pocket money for souvenirs and luxuries.

RALEIGH
207 Waterloo Road, London SE1 8XD
☎ (0)20 7183 1270
info@raleigh.org.uk
www.raleighinternational.org

Youth and sustainable development charity; a founding member of the Year Out Group. Raleigh inspires people of all ages, backgrounds and nationalities to take part in challenging environmental, community, and adventure projects around the world.

PROGRAMME DESCRIPTION: Participants aged 17–24 have the option of a 10-week or 5-week expedition. The longer expedition consists of 3 distinct project phases: community, environment, and adventure. With the 5-week expedition, participants choose either a community or environmental project plus a team-based adventure challenge. Sample projects include the building of a primary school in remote areas, providing running water to villages, conserving the world's smallest bear (the sun bear), or trekking through mountainous terrain. Volunteers over 25 can join Raleigh as volunteer managers and must commit to either 8 or 13 weeks.

DESTINATIONS: Costa Rica, Nicaragua, Malaysia (Borneo), and India.

PREREQUISITES: Applicants must be aged between 17 and 24 to join an expedition as a venturer, or 25–75 to join as a volunteer manager.

DURATION AND TIME OF PLACEMENTS: 5- or 10-week programmes run throughout the year, with start dates in spring, summer and autumn.

SELECTION PROCEDURES AND ORIENTATION:
Participants from all backgrounds and nationalities are

welcome. Participants receive training in the UK and on expedition. Volunteer managers are assessed.

COST: Expeditions for participants cost £2,995 for a 10-week programme and £1,750 for a 5-week programme. Prices include food, accommodation, medical insurance, training, and in-country travel, but exclude flights. Some young people may be eligible for a bursary (see website). Volunteer managers fundraise £1,350 for an 8-week expedition or £1,950 for 13 weeks.

REAL GAP EXPERIENCE
1 Meadow Road, Tunbridge Wells,
Kent TN1 2YG
☎ (0)1892 516 164
🖰 info@realgap.co.uk
🖳 www.realgap.co.uk

Leading gap year specialists, offering a comprehensive range of projects in 35 countries. ATOL and ABTA recognised for financial security. Provider of career breaks through www.gapyearforgrownups.co.uk.

PROGRAMME DESCRIPTION: Wide range of volunteer and travel options in 35 countries, including paid work placements, volunteering with wildlife, conservation, teaching, language courses, sports, expeditions, adventure travel, volunteering with children, communities, career breaks, learning new skills, and tailor-made gap years.

DESTINATIONS: 6 continents: Africa – Ghana, Kenya, Uganda, Namibia, Tanzania, South Africa, Zambia, Botswana, Zimbabwe, Mozambique, Swaziland; Australasia – Australia, New Zealand, Fiji; Asia – Thailand, Vietnam, Cambodia, Malaysia, India, Sri Lanka, Nepal, China; South America – Galápagos Islands, Ecuador, Peru, Bolivia, Brazil, Argentina; Central America – Guatemala, Costa Rica; North America – USA, Canada; Europe – Moldova, France.

PREREQUISITES: Most have none. Some programmes have visa requirements, and require basic level of fitness.

DURATION AND TIME OF PLACEMENTS: 2 weeks to 2 years. Programmes available year-round and gap year itineraries can be tailor-made.

COST: Prices from £349, depending on destination and duration.

RESTLESS DEVELOPMENT
7 Tufton Street, London SW1P 3QB
☎ (0)20 7976 8070
🖰 info@restlessdevelopment.org
🖳 www.restlessdevelopment.org

Restless Development, formerly SPW (Students Partnership Worldwide), is a youth-led development agency and non-profit making charity, currently working in Africa and South Asia. Its development model has been cited as a model of best practice by UNICEF, the World Bank, and others.

PROGRAMME DESCRIPTION: Range of tiered International Placements, which means assignments are appropriate to the volunteer's level of experience and skills and the placements provide structured and professional experience in the field of international development. European, American, and Australian volunteers aged 18–28 are recruited to work in partnership with counterpart volunteers from Africa and Asia. In pairs or groups, they live and work in rural communities for 5–9 months. Their input builds awareness and begins to change attitudes and behaviour on important health, social, and environmental issues among young people and communities. All volunteers take part in training which covers health, hygiene, sanitation, nutrition, and the environment, with a particular emphasis on HIV/AIDS prevention and care.

DESTINATIONS: Long-term community development placements in Uganda and Nepal.

NUMBER OF PLACEMENTS PER YEAR: 28 places for European, American, and Australian volunteers.

PREREQUISITES: Volunteers need to be physically and emotionally healthy, hard-working, open-minded, enthusiastic, and have good communication skills.

DURATION AND TIME OF PLACEMENTS: 5–9 months.

SELECTION PROCEDURES AND ORIENTATION: Every applicant is required to attend an information and selection day in London, where they can meet staff and previous volunteers. Applicants are then required to complete an application form and take a selection interview. All selected applicants will attend 3-day training prior to departure, with 1-month, in-country training at the beginning of their placement.

COST: Minimum donation of £3,600 to the charity. All costs are then covered by Restless Development, including open return flight, accommodation, basic living allowance, insurance, in-country work permit, UK briefings, and general administrative support, and extensive overseas training and support.

ROTARY INTERNATIONAL IN GREAT BRITAIN AND IRELAND (RIBI)
Kinwarton Road, Alcester, Warwickshire
B49 6PB
☎ (0)1789 765 411
🖰 enquiries@youthexchange.org.uk
🖳 www.youthexchange.org.uk/wp

PROGRAMME DESCRIPTION: Various long-term and other exchanges relevant to students aged 16–18½ are funded by the Rotary Club. Exchange students stay with families in host country and attend a place of academic or vocational learning. Another programme is called New Generation, whereby young people take up unpaid vocational placements for 3 weeks to 3 months.

NUMBER OF PLACEMENTS PER YEAR: 7,000 worldwide.

DESTINATIONS: See website – many countries.

PREREQUISITES: 16–18. All nationalities. Students need not be associated with a Rotarian, but are expected to get involved in the activities of their host Rotary Club.

DURATION AND TIME OF PLACEMENTS: 10–12 months. Also short-term exchanges in summer of 3–4 weeks.

COST: Students pay for costs of travel and insurance plus around £200 for orientation and sundries. Pocket money of £60 per month may be given.

SELECTION PROCEDURES AND ORIENTATION: Schools normally recommend candidates. Deadline for applications is the end of February. Interviews held in candidate's home with parents. Students should be from the top 10% of their school year in overall achievement. Weekend residential orientation in March and local orientation of half a day prior to leaving. Students receive orientation within 1 month of arriving in their host country. Exchangees have regular contact with, and access at all times to, an independent counsellor to ensure their safety and a successful experience.

CONTACT: Andrew Page.

SKI LE GAP
220 Wheeler Street, Mont Tremblant, Québec J8E 1V3, Canada
☎ (0)800 328 0345 (UK)
☎ 1 819 429 6599 (Canada)
info@skilegap.com
www.skilegap.com

PROGRAMME DESCRIPTION: Ski and snowboard instructor's programme in Québec, Canada, designed for gap year students from Britain. See entry in 'Directory of Sport and Activity Courses' and further details in *Canada* chapter.

STARFISH VENTURES
☎ (0)845 004 8010
enquiries@starfishventures.co.uk
www.starfishvolunteers.com

Not-for-profit gap year organisation; volunteers work closely with Thai partner organisations to provide range of volunteer services.

PROGRAMME DESCRIPTION: Volunteer programmes in teaching, community development, conservation, and medical.

DESTINATIONS: Surin and Rayong provinces, Thailand.

PREREQUISITES: Minimum age 18. All nationalities accepted. CRB check certificate essential for UK applicants; non-UK residents must provide evidence of no criminal record.

DURATION AND TIME OF PLACEMENTS: 2–12 weeks, longer placements can be arranged.

COST: From £400 for 2 weeks, including 2-night hotel stopover in Bangkok, transfers and accommodation.

CONTACT: Dan Moore, Founder, or Steve Williams, Director.

SUDAN VOLUNTEER PROGRAMME (SVP)
34 Estelle Road, London NW3 2JY
☎ (0)20 7485 8619
davidsvp@blueyonder.co.uk
www.svp-uk.com

PROGRAMME DESCRIPTION: Volunteer teaching programme in Sudan (mainly Khartoum and local area) for people aged 20+. See entry in 'Directory of Volunteering Abroad'.

THINK PACIFIC
Old Broadcasting House, Woodhouse Lane, Leeds, LS2 9EN
☎ (0)113 253 8684
info@thinkpacific.com
www.thinkpacific.com

The only gap year organisation to specialise in the South Pacific Islands. 2011 saw the first ever marine conservation project to take place in the Cook Islands, in partnership with the Pacific Islands Conservation Initiative and the Cook Islands Ministry of Marine Resources. Think Pacific's partners in Fiji are the Fijian Ministry and the Lomaiviti Provincial Council.

PROGRAMME DESCRIPTION: Volunteer-based team expeditions to Fiji and the Cook Islands. Fiji expeditions involve teams of up to 18 volunteers who achieve specific building, youth, teaching, and sports coaching aims while living in tiny traditional and impoverished villages. Volunteer projects are combined with sailing, trekking, and snorkelling excursions as part of each expedition. Marine conservation expeditions in the Cook Islands begin with three weeks of intensive diving and marine survey training on Rarotonga. Training to advanced PADI level is included alongside tutorials in marine conservation techniques by resident marine biologists from the Pacific Islands Conservation Initiative and Australian Universities. Volunteer teams then move to Aitutaki, where they undertake daily dive and snorkel surveys of the lagoon and surrounding reefs to collect and analyse vital data, while camping on a private beach. Each expedition ends with a long weekend of trekking, kiteboarding, and relaxation at the beach resorts of Rarotonga Island.

DESTINATIONS: Outer islands of the Lomaiviti province of Fiji; pre-and post-research activity in the Cook Islands takes place on the island of Rarotonga, while the research project is on a small atoll in the Aitutaki lagoon.

NUMBER OF PLACEMENTS PER YEAR: 140.

DURATION AND TIME OF PLACEMENTS: 5 or 10 weeks in Fiji, 6 or 10 weeks in Cook Islands.

PREREQUISITES: Minimum age 17, average age 20. No specific qualifications are required, but volunteers must have a real enthusiasm and drive to get the most from their project and achieve the local community development or conservation aims to the highest standard. No diving experience is required for marine expeditions as all training is provided in the Cook Islands, but a good level of fitness is required. Cook Island expeditions include PADI Open Water Certification training, PADI Advanced Open Water Certification, introductory course in marine survey techniques, and biodiversity assessment training. In Fiji, qualifications, skills, or experience in sports coaching, primary teaching, youth leadership, or building can be a real advantage.

SELECTION PROCEDURES AND ORIENTATION: Expeditions are oversubscribed and are usually filled 3 months in advance. Informal interviews, usually by telephone (or in person if participant prefers), take place in all cases. The aim of the interview is for Think Pacific to describe the expedition in detail, discuss challenging elements of the experience (eg the homestay accommodation in Fiji is likely to involve cold bucket showers, limited electricity, and pit toilets), and also to assess the volunteer's interests, their passion for volunteering, and their suitability for the project. A briefing and team meeting specific to each expedition is held at the University of Leeds one month before departure. Every Fiji expedition begins with a 5-day orientation on a remote island, and ends with a resort-based island safari through Fiji's 330 islands.

COST: Fiji volunteer expedition: 5 weeks for £1,595; 10 weeks for £2,595. Cook Islands diving and marine expedition: 6 weeks for £2,350; 10 weeks for £2,950. Expeditions include all food, accommodation, in-country travel, 24-hour leader support, training (including all dive and survey training), adventure activities such as diving, trekking, tall ship sailing, and snorkelling excursions, as detailed on each itinerary and a donation (£400 per person) to fund materials and resources for project partners. Additional costs are international flights and personal travel insurance.

CONTACT: Simon Darker, Co-Founder.

TICKET TO RIDE – GAP YEAR SURFING ADVENTURES
263 Putney Bridge Road, London SW15 2PU
☎ (0)20 8788 8668
✉ info@ttride.co.uk
🖥 www.ttride.co.uk

PROGRAMME DESCRIPTION: Ticket to Ride is a small company that organises Surfing Gap Years focusing on surf coaching and getting involved in community projects while travelling to various locations around Southern Africa and in Costa Rica. Surf course includes over 60 hours of professional instruction from elite surfers. Riders are on hand to teach or work with children in schools, local townships, and on the beach.

DESTINATIONS: South Africa, Mozambique, Kenya, and Costa Rica.

PREREQUISITES: Should have reasonable swimming ability. Some trips are for confident surfers.

DURATION AND TIME OF PLACEMENTS: 13-week programmes in Africa. Shorter courses elsewhere eg 6-week kitesurfing course at Diani Beach in Kenya and 6-week programme in Costa Rica.

SELECTION PROCEDURES AND ORIENTATION: Applications should be received at least a month in advance of departure. Riders are given a light fitness regime prior to the trip. Riders can qualify as SSA Level 1 Surf Instructors and SPA Surf Lifesavers (both qualifications are UK and internationally recognised).

COST: £5,295 for 13-week Africa gap year programme (2012). 6-week programme in Costa Rica costs £3,495.

TRAVELLERS WORLDWIDE
2A Caravelle House, 17/19 Goring Road, Worthing, West Sussex BN12 4AP
☎ (0)1903 502 595
✉ info@travellersworldwide.com
🖥 www.travellersworldwide.com

Travellers is a Founder Member of the Year Out Group.

PROGRAMME DESCRIPTION: 250+ voluntary projects in 20 countries, including care and community, teaching, sports, internships (see entry in 'Directory of Work

Experience'), conservation, marine, language courses, cultural courses, and drama, dance, and music.

DESTINATIONS: Argentina, Australia, Brazil, Cambodia, China, Ecuador, Ghana, Guatemala, India, Kenya, Malaysia, Mauritius, Mozambique, New Zealand, Peru, South Africa, Sri Lanka, Thailand, Zambia, and Zimbabwe.

NUMBER OF PLACEMENTS PER YEAR: 1,000+.

PREREQUISITES: No qualifications or previous experience are necessary, just a good dose of enthusiasm. All are welcome, whether gap year, undergraduate, or retired, and all nationalities. Minimum age 17.

DURATION AND TIME OF PLACEMENTS: From 1 week to 1 year, subject to visa requirements, with flexible start and finish dates all year.

COST: Prices start from £695 and include food, accommodation, airport pick-up, induction, orientation, 24/7 support on the ground and at home, but don't include international travel, visas or insurance.

CONTACT: Jennifer Perkes, Managing Director.

TRAVEL TO TEACH
47/1 Charunmuang Road, Soi 2, Muang Chiang Mai, 50000 Thailand
✍ apply@travel-to-teach.org
🖥 www.travel-to-teach.org

PROGRAMME DESCRIPTION: Travel to Teach is an international volunteer organisation, which provides affordable opportunities to volunteer in fields such as English and IT teaching, conservation, eco-tourism, and community development. Some placements offer the chance to participate in Buddhist observances.

DESTINATIONS: Thailand, Cambodia, Bali, China, Laos, Nepal, Vietnam, India, Costa Rica, Ecuador, El Salvador, Mexico, Peru, Ghana, and Uganda.

PREREQUISITES: No qualifications required. Must be adaptable, ie willing to live without modern plumbing, hot water, and electricity.

DURATION AND TIME OF PLACEMENTS: 2 weeks to 6 months, though fees quoted in blocks of 4, 8, 12, or 24 weeks.

SELECTION PROCEDURES AND ORIENTATION: Teacher training courses can be arranged in Thailand (with ECC Thailand).

COST: €550–€870 for 4 weeks (varies according to destination), €750–€1,170 for 8 weeks, €950–€1,470 for 12 weeks. All fees include an application fee of €250. Thailand and Cambodia are the cheapest countries; India is the most expensive. Fees are used to run the programmes and support different causes in host countries.

CONTACT: Charlotte Williams, International Programme Manager.

TRAVELWORKS
Muensterstr. 111, 48155 Muenster, Germany
☎ (0)844 576 5411 (UK)
☎ +49 2506 830 3299 (from outside UK).
✍ info@travelworks.co.uk
🖥 www.travelworks.co.uk

Member of WYSETC and WYSE Work Abroad. TravelWorks is a tour operator offering gap year volunteering projects and paid work programmes in over 30 countries around the world. Well-established in Germany, it began offering programmes to the English-speaking market in 2008.

PROGRAMME DESCRIPTION: Many programmes abroad for gappers, including hotel and farm work in Europe, working holidays in Australia and New Zealand, and volunteer work in Africa, Asia, Latin America, and Australasia. Volunteer work opportunities are in the fields of childcare, healthcare, education (English teaching), nature protection, wildlife conservation, maintenance/construction, and tourism.

DESTINATIONS: Worldwide.

DURATION AND TIME OF PLACEMENTS: 2 weeks to 1 year.

SELECTION PROCEDURES AND ORIENTATION: Comprehensive travel support offered in conjunction with partner organisations worldwide.

COST: £1,220 for 4 weeks, £1,790 for 8, £2,335 for 12 weeks; excluding airfares.

CONTACT: Laura Hoesman, Content Manager (lhoesman@travelworks.co.uk).

TUTORS WORLDWIDE
UK office: **Tutors Worldwide, Gaufron Villa, Gaufron, near Rhayader, Powys LD6 5PB**
☎ (0)1597 810 861
☎ (0)7768 191 437
✍ r.finney@xtra.co.nz
🖥 www.tutorsworldwide.org
New Zealand office: **Tutors Worldwide, 2/9 Majesty Plc, Half Moon Bay, Auckland 2012**
☎ +64 9 534 9999
☎ +64 21 995 553 (mobile)

PROGRAMME DESCRIPTION: School leavers are given the opportunity to work in an overseas school environment as a tutor at either a prep or secondary (high) school in New Zealand, and occasionally Australia or South Africa.

DESTINATIONS: New Zealand mostly, with some in Australia and South Africa (and the UK for New Zealanders, Australians, and South Africans).

PREREQUISITES: Must be students of the above nationalities. Initiative, enthusiasm, adaptability, flexibility, communication, commitment, motivation, reliability, and responsibility needed. Many posts involve a lot of sporting activities with children, including coaching and supervision.

DURATION AND TIME OF PLACEMENTS: One full academic year (July to July).

SELECTION PROCEDURES AND ORIENTATION: Application and referee support forms need to be completed and forwarded. Application deadline is early January. Extensive interview with each applicant to try to get the best match between overseas school and student assistant.

COST: £85 registration fee. Placement fee of £500 is charged only to candidates who are offered and accept a place overseas. All posts are residential, and board and lodging are provided.

CONTACT: Robin Finney.

UKSA THE MARITIME ACADEMY
West Cowes, Isle of Wight PO31 7PQ
☎ (0)1983 294 941
info@uksa.org
www.uksa.org

PROGRAMME DESCRIPTION: Gap year programmes last up to 1 year, covering range of watersports and work experience in UK and overseas.

COST: Fees ranges from £3,250 to £14,400 (see entry in 'Directory of Sport and Activity Courses').

VAE TEACHERS KENYA
UK office: Bell Lane Cottage, Pudleston, near Leominster, Herefordshire HR6 0RE
☎ (0)1568 750 329
harris@vaekenya.co.uk
www.vaekenya.co.uk
Kenya address: The Green House, Kairi Farm, PO Box 246, Gilgil, 20116 Kenya
☎ +254 50 50080

VAE runs two associated charities: Harambee Schools Kenya, providing educational infrastructure and materials (www.hsk.org.uk), and Langalanga Scholarship Fund, providing secondary education to bright children who would not otherwise be able to afford it (www.langalanga.org.uk).

PROGRAMME DESCRIPTION: British school leavers and graduates teach in poor rural schools based around the town of Gilgil in Kenya. Volunteers are placed only in schools with a shortage of teachers and resources, and must assume major responsibility as they become integrated and live as part of an African community. VAE is also involved with the local town's street children.

PREREQUISITES: Must have 3 good A levels, and extra-curricular interests such as sport, drama or music.

DURATION AND TIME OF PLACEMENTS: Preferred departure time January for 6 months or volunteers can spend 3–4 months from September or May. Places can sometimes be filled as much as two years in advance.

SELECTION PROCEDURES AND ORIENTATION: Applicants must supply 2 references and be interviewed.

COST: From £2,235 for 3-month stay to £3,155 for 6 months, excluding flight, visa and insurance.

CONTACT: Simon C D Harris, Director; Sophie Herring.

VENTURE CO WORLDWIDE
The Ironyard, 64–66 The Market Place, Warwick CV34 4SD
☎ (0)1926 411 122
mail@ventureco-worldwide.com
www.ventureco-worldwide.com
www.ventureco.org

The original gap year providers in South America, with itineraries that include volunteer projects, language learning, and expeditions. Also recruit volunteers to join the Book Bus crews to work with children in Malawi, Zambia, and Ecuador (www.thebookbus.org).

PROGRAMME DESCRIPTION: Various options in South America: Inca & Amazon Venture, Andes Adventure, Amazon Explorer, Inca & Patagonia Venture, Galápagos Conservation. Gap year students spend time learning Spanish, and attending cookery and dance classes, before taking part in volunteer projects, including for example the Book Bus Charity (a literacy outreach programme), and participating in expeditions such as trekking to Machu Picchu.

DESTINATIONS: Ecuador, Peru, Chile and Bolivia, Argentina and Tierra del Fuego. Detailed itineraries are available on website.

NUMBER OF PLACEMENTS PER YEAR: 200+.

PREREQUISITES: Must have motivation, enthusiasm and desire to be part of a Venture team.

DURATION AND TIME OF PLACEMENTS: 6–15 weeks, with departures year-round. Summer Ventures are available (1–3 months) in Peru, the Galápagos, Amazon, and

Andes departing July. Volunteer projects available lasting from 2 weeks in Africa and South America.

SELECTION PROCEDURES AND ORIENTATION: Attendance at an open evening, held in London on the first Tuesday of every month, can be booked by phone or online. There is an online application form. Preparation weekends are held in UK, and expedition skills training in-country.

COST: Venture costs range from £635 for a 2-week volunteer project, to £1,895 for a 6-week Summer Venture and from £4,700 for a full 15-week Gap Venture (plus contribution of £600 and local payment of £650). Flights, airport taxes, insurance, and visas are not included.

CONTACTS: David Gordon and Mark Davison, Directors.

VESL
Volunteers for Educational Support & Learning,
17 Silk Hill, Buxworth, High Peak, Derbyshire
SK23 7TA
☎ (0)845 094 3727
✎ info@vesl.org
✎ enquiries@vesl.org
🖥 www.vesl.org

VESL is a charity registered in the UK (no. 1117908) and as an NGO in Sri Lanka and Thailand.

PROGRAMME DESCRIPTION: Volunteers (and qualified teachers) are sent to run English language summer schools, and for longer periods in remote communities.

DESTINATIONS: India (Andhra Pradesh), Thailand (Chiang Rai Province), and Sri Lanka (Southern, Central and Uva provinces).

NUMBER OF PLACEMENTS PER YEAR: Up to 60.

PREREQUISITES: Minimum age 18, though most volunteers are older. Volunteers should be enthusiastic, motivated, and up for a challenge. TEFL experience and some experience overseas are helpful but not a requirement.

DURATION AND TIME OF PLACEMENTS: 3–6-month projects throughout the year, and 4–6-week summer programmes in July and August.

SELECTION PROCEDURES AND ORIENTATION: Applications accepted throughout the year. All candidates must be able to attend a selection day and training weekend (dates and places in the UK to be notified).

COST: Programme fee ranges from £900 for summer placement to £1,350 for 3 months, which covers cost of setting up the projects, training, orientation, insurance, accommodation, food, in-country travel, and comprehensive back up and support. VESL is run mainly by volunteers, so costs are kept to a minimum.

CONTACT: Tom Harrison, Programme Director.

VOLUNTEER MALDIVES PVT LTD
Unimoo Building, Orchid Magu, Male, Maldives
☎ +960 330 0609
✎ info@volunteermaldives.com
🖥 www.volunteermaldives.com

PROGRAMME DESCRIPTION: Volunteering in various locations in the Maldive Islands for 1–12 months. See entry in 'Directory of Volunteering Abroad'.

VOLUNTEER UGANDA
✎ ukteam@volunteeruganda.org
🖥 www.volunteeruganda.org/volunteering

PROGRAMME DESCRIPTION: Volunteer Uganda works in partnership with affiliate charities which have set up and run 4 primary schools, 1 secondary school, and a college. Volunteers are placed in 10 primary schools in rural south-west Uganda, and also work on outreach programmes teaching teenagers and young people about family planning and HIV avoidance. Programmes also include white-water rafting and a safari. Volunteers live together at the purpose-built Volunteer Uganda lodge on the edge of Bwindi National Park, home to 300 of the 600 remaining wild mountain gorillas.

NUMBER OF PLACEMENTS PER YEAR: 120 in 2011, 180 in 2012.

DESTINATIONS: South-western Uganda.

PREREQUISITES: Ages 18–25. All nationalities welcome, but should speak English fluently. Should be enthusiastic and outgoing. Volunteers should have A level or equivalent education.

DURATION AND TIME OF PLACEMENTS: 3 months, starting February and July.

SELECTION PROCEDURES AND ORIENTATION: Informal telephone interviews conducted to ensure programme is suitable. The first week in Kinkizi is an induction week, consisting of training sessions on teaching methods, learning theory, teaching observations, and practice peer teaching. Volunteers will also be given basic local language lessons. Training is run by experienced teachers and British group leaders.

COST: £2,400 for 3 months, including accommodation in a mountain lodge overlooking Bwindi Impenetrable Forest. Volunteers live together at the lodge, which has capacity for 36 volunteers. Adventure and wildlife activities included.

WARRIORS
46A Franschoek, Magoebaskloof, Limpopo
Province, South Africa
☎ +27 82 802 0880
✎ rudi@warriors.co.za
🖥 www.warriors.co.za

PROGRAMME DESCRIPTION: The Warriors programme can bridge 7 months or an entire gap year, and is designed for energetic and adventurous young adults looking for direction and purpose. Warriors offers huge range of timetabled hands-on learning, from basic climbing techniques to car maintenance, bush survival to cookery. The adventure and development programme places emphasis on coaching participants to develop emotional fitness and a self-reliant attitude towards life.

DESTINATIONS: Base Camp is situated in the Magoebaskloof area at the northern end of the Drakensburg Mountains of South Africa. Trips are made throughout the gap year including to Mozambique, game reserves, Graskop Gorge, etc.

NUMBER OF PLACEMENTS PER YEAR: 40–50.

DURATION AND TIME OF PLACEMENTS: 7 months, February to August. 2 short breaks allow participants to go home on a visit if desired.

PREREQUISITES: Minimum age 17, average age 19. Must have an adventurous spirit and total commitment to the programme.

SELECTION PROCEDURES AND ORIENTATION: Challenging course, both physically and mentally, so not all candidates who apply will be accepted. Deadline for applications is December, but preferred by the end of October. Applications are screened on the basis of a questionnaire and if needed a telephone or Skype interview can be arranged. UK participants need to apply for a study visa.

COST: £11,000 (which works out at about £50 a day). Shared accommodation in log cabins.

CONTACT: Rudi Viljoen, Programme Director and Owner.

WAVA
67–71 Lewisham High Street, Lewisham, London SE13 5JX
☎ (0)800 80 483 80
✎ smordarski@workandvolunteer.com
💻 www.workandvolunteer.com

PROGRAMME DESCRIPTION: 'WAVA' stands for 'Work and Volunteer Abroad', as Twin Work & Adventure Abroad was rebranded in 2010. WAVA offers 3 types of travelling experience: volunteering on projects in developing countries; internships in professional environments around the world; and seasonal paid and unpaid working holidays in developed economies.

DESTINATIONS: All over the world: North and South America, Europe, Africa, Asia, and Australasia.

NUMBER OF PLACEMENTS PER YEAR: 500+.

PREREQUISITES: All ages. All nationalities are accepted, subject to visa requirements. Specific skills may be

required, depending on the programme. Participants need to be enthusiastic, willing to get actively involved, have an open mind, and sometimes a sense of humour.

DURATION AND TIME OF PLACEMENTS: From 2 weeks to 1 year.

SELECTION PROCEDURES AND ORIENTATION: As part of WAVA's Responsible Travel Policy, it focuses heavily on responsibly matching participants to programmes. The company advises participants to apply at least 12 weeks before their intended start date, although in many cases WAVA can fast-track applications. The programme fee often includes a pre-departure briefing in London.

OTHER SERVICES: Because WAVA's programmes differ so much, a 'foot rating' system is in place to categorise programmes according to the level of comfort and accessibility.

COST: From £390. Fees include pre-departure and in-country induction/training, a donation to the project, in-country transportation, accommodation (volunteer house, on-project residence, or local hostel/lodge), and food.

CONTACT: Sally Mordarski, Travel Administrator (smordarski@workandvolunteer.com).

WORLDWIDE EXPERIENCE
The Oak Suite, Guardian House, Borough Road, Godalming, Surrey GU7 2AE
☎ (0)1483 860 560
✎ info@worldwideexperience.com
💻 www.worldwideexperience.com

PROGRAMME DESCRIPTION: Specialist conservation placements in Southern Africa that give participants the chance to get actively involved in conservation on various game reserves, animal rehabilitation centres, and ocean research projects. Other projects include community placements, game ranger courses, a wildlife film academy, and a sculpting course.

DESTINATIONS: Projects are located in South Africa, Kenya, Malawi, India, and Sri Lanka.

NUMBER OF PLACEMENTS PER YEAR: 400+.

PREREQUISITES: No particular skills needed. All nationalities accepted.

DURATION AND TIME OF PLACEMENTS: 2–12 weeks. Placements are available year-round (gap year, summer break, and sabbatical).

SELECTION PROCEDURES AND ORIENTATION: Applications accepted year-round. Interviews are informal and can be done by telephone. Open days are arranged throughout the year when Worldwide Experience crew meet potential volunteers. Full medical and personal checklist is supplied during preparation.

COST: From £599 for 2 weeks, inclusive of transfers, meals, accommodation (furnished and comfortable, shared between two), and placement activities.

YEAR IN INDUSTRY
The University of Southampton, Southampton SO17 1BJ
☎ (0)23 8059 7061
✎ info@yini.org.uk
🖥 www.yini.org.uk

Founding member of the Year Out Group. Major provider of gap year industrial placements throughout the UK. See entry in 'Directory of Work Experience in the UK'.

YEAR OUT DRAMA COMPANY
Stratford-upon-Avon College, Alcester Road, Stratford-upon-Avon, Warwickshire CV37 9QR
☎ (0)1789 417 255
✎ yearoutdrama@stratford.ac.uk

Founding member of the Year Out Group. 1-year course covers acting, directing, performance, voice work, movement, and design. See entry in 'Directories of Courses'.

YOMPS
10 Woodland Way, Brighton, East Sussex BN1 8BA
☎ (0)845 006 1435
✎ info@yomps.co.uk
🖥 www.yomps.co.uk

PROGRAMME DESCRIPTION: Volunteering, adventure, training courses, exploration, and cultural experiences.

DESTINATIONS: South Africa, Namibia, Malawi, Kenya, Botswana, Zambia, Zimbabwe, Mozambique, Mexico, Ecuador, Venezuela, Guatemala, Honduras, Chile, Peru, Argentina, Thailand, Fiji, USA, Australia, and Switzerland.

NUMBER OF PLACEMENTS PER YEAR: 200+.

DURATION AND TIME OF PLACEMENTS: 2 weeks to 2 years; average trip lasts 4–8 weeks but longer programmes are available.

PREREQUISITES: Open to people of all nationalities. Most participants are aged 18–40.

SELECTION PROCEDURES AND ORIENTATION: Online applications accepted throughout the year. Field manual provided pre-departure, and project orientation on arrival.

COST: From £649 for short trips, or more typically from £990 for 4 weeks volunteering in South Africa, to £4,225 for 6-month Venezuela Explorer. Prices include accommodation, which varies according to trip; for example, a chalet in Switzerland, tented camp in South

Africa, waterfront volunteer base in Mexico or Lake Malawi, overlanding vehicle in Southern Africa, host family in Guatemala, under the stars in Namibia, Amazonian rainforest research base in Ecuador, and camping out in the Patagonian wilderness of Chile.

CONTACT: Client co-ordinator.

YOUTH IN ACTION
See European Voluntary Service (EVS) above.

ZANZIGAP LTD
18 Melrose Road, Sheffield S3 9DN
☎ (0)114 249 1661
✎ enquiries@zanzigap.com
🖥 www.zanzigap.com

Zanzigap was set up in 2007, and is run by a group of teachers and ex-teachers in Sheffield, who are familiar with Zanzibeir in Tanzania and with experience of organising long-term visits.

PROGRAMME DESCRIPTION: Teaching English (or any preferred specialist subject) to GCSE level in secondary schools in Zanzibar.

DESTINATIONS: Zanzibar (Tanzania).

NUMBER OF PLACEMENTS PER YEAR: Up to 60.

PREREQUISITES: Minimum age 16, average age 19. Mainly but not exclusively British. GCSEs and/or A levels preferred.

DURATION AND TIME OF PLACEMENTS: 3–9 months, or full academic year (end of January to beginning of November).

SELECTION PROCEDURES AND ORIENTATION: Applications should be made 6 months to 1 year in advance. No interview needed. Pre-departure bonding weekend is part of programme. Full orientation given, including CD-ROM, risk assessment, packing list, and medical information. Support given in situ, lesson observation, training, and teaching practice. 24-hour hotline to UK.

COST: £1,950–£2,500 depending on duration of stay, includes comprehensive health and travel insurance, airfares, visa, accommodation, and living expenses. Local accommodation only, which may not have water or electricity. Mobile phone signal available in all locations.

CONTACT: John Errington MBE, Director.

See also directories at the end of the chapters on Volunteering, Work Experience, Au Pairing, and Courses for other organisations that welcome gap year students (among others).

BSES

James Borrell travelled to hot and cold climes on BSES expeditions before taking a university place.

At the age of 17, I was suddenly immersed in an unknown land of rainforests and lemurs. Completely by chance, a friend had introduced me to the British Schools Exploring Society (BSES), and without a second thought I embarked on an expedition to Madagascar. Living and working in such a remote and enchanting country was overwhelming; the kindness of the people was humbling. Over the course of our expedition, we helped initiate a tree-planting programme in an effort to reverse the rate of deforestation, conducted surveys to assess the lemur population, and most importantly, we learnt about an entirely different culture and about ourselves.

I found myself longing for the simplicity of the Malagasy way of life, inspired that in some small but significant way, a group of young people from half a world away could make a difference. They say that you might return a different person, and I think I did.

After finishing my A levels, I headed to the ice-capped mountains of Norway to complete the BSES Leadership Development Programme, in the hope of one day heading my own expeditions. As results day approached, a remote Scandinavian valley was the setting in which I was able to receive my grades, via satellite phone!

My experiences with BSES in Madagascar and Norway encouraged me to study Biology at the University of Exeter, while always on the look-out for the next expeditions. With a degree, I hoped that I could make an even greater contribution to conservation around the world. Now, with my course drawing to a close and finals rapidly approaching, my dream has come true, as I prepare to help lead a conservation expedition with BSES to a remote and pristine part of the Peruvian Amazon, departing the day after I graduate.

The BSES has not only opened my eyes to the opportunities available and given me friends for life - it has also given me the skills and confidence to rise to any challenge, and taught me that the only limits you have are the ones you set yourself.

EXPEDITIONS

Adolescence is a good time to discover tales of adventure from the literature of exploration, whether it is the casual descriptions of suffering by mountaineers or sailors, classics by Robert Byron or Freya Stark, or more recent works by authors and film-makers such as Benedict Allen and Bruce Parry.

Visiting a wild and woolly part of the world might seem an impossible dream for a 17-year-old with no money and no travel experience beyond a youth hostelling weekend in the Peak District. But a number of organisations cater specifically for gap year travellers looking for challenging adventures in remote places. These are open to anyone who is mentally and physically fit and who is prepared to raise funds for the fees (typically starting at £3,000 plus equipment, etc).

If you feel the need for a testing adventure or would like to show your friends and family what stern stuff you are made of, then a gap year is the perfect time to think about going on an expedition. In a Radio 4 interview, the director of the Wilderness Foundation tried to explain the value of spending time in wild places and why it fosters tolerance: *'Wilderness creates a sense of vulnerability... and vulnerability is the greatest way of finding a common sense of humanity between people.'*

EXPEDITIONS AND THE DUKE OF EDINBURGH'S AWARD

Students who have attended schools with a tradition of sending pupils on expeditions will be at an advantage in tracking down suitable opportunities for their gap year: an expedition forms part of the requirements to gain a Duke of Edinburgh's Award. Most people become involved through their local school or youth club, though it is possible to enlist through an Open Award Centre. Most take place in the UK (usually the Lake District or Wales), but some go abroad, eg on canoeing expeditions to Canada. The Duke of Edinburgh's Award Scheme (www.dofe.org) supports personal and social development of young people aged 14–25, and has links with companies and clubs that are Approved Activity Providers (see website).

HELPFUL ORGANISATIONS

The Royal Geographical Society with the Institute of British Geographers (1 Kensington Gore, London SW7 2AR; www.rgs.org) encourages and assists many British expeditions. The RGS-IBG keeps files of past expedition reports, guidebooks, and maps in the Foyle Reading Room for travellers.

The old Expedition Advisory Centre is now known as Geography Outdoors (www.rgs.org/GO). It hosts an annual weekend seminar called 'Explore' in November on expedition and fieldwork planning (www.rgs.org/explore), covering fundraising and budgeting for expeditions, as well as issues of safety and logistics in many different environments (attendance fee £75 for students, £110 otherwise). The directory of grant-awarding organisations from its publication *The Expedition Handbook* (2004, £16.99) is available online. Although many grants have set criteria (eg must live within eight miles of Exmouth Town Hall) it is certainly worth checking and applying as widely as possible.

The RGS-IBG's Leading and Learning programme (020 7591 3180; www.rgs.org/L&L) offers Gap Year Scholarships worth up to £4,000 to A level geography students, especially from challenging backgrounds, who would benefit from a bursary and mentoring to enable them to undertake a meaningful gap year overseas before undergraduate study in geography. An online toolkit, Gap Planning, is available to help students develop a safe and responsible programme of activities during their travels (www.rgs.org/Gap).

MY GAP YEAR: LYNN MUNRO

Lynn Munro was one of the fortunate recipients of the RGS's Gap Year Scholarship.

It was thanks to the Royal Geographical Society's Learning and Leading Gap Year Scholarship that I was able to fund my gap between May 2009 and September 2010. The scholarship provided a grant of £4,000, which I combined with sponsorship sought from local business owners and money made while working over the summers on either side of my trips. One of the most challenging parts was deciding on which country to go to and which activities to take on. I made the decision to travel in South Africa for three months, then return home in December to apply to Scottish universities, and plan the second phase of my gap experience in New Zealand, where I spent three and a half months.

When trying to decide where to go, I realised I'd always had an underlying interest in elephants and African wildlife and culture. With a love for the physical aspects of geography, I also settled on New Zealand, which seemed the ideal place to combine outdoor activities with all the geography I could ever dream of. I opted to travel independently, but created a safety net by paying to volunteer with the organisation Edge of Africa; I spent two weeks on an African 'Big Five' wildlife and conservation project, another two at a predator sanctuary, and finally four weeks on the 'Everything Elephant' project. I immediately made it my aim to get stuck in to each project and become involved with daily tasks such as cleaning elephant enclosures, planting trees, feeding cheetah, fencing, recording elephants from 7am until 5pm daily, plant studies, and cheetah tracking, along with extras such as visiting townships and working alongside a Rastafarian community. We also had continual weekend excursions, and I was able to visit the world-famous Cango caves, and Addo National Park, which has the highest concentration of African elephants. One experience I'll never forget was spending an hour sat at a watering hole visited by over 100 elephants. Africa taught me an endless amount, such as how to put my knowledge of fieldwork into practice. I had to show initiative during my month at this project, constantly giving feedback about how data was being recorded and changes that could be made.

Arriving in New Zealand in January, I spent the first two months on the South Island, where my dreams of travelling through the landscape studied in school were met. It was while hiking on the Kepler Track that I decided to accept my university offer to study Environmental Science and Outdoor Education. The most challenging part of the whole experience was coming home, back to reality and trying to carry forward who and what I had learnt while I was away. I wish I had known just how much I would fall in love with South Africa and New Zealand before I departed, as I would happily have stayed in both countries for a lot longer.

The benefit of the gap year for me was to return with new-found motivation and direction for future studies. Having spent time thinking about what was the biggest impact of this experience on me, I know it's the continual smile I have every time I talk about my experience. I think a smile says an endless amount: I have gained confidence, belief, and self-motivation as I'm now studying at university and have realised that the impossible is possible.

The Young Explorers' Trust (YET; www.theyet.org), affiliated to the RGS, is a registered charity that promotes safe and responsible expeditions. It offers advice and support to groups of students who wish to organise their own expedition during their gap year. YET does not offer pre-arranged expeditions, but instead an expert panel of advisers and assessors to evaluate expedition plans. Grant aid is available to YET-evaluated expeditions.

Raleigh International (www.raleighinternational.org) is a well-established youth and sustainable development charity that has over nearly three decades sent 35,000 people from all walks of life, nationalities, and ages on expeditions. Participants develop new skills and friendships, and make a difference to communities and environments across the world. Raleigh runs expeditions consisting of community, environmental, and adventure projects in which 17–24-year-olds can participate (and 25–75-year-olds can sign up as volunteer managers). When **Felicia Royaards** decided to take time out before starting university, she signed up to the Costa Rica expedition after hearing about Raleigh from a friend. She fundraised with support from friends and family, and got creative by selling her own jewellery designs at a local fair. Her enthusiasm for choosing a Raleigh expedition is boundless:

> Raleigh puts you in such a different situation; in a new environment, with new people, and in a new country with another language being spoken. It gives you a great opportunity to do three totally different things in one expedition: not only do you learn a lot about yourself through adventure, you get to appreciate the community and the environment. Changing groups every phase made me more confident and more independent. Furthermore, you get to know a lot of people from different kinds of backgrounds. My highlight has been finishing the Kamuk trek. It was a personal challenge: you push yourself to the limit and find out how strong you are. Raleigh changed me in positive ways, and I reckon it will help me in the future when I'm looking for a job after my degree.

Amy Walton graduated from Bournemouth University in 2009 with a degree in Tourism Management, but found that she was being turned down for graduate roles in the sector due to her lack of international experience. Amy decided that a Raleigh expedition was the perfect opportunity, and went on an expedition to Costa Rica and Nicaragua in summer 2010. Since returning from her expedition, Amy has now found her dream job working for Virgin Holiday Cruises.

> *I have learnt I have a lot more determination than I thought I did. I also learnt that I can make the best out of any situation, however challenging. I have had an amazing time throughout, not just because of what I have done to make it the best but also thanks to others. I have learnt I can easily make new friends and mix with people from different cultures with confidence. I am sure Raleigh has helped my employability and work skills hugely. I have further developed my leadership skills while on trek, and team-building skills gained during the environmental phase of the expedition. I can deal with unknown situations and meeting new people with confidence, which has been developed throughout being on Raleigh.*

The British Schools Exploring Society (see entry for BSES Expeditions, p214) organises an impressive range of expeditions that combine scientific research projects and adventurous activities. This youth development charity has been running wilderness expeditions for nearly 80 years. Visiting some of the world's most remote and challenging environments, from the Arctic to the Amazon, BSES offers the opportunity to explore and learn about environmental issues facing the world today. Expedition members take part in a UK-based training weekend so that they can meet the rest of the team and find out more about the science and adventure objectives. It is a chance to become familiar with kit and equipment and gain some of the essential skills required for living in an extreme environment.

MY GAP YEAR:
SARAH PHILLIPS

Sarah Phillips thinks that although her fundraising target was high, so were the rewards. She joined an Extreme Arctic Expedition to Svalbard through BSES two years ago. Being at such a high latitude (78 degrees north) means that the sun never sets during the spring and summer. The cold is unbelievable. At night, breath vapour condenses against the ceiling of tents where it instantly freezes and then falls on you as soon as a gust of wind hits the tent.

The total cost of the expedition came to around £8,000, which I felt was quite expensive for a gap year, but I would rather spend it on something like that where I am doing something completely different and unforgettable, than go around New Zealand, Thailand, and Fiji, which is commonplace with gap year students. Furthermore, the kit was very costly. But you have to get the right kit, because it is not something you can take a short cut with, and I didn't mind paying out for something that kept me alive!

We had some absolutely unforgettable days. Our leader Richard had managed to cast his mind back and relocate an untouched ice cave up a steep valley. He was concerned about the huge cornice overhanging the valley, especially since the snow was heavily piling up and the weather was vicious. So we ventured up the side of the valley in the relentless wind, which tries to knock you over as you wobble and sway up the incline.

We were lowered into the little slot of the cave, which opened up into a huge church-like cavern. It was stunning. The ceiling glistened and sparkled, secretly twinkling out of the corner of your eye. I really had the sense of it being the Snow Queen's forgotten lair. We excitedly ventured further in, coming across untouched spots of beauty, such as cascading water frozen delicately as it splashed to the floor, and fragile glass-like icicles of all sizes hanging from the starry ceiling.

We settled down to our scientific survey of the cave, planning to map it out by taking detailed measurements at frequent intervals along the 240m tunnel. We eventually hope to turn our results into a 3D model and assign tasks for future expeditions. When we reached the back of the cave, we turned off our head torches and simply appreciated the still darkness and utter silence. It was truly a special moment of meditating and appreciating these simple things. Richard reckoned there had been fewer people in the cave than on Everest. After five hours of hardcore science and spectacular adventure, we rugged up and braved the angry weather outside the cave. After a short while, we reached our beloved camp and escaped the harrowing wind. All in all, a magical day that can't really be described.

These highlights compensated for the downsides that Sarah encountered, such as not being in contact with anyone at home for three months and feeling uncomfortably isolated.

SAILING ADVENTURES

Several youth-oriented organisations and charities take young people on Sail Training expeditions. Fees vary, but most tend to be £60–£80 a day. The Association of Sail Training Organisations (ASTO) is the umbrella group for such organisations in the UK, and its website (www.uksailtraining.co.uk) is a useful link to member organisations, with more than 50 boats, including RTW racing yachts, gaff-rigged classics and large square-rigged ships. UK Sail Training organisations predominantly operate around European waters, with many taking part in the Tall Ships Races. A few vessels operate in the Caribbean or Canaries. ASTO not only organises but also funds a handful of short international exchanges in Australia and Canada for 18–25-year-olds who have sailed before on ASTO's member vessels.

MY GAP YEAR: CRAIG YOUNG

Craig Young's gap year was spent as a volunteer bosun on the Sail Training Ship *Leader*, an experience that changed the direction of his life.

Deciding on what to do for a gap year was a challenge: I was a keen hillwalker and dinghy sailor, and had recently been able to sail on a tall ship through my involvement with the Sea Cadets. I knew whatever I chose to do, I wanted it to be free or self-funding, as well as constructive. I wanted to develop skills and interests that I already had, rather than spending money travelling for the sake of it. I decided that I wanted to get involved in sailing a tall ship, and spent hours contacting ships that might be looking for crew. The largest stumbling block I came across was a lack of qualifications, and little money to obtain them. By Christmas, I was starting to lose hope, when I came across the website for the Association of Sail Training Organisations (www.uksailtraining.co.uk), which was advertising a vacancy for a seasonal volunteer on board one of the historic sailing trawlers operated by the Trinity Sailing Trust (www.trinitysailing.co.uk). This sounded exactly what I was after: a chance to learn and work as a volunteer, with food and board provided on a ship that would be sailing around the UK and European waters, based out of Brixham in Devon. I travelled down from Lancashire to Brixham for an interview in January, and two weeks later I returned to Devon to join the boats in Dartmouth, with little idea how the next eight months would turn out.

Trinity Sailing operates three historic sailing vessels: Leader, **Provident**, and **Golden Vanity**, all of which were built in Devon in a time before diesel engines and steel hulls. I would be working on **Leader**, the oldest, and biggest, of the fleet. Built in 1892, she is 110 tonnes and made entirely of wood and gaff-rigged, meaning the sails are hoisted on spars just as they would have been in the 19th century: very exciting for someone like me interested in traditional sailing! On deck, **Leader** looks much as she would have done in the age of sail, while below is fitted out for its modern dual role as both sail training vessel for young people and also for adult charter holidays. As a volunteer, referred to as the bosun, I would be working with the permanent crew (skipper, mate, and cook) to help with the sailing, maintenance, and domestic chores as needed. The first two months were spent in refit, which was a huge learning curve for me. Wooden boats need a lot of maintenance, and I acquired lots of practical skills from sanding, painting, and varnishing, to rigging work, cleaning, and even the plumbing. The days were long, and being outside in the winter, cold and often wet, but I was being given the grounding in skills that would be of great use during the sailing season. We lived onboard Provident during the refit, taking it in turns to cook and clean: it was my first taste of communal living, and was of massive use to me later on at university! With a succession of different groups such as young people from a school or youth service, people with learning difficulties or behavioural issues, or adult groups who had chartered **Leader** for a holiday, we sailed from Brixham to a variety of ports on the south coast or, when the weather allowed, across the Channel to Brittany, exploring the quiet French ports and fishing towns, or to Guernsey, Sark, or the Scilly Isles, to some amazingly remote spots with rare plants and wildlife.

That year, **Leader** took part in the Tall Ships Races, a fantastic annual series of festivals and races attracting tall ships from all over the world. We raced from Liverpool to Måløy in Norway, before spending several weeks cruising the Norwegian fjords with holiday guests, calling into some of the most remote and beautiful bays I could ever imagine, and having the chance to sail alongside dolphins, whales, and porpoises, before eventually returning to Scotland, via the rugged Orkney and Shetland Islands in September. The list of possible jobs was endless, and ranged from the fun (driving guests around in the small power-boat), to the adventurous (climbing the mast to fix a loose line), and the not-so-fun (keeping the boat's toilet systems functioning!) My responsibilities increased as the months went on, and by the time I left **Leader** in Scotland, I had achieved my RYA Watch Leader qualification, and had a much greater understanding of both people and boats.

I finish my degree this summer (2011) and have decided to return to sail training, at least for a few years. I have just been successful in obtaining a Trinity House Bursary (no connection to Trinity Sailing) that will pay for all the courses I need to become a fully qualified mate and, one day, skipper ... something I would never have dreamed of before deciding to take a gap year! It has however meant I have struggled with uni work - not grades as such, but the motivation to sit at a laptop all day when I know I could be outside fighting a sail in a storm or fixing something challenging instead. My time on **Leader** has made me a much more practical, hands-on person, and hours of journal reading has been a struggle!

The organisation At Sea Sail Training (www.atseasailtraining.com) co-ordinates crew placement for vessels taking part in an annual series of Tall Ships Races. More than half the trainees are obliged to be 18–25 and they are of mixed nationalities; some use the trip as the residential element of the Duke of Edinburgh's Gold Award. No experience is needed to join the crew. The full daily cost of a berth is £60–£90. For example, the youth cost of joining the whole Tall Ships Races 2011 from Ireland to Scotland, the Shetland Islands, Norway, and Sweden for nearly six weeks is £2,700. Those who would like to do a seven-week transatlantic crossing of an ocean and travel the world under sail can join the *Bark Europa* from Argentina to South Africa at a cost of £6,015.

FUNDRAISING

Expeditions tend to be among the most expensive among gap year placements, and some of the targets fixed by the major organisations are truly daunting. See the section on Fundraising in the chapter 'Before You Go' for ideas on how to earn, save, and persuade others to give you the necessary funds.

Those with a specialised project might discover that targeted funds are available from trusts and charities. However, many, like the Mount Everest Foundation (www.mef.org.uk/mefguide.htm), are earmarked for high-level expeditions undertaking first ascents, new routes, and scientific research on mountains, so that, according to the MEF's Honorary Secretary, 'gap year projects are extremely unlikely to be eligible for support'.

Relevant companies are sometimes willing to give equipment in lieu of a cheque, though most manufacturers of hiking and camping equipment are inundated with requests. Successful supplicants often present imaginative ways in which they plan to publicise their benefactors' products.

SPONSORED EXPEDITIONS FOR CHARITY

A large and growing number of charities in the UK now offer adventurous group travel to individuals who are prepared to undertake some serious fundraising on their behalf. Household names such as Marie Curie Cancer Care and Mencap organise sponsored trips, as do many less well-known good causes. Specialist agents such as Charity Challenge (www.charitychallenge.com) allow you to select your trip (most of which last no more than a fortnight) and which charity you would like to support. Participants are asked to raise £2,700 (say) for the charity and in return receive a 'free' trip. You are in a far stronger position to ask people for donations if you can say you are supporting the Children's Trust, British Heart Foundation, Whale Conservation Society, or whatever, than if you say you are trying to raise money for a holiday to Morocco, Patagonia, Borneo, etc. These trips are usually more attractive to older people looking for an interesting way to take a break than to school-leavers.

DIRECTORY OF EXPEDITIONS

BORDERS EXPLORATION GROUP
@borders-exploration-group.org.uk
www.borders-exploration-group.org.uk

Borders Exploration Group is a non-profit-making voluntary organisation which organises international and European expeditions for young people living in the Scottish Borders area.

DESTINATIONS: 2-week expedition to Ukraine (summer 2011) and 4-week expedition to Cuba (summer 2012).

NUMBER OF PLACEMENTS PER EXPEDITION: About 35 on an international expedition, 15 on a European trip.

PREREQUISITES: Must live in Scottish Borders catchment area. Ages 16–25.

CONTACT: Jono Ellis, Chair.

BRATHAY EXPLORATION CLUB
Brathay Hall, Ambleside, Cumbria LA22 0HP
☎ (0)1539 433 942
admin@brathayexploration.org.uk
www.brathayexploration.org.uk

Established 1947.

PROGRAMME DESCRIPTION: Mounts expeditions and expeditionary courses for young adults. Wide-ranging activities including adventure and environmental awareness.

DESTINATIONS: Worldwide, varying from year to year. 2011 expeditions included one in the summer to measure the Jostedal Glacier in Norway using GPS equipment.

NUMBER OF PLACEMENTS PER YEAR: 200.

PREREQUISITES: Ages 15–25, with most aged 16–21. No qualifications needed. People with disabilities welcome to apply.

DURATION AND TIME OF PLACEMENTS: 1–5 weeks, summer holiday period.

SELECTION PROCEDURES AND ORIENTATION: Briefing and pre-departure training sessions on outdoor skills and first aid.

COST: Up to £2,000 for a month-long overseas expedition (excluding airfares); less for trips in UK. Norway fee was £1,150–£1,300.

BSES EXPEDITIONS
Royal Geographical Society, 1 Kensington Gore, London SW7 2AR
☎ (0)20 7591 3141
info@bses.org.uk
www.bses.org.uk

The British Schools Exploring Society (BSES) is a youth development charity which was founded in 1932 by an original member of Captain Scott's ill-fated Antarctic Expedition of 1910–1913. It provides opportunities for young people to take part in challenging scientific expeditions to remote wild environments.

PROGRAMME DESCRIPTION: The expeditions aim to combine living in extreme and challenging conditions with valuable scientific and environmental research. Past expeditions have included climbing a 6,000m peak in India, protecting 30,000 turtle eggs from poachers by building artificial nesting sites in the Amazon, glaciology fieldwork through the Arctic winter in Eastern Greenland, sea kayaking in Alaska, and other expeditions in the Arctic. Future destinations include the Empty Quarter of Oman, the Extreme Arctic in Svalbard, elephant conservation in Namibia, and a return to the Amazon. Expeditions can count towards the Duke of Edinburgh's Gold Award Residential and Expedition sections.

DESTINATIONS: Arctic, jungle, desert, and mountain environments worldwide; for example, the Amazon rainforest, the Himalayas, Svalbard, Namibia, and Oman. Destinations change from year to year.

NUMBER OF PLACEMENTS PER YEAR: About 200.

PREREQUISITES: Must be aged between 16 and 23, be well motivated, and have a good level of fitness. However, no previous experience is necessary.

DURATION AND TIME OF PLACEMENT: Expedition lengths vary from 1 month in the summer holidays to 3 months for gap year expeditions.

SELECTION PROCEDURES AND ORIENTATION: Applicants will be interviewed regionally or by telephone. Places are allocated on a first come, first served basis, on completion of a successful interview. On accepting the offer of a place, Young Explorers take part in a briefing weekend before their expedition. Following the expedition, the BSES Annual Gathering Presentations take place in the Royal Geographical Society.

COST: £2,100–£5,200. BSES Expeditions offers lots of help and guidance on fundraising, including a bursary scheme. No-one showing appropriate commitment and effort in raising the contribution will be denied a place.

CORAL CAY CONSERVATION (CCC)
Elizabeth House, 39 York Road, London
SE1 7NJ
☎ (0)20 7620 1411
✉ info@coralcay.org
🖥 www.coralcay.org

CCC runs tropical forest and coral reef expeditions in the Philippines, Tobago, and Cambodia. Volunteers are trained to survey scientifically some of the world's most beautiful yet endangered tropical environments. For details, see 'Directory of Specialist Gap Year Programmes'.

GLOBAL VISION INTERNATIONAL (GVI)
UK Office: Third Floor, The Senate, Exeter
EX1 1UG
☎ (0)1727 250 250
✉ info@gvi.co.uk
🖥 www.gvi.co.uk
North American office: 66 Long Wharf, Suite
562 S, Boston, MA 02110
☎ +1 888 653 6028
✉ www.gviusa.com
Australian office: Suite 206, 530 Little Collins
Street, Melbourne, VIC 3000
☎ +61 1300 795013
✉ www.gviaustralia.com

PROGRAMME DESCRIPTION: Since 1998, GVI has been running overseas marine, rainforest, and other expeditions and projects in Africa, Latin America, and Asia.

DESTINATIONS: South Africa, Kenya, Seychelles, Ecuador, Mexico, Costa Rica, and Patagonia.

PREREQUISITES: None. Minimum age 18. All nationalities welcome. No special training or qualifications are required as all training will be provided in the field.

DURATION AND TIME OF PLACEMENTS: 4–12 weeks.

SELECTION PROCEDURES AND ORIENTATION: Online application plus application assessment.

COST: From £2,185 for 8-week rainforest expedition in Ecuador (2012).

JUBILEE SAILING TRUST YOUTH LEADERSHIP @ SEA SCHEME
JST, 12 Hazel Road, Woolston, Southampton
SO19 7GA
☎ (0)23 8044 9108
✉ sales@jst.org.uk
🖥 www.jst.org.uk

COURSES OFFERED: Leadership course on a sea voyage to develop communication, leadership and team skills, while building an understanding of disability.

PREREQUISITES: Ages 16–25. Must be prepared to act as a full part of a tall ship voyage crew for the duration of the voyage.

SELECTION PROCEDURES AND ORIENTATION: By written application; mark form with 'Youth Leadership @ Sea' and enclose short personal statement of 200–400 words, detailing why you think you should be chosen. Places are limited.

COST: Prices start from £425 for a 4-day voyage. This includes all accommodation, meals, and training. Subsidies of up to £300 are offered towards the cost of the Jubilee Sailing Trust Youth Leadership @ Sea Scheme.

LEADING EDGE EXPEDITIONS IN ASSOCIATION WITH THE DORSET EXPEDITIONARY SOCIETY
Lupins Business Centre, 1–3 Greenhill,
Weymouth, Dorset DT4 7SP
☎ (0)1305 777 277
✉ admin@leadingedge.org.uk
🖥 www.leadingedge.org.uk

Leading Edge Expeditions promotes adventurous opportunities for young people from throughout the UK. All expedition leaders are volunteers and company is non-profit-making. Duke of Edinburgh's Award has granted certificates as a Gold Residential and Gold Expedition Approved Activity Provider (status differs according to expedition).

PROGRAMME DESCRIPTION: Expeditions include trekking, mountain climbing, kayaking, white-water rafting, mountain biking, and safaris, and experience of other world cultures. Community project work and gap year or extended stays available working with the Okhle Village Trust in Nepal and the Dorset–Murugi link in Kenya.

DESTINATIONS: Europe, North and South America, Africa, India, and Asia, always to wilderness areas off the tourist track.

PREREQUISITES: Participants must be fit and healthy. Minimum age 15 for some expeditions, 16 or 18 for others.

DURATION AND TIME OF PLACEMENTS: 3–5 weeks for main expeditions, usually in the summer holidays. Longer stays from 3 to 7 months also available. Duke of Edinburgh's training and practice plus expedition up to 6 days. Weekend activities and skills training (mostly in the UK).

SELECTION PROCEDURES AND ORIENTATION: Selection weekend to choose suitable candidates for month-long expeditions. Gap year acceptance given after meeting with leader. Training courses for aspiring leaders are organised through the Dorset Expeditionary Society (dorsetexp@gmail.com; www.dorsetexp.org.uk), to gain nationally recognised qualifications such as Emergency Rescue First Aid Certificate, Single Pitch Assessment, Mountain Bike Leader, Cave Leadership, and Mountain Leadership Awards.

COST: £50 for the selection weekend plus expedition costs (roughly £400–£2,500). Weekends from £95. Duke of Edinburgh £295–£495. Guidance on fundraising is given.

CONTACT: Lucy Wyman, Secretary. Twitter/expeditions Facebook ID: 2229085667.

OASIS OVERLAND
The Marsh, Henstridge, Somerset BA8 0TF
☎ (0)1963 363 400
✉ info@oasisoverland.co.uk
🖥 www.oasisoverland.co.uk

Overland expedition company founded in 1997.

DESTINATIONS: South America, Africa, Middle East, Egypt.

NUMBER OF PLACEMENTS PER EXPEDITION: Purpose-built trucks carry up to 24.

DURATION: Large choice (see website) between 10 days and 40 weeks.

COST: From £110 a week plus £40 kitty on longest trips, rising to £165 plus £80 kitty in South America. Sample expedition 15 weeks Quito to Rio costs £2,395, plus $1,790 kitty paid locally.

CONTACT: Chris Wrede, Director.

RALEIGH
207 Waterloo Road, London SE1 8XD
☎ (0)20 7371 8585
✉ info@raleigh.org.uk
🖥 www.raleighinternational.org

Expeditions for young people aged 17–24, comprising a diverse mix of people including gap year students, graduates, and people from the expedition country. The aim is to make a positive contribution to the host countries – Costa Rica, Nicaragua, Malaysia (Borneo), and India. Participants are involved in adventure, community, and environmental projects. See listing in the 'Directory of Specialist Gap Year Programmes'.

REAL GAP EXPERIENCE
1 Meadow Road, Tunbridge Wells, Kent
TN1 2YG
☎ (0)1892 516 164
✉ info@realgap.co.uk
🖥 www.realgap.co.uk

PROGRAMME DESCRIPTION: Gap year adventure expeditions combining travel, adventure, and volunteer work in a range of destinations.

DESTINATIONS: Everest base camp, Ecuador, Peru, Venezuela, India, Indonesian Islands, Kenya, and Tanzania.

PREREQUISITES: None, except as limited by visas. Some programmes require basic level of fitness.

DURATION AND TIME OF PLACEMENTS: Everest trip is 35 days, most others last 4, 6, or 8 weeks.

COST: Everest expedition costs £1,999 for 5 weeks and includes some volunteering.

THE RONA SAILING PROJECT
Universal Marina, Crableck Lane, Sarisbury
Green, Southampton SO31 7ZN
☎ (0)1489 885 098
✉ office@ronatrust.com
🖥 www.ronatrust.com

Founded as the Rona Trust in 1960.

PROGRAMME DESCRIPTION: Sail training voyages for young people on three large sail training yachts. Older trainees sail in the two larger vessels and cross the Channel to France or the Channel Islands. Some crews are all women.

DESTINATIONS: South coast, France, or Channel Islands.

PREREQUISITES: For ages 16–19 and 18–25, and some for younger sailors.

DURATION AND TIME OF PLACEMENTS: Mostly 6 days.

SELECTION PROCEDURES AND ORIENTATION: Charity aims for broad social mix on each sailing. Most applicants come via recognised organisations such as scouts, sea cadets, youth clubs, schools, and colleges, but individuals may also book directly.

COST: £180 a week (because charitable project is subsidised).

CONTACT: Ann Bowers, Project Secretary.

SEA|MESTER PROGRAMS
PO Box 5477, Sarasota, FL 34277, USA
☎ +1 941 924 6789
info@seamester.com
www.seamester.com

Parent company (ActionQuest) has been operating experiential education programmes for youth for over 30 years and 'Sea I mester' programmes since 1998.

PROGRAMME DESCRIPTION: Educational adventures on an 88ft or 112ft schooner. Primary academic foci are oceanography, nautical science, communication, and leadership skills development. Students undertake research and service projects with local government and private organisations while working toward certification in sailing and scuba diving. Voyages are available in the Caribbean and worldwide destinations with ocean crossings.

NUMBER OF PLACEMENTS PER YEAR: About 200.

DESTINATIONS: Worldwide destinations include Mediterranean, Caribbean, South East Asia, Pacific, Australia, and ocean crossings.

PREREQUISITES: No experience necessary. Minimum age 17 (many students are pre-matriculates). All nationalities.

DURATION AND TIME OF PLACEMENTS: 80- and 90-day voyages during the autumn and spring. Also 20- and 40-day voyages during the summer.

COST: $22,970 for 90 days, $20,970 for 80 days, $9,870 for 40 days, $4,270 for 20 days.

CONTACT: Kyle Busacker, Admissions Co-ordinator, (kyle@seamester.com).

TALL SHIPS YOUTH TRUST
2A The Hard, Portsmouth, Hampshire PO1 3PT
☎ (0)23 9283 2055
info@tallships.org
www.tallships.org

Youth charity dedicated to the personal development of young people through crewing on its 60m^2 rigged ship *Stavros S Niarchos*.

PROGRAMME DESCRIPTION: Tall ships adventures and adventure sail training voyages, mostly lasting 7 days. These take place year-round in the waters around the UK and Northern Europe in the summer.

PREREQUISITES: Minimum age 16, with an upper age limit of 25 on youth voyages, 18–75 for adult voyages.

SELECTION PROCEDURES AND ORIENTATION: No previous sailing experience needed. Enthusiasm and an ability to work well with others is all that is required.

COST: £499 for 7 days, or £399 on different vessel, which may be reduced to £299 or £249 with bursaries.

THINK PACIFIC
Old Broadcasting House, Woodhouse Lane, Leeds, LS2 9EN
☎ (0)113 253 8684
info@thinkpacific.com
www.thinkpacific.com

Marine conservation expeditions in the Cook Islands that begin with PADI dive training and finish with trekking, kite boarding, etc on Rarotonga Island. Fiji expeditions volunteering in tiny rural villages combined with sailing, trekking, and snorkelling in some of Fiji's 330 islands. See entry in 'Directory of Specialist Gap Year Programmes'.

YORKSHIRE SCHOOLS EXPLORING SOCIETY
579 Denby Dale Road, Calder Grove, Wakefield, Yorkshire WF4 3DA
☎ (0)1924 267 144 (answering machine)
info@yses.org.uk
www.yses.org.uk

PROGRAMME DESCRIPTION: Expeditions are organised to wilderness areas, most recently to Sinai, Mongolia, and South Africa. Young leaders are needed to assist with the expeditions.

DESTINATIONS: Vary from year to year.

NUMBER OF PLACEMENTS PER YEAR: Around 70/80.

PREREQUISITES: Students on the expeditions must be in full-time education in Yorkshire (aged 14–19). Leaders can come from anywhere and need not be in full-time education.

DURATION AND TIME OF PLACEMENTS: 4–5 weeks in summer.

WORK EXPERIENCE

Focused school leavers who have a clear idea of what career path they intend to follow can try to build into their gap year a component of working in a related field, which will also feed into their university course. This works better with engineering than English literature, say, but in all cases will look impressive on future CVs. Work experience considered in its broadest terms applies to any experience of the world of work, which can also be in a developing country, and is very often unpaid.

With graduate unemployment at a 17-year high and one in 10 graduates unable to find a job within a year of graduating, unpaid work experience placements may be all that a new graduate can aspire to. The new buzzword in this context is 'intern' as a means of kickstarting careers, and the UK government's Department for Business, Innovation and Skills sponsors a service and website to match graduates with businesses.

GRADUATES' TIP

The Graduate Talent Pool (http://graduatetalentpool.direct.gov.uk) is a government initiative that helps recent graduates get internships with companies; registration is free.

Experience in a working environment, preferably in your chosen career field, is a valuable asset for any serious job search. And if this can be combined with cultural immersion and the chance to cope with a foreign working environment, your profile will be enhanced even more. The troubled economy is predicted to send more students and graduates to untraditional places, from China to California, searching for an opportunity to extend their CVs and provide potential for future job references. Even if an overseas work placement is irrelevant to your future career plans, it will at least provide a useful introduction to how companies or organisations function in a different culture. This applies to people taking a pre- or post-university gap year.

Although all Year 10 students are obliged to undertake a 10-day work experience placement in the summer term, a longer period spent working in a particular area gives a much clearer idea of what a job is about and whether it is of interest to you as a potential career. Work placements are looked on favourably by university admissions officers; experience of the 'real world' often helps students to develop a more mature outlook on life which enables them to do relatively better at university than their peers, who come straight from school or a Thai island. Similarly, employers view students with work experience as more desirable. There is less risk for an employer in choosing someone who has already had some exposure to a particular career, and also less expense in training.

Employers, especially in companies with an international profile, look for employees who have demonstrated that they are open-minded and can adapt to different cultures. One way to impress these employers is with a CV that shows that you have successfully completed a period of work experience abroad. This is particularly impressive if the student uses or learns a foreign language as part of this experience. However, experience in the USA or Australia will also boost your CV.

Nowadays, the demand for many careers often outweighs supply, and exam qualifications no longer seem to be enough to get a job. Work experience can be used as a means of getting a foot in the door with particular companies and occupations. If you are interested in gaining experience in a competitive field such as the media, publishing, broadcasting, museology, medicine, veterinary science, wildlife conservation, etc, you may find it very difficult to obtain paid work.

If you are serious about enhancing your CV or simply getting a taste of what it will be really like, you should be prepared initially to work on a voluntary basis, which is now standard practice in many professions such as conservation. Some UK companies specialise in arranging work experience abroad in fields allied to medicine, journalism and others; see entries below for Global Volunteer Projects and Learn Overseas and also see the Work the World website (www.worktheworld.co.uk), which organises placements for student medics, nurses, dentists, and physiotherapists to gain experience working in Ghana, Tanzania, Nepal, Sri Lanka, and Argentina. Gap Medics (www.gapmedics.co.uk) has placements in India, Tanzania, and the Caribbean.

If you foresee yourself working in business, engineering, banking, accountancy, or industry after graduation, you may be able to arrange a relevant paid work experience placement in your year between school and university. Not only are you likely to be able to earn and save money, but with luck a firm will like you enough to offer you future vacation jobs or even a permanent career. **Nicky Stead** from West Yorkshire found herself in the unwelcome position of being forced to take a gap year when her A level results were worse than expected. Undaunted, she decided to work locally before embarking on some world travels:

> *I had to get a job and decided that to make the best of things I should get one that was relevant to my preferred career and would look good on my CV, as well as raise money for travelling. I got a job inputting mortgage applications for Skipton Building Society for six months, which I really enjoyed. I made so many friends and I loved the business environment. I felt grown up, and it was great. My appraisal was good and they encouraged me to stay.*

FINDING A PLACEMENT

Several companies that take students for work placements for a substantial period are listed at the end of this chapter. It is worth visiting the local Connexions office for the names of local companies that might take on students. Students can also write directly to companies enclosing a CV to ask whether they offer work placements, although the ratio of replies (let alone favourable ones) to letters sent is likely to be discouraging. The direct approach is more personal and likely to please potential employers, especially if there is a particular aspect of the company which students can say has attracted them.

Much can be achieved by confidently and persistently asking for the chance to help out in your chosen workplace unpaid. **Laura Hitchcock** from the USA managed to fix up two three-month positions in the field of her career interest by agreeing to pay her own expenses if they would take her on and help her find accommodation in local homes. Her jobs were in the publicity departments of the Ironbridge Museums and then in a theatre arts centre in East Anglia. Laura discovered that if you are willing to help yourself people can be helpful and encouraging.

Specific gap year programmes offered by big companies are generally fiercely competitive. If applying for one of these competitive schemes, such as the ones offered by Deloitte or KPMG, be prepared to undergo psychometric tests and other rigorous selection procedures. At interview, you will be expected to talk about market issues in the financial world affecting the service line for which you are applying, ie tax or assurance/audit. Also, you should have an example prepared that demonstrates how you solve problems in a team. And of course they will want to know your reasons for taking a gap year. Whatever the question, use it to demonstrate a strength of yours, not a weakness.

The fortunate few who are successful are usually paid a reasonable salary and many other benefits. The companies offer these schemes in order to attract the best possible candidates to join their companies after university. They tend to make their programmes interesting and varied to impress students. For example, the Accenture Horizons Gap Year Scheme is a programme that lasts eight months from September and combines training with paid work experience. Accenture pays £20,000 (pro rata, so equivalent to more than £13,000 for the eight months) plus a relocation bonus. The early finish date leaves plenty of time and money for travelling before university in the autumn.

MY GAP YEAR: ROBERT NOESSLER

Robert Noessler, from Leipzig, spent a gap year in Chile and is sold on the idea of going abroad to do work experience, even if he found it financially challenging. From September 2010 to February 2011, he did an internship in marketing and public relations at the agency Chile Inside in Santiago, where most of the interns taken on are aged 19–24.

The decision to take a gap year was actually taken jointly with my girlfriend Corinna. Since she had plans to study for one semester in South America (to improve her language skills for her Spanish studies), and I was always interested in working or studying in another country (but didn't use the opportunities during my Journalism and English course at university), we took the chance to go abroad together. The main motives for me were the cultural, social and personal experiences I expected to collect during a longer time away from home. The pros were also the chance to discover a new job field, to orientate myself professionally, and last but not least to give my CV a special touch with experience abroad. New creative influences were an important aspect for me, as well, since I am making music as a singer-songwriter, and hoped to get a lot of new impressions.

Internships in South America, even in such developed countries as Chile, are in most cases not paid. So I had to find another way to finance my trip. Apart from that, I was at first a bit worried about finding my way in a new language (Spanish), which I was just starting to learn. But there was no need for the insecurity, as it turned out. I started my gap year with a two-week Spanish course at the ECELA Language School on arrival, which was a really good opportunity to improve my language skills and to get in touch with other people.

Chile Inside arranges volunteer and intern positions for a fee, but instead of participating in one of their programmes I found the idea very interesting to work directly in such an international and multilingual agency. In the office, I worked in the areas of marketing, public relations and translation. This was a good opportunity for me to discover a new branch of employment and at the same time to apply my journalistic and language skills. My main task was to write texts in different languages, such as guides for different countries in

South America or programme descriptions for the website and other publications. The working conditions and atmosphere in the agency were very friendly and helpful. Since the work was computer-based, I had my own desk with PC and internet access in the office. Because Chile Inside is a small company, it was always possible to ask colleagues and bosses when there was a question. Moreover, the agency arranged the language course as well as housing for my girlfriend and me.

Travelling throughout South America after my internship in Santiago was not only the highlight of my gap year, but also of recent years. In general, the mix of learning a language in a foreign country, applying it during an internship, followed by a longer period of travel, was in my eyes a perfect way to look beyond one's own nose. I can absolutely recommend it.

Other gap year schemes, such as the one run by IBM, are hanging in there, although Pricewaterhouse Coopers cancelled its programme for gap year students in 2009, blaming the economic downturn. Many students seeking work experience will entertain more modest ambitions than these gold-plated companies. Agency temping experience in different kinds of office can be a useful stepping stone not only to well-paid holiday work in the future but also to acquiring a broad acquaintance with the working world.

You could also try WEXO (Work Experience Online; www.wexo.co.uk), a networking community for those requiring or offering work experience, internships, and jobs. In the current climate, there are far more internship-seekers registered than there are offers from companies. The majority of work experience placements are designed for university students, typically in their third year, and many university careers services have excellent databases of prospective companies. Individual universities cater mainly to their own students, but their careers webpages can be worth searching. The Windsor Fellowship (www.windsor-fellowship.org) offers sponsorship to high-achieving undergraduates (first or second year) from African, African-Caribbean, and Asian communities in the UK. For example, the Leadership Programme involves a work placement with a private or public sector employer, as well as community involvement. Similarly, Sponsors for Educational Opportunity (SEO), a non-profit organisation based in London, assists exceptional undergraduates from under-represented ethnic minority backgrounds to find summer internships with banks, corporate law firms, and other UK businesses.

YEAR IN INDUSTRY

The Year in Industry (YINI) is a leading provider of gap year work placements throughout the UK and is run by the educational charity, the Engineering Development Trust (EDT). Last year, around 500 students took part in the scheme, gaining skills and experience to enhance their degree course while earning a real salary. The Year in Industry is this year (2011) celebrating 25 years of helping students realise their potential and has provided placements for around 12,000 students over the years.

There are opportunities in all branches of engineering, science, technology, IT, business, and other fields. Placements generally last 10–12 months from August/September to June/July and are paid, so students get valuable work experience while saving for university or travels. It's a great chance for students to confirm their degree choice and get a feel for the working world before starting university.

Students develop skills that will enhance their university education and maximise their graduate employment prospects. Many companies view the Year in Industry as a part of their graduate recruitment programme, and go on to sponsor placement students through university or offer vacation work. Around one in four students goes on to receive financial support from his or her company throughout university, and many students are subsequently offered jobs on graduation.

When **Oliver Taylor** took a gap year with the Year in Industry, he was placed with the underwater systems business, Qinetiq, a British defence technology company (now Atlas Elektronik). Now at Nottingham University, Oliver commented, '*I am always noticing the difference between myself and other students that has come about from doing my YINI placement. I'm getting a lot more out of my uni experience, having gained the experience in independence from the year out.*'

WORK EXPERIENCE ABROAD

Anyone with sufficient determination and patience has a good chance of persuading a company or organisation overseas that they could use an unpaid assistant keen to gain exposure to that particular profession. **Kate Day** wanted to travel after university while advancing her ambition of becoming a journalist:

> *I spent a year getting a range of work experience after graduating from university. I had decided I wanted to be a journalist rather late and was ill during my undergraduate degree so had no journalism experience when I graduated. I worked on a couple of local papers in this country and then went out to California for three months last March where I was a reporter for a tiny paper called the* **Los Altos Town Crier** *in Silicon Valley. I then went to India last summer with Projects Abroad and stayed on in the country after my placement finished to travel a little bit and spent a week at* **The Hindu** *office in Chennai at the end. I am now doing a newspaper journalism diploma at City University in London and spent the Christmas holidays working for* **Times Online.**

In order to fix up the internship near San Francisco, Kate says she did endless Googling (journalism jobs/internships), and concentrated her efforts on small local papers. She didn't hear back from most of them but did succeed with one. Getting paid was out of the question for visa reasons. After signing up with a gap year agency to arrange a placement in south India, she says now that she was naïve in expecting everything to be laid on, because it wasn't. Undaunted, she made a private arrangement to do some work shadowing at the main Indian daily *The Hindu*, experience that must have counted in her favour when she was applying for work experience in London later.

Work experience is also one of the fastest-growing sectors in the youth travel industry. Projects Abroad is just one of many fee-charging placement agencies. The international association of work experience providers called WYSE Work Abroad (www.wyseworkabroad.org) has more than 150 member organisations around the world, many of which are affiliated to language schools that provide a preparatory language course before assignment to a workplace. WYSE Work's stated aim is to '*facilitate and increase international youth travel and exchange through the promotion of culturally-oriented work exchange and work experience activities*'. Its website includes links to its members and is a good starting place for anyone interested in fixing up work experience abroad, almost all of which is unpaid. Most mediating organisations charge a substantial fee for their services, usually between €750 and €1,500, which may not include living expenses.

Students and recent graduates in business, management, marketing, accounting, finance, computing, education or economics may be interested in an organisation run by a global student network based in 90 countries. AIESEC, a French acronym for the International Association for Students of Economics and Management (www.aiesec.co.uk), can organise placements in any of its member countries, aimed at giving participants an insight into living and working in another culture. IAESTE stands for the International Association for the Exchange of Students for Technical Experience. It provides international course-related vacation training for thousands of university-level students in 80 member countries. Placements are available in engineering, science, agriculture, architecture, and related fields. British undergraduates should apply directly to IAESTE UK at the British Council (www. iaeste.org.uk). The US affiliate is the Association for International Practical Training or AIPT (+410 997 3069; www.aipt.org), which can arrange long- and short-term placements for graduates and young professionals as well as college students in related fields.

WORKING IN EUROPE

Legislation has existed for many years guaranteeing the rights of all nationals of the European Union to travel, reside, study, and work in any member country. The accession of two new countries to the European Union in 2007 (Bulgaria and Romania), in addition to the 10 new countries that joined in May 2004, means that the EU now consists of the original 15 member states (Austria, Belgium, Denmark, Finland, France, Germany, Greece, Ireland, Italy, Luxembourg, the Netherlands, Portugal, Spain, Sweden, and the UK) plus Hungary, Poland, the Czech Republic, Slovakia, Slovenia, Estonia, Latvia, Lithuania, Malta, Cyprus, Romania, and Bulgaria. However, some transitional barriers to the full mobility of labour linger on.

The computerised, pan-European job information network EURES (EURopean Employment Service) is accessible through JobcentrePlus offices around the UK and all national employment services in Europe. Throughout Europe, hundreds of specially trained EuroAdvisers can offer help and information about vacancies within Europe. It is also possible to access the EURES database online via the EURES portal http://ec.europa.eu/eures to see the kinds of vacancies available from Iceland to Greece. Registered vacancies are usually for six months or longer, and are often in hotels and catering, personal services, or for skilled, semi-skilled, and (increasingly) managerial jobs. Naturally, language skills are very often a requirement.

A number of special exchanges and youth programmes help young Europeans move easily across borders for short and longer periods. Some of these projects cannot be applied for directly by the student, but must be supported by their school, university, or local youth agency. The aim of the EU's Leonardo da Vinci scheme is to improve the quality of vocational and language training in Europe. It grants students and recent graduates mobility and in some cases full funding to undertake overseas work placements of between three and 12 months (for students) or between two and 12 months (recent graduates). Applications for Leonardo funding must be submitted by organisations, not individuals. Details are available from university placement offices or International Relations Offices, or directly from ECOTEC, acting as the Leonardo UK National Agency in Birmingham (0845 199 2929; leonardo@ecotec.com; www.leonardo.org.uk). The terms of the programme are quite prescriptive (eg they cover 'linguistic preparation' but not 'language courses'), so candidates must be prepared to conform to the specifications.

The well-established Erasmus student exchange incorporates an Internship in Europe component which is integrated throughout the EU. Students from all the participating countries can do an Erasmus internship somewhere in the European Union, plus Norway, Iceland, Liechtenstein, and Turkey. The Erasmus internship should last at least three months, but no more than 12, and it should be relevant to the trainee's degree studies.

POST-UNIVERSITY GAPPERS' TIP

High fliers who would like to work for the European Commission as administrators, translators, secretaries, etc must participate in open competitions to do so (http://ec.europa.eu/stages). (See entry p232.)

DIRECTORY OF WORK EXPERIENCE IN THE UK

ACCENTURE HORIZONS GAP YEAR SCHEME
40 Fenchurch Street, London EC3M 3BD
☎ (0)500 100 189 (recruiting helpline)
✆ ukgraduates@accenture.com
✆ UKI_peopleline_HR@accenture.com
💻 https://microsite.accenture.com/UK_
graduate_joiners/Where_will_I_fit_in/
Internships_and_placements/Pages/
Horizons.aspx

PROGRAMME DESCRIPTION: Provides students looking to take a gap year with a combination of training, work experience, and the opportunity to travel before going to university. The job involves working alongside high-profile clients to deliver technology and management consultancy solutions. Upon successful completion of the placement, an opportunity is given to do further paid summer vacation work while at university, and potentially an offer of a permanent position on graduation.
DESTINATIONS: London base; however, the work may require travel to client sites across the UK.
PREREQUISITES: Must be an A level student currently in the upper sixth, with a keen interest in business and technology. A strong record of academic achievement is important with good grades in Maths and English at GCSE and a minimum of 340 UCAS points (AAB at A level) or 5 Bs at Scottish Highers predicted. Candidates should be confident, enthusiastic, and mature, with excellent communication and team working skills.
DURATION AND TIME OF PLACEMENTS: 8-month internships from early September to April.
SELECTION PROCEDURES AND ORIENTATION: All applications should be made online. Applications are open between 1 September and 31 December. Interviews will be held from the September of the candidate's final year at school.
REMUNERATION: Candidates are paid the pro rata equivalent of £20,000 per year, with a £500 relocation bonus. Depending on performance, the chance to come back and work during summer holidays is extended.
CONTACT: Emma Bell, Schemes Recruiter.

BBC WORK EXPERIENCE PLACEMENTS
✆ careers@bbchrdirect.co.uk
💻 www.bbc.co.uk/workexperience

PROGRAMME DESCRIPTION: A chance for people to see what the working life of the BBC is like for a few days or up to 4 weeks.
NUMBER OF PLACEMENTS: 150+ placement areas from which to choose, based at various UK locations.
PREREQUISITES: See searchable database of opportunities online for specific criteria.
REMUNERATION: None.
SELECTION PROCEDURES AND ORIENTATION: Deadlines vary according to business area (eg production, business management and support, journalism). Up to 3 months needed to process applications, and applications accepted up to 6 months before proposed start date.

CIVIL SERVICE CAREERS
💻 www.civilservice.gov.uk/jobs/entry/
Undergraduates-Graduates-Work-
Experience.aspx

More than 170 departments and executive agencies, employing nearly half a million people, make the Civil Service one of the largest employers in the UK. Very few government departments and agencies offer vacation opportunities for graduates and undergraduates in relevant fields, and those that have been run in the past are being slashed. For example, the Government Legal Service (www.gls.gov.uk) has announced: '*Unfortunately, the GLS will not be operating a Vacation Placement Scheme in 2011. At a time when departments are required to make a number of efficiency savings, the cost of operating the VPS is one that departments are currently unable to meet.*' The Civil Service Fast Stream, however, runs a Summer Diversity Internship Programme (http://faststream.civilservice.gov.uk/Summer-Diversity-Internships/Programmes-and-Schemes) lasting 6–9 weeks for ethnic minority students and candidates from lower socio-economic backgrounds.

CORAL CAY CONSERVATION (CCC)
Elizabeth House, 39 York Road, London
SE1 7NJ
☎ (0)20 7620 1411
✆ info@coralcay.org
💻 www.coralcay.org

Founding member of the Year Out Group. CCC sends hundreds of volunteers to assist in conserving endangered tropical marine and terrestrial environments in the Philippines, Tobago, and Cambodia (see 'Directory of Specialist Gap Year Programmes').

PROGRAMME DESCRIPTION: Opportunities for PR, sales, and marketing interns to work at London head office. Positions are part-time (2 days a week) and unwaged, but travel and other expenses are paid. Marketing interns may be asked to attend gap year and careers fairs, exhibitions, and networking events.

CONTACT: Lorrae Guilfoyle, PR & Communications Co-ordinator (lg@coralcay.org).

DELOITTE
Stonecutter Court, 1 Stonecutter Street, London EC4A 4TR
☎ (0)20 7303 7019
toliver@deloitte.co.uk
💻 www.deloitte.co.uk/scholars

PROGRAMME DESCRIPTION: Scholars Scheme offers financial sponsorship and work experience in the financial industry to high-calibre students from the start of a gap year through to when they graduate from university. Alternative programme is BrightStart Deloitte School Leaver Programme for Audit Tax & Corporate Finance (www.deloitte.co.uk/graduates/brightstart) in multiple locations, where students get on-the-job training over 5 years instead of going to university.

NUMBER OF PLACEMENTS PER YEAR: 40.

DESTINATIONS: Placements offered in a number of regional offices (including St Albans, Reading, Bristol, Cambridge, Birmingham, Nottingham, Manchester, Leeds, Edinburgh, and Glasgow) as well as London office (on the Strand) and others.

PREREQUISITES: Good A levels (any subject) with intention to go on to study at a top UK university after their gap year. Must have achieved at least B in GCSE Maths and C in English language, be predicted 320 UCAS tariff points in first 3 A levels excluding General Studies. Should have interest in business/finance.

DURATION AND TIME OF PLACEMENTS: Gap year placements last 30 weeks from the end of August. Successful candidates remain involved in the scheme throughout their university education.

SELECTION PROCEDURES AND ORIENTATION: Applications open on 1 July (13 months before scheme begins); no closing date since the scheme remains open until places are filled with suitable candidates on a first come, first served basis. Applications are made online via website above.

REMUNERATION: Scholars receive a competitive salary and receive £1,500 travel bursary to spend in the remainder of their gap year. Once at university, they receive £1,500 academic bursary each year and return to Deloitte for at least 4 weeks a year in their holidays for further paid work.

CONTACT: Tarrilyn Oliver, Early Identification Administrator.

EARTHWATCH INSTITUTE (EUROPE)
Mayfield House, 256 Banbury Road, Oxford OX2 7DE
☎ (0)1865 318 838
info@earthwatch.org.uk
💻 www.earthwatch.org/europe

Earthwatch is an international environmental charity which engages people worldwide in scientific field research and education, to promote the understanding and action necessary for a sustainable environment. Earthwatch's vision is a world in which we live within our means and in balance with nature.

PROGRAMME DESCRIPTION: Various unpaid internship positions are available in the Oxford office, offering useful experience to those wishing to enter the charity/environmental sector. Positions are advertised as and when available. Internships are also offered at the Earthwatch office in Boston, USA (to which interested people can apply at any time).

DURATION AND TIME OF PLACEMENTS: 4–6 months.

SELECTION PROCEDURES AND ORIENTATION: Internship candidates in the UK must submit a CV and covering letter and are selected subject to interview. Internship candidates in the USA must submit a writing sample.

GLOBE EDUCATION
International Shakespeare Globe Centre, Globe Education, 21 New Globe Walk, London SE1 9DT
☎ (0)20 7902 1433
💻 www.shakespearesglobe.com/about-us/opportunities/internships

PROGRAMME DESCRIPTION: Paid gap year student internships to run the 'Lively Action Schools Programme' (the theatre's workshop and lecture programme caters for 45,000 students annually). Shorter unpaid administrative work experience placements in various departments: exhibitions, appeals/fundraising, and communications. Students will be able to work on special projects and events and act as stewards during the summer.

NUMBER OF PLACEMENTS: 2 paid internships for school leavers who want to develop a career in arts or education administration. Possibility of 30 short internships.

DURATION AND TIME OF PLACEMENTS: 12 months from 1 September for internship. 1–2 weeks' work experience (or longer if gap year placement), or minimum 3 months' unpaid internship.

REMUNERATION: Stipend paid with 25 days' holiday, free access to the majority of Globe Education events, and some free theatre tickets. No wage paid for short work experience placements, and travel expenses are not covered.

SELECTION PROCEDURES AND ORIENTATION: Due to the large volume of unsolicited enquiries received, they reply only to applications for positions advertised on their website.

CONTACT: Rob Norman, Personnel Manager (robert.n@shakespearesglobe.com).

IBM UK
PO Box 41, North Harbour, Portsmouth
PO6 3AU
☎ (0)23 9256 4104 (student recruitment hotline)
✍ ibmstudent@uk.ibm.com
💻 www-05.ibm.com/employment/uk/futures

PROGRAMME DESCRIPTION: IBM Futures Programme is a gap year scheme for academically outstanding students. Choice of business or technical strands. Pre-university employment (eg in technology, marketing, consulting, and human resources) lasts 9 months, followed by 3 months doing what you like, including the possibility of working with Raleigh (see entry in 'Directory of Specialist Gap Year Programmes'). The Raleigh expedition complements the competencies that IBM recruits against and the firm will be flexible (business permitting) to support any student wishing to pursue this unique opportunity.

PREREQUISITES: Selection against a number of competencies based on tangible evidence. Must have a deferred place or be planning a deferred place at university.

DURATION AND TIME OF PLACEMENTS: 9–12 months starting in August/September. Deadline for applications is May.

SELECTION PROCEDURES AND ORIENTATION: Assessments centres set up in September of year preceding gap year.

OTHER SERVICES: Residential induction course at beginning of year. Salary of £15,000 pro-rata and up to £1,000 performance-related bursary awarded at end of the initial 9-month contract, depending on performance against key objectives.

INDEPENDENT TELEVISION
See below for contact details.

PROGRAMME DESCRIPTION: A limited number of work experience placements is sometimes available with the regional ITV companies. Vacancies are rarely known in advance and demand constantly outstrips supply.

PREREQUISITES: Applicants must be students on a recognised course of study at a college or university; their course must lead to the possibility of employment within the television industry (ideally, work experience would be a compulsory part of the course); and the student must be resident in the transmission area of the company offering the attachment, or in some cases, attending a course in that region. However, opportunities occasionally exist for students following computing, librarianship, finance, legal, administrative, or management courses.

DURATION AND TIME OF PLACEMENTS: Placements vary in length from half a day to several weeks or months, depending on the work available and the candidate's requirements.

REMUNERATION: Students do not normally receive payment, although there is a possibility that expenses will be paid. Students from sandwich courses who are on long-term attachments may be regarded as short-term employees and paid accordingly.

CONTACT General information on working in media can be obtained from the Sectors Skills Council for Creative Media (broadcast, film, video, interactive media, and photo imaging) on www.skillset.org. Their careers service, Skillset Careers, offers media careers information, advice, and guidance to anyone wanting to enter or progress in the media industry. Visit www.skillset.org/careers/work_experience or call one of the free helplines – (0)8080 300 900 in England, (0)8458 502 502 in Scotland or (0)800 0121815 in Wales.

KPMG LLP
✍ ukfmgraduate@kpmg.co.uk
💻 www.kpmgcareers.co.uk (search for A Level Trainees and then the Gap Programme)

PROGRAMME DESCRIPTION: Gap Year Programme in Audit or Risk & Compliance department, which provides hands-on commercial experience and an understanding of the professional services industry. May involve travel to clients' premises.

DESTINATIONS: Offices throughout the UK.

PREREQUISITES: Must have already obtained or have predicted at least 320 UCAS tariff points and minimum grade B in GCSE Maths and English. Must be pro-active individual who can demonstrate commitment to their chosen team.

DURATION AND TIME OF PLACEMENTS: 6 months from October to April.

SELECTION PROCEDURES AND ORIENTATION: Online application in first instance. Acceptance is very competitive at the next stages of online numeracy and verbal reasoning tests followed by a competency-based interview. Chosen candidates are then given a 1-week induction, and then assigned to a mentor for informal support and guidance, a manager who oversees the day-to-day work, and a senior manager who will review performance.

METASWITCH NETWORKS
100 Church Street, Enfield EN2 6BQ
☎ (0)20 8366 1177
🖰 careers@metaswitch.com
🖥 www.metaswitch.com/careers/internships/
pre-university

Metaswitch Networks is a leading technology company.

PROGRAMME DESCRIPTION: Vacation work and year-long placements are offered to exceptional pre-university and university students with an interest in the development of complex software. The company provides challenging programming assignments, while offering help and support.

PREREQUISITES: Successful applicants usually have all A grades at A level or equivalent. Computing experience not required, but must have a real interest in technology.

DURATION AND TIME OF PLACEMENTS: Minimum of 8 weeks over the summer or for a gap year.

SELECTION PROCEDURES: Recruitment takes place year-round. 1-stage interview process with results known within 3 days.

REMUNERATION: A salary of £1,100 per month for pre-university students. Also subsidised accommodation in the company house, a few minutes' walk from the office.

CONTACT: The Recruitment Team.

OXFAM
Volunteering Team, Oxfam House, John Smith Drive, Cowley, Oxford OX4 2JY
☎ (0)1865 473 252
🖰 internship@oxfam.org.uk
🖥 www.oxfam.org.uk/get_involved/volunteer/
interns.html

PROGRAMME DESCRIPTION: Voluntary internship scheme in NGO sector. Successful candidates can contribute to Oxfam's goal of reducing poverty and suffering worldwide by volunteering in a variety of divisions, such as Campaigns, Humanitarian, or Trading. Opportunities for specific training if relevant to assigned project, eg project management, time management, negotiation skills.

DESTINATIONS: UK only.

PREREQUISITES: Required skills and experiences vary depending on the specific role. Open to any age group, though some offices are restricted to taking interns 18 years and over.

DURATION AND TIME OF PLACEMENTS: Up to 3 days per week for 3 to 6 or 12 months, depending on position. Recruitment is ongoing throughout the year.

REMUNERATION: Positions are unpaid. Lunch and reasonable travel expenses are reimbursed in line with Oxfam's policy.

PRICEWATERHOUSECOOPERS
🖥 www.pwc.com/uk/careers

The member firms of the PricewaterhouseCoopers network (www.pwc.co.uk) provide assurance, tax, and advisory services to clients and their stakeholders in 154 countries.

PROGRAMME DESCRIPTION: PricewaterhouseCoopers' gap year programme was cancelled in 2009; however, it offers internships to penultimate-year undergraduates and graduates.

ROYAL OPERA HOUSE
Covent Garden, London WC2E 9DD
🖥 www.roh.org.uk/workhere/workexperience/
index.aspx

PLACEMENTS OFFERED: Work placements as part of 'First Stage' programme offered across the organisation, but predominantly in technical and production areas (for example model room, costume production, or sound and lighting).

PREREQUISITES: Selection criteria and minimum age limits vary, depending on the placement type. Applications accepted from UK residents only. Minimum age 18. Students should have an interest in ballet, opera, or music, with a view to working in the arts.

DURATION OF COURSES: Depends on placement type, from 2 days to several months, though most of no more than a couple of weeks.

CONTACT: Lowri Jones, Work Experience Administrator.

SIR ROBERT MCALPINE
Eaton Court, Maylands Avenue, Hemel Hempstead, Hertfordshire HP2 7TR
☎ (0)1442 412 909
🖰 www.sir-robert-mcalpine.com

A long-established building and civil engineering contractor, which has suspended its gap year scheme, but will review the decision in autumn 2011.

STEP
STEP Enterprise House, 14–16 Bridgford Road, West Bridgford, Nottingham NG2 6AB
☎ (0)844 248 8242
🖰 students@step.org.uk
🖥 www.step.org.uk

Initiative formerly sponsored by Shell UK to match undergraduates and new graduates with small and medium-sized businesses and community organisations for work projects.

PROGRAMME DESCRIPTION: Work experience projects, mostly in the summer, for second- and higher-year university students and new graduates in science, technology, and engineering subjects.

NUMBER OF PROJECTS: About 600.

PREREQUISITES: Must be studying full-time at a UK university, in either second or penultimate year, or recent graduates. No age restrictions.

DURATION AND TIME OF PLACEMENTS: 8–12 weeks.

SELECTION PROCEDURES AND ORIENTATION: Application can be made online. Deadline for summer placements falls in the second week of June.

REMUNERATION: Summer students receive £210 per week. Travelling expenses are paid at the employer's discretion.

TATA STEEL PLACEMENT SCHEME
Tata Steel Graduate Recruitment, Ashorne Hill, Leamington Spa, Warwickshire CV33 9PY
☎ (0)1926 488 025
🖰 graduate.recruitment@tatasteel.com
🖥 www.tatasteelcareers.com

PROGRAMME DESCRIPTION: Tata Steel recruits placement students into the following fields in the UK: manufacturing, engineering (mechanical, electrical, civil, chemical, and environmental), metallurgy, R&D, process control and automation, commercial, logistics & supply chain, finance, and human resources.

DESTINATIONS: Vacancies are based across the UK, with main locations including Hartlepool, York, Scunthorpe, Rotherham, Corby, Llanwern, Port Talbot, Trostre, and Shotton.

DURATION AND TIME OF PLACEMENTS: 3 months and 12 months.

PREREQUISITES: A relevant degree is required for the technical functions. Ideally, undergraduates would be on track to receive at least a 2.1.

SELECTION PROCEDURES AND ORIENTATION: Applications should be made online between beginning of February and mid-March via www.tatasteelcareer.com.

REMUNERATION: Up to £16,000 per year. Upon successful completion of a placement, there is the possibility of receiving sponsorship for following academic year.

YEAR IN INDUSTRY
University of Southampton, Southampton SO17 1BJ
☎ (0)23 8059 7061
🖰 info@yini.org.uk
🖥 www.yini.org.uk

Founding member of the Year Out Group. The Year in Industry, founded 25 years ago, is a major provider of gap year industrial placements throughout the UK and is administered by EDT (www.etrust.org.uk).

PROGRAMME DESCRIPTION: The Year in Industry programme provides paid, structured, and fully supported work experience from which students gain career and personal development, confirm their career choices and prepare for their degrees. Participants are encouraged to enter an end-of-year competition with cash prizes.

NUMBER OF PLACEMENTS PER YEAR: 500–600.

PREREQUISITES: Students should be interested in gaining experience in industry, and must be intending to go to university. Most participants are intending to study engineering, science, technology, or business, although opportunities are available for other disciplines.

DURATION AND TIME OF PLACEMENTS: Placements generally last 10–12 months, from August/September to May/July. Placements that finish early can be combined with travel abroad, with YINI's gap year partners Coral Cay Conservation, BUNAC, Raleigh International, and Projects Abroad.

SELECTION PROCEDURES AND ORIENTATION: All applicants will be interviewed by the Year in Industry. Participants are also offered university-level maths course and leadership training.

REMUNERATION: Students earn competitive salaries during their placements.

DIRECTORY OF WORK EXPERIENCE ABROAD

AGRIVENTURE

International Agricultural Exchange Association (IAEA), UK AgriVenture Global Office, Long Clawson, Melton Mowbray, Leicestershire LE14 4NR

☎ (0)1664 822 335
🖰 post@agriventure.com
💻 www.agriventure.com

PROGRAMME DESCRIPTION: International agricultural and horticultural work placements for British and EU participants.
DESTINATIONS: Placements for UK and European participants in the USA, Canada, Australia, New Zealand, and Japan.
PREREQUISITES: Must be aged 18–30 with an aptitude for or interest in working in agriculture or horticulture.
DURATION AND TIME OF PLACEMENTS: Placements in the USA and Canada begin in February and April and last for 7 or 9 months. Placements for Australia and New Zealand run throughout the year and last 4–12 months. Placements in Japan begin in April and last 4–12 months. They also offer a Workabout programme in Canada, Australia, and New Zealand where you have short-term placements as you travel round. There are also several round-the-world itineraries, which depart in the autumn to the southern hemisphere for 6–7 months, followed by another 6–7 months in the northern hemisphere.
SELECTION PROCEDURES AND ORIENTATION: Selection by interview. Pre-departure information meeting and orientation seminar on arrival.
COST: Participants pay between £2,030 and £4,500, which includes airline tickets, visas, insurance, orientation seminar, back-up, and board and lodging throughout, with an approved hosting enterprise. Trainees are paid a realistic wage.

AIL MADRID SPANISH LANGUAGE IMMERSION SCHOOL IN SPAIN

C/Nuñez de Balboa 17, 2°D, 28001 Madrid, Spain

☎ +34 91 72 56 350
🖰 info@ailmadrid.com
💻 www.ailmadrid.com/gap year/home

PROGRAMME DESCRIPTION: 12-week Spanish language course in Madrid and other cities in Spain with work placement options.
PREREQUISITES: Minimum age 17, average age 22.
DURATION AND TIME OF PLACEMENTS: 12–48 weeks with flexible start dates.
COST: 12-week programme from €3,500.
CONTACT: Maya Bychova.

AUSTRALIAN INTERNSHIPS

Suite 1, Savoir Faire, 20 Park Road, Milton, Brisbane, Queensland 4064, Australia

☎ +61 7 3305 8408
🖰 info@internships.com.au
💻 www.internships.com.au

PROGRAMME DESCRIPTION: There are 2 programme options for candidates interested in seeking international hands-on experience: Professional Internship Programme and Hospitality Internship Programme. Former offers hands-on experience in most fields (apart from medicine) especially administration, education, engineering, finance, government, graphic design, journalism, marketing, and trade. Latter offers paid positions for hospitality students willing to work in hands-on fields such as cookery, food and drink, and housekeeping. Candidates should be flexible with their destinations as positions vary from capital cities to islands and resorts in remote locations.
DESTINATIONS: Throughout Australia.
NUMBER OF PLACEMENTS: 600–1,000.
PREREQUISITES: Ages 18–30, mostly current students and recent graduates. Pre-university students are eligible but will be placed in entry-level roles.
DURATION AND TIME OF PLACEMENTS: 6–52 weeks, but usual maximum is 6 months.
SELECTION PROCEDURES AND ORIENTATION: All details for the internship are confirmed, with each candidate in a formal training agreement, which defines the terms and conditions for their training in Australia. All interns must be interviewed by telephone.
REMUNERATION: Hospitality interns are paid according to the Australian standard: the minimum hourly rate is A$13.
COST: Sample fees for professional internship placements are A$1,950 for 7–12 weeks, A$2,700 for

21–26 weeks; and for hospitality interns A$3,340 for 26 weeks, A$3,750 for 38 weeks, and A$4,150 for 52 weeks. Agency can arrange homestay and other accommodation at extra cost.

CONTACT: Rebekah Gilchrist, Marketing Manager.

BOLIVIAN EXPRESS
Departamento 17E, Edificio 20 de Octubre, Calle 20 de Octubre, La Paz, Bolivia
☎ +591 2 242 3043
☎ +591 783 431 6847 (from UK)
info@bolivianexpress.org
www.bolivianexpress.org

PROGRAMME DESCRIPTION: Bolivian Express offers participants the possibility of working as part of a team who produce a monthly English-language publication distributed in print and online in Bolivia and abroad. *Bolivian Express* covers a range of topics such as music, folklore, nightlife, sport, and literature. Participants are encouraged to interact with locals and produce fresh pieces of research by exploring the country and its people.

DESTINATIONS: Bolivia.

NUMBER OF PLACEMENTS PER YEAR: Up to 8 at one time; around 50 per year.

DURATION AND TIME OF PLACEMENTS: 1 month to 1 year. Participants typically stay for 2–3 months, though some stay on longer and take on greater responsibilities including management and general editing.

PREREQUISITES: All ages. Gap year students welcome. Candidates must have a basic level of Spanish and must have finished secondary education (pre-university). All nationalities are accepted, but it is the applicant's responsibility to make their own travel and visa arrangements to come to Bolivia. Applications encouraged from those who have a proven interest in photography, design, marketing, publicity, journalism, and other forms of writing. Candidates should also demonstrate cultural sensitivity, and openness to communicate and interact with Bolivian locals and people from other nationalities who take part in the programme.

SELECTION PROCEDURES AND ORIENTATION: Applications are received all year round but with more pressure on places June–September. Application procedure involves writing a short personal statement and uploading a CV. Selected candidates are then interviewed for 20 minutes over the phone. Successful candidates must pay a deposit within a month of their offer being made to secure a place on the programme. To support interns after arrival, lessons are provided in Spanish, journalism, photography, and design. Those taking part

learn about the entire process involved in producing a professional publication.

COST: Programme costs £800 for the first month (which includes tuition in various areas) and £400 per month thereafter. Fee includes shared accommodation in a penthouse in the centre of the capital, La Paz, which has a computer (shared), wi-fi internet and a fully equipped kitchen.

OTHER SERVICES: Participants are collected from the airport upon arrival and given a full induction into the publication and local amenities (safety, transport, etc). For safety and ease of communication, participants are given a mobile phone with a Bolivian number for use during their stay.

CONTACT: Amaru Villanueva Rance, Director.

CEI/CLUB DES 4 VENTS
1 Rue Gozlin, 75006 Paris, France
☎ +33 1 43 29 17 34
☎ +33 1 40 51 11 86
wif@cei4vents.com
www.cei4vents.com

PROGRAMME DESCRIPTION: Paid job and internship placement service.

PREREQUISITES: Ages 18–30.

DURATION AND TIME OF PLACEMENTS: Flexible lengths for interns from Europe, 3 months for non-European students. Placements available year-round.

COST: €620 job placement for EU nationals, €825 for nationalities that do not require a visa, €980 for nationalities that require a visa for France. Internships for European students cost €580, and €810 for all other nationalities.

OTHER SERVICES: CEI offers homestay and residential summer French courses for young people aged 12–18 in a number of places, including Paris. Runs residential language courses in Paris at the French school, Paris Langues (www.parislangues.com).

CONTACT: José Luis Ponti, Incoming Programmes Manager.

CHILE INSIDE
Andrés de Fuenzalida 17, Oficina 51, Providencia, Santiago, Chile
☎ +56 2 335 9072
info@chileinside.cl
www.chileinside.cl

PROGRAMME DESCRIPTION: Internships, working holidays, volunteer work, farm stays, Spanish language courses (see separate entry p331), and accommodation throughout Chile.

NUMBER OF PLACEMENTS PER YEAR: 500 for all programmes. Also a handful of interns aged 19+ work in the Chile Inside office in the areas of marketing, public relations and translation.

DESTINATIONS: Chile.

PREREQUISITES: Minimum age 18, average age 21–25. All nationalities accepted. Programmes tailored to individual backgrounds, interests, and education. Interns in the Chile Inside office should have good computer skills, and some knowledge of Spanish (and/or German) as well as English.

DURATION AND TIME OF PLACEMENTS: Programmes last between 6 weeks and 6+ months.

SELECTION PROCEDURES AND ORIENTATION: No special selection criteria. Candidates need to send CV and fill in registration form. Applications should be sent 4–10 weeks prior to programme start date. Orientation talk will be held upon arrival in Chile. Personal assistance and regular participants' meetings and activities arranged throughout stay in Chile. Participants are given a programme handbook and guide/map to Santiago. 24-hour support available.

COST: $75 registration fee and programme fees range from $180 to $800.

ACCOMMODATION: Host family, shared apartment, student residences, furnished rooms.

CONTACT: Marion Ruhland, Founder and Executive Director.

CRCC ASIA
106 Weston Street, London, SE1 3QB
☎ (0)20 7378 6220
🖊 internships@crccasia.com
💻 www.crccasia.com

A consulting company that runs China Internship Programmes and finance, legal, and Mandarin courses in Beijing and Shanghai.

PROGRAMME DESCRIPTION: 1- or 2-month internships in a variety of company sectors in China's two biggest cities, including legal, financial, technology, marketing, and PR. Programme includes arrangement of business visas, accommodation, Chinese business culture training, language induction, English-speaking mentor within company, and full support. Also offer various courses (see 'Directory of Courses').

DESTINATIONS: Beijing and Shanghai.

PREREQUISITES: All fluent English speakers. Must be enrolled or graduated from a degree course, have interest in China, and be diligent, independent, and enthusiastic.

DURATION AND TIME OF PLACEMENTS: 1 or 2 months. 9 departures annually, spread throughout the year.

SELECTION PROCEDURES AND ORIENTATION: Applications accepted year-round. Telephone interview arranged within a week of application.

COST: 1 month: £1,495 in Beijing, £1,595 in Shanghai; 2 months: £1,995 in Beijing, £2,195 in Shanghai; includes accommodation and visa application cost.

DAKTARI BUSH SCHOOL & WILDLIFE ORPHANAGE
Bona Ingwe Farm, Harmony 81, Hoedspruit 1380, South Africa
☎ +27 82 656 2969
🖊 info@daktaribushschool.org
💻 www.daktaribushschool.org

The mission of the private game reserve, Daktari, is to educate underprivileged children to care for the environment through the medium of a wildlife orphanage. See entry for paying volunteers in 'Directory of Volunteering Abroad'.

PROGRAMME DESCRIPTION: Volunteers come for 6–12 months to act as office assistant or volunteer co-ordinator. Director's assistant provides administrative support, including drafting writing proposals, marketing, fundraising, writing newsletters, orders for suppliers, reception of food deliveries, and taking care of orphaned animals when necessary. Volunteer co-ordinator greets, trains, and oversees paying volunteers, and contributes to their morale.

DESTINATIONS: Bush school is located near Kruger National Park, South Africa.

NUMBER OF PLACEMENTS PER YEAR: 2–4.

DURATION AND TIME OF PLACEMENTS: 6–12 months.

PREREQUISITES: Minimum age 20. Must be willing to accept quite a bit of responsibility, especially during director's occasional absences.

COST: Free food and accommodation. Spending money needed for time off (weekends and one week in eight).

CONTACT: Michele Merrifield, Director.

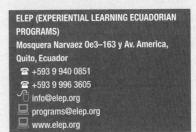

ELEP (EXPERIENTIAL LEARNING ECUADORIAN PROGRAMS)
Mosquera Narvaez Oe3–163 y Av. America, Quito, Ecuador
☎ +593 9 940 0851
☎ +593 9 996 3605
🖊 info@elep.org
💻 programs@elep.org
💻 www.elep.org

PROGRAMME DESCRIPTION: Customised internships in many fields, eg audit/finance, accounting, human resources, foreign trade, marketing/PR, IT, graphic design, engineering, architecture, medicine, environment, journalism, psychology, agriculture and natural resources, law, and social work. Also arranges placements in humanitarian and ecological volunteer sector: childcare, HIV/AIDS, human rights, teaching English, healthcare/nursing, micro-enterprise, building/construction work, organic farming and agroforestry, animal care and veterinary medicine, etc. Spanish language training is available for beginners, intermediate and advanced individuals and groups.

DESTINATIONS: Throughout Ecuador, including highlands, coastal areas, Amazonia, and the Galápagos Islands.

PREREQUISITES: Good knowledge of Spanish is required for the internships and basic knowledge for the volunteer work. Must have an open mind and be able to adapt to different culture.

DURATION OF PLACEMENTS: 2 weeks to 6 months for volunteer programme. From 4 weeks to 6 months for internships (depending on field). Available any time of year. No special visa needed for stays of less than 6 months.

COST: Application fee $100. Internship programme fee of $635 for 4 weeks. Fee includes transfer from airport to host family, accommodation and in-country support. Volunteer programme fee $420 for 2 weeks. Private language lessons cost $6.50 an hour (20 hours a week). Special offers include 20 hours of Spanish plus 4 weeks volunteering or interning plus accommodation for $750; 40 hours of language lessons plus 8 weeks of internship or volunteering for $1,100; 4 weeks of Spanish lessons plus 8 weeks internship or volunteering for $1,620.

ACCOMMODATION: Accommodation with host families in private room costs $105 a week on the mainland, $175 on the Galápagos. 3 meals a day and laundry service included.

CONTACT: Patricia Parrales, Programme Consultant; Kleber Parrales, Programme Officer; Patricio Fernández, Managing Director.

EUROINTERNS
Solano 11, 3°-C, Pozuelo de Alarcon, 28223 Madrid, Spain
☎ +34 637 543 900
☎ +34 91 711 6319
✍ info@eurointerns.com
🖥 www.eurointerns.com

PROGRAMME DESCRIPTION: Internships in Spanish and Belgian firms for practical language enhancement and work experience.

DESTINATIONS: Spain, Italy, and Belgium (Brussels).

NUMBER OF PLACEMENTS PER YEAR: 100.

PREREQUISITES: Ideal candidates will have professional or academic experience in the area chosen for the internship as well as intermediate language skills in Spanish, Italian, or French, except in the case of English-speaking companies.

DURATION AND TIME OF PLACEMENTS: 2–6 months.

SELECTION PROCEDURES AND ORIENTATION: 2–4 weeks' intensive language training in Spanish, Italian, or French is recommended unless candidates have advanced knowledge of the language.

COST: €1,100 fee.

CONTACT: Suzanne Diez, Internship Co-ordinator.

EUROPEAN COMMISSION
Traineeship Office/Bureau des Stages, 200 Rue de la Loi, 1049 Brussels, Belgium
☎ +32 2 295 5344
✍ eac-stages@ec.europa.eu
🖥 http://ec.europa.eu/stages/index_en.htm

The scheme is open to university graduates from all over the world and is administered by the Training Office at the European Commission's Directorate General for Education and Culture.

PROGRAMME DESCRIPTION: Twice a year, the Commission organises in-service training periods to give trainees a general idea about the objectives and problems of European integration and provide them with practical knowledge of the workings of the Commission's departments. Traineeships are available in the Directorate General for Translation or in Administration.

DESTINATIONS: Most are in Brussels, some in Luxembourg, and in Representation Offices in the Member States.

NUMBER OF PLACEMENTS PER YEAR: Approximately 600 per period (out of 7,000 applications), ie 1,200 per year.

PREREQUISITES: Applicants must have a thorough knowledge of one other EU official language in addition to their mother tongue. Applicants must also have completed their degree.

DURATION AND TIME OF PLACEMENTS: 3 or 5 months. Training periods begin in first week of March or October every year.

SELECTION PROCEDURES AND ORIENTATION: Application forms must be submitted online. Deadlines are 1 September and 31 January.

REMUNERATION: All official trainees are paid a grant of €1,071 per month and their travel expenses.

GLOBAL NOMADIC
84 Finchley Lane, Hendon, London NW4 1DH
☎ (0) 20 7193 2652
📧 jeremy@globalnomadic.com
📧 info@globalnomadic.com
🖥 www.globalnomadic.com

Global Nomadic is a company and website that promotes volunteer placements and internships from around the world. See main entry in 'Directory of Specialist Gap Year Programmes'.

PROGRAMME DESCRIPTION: Worldwide placements in many fields from media and journalism to NGO management and teaching. These placements are designed to build careers and give people (mainly in their 20s) the opportunity to gain real working experience in their chosen field.

CONTACT: Jeremy Freedman, Director.

GLOBAL VISION INTERNATIONAL (GVI)
UK office: **Third Floor, The Senate, Exeter, EX1 1UG**
☎ (0)1727 250 250
📧 info@gviworld.com
🖥 www.gvi.co.uk/internships-abroad
North American office: **66 Long Wharf, Suite 562 S, Boston, MA 02110**
☎ +1 888 653 6028
🖥 www.gviusa.com

PROGRAMME DESCRIPTION: GVI offers those seeking practical experience in a specific field a unique opportunity to develop new skills, practical experience and opportunities. Main fields are marine biology and conservation, environmental research, and conservation, with coral reefs, monkeys, lions, turtles and other species, teaching in developing communities, childcare, English language teaching, and organic farming.

DESTINATIONS: Africa, Latin America, Europe, and Asia. Sample internships include training to become a safari field guide in South Africa, marine biology and conservation in Mexico and the Seychelles, and childcare in indigenous communities in Latin America.

DURATION AND TIME OF PLACEMENTS: Short- and long-term placements, from 2 weeks to 1 year.

GLOBAL VOLUNTEER PROJECTS
7–15 Pink Lane, Newcastle upon Tyne NE1 5DW
☎ (0)191 222 0404
📧 info@globalvolunteerprojects.org
🖥 www.globalvolunteerprojects.org

PROGRAMME DESCRIPTION: Specialise in work experience projects for people hoping to go into medicine or the subjects allied to medicine, such as physiotherapy, dentistry, and nursing, and people looking for work experience in journalism. Placements are available in Ghana, Tanzania, India, China, Cambodia, Mexico, and Romania. See entry in 'Directory of Specialist Gap Year Programmes'.

GLS SPRACHENZENTRUM BERLIN
Kastanienallee 82, 10435 Berlin, Germany
☎ +30 78 00 89 15
📧 german@gls-berlin.de
🖥 www.gls-berlin.de

PROGRAMME DESCRIPTION: Minimum 4-week language course followed by an internship lasting 6, 8, or 12+ weeks in a company in or near Berlin. Traineeships available in range of fields such as marketing, government, architecture, social work, and banking.

PREREQUISITES: Students should have at least B1 certificate (intermediate) by the time the internship starts, ie be able to express themselves in German and understand everyday conversations. Must also show initiative. Minimum age 18/19.

COST: Placement fee is €600.

OTHER SERVICES: The GLS campus is a leading centre in Berlin for teaching German as a foreign language and is a key member of WYSE Work Abroad. GLS offers 50 studio-apartments and a restaurant on-site.

CONTACT: Anna Bartnikowska (anna.bartnikowska@gls-berlin.de).

INTERN OPTIONS
159–161 Temple Chambers, 3–7 Temple Avenue, London EC4Y 0DA
☎ (0)20 7353 7699
📧 info@internoptions.com
🖥 www.internoptions.com

PROGRAMME DESCRIPTION: Unpaid internships in many industries, especially hospitality, horticulture, and travel. Entry-level admin jobs available to school leavers.

NUMBER OF PLACEMENTS PER YEAR: 30–60+.

DESTINATIONS: Sydney and Melbourne, mainly. Placements also available elsewhere in Australia and New Zealand.

PREREQUISITES: Students and graduates aged 18–30 (in order to qualify for a working holiday visa). Candidates should be looking for a work experience placement in their field of study or experience.

DURATION AND TIME OF PLACEMENTS: 6 weeks to 1 year, though most last 10–26 weeks. Summer internships (June to September) are available.

COST: Various fees: eg. £800 for an unpaid training internship in Sydney, £399 for Australia Horticulture Jobs Programme, £950 for a paid hospitality internship in New Zealand and £750 for a paid dairy farming placement.

CONTACT: Jonathan Carroll, Director.

IST PLUS
Churcham House, 1 Bridgeman Road, Teddington, Middlesex TW11 9AJ
☎ (0)20 7788 7877
✉ info@istplus.com
🖥 www.istplus.com

PROGRAMME DESCRIPTION: Work and teaching abroad programmes, including Work & Travel USA, Camp USA, Internship USA, Work & Travel Australia, Work & Travel New Zealand, Teach in China, and Teach in Thailand. New working holidays in Singapore for self-funding students.

DESTINATIONS: USA, Australia, New Zealand, China, Thailand and Singapore.

PREREQUISITES: Different eligibility requirements for each programme. To work in the USA, the participant must either be a student, graduate or young professional. To work in Australasia, they must be over 18. To teach in Asia, they must be a degree-holder.

DURATION AND TIME OF PLACEMENTS: Anything from a few weeks up to 18 months. The Work & Travel USA summer programme is open between June and October. Internship USA can last up to 18 months and runs all year round. Students bound for Australia and New Zealand can go out for 12 months at any time of year. 5- or 10-month contracts for Teaching in China start in August or February, and for Thailand they begin in May or October.

SELECTION PROCEDURES AND ORIENTATION: The application deadlines are the end of June for Work and Travel USA, mid-November or early May for Teach in China, and mid-February and mid-July for Thailand. Participants receive 7 days of orientation in Shanghai or Bangkok, covering the essentials of TEFL and an introduction to Asia, its culture and language. Students participating in Work and Travel USA receive a pre-departure orientation.

COST: Teach in China and Thailand programme fee from £995–£1,095 plus flights. Participants receive a local wage which allows for a comfortable lifestyle, and on completion of a 10-month contract have their return

flight reimbursed. Work & Travel USA fee starts from £460, which includes insurance, US government SEVIS fee, and all support services. Singapore programme fee is £675 plus approx £335 per month to cover expenses.

JUNIOR EXPAT
PT JuniorExpat Indonesia, Graha Wahid Blok, Sydney No C6, Semarang, Java, Indonesia
☎ +6 22 49 124 4068
✉ iexperience@juniorexpat.com
🖥 www.juniorexpat.com

Registered in the Netherlands (JuniorExpat Netherlands), Indonesia (PT JuniorExpat Indonesia), Hong Kong (JuniorExpat Hong Kong Ltd), and the USA (JuniorExpat LLC).

PROGRAMME DESCRIPTION: iExperience Program China/Indonesia provides internship/work experience opportunities in many areas of personal development and education, such as marketing, business, finance, hospitality, and information technology. Internship possibilities are also available for junior teachers, product development and design students, and event management students.

DESTINATIONS: Shanghai, Beijing, Hong Kong, Jakarta, Bali, and Semarang (Indonesia).

NUMBER OF PLACEMENTS PER YEAR: 300.

PREREQUISITES: Minimum age 18. Students must be about to start, or part way through higher education. Candidates with bachelor's and master's degrees accepted too. Open to all nationalities, but must be English-speaking; most participants are from UK, France, Netherlands, Belgium, Germany, USA, Canada, Australia, and New Zealand.

DURATION AND TIME OF PLACEMENTS: Normally 3–6 months, starting throughout the year.

SELECTION PROCEDURES AND ORIENTATION: Pre-arrival intake interview and assistance given with visa sponsorship, contracts, finding accommodation, etc. JuniorExpat has western-style accommodation available through its partners in all locations.

REMUNERATION: The majority of internships are unpaid; however, companies provide lunch and local transport for foreign interns. Most internships in China are paid a monthly remuneration of €150–€500.

COST: iExperience Program Indonesia fee €495 and iExperience Program China fee €695 (2011).

CONTACT: Azzan Goeting, International Relations Manager.

Language Courses Abroad Ltd is a UK-based language travel agency, offering in-country full immersion language courses at more than 100 schools. Trading name is Apple Languages (www.applelanguages.com).

PROGRAMME DESCRIPTION: Work experience placements in range of countries. Any type of work experience can be provided as long as the student has relevant qualifications. A few work placements available in company's own schools.

DESTINATIONS: Spain, Latin America, France, Germany, and Italy.

NUMBER OF PLACEMENTS PER YEAR: 100–200.

PREREQUISITES: Work placements require at least an intermediate level of the language. Most work placements are preceded by a 4-week in-country language course (see entry in 'Directory of Language Courses').

DURATION AND TIME OF PLACEMENTS: 4 weeks minimum, normally 8–16 weeks.

SELECTION PROCEDURES AND ORIENTATION: Applications should be sent at least 8 and preferably 12 weeks in advance. Personal monitor is appointed to oversee work placement.

COST: Work placements not normally paid, except those in the hotel and catering industry, for which students normally receive free board and lodging, and sometimes also payment at national minimum wage levels. Fees included on company website.

CONTACT: Scott Cather, Language Travel Adviser.

PROGRAMME DESCRIPTION: Work experience available along with other gap year placements in India. Specialists in placements for students applying for medicine and related fields, or wanting to complete research projects. Mixture of hands-on, observation, and work-shadowing experience in Delhi.

DESTINATIONS: Delhi, India

PREREQUISITES: Ages 17+.

DURATION AND TIME OF PLACEMENTS: From 2 weeks to 4 months throughout the year.

COST: From £995 for short placements, including transport within the country, full board and lodging, and weekend breaks, but excluding airfares and insurance.

CONTACT: Poonam Puri.

Promotes linguistic and cultural exchanges within Europe.

PROGRAMME DESCRIPTION: Organises work experience abroad for European students aged 16–18/20.

DESTINATIONS: Mainly Brussels; also Lübeck for students of German.

NUMBER OF PLACEMENTS PER YEAR: 100–200.

PREREQUISITES: Language skills (French or German), organisation, enthusiasm, and self-motivation are needed. Students ought to have studied French or German at school.

DURATION AND TIME OF PLACEMENTS: 1 or 2 weeks, occasionally longer if requested throughout the year.

SELECTION PROCEDURES AND ORIENTATION: A CV is required, but interviews are not essential.

COST: Work experience fees are €300 for 1 week between October and May, and €375 in July and August. Fortnight-long placements cost €450 in winter, €475 in summer.

CONTACT: Xavier Mouffe, Manager (xavier.mouffe@telenet.be).

PROGRAMME DESCRIPTION: Professional internship programme offering year-round work placements in Shanghai, Beijing, Hong Kong and Mumbai. Placements may be found in many fields such as architecture, art, design, finance, IT, engineering, journalism, law, medicine, pharmaceuticals, advertising, marketing, and public relations. Links with big companies such as McCann Group, Publicis, CIBA, *China Daily*, *Shanghai Business Review*, Wieden & Kennedy, and more.

NUMBER OF PLACEMENTS PER YEAR: 100.

DESTINATIONS: China, Hong Kong, and India.

PREREQUISITES: Ages 18–35. Must be fluent in English, have motivation, good-quality CV, and interest in professional career-geared programme.

DURATION AND TIME OF PLACEMENTS: 1–6 months. Participants choose their start date, length of stay, and field of placement.

SELECTION PROCEDURES AND ORIENTATION: Online application at least 2 months (preferably 3) before proposed arrival. 3 hours per week of Mandarin lessons are part of programme. Monthly career and professional meeting with an executive recruiter at Next Step Connections office, to carry out programme monitoring and overview. Each meeting tackles a different topic, and provides a better insight into the Asian job market and how to improve a CV.

REMUNERATION: None.

COST: £1,750 for 1 month, £5,650 for 6 months, including internship placement, housing, insurance, airport transfers, and back-up.

CONTACT: Jerome Le Carrou, Director.

NYQUEST TRAINING AND PLACEMENT
571 Roselawn Avenue, Toronto, Ontario, M5N 1K6, Canada
☎ +416 932 1370
📧 info@go-nyquest.com
🖥 www.go-nyquest.com

PROGRAMME DESCRIPTION: The Canadian Camp Experience programme trains and places leaders for work experience at day and residential summer camps in Canada, working and living with children aged 7–16. Camp counsellors work directly with children, leading activities and supervising campers. Support staff work behind the scenes setting up the camp, maintaining camp facilities and helping out in the dining hall and kitchen.

DESTINATIONS: All over Canada.

NUMBER OF PARTICIPANTS: 300+.

PREREQUISITES: Ages 19–26, average age 20–23. Should have leadership qualities and an interest in travel and outdoor education. Gap year students must submit very strong applications and have some experience teaching and supervising children.

DURATION AND TIME OF PLACEMENTS: Minimum work period 8 weeks between mid-June and the end of August, or from the end of August to the beginning of November. Many participants work for 6 months at camps from May to October and then travel or start working at a winter resort in Canada.

SELECTION PROCEDURES AND ORIENTATION: British applicants must apply through CCUSA (see entry p177). Provides training, work placement assistance, and ongoing support. NYQUEST will arrange work permits and provide health insurance, free Canadian bank account, Canadian Social Insurance Number (SIN), 2 nights' accommodation and 1-day orientation in Canadian host city, internet access and free phone card, transport from airport to accommodation in host city, and on to camp placement.

COST: C$300–C$500 excluding flights; CCUSA fee for Britons is £299 for early applicants; £399 for later ones.

CONTACT: Jonathan Nyquist, Founder and Operations Director.

PROJECTS ABROAD
Aldsworth Parade, Goring, West Sussex BN12 4TX
☎ (0)1903 708 300
📧 info@projects-abroad.co.uk
🖥 www.projects-abroad.co.uk

Projects Abroad arranges unpaid work experience in many countries, as well as placing fee-paying volunteers in a variety of projects.

PROGRAMME DESCRIPTION: Voluntary work experience opportunities in selected destinations for business, conservation, and other fields, including archaeology, care, medical, media/journalism, and supervised dissertations for degree courses.

DESTINATIONS: Argentina, Bolivia, Cambodia, China, Costa Rica, Ethiopia, Ghana, India, Jamaica, Mexico, Moldova, Mongolia, Morocco, Nepal, Peru, Romania, Russia, Senegal, South Africa, Sri Lanka, Tanzania, and Thailand. Destinations and programmes can be combined.

NUMBER OF PLACEMENTS: 4,000 in total, of which 75% are project placements and 25% teaching.

PREREQUISITES: Minimum age 16.

DURATION AND TIME OF PLACEMENTS: Very flexible, with departures year-round and varying lengths of placement.

COST: Placements are self-funded and the fee charged includes insurance, food, accommodation, and overseas support. 3-month placements cost between £1,395 and £2,595, excluding travel costs.

RESTLESS DEVELOPMENT
7 Tufton Street, London SW1P 3QB
☎ (0)20 7976 8070
📧 info@restlessdevelopment.org
🖥 www.restlessdevelopment.org

PROGRAMME DESCRIPTION: An international development charity, formerly SPW, that recruits young people aged 18–28 to volunteer and work in rural communities on placements that provide structured and professional experience in the field of international development, with a special focus on HIV/AIDS prevention and care. Also offers technical assistant placements for skilled and high-capacity young professionals in one of the charity's offices in Africa or Asia.

DESTINATIONS: Nepal and Uganda for community development placements. Technical assistant placements are made in India, Nepal, Sierra Leone, South Africa, Tanzania, Uganda, Zambia, and Zimbabwe.

CONTACT: Beth Goodey, International Placements Co-ordinator.

SPANNOCCHIA FOUNDATION FARM INTERNSHIP PROGRAMME
Tenuta di Spannocchia, 53012 Chiusdino, Siena (SI), Italy
☎ +39 057 775 2611
✆ internships@spannocchia.org
💻 www.spannocchia.org

PROGRAMME DESCRIPTION: Hands-on internships on a 1,200-acre community organic farm and education centre in the hills of Tuscany, about 30 minutes from Siena; 7 farm interns spend three-quarters of time working alongside Italian farm staff in the vegetable garden, vineyards, olive groves, forestry operations, etc. The Spannocchia Guest Services Internship Programme accepts 1 intern per session, who works in the guest services operation, setting up breakfast, bottling and labelling products, assisting with grounds maintenance, helping in kitchen when needed, etc. The rest of the interns' time is devoted to structured courses, particularly in Italian language and culture.

NUMBER OF PLACEMENTS: 8 per session, 24 per year.

PREREQUISITES: All nationalities welcome to apply, although programme and agriturismo attract a mostly American clientele. A very strong interest in manual labour and community living and a positive attitude are essential.

DURATION AND TIME OF PLACEMENTS: 3-month internships each year in spring, summer, and autumn.

COST: One-time $250 education fee, plus student membership of Spannocchia Foundation ($30). Interns are responsible for their airfare to Italy, plus international health insurance coverage and spending money.

OTHER SERVICES: Accommodation and meals are provided in exchange for 30 hours per week of farm work.

CONTACT: Katie Phelan, Education Director.

SUBWAY WATERSPORTS
Brick Bay, Roatan, Bay Islands, Honduras, Central America
✆ internship@subwaywatersports.com
💻 www.subwaywatersports.com/Courses/internship.htm

PROGRAMME DESCRIPTION: Internship working in a dive shop while training towards a professional PADI Divemaster qualification (see entry in 'Directory of Sport and Activity Courses').

THAILAND GAP INTERNSHIPS
GPO Mae Haad, Koh Tao, Suratthani 84360, Thailand
☎ +66 86 271 2212
☎ +66 86 059 1590
✆ darius@gapinternshipsthailand.com;
✆ info@gapinternshipsthailand.com
💻 www.gapinternshipsthailand.com

Thailand Gap Internships was set up at the beginning of 2009, by divers who have been living and training divers on Koh Tao island for many years.

PROGRAMME DESCRIPTION: Internship programmes on this beautiful island in the Gulf of Thailand include professional-level scuba training (divemaster or instructor), professional underwater videographer, freediver (master freediver/apnoea), Muay Thai training, sailing internships, trapeze performance (1 month), and marine conservation.

NUMBER OF PLACEMENTS PER YEAR: 20+ per month.

PREREQUISITES: Most interns are aged 18–25.

DURATION AND TIME OF PLACEMENTS: Variable, but 1–7 months is ideal, depending on programme.

COST: 7-month package that includes everything except food will cost about 45,000 Thai baht (£920) per month. 3-month Muay Thai internship can be done for less than 25,000 Thai baht per month (£500). Clean comfortable accommodation with a fan and private hot water bathroom is included in the price.

CONTACT: Darius Moazzami and Gary Bain, Co-owners.

TRAVELLERS WORLDWIDE
2A Caravelle House, 17/19 Goring Road, Worthing, West Sussex BN12 4AP
☎ (0)1903 502 595
✆ info@travellersworldwide.com
💻 www.travellersworldwide.com

Travellers is a Founder Member of the Year Out Group.

PROGRAMME DESCRIPTION: A wide range of professional work experience internship placements across the world, available in architecture, law, journalism, medicine, physiotherapy, radio, TV, tourism, veterinary medicine, web design, and many more. Placements are tailored to preferences and experience and are open to everyone, from students to professionals or those on career breaks.

DESTINATIONS: Argentina, Australia, China, Ghana, Guatemala, India, Kenya, Malaysia, New Zealand, South Africa, Sri Lanka, and Zambia.

NUMBER OF PLACEMENTS PER YEAR: 1,000+.

PREREQUISITES: Qualifications required depend on the chosen placement. Some require little or no relevant experience or qualifications; others do. Staff can advise on the most beneficial placements for individuals.

DURATION AND TIME OF PLACEMENTS: From 1 week to 1 year, subject to visa requirements, with flexible start and finish dates all year round.

COST: Prices start from £695, and include food, accommodation, airport pick-up, induction, orientation, 24/7 support on the ground and at home, but don't include international travel, visas, or insurance.

CONTACT: Jennifer Perkes, Managing Director.

WAVA
67–71 Lewisham High Street, Lewisham, London SE13 5JX
☎ (0)800 80 483 80
✍ smordarski@workandvolunteer.com
🖥 www.workandvolunteer.com

PROGRAMME DESCRIPTION: 'WAVA' stands for 'Work and Volunteer Abroad', rebranded in 2010 from 'Twin Work & Adventure Abroad'. Among its 3 strands, it organises internships in professional environments around the world. For more information, see entry in 'Directory of Specialist Gap Year Programmes'.

DESTINATIONS: France, Germany, India, Canada, Australia, and Ghana.

PREREQUISITES: All ages and nationalities are accepted, subject to visa requirements. Specific skills may be required depending on the programme.

DURATION AND TIME OF PLACEMENTS: Minimum 4, 6, or 8 weeks.

COST: From £390.

CONTACT: Sally Mordarski, Travel Administrator (smordarski@workandvolunteer.com).

WORKTRAVELSA.ORG
PO Box 3288, Somerset West, 7129, Cape Town, South Africa
☎ +27 21 851 9494
✍ info@worktravelsa.org
🖥 www.worktravelsa.org

PROGRAMME DESCRIPTION: General internship placements, hospitality programme offering internships in hotels and safari lodges in South Africa, and a medical internship programme. Customised internship placements can be made according to the client's abilities and requirements. Also offer placements in a provincial hospital project where volunteers can job shadow and medical students can do an elective.

DESTINATIONS: Majority of placements in the Western Cape region of South Africa.

NUMBER OF PLACEMENTS PER YEAR: 500+.

DURATION AND TIME OF PLACEMENTS: 6 weeks to 6 months. Hospitality positions are for 3 months.

PREREQUISITES: No experience needed for general internships, so open to school leavers aged over 18. Highly specialised placements also available for university students, graduates, and young professionals.

COST: Available on request.

CONTACT: Amy Wyness, Office Administrator.

YOU VOLUNTEER
1 Riverside Close, Oundle, Peterborough PE8 4DN
☎ (0)1832 275 038
✍ nick@youvolunteer.org
🖥 www.youvolunteer.org

Part of the Great Aves non-profit organisation. Internships also available in UK, people living within reach of Peterborough who are willing to raise funds and equipment for projects in Ecuador, mainly working from home.

PROGRAMME DESCRIPTION: Great Aves offers administrative internships in its office in Puyo, Ecuador. Tasks include marketing, fundraising, web design, human resource management, networking, and operations management.

DESTINATIONS: Ecuador.

DURATION AND TIME OF PLACEMENTS: 8–12 weeks. 15–20 hours a week.

COST: Unpaid placement. Total cost of accommodation and food about $1,000 plus $75 for transport.

CONTACT: Nick Greatrex, Operations Manager.

PROJECT TRUST

Project Trust is an educational charity specialising in sending 17–19-year-old school leavers overseas for long-term placements of eight or 12 months. Currently operating in more than 20 countries across Africa, Asia, and the Americas, its projects include teaching, social care, medical work, and Outward Bound instructing. All of these projects are vetted to ensure that volunteers add to the community in a positive way rather than taking roles that could be filled by locals. This enables our volunteers to really integrate and become valued members of the communities that they work in.

Established in 1967 and based on the Isle of Coll in the Inner Hebrides off the west coast of Scotland, the Trust invites all applicants to attend a selection course on the island. This is a four-day residential course in which volunteers participate in both indoor and outdoor group activities, talk to members of staff about what they would like to do during their year out, and eventually make a decision about where they would like to go. We feel that it is vital we meet volunteers over these four days in order to partner them with a project that is suitable for them. Without knowing the volunteers' individual skills and interests, we would be unable to do this.

Heather Arnold travelled to Uganda last year to work at a secondary school called Queen of Peace. It involved basic living and was incredibly rural. Heather compares the experience to standing on a plank of wood 145ft above the Nile:

That was the first time I have ever bungee-jumped off anything; immediately afterwards, the only thing I could say about it was that it was the most terrifying but rewarding experience I have ever had. Apart from the decision I made to go away with Project Trust.

There are many similarities in the decision to live in a brand new place for 12 months and the decision to throw yourself off a cliff. As soon as you make the decision and sign up, you get ridiculously excited. All you talk about for a long time is the jump (whether it's a jump into a river or a jump into a new way of life); every time you stop to daydream, it's the first thing that enters your head, and you imagine what it'll be like. The nearer it gets to departure, the more excited you get; even after the worry hits you. This is when you suddenly realise what you've signed up for (though with hindsight you really have no idea what's ahead of you).

Then, before you know it, you're on the edge, about to leave the familiar jumping pad and launch yourself into a river, miles away from everything familiar to you. Some people just go, jump, showing no fear whatsoever; others scream and shout in a mixture of joy and fear and some, like me, just cry. Cry, shut my eyes, and fall off the edge. Then you are hurtling ridiculously quickly into something completely new and it is nothing short of amazing.

Everything changes: how you see things, hear things, the way the world moves around you. And you curse yourself for having closed your eyes and missing a single moment of it all. Finally, plunged into the water, just as all this newness becomes normal, you get a second wave of shock when you realise exactly what you're doing and what you've just done – how terrifying it was yet you did it anyway (you hope with style) and how much you've gained. You feel really, truly and honestly proud of yourself.

You've bounced back up and again you can appreciate things around you – dangling there trying to absorb every moment before you're taken down and returned to those who had cheered you on through the entire thing.

Going away with Project Trust was not only the most terrifying and most rewarding decision I've ever made, but unarguably the best.

For more information visit www.projecttrust.org.uk
or www.facebook.com/ProjectTrustVolunteers.

AFRICAN CONSERVATION EXPERIENCE

Leanne Parsons, an African Conservation Experience volunteer at Khulula Wild Care, 2011, had unforgettable experiences on her gap year, sleeping under the stars and hand-rearing a rhino.

I never thought that I would have felt so at home after travelling alone over 5,000 miles away from England, but at Khulula Wild Care, I did. My passion for wildlife conservation and a desire to work with animals got me involved with the African Conservation Experience.

My time at the centre saw the arrival of several baby ostriches, and a baby white rhino, who we called Bobby. After Bobby, who was around three months old, had settled in, we arranged shifts between us to keep him company. He had come to the centre after his mother was poached and he was left to fend for himself. He hated remaining alone, and the volunteers became his family. Day and night shifts ensued. On one night of heavy rain, thunder and lightning, we had to move Bobby into the next enclosure ... Two humans trying to move a 150-pound baby rhino in the dark is even harder than you would think!

Not a day or night went by when I didn't appreciate the animals I was surrounded by, the sky being completely filled with twinkling stars or perfect sunsets.

www.ConservationAfrica.net

VOLUNTEERING

Voluntary work is not only fulfilling and satisfying in itself but can provide a stepping stone to interesting possibilities later on. By participating in a project such as digging wells in a Turkish village, playing football with Ghanaian kids or just helping out at a youth hostel, gap year volunteers have the unique opportunity to live and work in a remote community, and the chance to meet young people from many countries. You may be able to improve or acquire a language and learn something of the customs of the society in which you are volunteering. You will also gain practical experience, for instance in the fields of construction, archaeology, museums, or social welfare, which will later stand you in good stead when applying for paid work. Less tangible but equally marketable benefits include the acquisition of new skills like problem solving, leadership, relationship building, communication skills, and general self-development. Research based on findings of the recruitment group Reed Executive showed that three-quarters of employers in business prefer applicants with experience of volunteering.

With its commitment to the so-called 'Big Society', the current UK government strongly supports the ethos of volunteering, especially among young people. Despite the devastating cutbacks in so many government-funded programmes, the new International Citizen Service programme (www.dfid.gov.uk/ics) has been launched in 2011, which aims to bring global volunteering experiences within reach of young people aged 18–22 whatever their background. Means-tested funding is available. In this pilot year, up to 1,250 ICS volunteers will live and work with other youth volunteers in a developing country for up to three months. Arrangements are made through six approved agencies, including VSO, who will oversee the selection of suitable volunteers and worthwhile placements. (See 'Directory of Specialist Gap Year Programmes' for more details).

Although this book is devoted largely to canvassing options abroad, do not discount the possibility of spending some of your gap year in the UK doing something worthwhile away from home. Last year, London Mayor Boris Johnson launched a new stay-at-home volunteer scheme called City Year London to encourage gappers to tackle the 'urban jungle' of deprived parts of London. A number of such organisations are listed in the UK Directory below. Unlike placements abroad, you are unlikely to be out of pocket at the end of an attachment to British organisations, which sometimes pay your travel and living expenses and may even pay an allowance. Also, your carbon footprint will be much lighter. Note that volunteer organisations taking on people to work with children or vulnerable adults have a statutory obligation to run a police check on new volunteers. It is the responsibility of the organisation rather than the individual to apply to the Criminal Records Bureau (www.crb.gov.uk).

The Rank Foundation runs a Gap Award Scheme open to volunteers aged 17–24 who are recommended by their school/college or already active in a member charity in the Rank Charities network. Up to 40 volunteers are selected to work full-time in the UK for 6–9 months and receive board and lodging, training, travel, and a personal allowance, a bonus on completing the scheme of £750–£1,200, plus a certificate that carries some weight in youth work (details from Youth Projects, Rank Foundation, 28 Bridgegate, Hebden Bridge, West Yorkshire HX7 8EX; www.rankyouthwork.org/gap/index.htm).

COMMUNITY SERVICE VOLUNTEERS

Community Service Volunteers (CSV) provides volunteering and training opportunities throughout the UK to those aged 18 to 35 who commit themselves to volunteer full-time away from home for either six or 12 months. As many as 1,000 volunteers throughout the UK receive £35 a week pocket money in addition to accommodation and meals. Details can be obtained from CSV (contact details below). CSV produces oodles of persuasive literature demonstrating how worthwhile a stint as a volunteer can be. Projects are usually with people who need help, such as children with special needs, adults with learning difficulties, teenagers at risk of offending and homeless people. Interestingly, two-thirds of volunteers are women and one-third are men. The scheme is also open to qualifying volunteers from the

European Union and from a dozen other countries with a partner agency, ie Austria, Canada, Colombia, Costa Rica, France, Germany, Honduras, Japan, Korea, Mexico, Taiwan, Turkey, and the USA.

Elizabeth Moore-Bick volunteered with CSV just after graduating from Cambridge. Studying for a degree in Classics had meant that she had led a fairly rarefied existence, and she decided it was time to develop her 'people skills'. Despite initial doubts, she decided to take the plunge and did a placement supporting a woman who had been left paralysed by a car accident 20 years before.

CSV has links with disability services at most British universities and a stint supporting a student might provide a useful initiation, as it did for 19-year-old **Jo Scluz**, who supported three students at Loughborough University for her year between school and university:

> *After finishing A levels, I wanted to have a break from study and give something back. Being on placement at a university means that everyone is my own age. I've made so many friends. The other students think it is really great that I get to have all the perks of student life without having to do all the study, but of course I've got that to look forward to next September when I start my geology course. Being a CSV has been a crash course in university life.*

EUROPEAN VOLUNTARY SERVICE

Thousands of young people aged 18–30 are eligible to take up fully funded placements lasting six, but preferably 12, months in Europe or beyond through the EU-funded European Voluntary Service (EVS) programme. Full details are available from Youth in Action at the British Council (see entry for European Voluntary Service in the 'Directory of Specialist Gap Year Programmes'). The programme is generally regarded as excellent, although the usual entry route is slightly complicated. After making contact with a national agency, you have to find a sending organisation from the list of youth exchange and other participating voluntary organisations supplied by the EVS department. Alternatively, you can ask a group that you already work or volunteer for (eg a youth centre, women's refuge, etc) to become your sending sponsor. When you have found a sending organisation, they will give you a password for the database of host projects across Europe. These are extremely varied, from conference centres to film workshops, orphanages to environmental projects, though all are socially based with the aim of making contacts across Europe and of benefiting the community.

The programme is open to European nationals of all social and educational backgrounds. In fact, young people from disadvantaged situations are especially encouraged. Participants pay nothing. Both the sending and the host organisations receive funding from the European Youth in Action programme (with a budget allocated until 2013), and the volunteers get their travel costs, insurance, board and lodging, language classes, pocket money, orientation, and mid-term programme all provided free. There is also a tutor in each project who is available to help with any difficulties and guide the volunteer.

VOLUNTEERING ABROAD

The burgeoning of interest in volunteering abroad has been astonishing in recent years. While working for Daktari, a wildlife and education charity in South Africa with an entry below, **Kirsten Shaw** was responsible for running the marketing and social media programmes. Her eyes were opened to how popular volunteering has become as a form of holiday over the past few years. There are websites in every language, for every country, for every type of volunteering, to suit every individual taste. According to Kirsten, '*Volunteering has become a phenomenon – like recycling!*' She found her own voluntary position through independent research:

> *I am glad I never went through any mediating agency, I prefer to take charge of things myself, rather than let others do it for me. A volunteering choice is personal, and just the simple fact of communicating with the director of Daktari before my arrival, booking my own tickets, and finalising details made the experience more my own. Also, I know of agencies that charge exorbitant registration and process fees to unsuspecting 18-year-olds.*

PROJECTS ABROAD

Peter Browning went to Morocco with Projects Abroad on a Care project. He was able to make a significant impact on the lives of the children there and also gained invaluable experience.

No amount of research can truly prepare you for your time in Morocco. Morocco is itself a country of contradictions: it can feel both European and Middle Eastern, yet it is in Africa. The rich are very rich, the poor very poor. The pace of life is laid back, but in a strangely chaotic way – of all the places I've been, Morocco is certainly the most challenging, that is to say, the most culturally shocking.

I spent my time in Morocco working in a centre for underprivileged children. I ended up also teaching music, art, English, French, and maths, and even took part in sports activities. Such is the keenness to learn and experience new things that these children have, you have to be ready to adapt to anything. The children who come to the centre live in conditions I'd not have believed had I not seen them for myself.

By volunteering in a centre like this you have the opportunity to change these children's lives. As a volunteer, your role is manifold: not only do you have the opportunity to furnish these children with practical skills – English, maths, people skills – that will help them later on in life, but your being there makes a big statement.

Projects Abroad's dedication to this centre is witness to the fact that these children are far from being a 'lost cause', and while you play games, run around and have fun with the children, making them smile and laugh, you are not only helping them in that moment, you are also making more privileged Moroccans wake up and take note of the situation they're so used to ignoring.

By taking an active interest in Morocco's underprivileged children, you let everyone know that they, although so often ignored, are just as deserving of education, are just as important to society, and are just as valuable human beings as anyone else.

The impulse to want to help in distant parts of the world is almost always a worthy one, although as has been discussed in the chapter on 'Specialist Gap Year Programmes', there are plenty of greedy companies trying to cash in on this impulse. **Helen Reid**, who worked for about half a dozen different good causes in Africa and throughout South America during her gap year, fixed them up through independent research and after using the services of Volunteer Latin America (see entry below), which cost only £25.

Time spent in an Ecuadorian orphanage, an orang-utan rehabilitation centre or working with street children in India can be a wonderfully liberating release from the struggle with exams, whether at school or university, a welcome break before entering the fray for a job. The spirit to help others may be willing but the cash flow may be weak. While charities in the UK might be able to cover their volunteers' basic costs, this is almost never the case abroad. We have already seen how expensive specialist gap programmes can be. The organisations listed in this chapter do not specialise in gap year students, and the initial outlay for joining one of these organisations will usually be less than for the high-profile specialist agencies. As a consequence, they may not be so geared up for integrating volunteers as young as 18, which is not usually a problem if the volunteer does not carry unreasonable expectations.

Most voluntary jobs undertaken abroad will leave the volunteer seriously out of pocket, which can be disillusioning for those who think that a desire to help the world should be enough. After participating in several prearranged voluntary projects in the USA, **Catherine Brewin** did not resent the fee she had paid to Involvement Volunteers:

> *The whole business of paying to do voluntary work is a bit hard to swallow. But having looked into the matter quite a bit, it does seem to be the norm. While it may be a bit unfair (who knows how much profit or loss these voluntary organisations make or how worthy their projects?) most people I've met did seem to feel good about the experience. The group I was with did make the odd comment about it all, but did not seem unduly concerned. However, I should mention that most were around 18 years old and their parents were paying some if not all the costs.*

SOURCES OF INFORMATION

The website of Volunteering England (www.volunteering.org.uk) has a great deal of other information about volunteering generally. The revolution in information technology has made it easier for individuals to become acquainted with the amazing range of possibilities. There are some superb websites with a multitude of links to organisations big and small that can make use of volunteers. WorldWide Volunteering (WWV) is a non-profit organisation that maintains an extensive database of opportunities (www.wwv.org.uk) and www.independentvolunteer.org is international in scope.

Another online directory, www.traveltree.co.uk, covers gap year ideas and volunteering opportunities worldwide as well as internships, educational travel, and related matters. University careers websites often carry a page of gap year volunteering listings, for example, www.bath.ac.uk/careers/earlybird/cvgy.pdf.

Hosted by Action Without Borders, www.idealist.org is an easily searchable site that will take you to the great monolithic charities such as the Peace Corps as well as to small grassroots organisations in Armenia, Tenerife, or anywhere else. It lists 60,000+ organisations in more than 100 countries. When planning her gap year, **Katie White** says she spent hours browsing the amazing opportunities on www.idealist.org and www.goabroad.com and felt '*like a kid in a candy shop*'.

Students with a church affiliation and Christian faith have a broader choice of opportunities since a number of mission societies and charities are looking for young Christians (see the separate listing of Religious Organisations at the end of this chapter). Whereas some religious organisations focus on practical work, such as working with street children, orphans, in schools, building libraries, etc, others are predominantly proselytising or church planting, which will appeal only to the very committed. Christian Vocations (St James House, Trinity Road, Dudley, West Midlands DY1 1JB; 0121 288 0854;

www.christianvocations.org) publishes a searchable online directory of short-term opportunities with Christian agencies.

AVOIDING PROBLEMS

It is impossible to predict the circumstances in which you will find yourself. Whereas some gappers have a ready-made social life because of their location, others will find themselves fairly isolated. The picture on the brochure of the smiling volunteer teacher at the blackboard addressing some bright-eyed students might not be your day-to-day experience. **Abi Cooke** found herself the only European in a Thai village and had to get used to everyone shouting and pointing, stopping and staring.

The teaching itself had its ups and downs. Some days when the kids were keen and the weather not too sticky were great, and the enthusiasm you receive makes the effort worth the while. It is difficult, though, when you are faced with a class of 50 and half the kids are unable to read and write in their own language, never mind in English. The time I spent with the English Club I started was my favourite, when I met kids who really wanted to learn and weren't afraid to voice the few words they knew. In class, it was very difficult to have individual conversations with separate kids.

Bear in mind that voluntary work, especially in the developing world, can be not only tough and character-building, but also disillusioning. Misunderstandings can arise, and promises can be broken just as easily in the context of unpaid work as paid work. If you are in any doubt about an organisation you are considering working for, ask for the names of one or two past volunteers whom you can contact for an informal reference. Any worthy organisation should be happy to oblige.

WORKCAMPS/VOLUNTEER PROJECTS

Voluntary work in developed countries often takes the form of workcamps, which accept unskilled short-term labour. The term 'workcamp' is falling out of favour and is often replaced by 'volunteer project'. These short-term projects are an excellent introduction to travelling for 18–21-year-olds who have never before been away from a family-type social structure. Certain projects in the UK are open to 16- and 17-year-olds. As part of an established international network of voluntary organisations, they are not subject to the irregularities of some privately run projects. As well as providing gap year and other volunteers with the means to live cheaply for two to four weeks in a foreign country, workcamps enable volunteers to become involved in what is usually useful work for the community, to meet people from many different backgrounds, and to increase their awareness of other lifestyles, social problems, and their responsibility to society.

Within Europe, and to a lesser extent further afield, there is a massive effort to co-ordinate workcamp programmes. This usually means that the prospective volunteer should apply in the first instance to the appropriate organisation in his or her own country, or to a centralised international headquarters. The vast majority of camps take place in the summer months, and camp details are usually published online in March/April, with a flurry of placements made in the month or two following. It is necessary to pay a registration fee, which has become standard across the different agencies recruiting volunteers; usually £150 for a project in Europe, £180 for one in a developing country to help finance future projects or to pay for specialised training. The fee covers board and lodging but not of course travel.

The umbrella body for workcamps organisations is Service Civil International (www.sciint.org) with branches in 41 countries. The UK branch is International Voluntary Service (IVS-GB) in Edinburgh (0131 243 2745; info@ivsgb.org). The cost of registration on IVS workcamps outside the UK is £190, which includes £35 IVS membership fee. IVS has linked with the four other main agencies listed below to form VINE-UK (www.vineuk.co.uk), all of whom organise international volunteer exchange programmes. The other organisations in the network are:

Concordia International Volunteers, Brighton BN41 1DH (01273 422 218; www.concordia volunteers.org.uk). Programme of workcamps in 30 countries worldwide. Registration fee £180. (For projects in Latin America, Asia, Middle East, and Africa, volunteers pay an extra fee of about £150 to cover food and accommodation, etc.)

UNA Exchange, Cardiff (029 2022 3088; www.unaexchange.org). Membership costs £12 plus £150 for European projects, £175 for workcamps in the developing world, and £200–£300 for longer-term ones.

Voluntary Action for Peace/VAP, London SE22 0PH (0844 209 0927; www.vap.org.uk). Work-camps held in many countries in Western and Eastern Europe, plus Mexico, the Middle East, and Bangladesh.

Xchange Scotland, Glasgow (www.xchangescotland.org).

ARCHAEOLOGY

Taking part in archaeological excavations is another popular form of voluntary work, especially among those on gap years planning to study a related subject at university. Volunteers are almost always expected to make a contribution towards their board and lodging. Also, you may be asked to bring your own trowel, work clothes, tent, etc. (see directory entry for *Archaeology Abroad*, p255). *Archaeology Abroad* subscribers are eligible to apply for fieldwork awards of up to £500 to help with their dig expenses. Excavations applied for must be listed in the annual *Archaeology Abroad* bulletin or in one of its email updates.

For those who are not students of archaeology, the chances of finding a place on an overseas dig will be greatly enhanced by having some digging experience nearer home. Anyone who wants to participate on an archaeological dig should read information available from the Council for British Archaeology (CBA) in York; some of its fieldwork listings are freely available on its website (www.britarch.ac.uk/briefing/field.asp). Otherwise, you can subscribe to CBA's briefings, which list the archaeological digs to which volunteers can apply.

Anthony Blake joined a dig sponsored by the University of Reims in France and warns that '*archaeology is hard work, and applicants must be aware of what working for eight hours in the baking heat means!*' Nevertheless, Anthony found the company excellent, and the opportunity to improve his French welcome.

Israel is probably the country with the most active archaeology digs. Information on volunteering at archaeological digs in Israel is available on the website of the Israeli Ministry of Foreign Affairs (though it's a little difficult to locate; try Googling 'mfa digs 2012'). After choosing an excavation of interest, you directly contact the person in charge of the research. Some of them are in the Department of Classical Studies at Tel Aviv University, and others at universities elsewhere in Israel or abroad.

Volunteers are needed to do the mundane work of digging and sifting on a range of archaeological digs. In Israel, volunteers normally have to pay a daily fee of $35–$50+ to cover food and accommodation and sometimes considerably more, plus a registration fee (typically $50–$75). Most camps take place during university holidays between May and September, when temperatures soar. Volunteers must be in good physical condition and able to work long hours in hot weather. Valid health insurance is required.

CONSERVATION

People interested in protecting the environment can often slot into conservation organisations abroad. To fix up a short conservation holiday, contact BTCV, the British Trust for Conservation Volunteers (http://shop.btcv.org.uk), which runs a programme of UK and international projects in a dozen countries including Iceland, Slovakia, Bulgaria, the USA, and Cameroon. Accommodation, meals and insurance are provided; sample prices are £495 for a week of nest-building on the Black Sea, to £690 for two weeks' planting trees in a Cameroonian village, excluding flights.

The international system of working-for-keep on organic farms is another good way of visiting unexplored corners of the world cheaply (see entry for World Wide Opportunities on Organic Farms/WWOOF, p275). Of the several thousand WWOOF members in the UK, about half are aged 18–25.

Other internet-based exchanges of work-for-keep volunteers can be found at www.helpx.net where more that 1,300 Australian and New Zealand hosts are listed, with a growing number in Europe and worldwide as well. The site www.workaway.info run from Spain has up-to-date rural job listings worldwide, which potential work-for-keep volunteers can access by paying a fee of €22 for two years, €29 for a couple.

Several organisations assist scientific expeditions by supplying fee-paying volunteers, in addition to Earthwatch (see entry below, p259). For details of scientific expedition organisations which use self-financing volunteers, investigate Biosphere Expeditions (0870 446 0801; www.biosphere-expeditions.org) and Coral Cay Conservation, Gapforce, and Frontier in the 'Directory of Specialist Gap Year Programmes'.

THE GREAT PROJECTS

Your gap year is a fantastic opportunity to take part in volunteer work abroad; this allows you to spend part of your gap year truly making a difference.

Working with animals is an incredibly popular form of volunteering. Whether you are looking to help rehabilitate orphan orang-utans or research lions in the great African bush, you can always find a project that suits you, and all that is necessary is a passion for animals.

The Great Projects is a responsible travel company, twice winner of the Responsible Tourism Awards, allowing volunteers to travel and make a difference abroad on short-stay conservation volunteering programmes. On a Great Project such as the Great Orangutan Project in Borneo, the Great Gorilla Project in Uganda, or the Great Lion Project in South Africa, you get involved in the conservation process and immerse yourself in the local efforts to help save these endangered animals.

Daniel Murray shares his experience working with orang-utans in Borneo.

I spent a month on the Great Orangutan Project working with animals at Matang Wildlife Centre at Kubah National Park in Sarawak, Malaysian Borneo.

I really enjoyed all of the different work we took part in at the Centre, whether it was construction, enrichment, or the cleaning of the animal pens. It was satisfying to know that what we were doing was going to help directly, and that we would be there to see the benefits for the animals ourselves.

All of the volunteers I was with got on well, and we have all stayed in touch. I wasn't expecting to make as many good friends as I did but everyone had a good sense of humour, which is pretty much a prerequisite for life in the jungle!

My unforgettable moments on the Great Orangutan Project were when a female orang-utan swung through the forest towards the feeding platform with her baby holding on to her side, watching three orang-utans all playing in the pool that we helped to finish, learning to speak some Malay, and spending a day at the sun bear enclosure, among many others. I didn't want to leave Matang Wildlife Centre. Don't hesitate for a second in deciding whether or not to go, you'll love every second of it.

Visit www.thegreatprojects.com or find us on Facebook – The Great Orangutan Project.

OYSTER WORLDWIDE

After having had the most amazing experience of my life working with bears in Romania through Oyster Worldwide, I decided to jet a bit further afield to work with turtles on the Pacific Coast of Costa Rica.

Expectations were high after such a positive experience before, and I was not to be disappointed.

I was to be spending five weeks in small village communities nestled between stunning expanses of white sand beaches and dense rainforests, boasting more plant and animal life than I could possibly imagine. Grassy plains lead into tree-covered mountains shrouded in mist, and exotic bright flowers and plants dashed additional colour on the rich blanket of greens. It felt like I had landed in the set for *Lost*.

I was there during the rainy season, which generally meant sunny mornings and rainy afternoons. With the sun out it was absolutely glorious. The heat was intense, the sunlight danced through the leaves of the banana plants, and the children all came out to play in the centre of the village. On these days, you could stroll along the coastal roads, up into the mountains, or explore the rainforests. You could climb waterfalls, swim in their luscious pools and get an intense massage from the falling water, go horse riding along the beach in the sunset, learn to surf, go out for lunch or drinks or just sunbathe on the beach. The lifestyle was completely appealing, living immersed in Costa Rican culture (my Spanish improved in leaps and bounds!) in tiny little communities where you become an important member, helping out teaching English at the schools and educating people on turtle conservation.

Pacific Coast turtles are massively in decline in Costa Rica due to poaching, predation, and industrial fishing. Working with a local charity collecting the turtle eggs and transporting them to a hatchery means that they have a higher chance of hatching. We would patrol the beach every evening, and on a clear night we wouldn't even need the aid of a torch, for the Milky Way would shine down on us so brightly that you could see far ahead. You would never get such a beautiful sight back at home: straggling palm trees lining a wild ocean with ghostly star shadows. And then a turtle emerges from the waves, pulling herself up the sands where she will manoeuvre herself to dig a nest for her eggs. Once this is dug, she will lay around 100 eggs before making her way back to the sea. Around 50 days later, the vast majority of those eggs will hatch, releasing tiny scuttling baby turtles, who fall over each other in their eagerness to make it to the ocean. Watching a wave of a hundred baby turtles is one of the most beautiful sights I have ever seen.

DEVELOPING COUNTRIES

Commitment, no matter how fervent, is not enough to work for an aid organisation in the developing world. You must be able to offer some kind of useful training or skill. However, if you are travelling in underdeveloped countries and take the time to investigate local possibilities, you may discover wildlife projects, children's homes, special schools, etc, in which it is possible to work voluntarily for a short or longer time. You may simply want to join your new Vietnamese, Sri Lankan, or Ecuadorian friends wherever they are working. You may get the chance to trade your assistance for a straw mat and simple meals but more likely the only rewards will be the experience and the camaraderie.

MY GAP YEAR: SUSAN MOLLOY

Susan Molloy volunteered through Project Trust at Thembelihle in South Africa. She explains more about the place she made home for a year.

Because Thembelihle Home is a place of safety, the children cannot go to local schools. The home has a small classroom in the backyard where schooling takes place five days a week. My project partner and I were the only teachers (for up to 30 children of ages between five and 18), and wrote and set up the lesson plans, curriculum, and exams. Without Project Trust volunteers, the home school would not run, and therefore the children would be without education. Thembelihle could not afford to employ fulltime teachers, let alone those who would agree to live on-site 24/7 and be social care workers, friends, and listeners!

Not only do the volunteers run the school and support the children when they need it, but they are also a huge support for the other staff members. Resources are scarce, but the available materials are cherished and loved, just like all those, including children and staff, who are involved in the success and triumph of such a small home.

I have definitely matured in leaps and bounds since returning from South Africa. I feel like I have a better understanding of how difficult life is for people and how I have been handed everything I have ever wanted on a silver plate. I am now more grateful for everything I have. Nothing should be taken for granted. My year has opened my eyes to what really matters and what I want from my life now. I learnt to have patience and an understanding of how other people live.

I think life in South Africa is at a pace slower than the UK, but that's not a bad thing. I learnt to take things one at a time. Try to enjoy things more. Before I left for South Africa, my life was a rat race of deadlines and things to be done and places to be. Now, I have learned to relax, to slow down, to enjoy things, and realise what really matters and what things don't. Never again will I be ungrateful for anything I receive.

DIRECTORY OF VOLUNTEERING IN THE UK

L'ARCHE
10 Briggate, Silsden, Keighley, West Yorkshire
BD20 9JT
☎ (0)1535 656 186
✉ info@larche.org.uk
🖥 www.larche.org.uk

PROGRAMME DESCRIPTION: L'Arche is a worldwide network of communities where assistants help people with learning disabilities to live in a congenial atmosphere. The aim is to provide a real home, with spiritual and emotional support. Volunteers in their gap year are accepted.

DESTINATIONS: 9 centres in the UK: Kent, Liverpool, Inverness, Lambeth, Bognor Regis, Ipswich, Brecon, Edinburgh, and Preston.

NUMBER OF PLACEMENTS PER YEAR: 190–200.

PREREQUISITES: Assistants need an ability and willingness to live communally and to share life with people with learning disabilities.

DURATION AND TIME OF PLACEMENTS: Generally 12 months, although shorter and longer stays are sometimes acceptable.

SELECTION PROCEDURES AND ORIENTATION: Enquirers are sent an information pack along with a detailed application form. They are invited to visit the community, meet the members and have an informal interview with house leaders, assistants, and co-ordinators. All assistants work for a probationary period and receive a one-to-one induction with the community leader.

COST: Assistants must pay their own travel costs and personal insurance. Free board and lodging are provided and a modest allowance is paid.

CSV – COMMUNITY SERVICE VOLUNTEERS
Fifth Floor, Scala House, 36 Holloway Circus,
Birmingham B1 1EQ
☎ (0)800 374 991
☎ (0)121 643 7690
✉ volunteer@csv.org.uk
🖥 www.csv.org.uk/fulltimevolunteering

CSV is the UK's leading volunteering and training organisation. CSV's gap year opportunities are open to those aged 18–35 who commit to volunteer full-time and away from home for 6–12 months.

PROGRAMME DESCRIPTION: Volunteers help people throughout the UK in a huge range of social care projects, eg working with the homeless, mentoring young offenders, supporting children in special schools, or helping the disabled to live independently in their homes, and at the same time learn new skills. Volunteers can be placed anywhere within the UK.

NUMBER OF PLACEMENTS PER YEAR: 1,000.

PREREQUISITES: No specific qualifications or experience are needed. Open to UK or EEA citizens who are residents in the UK. Other international volunteers can participate provided they apply through one of CSV's international partnerships (details from www.csv.org/gapyear).

SELECTION PROCEDURES AND ORIENTATION: Volunteers receive regular supervision and support from their project and local CSV office.

COST: CSV volunteers receive accommodation and subsistence, including £35 per week towards day-to-day expenses; plus food (or up to £40 per week to buy food). Travel expenses are also provided.

HESSE STUDENT SCHEME
Aldeburgh Festival, Aldeburgh Music, Snape
Maltings Concert Hall, Snape, Saxmundham,
Suffolk IP17 1SP
☎ (0)1728 687 127
✉ jalexander@aldeburgh.co.uk
🖥 www.aldeburgh.co.uk

PROGRAMME DESCRIPTION: Volunteers assist in the day-to-day running of the Aldeburgh Festival of Music and the Arts in June and prepare for the weekly Hesse Students Concert. Duties include selling programmes, conducting shuttle buses, page turning, and assisting Aldeburgh staff with a variety of light tasks. Students are also expected to devise and perform a concert as part of the festival events.

NUMBER OF PLACEMENTS PER YEAR: 2 sets of 10 students are chosen for each half of the festival.

PREREQUISITES: Ages 18–25. Must be a music lover, willing to help with the general running of the festival and have a cheerful disposition and a professional approach.

DURATION AND TIME OF PLACEMENTS: 1 week during the festival, which runs over the middle 2 weeks in June.

COST: Volunteers receive bed and breakfast accommodation and tickets to festival events.

CONTACT: Jane Alexander (jalexander@aldeburgh.co.uk).

OXFAM
Oxfam House, John Smith Drive, Cowley, Oxford OX4 2JY
☎ (0)300 200 1266
✒ stewards@oxfam.org.uk
💻 www.oxfam.org.uk/stewarding

PROGRAMME DESCRIPTION: Volunteer stewards recruited for various summer musical festivals including Glastonbury, Latitude, and WOMAD.

NUMBER OF PLACEMENTS PER YEAR: 5,000.

SHAD – SUPPORT AND HOUSING ASSISTANCE FOR PEOPLE WITH DISABILITIES
SHAD Wandsworth, 5 Bedford Hill, London SW12 9ET
☎ (0)20 8675 6095
✒ volunteering@shad.org.uk
💻 www.shad.org.uk

SHAD enables tenants with physical disabilities to live in their own homes. Volunteers are needed to act as the tenants' arms and legs, following their instructions.

DURATION AND TIME OF PLACEMENTS: Minimum 3–4 months, maximum 12 months. Work is on a rota basis: volunteers can expect a minimum of 4 days off a fortnight. A shift system is worked by volunteers allowing plenty of free time to explore London.

PREREQUISITES: No experience is necessary and support is guaranteed. Opportunity to gain good work experience in a friendly and supportive environment, and to live and work with people from all over the world. Volunteers from overseas welcome.

SELECTION PROCEDURES AND ORIENTATION: Through application form, interview and suitable references. Induction and safe manual handling training is provided.

REMUNERATION: Volunteers receive an allowance equivalent to £60 a week and free accommodation (shared with other volunteers). Certificates and references provided on successful completion of a placement.

V-INSPIRED
Fifth Floor, Dean Bradley House, 52 Horseferry Road, London SW1P 2AF
☎ (0)800 089 9000
☎ (0)20 7960 7000
✒ info@vinspired.com
💻 www.vinspired.com

This is the National Youth Volunteers Service, a public-funded body with a budget of £48 million.

PROGRAMME DESCRIPTION: UK-wide initiative provides opportunities for volunteers aged 16–25 in the UK.

DESTINATIONS: Throughout the UK regions.

NUMBER OF PLACEMENTS PER YEAR: Unlimited.

COST: Out-of-pocket expenses covered.

VITALISE (FORMERLY WINGED FELLOWSHIP TRUST)
Shap Road Industrial Estate, Shap Road, Kendal, Cumbria LA9 6NZ
☎ (0)845 330 0148
☎ (0)1539 814 682
✒ volunteer@vitalise.org.uk
💻 www.vitalise.org.uk

Charity that provides essential breaks for disabled people and carers and inspirational opportunities for volunteers.

PROGRAMME DESCRIPTION: Volunteers are recruited to support people with disabilities and carers on holiday.

DESTINATIONS: Centres in Southampton, Chigwell, and Southport.

PREREQUISITES: Minimum age 16. No experience necessary.

DURATION AND TIME OF PLACEMENTS: Year-round availability (especially spring and autumn). Anything from 1 week (most common) to 1 year.

SELECTION PROCEDURES AND ORIENTATION: Booking form, references, CRB check. Trained care staff are always around, and induction training and ongoing support are given.

COST: Completely free. All board, lodging, and travel to centres is paid.

CONTACT: Val Allen, Senior Volunteers Administrator.

PROGRAMME DESCRIPTION: WORLDwrite is an educational charity that uses documentary film-making as a medium for campaigning on domestic and global issues, and uses lots of London-based volunteers for varying periods. Their news channel WORLDbytes (www.worldbytes.org), run by young volunteers, covers a lot of domestic as well as international issues.

SELECTION PROCEDURES AND ORIENTATION: Volunteers should be passionate about the cause and not just submit CVs. WORLDwrite hosts occasional drop-in open evenings in Hackney.

CONTACT: Patrick Hayes, Volunteer Co-ordinator; Ceri Dingle, Director; Viv Regan, Assistant Director.

Helps people interested in organic farming to exchange their manual labour for a stay on farms throughout the UK and Ireland. Membership costs £20 for 1 person, £30 for 2 for a year. Access to about 400 UK properties that accept working volunteers. See also entry in 'Directory of Volunteering Abroad'.

DIRECTORY OF VOLUNTEERING ABROAD

African Impact facilitates conservation and community development volunteer programmes, internships, and small group adventures in Southern and East Africa.

PROGRAMME DESCRIPTION: Voluntourism opportunities on community projects (teaching, medical, and sports), and on lion conservation projects. Internships and professional courses also available.

DESTINATIONS: Zambia, Zimbabwe, South Africa, Zanzibar, Mozambique, Kenya, etc.

NUMBER OF PLACEMENTS: 1,200.

PREREQUISITES: Minimum age 18.

DURATION AND TIME OF PLACEMENTS: Typically 2–8 weeks on community projects, 2–4 weeks on lion projects, preferably starting on the first or third Monday of every month.

SELECTION PROCEDURES AND ORIENTATION: Telephone interviews are conducted for more complex and sensitive placements; otherwise, a CV is sufficient.

COST: Sample prices £1,045 for fortnight volunteering with lions in Livingstone, £1,725 for 6 weeks teaching in Kenya (2011 rates).

CONTACT: Kylie Taute, Destination Manager.

PROGRAMME DESCRIPTION: Runs its own community surf volunteer, and wildlife volunteer projects in Jeffreys Bay and co-operates with partner organisations elsewhere in South Africa to offer other volunteer opportunities.

DESTINATIONS: South Africa.

NUMBER OF PLACEMENTS PER YEAR: 50–100.

DURATION AND TIME OF PLACEMENTS: 1–3 months.

PREREQUISITES: Average age 16–45. All nationalities accepted. No specific qualifications needed, only life skills.

SELECTION PROCEDURES AND ORIENTATION:
Applications due at least 4 weeks in advance of arrival.
COST: Varies with programme. Volunteer fee covers
meals, lodging, and programme sponsorship. Accommodation is in volunteer lodge (for community project),
or log cabins in game area (for wildlife project).
CONTACT: Tyron van Tonder, Company Owner.

ALL OUT AFRICA
PO Box 153 Lobamba, Swaziland
☎ +268 416 2260
🖰 info@alloutafrica.com
🖥 www.alloutafrica.com

Travel organisation that offers packages combining
volunteering and tourism.
PROGRAMME DESCRIPTION: Projects are aimed at
engaging people from around the world in research and
action for a sustainable Africa. Social projects include
orphan care, teaching, sports development and building
in Swaziland; teaching, childcare, and medical/social
work project in Cape Town; and childcare or teaching in
Botswana and Mozambique. Conservation projects focus
on research and monitoring of marine and onshore wildlife, with some hands-on conservation action. Volunteers
help to collect and analyse field data on whale sharks,
humpback whales, turtles, coral fish, Marabou storks,
tortoises, rodents, bats, and vultures in Mozambique and
Swaziland.
DESTINATIONS: Swaziland, South Africa, Botswana, and
Mozambique.
DURATION AND TIME OF PLACEMENTS: Standard
length of stay is 4 weeks, though 2, 6, 8, or 12 weeks (or
longer) are also possible. Arrival day is the first Monday
of each month.
PREREQUISITES: Ages 18–65. No special skills needed,
except for medical project in Cape Town. Attempts are
made to match a volunteer's skills to a particular project.
SELECTION PROCEDURES AND ORIENTATION: Appli-
cations should be submitted at least a month before start
date. Volunteers receive project briefs and a travel pack
in advance and an orientation tour on arrival. The whale
shark marine project incorporates a scuba dive course.
COST: From £993 upwards. In Swaziland and Cape
Town, volunteers stay in backpacker lodges, in
Mozambique in a beach volunteer house, and in
Botswana with host families, all on-site. Private accom-
modation can be organised subject to availability.
CONTACT: Gabby Lee, Bookings Officer.

AMERICAN CONSERVATION EXPERIENCE (ACE)
2900 N Fort Valley Road, Flagstaff, AZ 86001,
USA
☎ +1 928 226 6960
🖰 cbaker@usaconservation.org
🖰 intern@usaconservation.org
🖥 www.usaconservation.org

PROGRAMME DESCRIPTION: Environmental conservation projects in America's National Parks and public
lands. Typical projects include walking track construction,
revegetation, weed eradication, fencing, habitat surveys,
erosion control, and watershed restoration.
DESTINATIONS: Grand Canyon, Zion, Bryce,
Canyonlands, Arches, Yosemite, Sequoia, and many
other National Parks throughout America's west.
NUMBER OF PLACEMENTS: 250.
PREREQUISITES: All nationalities. Minimum age 18
(average 23).
DURATION AND TIME OF PLACEMENTS: 8, 10, or
12 weeks.
SELECTION PROCEDURES AND ORIENTATION:
Applications must be sent to partner agent, eg BUNAC in
the UK (www.bunac.org/volunteer/usa).
COST: BUNAC fee is £295 for 10 or 12 weeks, £475 for
8 weeks. Volunteers must fund their airfares to Phoenix or
San Francisco, plus pay for food on their days off. Dorm
accommodation and meals while on project are provided.
CONTACT: Chris Baker, Director.

AMERISPAN STUDY ABROAD
PO Box 58129, Philadelphia, PA 19103, USA
☎ +1 800 879 6640
☎ +1 215 751 1100
☎ (0)20 8123 6086 (UK)
🖰 info@amerispan.com
🖥 www.amerispan.com/volunteer_intern

Travel organisation with expertise in arranging language
courses, voluntary placements, and internships
throughout South and Central America, as well as other
languages in Europe and English-language placements
in Africa and Asia.
PROGRAMME DESCRIPTION: The volunteer/internship
programme is designed to provide in-depth experience
in an area of participant's interest, with the option of
language courses and homestays in most locations.
All projects are listed on website. A typical programme
would be a 2-week language course followed by a
4-month volunteer placement in healthcare, education,
tourism/marketing, national parks, or social work.

PREREQUISITES: Open to all nationalities. Some minimum requirements may apply, depending on project.

COST: Fees start at $1,345 for a 4-week placement in Guatemala which includes homestay, language lessons, and volunteer placement.

AMIGOS DE IRACAMBI – SAVING FORESTS, CHANGING LIVES

Caixa Postal No 1, Rosário da Limeira, 36878–000, Minas Gerais, Brazil

☎ +55 31 3956 0454

✆ volunteers@iracambi.com

💻 www.iracambi.com

Organisation working at the cutting edge of conservation and sustainability to make the conservation of the rainforest more attractive than its destruction, in one of the world's top five biodiversity hotspots, the Atlantic Forest in south-eastern Brazil.

PROGRAMME DESCRIPTION: Volunteers take part in the Citizen Science Programme, monitoring forests and streams as part of overall ecosystem monitoring. Support activities include working in the forest nursery, trail maintenance, GIS, marketing, fundraising, and administrative support.

NUMBER OF PLACEMENTS PER YEAR: 110.

PREREQUISITES: Volunteers must be enthusiastic, flexible, self-motivated people who want to make a valid contribution.

DURATION AND TIME OF PLACEMENTS: Minimum stay 1 month.

SELECTION PROCEDURES AND ORIENTATION: Rolling acceptance year round. After receiving application and CV, volunteer's skills are matched with programme needs. Support and advice available throughout stay.

COST: R$1,200 (£470) for first month, R$1,150 (£450) for second month, R$1,100 (£430) for third and subsequent months. Cost includes full board accommodation in shared housing.

CONTACT: Volunteer Co-ordinator.

APES (ANIMAL PROTECTION AND ENVIRONMENTAL SANCTUARY)

PO Box 433 (Greytown, 3250 KwaZulu-Natal), South Africa

☎ +27 072 306 5664 (mobile)

✆ apes1@gom.co.za

💻 www.apes.org.za

APES is a non-profit organisation specialising in primate rehabilitation, rescue, and animal care.

PROGRAMME DESCRIPTION: Committed volunteers accepted year-round to work with the animals, especially vervet monkeys. Tasks may include snare/trap clearing; game counts, and environmental management. Project list available on request. APES also promotes community development and environmental education in local Zulu schools.

DESTINATIONS: Khobotho and Umpalazi Reserves, KwaZulu-Natal. Also other venues by arrangement.

DURATION AND TIME OF PLACEMENTS: Discretionary.

COST: £610 per month, including full board and lodging.

CONTACT: Dawn Magowan, Founder, and Rodney Pendleton, Co-Founder.

ARCHAEOLOGY ABROAD

31–34 Gordon Square, London WC1H 0PY

☎ (0)20 8537 0849

✆ arch.abroad@ucl.ac.uk

💻 www.britarch.ac.uk/archabroad

Established in 1972 with official base at University College London.

PROGRAMME DESCRIPTION: Provides information about archaeological fieldwork opportunities outside the UK through its annual publication *Archaeology Abroad* (available on CD-ROM or via email) and via occasional email updates throughout the year. Free factsheets, including *Digging Abroad in a Gap Year*, available in exchange for a large, stamped, self-addressed envelope.

DESTINATIONS: Worldwide (outside the UK).

NUMBER OF PLACEMENTS PER YEAR: 500+.

PREREQUISITES: Archaeological fieldwork involves physical labour. Volunteers need to be fit and healthy and enjoy working as part of a team. Previous experience useful, though not essential.

DURATION AND TIME OF PLACEMENTS: From 1 week.

SELECTION PROCEDURES AND ORIENTATION: People with a definite interest in the subject are generally though not always preferred. Basic training is usually offered to those with no excavation experience.

COST: Annual subscription to *Archaeology Abroad* costs £20 electronically or for a CD-ROM £25 (£27 in Europe, £29 elsewhere). Subscribers eligible for fieldwork awards towards cost of joining excavation projects listed in *Archaeology Abroad*.

CONTACT: Wendy Rix Morton, Honorary Editor and Secretary.

THE BACKPACK & AFRICA TRAVEL CENTRE

74 New Church Street, Tamboerskloof, Cape Town, South Africa

☎ +27 21 423 5555

✆ toni@backpackers.co.za

💻 www.backpackers.co.za

PROGRAMME DESCRIPTION: No set volunteer programme, but volunteer teaching assistants are needed to teach maths, science, and English in a local primary school during school hours. Also option of assisting sport coaches after-school, with gardening project or in new library.

DESTINATIONS: Cape Town.

PREREQUISITES: Minimum age 18. Mature individuals needed, who are passionate about teaching children how to read or play sport.

SELECTION PROCEDURES AND ORIENTATION: Backpackers' introduction to Cape Town given.

CONTACT: Toni Shina, Co-owner.

BIMINI BIOLOGICAL FIELD STATION
9300 SW 99 Street, Miami, FL 33176 2050, USA
☎ +1 305 799 9048 (mobile)
📧 sgruber@rsmas.miami.edu;
📧 bbfsshark-lab@gmail.com
💻 www.miami.edu/sharklab

Privately owned marine biological research station in the Bahamas.

PROGRAMME DESCRIPTION: Active field research on lemon sharks and other marine animals. Studies consist of genetics, behaviour, telemetry-tracking, etc. Volunteers perform all tasks including research, plus routine maintenance, and occasional cooking.

DURATION AND TIME OF PLACEMENTS: Minimum 1 month from the 15th of the month, renewable monthly.

NUMBER OF PLACEMENTS: About 20 per year (5–7 volunteers at any one time).

PREREQUISITES: Must speak English, have taken some courses in biology, and possess a keen interest in sharks.

SELECTION PROCEDURES AND ORIENTATION: Applications via email accepted year-round. Two academic references must be submitted.

COST: $695 per month to cover meals and housing.

CONTACT: Professor Samuel H Gruber, Director.

BOTTLENOSE DOLPHIN RESEARCH INSTITUTE (BDRI)
Via A. Diaz 4, Golfo Aranci, Olbia-Tempio, Sardinia 07020, Italy
☎ +39 0789 183 1197
☎ +39 338 469 5878
☎ +39 346 081 5414 (mobile)
📧 info@thebdri.com
💻 www.thebdri.com

PROGRAMME DESCRIPTION: Boat-based field work, marine conservation, and dolphin research project for paying volunteers.

NUMBER OF PLACEMENTS PER YEAR: 75.

DESTINATIONS: Emerald Coast of northern Sardinia.

PREREQUISITES: All welcome.

DURATION AND TIME OF PLACEMENTS: Minimum 6 days; standard stay 13 days. No maximum.

COST: €75–€100 per day.

CONTACT: Bruno Diaz Lopez, Chief Biologist and Director.

BRIDGE VOLUNTEERS
915 S. Colorado Boulevard, Denver, CO 80246, USA
☎ +1 888 825 3454
📧 bvbookings@bridge.edu
💻 www.BridgeVolunteers.org

Affiliated to Bridge TEFL (www.bridgetefl.com).

PROGRAMMES OFFERED: Volunteers can choose to work in the areas of community development, conservation, public health, sports coaching, construction, youth outreach, or English teaching in many countries in Africa, Asia, and Latin America. Teacher training, language courses, and host families are also available on many projects.

DESTINATIONS: Africa (Zambia, Mozambique, South Africa, Swaziland), Asia (India, China), Central and South America (Argentina, Brazil, Chile, Peru, Ecuador, Honduras), and Europe (Albania, Turkey).

DURATION OF PROGRAMMES: Variable. From 1 week to 1 year. Average project length is 2 weeks, though there are some that last 4 weeks and longer.

ACCOMMODATION: Local host families, hostel, or volunteer housing.

OTHER SERVICES: TEFL Online training for volunteer teaching projects, language immersion courses, activities, and excursions to get to know the local culture.

COST: Sample costs would be $1,345 for a fortnight in youth outreach work in Albania, $2,376 for 4 weeks teaching in Zambia.

BUENOS AIRES VOLUNTEER (BAV)
Pas. Rivadavia 2431, Third Entrance, 4 floor, office 9, (C1034ACD) Ciudad Autónoma de Buenos Aires, Argentina
☎ +54 11 4952 4779
📧 info@bavolunteer.org.ar
💻 www.bavolunteer.org.ar

BAV is a programme run by Amartya, a social enterprise based in Argentina with a branch in Scandinavia.

PROGRAMME DESCRIPTION: Organises and co-ordinates volunteer work projects for people from all over the world with the objective of strengthening social organisations in Argentina, focusing on child services development, arts and development, social inclusion, poverty relief, and micro-enterprises.

NUMBER OF PLACEMENTS PER YEAR: 40.

DESTINATIONS: BAV works with over 50 grassroots and other organisations of different types in and around Buenos Aires, as well as in different provinces of Argentina.

PREREQUISITES: Minimum age 18. Average age 24. Volunteers should know basic Spanish. Should be flexible and pro-active.

DURATION AND TIME OF PLACEMENTS: Minimum 3 months.

SELECTION PROCEDURES AND ORIENTATION: Applications accepted year-round.

COST: Programme fee $800 includes assistance with finding homestay or private accommodation, intensive Spanish course, information about cultural events, bi-weekly meetings and seminars, etc.

CENIT (CENTRE FOR THE WORKING GIRL)
Calle Huacho 150 y Jos Peralta, Barrio El Camal, Quito, Ecuador
☎ +593 2 265 4260
contact@cenitecuador.org
volunteer-office@cenitecuador.org
www.cenitecuador.org

PROGRAMME DESCRIPTION: CENIT relies heavily on volunteers from all over the world to help achieve its aim to allow families to send their children to school rather than have them working on the streets. Volunteers work in projects such as street outreach, English classes, the medical clinic, dental programme, literacy classes, art and jewellery-making workshops, and drop-in tutoring centres, mainly in south Quito.

NUMBER OF PLACEMENTS: 40–60, usually for short periods, although longer-term volunteers are preferred, and are able to take on more responsibilities at the project.

DURATION AND TIME OF PLACEMENTS: Minimum 2 months. Placement depends on the amount of time committed and level of Spanish.

PREREQUISITES: All ages. Basic knowledge of Spanish required. Volunteers should be outgoing and self-motivating, and (for some projects) willing to work with children who have suffered severe neglect or abuse.

COST: One-time administrative fee of $75. Volunteers are responsible for finding (and funding) their own accommodation, though advice on homestays and hostels is available from CENIT; the latter will cost $80–$150 a month.

CONTACT: Vail Miller or Gladys Pérez, Volunteer Co-ordinators.

CHILE INSIDE LTDA/SOUTH AMERICA INSIDE
Andrés de Fuenzalida 17, Oficina 51, Providencia, Santiago, Chile
☎ +56 2 335 9072
info@southamerica-inside.com
www.southamerica-inside.com

PROGRAMME DESCRIPTION: Volunteering placements, working holidays, internships, wildlife and nature projects, farm stays, teaching English programmes, and language courses throughout Latin America.

NUMBER OF PLACEMENTS PER YEAR: 500 total.

DESTINATIONS: Throughout Latin America.

PREREQUISITES: Minimum age 18. All nationalities accepted.

DURATION AND TIME OF PLACEMENTS: Programmes last between 2 weeks and 6+ months.

SELECTION PROCEDURES AND ORIENTATION: No special selection criteria. Candidates need to send CV and registration form 3–10 weeks in advance.

COST: Programme cost depends on each programme and the length of stay, from about $160 for 2 weeks volunteer work or language course.

ACCOMMODATION: Host family, volunteer house.

CONTACT: Marion Ruhland, Founder and Executive Director.

CONCORDIA
19 North Street, Portslade, Brighton, Sussex BN41 1DH
☎ (0)1273 422 218
info@concordiavolunteers.org.uk
www.concordiavolunteers.org.uk

Concordia is a small, not-for-profit education charity (no. 305991) committed to international youth exchange and established in 1943; it aims to bring people from different countries together to break down cultural stereotypes and promote greater international understanding and peace.

PROGRAMME DESCRIPTION: Programme of short-term international volunteer projects in more than 60 countries. Projects range from nature conservation, renovation, construction, and archaeology to social work, including working with adults and children with learning or physical disabilities, children's playschemes, youth work, and teaching.

DESTINATIONS: Western, Central and Eastern Europe, Russia, Japan, South Korea, Africa, the Middle East, South East Asia, India and North, Central, and South America.

PREREQUISITES: Aged 18+ and resident in the UK. A selection of projects is available for teenagers aged 16 and 17. No experience or specific skills needed, though motivation is essential. For projects in Asia, Latin America, and Africa volunteers must attend a preparation weekend in Brighton; dates are set in February, June, July, and October, and the participation fee is from £40.

DURATION AND TIME OF PLACEMENTS: 2–4 weeks, mainly between June and September with a smaller winter/spring programme. Some longer term placements for 3–12 months available.

COST: Volunteers pay a registration fee of £180 and fund their own travel and insurance. Board and accommodation are free of charge for projects in Europe, North America, Japan, and South Korea. For projects in Latin America, Asia, Middle East and Africa, volunteers pay a fee on arrival of around £150 that covers food and accommodation, as well as funding the programme in the country.

CONTACT: Francesco Bonini, International Volunteer Co-ordinator.

CROSS-CULTURAL SOLUTIONS
UK Office: Tower Point, 44 North Road, Brighton BN1 1YR
☎ (0)845 458 2781/2
info@uk@crossculturalsolutions.org
www.crossculturalsolutions.org
See website for US address

A not-for-profit international volunteer organisation founded in 1995 and a registered charity in the UK (no. 1106741).

PROGRAMME DESCRIPTION: Opportunity for participants to support sustainable community development abroad working side-by-side with local people on community-led initiatives and engaging in cultural exchange.

DESTINATIONS: Africa, Asia, Eastern Europe, and Latin America.

NUMBER OF PLACEMENTS PER YEAR: 3,000+.

PREREQUISITES: No language or specialist skills are necessary. All nationalities welcome. No upper age limit.

DURATION AND TIME OF PLACEMENTS: 1–12 weeks. Start dates are offered year-round.

COST: Programme fees start at £1,207 for 1 week. Fees cover the cost of lodging, meals, safe drinking water, and in-country ground transport, plus individual attention and guidance from an experienced programme manager, co-ordination of the placement, cultural and learning activities, a 24-hour emergency hotline, medical insurance, and more. Airfares not included.

DAKTARI BUSH SCHOOL & WILDLIFE ORPHANAGE
Bona Ingwe Farm, Harmony 81, Hoedspruit 1380, South Africa
☎ +27 82 656 2969
info@daktaribushschool.org
www.daktaribushschool.org

The mission of the private game reserve Daktari is to educate underprivileged local children to care for the environment through the medium of a wildlife orphanage.

PROGRAMME DESCRIPTION: Hands-on volunteering experience with injured and orphaned wild animals while educating local children, with a view to giving them both a brighter future. Animals include impala, kudu, wildebeest, zebra, giraffe, hyena, and leopard. Longer-term opportunities exist for director's assistant and volunteer co-ordinator (see entry in 'Directory of Work Experience').

DESTINATIONS: 700-hectare wildlife reserve is located near Kruger National Park, South Africa.

NUMBER OF PLACEMENTS PER YEAR: 70 volunteers a year.

DURATION AND TIME OF PLACEMENTS: 1–12 weeks starting any time of year. Average stay is 1 month. For stays exceeding 90 days; participants must obtain a volunteer visa.

PREREQUISITES: Minimum age 18. All nationalities welcome. No qualifications/skills necessary, only enthusiasm.

SELECTION PROCEDURES AND ORIENTATION: Volunteers have a welcome meeting to explain the project and the rules of life in the bush. Meeting held every evening to discuss the organisation of the following day. Solar power used since there is no electricity on the farm.

COST: 1 week £390, 2 weeks £550, 3 weeks £790, 4 weeks £990, and so on, up to 12 weeks £2,790. Accommodation in on-site chalets or in the main house of the director.

CONTACT: Michele Merrifield, Director.

DEVELOPMENT IN ACTION
78 York Street, London W1H 1DP
☎ (0)7813 395 957
info@developmentinaction.org
www.developmentinaction.org

Formerly Student Action India.

PROGRAMME DESCRIPTION: Arrange voluntary attachments to various local development NGOs in India. Partner organisations require volunteers to work in a wide variety of areas: from non-formal education, working with vulnerable children or deaf and blind children, to fieldwork and research, working on solar energy projects, and administrative and office work.

DESTINATIONS: India, with projects in the Mumbai area (rural placements), Pune, Indore, Bhopal, and Pondicherry.

PREREQUISITES: Energy and enthusiasm, a commitment to volunteering, and an interest in grassroots development. All ages welcome.

DURATION AND TIME OF PLACEMENTS: 2-month summer placements (July-August) or year-out 5-month placements (September-February).

SELECTION PROCEDURES AND ORIENTATION: University recruitment talks/careers fairs take place October to March (see website). Application deadlines in March and April; interviews held in March and May. Pre-departure training over one weekend plus orientation on arrival. Sessions led by recently returned volunteers, and include some basic Hindi language training.

COST: £800 for summer; £1,600 for 5 months (covers placement, training, support, and accommodation). Flights, insurance, visa, and subsistence costs are extra.

CONTACT: Michelle Leeder, UK Co-ordinator.

THE DODWELL TRUST
16 Lanark Mansions, Pennard Road, London W12 8DT
☎ (0)20 8740 6302
✉ dodwell@madagascar.freeserve.co.uk
🖥 www.dodwell-trust.org

PROGRAMME DESCRIPTION: Hands-on experience in English teaching, working with children, French-language conversation tuition, conservation, research, or zoology (depending on time of year).

DESTINATIONS: Madagascar.

NUMBER OF PLACEMENTS PER YEAR: 60–70.

DURATION AND TIME OF PLACEMENTS: 3 weeks to 8 months. Flexible timing.

PREREQUISITES: No skills required. All nationalities welcome provided English is spoken, and programme open to gap year students and career breakers. Placements matched with volunteers' skills and interests where possible; for example local radio, French practice, tennis, song groups, conservation, and animal studies at zoo.

SELECTION PROCEDURES AND ORIENTATION: Interviews not essential, though frequent optional meetings and briefings are held in London. Two-day training and orientation course on arrival in Madagascar at placement.

COST: In-country placement costs from £670 for 3 weeks, £1,340 for 12 weeks. Self-contained accommodation with cooking facilities provided, in quaint small towns in highlands, rainforest, or seaside. Volunteers usually placed in pairs. Volunteers are responsible for obtaining their own visas and health insurance.

CONTACT: Christina Dodwell, Head of Projects.

DRAGONFLY COMMUNITY FOUNDATION
1719 Mookamontri Soi 13, A. Meuang Nakhon Ratchasima 30000, Thailand
✉ dan@thai-dragonfly.com
🖥 www.thai-dragonfly.com

PROGRAMME DESCRIPTION: Charitable foundation in Thailand working on building, orphanage, and education projects. Volunteers are recruited to help with English teaching in schools and orphanages, and to build mud-brick buildings as an affordable and environmentally friendly alternative to standard concrete buildings.

DESTINATIONS: Thailand.

NUMBER OF PLACEMENTS PER YEAR: 50.

PREREQUISITES: Good working knowledge of English (or Thai!), flexibility, and an open mind.

DURATION AND TIME OF PLACEMENTS: Teaching project requires a minimum 2-month commitment, up to 4 months. Building projects are more flexible and any help that can be given is accepted if possible.

SELECTION PROCEDURES AND ORIENTATION: Preliminary contacts online; application forms processed by email followed by Skype interview.

OTHER SERVICES: TEFL courses through local providers for teaching volunteers; choice of online option and courses based in beach towns in Thailand.

COST: Teaching project training fee 3,000 Thai baht (£65); lunches and accommodation normally provided by schools. For building projects, volunteers must cover their own costs. Donations to various projects gratefully accepted.

CONTACT: Dan Lockwood, Volunteer Projects Co-ordinator.

EARTHWATCH INSTITUTE (EUROPE)
Mayfield House, 256 Banbury Road, Oxford OX2 7HT
☎ (0)1865 318 838
✉ info@earthwatch.org.uk
🖥 www.earthwatch.org/europe

Founded in 1971, Earthwatch is an international environmental charity that offers conservation volunteering opportunities on scientific research expeditions worldwide, not eco-tourist trips.

PROGRAMME DESCRIPTION: Earthwatch currently supports hundreds of expeditions on 61 projects in 29 countries. To ensure research addresses pressing global environmental issues, Earthwatch preferentially funds projects that fit the focus of one or more of the following priority research areas: climate change, oceans, ecosystem services, and cultural heritage. As an environmental charity, it engages volunteers to help gather data. Expeditions are designed at the request of scientists who are trying to find solutions to pressing environmental problems. (Earthwatch also offers internships in its Oxford and Boston offices; see *Work Experience* chapter.)

DESTINATIONS: Volunteer field assistants needed throughout Europe and worldwide. European projects include monitoring whales and dolphins in Scotland and contributing to climate change research in Oxford's Wytham Woods. International projects range from turtle conservation and coral reef research to protecting wildlife in Kenya or the Peruvian Amazon.

NUMBER OF PLACEMENTS PER YEAR: Approximately 4,000.

PREREQUISITES: Normal age limit is 18+ with no maximum; also some teen teams (for ages 16–18). All nationalities accepted.

DURATION AND TIME OF PLACEMENTS: Projects last 1–22 days throughout the year (see www.earthwatch. org/europe for expedition dates).

SELECTION PROCEDURES AND ORIENTATION: No previous experience or special skills necessary. Volunteers fill out a questionnaire and health form before participating on the project; no interview is required. All volunteers receive a briefing pack prior to joining an expedition, giving detailed information about the project, logistics, and general information about the area. All volunteers also receive training at the expedition site before they begin assisting the scientists.

COST: From £195 to £2,195, given as a charitable donation to support the research. Cost covers training in the field, food, accommodation, medical emergency evacuation, and the offsetting of greenhouse gases. Accommodation provided, from study centres at the Arctic's edge to tents in the rainforest or wildlife lodges in Kenya. Fee does not include travel to the rendezvous site.

The Trust promotes creative change in Russia through youth, ecology, and education, working closely with the Kitezh Community of foster families.

PROGRAMME DESCRIPTION: Volunteer programme ideal for those on gap years at the Kitezh Children's Community for orphans in Kaluga region, western Russia, where they live with families, interact with children, and take part in community life. Russian language is not essential, although students of Russian will quickly become fluent. Intensive Russian language courses are offered in spring and summer.

DESTINATIONS: Kaluga, Russia.

NUMBER OF PLACEMENTS PER YEAR: 16.

PREREQUISITES: Minimum age 18; most are 18–35. Reasonable knowledge of Russian language, TEFL, or experience teaching English as a foreign language, experience working with children (sports, arts and crafts, music, drama), building, cooking, and gardening. An interest in children and a willingness to participate fully in the life of the community are essential.

DURATION AND TIME OF PLACEMENTS: 1–3 months; additional months are at the discretion of the Kitezh Council.

SELECTION PROCEDURES AND ORIENTATION: Introductory questionnaire followed by telephone interview required. Police check in country of residence required. Extensive preparatory materials are sent, including feedback from previous volunteers. Informal orientation given on arrival, weekly meeting with volunteer supervisor, and ongoing support from Ecologia Youth Trust via email.

COST: 1 month costs £1,105, 2 months £1,320, 3 months £1,450. Costs include visa support, visa registration, transfer Moscow to Kitezh return, and accommodation and food in Kitezh. Insurance, consular fee, and airfare are not included; flight costs from £220 from London. Cost of extended stay £130 per month.

CONTACT: Liza Hollingshead, Director.

Ecoteer is a non-profit organisation.

PROGRAMME DESCRIPTION: Ecoteer is a collection of around 150 projects worldwide that need volunteers and are willing to provide food and accommodation at no, or at little, cost. Volunteer openings are at eco-lodges, conservation projects, farms, teaching, and humanitarian projects. Ecoteer provides contact information to members so they can organise their placement directly with the projects.

DESTINATIONS: Worldwide.

NUMBER OF PLACEMENTS: 180.

PREREQUISITES: Varies between projects. Most of the projects are remote, so require volunteers to be tolerant with a willingness to participate.

DURATION AND TIME OF PLACEMENTS: Minimum 1 month; no maximum.

COST: Membership is £15 per year, £25 for a lifetime membership. Membership gives access to contact details for NGOs etc registered with Ecoteer, access to Ecoteer forums, and the chance to advertise yourself as a volunteer.

CONTACT: Daniel Quilter, Owner.

EDGE OF AFRICA
Suite 88, Private Bag X31, Knysna 6570, South Africa
☎ +27 72853 2753
✆ info@edgeofafrica.com
🖥 www.edgeofafrica.com

Winner of the 2010 Welcome Awards for best South African tour operator.

PROGRAMME DESCRIPTION: Volunteer experiences along the Garden Route. Wide range of wildlife, environmental, sports, medical, and community projects. One project, Everything Elephant, involves volunteers in recording elephants' behaviour, cleaning their enclosures, and taking a trip to Addo National Park famed for its elephant population.

DESTINATIONS: South Africa.

NUMBER OF PLACEMENTS PER YEAR: 200.

DURATION AND TIME OF PLACEMENTS: 2–8 weeks.

PREREQUISITES: All ages and nationalities.

COST: 3,500 rand to 1,750 rand per 4 weeks, depending on the project. Dorm-style accommodation in a comfortable house. Edge of Africa is privately run and funded solely by volunteers' contributions.

CONTACT: Dayne Davey, Managing Director.

EDUCATORS ABROAD LTD
15 Palmer Close, Redhill, Surrey RH1 4BU
☎ (0)1737 768 254
✆ craig@educatorsabroad.org
🖥 www.educatorsabroad.org

Company that manages and operates the English as a Foreign Language teaching assistant programme for students and adults from the UK and other countries.

PROGRAMME DESCRIPTION: Volunteer participants assist teachers and students in ESL and EFL classes by bringing their native fluency in English to schools around the world.

DESTINATIONS: Over 25 countries on all continents.

DURATION AND TIME OF PLACEMENTS: 4 or 10 weeks throughout the year.

COST: $500 placement fee plus $2,300-$4,200, depending on programme option, plus travel, and in some cases room and board. Host schools assist with arrangements for accommodation and board.

CONTACT: Dr Craig Kissock, Director.

THE ELEPHANT MAHOUT PROJECT
88/10 Mubaan Kunsook 1,Bangsaray, Sattahip, 20180 Thailand
☎ +66 89 060 4075
☎ (0)1484 854 990 (UK)
✆ info@theelephantmahoutproject.com
🖥 www.theelephantmahoutproject.com

Organisation that works with tourist camps.

PROGRAMME DESCRIPTION: Placement of paying volunteers to work with and care for elephants as an alternative to tourist rides, which harm the animals' backs. Volunteers walk the elephants into the forest to graze, wash the elephants, keep their enclosures clean, etc.

DESTINATIONS: Tourist camps are mostly located in the Sattahip district, south of Bangkok.

DURATION AND TIME OF PLACEMENTS: Minimum 2 weeks, average 2–4 weeks.

PREREQUISITES: All ages; roughly a third of visitors are on gap years. Should have a love of animals and the environment, an interest in other cultures, a willingness to 'muck in', and a sense of adventure.

SELECTION PROCEDURES AND ORIENTATION: Last-minute applications may be possible, but one week's notice is preferred.

COST: £450 per week, including accommodation, most meals (except weekends), insurance and transport, plus project fees to camp and mahout (elephant handler). Volunteers stay in shared, western-style houses approximately 5 minutes from the camp with internet access.

CONTACT: Sam Clarke, Founder.

EUROPEAN VOLUNTARY SERVICE (EVS)
Youth in Action, British Council
🖥 www.britishcouncil.org/youthinaction

PROGRAMME DESCRIPTION: EVS gives young people aged 18–30 the opportunity to spend time in a European country (including Eastern Europe) as full-time volunteers on a social project, eg working with children with special needs. Volunteers do not have to pay for their placement. Further details in the 'Directory of Specialist Gap Year Programmes'.

EXPERIENCE MEXECO LTD
UK office: 38 Award Road, Fleet, Hampshire, GU52 6HG
☎ (0)1252 629 411
Mexico office: #59 Valentin Gómez Farías, San Patricio Melaque, Jalisco
☎ +52 1 315 355 7027
✆ info@experiencemexeco.com
🖥 www.experiencemexeco.com
🖥 www.mex-ecotours.com

PROGRAMME DESCRIPTION: Sea turtle conservation, English teaching projects, community fundraising for special needs schools, physiotherapy placements, and other community-based projects.

DESTINATIONS: Pacific coast of Mexico.

NUMBER OF PLACEMENTS PER YEAR: 30–35.

PREREQUISITES: All nationalities and ages; average age 19–26. All backgrounds welcomed, as any necessary training is provided. Spanish is not a necessity as local staff speak English and Spanish.

DURATION AND TIME OF PLACEMENTS: 1–3 months.

SELECTION PROCEDURES AND ORIENTATION: Applications should be received no less than 1 month before desired start date, though earlier preferred. Interview not required.

COST: £799–£899 for 1 month, £1,899–£1,999 for 3 months; covers accommodation (homestay, private, or small tents, on turtle project) and food throughout placement, plus insurance and 24-hour in-country support, but excluding flights.

CONTACT: Daniel Patman, Director.

FUNDACION JATUN SACHA
Eugenio de Santillán N34 248 y Maurián, Casilla 17 12 867, Quito, Ecuador
☎ +593 2 432 240
☎ +593 2 432 246
✆ volunteer@jatunsacha.org
🖥 www.jatunsacha.org

Jatun Sacha Biological Station is a 2,200-hectare tropical rainforest reserve. All reserves protect endangered ecosystems critical to Ecuador, and are located in all four regions of the country.

PROGRAMME DESCRIPTION: Volunteers and interns participate in research, education, community service, station maintenance, plant conservation, and agroforestry.

DESTINATIONS: Amazonian Ecuador and the Galágapos.

NUMBER OF PLACEMENTS PER YEAR: 800 on different projects.

PREREQUISITES: Minimum age 16 (with parental permission), average age 23.

DURATION AND TIME OF PLACEMENTS: Minimum 15 days at any reserve, though the majority stay for 1 month, and some stay 3, 6, or 12 months.

COST: $47 or $67 application fee, plus reserve fees (including lodging and meals) of $475 for the first month $380 afterwards; some reserves are more expensive.

CONTACT: Santiago Paz y Miño, Volunteer Programme Co-ordinator.

GLOBALTEER
Globalteer House, TheaChamrat Road, Wat Bo Village, Salakamroeuk Commune, Siem Reap, Cambodia
☎ +855 6376 1802
✆ info@globalteer.org
🖥 www.globalteer.org

PROGRAMME DESCRIPTION: Globalteer provides financial support and volunteers, to teach and assist in the daily running of its partner in-country projects in 5 countries. In Cambodia, volunteers work with 4 projects in Siem Reap to assist over 800 underprivileged Khmer children and build water filters for rural communities. In Mondulkiri, Cambodia, the projects assist the indigenous Bunong hill tribe people and elephants, and conserve the forest. There are also projects to help orphaned and street children in Peru and Colombia, and projects working with wildlife in Thailand and Indonesia.

DESTINATIONS: Cambodia, Thailand, Indonesia, Peru, and Colombia.

PREREQUISITES: Minimum age 18. Should be fit and healthy, and be able to speak English.

DURATION AND TIME OF PLACEMENTS: 1 week to 3 months.

SELECTION PROCEDURES AND ORIENTATION: Applications should be sent at least 2 months in advance. Late applications accepted where there is availability. Each project has a volunteer co-ordinator to liaise with local staff.

COST: Each project asks for a donation for the volunteer placement depending on duration, which helps to fund the project. Donations (as listed on website) cover accommodation, airport pick-up, in-country support, administration costs, and a direct donation to the project.

CONTACT: Each of the 9 projects across 5 countries has a separate email contact, available from info@globalteer.org.

GLOBAL VOLUNTEER NETWORK
PO Box 30–968, Lower Hutt 5040, New Zealand
☎ +64 4 569 9080
✆ info@volunteer.org.nz
💻 www.globalvolunteernetwork.org

PROGRAMME DESCRIPTION: Volunteers recruited for a variety of educational, community aid, health/medical, environmental/conservation, construction, wildlife programmes, and cultural homestays in 22 countries. Fundraising treks are also offered to Everest Base Camp, Mount Kilimanjaro, and Machu Picchu.

DESTINATIONS: Cambodia, China, Costa Rica, Ecuador, Ethiopia, Ghana, Guatemala, Honduras, India, Kenya, Nepal, New Zealand, Peru, Philippines, South Africa, Thailand, Uganda, Vietnam, and USA (South Dakota).

DURATION AND TIME OF PLACEMENTS: 2 weeks to 12 months, depending on the placement. Applications accepted year-round.

NUMBER OF PLACEMENTS PER YEAR: Around 2,000.

PREREQUISITES: Minimum age 18, average age 19–23. No special skills or qualifications needed in most cases. All nationalities placed, although projects in China accept only Australians, Canadians, Europeans (including Irish and British), Americans, and New Zealanders.

COST: US$350 application fee to GVN covers personal staff support, programme guide, fundraising guide and software, access to online journal, and online video 'Preparing for your trip'. Programme fees start at US$597 per month in China. Fees cover training, accommodation, and meals during training and placement, supervision, and project transport (but not international airfares).

CONTACT: Colin Salisbury, Founder and President

GLOBAL XCHANGE PROGRAMME
27a Carlton Drive, London SW15 2BS
☎ (0)20 8780 7500
✆ enquiry@globalxchange.org.uk
💻 www.globalxchange.org.uk

VSO's Global Xchange (GX) programme gives young volunteers the opportunity to gain volunteering experience and develop skills in an international setting.

PROGRAMME DESCRIPTION: VSO's development projects involve working on a range of issues including HIV and AIDS awareness, education, youth leadership, active citizenship, and climate change. Work will involve activities such as educating other young people on health issues, helping conduct community research projects, or supporting local campaigns for change.

DESTINATIONS: Dozens of countries, from Nigeria to Pakistan.

DURATION AND TIME OF PLACEMENTS: Choice of spending 3 months on the Youth Action programme working in a group with local youth volunteers on community action projects, or 6 months on Youth Xchange, an exchange programme with 3 months each in the UK and abroad. A series of Youth Actions will be departing in January and April 2012 (application deadlines 1 November 2011 and 1 February 2012 respectively).

PREREQUISITES: Participants must be aged between 18 and 22 on 30 June and they must be either a UK citizen with a current UK address, an EEA citizen currently residing in the UK, or have indefinite leave to remain in the UK. They must be committed to volunteering, and demonstrate that they have the right skills to contribute to a team working overseas. They should also be interested in longer-term involvement in development work, either in the UK or overseas.

SELECTION PROCEDURES AND ORIENTATION: Applicants take part in a competitive assessment process. Selected volunteers are matched to placements developed by VSO programme offices in 14 different countries. All volunteers complete pre-departure training to help them explore their motivation to volunteer, increase their understanding of cross-cultural issues, and help develop their existing skills for working in a development context.

COST: All volunteers are expected to fundraise, but targets are dependent on annual household income: none if income is less than £25,000; £1,000 if income is £25,000-£40,000; and £2,000 if income is more than £40,000.

GO DIFFERENTLY
Flat 1, The White House, 24 Third Avenue, Hove BN3 2PD
☎ (0)1273 451 372
✆ info@godifferently.com
💻 www.godifferently.com

PROGRAMME DESCRIPTION: Several volunteering programmes throughout Thailand, including working with elephants, langurs (monkeys), teaching English, and providing assistance with various local village projects (eg tsunami recovery, supporting local craft workshops, etc). Participants at the elephant project learn to ride and care for elephants and about the traditional life of the mahouts. Educational projects involve teaching English to village children while living with a family and helping with household and farm duties. Also 'voluntourism' tours lasting 2 weeks, which combine short-term volunteering with some adventure and exploration.

NUMBER OF PLACEMENTS PER YEAR: 200–300.

DESTINATIONS: Elephant Project is in Pattaya (southern Thailand), while teaching takes place among Karen tribal people in Um-Phang (in mountainous Tak province), or in Andaman villages in southern Thailand.

PREREQUISITES: Volunteers should be willing to respect Thai culture (guidance will be given), be open-minded, and have a sociable attitude towards the local people. All ages are welcome.

DURATION AND TIME OF PLACEMENTS: 1–4 weeks (elephants/langurs), 1 week to 6+ months (teaching), 2 weeks voluntourism tours.

SELECTION PROCEDURES AND ORIENTATION: Visits can normally be arranged at short notice.

COST: Average cost for 2 weeks including accommodation and meals but excluding flights is £840 per person, which includes homestay accommodation. Part of fees supports sustainable tourism in the villages.

CONTACT: Nikki Bond, Director.

GREENPEACE
Canonbury Villas, London N1 2PN
☎ (0)20 7865 8100
🖰 info.uk@greenpeace.org
💻 www.greenpeace.org.uk/what-you-can-do/jobs-and-volunteering
💻 www.greenpeace.org/international/about/worldwide (worldwide address list)

Greenpeace has offices around the world and volunteer participation is sometimes welcomed locally. Greenpeace UK regrets that it is unable to offer work experience, nor does it offer sponsorship, but interns and voluntary input are occasionally needed at London office, and Greenpeace has groups of volunteers around the UK.

HANDS FOR HELP NEPAL
Baluwatar Kusum Galli, Kathmandu, Nepal
☎ +977 98510 517 36 (mobile)
☎ +977 1444 0652
🖰 hforh@wlink.com.np
💻 www.handsforhelp.org.np

PROGRAMME DESCRIPTION: Teaching in schools, orphanage assistance, environmental and conservation work, health and first aid, community building, and various internship programmes.

NUMBER OF PLACEMENTS PER YEAR: 300.

PREREQUISITES: All nationalities welcome. Most volunteers are aged 19–28. Applicants must have at least high school education and ability to communicate in English.

DURATION AND TIME OF PLACEMENTS: 1 week to 5 months, though average is 2 months. Applications should be sent at least a month in advance for start dates throughout the year.

SELECTION PROCEDURES AND ORIENTATION: Orientation provided, plus training lasting from 1 to 7 days on cultural adjustment, personal safety, health, Nepali language, project description, and travel information.

COST: €400 for first month; €180 for subsequent months, including host family accommodation.

ICYE-UK: INTER-CULTURAL YOUTH EXCHANGE UK
Latin American House, Kingsgate Place,
London NW6 4TA
☎ (0)20 7681 0983
🖰 info@icye.org.uk
💻 www.icye.org.uk

ICYE is a registered charity and user-led organisation facilitating cultural exchanges throughout the world. ICYE-UK is a member of the international ICYE Federation, with over 60 years of volunteering experience.

PROGRAMME DESCRIPTION: ICYE's core programme is a reciprocal 6–12-month exchange programme. Recently it has introduced a short-term programme (STePs) to give applicants more flexibility. All ICYE programmes place an emphasis on intercultural understanding and integration into local communities, and the vast majority of ICYE volunteers live with host families. Many ICYE projects are social and community-based, such as working with street children, HIV/AIDS education, working in disability support, or volunteering as a teaching assistant. Eco-projects such as conservation work and caring for animals are also available in some partner countries.

DESTINATIONS: Throughout Africa, Asia, Latin America, and Eastern Europe (see website).

NUMBER OF PLACEMENTS PER YEAR: 80 volunteers sent overseas; UK hosts about 45 international volunteers.

PREREQUISITES: No formal qualification or previous experience is necessary, but applicants must be open-minded and committed to intercultural learning and volunteering. ICYE's long-term programme is open to

18–30-year-olds. The STeP is open to volunteers of any age over 18.

DURATION AND TIME OF PLACEMENTS: The long-term programme begins in August and January and lasts 6 or 12 months. The STeP offers year-round departures (starting the first Monday of every month), and placements last 3–16 weeks.

COST: ICYE's programme fee includes return flights, insurance, visa support, accommodation, daily meals, pocket money (long-term only), pre-departure and on-arrival training, language course (long-term only), full international administration, and ongoing support. The 12-month programme fee is £4,495, and 6 months is £3,795. The STeP starts from £1,600 for four weeks, and varies according to country and length of stay. ICYE offers full fundraising support. Volunteers also have the opportunity to apply for bursaries of £750–£1,500.

CONTACT: Jenny Williams, Long-term Co-ordinator; Sarahgwen Sheldon, Short-term Co-ordinator for Latin America, Asia, and Europe; Charlotte Dando, Short-term Co-ordinator for Africa.

INSPIRE VOLUNTEERING
Futuresense Ltd, Town Hall, Market Place, Newbury RG14 5AA
☎ (0)800 323 350
✆ info@inspirevolunteer.co.uk
🖥 www.inspirevolunteer.co.uk

Inspire provides ethical and sustainable volunteer opportunities overseas. Volunteers' skills and aspirations are matched to projects in genuine need, ensuring that volunteers maximise their impact and experience.

PROGRAMME DESCRIPTION: Inspire volunteer programmes support underprivileged communities by deploying volunteer resources where the need is greatest. Volunteers are profiled and matched to specific projects, where they support teaching, childcare, healthcare, livelihood support, community work, and conservation. Volunteers work closely with local communities, NGOs, and charities to achieve the long-term development goals of UK registered charity, the FutureSense Foundation.

DESTINATIONS: India, Tanzania, Nepal, Sri Lanka, Romania, South Africa, Ecuador, Chile, the Gambia.

NUMBER OF PLACEMENTS PER YEAR: Around 200.

PREREQUISITES: Volunteers must be aged 18 or over. All nationalities accepted. Business experience necessary for business development programmes. Relevant experience useful for other programmes, but not essential. Volunteers must have enthusiasm, flexibility, and good communication skills.

DURATION AND TIME OF PLACEMENTS: Programmes last from 2 weeks to 6 months with flexible start dates year-round.

SELECTION PROCEDURES AND ORIENTATION: Application can be made online or by phone, with acceptance subject to an informal interview and receipt of references. Volunteers are provided with pre-departure briefing and given local orientation by our in-country teams on arrival.

OTHER SERVICES: Inspire offers specialised travel programmes in India, Nepal, and Tanzania. Trips include treks, safaris, and cultural tours, and are fully guided.

COST: Costs vary depending on location, but start from £795 for a 1-month placement. All accommodation and some meals are included.

CONTACT: Katie Guy, Volunteer Co-ordinator.

INTERNATIONAL SOCIETY FOR ECOLOGY AND CULTURE
PO Box 9475, Berkeley, CA 94709, USA
☎ +1 510 548 4915
✆ infoUSA@isec.org.uk
🖥 www.localfutures.org/ladakh-project/
learning-from-ladakh/learning-from-ladakh

PROGRAMME DESCRIPTION: 'Learning from Ladakh' is an experiential education programme that provides the opportunity to understand the pressures being exerted on rural communities worldwide, and to learn about innovative strategies to strengthen traditional cultures and local economies. Participants live with a Ladakhi farming family, help with farm and household work, and participate in educational workshops.

DESTINATIONS: Ladakh, India.

PREREQUISITES: Should be in good health, to withstand the risks of living and working at high altitude. All nationalities accepted.

DURATION AND TIME OF PLACEMENTS: 1 month – July or August.

SELECTION PROCEDURES AND ORIENTATION: Applications accepted on a rolling basis.

COST: £430 ($700) for 1 month.

CONTACT: Victoria Clarke, LFL Programme Administrator.

INVOLVEMENT VOLUNTEERS ASSOCIATION INC (IVI)
PO Box 334, Diamond Creek, Victoria 3089, Australia
☎ +61 3 9438 6007
✆ ivworldwide@volunteering.org.au
🖥 www.volunteering.org.au

Involvement Volunteers was established in 1988, with the original aim of making volunteering available to young people wanting to assist and learn from volunteer experiences.

PROGRAMME DESCRIPTION: IVI arranges individual volunteer placements worldwide lasting at least 2 weeks (up to 52). Projects are concerned with conservation, the environment, animal welfare, social and community service, medicine, education, and childcare.

DESTINATIONS: Dozens of countries worldwide.

PREREQUISITES: Minimum age 18, although minimum age rises to 21 for some projects.

DURATION AND TIME OF PLACEMENTS: 2–6 weeks, with chance to arrange series of back-to-back placements. A series of one or more projects can be arranged lasting up to 1 year for a multicultural round-the-world experience.

COST: The one-placement package cost is A$1,200; two-placement package is A$2,070 and so on.

KIBBUTZ PROGRAM CENTER
Volunteer Department, 6 Frishman Street, Corner of Hayarkon Street, Tel Aviv 61030, Israel
☎ +972 3 524 6154/6
🖐 kpc@volunteer.co.il
💻 www.kibbutz.org.il/volunteers

The office is open Sunday to Thursday 8.30am–2.30pm. The buses needed to reach the office are: number 475 from the airport, 10 from the railway station, and 4 from the Central Bus Station.

PROGRAMME DESCRIPTION: Placements on 27 kibbutzim throughout Israel.

DESTINATIONS: Throughout Israel. Most kibbutzim are situated in the fertile lands of northern and southern Israel. The north can be cold and rainy in winter, whereas the Jordan Rift Valley can be one of the hottest and driest places in the world.

PREREQUISITES: Age range accepted is 18–35. Must be free to stay for a minimum of 10 weeks.

DURATION AND TIME OF PLACEMENTS: 2¹/₂–6 months.

SELECTION PROCEDURES AND ORIENTATION: For visa reasons, volunteers cannot be assigned to a kibbutz after arrival in Israel. They must register in advance through the website and then arrive at the KPC office with a passport, photocopy of passport, medical certificate, airline ticket out of Israel, and fees.

COST: $260 to cover registration fee, visa fee, and health insurance fee, payable to the KPC.

KIYA SURVIVORS
41–43 Portland Road, Hove, East Sussex BN3 2DQ
☎ (0)1273 721 092
🖐 volunteer@kiyasurvivors.org
💻 www.kiyasurvivors.org

PROGRAMME DESCRIPTION: Volunteers at the Kiya centre in Peru help to provide love, support, education, and therapy to children and young people who have special needs or have been abused or abandoned. Volunteers work as teaching assistants and in workshops on art, drama, and cooking, or get involved with sporting and theatre events. Opportunities to shadow a trained physiotherapist, social worker, or psychologist.

NUMBER OF PLACEMENTS PER YEAR: Up to 12 at any one time.

DESTINATIONS: The Rainbow Centre educational day centre and Rainbow House children's home in Urubamba, near Cusco, Peru.

PREREQUISITES: The only prerequisite is that you are enthusiastic, caring, and passionate. No experience is needed as volunteer's skills and interests are matched to the needs of the centre. Knowledge of basic Spanish is encouraged.

DURATION AND TIME OF PLACEMENTS: 1- to 6-month placements. Longer placements may be possible on request and start dates are available throughout the year.

SELECTION PROCEDURES AND ORIENTATION: Selection is based on completion of an application and criminal records check. Optional 2-day training is available in the UK before departure, including one day working at a special needs school. Full orientation given, on arrival in Peru, of Urubamba, the centre and its work. Spanish classes are also available.

COST: £817–£3,374, depending on programme and length of stay.

CONTACT: Mipsie Marshall, Volunteer Programme Co-ordinator (mipsie@kiyasurvivors.org).

LANGUAGECORPS
53 Whispering Way, Stow, MA 011775, USA
☎ +1 978 562 2100
🖐 info@languagecorps.com
🖐 jan.patton@languagecorps.com
💻 www.languagecorps.com
💻 www.languagecorps.org

PROGRAMME DESCRIPTION: English teaching programmes in various countries, all of which include an intensive 4-week TESOL training and certification course, pre-departure support, and assistance finding a paid teaching position.

NUMBER OF PLACEMENTS PER YEAR: 500–600.
DESTINATIONS: Latin America, Asia, and Europe.
PREREQUISITES: Minimum age 19, average age 25. Some countries require a college degree in addition to the TESOL certification. If someone between school and university demonstrates a solid level of maturity and independence, they may qualify. Applicants must be native English speakers, or have native-level English speaking skills.
DURATION AND TIME OF PLACEMENTS: 6–12 months for most paid positions. Short-term volunteer programmes available in Thailand, Vietnam, and Cambodia.
SELECTION PROCEDURES AND ORIENTATION: Applications welcomed 2–6 months in advance. A phone interview is required for some programmes. Some include local language and cultural training, medical insurance, accommodation, excursions, and other support services.
COST: $1,695–$3,495.
CONTACT: Jan Patton, Programmes Director.

MONA FOUNDATION GIRONA
Carretera de Cassà, s/n - 17457 Girona, Spain
☎ +34 972 477 618
✆ info@fundacionmona.org
🖥 www.fundacionmona.org

PROGRAMME DESCRIPTION: Volunteers help with the daily care of the primates living in the centre (chimpanzee and Barbary macaque). Tasks include food preparation, cleaning facilities, feeding, enrichment preparation, and helping with rehabilitation. Other activities may include behavioural observation, or building facilities for the animals, such as platforms, towers, and hammocks.
NUMBER OF PLACEMENTS PER YEAR: 8 long-term volunteers per year.
DURATION AND TIME OF PLACEMENTS: 6 months.
PREREQUISITES: Minimum age for long-term volunteers is 21 years; minimum for students is 18 years. Most student volunteers are studying primatology, biology, veterinary medicine, psychology, anthropology, or related subjects. All nationalities who are eligible for a visa and who have a good knowledge of Spanish and/or English. Volunteers should be motivated, interested in animal protection issues, cheerfully willing to work 5 days a week (which may include weekends), and be prepared to do tasks that may be monotonous but contribute to rewarding work with primates.
SELECTION PROCEDURES AND ORIENTATION: Applications are accepted at any time throughout the year.

Two selection processes take place annually. Training provided at the centre. Volunteers are not ready to work independently until at least 2 months after arrival.
COST: None, but no food or accommodation is provided.
CONTACT: Olga Feliu, Director (o.feliu@fundacionmona.org).

ORIGINAL VOLUNTEERS
Riverside House, 5 Lovelstaithe, Norwich NR1 1LW
☎ (0)800 345 7582
☎ (0)1603 627 007
✆ contact@originalvolunteers.info
🖥 www.originalvolunteers.co.uk

PROGRAMME DESCRIPTION: Social care and conservation placements throughout the world.
DESTINATIONS: Mexico, Guatemala, Costa Rica, Honduras, Ecuador, Peru, Argentina, Brazil, Paraguay, Ghana, Kenya, South Africa, Tanzania, India, Nepal, Thailand.
NUMBER OF PLACEMENTS PER YEAR: 3,000.
DURATION AND TIME OF PLACEMENTS: 14 weeks, with possibility of combining 2 or more placements.
PREREQUISITES: All ages and backgrounds accepted.
SELECTION PROCEDURES AND ORIENTATION: Informal training given on arrival by local staff or long stay volunteers.
COST: One-off registration fee of £125, plus £20–£60 per week to cover room and board on-site. Accommodation is usually self-catering in shared houses or apartments with other volunteers, 2/3 volunteers to a room. Sample prices: from £47 for 4 weeks in Latin America, to £100 one-off payment in Thailand, and free accommodation provided in Paraguay and at rural school in Tanzania.

OTRA COSA NETWORK
Las Camelias 431, Huanchaco Trujillo, Peru
☎ +51 44 461302
✆ otracosanetwork@gmail.com
🖥 www.otracosa.org

PROGRAMME DESCRIPTION: Projects include teaching English to locals who cannot afford to learn otherwise, working with children at a day care centre, helping out at an organic coffee and sugar farm, supporting animal refuges, and many others.
NUMBER OF VOLUNTEERS PER YEAR: 25.
DESTINATIONS: Most projects are in and around Huanchaco and Trujillo, but also some opportunities in northern Peru and near mountains.
PREREQUISITES: Knowledge of Spanish not essential; cheap lessons can be arranged.

267

COST: €85 (400 soles) for administration fee that covers a stay of up to 3 months.

CONTACT: Najin Kim and Diego Velasquez, Local Team.

PAN AFRICAN CLIMATE EDUCATION (PACE)
Ghana office PO Box CT, 5671 Cantonments, Accra, Ghana
☎ +24 329 0039
✎ pacecentreafrica@gmail.com
Cameroon office: ICEYOM (International Centre for Education Youth Orientation and Mobilisation), c/o Cameroon Vision Trust, PO Box 1075, Limbe, South West Province, Republic of Cameroon
☎ +237 7419 0403
☎ +237 9958 0292
✎ sweetafrica09@gmail.com
🖥 www.worldpulse.com

Several charities under single leadership, including one in Monrovia, Liberia, the Society for Women Empowerment Education and Training (SWEET) (+231 624 2236).

PROGRAMME DESCRIPTION: Placements for all kinds of voluntary service including hospitality, conservation, climate change, sports, community service, and fundraising.

NUMBER OF VOLUNTEERS PER YEAR: 100.

DESTINATIONS: Liberia, Cameroon, Ghana, Nigeria, Malawi, Tanzania, Kenya, Uganda, Republic of Congo, Equatorial Guinea, Rwanda, etc.

PREREQUISITES: Minimum GCSEs or high school graduation. Gap year students welcome.

DURATION AND TIME OF PLACEMENTS: Minimum 6 months, maximum 2 years, with option to extend.

SELECTION PROCEDURES AND ORIENTATION: Applications accepted year-round.

COST: £350 ($500/€400). Projects usually provide accommodation, holiday schemes, in-country transport and some allowance depending on placement.

CONTACT: Rosemary Olive Mbone Enie, International Co-ordinator.

PASSAGE INTERNATIONAL
Study Abroad , Experiential Education Program In South Asia, GPO 8974, CPC 373, Kathmandu, Nepal
☎ +977 1 437 1414
☎ +977 1 465 0723
✎ info@passageinternational.com
🖥 www.passageinternational.com

PROGRAMME DESCRIPTION: Passage International creates opportunities for students to live and learn abroad, as part of an international exchange to foster global awareness. Cultural immersion through home-stays, internships, seminars, excursions, and language study.

DESTINATIONS: Nepal and some parts of India.

DURATION AND TIME OF PLACEMENTS: Programmes run year-round: 12-week spring and autumn semesters, and 6-week summer sessions. 12-week semester stays from late February or mid-September. Personal passages can be arranged year-round, lasting 6–20 weeks in Nepal, and 6–24 weeks in India.

PREREQUISITES: Ages 18+. No qualifications needed, but participants should be sensitive to others' beliefs and cultures.

SELECTION PROCEDURES AND ORIENTATION: Application and medical forms to be sent by email. Deposit of $500 and signed waiver form to be sent after selection process. Application deadlines normally two months before programme begins.

CONTACT: Tsering Choden, Marketing and Administrative Director.

PERU'S CHALLENGE
Urb. Ingenieros D-2-12 Los Saucos, Larapa, San Jeronimo, Cusco, Peru
☎ +51 84 272 508
✎ volunteer@peruschallenge.com
🖥 www.peruschallenge.com

Peru's Challenge was awarded a highly commended for Best Volunteering Organisation at the international Virgin Holidays Responsible Tourism Awards in 2009, and shortlisted in 2010.

PROGRAMME DESCRIPTION: Peru's Challenge programme combines tours with volunteering to give people the opportunity to travel and see the best of Peru while also doing something positive for local communities. Volunteering projects in the fields of creating sustainable schools, education, construction, health, nutrition, and welfare. Tour of Peru includes some or all of the following (depending on length of programme): return flight Lima-Cusco, shared accommodation in Volunteer House, Spanish language lessons, choice of 4-day Inca Trail trek or 2-day train trip to Machu Picchu, horse riding, 3-day tour to Lake Titicaca, and 3-day tour to Arequipa and Colca Canyon.

DESTINATIONS: Based in Cusco, but programme travels all around Peru.

DURATION AND TIME OF PLACEMENTS: 3, 6, 8, weeks or longer.

PREREQUISITES: All skills and experience can be put to good use for teaching English, art, sport, music, dance, or computers, painting and renovating, etc. All nationalities welcome.

SELECTION PROCEDURES AND ORIENTATION: Placements tend to be booked up 3–6 months in advance. On-site volunteer manager carries out a phone interview with applicants to discuss expectations, etc.

COST: Tour and volunteer prices are quoted separately: tour costs from $1,950 for 3 weeks to $2,700 for 6 weeks. Volunteer component costs from $450 for 3 or 4 weeks to $800 for 6 weeks.

CONTACT: Jane Gavel, President and Founder.

QUETZALTREKKERS
Casa Argentina, 12 Diagonal, 8–37, Zona 1,
Quetzaltenango, Guatemala
☎ +502 7765 5895
info@quetzaltrekkers.com or
quetzaltrekkers@gmail.com
💻 www.quetzaltrekkers.com

Non-profit trekking company that relies on volunteer guides and uses trekkers' fees to assist free school and activity programme for local street children.

PROGRAMME DESCRIPTION: Volunteer guides recruit customers for treks, prepare food and equipment, maintain and clean equipment, and guide treks. Volunteers also needed for street school and dormitory in Las Rosas.

DESTINATIONS: Quetzaltenango and environs in Guatemala, plus programme in Nicaragua.

NUMBER OF PLACEMENTS: 60.

PREREQUISITES: Must know intermediate Spanish. Training given in any skills that are lacking.

DURATION AND TIME OF PLACEMENTS: Volunteer guides work at least 3 months. Volunteers working with children stay at least 3 months.

COST: Guides receive all expenses and food on treks, and discount on room in Casa Argentina. Rent charged to volunteers is 100 quetzals (less than $14) per month, and food will be on top of that, although shared meals are often covered by tips from generous clients.

SKIP (SUPPORTING KIDS IN PERU)
volunteering@skipperu.org
💻 www.skipperu.org

PROGRAMME DESCRIPTION: Non-profit organisation providing holistic support to economically disadvantaged children in the district of El Porvenir, located on the north coast of Peru. SKIP works to strengthen and empower families so they can enable children to realise their right to an education. Projects include teaching in both English and Spanish, youth work, social work, psychology, including group and individual work with children, young people, and parents.

DESTINATIONS: El Porvenir, Trujillo, Peru

PREREQUISITES: Minimum age 18. SKIP can provide training suitable for volunteers who want to learn about working in an NGO. Volunteers must be comfortable working with and around children.

DURATION AND TIME OF PLACEMENTS: Minimum 1 month.

SELECTION PROCEDURES AND ORIENTATION: Rolling applications accepted year-round. Specific vacancies are advertised on idealist.org. Telephone interviews held in some cases.

COST: $350 per month for the first two months, $250 for 3–5 months, $180 for 6–8 months and $125 for 9–12 months. Accommodation in the volunteer house (for up to 22 volunteers) or with a host family is included, but not food and travel.

CONTACT: Liz Wilson, Director.

SOFT POWER EDUCATION
PO Box 1493, Jinja, Uganda, East Africa
☎ +256 774 162 541
info@softpowereducation.com
💻 www.softpowereducation.com

British registered non-religious charity to enhance the education facilities for hundreds of Ugandan children.

PROGRAMME DESCRIPTION: Volunteers needed for a range of projects in the Jinja area: 2 pre-schools for orphans and vulnerable children, a school refurbishment programme, to assist with hands-on learning experiences at the Amagezi Education Centre used by upper primary pupils from 26 partner schools, a special needs project, and the Murchison Project, which brings conservation education to the communities surrounding the National Park. Particular areas of interest among grown-up volunteers are for TEFL teachers and those with experience in working with children with special educational needs.

NUMBER OF PLACEMENTS PER YEAR: About 100 independent volunteers and 150+ in student groups.

PREREQUISITES: Minimum age 18, no maximum. Summer groups are mainly university students. No qualifications needed. All nationalities accepted. Soft Power is looking for highly independent and motivated individuals who want a grassroots volunteering experience where they can be involved in a wide range of activities.

DURATION AND TIME OF PLACEMENTS: 1 day to 12 months. Volunteers accepted year-round.

SELECTION PROCEDURES AND ORIENTATION: Arrival should be arranged at least a month in advance. Airport collection and accommodation are organised, but volunteer covers those costs. Volunteer co-ordinator meets volunteers soon after arrival and gives orientation on all projects.

COST: Volunteers must cover their own living and travel expenses as well as a donation to the charity (minimum £75 a week).

ACCOMMODATION: Everything from camping to living with local community family to staying in a 5-star lodge.

CONTACT: Sharon Webb, General Manager.

SUDAN VOLUNTEER PROGRAMME
34 Estelle Road, London NW3 2JY
☎ (0)20 7485 8619
✉ davidsvp@blueyonder.co.uk
🖥 www.svp-uk.com

PROGRAMME DESCRIPTION: SVP works with undergraduates and graduates who are native English speakers and wish to teach English in Sudan. Teaching tends to be informal in style, with only 4–5 hours of contact a day. Volunteers can plan their own teaching schemes, such as arranging games, drama, competitions, and tests for assessing skills learned by the students.

DESTINATIONS: Sudan, mostly in and around Khartoum area, and especially Omdurman.

PREREQUISITES: TEFL certificate, experience of travelling in developing countries, and some knowledge of Arabic are helpful but not obligatory. Volunteers must be in good health and native English speakers, and have experience of living away from home.

DURATION AND TIME OF PLACEMENTS: Preferred minimum 8 months from September or early January. Shorter summer placements are possible.

SELECTION PROCEDURES AND ORIENTATION: Applications accepted year-round. Two referees are required. Prior to departure, medical check-up required plus selection interviews, orientation, and briefings take place. Volunteers are required to write a report of their experiences and advise new volunteers.

COST: Volunteers must raise the cost of the airfare to Sudan (currently £485), plus £65 (cost of the first 3 months' insurance). Volunteers must be able to support themselves for the first 3–4 weeks in Khartoum while their permits are obtained prior to travelling, and the first month in their placement town as most universities pay the allowance in arrears. Accommodation is provided in flats shared with other volunteers.

CONTACT: David Wolton (at email above).

TEACHERS FOR VIETNAM
159 Piermont Avenue, Piermont NY 10968, USA
☎ +1 845 680 6560
✉ info@teachersforvietnam.org
🖥 www.teachersforvietnam.org

PROGRAMME DESCRIPTION: Recruits teachers of ESL for university posts in Vietnam, to further Vietnam's educational development by increasing fluency of spoken English, and to build bridges between people in Vietnam and the west, particularly the USA.

NUMBER OF PLACEMENTS PER YEAR: 5.

PREREQUISITES: Must be university graduate, so most volunteers are over 21. Some experience and/or training in TESL needed, plus eagerness to live and work in Vietnam.

DURATION AND TIME OF PLACEMENTS: Academic year, late August to May.

SELECTION PROCEDURES AND ORIENTATION: Deadline for applications is 1 April. Face-to-face interviews preferred but can be done by phone. In-country orientation session provided, which covers cultural issues as well as practical matters for foreigners newly arrived in Vietnam.

COST: Application fee $50. Programme pays for airfare, health insurance, and travel during Tet holiday. Host universities pay a cost-of-living salary and in most cases provide free housing, usually a room or suite in a campus guesthouse.

CONTACT: John Dippel, Executive Director.

THAI-EXPERIENCE.ORG
1133/4 Kaewworrawut Road, Moo 1, Meaung District, Nongkhai 43000, Thailand
☎ +66 8444 92022 (mobile)
🖥 www.thai-experience.org

PROGRAMME DESCRIPTION: Teaching English, computer skills, or vocational skills to disadvantaged children and/or adults in Thailand. Maintaining computers.

NUMBER OF PLACEMENTS PER YEAR: 80.

DESTINATIONS: Mainly north-eastern Thailand (Isan province).

PREREQUISITES: Minimum age 18. Good command of English language. Computer teachers need IT skills, open mind, and patience to deal with different environment. No TEFL certificate needed as volunteers do not replace teachers but assist them, encouraging students to use their English language skills to speak and practise, and motivate them to learn more.

DURATION AND TIME OF PLACEMENTS: 1 week to 1 year; typically 2–3 months.

SELECTION PROCEDURES AND ORIENTATION: Application can be made online. Volunteers can be placed at short notice, but 2–3 months' advance warning preferred.

COST: €350 for 1–2 weeks, €450 for 3 weeks, €500 for 1 month, €1,380 for 24 weeks. Fees include orientation, pre-arranged accommodation, travel within the project, cultural outings, and support, before and during the stay.

CONTACT: Sabine Lindemann, Project Manager.

TRAVELLERS WORLDWIDE
2A Caravelle House, 17/19 Goring Road,
Worthing, West Sussex BN12 4AP
☎ (0)1903 502 595
✆ info@travellersworldwide.com
🖥 www.travellersworldwide.com

Travellers is a Founder Member of the Year Out Group.
PROGRAMME DESCRIPTION: 250+ voluntary projects
in 20 countries, including care and community, teaching,
sports, internships (see entry in 'Directory of Work Experience Abroad'), conservation, marine, language courses,
cultural courses, and drama, dance, and music.
DESTINATIONS: Argentina, Australia, Brazil, Cambodia,
China, Ecuador, Ghana, Guatemala, India, Kenya,
Malaysia, Mauritius, Mozambique, New Zealand,
Peru, South Africa, Sri Lanka, Thailand, Zambia, and
Zimbabwe.
NUMBER OF PLACEMENTS PER YEAR: 1,000+.
PREREQUISITES: No qualifications or previous experience are necessary, just a good dose of enthusiasm. All
are welcome whether gap year, undergraduate or retired,
and all nationalities. Minimum age 17.
DURATION AND TIME OF PLACEMENTS: From 1 week
to 1 year, subject to visa requirements, with flexible start
and finish dates all year.
COST: Prices start from £695 and include food, accommodation, airport pick-up, induction, orientation, 24/7
support on the ground and at home, but don't include
international travel, visas, or insurance.
CONTACT: Jennifer Perkes, Managing Director.

TREK TO TEACH
Corvallis, Oregon, USA
☎ +1 619 405 8818
✆ Brad@trektoteach.org
🖥 www.trektoteach.org

PROGRAMME DESCRIPTION: Programme combines
teaching in Nepal with a family stay and trekking.
DESTINATIONS: Himalayan Nepal.
NUMBER OF PLACEMENTS PER YEAR: 3–7 (because
programme is new).
DURATION AND TIME OF PLACEMENTS: 1–8 months.
PREREQUISITES: Minimum age 22. Schools want
teachers who can teach English, maths, and computers,
while the Nepali students want teachers who can teach
them new hobbies and new ways of looking at the world.
Candidates should be academically able, with a degree
or heading towards one, and be passionate about life.
SELECTION PROCEDURES AND ORIENTATION: No
deadline. Applications must be in at least 1 month prior

to expected teaching date. Nepali school year is April–
December. Telephone interviews necessary.
COST: First month, $1,600; second and third months,
$600; fourth to eighth months, $500.
CONTACT: Brad Hurvitz, Founder (brad.hurvitz@gmail.
com).

LA UNION CENTRO LINGUISTICO
1A Avenida Sur No. 21, Antigua, Guatemala
☎ +502 7832 7337
✆ info@launion.edu.gt
🖥 www.launion.edu.gt

Organisation for sharing Spanish language and
Guatemalan culture, run by a group of experienced
Guatemalan Spanish teachers.
PROGRAMME DESCRIPTION: Voluntary placements in
a day care centre (for the children of single impoverished
mothers), in a hospital, in a home for elderly people,
rebuilding homes, and (for longer stays) as assistants in
schools. Trips around Guatemala can also be organised
through partner tour operator.
NUMBER OF PARTICIPANTS: No limit.
DURATION OF COURSES: Flexible; from 1–2 weeks to
many months.
COST: $25 weekly when not taking lessons, or none
when volunteers take Spanish lessons, though volunteers
pay for their accommodation and other expenses.
ACCOMMODATION: Homestays with full board (3 meals
a day Monday to Saturday and 7 nights' lodging) cost
$95 a week when taking lessons and/or doing volunteer
job, or $115 when just visiting.
CONTACT: Juan Carlos Martinez, General Director.

UNIPAL
BCM Unipal, London WC1N 3XX
✆ info@unipal.org.uk
🖥 www.unipal.org.uk

PROGRAMME DESCRIPTION: The Universities' Trust
for Educational Exchange with Palestinians operates
an educational and cultural exchange with Palestinian
communities and accepts summer volunteers to teach
English, crafts, music, or drama.
DESTINATIONS: West Bank and Lebanon. The political
situation has made it impossible for projects to continue
in Gaza and the other Palestinian territories.
NUMBER OF PLACEMENTS PER YEAR: 30.
DURATION AND TIME OF PLACEMENTS: 5-week
contracts, from the end of June/early July.
PREREQUISITES: Minimum age 20. Native English
speakers. Experience with children or teaching. TEFL

a bonus. Should be fit, since work is in a very hot climate. Sensitivity, tolerance, adaptability, readiness to learn, political awareness, and tenacity also needed, and volunteers must work well in teams.

SELECTION PROCEDURES AND ORIENTATION: Application forms due by the end of February, with interviews in March. Compulsory training days in mid-April and June.

COST: Volunteers pay £550 for flight, accommodation, food, insurance, etc.

CONTACT: Brenda Hayward, Director.

VILLAGE-TO-VILLAGE
Callmate House, 1 Wilton Street, Bradford BD5 0AX
☎ (0)1274 397 830
✎ enquiries@village-to-village.org.uk
🖥 www.village-to-village.org.uk

Village-to-Village is a charity which has been working to reduce poverty in Tanzania for over 10 years. Member of the Year Out Group.

PROGRAMME DESCRIPTION: Volunteers are sent to the Kilimanjaro region to assist on various projects including teaching English in primary schools and orphanages, teacher training, as well as construction and sustainable agriculture projects.

NUMBER OF PLACEMENTS PER YEAR: 40.

DESTINATIONS: Tanzania.

PREREQUISITES: Minimum age 16 (with parental consent). Most are gap year and university students. All nationalities welcome, provided volunteers can speak English or Swahili.

DURATION AND TIME OF PLACEMENTS: Minimum 2 months for teaching placements starting year-round; otherwise timing is flexible.

SELECTION PROCEDURES AND ORIENTATION: Volunteers are required to attend an induction day before their placement, which will offer some Swahili language training. Orientation will be held on arrival in Tanzania. Volunteers are required to obtain a B3 class visa prior to travel.

COST: Typical 8-week placement requires a minimum donation of £1,450 (excluding international flights). The third and fourth months are charged at £300 each, and the following two months at £150 each. Accommodation is provided in volunteer centre or homestay.

CONTACT: Libby James, UK Programme Director (libby@village-to-village.org.uk).

VOLUNTEER AFRICA
PO Box 24, Bakewell, Derbyshire DE45 1YP
✎ support@volunteerafrica.org
🖥 www.volunteerafrica.org

PROGRAMME DESCRIPTION: UK charity recruits volunteers to work on community projects in Tanzania, eg in rural development or working with children. Other vacancies in Africa with various charities and aid agencies are posted on the same website.

DESTINATIONS: Singida region of Tanzania.

PREREQUISITES: All ages accepted over 18.

DURATION AND TIME OF PLACEMENTS: 2, 4, 7, 10, 11, or 12 weeks.

COST: Fees are £600 (2 weeks), £1,050 (4 weeks), £1,380 (7 weeks), £1,710 (10 weeks), £1,950 (11–12 weeks), a proportion of which is a donation to the host programme.

CONTACT: Moya Cutts, Volunteer Co-ordinator.

VOLUNTEER LATIN AMERICA
Office 1728, PO Box 6945, London W1A 6US
☎ (0)20 7193 9163
✎ info@volunteerlatinamerica.com
🖥 www.volunteerlatinamerica.com

PROGRAMME DESCRIPTION: Volunteer Latin America is an advisory service enabling clients to set up their own volunteer placement in environmental or humanitarian projects in Central and South America, and also to find Spanish and Portuguese language schools in the region. Volunteers are directed towards environmental projects in Latin America ranging from organic farming to monitoring big cats such as jaguar, as well as working with a diverse range of species and habitats. Other projects provide humanitarian assistance to disadvantaged communities by means of child welfare, community development, education, and health programmes.

NUMBER OF PLACEMENTS PER YEAR: 1,000.

DURATION AND TIME OF PLACEMENTS: 1 week to 1 year.

COST: The projects offered either require the volunteer to make a small financial contribution (participation fee), are free but leave volunteers responsible for covering their living expenses, or provide complimentary accommodation and/or food. Volunteer Latin America charges clients for its advisory service: £25 for a volunteer guide, which includes information on Spanish and Portuguese language schools throughout the region.

CONTACT: Stephen Knight, Manager.

VOLUNTEER MALDIVES PVT LTD
Unimoo Building, Orchid Magu, Male, Maldives
☎ +960 330 0609
✎ info@volunteermaldives.com
🖥 www.volunteermaldives.com

PROGRAMME DESCRIPTION: Volunteering in various locations in the Maldive Islands, mainly teaching and sports programmes.

DESTINATIONS: Many islands of the Maldives.

NUMBER OF PLACEMENTS PER YEAR: 500+.

DURATION AND TIME OF PLACEMENTS: Minimum 1 month, preferred stay 2–3 months. Possible to stay up to 12 months. Start dates throughout the year.

PREREQUISITES: Minimum age 18. English reading and writing skills must be good. Background in teaching not essential, though trainee teachers and qualified teachers are in great demand. Non-qualified, enthusiastic volunteers can help teachers in the classroom, or may work at pre-schools.

SELECTION PROCEDURES AND ORIENTATION: Candidates must supply police check. Volunteer Maldives looks after visas. Possible extra activities include snorkelling trips, visits to uninhabited islands for swimming and sunbathing, and night fishing with the locals.

COST: 4 weeks US$950, subsequent months $700. If volunteer stays for 9 months, the next 3 months are free. Discount of 10% for booking 6 months in advance, of 20% for paying 6 months in advance, and of 25% for the second person. Price includes accommodation (homestay or shared in volunteer house), meals, return transfer between Male Airport and the island, visa, welcome pack, T-shirt, and local sim card with small amount of credit, but excludes flights and insurance (which is compulsory).

CONTACT: Michelle Flake and Yvonne Habeeb, Company Founders.

VOLUNTEER NEPAL NATIONAL GROUP
Jhaukhel 4, Bhaktapur, Nepal
☎ +977 1 509 0524
✆ info@volnepal.np.org
✆ volunteer_nepal2002@yahoo.com
🖳 www.volnepal.np.org

Community-based non-profit organisation that co-ordinates local and international work camps to empower community self-help initiatives.

PROGRAMME DESCRIPTION: Placements for volunteers in schools, colleges, and universities. Volunteers help with sports, music, extracurricular activities, English teaching, and other administrative and social welfare work. Also arrange internships in fields of medicine, media, conservation, etc.

NUMBER OF PLACEMENTS PER YEAR: 100.

DESTINATIONS: Kathmandu Valley near the historic city of Bhaktapur.

PREREQUISITES: Minimum age 18.

DURATION AND TIME OF PLACEMENTS: 2 weeks to 5 months, starting January, April, August, and November.

SELECTION PROCEDURES AND ORIENTATION: Application form, CV, and references needed.

COST: Volnepal programme fee is $450 for up to 8 weeks, $750 for 18 weeks; includes pre-service training, language instruction, homestay, and meals, trekking, rafting, jungle safari, and volunteering. Sample costs are $550 for first month for medical interns (includes donation to hospital), $450 for school and orphanage volunteers. Second and third months cost $150–$200.

CONTACT: Anish Neupane, Director.

VOLUNTEERS AUSTRALIA
Suite 1, Savoir Faire, 20 Park Road, Milton, Brisbane, Queensland 4064, Australia
☎ +61 7 3305 8408
✆ info@volunteersaustralia.com.au
🖳 www.volunteersaustralia.com.au

PROGRAMME DESCRIPTION: Indigenous volunteer programme offers projects arranged in co-operation with indigenous organisations and communities, to create a structured and well-organised experience for participants. Examples include a linguistics project in remote Queensland, or helping children with literacy in a suburb of Brisbane.

DESTINATIONS: Selected indigenous communities throughout Australia.

PREREQUISITES: Minimum age 18. Open to all candidates on a tourist, working holiday, or student visa.

DURATION AND TIME OF PLACEMENTS: 3–12 weeks.

SELECTION PROCEDURES AND ORIENTATION: 3-day orientation session on arrival at project.

COST: Prices range from A$1,906 for 3 weeks to A$4,156 for 12 weeks. Optional extras include insurance (A$18.20 a week) and airport reception (A$115).

CONTACT: Rebekah Gilchrist, Marketing Manager.

VOLUNTHAI: VOLUNTEERS FOR THAILAND
86/24 Soi Kanprapa, Prachacheun Road, Bahng Sue, Bangkok 10800, Thailand
☎ +1 202 403 1540
✆ info@volunthai.com
🖳 www.volunthai.com

PROGRAMME DESCRIPTION: Volunteer teaching in 20 target schools with homestay. Volunteers teach conversational English in the classroom for 3–4 hours a day.

DESTINATIONS: Rural areas in remote provinces of Thailand.

NUMBER OF PLACEMENTS PER YEAR: 100.

DURATION AND TIME OF PLACEMENTS: 2–4 weeks minimum.

PREREQUISITES: Ages 21–70. Degree required. Must be speaker of English (native or non-native). Must be willing to live with and learn from the locals.

SELECTION PROCEDURES AND ORIENTATION: Rolling admissions. Online interviews. Volunteers are met in Bangkok for an introduction, and then go to the headquarters in rural Chaiyaphum for a brief training in Thai culture and language. A Thai teacher is available at the homestay to help with questions.

COST: Modest monthly fee ($325 for first month, $150 for subsequent months) to cover comfortable homestay and meals. Volunteers pay for their own travel costs.

CONTACT: Michael Anderson, Founder.

WAVA
67–71 Lewisham High Street, Lewisham, London SE13 5JX
☎ (0)800 80 483 80
smordarski@workandvolunteer.com
💻 www.workandvolunteer.com

PROGRAMME DESCRIPTION: WAVA stands for 'Work and Volunteer Abroad', having been rebranded in 2010 from Twin Work & Adventure Abroad. Among other programmes, WAVA offers volunteer placements on projects in developing countries.

DESTINATIONS: All over the world: North and South America, Europe, Africa, Asia, and Australasia.

PREREQUISITES: All ages and nationalities.

DURATION AND TIME OF PLACEMENTS: From 2 weeks to 1 year.

COST: From £390. Fees include pre-departure and in-country induction/training, a donation to the project, in-country transportation, accommodation (volunteer house or on-project residence or local hostel/lodge), and food.

CONTACT: Sally Mordarski, Travel Administrator (smordarski@workandvolunteer.com).

WLS INTERNATIONAL LTD
29 Harley Street, London W1G 9QR
☎ (0)203 384 4058
info@GapYearInAsia.com
💻 www.GapYearInAsia.com.

PROGRAMME DESCRIPTION: Affordable volunteering programmes in Asia.

DESTINATIONS: China, Cambodia, India, Nepal, the Philippines, Thailand, and Vietnam.

NUMBER OF PLACEMENTS PER YEAR: 350.

DURATION AND TIME OF PLACEMENTS: 1–12 weeks.

PREREQUISITES: All nationalities welcome. Most participants are aged 20–35, but there is no limit. Volunteers must have enthusiasm, flexibility, and a willingness to help. Candidates should be willing to prepare ideas for English lessons in advance of their trip.

SELECTION PROCEDURES AND ORIENTATION: Most candidates book a month in advance, but last-minute placements are available.

COST: Sample prices: £505 for 4 weeks in Nepal (plus £50 for each extra week), and £585 per 4 weeks in the Philippines (plus £55 per extra week). Accommodation in guest house or as homestay.

CONTACT: Matt Jones, Programme Manager.

WorkTravelSA.org
PO Box 3288, Somerset West, 7129, Cape Town, South Africa
☎ +27 21 851 9494
info@worktravelsa.org
💻 www.worktravelsa.org

PROGRAMME DESCRIPTION: Choice of wildlife conservation experience programme, and humanitarian and social programme. The former enables volunteers to offer valuable practical assistance to local conservation staff, field researchers, and game reserve managers. Volunteers receive hands-on experience in game reserve management, conservation work, environmental and wildlife care. Volunteers in the social programme choose from range of projects, eg working with babies and toddlers at an AIDS orphanage and improving the lives of young children in a township community. WorkTravelSA also have a general internship programme, a hospitality programme offering internships in hotels and safari lodges in South Africa, and a medical internship programme (see 'Directory of Work Experience Abroad').

DESTINATIONS: Comfortable bush camps with electricity, hot water, flush toilets, internet, and TV located inside the game reserve or national park (Kruger NP, Addo NP, Welgevonden Private Reserve). Furnished apartments in Stellenbosch and a volunteer house in Somerset West, both near Cape Town.

NUMBER OF PLACEMENTS PER YEAR: 500+.

DURATION AND TIME OF PLACEMENTS : 4–12 weeks for most; hospitality positions are for 3 months.

PREREQUISITES: Minimum age 18, average age 22. English speakers of all nationalities.

SELECTION PROCEDURES AND ORIENTATION:
Applications accepted at short notice for conservation and social programmes; telephone interview a month in advance for professional internships. 5-day local orientation is provided with appropriate manuals. For the conservation projects, the arrival orientation and safety inductions are followed by a compulsory 7-day bushcraft training course to familiarise volunteers with procedures for living in the African bush.

COST: £1,110 for 4 weeks of conservation volunteering, £1,225 for 8 weeks of humanitarian volunteering. Hospitality interns are given free accommodation and meals, plus a monthly personal allowance and time to explore the area.

CONTACT: Amy Wyness, Office Administrator.

WWOOF – WORLD WIDE OPPORTUNITIES ON ORGANIC FARMS
💻 www.wwoof.org
💻 www.wwoofinternational.org

The International WWOOF Association (IWA) website has links to both the national organisations in the countries that have a WWOOF co-ordinator and to those that do not, known as WWOOF Independents. National WWOOF co-ordinators compile a list of member farmers willing to provide bed and board in a non-monetary exchange with volunteers, who help out and are genuinely interested in furthering the aims of the organic movement.

PROGRAMME DESCRIPTION: Visitors are expected to work around 6 hours per day in return for free accommodation and food. Visitors have the opportunity to learn about the organic growing of crops and food.

DESTINATIONS OFFERED: Worldwide.

PREREQUISITES: Minimum age 18. Should be prepared to work hard and have an interest in organic growing and environmental issues.

DURATION AND TIME OF PLACEMENTS: Anything from a few days upwards.

SELECTION PROCEDURES AND ORIENTATION:
Most WWOOF organisations have an online application process.

COST: Varies according to which WWOOF you wish to join. WWOOF UK membership costs £20. Individual national WWOOF organisations have to be joined separately (eg Denmark, Sweden, Germany, Switzerland, Austria, Italy, Australia, New Zealand, Canada, Ghana, Japan, Korea, and many more – some are mentioned in country-by-country chapters).

YOU VOLUNTEER
1 Riverside Close, Oundle, Peterborough PE8 4DN
☎ (0)1832 275 038
🖱 nick@youvolunteer.org
💻 www.youvolunteer.org

Part of the Great Aves non-profit organisation (registered charity no. 1133399).

PROGRAMME DESCRIPTION: Arajuno Road Project (www.arajunoroadproject.org) offers volunteers the opportunity to work and teach in schools in Ecuador.

DESTINATIONS: Amazon jungle of central Ecuador.

COST: US$290 for 2 weeks, $500 for 4 weeks, $105 for subsequent weeks.

CONTACT: Nick Greatrex, Operations Manager.

DIRECTORY OF RELIGIOUS ORGANISATIONS

BMS WORLD MISSION
PO Box 49, Baptist House, Didcot, Oxfordshire OX11 8XA
☎ (0)1235 517 653
🖱 opportunities@bmsworldmission.org
💻 www.bmsworldmission.org/actionteams

PROGRAMME DESCRIPTION: Action Teams enable young people to spend 6 months living and working alongside BMS mission workers or a partner organisation involved in church work, community development, basic TEFL teaching, youth and children's work, and drama and music outreach.

DESTINATIONS: Asia, Europe, Africa and South America.

NUMBER OF PLACEMENTS PER YEAR: 40 or more.

PREREQUISITES: Ages 18–23. Must be a committed Christian with support from local UK church. Health clearance required.

DURATION AND TIME OF PLACEMENTS: 10 months, including 1 month's training (September), 6 months overseas (October-April) and a 2-month tour (April-June) of UK churches upon return, to share experiences and inspire others for mission.

SELECTION PROCEDURES AND ORIENTATION: Interviews are held over a weekend at BMS International Mission Centre in Birmingham. A 1-month period of training and preparation follows. Debriefing is given on return.

COST: Contribution of approximately £3,950 to include flights, accommodation, and living expenses overseas, insurance, visas, and training.

CONTACT: Sarah Lewney, Mission Teams Administrator.

BOSCO VOLUNTEERING ACTION (BOVA)
Savio House, Ingersley Road, Bollington, Cheshire SK10 5RW
- ☎ (0)1625 560 724
- ✎ bova@salesianyouthministry.com
- 🖥 http://boscovolunteeraction.co.uk

BOVA is the overseas volunteering group of the Salesians of Don Bosco in the UK, a Catholic Religious order focusing on serving the young and the poor.

PROGRAMME DESCRIPTION: Volunteer programmes in Salesian communities around the world, assisting in their work with the young and the poor while experiencing life in other countries. Previous volunteers have assisted in schools, vocational training centres, youth centres and residential centres, done office work and administration, coached sport, led music, taught maths, ICT (computers), and English.

NUMBER OF PLACEMENTS PER YEAR: 25.

DESTINATIONS: Don Bosco works in 130 countries. So far, BOVA volunteers have lived and worked with host communities in Bolivia, Ghana, India, the Philippines, Sierra Leone, Tanzania, Kenya, Azerbaijan, the Solomon Islands, Swaziland, El Salvador, and Nigeria. BOVA aims to match volunteers to communities' needs, so cannot guarantee a placement in a particular country.

PREREQUISITES: Minimum age 18. BOVA accepts non-Catholics and people of no faith who are willing to work in a Catholic context.

DURATION AND TIME OF PLACEMENTS: 1 month to 2 years.

SELECTION PROCEDURES AND ORIENTATION: Reference check and CRB check. Two pre-departure training weekends organised (at volunteers' own expense).

COST: £25 administration charge, £100 for 2 training weekends, £50 training fee. Volunteers cover airfares, insurance, visas, and spending money; host community provides lodging and food.

CONTACT: James Trewby.

CHRISTIAN AID VOLUNTEER YOUTH INTERNSHIP
Churches and Young People's Team, Christian Aid, 35 Lower Marsh, London SE1 7RL
- ☎ (0)20 7523 2012
- ☎ (0)20 7523 2025
- ✎ internship@christian-aid.org
- 🖥 www.christianaid.org.uk/getinvolved/ volunteer/gapyear/gap_year.aspx

Christian Aid is a non-governmental development charity. It is not evangelistic, but its mission is to help eradicate poverty and challenge the root causes of poverty.

PROGRAMME DESCRIPTION: Gap year scheme involves working in a regional office in the UK and getting local teenagers, university students, and youth leaders interested and engaged in Christian Aid's global campaigns and activities. Overseas trip will be included. Role involves fundraising and visiting up to four summer festivals to promote the work of Christian Aid.

NUMBER OF PLACEMENTS: 20.

PREREQUISITES: Minimum age 18, average age 22. Christian Aid works with people of all faiths and none, although much of the youth work is undertaken with church-connected young people. A passion for global justice is essential.

DURATION AND TIME OF PLACEMENTS: 10 months.

SELECTION PROCEDURES AND ORIENTATION: Application deadline is 31 March. Briefing and interview days are held in the spring and placements are agreed by the end of June. Extensive on-the-job training given.

COST: Subsistence allowance provided by Christian Aid. Christian Aid gap year volunteers are usually placed with a family or in a shared house close to the area office where they work.

CONTACT: Claire Ford or Chris Mead.

CMS (CHURCH MISSION SOCIETY)
Watlington Road, Cowley, Oxford OX4 6BZ
- ☎ (0)1865 787 400
- ✎ vro@cms-uk.org
- 🖥 www.cms-uk.org

PROGRAMME DESCRIPTION: CMS short-term placements provide an experience of mission service alongside Christians in other cultures. Examples include youth worker in Brazil, nursing assistant in Nepal, English teacher in Uganda, working with visually or hearing-impaired children in Lebanon, church planting in France.

DESTINATIONS: Various countries in Africa, Asia, Europe, the Middle East, and South America.

PREREQUISITES: Christians aged 18+ living in Britain, who are involved with their local church, interested in learning about and sharing in cross-cultural mission.

DURATION AND TIME OF PLACEMENTS: 4 months to 2 years. Placements can start after core training in January or July each year. Short encounters of 2–4 weeks also available.

SELECTION PROCEDURES AND ORIENTATION: Application form, interview process, CRB, and medical check. 12-day preparatory training and debrief.

COST: Volunteers must be self-financing, though CMS can advise on fundraising.

CONTACT: Rebecca Thomlinson, Vocational Recruitment Officer (for individuals); Debbie James, Discipleship Team Leader (for groups).

LATIN LINK STEP & STRIDE PROGRAMMES
87 London Street, Reading, Berkshire RG1 4QA
☎ (0)118 957 7100
✆ step@latinlink.org or stridelatinlink.org
🖥 www.latinlink.org

PROGRAMME DESCRIPTION: Step is a self-funded team-based programme, involved in small-scale building projects and church work in Latin America for committed Christians only. Stride arranges individual placements in Latin America using participants' specific skills and gifts according to the needs of the Latin American church. Opportunities include school and TEFL teaching, children's work, church work, agricultural and engineering work, project development, and prison ministry. Stride also provides opportunities for short-term medical electives and Bible college placements, from a minimum of 8 weeks.

DESTINATIONS: Argentina, Bolivia, Brazil, Cuba, Costa Rica, Ecuador, Guatemala, Nicaragua, Peru, and Spain.

NUMBER OF PLACEMENTS PER YEAR: Step: 150; Stride: 25–30.

PREREQUISITES: Minimum age 17 years for 3-week to 6-month Step programme; minimum age 18 for 6-month to 2-year Stride programme. Volunteers must have an active Christian faith. Applicants need to be flexible, have initiative, and be open to learning. Knowledge of Spanish or Portuguese is not essential but it is a great help. It is suggested that volunteers attend evening classes to prepare for the project.

DURATION AND TIME OF PLACEMENTS: Step: spring projects run from March to July, and summer ones during July and August (7 weeks). Stride: orientation and departures in September and January.

COST: Step: From £1,500–£2,000 in total; details on application. The cost of the Stride programme varies from country to country, but is around £1,950 for initial costs, followed by £450 per month. As with Step, the cost includes flights, insurance, training, debriefing, food, and accommodation, but not language lessons and visa costs.

OASIS UK
75 Westminster Bridge Road, London SE1 7HS
☎ (0)20 7921 4200
✆ enquiries@oasisuk.org;
🖥 www.oasisuk.org

In operation since 1985.

PROGRAMME DESCRIPTION: Global Action Teams and Short-term Summer Teams. Practical projects run alongside local Christian groups and churches to help transform communities in some of the poorest areas of the world. Activities vary from children's holiday clubs to teaching English, community health work with those affected/orphaned by HIV/AIDS, to youth discipleship, drama, music, and projects with slum-dwellers.

DESTINATIONS: Uganda, Bangladesh, and other developing countries.

NUMBER OF PLACEMENTS PER YEAR: 250.

PREREQUISITES: Minimum age 18. Applicants should be committed Christians and in sympathy with the aims of the Oasis Trust.

DURATION AND TIME OF PLACEMENTS: Gap Year (Global Action) Teams depart twice a year for 3–6 months. Summer teams last 2–6 weeks.

COST: From £3,000 for 3-month Global Action Team; £4,250 for 4 and a half months. From £2,000 for 2–6 week Short-Term Summer Teams.

SALESIAN VOLUNTEERS
Ingersley Road, Bollington, Macclesfield
SK10 5RW
☎ (0)1625 573 256
✆ jessicabarnett@saviohouse.org.uk
🖥 www.virtualsavio.com

PROGRAMME DESCRIPTION: Gap year scheme for living and working in a Catholic residential community with other volunteers, doing hands-on youth work for various projects including residential retreat programmes, outreach, and day retreats.

PREREQUISITES: Committed Christians aged 18–30.

DURATION AND TIME OF PLACEMENTS: September to July.

SELECTION PROCEDURES AND ORIENTATION:
Interview, including week's residential experience. All new volunteers are given in-house and external training and preparation, and ongoing developmental personal and professional support.

COST: None. Weekly allowance is paid.

CONTACT: Jessica Barnett, Retreat Team Leader.

TEARFUND
100 Church Road, Teddington, Middlesex
TW11 8QE
☎ (0)20 8943 7777
transform@tearfund.org
www.tearfund.org/Transform

A Christian charity working with local church partners to bring justice and transform lives by overcoming global poverty.

PROGRAMME DESCRIPTION: 'Transform Teams' work practically supporting Tearfund partners overseas with their projects, mainly with children and the vulnerable, holiday clubs, AIDS education, etc.

DESTINATIONS: Kenya, Burundi, Malawi, Rwanda, Zambia, Tanzania, Burkina Faso, Uganda, South Africa, Bangladesh, Cambodia, Thailand, India, and Peru.

DURATION AND TIME OF PLACEMENTS: 2- to 4-month trips leave in March and April. 4- to 6-week teams leave July and August.

COST: 4- to 6-week trips from £1,300; 2-month trips from £1,600; 3- to 4-month team from £2,500. All trip costs exclude flights and visas.

TIME FOR GOD (TFG)
Community House, 46–50 East Parade,
Harrogate, HG1 5RR, North Yorkshire
☎ (0)1423 536 248
office@timeforgod.org
www.timeforgod.org

One of the most longstanding organisations in the UK working in the field of voluntary service, gap years, and career breaks.

PROGRAMME DESCRIPTION: Gap year and career break organisation with an interdenominational and international focus. UK placements include but are not limited to inner-city projects with the homeless and disadvantaged, caring for children with special needs,

assisting the ministry team in a church, children's and youth work, youth retreat centres/outdoor activity centres, drug and alcohol rehabilitation centres, and more.

NUMBER OF PLACEMENTS PER YEAR: 150.

DESTINATIONS: UK, Europe, USA, Canada, Hong Kong, and South Korea.

PREREQUISITES: Minimum age 18. Must be open to explore the Christian faith.

DURATION AND TIME OF PLACEMENTS: 3–12 months from September or January.

COST: Fees vary according to programme selected, and range from a free gap year in Europe for UK young adults (subject to approval through EVS – see entry in 'Directory of Specialist Gap Year Programmes), to £1,550 for a year in Hong Kong, the USA, or South Korea, excluding travel expenses, insurance, visa, and immunisation fees. Includes orientation and re-entry training, ongoing training and support while in placement, accommodation, food expenses, and pocket money.

CONTACT: Susann Haehnel, Field Team Leader.

WYCLIFFE BIBLE TRANSLATORS
Wycliffe Centre, Horsleys Green, High
Wycombe, Buckinghamshire HP14 3XL
☎ (0)1494 682 256
recruitment_uk@wycliffe.org
www.wycliffe.org.uk

PROGRAMME DESCRIPTION: Programme with opportunities to tutor missionaries' children who are being home-schooled, or work as classroom assistants in mission schools. Possibilities in IT or IT training for those with suitable qualifications.

DESTINATIONS: Worldwide, but mainly Africa and Asia.

DURATION AND TIME OF PLACEMENTS: 3 months to 2 years abroad.

PREREQUISITES: Minimum age 18.

COST: Variable, but normally £400–£450 a month to cover living costs, medical insurance, etc, not including airfares.

CONTACT: Katharine Fairbairn, Recruitment Co-ordinator.

YEAR FOR GOD
YMAM, Holmsted Manor, Staplefield Road,
Cuckfield, West Sussex RH17 5JF
☎ (0)1444 440 229
☎ (0)7805 154 486 (mobile)
yfg@holmsted.org.uk
www.yearforgod.co.uk

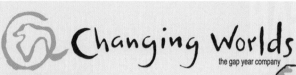

Gap Year South America

Learn – Give – Live

Adventures from
2 to 15 weeks

www.ventureco-worldwide.com

There's Work Experience and there's World Experience...

(We can offer you both)

Are you looking to improve your future prospects, gain valuable work experience, make a difference and see more of the world?

To discover the benefits of **8-12 months** volunteering in **Africa**, **Asia**, or the **Americas**, please visit **www.projecttrust.org.uk** or give us a call on **01879 230444**

 www.facebook.com/ProjectTrustVolunteers

prO**ject** TRUST *Since 1967*

Changing lives. year in. year out...

Registered as a Charity in Scotland. No. SCO25668

TEACHING | **SOCIAL CARE** · **OUTWARD BOUND** · **JOURNALISM**

ive life out **loud**

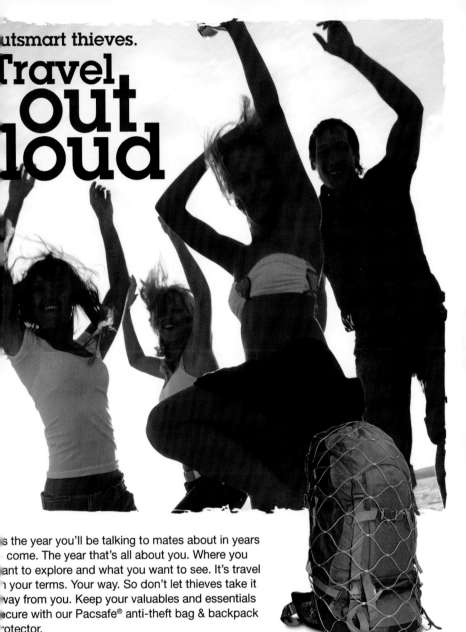

utsmart thieves.

Travel
out
loud

s the year you'll be talking to mates about in years
come. The year that's all about you. Where you
ant to explore and what you want to see. It's travel
1 your terms. Your way. So don't let thieves take it
vay from you. Keep your valuables and essentials
ecure with our Pacsafe® anti-theft bag & backpack
rotector.

ith its lightweight, slashproof eXomesh® cage
stem, you'll be able to lock and leave your gear to
secure fixture while you focus on getting out there
way out there. No worries. No inhibitions and
ore importantly, no holding back.

**anti-theft backpack
& bag protector**
pacsafe™ 85L

pacsafe®
smart travel gear

rww.pacsafe.com

clic ... just clic!

Spanish Courses

in Seville and Cadiz

*amar, vivir
y sentir
en español*

Teacher Training Institute

English Teacher Training

CELTA and DELTA

Seville T 954 502 131
Cadiz T 956 255 455

www.clic.es   clic@clic.es   www.tefl.es

 International House Sevilla y Cádiz
A MEMBER OF THE INTERNATIONAL HOUSE WORLD ORGANISATION

PROGRAMME DESCRIPTION: Year For God is a gap year programme of Youth With A Mission, for Christians 18+ wanting to take a year to develop their relationship with God and to serve Him through overseas missions in a cross-cultural setting.

NUMBER OF PLACEMENTS PER YEAR: 20–30.

DESTINATIONS: Bolivia, India, Indonesia/Malaysia, Singapore, Tanzania, and Uganda.

PREREQUISITES: The year will be challenging and life changing, so the YFG co-ordinators are looking for committed people with enthusiasm, initiative, and a desire to know God more and serve Him. YFG is also a good starting point for those considering being involved in missions in the future.

DURATION AND TIME OF PLACEMENTS: 12 months starting either in August or February (2 intakes per year).

SELECTION PROCEDURES AND ORIENTATION: Application form with references. Informal interview at Holmsted. Orientation week at start of the year.

COST: £3,500 (India), £5,000 (Bolivia and Uganda), £8,900 (Singapore). This includes airfare, food and accommodation, medical insurance, immunisations, visas, and DTS (Discipleship Training School) fees. Extra needed for personal spending money.

CONTACT: Gary and Caroline Morgan, YFG Co-ordinators (YWAM England).

YOUTH WITH A MISSION
Highfield Oval, Harpenden, Hertfordshire
AL5 4BX
☎ (0)1582 463 216
✉ enquiries@oval.com
🖥 www.ywamengland.org

Founded in 1960, Youth With A Mission is an international, interdenominational missionary movement of Christians. It currently has more than 17,000 full-time volunteers working in more than 170 countries, and sends out 25,000 short-term missionaries each year.

PROGRAMME DESCRIPTION: Gap year programmes include life-changing training and outreach that gathers together people from many nations with a desire and commitment to express God's heart to the world. Courses consist either of a 3-month lecture phase followed by a 2- or 3-month outreach; or an 11-month option that combines training with outreach. Extensions beyond 6 months working in a variety of ministries, depending on location.

DESTINATIONS: Urban and youth settings within the UK and in the rest of the world including Europe, Malaysia, Indonesia, Philippines, East Africa, South America, India, Far East, Egypt, and South Africa.

NUMBER OF PLACEMENTS PER YEAR: 30–40.

DURATION AND TIME OF PLACEMENTS: 5–12 months, starting at various times of the year. Short-term 'taster' opportunities of a month or less are also available.

PREREQUISITES: Volunteers must be Christian and support Youth With A Mission mission's stated aim. Its motto is 'To Know God and Make Him Known'.

SELECTION PROCEDURES AND ORIENTATION: Application forms can be downloaded from the website. Interviews are not always required. For some courses, enquiry weekends are run for interested applicants.

COST: Fees vary from £1,600 to £4,000, plus outreach expenses.

CONTACT: Natalie Edwards (enquiries@ywamengland.org).

A YEAR OFF FOR NORTH AMERICANS

Once completely unknown in North America, the concept of and even the term gap year is catching on. Colleges are gradually getting to grips with the concept of deferred entry, though it is still an alien notion to some. To take just one example, the number of gap years doubled between one year and the next at prestigious Swarthmore College, where students who want to defer their admission have to write an essay on what they plan to do with their year out. It has long been recognised that the scramble to get into a good university dominates every waking minute of young people's lives from the age of about 14, so that everything they do is done with an eye to their college application. The Swarthmore Dean of Admissions was quoted as saying that he thinks that the gap year is the new summer for ambitious American students, since '*Summers have disappeared, sadly, because so many students are doing what they think will look good on college applications*'. Be aware that some institutions will grant a deferral, but require the student to sign a pledge that they will not apply elsewhere.

The trend may have started with an article published by the Admissions Office of Harvard University, and which continues to have wide circulation, entitled 'Time Out or Burn Out for the Next Generation'. It argued strenuously for having a break from the intense pressures affecting students trying to get into the top universities. More recently, Princeton University has created a programme by which up to 10% of its intake participate in a year of social service abroad before they arrive. The university's president is quoted as citing the advantages of giving students a more international perspective, adding to their maturity, and providing them with a break from academic pressures.

Two American gap year programmes, Dynamy and Thinking Beyond Borders, now co-sponsor a national circuit of Gap Year Fairs (www.usagapyearfairs.org) in nearly 20 states, and with 42 gap year programmes. So far the fairs have been quite small, attracting between 70 and 200 people, but they are hoping to expand.

After finishing high school in his hometown of Flagstaff, Arizona, **Kellen Brandel** knew that he wanted to take a year out in 2010–11. In his search for something affordable that would let him work on his Spanish, he settled on an NGO in the capital of El Salvador (see details for CIS in the 'Directories of Courses'), which teaches English to local people, and also supports some social justice projects around the country. Kellen spent a total of seven months in Central America and reflects on the benefits:

> The rewards of teaching and volunteering at CIS in San Salvador were too numerous to count. This experience helped give me confidence in teaching and more comfort in my native tongue, as well as to see the world in a different way than I would have before. This particular NGO works heavily with social justice, which for me was the best part. It is an organisation that is so involved in giving back to the community, it was incredible to be a part of it.
>
> I loved my gap year abroad, which made me realise the importance of a university degree. I will start school shortly, doing Sociology for my major, with the intent of working in structuring NGOs and system organisation. My gap year helped me experience the 'real world' outside, which is a lot better than a lot of my friends, who went straight into university from high school. While they've been undecided studying, I've been able to get a feel for real passions, and connect a major to a career. It was nice because I met many recent graduates who all helped comfort me, advise me on what to study, and told me how much they wished they had done what I was doing. My gap year has helped me decide what I want to do in the future.

Post-college gap years are more common in North America, though even here there is pressure on many new graduates to get immediately on to the career ladder. Yet those who have never travelled outside their home continent may leave college with a nagging feeling that their horizons need broadening.

Canada has definitely seen an upsurge of interest in taking a year off before university. The national student travel agency Travel CUTS, and its work abroad programmes entitled SWAP, have launched a website called www.gapyearabroad.ca. **Graham Milner** from Victoria, British Columbia, took advantage of a gap year scheme and spent a happy year at a residential school between London and Cambridge. He soon realised his school was not far from Stansted Airport and became an aficionado of cheap European flights with no-frills airlines, which he could afford even on his modest salary. In order to find a travelling companion, he simply sent a round-robin email to the other participants from Canada, offering to search out the cheapest flights and accommodation. As a result, he and a young woman gapper spent a long weekend in Milan not long after they both arrived in England.

Halael Craig from Vancouver wanted to spend the second half of her gap year in England, because she had enjoyed a year in Cambridge previously when her family was on sabbatical. Partly because she had family contacts, she wanted to fix her gap year up independently. However, when she gradually realised that she was not going to be able to pin down either a job or accommodation in advance, she began to lose heart. But she had managed to save C$5,000 by working at a chain clothes store, and decided to go for it anyway, arriving in cold and rainy February:

Moving to England by myself without any parental assistance really showed me what I was capable of doing (although I do fully recognise all those who were very helpful during my initial period there). However, the fact that I was able to find a room to rent and a job all by myself without going broke was very satisfying, and gave me confidence in my capabilities. I really enjoyed my job at Laura Ashley, where there were some really nice girls who worked part-time and with whom I would go out for drinks or dinner. The low points of my year out were the drudgery of working for five months in Canada. I was only able to get part-time work, which meant that I was quite bored and my parents would nag at me to do something helpful . . . blah blah.

Having a year out from school was one of the best decisions I've ever made. My experiences gave me more confidence and maturity as I arrived at university. I had travelled and been in situations where I had to meet complete strangers, and these experiences helped me overcome shyness and gave me confidence when faced with this new rather daunting social experience. Throughout the six months I was in Britain and Europe, I managed to save money so that after all travel, rent, and food payments had been made, I had still saved money that would go to university expenses. It was an excellent year out and I look back on it fondly.

One changing trend is for British gap year organisations to accept more clients from North America. It seems that the increase in competition among the companies has prompted many of the British agencies to stop worrying about the reputed litigiousness of Americans and to start not just welcoming but actively recruiting Americans on to their programmes. Several, such as Global Visions International, i-to-i, and Projects Abroad, have offices in the USA.

Of course, many Americans taking a gap year do not leave the shores of their country. Some who are undecided about the next step join AmeriCorps, the national service programme instituted by President Clinton in 1993, which has been described as a domestic Peace Corps. In exchange for 1,700 hours of community service over a 10-month period, AmeriCorps volunteers aged 17–24 receive an education voucher worth up to US$5,350, and a living allowance of US$100 or more a week. The Federal Work Study programme is another scheme that encourages a volunteering culture with monetary rewards: financial assistance is given to students in financial need who work in community service positions during term-time or while on holiday, eg working with deprived children to raise literacy rates. Proponents of the Big Society in the UK are attracted to such incentives, and similar schemes come under consideration from time to time in Britain.

MY GAP YEAR:
LAURA WERNER

Laura Werner turned to mediating agencies after graduating from Harvard, as access to Europe is not as easy for American students as for EU nationals. After carrying out quite a lot of detailed research, she opted for a gap year internship arranged by Adelante (listed below) and wrote from Spain several months into the experience.

I spent the entirety of my senior spring stressing over what to do after college. I was worried because I couldn't find anything that I wanted to pursue wholeheartedly. Instead, I ended up in my hometown working for a marketing and distribution company. I knew I was meant to do more and see more of the world. I found my mind turning back to one idea, that I wanted to travel. I had studied Spanish in college and wanted to expand on my language set. Since there are so many programmes, it's hard to know which ones are reliable unless you've met somebody who's already been through it. Adelante offers to help you find an internship in several cities in Spain, lasting one to six months plus housing and assistance with visas. It seemed right on target with what I wanted: to live abroad, to work on my Spanish, and to try a new job without the pressures of a contract. The only drawback, aside from my family and best friends being so far away, was financial. As a recent graduate, I had not managed to save much. So, I decided to take out a loan calculated to cover my six months in Barcelona. I didn't really think about what would happen when I came home or if I ran out of money. I just wanted to go!

I was very excited on arrival in Barcelona and was lucky to be placed in an apartment with an outgoing and helpful woman from the city studying for her master's. My other room-mate was also on the Adelante programme and we were at the same point in our lives, recent grads, unsure of our futures. The first two weeks, we went to the Kingsbrook Language School, which was a great way to reintroduce yourself to the language and start to understand the colloquial speech of Barcelona; however, the lack of structure made it tough to improve by leaps and bounds as you might wish.

From the stories I had heard, I thought I could find ways of earning money, even though I wasn't legally permitted to work in Spain. Unfortunately, this was only partially the case. I found work babysitting, but the income was hardly enough to cover my needs, as I had not anticipated so many extra expenses such as public transport, internet, cell phone and water (which isn't free, like in the States). I didn't live like a rock star, but I certainly learned how much money you need if you want to live abroad. If you haven't saved up a lot, you probably shouldn't be doing an unpaid internship (as I did).

After the course, I started my five-month internship with a small publishing company called ACV Global. The company is absolutely wonderful! The atmosphere is bright and welcoming and the employees are very friendly. The friends that I made through my internship, as well as my room-mates, helped pull me out of occasional spells of homesickness. The small company gave me the opportunity to participate in a variety of projects, and I am thrilled with my work in the design and communication sector. Since my experience has been so positive, I feel that I have strengths that have been revealed by this trip and I certainly plan on emphasising them in the job search. I've already started making contacts in NYC and sent some CVs to a few companies. I hope that my transition into the working world will be a lot smoother than it might have been otherwise!

ADVISORY SERVICES

There are companies that maintain databases of gap year semester programmes and a wealth of opportunities (mostly unpaid), which offer personalised consultations to fee-paying clients (often young people aged 16–25) and attempt to match them with a suitable work, volunteer, or study placement abroad:

Center for Interim Programs LLC, Princeton (+1 609 683 4300; www.interimprograms.com). Consulting service with offices in Princeton and Northampton, Massachusetts, aimed primarily at pre-university and university students looking to arrange an internship or volunteer work. Consulting fee US$2,300.

Horizon Cosmopolite, Montréal, Canada (+1 514 935 8436; www.horizoncosmopolite.com). Database of volunteer work, internships, and Spanish immersion in 30+ countries around the world. Tries to match clients with suitable placements. Participation fee to Horizon Cosmopolite on sliding scale, from about C$350 for three weeks to C$800 for 12 weeks. Varying programme fees are in addition.

LEAPNow, Calistoga, California (+1 888 424 5327; www.leapnow.org/gapyear.php). Various internships and experiential programmes in 126 countries. Prices from $8,400 for semester-long Service in India programme.

Taking Off: Gap Year Consultants, Boston (+1 617 424 1606; www.takingoff.net). Taking Off provides ongoing personal assistance to those looking for international experiences that include volunteer work, internships, and custom-designed situations (not paying jobs). Initial consultation costs $50; full service consulting fee is US$2,100.

KEY NORTH AMERICAN ORGANISATIONS

Of the thousands of organisations large and small throughout North America that are involved with student exchanges and assisting young people to undertake worthwhile projects or internships abroad, paid or voluntary, here is a small selection.

Abroader View (www.abroaderview.org). 180 affordable volunteer projects in 21 countries including the Philippines and Rwanda as well as the usual suspects.

Adelante LLC (www.adelanteabroad.com). Internships, volunteer placements, teaching abroad and semester/summer study opportunities from 1–12 months in Spain (several cities), Costa Rica (San José), Mexico (Oaxaca), Chile (Vina del Mar/Valparaiso), and Uruguay (Montevideo). New Observational Research Assignments in Scotland with various organisations (6 weeks in summer).

AFS International Youth Development (www.afsusa.org). Search for 'gap year' on website. Full intercultural programme lasting 4/6–12 months in 28 countries, including many in Europe, for volunteers aged 18–29. Most programmes include language training prior to volunteer placement, homestay accommodation and participation in local voluntary projects.

Agriventure (International Agricultural Exchange Association), Alberta, Canada. www.agriventure.com. Details of the international farm exchange may be found in the chapter on work experience.

AIDE (Association of International Development and Exchange) (+1 866 6-ABROAD (227623); reinventyourself@aideabroad.org; www.aideabroad.org). Variety of overseas placements in volunteer, internship, work, and teach abroad programmes, lasting 2 weeks to 12 months, in Argentina, Australia, Chile, China, Costa Rica, Ecuador, England, Guatemala, India, Ireland, Peru, South Africa, Spain, and the USA. Participants pay a programme fee to cover placement, airport pick-up, accommodation, meals, local support, medical insurance, and optional language courses. Programmes can also include cultural and adventure tours.

AIPT (Association for International Practical Training) (www.aipt.org, or www.iaesteunited states.org). Short- and long-term placements in more than 80 countries through the International Association for the Exchange of Students for Technical Experience (IAESTE), available to students in science, engineering, math, agriculture, or architecture. Other work exchange schemes with selected countries.

Amerispan Unlimited, Philadelphia (+1 800 879 6640; info@amerispan.com). Specialist Spanish-language travel organisation with expertise in arranging language courses, voluntary placements and internships throughout South and Central America.

Amigos de las Americas, Houston (+1 800 231 7796; www.amigoslink.org). Summer training programme for 700+ high school and college student volunteers mostly in community health projects throughout Central and South America. Participation fee is $4,700, including travel from the USA. All volunteers must have studied Spanish at school or university and undergone training.

ArchaeoSpain, Connecticut (+1 866 932 0003; www.archaeospain.com). Summer archaeological programmes for anyone over 18 in Spain and Italy. Sample cost $2,690 for a month working on a Roman excavation in Spain.

British American Education Foundation (+1 201 261 4438; www.baef.org). Offers students from North America the opportunity to spend a term or a year in a British boarding school following the normal sixth-form curriculum. Cost $35,000-$45,000.

Brown Ledge Gap Year (+1 888 74-FOCUS (36287); www.brownledgegapyear.org). 4-month programme August to Christmas; first phase is 4 weeks' documentary film training at camp in Vermont, then road trip to Salt Lake City for a 6-week internship or community service; on to New Orleans for the last phase. Participants identify subjects for documentaries along the way. Costs $14,500.

BUNAC USA (+1 203 264 0901; www.bunac.org). Administers a number of programmes for US students and young people including Intern in Britain, Work in Ireland, Work in France, Work Australia, Work in France, Work New Zealand, Work Canada, Volunteer South Africa, Volunteer Peru, and Volunteer Cambodia. Note that the former Work in Britain programme was cancelled due to UK visa changes in 2009.

Castle Rock Institute (www.castle-rock.org). Educational organisation in the Blue Ridge Mountains of North Carolina, devoted to balancing academic study of the humanities and outdoor adventure. Semester tuition and living expenses from $15,250.

CCI – Center for Cultural Interchange, Chicago. www.cci-exchange.com. Language courses, homestays, internships lasting 1–3 months and volunteering programmes in many countries worldwide. English teaching in Georgia, Korea, China, and Thailand.

CCUSA (Camp Counselors USA) (www.ccusa.com). Work experience programmes in Australia/New Zealand, teaching in China, and summer camp counsellors in Russia and Croatia.

CDS International (+1 212 497 3500; www.cdsintl.org). Practical training internships for American students or recent graduates mainly in Germany but also in Spain, Argentina, Chile, and Switzerland.

CIEE-Portland (toll-free +1 800 40 STUDY; www.ciee.org/hsabroad/gap/index.html). Gap years or gap semesters for pre-university students arranged in China, Japan, Chile, the Dominican Republic, France, and Spain. Programme includes housing and meals with local families, language classes, and English teaching internship or community service. Prices from about US$12,000 for one semester. Also organise teach abroad programmes for graduates in Chile, China, Korea, Vietnam, Thailand, Spain, and the Dominican Republic (www.ciee.org/teach).

City Year (www.cityyear.org). Community service and leadership development for young people of all backgrounds, ages 17–24, for a demanding year of community service in 19 US communities and in Johannesburg, South Africa.

Cross-Cultural Solutions, New Rochelle, New York (+1 800 380 4777; www. crossculturalsolutions. org). Volunteers work side-by-side with local people on community-led initiatives in the areas of care-giving, teaching, healthcare, and community development in Africa, Asia, Eastern Europe, and Latin America.

Cultural Embrace, Austin, Texas (+1 512 469 9089; www.culturalembrace.com). Internships, volunteer teaching, and work programmes in lots of countries.

Dynamy, Worcester, Massachusetts (+1 508 755 2571; www.dynamy.org). Residential internship year for up to 40 people aged 17–22; Outward Bound expedition, community service and optional college credit. Tuition for 9-month programme is $18,000 plus housing $7,000+; for one semester fees are half as much. Scholarships are available.

Earthwatch Institute (+1 800 776 0188; www.earthwatch.org). An international environmental charity that engages people worldwide in scientific field research and education to promote the understanding and action necessary for a sustainable environment. Earthwatch recruits 3,000 volunteers a year to assist scientific field research projects around the world. Prices range from $759 to $5,750, excluding travel to the location.

Educators Abroad (www.educatorsabroad.org). English as a Foreign Language Teaching Assistant placement programme open to gap year students among others. Participants are sent to 25 countries on all continents for 4–10 weeks throughout the year. Total costs from $3,000 for 4 weeks, plus $500 placement fee. Host schools assist with arrangements for accommodation and board.

EIL (Experiment in International Living), Vermont (+1 800 345 2929; www.experiment international.org). Programmes lasting 3–5 weeks include some language training.

Experiential Learning International, Denver, Colorado (+1 303 321 8278; www.eliabroad.com). Immersion, intern, and volunteering programmes in 22 countries in South and Central America, Africa, Asia, and Europe.

Explorations in Travel, Guildford, Vermont (www.volunteertravel.com). International volunteers for rainforest conservation, wildlife, community, and many other projects worldwide.

Foundation for Sustainable Development, San Francisco, California (+1 415 283 4873; www.fsdinternational.org). Short summer and longer-term internships for anyone over 18 in the field of development in Argentina, Bolivia, India, Kenya, Nicaragua, and Uganda. Volunteers in Latin America will be usually expected to converse in Spanish. Prices from $4,100 for 9 weeks.

GeoVisions, Connecticut (www.geovisions.org). Volunteer or teach abroad in range of countries from Russia to Jordan.

Global Citizens Network, Minneapolis (+1 800 644 9292; www.globalcitizens.org). Volunteer vacations in Kenya, Nepal, Mexico, Guatemala, Peru, Tanzania, and others.

Global Crossroad, Irving, Texas (+1 866 387 7816; www.globalcrossroad.com). Volunteer teaching and internships in 23 countries. Paid teaching in China (1–12 months). Application fee of $350 plus placement fees, eg $1,024 for 6 weeks in China.

Global Experiences, www.globalexperiences.com. Range of customised international internships for university-level students and recent graduates in Ireland, Italy, France, Spain, UK, and Australia. Internships are available in nearly all career fields and include accommodation, for-credit components, on-site support, and more. Sample price 12 weeks in Florence for $8,490 (autumn 2011).

Global Intern (+1 973 537 6800; www.theglobalintern.com). Professional internships arranged in UK, Israel, Italy, and China. Placement fees $2,300 excluding accommodation.

Global Learning Across Borders (+1 800 984 4522; www.global-lab.org). International cultural immersion, experiential education, and community service programmes for young adults aged 16–22 and others. Semester programmes in Morocco, India, China/Tibet, and Greece.

Global Routes, Northampton, Massachusetts (+1 413 585 8895; www.globalroutes.org). Offers 12-week voluntary internships to students over 17 for teaching English and other subjects in village schools in Kenya, Costa Rica, Ecuador, and India. Participation fee $5,950 (6 weeks) to $9,750 (12 weeks).

Global Service Corps, San Francisco (+1 415 551 0000; www.globalservicecorps.org). Co-operates with grassroots organisations in Thailand, Cambodia, and Tanzania, and sends volunteers and interns for two or three weeks or longer.

Global Visions International, Boston, Massachusetts (+1 888 653 6028; www.gviusa.com). Large range of expeditions and volunteer projects worldwide (see entry in 'Directory of Specialist Gap Year Programmes').

Global Volunteers, St Paul, Minnesota (+1 800 487 1074; www.globalvolunteers.org). 'Granddaddy of the volunteer vacation movement'.

ICADS, San José, Costa Rica (+1 506 2225 0508; www.icads.org). Institute for Central American Development Studies, which combines study of the Spanish language and development issues with structured internships in Costa Rica and Nicaragua lasting a semester ($10,950) or a summer ($4,650).

Institute for Cultural Ecology, Hilo, Hawaii (+1 808 854 9806; www.cultural-ecology.com). Academic internships in Fiji, Thailand, Hawaii, and others, working on marine biology projects, environmental advocacy or custom-designed projects in student's major. 4, 6, 8, or 12 weeks. Sample fees: $1,895 for 4 weeks, $3,850 for 12 weeks, eg reef protection on the Fiji coast.

InterExchange, New York (+1 212 924 0446; www.interexchange.org). Homestay tutors in Spain; au pair placements in France, Germany, Netherlands, Spain, Norway, Turkey, Australia, and New Zealand; short-term work in Australia and New Zealand; volunteer opportunities in Ghana, India, Peru, Ecuador, Costa Rica, Argentina, and Australia. Fees from $495 for au pair placements.

International Co-operative Education, Menlo Park, California (+1 650 323 4944; www.icemenlo.com). Arranges paid and unpaid summer internships in England, Germany, Switzerland, Belgium, Singapore, Japan, China, Australia, Tanzania, Mongolia, Argentina, etc. Jobs include retail sales, banking, computer technology, hotels and restaurants, offices, etc.; most require knowledge of relevant language. Placement fee is $1,250 plus application fee of $250.

International Cultural Adventures (+1 888 339 0460; www.ICAdventures.com). Cultural, educational and volunteer service experiences in Peru and Nepal. Fees for 6-week summer programmes from $3,900 and from $5,450 for 12-week extended programmes beginning in February/March and September.

Kibbutz Program Center, New York (+1 212 462 2764; www.kibbutzprogramcenter.org). Volunteer placement service for candidates aged 19–35 on Israeli kibbutzim, $600 fee.

Knowledge Exchange, New York (+1 800 831 5095; www.keiabroad.org). Study and intern abroad programme for students including pre-college. Subject-specific internship placement and professional opportunities available in many countries.

Living Routes, Amherst (+1 888 515 7333; www.LivingRoutes.org). Semester, summer, and year-abroad programmes based in eco-villages around the world, that help people of all ages gain the knowledge, skills, and inspiration to build a sustainable lifestyle. Current programmes in India, Scotland, Israel, USA, Mexico, Brazil, Peru, Costa Rica, and Australia.

Map the Gap International, Connecticut (+1 203 672 5950/866 356 7120 (toll-free); www.map thegapinternational.com). Programmes in Italy ($13,450), Nicaragua, and Mexico.

Mountbatten Internship Programme, New York (+1 212 557 5380; www.mountbatten.org). Postgraduate Certificate in International Business Practice offered in London, combined with internships; open to American graduates. 12 months. Participation fee is $10,000.

Nikitas Language Abroad Schools, New York (+1 646 502 8677; www.nik-las.com). Internship and language study programmes in Italy, Spain, Portugal, and France.

Pacific Challenge, Eugene, Oregon (www.pacificchallenge.org). 56-day travel programmes through New Zealand/Australia.

Peace Corps, Washington, DC (+1 800 424 8580; www.peacecorps.gov). Sends volunteers on 2-year assignments to 70 countries.

Projects Abroad, New York (toll-free +1 888 839 3535; info@projects-abroad.org). US office of British counterpart (see 'Directory of Specialist Gap Year Programmes').

ProWorld Service Corps (+1 877 429 6753; www.proworldvolunteers.org). Offers a range of internships in fields from business to journalism, lasting 2–26 weeks with aid agencies in Peru, Belize, Mexico, Brazil, India, Thailand, and Ghana. Fees start at $1,895 which include project work with local NGOs, language training, room and board, and cultural activities. ProWorld has a UK contact number +44 (0)1865 596289.

SCI-IVS (Service Civil International-International Voluntary Service) (+1 206 350 6585; www.sci-ivs.org). International workcamps.

SWAP (Student Work Abroad Program) (+1 416 996 2887; swapinfo@swap.ca, www.swap.ca). Administered by the Canadian Federation of Students. Co-ordinates a working holiday programme for Canadian students and non-students in the UK, Ireland, France, Germany, Austria, New Zealand, Australia, Japan, and South Africa. Has a dedicated website – www.gapyearabroad.ca.

Thinking Beyond Borders (www.thinkingbeyondborders.org). Programme designed for gap year students to explore international development through global service learning and academic study. $39,000 for 35-week programme. Also offer gap semester in Ecuador ($19,000).

United Planet, Boston, Massachusetts (+1 800 292 2316; www.unitedplanet.org). International volunteering opportunities lasting up to 12 weeks or 6–12 months.

Visions Service Adventures (+1 800 813 9283; www.visionsserviceadventures.com). Summer volunteering programmes for people aged 16–25 in the Dominican Republic, Guadeloupe, the British Virgin Islands, and many other countries, which cost from $4,900 for one month.

Volunteers for Peace (www.vfp.org). Annual membership $30. Volunteers For Peace publishes an online International Workcamp Directory with more than 2,500 listings in nearly 100 countries, available from early April. Registration for most programmes is $300 ($500+ if under 18).

Where There Be Dragons, Boulder, Colorado (+1 800 982 9203; www.wheretherebedragons.com). Gap year semester programmes (12 weeks starting February or September) in Asia, Africa and Latin America (aimed at 15–22 years olds). Also 6-week summer programmes for ages 15–18 in a range of developing countries.

Wildlands Studies (+1 831 477 9955; www.wildlandsstudies.com). Conservation projects lasting 6 weeks in the USA (including Alaska and Hawaii), Belize, Thailand, Nepal, etc.

WISE (Worldwide International Student Exchange) (+1 731 287 9948; www.wisefoundation. com). Academic year abroad (ages 15–18) in Germany, Austria, Denmark, Japan, and Brazil for 5 or 10 months.

World Endeavors, Minneapolis, Minnesota (+1 612 729 3400; www.worldendeavors.com). Volunteer, internship, and study programmes lasting 2 weeks to 3 months in many countries. Sample price for volunteer teaching in India: $1,795 for 8 weeks.

WorldTeach Inc, Cambridge, Massachusetts (+1 617 495 5527; www.worldteach.org). Nonprofit organisation that provides college graduates with one-year English teaching contracts in American Samoa, Bangladesh, Chile, China, Costa Rica, Ecuador, Guyana, Kenya, the Marshall Islands, Mongolia, Namibia, Pohnpei, Rwanda, South Africa, and Venezuela. 8-week summer programmes in Bulgaria, China, Costa Rica, Ecuador, Namibia, Poland, and South Africa. Participants pay a volunteer contribution ranging from $500 to $7,990, but several programmes are fully funded by the host country.

Your World to Discover, Richmond Hill, Ontario (www.yourworldtodiscover.ca). Range of gap year and volunteering programmes.

Youth Challenge International, Toronto, Canada (+1 416 504 3370; www.yci.org). Teams of volunteers carry out community development projects lasting from 5–12 weeks in Costa Rica, Guyana, Nicaragua, and a number of others. Sample fundraising required: C$3,100 for 5 weeks in Guyana, C$3,800 for 10 weeks in Ghana.

Youth International (Experience the World), Gravenhurst, Ontario, Canada (+1 416 538 0152; www.youthinternational.org). One-semester programmes to Asia, Africa and South America for people 18–25 of any nationality; US$9,900.

The first organisation that American volunteers think of is the Peace Corps (www.peacecorps.gov), which sends both skilled and unskilled volunteers on two-year assignments to scores of countries. **Kristie McComb** was posted to Burkina Faso and gradually concluded that the Peace Corps programme places less emphasis on development than on cultural exchange, ie sharing American culture with the host country nationals, and then sharing the culture of the host country with Americans on their return home:

> *The cool thing for Americans is that you don't have to be qualified in anything to be accepted by the Peace Corps. There are many generalist programmes where you can learn what you need to know once you get there through the three-month pre-service training. I would encourage interested parties to be honest about what they can and cannot tolerate since not all volunteers are sent to live in mud huts. In a world changed by terrorism it is comforting to know how much of an active interest the US government takes in the safety and well-being of its citizens abroad. However, some people might find this stifling and not adventurous enough. How well the Peace Corps keeps tabs on volunteers in any given country depends on the local Corps leadership but, regardless, you are still in a high-profile group of well locatable people. Risk reduction is the buzzword in Washington these days.*
>
> *Overall, I am happy with my experience, though I am often frustrated by the inertia, the corruption and bureaucracy that makes me question whether anything will ever change. But you do gain a lot by (if nothing else) witnessing poverty on a regular basis. You quickly learn to recognise the difference between a problem and an inconvenience, and to see how lucky we are as Americans to have some of the 'problems' we have.*

LANGUAGE COURSES FOR NORTH AMERICANS

At a time when Americans seem to be reaching out under Barack Obama, going abroad to learn or improve a foreign language may have special appeal. Classroom learning has its place. But it is axiomatic that the fastest progress will be made when you are forced to use a language in everyday situations, both at home and work. Programmes that combine structured study of a language or culture with volunteering are arguably a paradigm of the kind of foreign travel experience, which can more than justify taking a year out before proceeding to college. Many organisations, both international and local, can arrange such placements, often in conjunction with a homestay to maximise exposure to the language.

Using a mediating agency simplifies the process of choosing a language school, since they tend to deal with well-established schools and programmes on the ground. These agencies also provide a useful back-up service if something goes wrong. An effective US-based search engine for locating courses is provided by the Institute of International Education at www.iiepassport.org. Alternatives are www.abroadlanguages.com and www.worldwide.edu.

Here is a list of language course providers and agents of possible interest to North Americans planning a gap year.

AmeriSpan (+1 800 879 6640; www.amerispan.com). Language training organisation that started as a Latin America specialist, but now offers programmes worldwide learning 10 languages.

Bridge-Linguatec (www.bridge.edu). Language courses in nearly 50 cities around the world.

Center for Cultural Interchange, Chicago (+1 888-ABROAD (227623) 1; www.cci-exchange.com). Language courses, volunteering and internship programmes in many countries. High-school semester or year abroad in Australia, and a number of European countries.

Eduvacations, Washington, DC (+1 202 857 8384; www.eduvacations.com). Travel company specialising in customised language courses combined with sports, art instruction, etc, throughout Europe, Latin America, the Caribbean, Russia, the USA, etc.

Language Liaison (+1 800 284 4448; www.languageliaison.com). Total immersion language/culture study programmes and leisure learning courses.

Language Link (+1 800 552 2051; www.langlink.com). Long-established agency that represents dozens of Spanish language schools in Spain and Latin America.

The Learning Traveller, Toronto, Canada (+1 888 386 1411; www.learningtraveller.com). Agent for many language schools worldwide.

Lexia International, Hanover, New Hampshire (+1 800 775 3942; www.lexiaintl.org). Overseas academic programmes, which include intensive language study, civilisation course, research methodology course, academic research project, elective course, internships, and community service projects in Barcelona, Berlin, Budapest, Buenos Aires, Cape Town, Chiang Mai, Istanbul, Krakow, London, Paris, Prague, Rome, Shanghai, and Venice.

Lingua Service Worldwide, Connecticut (+1 800 394 5327; www.linguaserviceworldwide.com). Represents range of private language schools at all levels.

National Registration Center for Study Abroad, Milwaukee (414 278 0631; ww.nrcsa.com). Full language and culture immersion and other courses offered at 125 language schools and universities in 42 countries. Varying lengths of stay. Gap year students going on to university may be able to gain credit.

University Studies Abroad Consortium, University of Nevada, Reno (+1 775 784 6569; http://usac.unr.edu). University-accredited courses in Spanish, Basque, Chinese, Danish, and many other languages, plus art history, business, communications, etc.

PAID SEASONAL JOBS

ANYWORK ANYWHERE

Anywork Anywhere provides an online Job Search, Volunteer Guides and Resources for Work & Travel throughout Europe and Worldwide, via the website www.anyworkanywhere.com.

It is free to search and apply for jobs, as well as to access the resources sections, with no need to register first. Many jobs provide accommodation and sometimes meals as well. You may need to turn up for a face to face interview, but many employers are willing to interview over the phone, accompanied by a solid CV and checkable references.

Whilst the majority of positions are full-time temporary, with contracts running from a couple of weeks to 12 months, there are also a handful of advertised permanent positions, and it's not unlikely – where the employee/employer relationship has been good – for some 3/5-month summer/winter positions to turn into long-term working relationships.

You could find work in Summer Resorts, Ski Resorts, Fruit Picking & Packing, Pubs & Bars, Catering, TEFL, Education, Hotels, Entertainment, Activity Centres, Voluntary & Conservation, Holiday & Theme Parks, Care Work, Childcare and other varied and exciting opportunities we come across which we feel are interesting and of value to the site…

If you fancy something with a little moral depth, there are an abundance of Voluntary opportunities, with a wide range of fees to suit all budgets. Either going via a mainstream "Western World" based organisation, many of which you would have heard of already, or for the more adventurous, going direct to a local NGO or even smaller project on the ground, we try to maintain a balance of the two, knowing that everyone has their own ideal environment for this kind of expeditionary experience.

The site is vast. As well as listing Jobs or Voluntary opportunities, our comprehensive Guides section has lots of helpful info on Visas, Working Holiday Visas and other varied Work & Travel resources. From our embassy directory, listed by host country, easy to navigate map links, country specific links sections, voluntary guides and training & courses from snowboarding to cookery – find all this and much, much, more.

The fastest way to save money is of course to live at home, and find a job that pays more than the national minimum wage and has scope for working lots of overtime. Some students register with a local temp agency and request as many hours as possible, or simply find the highest paying job locally that will involve the least expenditure. In addition to allowing you to save for your gap year project, doing a dull, unskilled job might have other benefits, as **Alice Mundy** discovered when she spent months at a motorway services working in the restaurant area; as it was a short walk from her home, it required no outlay in petrol, and helped her save for a snowboard instructor's course in Canada:

Probably the lowest point of my gap year was working in certain jobs where there were a lot of people who didn't enjoy their work and so didn't put much effort in, but at the same time lacked either the resources or the ambition to do anything about changing it. However, on the positive side of that, my gap year has certainly highlighted for me just how lucky I am to have the opportunity of higher education, a privilege that a lot of people in the world don't have. This has definitely encouraged me to make the most of the next three years at university.

The majority of gappers work locally in the autumn to fund travels or foreign projects after Christmas. With dedication and self-denial, it is amazing how fast you can hit your target, as **Melissa Evans** testifies: '*Financing my gap year was fairly difficult, and it required long hours and very minimal spending. I had two jobs that I worked full-time, one in a call centre 9–5 Monday to Friday, and any overtime; then a job in a pub as a barmaid on Saturdays and Sundays in addition to three or four other shifts during the week. I worked approximately 13 hours a day 5 days a week, and also weekends. This allowed me to raise the money I needed quickly. I started the jobs in the September and by December I had paid for my flights and travel for 7 months away from home.*'

If you can manage to do it the other way round, you will probably find it much easier to land a job. For example, **Ed Fry** scraped and borrowed to fund a sailing course in Australia between September and January and then returned to London, where he found that so many of his contemporaries had taken off on their own gap years that finding a job was a piece of cake.

If the time comes when you can't stand the sight of the same old high street or the same old workmates, and want a complete break while still earning, you might want to consider some of the suggestions canvassed in this chapter. Although it is more difficult to save if working away from home, hotel work sometimes comes with meals and accommodation, and can be a more interesting way to save than the usual range of local jobs in stores, restaurants, and offices. **Mark Smith** ended up really enjoying the saving part of his gap year:

I worked at the Gleneagles Hotel in Perthshire. I wanted somewhere that I could both work and stay so I thought big hotels were a good idea. It was fantastic. I found that this was a great way to make money without having to spend a lot. They always need staff, you can stay in staff accommodation for really cheap, and just earn loads of money while having a great experience too. I hunted around a few other hotels and it can be a bit tedious applying, but there are loads of them about and a lot of the staff are temporary, only staying for six months or so at a time. This was all part of the gap year experience for me. I always thought this would be the boring bit that I had to endure in order to go on my travels but it turned out to be just as fun and rewarding as the trip itself. Living and working away from home was an absolute blast, and I made good friends and gained valuable experience.

Depending on the time of year, you may be able to arrange a short sharp change of routine by, say, working at a Scottish country house hotel over Christmas or going to pick grapes in France or Switzerland in September. The possibilities are so numerous that this chapter can only skim the surface. For much more comprehensive listings of seasonal jobs, look at *Work Your Way Around the World 2011/12*.

While opening up an enormous range of possibilities, the internet can be a bewildering place to hunt for a job. One of the best specialist recruitment websites is www.seasonworkers.com, a site that has been designed to help people find a summer job, outdoor sports job, gap year project, or ski resort job quickly and easily. Another website that can prove invaluable for job-seeking travellers is the free and non-commercial Jobs Abroad Bulletin website (www.jobsabroadbulletin.co.uk), which will send a free monthly jobs listing by email to subscribers. A sample issue from summer 2011 included advertisements for maintenance staff for a villa in the south of France, volunteers to earn a free holiday in Poland by speaking English to Polish businesspeople, and a range of teaching, au pairing, and other vacancies worldwide.

Otherwise, try www.anyworkanywhere.com, www.gapwork.com, www.kareeve.com, www.job monkey.com (especially for North America), www.hotrecruit.com, and so on. Everywhere you look on the internet, potentially useful links can be found. A surprising number of company home pages feature an icon you can click to find out about jobs, recruitment, or careers. The site www.euro summerjobs.com is a search engine for summer jobs abroad. Registration on sites such as www. justjobs4students.co.uk is usually free of charge . . . but you will soon see your inbox cluttered up with quite a high proportion of unsuitable jobs!

Among the kinds of firm that recruit quite aggressively (possibly because there is such a high turnover) are 'charity fundraising' firms. Ads may catch your eye, such as 'The Ultimate Gap Year Job – Charity Fundraising with Wesser – earn £1,400 a month'. Wesser (www.wesser.co.uk) has teamed up with some gap year agencies to offer a combined programme whereby students work for Wesser in the UK to fund a gap year scheme abroad (www.thegapyearjob.co.uk).

The commercial companies hired by both mainstream and smaller charities to raise money on the streets of British cities or door-to-door take a very significant cut from the sign-ups, which some young recruits have found disillusioning. Flow Caritas (www.flowcaritas.co.uk), Inspired People (www. inspiredpeople.org), Tim Lilley Fundraising (www.tlfc.org/fundraising-jobs), and others use worthy-sounding lines such as 'championing the search for a better world' in their bid to hire an army of young people to accost passers-by and try to persuade them to sign direct debit donation forms. This activity has been dubbed 'charity mugging', and hence employees are sometimes referred to as 'chuggers'. Unless you are a gifted salesperson, it is very difficult to get into the high-earning area, and in fact it is possible to make a loss. In some cases, if you don't meet your target of 20 sign-ups a week, then you don't get your basic salary and you have to pay the accommodation charge. If considering this job, check out feedback online, such as on Facebook or www.thestudentroom.co.uk.

Employees are moved from town to town and given shared accommodation, so it can suit a foreigner on a working holiday. Eighteen-year-old **David Cox** from Ontario was hired soon after arriving in London. He was invited to attend a day's training in Oxford before being dispatched to his first location, and looked forward to a chance to see different places:

The last three weeks have been very interesting, but I'm starting to get into the swing of things. So far I've been posted in Brighton, Portsmouth, and Newcastle, and am leaving for Manchester tonight. I love the job but it's literally 7 days a week and can be very stressful, so I'm looking forward to time off; I'm going to Norway in 2 weeks.

Not everybody ends up loving the job by any means. **Anna Ling** was attracted partly by idealism to do this job in Bristol, but came to consider it iniquitous since so much of the money raised goes to the 'middle-men'. She was paid £4 an hour plus a commission per donor.

Working for a local employer abroad is arguably one of the best ways of getting inside a culture, though the kind of job you find will determine the stratum of society that you experience. The student who spends a few weeks picking fruit in Canada will get a very different insight into North American culture from the one who looks after the children of a Texan millionaire. Yet both will have the chance to participate temporarily in the life of a culture and get to know one place well.

Most gap year students looking for holiday jobs abroad will have to depend on the two industries that survive on seasonal labour: tourism and agriculture. School leavers and their parents will probably feel happier with a pre-arranged job, possibly with a British tour operator, but that does limit the choice. Like job-hunting in any context, the competition for seasonal work will be hard to beat unless you are available for interview. If looking for farm work or a berth on a transatlantic yacht, a visit to a village pub frequented by farmers or yachties is worth dozens of speculative applications from home.

The other major fields of paid overseas employment for students are au pairing (see separate chapter) and English teaching (discussed below, and also in the relevant country chapters). The more unusual and interesting the job the more competition it will attract. For example, it is to be assumed that only a small percentage of applicants for advertised jobs actually gets the chance to work as underwater photographic models in the Caribbean, guides for a European tour company or assistants at a museum bookshop in Paris.

TOURISM

Hotels, restaurants, pubs, and campsites from Cannes to Canada depend on transient workers. Anyone with some home-town restaurant experience and perhaps some knowledge of a second language should be able to fix up a summer job in a European resort. If you secure a hotel job without speaking the language of the country and lacking relevant experience, you will probably be placed at the bottom of the pecking order, eg in the laundry or washing dishes.

Even if the job is fairly grim, you will probably collect some good anecdotes, as **S C Firn** did in an upmarket restaurant in Oberstdorf in the Bavarian Alps:

I had to peel vegetables, wash dishes, prepare food, clean the kitchen and sometimes serve food. Everything was done at a very fast pace, and was expected to be very professional. One German cook aged 16, who didn't come up to standard, was punched in the face three times by the owner. On another occasion, the assistant chef had a container of hot carrots tipped over his head for having food sent back. During my three months there, all the other British workers left, apart from the chef, but were always replaced by more.

So if you can't stand the heat . . . read on.

AGENCIES AND WEBSITES

The earlier you decide to apply for seasonal hotel work, the better are your chances. Hotels in a country such as Switzerland recruit months before the summer season, and it is advisable to contact as many hotel addresses as possible by March, preferably in their own language. A knowledge of more than one language is an immense asset for work in Europe. Those who have a GCSE or A level in German are at a particular advantage since many tourist resorts in Spain, Italy, and Greece cater mainly to a German clientele, so they like their staff to be able to communicate. Do not put too much faith in sending out a shower of speculative emails since these are routinely ignored by employers.

Specialist recruitment websites can be invaluable, such as those mentioned above, eg www.seasonworkers.com. Dozens of other sites may prove useful such as www.seasonal-jobs.com (formerly www.voovs.com), www.resortjobs.co.uk, and www.natives.co.uk.

Wherever there is a demand for jobs, there will be an agency charging clients to make the necessary arrangements. Air-Pro Working Holidays in Wembley (020 8123 7693; www.air-pro.co.uk) arranges for sun-worshipping party types to find work in Tenerife, Magaluf, Ibiza, and the other usual suspects (Malia and Ayia Napa in Cyprus). Punters pay £68 to register, and from £329 low season to £439 high season for a 'resort and reps' fee' to cover four weeks' accommodation plus assistance with the job hunt (but no guarantees).

On the other hand you might not be able to plan so far ahead, or you may have no luck with advance applications, so it will be necessary to look for work once you've arrived in a foreign country. All but the most desperate employers are far more willing to consider a candidate who is standing there in the flesh than one who sends in a CV out of the blue.

Two of the most useful tools in the jobseeker's repertoire are the free community noticeboards gumtree and Craigslist; the latter started in San Francisco in 1995, but has spread to hundreds of cities from Auckland to Buenos Aires, Moscow to Cairo. With notification of about half a million new job ads a month, it is probably the biggest job board in the world, as well as carrying accommodation listings and everything else. It also lists many unpaid jobs, internships, and pseudo-jobs (eg exchanging labour for accommodation).

Hotels represent just one aspect of the tourist trade, and many more interesting venues exist for cooking and serving, including luxury yachts, prawn trawlers, holiday ranches, safari camps, and ski chalets. People with some training in catering will find it much easier to find a lucrative job abroad than most. When applying for jobs which are not seasonal, you should stress that you intend to work for an indefinite period, make a career of fast food catering, etc. In fact staff turnover is usually very high. This will also aid your case when you are obliged to badger them to give you extra hours.

A good way of gaining initial experience is to work for a large organisation with huge staff requirements, such as PGL Adventure (www.pgl.co.uk/recruitment) in Britain and Europe, and Village Camps (www.villagecamps.ch) in Europe. Since they have so many vacancies (most of which pay only pocket money), the chances of being hired for a first season are reasonably good.

Mark Warner (020 7795 8375; www.markwarner.co.uk/recruitment) is a leading tour operator with resort hotels located around the Mediterranean and Aegean, and chalet hotels in top ski resorts in the Alps. The company recruits staff to work in Greece, Turkey, Corsica, Sardinia, and Italy for the summer season, and in Austria, France and Italy for the ski season. Positions are open for chefs, restaurant and bar staff, nursery nurses and children's activity leaders, watersport, tennis and aerobics instructors, pool attendants, customer service and shop staff, ski hosts, and many others. Employees are provided with a competitive package including full board, medical insurance, travel expenses, use of watersport and activity facilities (summer) and ski pass, skis and boots (winter).

CAMPSITE COURIERS

British camping holiday firms hire large numbers of people to remain on one campsite throughout Europe for several months. Holidaybreak (www.holidaybreakjobs.com) alone recruits about 1,800 campsite couriers and children's couriers for the self-drive camping brands Eurocamp and Keycamp. The courier's job is to clean the tents and caravans between visitors, greet clients, deal with difficulties (particularly illness or car breakdowns), and introduce clients to the attractions of the area, or even arrange and host social functions and amuse the children. All of this will be rewarded with, on average, £135 a week, in addition to free tent accommodation. Many companies offer half-season contracts April to mid-July and mid-July to the end of September. The massive camping holiday industry generates winter work as well; see France chapter for description of work with Brad Europe.

Some camping holiday and tour operators based in Britain are as follows (also listing the European countries in which they are active):

Canvas Holidays, Dunfermline, Scotland (01383 629 012; www.canvasholidaysrecruitment.com). Mainly France but also Germany, Switzerland, Italy, Netherlands, and Spain.

Club Cantabrica Holidays, St Albans, Hertfordshire (01727 866 177; www.cantabrica.co.uk). France, Austria, and Spain. Summer and winter positions.

Eurocamp (Overseas Recruitment Department) (01606 787 525; www.holidaybreakjobs.com). Up to 1,500 staff for 200 campsites in most European countries. Applications accepted from October. Interviews held in Hartford, Cheshire, over the winter.

Keycamp Holidays, Overseas Recruitment Department, Northwich, Cheshire (01606 787 525; www. holidaybreakjobs.com). Operate in most European countries.

Siblu Holidays (HR Department), Hemel Hempstead (01442 293 230; www.siblu.com). Park reps and children's courier staff for France.

Vacansoleil, Eindhoven, Netherlands (+31 040 844 7748; camping-jobs@vacansoleil.com; www.campingjobs.nl (in Dutch only)). Supplies summer staff to campsites around France, Spain, Italy, Denmark, Belgium, Holland, and many others.

Caroline Nicholls' problems at a campsite in Brittany included frequent power failures, blocked loos, and leaking tents, though most of the sites belonging to the established companies are well-managed with clean and functioning facilities:

> *Every time there was a steady downpour one of the tents developed an indoor lake, due to the unfortunate angle at which we had pitched it. I would appear, mop in hand, with cries of 'I don't understand. This has never happened before.' Working as a courier would be a good grounding for an acting career.*

Caroline goes on to say that despite enjoying being around the client families, she was glad to have the use of a company bicycle to escape the insular life on the campsite every so often. Some companies guarantee one day off-site, which is considered essential for maintaining sanity. The companies do vary in the conditions of work, and some offer much better support than others. For example, a company for which **Hannah Start** worked ignored her pleas for advice and assistance when one of her clients had appendicitis.

The big companies interview hundreds of candidates and have filled most posts by the end of January. But there is a very high drop-out rate (over 50%), and vacancies are filled from a reserve list, so it is worth ringing around the companies as late as April for cancellations. Despite competition, anyone who has studied a European language and has an outgoing personality stands a good chance if he or she applies early and widely enough.

ACTIVITY HOLIDAYS

UK SAILING ACADEMY

The Watersports Industry Needs You!

There is an increasing demand for enthusiastic and skilled watersports instructors, with supply currently failing to keep up with demand. People with the right attitude and qualifications can gain employment in destinations across the world, including the Mediterranean, Caribbean, and Red Sea, with plentiful opportunities for promotion to watersports and resort managers.

The UK Sailing Academy (UKSA) is a non-profit organisation aimed at supporting young people from all social environments to gain the skills and qualifications needed for a rewarding and fun career on the water. Our Watersports Instructor Training course is one of the many career-training paths designed for anyone seeking an exciting job that could take them around the world, or for those who are looking to take their passion for watersports to instructor level. Our students are drawn from a wide range of backgrounds, including the underprivileged, those sponsored by the Prince's Trust, mature students who want a change of lifestyle, and those with learning difficulties such as dyslexia, who often have excellent communication skills, a quality essential for those wishing to get a job in the watersports industry.

The Watersports Instructor Training course is an 11-week programme, based in either the UK or Egypt, and allows you to train as an instructor in a range of disciplines such as dinghy sailing, kayaking, and windsurfing. The opportunity to train overseas will help prepare you for work in a different country, while training on the Isle of Wight will provide great opportunities and access to a variety of locations and water conditions, whatever the weather!

The UKSA is a world leader in instructing and coaching watersports, giving you access to the best equipment and instructors. We offer personal mentoring and careers guidance, giving industry-specific, one-to-one advice on CV preparation and interview techniques. Our 3.5-acre site at Cowes offers accommodation for up to 170 people, with wi-fi access and en-suite facilities for those on residential courses. The Nelson's bar, overlooking the waterfront, is a busy hub of activity, screening sporting events and featuring live bands throughout the year, giving you the chance to relax and socialise with like-minded people. All courses include food and accommodation and access to the best facilities.

Other courses offered by the UKSA include our Watersports Internship, training you to instructor level in multiple disciplines, and providing you with your first season's experience, paid and under instructor guidance. This gives you the opportunity to upgrade your qualifications to teach higher-level courses, while working as part of one of Europe's largest residential sailing centres. Our Kitesurf Instructor Training will help you to develop your passion in this extreme sport to BKSA instructor level in five weeks. Growth in the popularity of kitesurfing has led to a huge increase in demand for skilled instructors worldwide who excel at this high-adrenaline sport.

Some of the UKSA's recent graduates are now instructing in locations such as Australia, Thailand and the Caribbean. Watersports Instructor Training is not only great for a gap year or career break, but for those who have decided not to go on to university. What better way to travel and get paid throughout the long summer holidays? Simon Davies, UKSA's Director of Youth Development, comments: 'You're doing what you love doing and every day is different. The people change and the wind and weather are never the same on two consecutive days.'

www.uksa.org/yourgapyear

FLYING FISH

19-year-old James from Chepstow spent his gap year on the beach, getting paid to windsurf.

After windsurfing on holiday, I thought it would be fun to become an instructor during my gap year. The Flying Fish course in Sydney was particularly appealing, as it gave me the chance to do much more than just windsurf.

I had maybe four weeks' windsurfing experience when I joined the course, although several people in my group had never windsurfed before and still passed. It doesn't matter if you don't have any experience, although I would recommend you try the sport first to make sure you like it!

Living in Manly was awesome. We were really close to the RYA [Royal Yachting Association] centre where we were training, it was only a 10-minute ferry ride to Sydney city centre, and a short walk to one of the top surfing beaches. The people I was staying with were also really cool, there was a great mix of people, from gappers like me to folk considering a career change after working in the City for a few years.

Our Flying Fish instructor was an outstanding windsurfer and coach, and windsurfing around Sydney Harbour was amazing. Learning to drive a powerboat past the Sydney Opera House and under Sydney Harbour Bridge, then having lunch opposite the Opera House on our own beach, are moments I don't think I will ever forget.

Obviously the qualification was valuable to my CV and employability but the experience of windsurfing and surfing every day with a brilliant group of people in one of the greatest cities in the world has to really be the most valuable thing I gained.

After I qualified, I applied for a job through the Flying Fish website, and immediately received an email asking me to come to an interview. I was offered the job at Mark Warner as a Windsurfing Instructor and given a choice of where I wanted to go.

Having spent a brilliant summer in Greece, I have come back to the UK to read Economics at the University of Birmingham. Next summer I plan to work in Egypt or Vass as a windsurfing instructor – or start an internship in the City. I think the internship may have to wait for another year!

Many specialist tour companies employ leaders for their tours, whether their clients are children or adults, on walking, cycling, and watersports holidays, etc. Any competent sailor, canoeist, diver, climber, rider, etc. should have no difficulty marketing their skills in the UK and abroad. Try, for example, Acorn Adventure (www.jobs-acorn.co.uk) or In2action based on the Isle of Wight (recruitment@in2action.co.uk), which recruit action teams to lead children in sports and activities at First Choice holiday resorts from Turkey to Tenerife. For more ideas, check the website www.adventurejobs.co.uk.

If you would like to do a watersports course with a view to working abroad, see the entries for Flying Fish and UK Sailing Academy in the 'Directory of Sport and Activity Courses'. They offer training as instructors in windsurfing, diving, dinghy sailing, and yachting, followed by a job recruitment service.

UK SAILING ACADEMY

Lucky William Satterly turned his talent and passion for watersports into a fantastic career, getting paid to travel to some of the most beautiful and exotic locations in the world.

Will was awarded a Prince's Trust scholarship with the UKSA, and successfully graduated from the Watersports Instructor Training course in Egypt as a 'windsurfing guru', in the words of his mentor.

Will spent four seasons at the UKSA as part of the watersports team, progressing to become the Senior Dinghy and Windsurfing Instructor. After two successful years as Senior Instructor, Will was promoted to Chief Instructor.

Will is now the Watersports Manager aboard a luxury superyacht, and is paid to travel to some of the most beautiful and exotic destinations worldwide, enjoying crystal clear waters, white sandy beaches, and always following the sun. With the help of the UKSA, Will realised his potential and talent on the water, turning his skills into a successful career with many opportunities, which surely beats a dull day stuck in an office.

www.uksa.org/yourgapyear

SKI RESORTS

OYSTER WORLDWIDE

I had always loved skiing and had a ski season on my to-do list for several years, so the opportunity to work with kids in one of the best ski resorts in North America and become a qualified ski instructor seemed too good to be true.

But it wasn't, so last year I found myself in Whistler, British Columbia, with 23 other 'Oysters', enthusiastically entering into the season.

We had training before being let loose on the mountain responsible for making skiers out of the little people in our charge. Everyone started out by teaching the 'never-evers' (kids that hadn't skied before), but by the end of the season we were teaching kids who could ski blue runs in parallel better than some of us may have started out!

Our days started with a morning meeting at 8.15am before the kids piled in. We'd then entertain them for a bit and give them a snack before following the rule of 'No pee, no ski'! Then we got out and began the skiing using our silliness and imaginations as much as possible to hold the kids' attentions and keep them having fun on their holidays! The day wound up at around 3.30pm, leaving time for a run or two before the lifts closed.

The work was great. We had a great team and I got on well with everyone I worked with. The supervisors were brilliant. They really cared how you were getting on, and supported you in your lessons if you had any worries. We had quite a few socials, and the training was amazing. You could have free lessons at any point in the season, as well as prep sessions for the certifications that you were thinking about doing. Pretty much everyone took their Level 1 ski instructor exam in early January, which meant that we were able to take the kids up on the chairlifts and get higher ability groups.

Compared to a ski instructor course, this trip wins hands–down. It worked out a lot cheaper – you could earn money at the same time and know that when you took your course you were ready and able to take and pass it. We also had a guaranteed job and accommodation, as well as access to some of the best instructors on the mountain.

Overall, I had an amazing time in Canada, and would highly recommend it to anyone thinking of doing a ski instructor course or a ski season abroad. Coming through Oyster was the only way we would have been able to get a job anywhere as a ski instructor without first having the qualification, so it was a fantastic placement. We had really good preparation, and it was great to have Tory, our rep, out there in case anything happened. I made some brilliant friends out there, lived and worked in another country, improved my skiing so much as well as fulfilling my ambition to work with kids in some way.

Thank you Oyster!

The winter season in the European Alps lasts from about Christmas until late April or early May. Between Christmas and New Year is a terrifically busy time, as are the middle two weeks of February during half-term. Because jobs in ski resorts are so popular among the travelling community, wages can be low. So many on gap years, as well as older students, are (or become) such avid skiers that in their view it is recompense enough to have easy access to the slopes during their time off. One of the best ways to improve your chances of being hired is to do a catering course, some of which specialise in ski chalet cooking (see 'Directory of Cookery Courses').

Specialist ski recruitment websites can be extremely helpful. Four excellent recruitment websites are www.natives.co.uk, www.seasonworkers.com, www.ski-jobs.co.uk, and www.freeradicals.co.uk, all of which describe themselves as one-stop shops for recruitment of winter staff for Europe or worldwide. Also check out www.snowworkers.com, which recently carried a number of ski resort jobs in Japan. Qualified or experienced nannies are especially sought after in the Alps and other resorts around the world.

You can either try to fix up a job with a British-based ski tour company before you leave (which has more security but lower wages and tends to isolate you in an English-speaking ghetto), or you can look for work on the spot. In the spring preceding the winter season in which you want to work, try to research ski tour companies (some of which are listed below). Their websites will describe the range of positions they wish to fill. These may vary slightly from company to company, but will probably include resort representatives (who may need language skills), chalet staff (who must be able to cook to a high standard), odd-jobbers, and ski guides/instructors. An increasing number of companies are offering nanny and crèche facilities, so this is a further possibility for the suitably qualified.

Listed below are some of the major ski tour companies in the UK. Some have a limited number of vacancies, which they can fill from a list of people who have worked for them during the summer season or have been personally recommended by former employees. So you should not be too disappointed if you are initially unsuccessful.

Hotelplan UK Group (which combines Inghams, Ski Esprit, and Ski Total), London SW15 (020 8780 4400; www.workaseason.com). Hundreds of chalets and chalet hotels requiring staff for winter season in France, Italy, Austria, and Switzerland. Perks include free ski pass, ski and boot hire, meals, accommodation, and return travel from the UK.

NBV Leisure, Bromley, Kent BN3 6BD (0870 220 2148; www.nbvleisure.com/recruitment.html). Catered chalet summer and winter holidays in France and Austria.

Neilson Overseas, Brighton BN2 5HA (www.neilson.co.uk/Recruitment-Overseas.aspx). Part of Thomas Cook Group. Resorts in Andorra, Austria, Bulgaria, Scandinavia, France, Italy, Switzerland, Canada, and the USA.

Powder Byrne, London SW15 6TG, (020 8246 5342; www.powderbyrne.com). Upmarket company operating in Switzerland, France, Italy, and Austria. Also recruits staff for summer resorts programme in Cyprus, Tunisia, etc.

Scott Dunn, London SW17 7PH, (www.scottdunn.com). Established in 1986; offers both summer and winter season recruitment.

Skibound (recruitment@tuiactivity.com; www.skibound.co.uk). Snow sports holidays for school parties.

Skiworld, London W6 9NU, (www.skiworld.ltd.uk). Catered chalet and hotel holidays in France, Austria, Switzerland, Canada, USA, and others.

Supertravel Ski (020 7962 9933; http://ski.supertravel.co.uk/seasonaljobs.aspx). Takes on winter staff for France, Switzerland, and Austria. All applicants must hold an EU passport and have a National Insurance number.

TUI Travel (020 8541 2223; www.jobsinwinter.co.uk). Three brands – Crystal Holidays, Thomson, and First Choice – make up the winter programme of mass tour operator TUI. Thousands of resort reps and chalet/hotel staff are hired for 140 ski resorts in Europe (especially France, Austria, and Italy) and North America (visa required).

VIPSki (www.vip-chalets.com). Employs scores of staff, especially in childcare. Usual minimum age 21.

You could attend the Metro Ski and Snowboard Show held each October at Olympia in London at which some ski companies hand out job descriptions and application forms. An added bonus is that you can attend the Natives Jobs Fair free at the same time.

A classic job for the gap year is as a 'chalet girl' or 'chalet boy'. The number of chalets in the Alps has hugely increased in recent years, with the biggest areas of expansion for British holidaymakers being Méribel, Courchevel, and Val d'Isère in France, Verbier in Switzerland, and St Anton in Austria. Clients in chalets are looked after by a chalet girl, or boy as is increasingly the case. The chalet host does everything (sometimes with an assistant), from cooking first-class meals for the 10 or so guests to clearing the snow from the footpath (or delegating that job). They are responsible for keeping the chalet clean, preparing breakfast, packed lunches, tea, and dinner, providing ice and advice, and generally keeping everybody happy.

Although this sounds an impossible regimen, many chalet hosts manage to fit in several hours of skiing in the middle of each day. The standards of cookery required vary from company to company according to the degree of luxury (ie the price) of the holidays. In most cases, you will have to cook a trial meal for the tour company before being accepted for the job, or at least submit detailed menu plans. Average pay for a chalet host starts at about £75 a week, plus perks including accommodation, food, and a ski pass (worth about £1,000 for the season). Recruitment of the 1,000+ chalet hosts needed in Europe gets under way in May or June, so early application is essential.

Eighteen-year-old **Dan Hanfling** baked a creditable cake for his interview in the autumn, and was pleased to be offered a chalet job. But on arriving in the Alps, he learned that chalet staff in their first season are not always assigned their own chalet, but are expected to service a number of them by carrying supplies, cleaning toilets, etc. This job was a lot less glamorous than he had imagined, and he returned to England after just a few weeks (to the consternation of his parents, who had booked a Christmas holiday in the same resort).

If you wait until you arrive to look for a ski resort job in the Alps, be prepared for lots of refusals. The situation is not as tight in resorts in Canada and New Zealand, so if you have a working holiday visa for those countries, you might try resorts like Whistler, Banff, and Queenstown (see chapters on the respective countries).

If you are already a good skier and interested in qualifying as an instructor, contact the British Association of Snowsport Instructors (BASI), or one of the gap year instructor courses such as Ski Le Gap, Peak Leaders, or the International Academy (see 'Directory of Sport and Activity Courses'). The recent explosion in snowboarding has resulted in many young people qualifying as instructors, though with not much demand, since snowboarders tend to be self-taught.

FARM WORK

Itinerant workers have traditionally travelled hundreds of miles to gather in the fruits of the land, from the tiny blueberry to the mighty watermelon. Living and working in rural areas is often a more authentic way of experiencing another culture than working in the tourist industry. The availability of harvesting work in Europe has been greatly reduced by the large numbers of Slovaks, Romanians, Albanians, etc. who have moved into every corner of Europe trying to earn the money their own struggling economies cannot provide.

To find out which farmers are short of help, check www.pickingjobs.com, with farm vacancies in the UK and Australia or, if already on the road, ask in the youth hostel, campsite or local café/pub. (According to one experienced traveller, this is great for people who are good at meeting prospective employers in pubs; unlike him, who just gets drunk and falls over.) The great advantage of job-hunting in rural areas rather than in cities is that people are more likely to know their neighbours' labour requirements, and are often more sympathetic and helpful in their attitudes.

Picking fruit may not be as easy as it sounds. If you are part of a large team, you may be expected to work at the same speed as the most experienced picker, which can be both exhausting and discouraging. Having even a little experience can make the whole business more enjoyable, not to mention more financially worthwhile if you are being paid piece work rates. The vast majority of picking jobs is paid piece work (with the notable exception of grape harvests in Europe), though a minimum level of productivity will be expected, particularly if you are being given room and board.

Anyone with a farming background could consider placing an advert in a farmers' journal or small town newspaper in your favoured destination. Something along the lines of this might work: '19-year-old Briton taking a year out before university seeks farm work. Willing to exchange labour for board and lodging and chance to get to know the country.' The usual caution must be exercised when considering any replies: if possible, talk to your prospective employer on the telephone and ask them for a reference. Always try to obtain the terms of employment in writing.

IEPUK (01572 823 934; www.iepuk.com), the rural employment specialist, places suitable applicants in all rural industries, including agriculture, horticulture, and wine-making. For people with relevant equine experience, live-in vacancies in dozens of countries in Europe and worldwide can be tracked down.

Some European countries have programmes whereby young people spend a month or two assisting on a farm, eg Norway and Switzerland (see chapters on respective countries). A farming background is not necessary for participating in these schemes, though of course it always helps. The work-for-keep exchange on organic farms known collectively as World Wide Opportunities on Organic Farms (WWOOF) is described in the chapter on *Volunteering*.

TEACHING ENGLISH

The English language is the language that literally millions of people around the world want to learn. There are areas of the world where the boom in English language learning seems to know no bounds, from Ecuador to China, Lithuania to Vietnam. People who are lucky enough to have been born native speakers of English find their skills universally in demand, though it is far easier to land a teaching job in a language school once you have a university degree.

As is obvious by the programme descriptions of the major gap year placement agencies in the earlier chapter, a high percentage of all gap year volunteer placements revolve around teaching English to young children, in secondary schools, and to adult learners. One of the best sources of information about the whole topic of English teaching (if I may be permitted to say so) is *Teaching English Abroad* by Susan Griffith (Vacation Work/Crimson Publishing, £14.99; new edition due in 2012), which covers in great detail training courses and recruitment agencies, and lists individual language schools around the world.

Your chances of gaining employment in a gap year are much stronger if you have undergone some training, preferably the four-week certificate course (see *Courses* chapter for further information).

JOB-HUNTING

Printed advertisements have been almost entirely replaced by the internet. The majority of employers advertise vacancies between February and June; most are looking for teachers who have some training or experience, but in some cases, a carefully crafted CV and enthusiastic personality are as important as EFL training and experience, especially for tutoring jobs at children's summer camps.

Arguably, it has become a little too easy to advertise and answer job adverts online. At the push of a button, your CV can be clogging up dozens, nay, hundreds of computers. But everywhere you look

LANGUAGE LINK

A 100-hour TEFL course led to Ho Chi Minh City, the Gobi Desert, and the Great Wall . . . and an enviable career along the way.

Enda Harty's modesty belies his success. He is talented, charming, and unavoidably likeable. We caught up with him as he launched the TEFL Express Online business.

Enda, tell me how your career started?
I'd finished college, done some travelling, and knew I'd like to see more of the world. I did a TEFL course in 2000, though without any teaching experience or long-term plan.

It seems to have led you down an interesting road.
Yeah, first stop Vietnam. My first teaching job did take a few months; an internship would have made things easier. I taught both adults and children in various centres in Vietnam and China over the next six years. My experience in reputable schools was invaluable when I moved somewhere new. In 2003, I was offered Director of Studies at Language Link, Beijing, and then moved on to overseeing the running of 12 schools in China. I also developed new courses for teens, which were very popular.

You enjoyed life in Asia?
Absolutely loved it! Vietnam is amazing - a unique culture and fantastic people. I had loads of fun and made great friends. China was intriguing and where most of my professional development happened. While I was based there, I saw Cambodia, Laos, Mongolia, Thailand, Japan, and North Korea - deeply enriching cultural experiences. Especially Laos and the Gobi Desert – what a place!

I believe you got an award in China. Why did you leave?
The City of Beijing gave me a Great Wall of Friendship Award for my contribution to Beijing's society and growth. They have a big emphasis on learning English. Hungry for teachers! I'd started developing more courses and was interested in broadening the availability through the web when a beautiful Spanish girl lured me to Majorca! Now I'm based between the UK, Ireland, and Majorca, and really excited about taking online teaching where it hasn't gone yet.

on the internet, potentially useful links can be found, especially the long established Dave's ESL Café (www.eslcafe.com), which dominates the field, along with www.tefl.com. 'Dave' provides a mind-boggling but well-organised amount of material for the future or current teacher, including accounts of people's experiences of teaching abroad (but bear in mind that these are the opinions of individuals). It also provides links to specific institutes and language school chains in each country.

Native speaker teachers are nearly always employed to stimulate conversation rather than to teach grammar. Yet a basic knowledge of English grammar is a great asset when pupils come to ask awkward questions. The book *English Grammar in Use* by Raymond Murphy is recommended for its clear explanations and accompanying student exercises.

Most schools practise the direct method (total immersion in English), so not knowing the language shouldn't prevent you from getting a job. Some employers may provide nothing more than a scratched blackboard. and will expect you to dive in using the 'chalk and talk' method. If you are very alarmed at this prospect you could ask a sympathetic colleague if you could sit in on a few classes to give you some ideas. Brochures picked up from tourist offices or airlines can be a useful peg on which to hang a lesson. If you're stranded without any ideas, write the lyrics of a pop song on the board and discuss them.

Whatever the kind of teaching you find, things probably won't go as smoothly as you would wish. After a year of teaching English in Italy, **Andrew Spence** had this sensible advice:

> *Teaching is perhaps the best way there is of experiencing another country, but you must be prepared for periods when not all is as it should be. The work is sometimes arduous and frustrating, or it can be very exhilarating. Be prepared to take the very rough with the fairly smooth.*

AU PAIRING

Gap year students who choose to become au pairs are generally looking for an affordable way to improve their knowledge of a country's language and culture. For several generations, female school leavers have been flocking to the continent, and more recently to the USA and even Australia, attracted by the safe and stable environment that a family placement can provide. When the au pair arrangement works well, it is ideal for young, under-confident and impecunious students who want to work abroad. Occasionally, young men can find live-in jobs, but the number of families and therefore agencies willing to entertain the possibility of having a male au pair is still painfully small.

The terms 'au pair', 'mother's help' and 'nanny' are often applied rather loosely, since all are primarily live-in jobs concerned with looking after children. Nannies may have some formal training and take full charge of the children. Mother's helps work full-time and undertake general housework and/or cooking as well as childcare. Au pairs are supposed to work for no more than 30 hours a week and are expected to learn a foreign language while living with a family. Although the term au pair is used in the American context, the hours are much longer and there is no language learning element for British au pairs (see *USA* chapter).

One of the great advantages of these live-in positions generally is that they are relatively easy to get (at least for women over 18). After proving to an agency or a family that you are reasonably sensible, you will in the majority of cases be able to find a placement, though it is much easier and quicker in some countries than others, eg easy in France, Switzerland, and Italy, but more difficult in Scandinavia and Portugal. Furthermore, au pairs can usually benefit from legislation that exempts them from work permit requirements.

The minimum age can be a stumbling block for some school leavers who are not yet 18. The majority of agencies prefer to accept applications only from candidates over 18, as **Camilla Preeston** discovered:

> *I had decided even before I had finished school that I would take a year off before university, and au pairing seemed like the perfect way to do this. Being 17-and-a-half made things much more difficult in the beginning, though I sent off endless letters to agencies in Britain and overseas. Most flatly replied that I was too young, though a couple said that they would try anyway. I eventually had success with a foreign agency. The reason they didn't turn me away may have been because the fee they levy is paid upfront before a family is found. By the time they had found me a family in Calais, four months of my year off had already gone by and I was almost ready to give up. I immediately accepted the offer, perhaps a little hastily. However, had I refused it, I might not have found another family willing to accept me, because of my age, and it was the first family offer I had received in the four months I had been trying.*

Camilla's youth did not prevent her from coping with what turned out to be a difficult situation, in which she was expected to accept a lot of responsibility for the children (including a newborn baby) and the running of the household, while the mother was away for five days and two nights a week.

The standard length of au pair stays is for one academic year, typically September to June. Summer stays can also be arranged to coincide with the school holidays, and there is some inevitable turnover at Christmas when homesick au pairs go home to their families and then decide not to return. The advantage of a summer placement is that the au pair will accompany the family to their holiday destination at the seaside or in the mountains; the disadvantage is that the children will be your responsibility for more hours than they would be if they were at school, while most language classes will also close for the summer. Make enquiries as early as possible, since there is a shortage of summer-only positions.

PROS AND CONS

THE GROUND RULES REGARDING AU PAIRING IN EUROPE

The Council of Europe guidelines stipulate that au pairs should be aged 18–27 (though these limits are flexible); should be expected to work about five hours a day, five days per week, plus a couple of evenings of babysitting; must be given a private room and full board, health insurance, opportunities to learn the language, and pocket money. The standard pocket money paid to au pairs in Europe is €260 a month, though it can be more, for example in Switzerland.

The relationship between au pair and family is not like the usual employer/employee relationship; in fact, the term au pair means 'on equal terms'. The terminology used is of 'host family' rather than 'employer'. Therefore, the success of the arrangement depends more than usual on whether individuals hit it off, so there is always an element of risk when living in a family of strangers.

Once you have arrived in the family, it is important to clarify immediately what your hours and duties will be, which day you will be paid, whether you can expect a rise, and how much notice either party must give if they wish to terminate the arrangement. This gets everyone off to a business-like start. But no matter how well-defined your duties are, there are bound to be occasions when your extra services will be taken for granted. It may seem that your time is not your own. So the standard working hours can soon turn into an unofficial string of 14-hour days. Whether you can tolerate this depends entirely on your disposition and on the compensating benefits of the job, eg free use of car and telephone, nice kids, good food, lots of sunshine, etc.

Gillian Forsyth's au pairing experience in Bavaria was a great success:

> *I had no official day off or free time, but was treated as a member of the family. Wherever they went, I went too. I found this much more interesting than being treated as an employee, as I really got to know the country and the people. In the evenings I did not have to sit in my room, but chatted with the family. Three years later, we still keep in close contact, and I have been skiing with them twice since, on an au pair/friend basis.*

If you do not have such a friendly arrangement with your host family, you may feel lonely and cut off in a foreign country. Many au pairs make friends at their language classes. Some agencies issue lists of other au pairs in the vicinity.

Most au pairs' duties revolve around the children. For some, taking sole responsibility for a child can be even more alarming than cooking for the first time. You should be prepared to handle a few emergencies (for example, sick or lost children) as well as the usual excursions to the park or collecting them from school. The agency questionnaire will ask you in detail what experience you have had with children and whether you are willing to look after infants, etc, so your preferences should be made known early.

APPLYING

Many au pair agencies now operate only as online matching services. The old-fashioned one-woman agency that used to arrange family placements with the help of a partner agency in France, Germany, Italy, etc has all but disappeared. This is primarily due to UK legislation which makes it illegal for any au pair agency to charge au pairs a fee for finding them work, either in the UK or abroad. As a result, agencies which at one time sent many British girls abroad are now concentrating exclusively on placing foreign girls with paying client families in the UK.

If you are already abroad, check in the local English language newspaper or visit an au pair agency office in the country where you are (addresses provided in country chapters). Many European agencies charge a substantial fee of €200+, which they claim is necessary to guarantee a minimum quality of service.

Many leading au pair agencies and youth exchange organisations in Europe belong to IAPA, the International Au Pair Association, a body trying to regulate the industry. The IAPA website (www.iapa.org) has links to its member agencies around the world. Agencies that specialise in one country are mentioned in the country-by-country chapters.

Other ways of hearing about openings are to check the noticeboards at the local English-speaking churches or ask the headteacher of a junior school if they know of any families wanting an au pair. One tip for finding babysitting jobs in resorts is to introduce yourself to the *portière* or receptionist on the desk of good hotels and ask them to refer guests looking for a babysitter to you, possibly offering them a small commission. With more suspicion around these days, informal arrangements like this are less likely to succeed; some potential clients might be reassured if you have good references.

THE INTERNET

Cyberspace buzzes with an exchange of information about live-in childcare. Finding agency details is very easy with several clicks of a mouse. Au pair placement was something that was always done by telephone and correspondence rather than requiring a face-to-face interview, so it is an activity that is well suited to an online database. Among the most popular sites are aupair-agency.com, greataupair.com, findaupair.com, au-pair-box.com and aupair-world.net (German-based), aupairconnect.com (US-based), which charges $45 for 3 months, and aupair-select.com.

Internet agencies enable families and applicants to engage in DIY arrangements. They invite prospective au pairs to register their details, including age, nationality, relevant experience, and in many cases a photo, to be uploaded onto a website which then becomes accessible to registered families. The families then make contact with suitable au pairs after paying an introduction fee to the web-based agency. Registration is invariably free for the jobseeker.

One problem identified by the traditional agencies is that this method makes it very difficult to carry out any effective screening of either party. On the other hand, the same could be said for 'situations vacant' advertising in the conventional way (see below). If relying on the internet, it is essential to ascertain exactly the nature of the situation and the expectations of your new employer. Work out in your mind what you will do in the event the arrangement does not work out; if the agency is simply a database-provider, they will be able to offer no back-up. **Jean-Marc Cressini**, director of the French agency Oliver Twist, thinks that this book '*should really warn applicants about free websites, as we have just been informed by Interpol that some girls have paid large amounts of money to families who do not exist. A person pretending to be a family has been arrested in England for asking applicants for large bank transfers*'. You should always be suspicious of any individual, family, and even company that asks for money upfront.

Jayde Cahir turned to the internet, found an agency, was emailed several families' portfolios from which she was able to make direct contact, and eventually chose a family in Germany. In initial discussions with the host family, she was misled on several counts, and found that she was expected to be more a paid companion for the neglected wife than an au pair. Even though she did develop a good relationship with the wife and boy, the husband took against her and unceremoniously dismissed her: '*I left the house within two hours of receiving his note asking me to leave or he would "throw me out". So I was left in a foreign country, unable to speak the language, with nowhere to live. In most cases, the agencies are there to support you; however, mine never returned my phone calls. This ended up being a very expensive experience as I am still owed unpaid wages.*'

COURSES

After the rigours and stresses of sitting A levels, many school leavers aspire to spend the following 15 months reading nothing more challenging than *The Beach* by Alex Garland, set on a fantasy Thai island. But after a decent recovery period has elapsed after exams, the idea of studying something either for fun or with a view to your future at university or in a career may come to seem more bearable. Whatever course is embarked on, extra qualifications and skills are viewed favourably by universities and potential employers, and students will gain practical knowledge for use at university and in later life.

Several course providers, principally Objective Gap Safety, Safetrek and Ultimate Gap Year, offer short preparatory courses for gap year students embarking on expeditions and world travel. See entries under 'Gap Year Safety and Preparation', below. One of the course organisers describes a potentially lethal situation for which his course prepared the clients well:

We once trained a group going off to Belize. On arrival, they went to pick up the two four-wheel drives they had arranged (through Avis), and found one of them to be seriously substandard. They were told that there was no alternative but that the vehicle would be replaced the next day, and so they reluctantly took it. Before they signed their life away though, they took very thorough photos of all aspects of the vehicle. Halfway through their journey, the rear axle sheared and the vehicle rolled off the road. Thanks to sensible planning, they only had the two team leaders in the 'dodgy' vehicle and all the gear. The two escaped with only bad scrapes, thanks to the kit being correctly packed, and stopped the vehicle from being squashed too much. On return to the car hire company, they were given short shrift and so went straight to the police with the photographs. On return to the shop, they got a much better response!

RANGE OF COURSES

Depending on how you have decided to divide up your gap year, you may find yourself spending a good chunk at the beginning trying to earn money in a less-than-stimulating workplace such as a supermarket or rowdy pub. If most of your friends have gone off to university or travelling, you may have the leisure to take a course locally (see section below). This can provide an ideal chance to get your driving licence, obtain a life-saving qualification, or sports instructor certificate, etc.

If you go abroad later in the year with no pre-arranged placement, it is a good idea to take documentary evidence of any qualifications you have earned in case you have the chance to work as an office temp in Sydney or spend a week cooking on a private yacht. A multitude of short leisure courses can be searched on the very good search engine supported by GoLearnTo (www.golearnto.com; 0844 502 0445), anything from beginners' Chinese in Beijing to yoga and photography combined in Costa Rica.

Georgina Nightingall is clearly a very focused young woman. Although she didn't have her gap year all mapped out in advance, she was determined not to waste a minute of it, and to fill it with a succession of worthwhile experiences. Looking back on it, her assessment is that 'As the year progressed, every experience/course seemed to get better and better.' In the autumn, she did a static line parachuting course, followed by a four-week 'Basic to Brilliant' cookery course (see her comments below), and then a short first aid course. The high point was going abroad to do the John Hall Venice pre-university history of art course, which she describes in the chapter on Italy. And most gappers feel pleased with themselves if they learn to drive!

LANGUAGE COURSES

The gap year is an ideal opportunity for students to brush up on a barely-remembered GCSE language or even start from scratch with a new one. Most employers will view this as a very constructive use of time, and anyone with competence in another language has an advantage in many job hunts. Even people who are not planning to study modern languages at university should consider the advantages of getting to grips with one of the main European tongues. Evening language classes offered by local authorities usually follow the academic year and are aimed at hobby learners. Intensive courses offered privately are much more expensive. If you are really dedicated, consider using a self-study programme with distance learning courses online or books and CDs, though discipline is required to make progress. Hold out a carrot to yourself of a trip to a country where your target language is spoken. Even if you don't make much headway with the course at home, take the books and tapes with you, since you will have more incentive to learn once you are immersed in a language.

Although many people have been turning to the web to teach them a language, many conventional teach-yourself courses are still on the market, for example the *Take Off in* . . . series from Oxford University Press (www.askoxford.com/languages) for £25 including mp3 downloads, the BBC (www.bbc.co.uk/languages), Linguaphone (0800 136973; www.linguaphone.co.uk), and Audioforum (www.audioforum.com). Linguaphone recommends half an hour of study a day for three months to master the basics of a language. A more enjoyable way of learning a language (and usually a more successful one) is by speaking it with the natives. Best of all is if you acquire a boyfriend or girlfriend who speaks the language you want to learn.

Numerous British companies represent a range of language schools abroad offering in-country language courses. They are very familiar with differences between schools, qualifications, locations, etc and what is most suitable for clients. CESA Languages Abroad, Caledonia, Cactus Language, and Language Courses Abroad, among others, all have wide-ranging programmes in Europe and beyond. These agencies also provide a useful back-up service if the course does not fulfil your requirements in any way (see list at the beginning of the 'Directory of Language Courses' later in this chapter).

Of course, it is also possible to book a course directly with a language school abroad, which is the route that **Annabel Iglehart** from Edinburgh chose in her post-university gap year:

> *After completing my university degree, I decided to take a year (or two) out to gain new skills and participate in interesting activities around the world. After working in a variety of jobs at home, I went to Salamanca to do a three-month intensive Spanish language course with Mester. I planned and paid for my course and accommodation directly through Mester and this saved me a lot of money; it was by far the most economical way to organise the trip. The course was fantastic. The classes were fast-paced and the teachers excellent. I lived with a Spanish family for a while, and then moved to a flat with other students. I met loads of people with whom I am still in touch.*

While learning a language at secondary school, you usually have two or three hours of classes a week which could work out at as little as 80 hours a year. While doing an eight-week intensive course, you might have 240 hours – the equivalent of three years of school instruction – plus you will be speaking the language outside the classroom, so progress is usually very quick.

Literally thousands of language schools around the world would like your business, so care needs to be taken in choosing one that suits individual needs. Possible sources of language school addresses on the web are http://language.studyabroad.com, http://languagestudy.goabroad.com/search.cfm, and http://language.shawguides.com. After considering the obvious factors such as price and location, when choosing a language school, also try to find out the average age and likely nationalities of your fellow learners, whether there will be any one-to-one tuition, and whether the course concentrates on oral or written skills, whether there are extracurricular activities and excursions included in the fee, and generally as much as you can. One key factor is whether or not a school prepares its students for exams. If they do and you are there only for the fun of it, you may find that lessons are not suitable (and vice versa).

Whereas some language schools run purely recreational courses, others offer structured courses leading to respected qualifications. The Council of Europe has been working for many years to set up a system of validating and assessing language ability, and the six levels of the Common European

Framework of Reference for Languages (CEFR) are becoming widely accepted across the continent. The levels range from A1 for beginners to C2 for language skills at near-fluent level. The mainstream providers of language qualifications such as the Alliance Française and Goethe Institut administer their own language exams which correspond to the CEFR. At the other end of the spectrum, some schools offer nothing more than a certificate outlining the period of study, and perhaps the level of language reached or work covered in the course, which may be of limited value if you ever need to show proof of linguistic attainment.

Serious language schools on the continent usually offer the possibility of preparing for one of the internationally recognised exams. In France, the qualification for aspiring language learners is the DELF (*Diplôm Elémentaire de Langue Français*) while the Spanish counterpart is the DELE (*Diploma de Español como Lengua Extranjera*), both of which are recognised by employers, universities, officialdom, etc. The DELE is split into three levels: *Certificado Inicial de Español*, *Diploma Básico de Español*, and the *Diploma Superior de Español*. Most schools say that even the Basic Diploma requires at least eight or nine months of study in Spain. A prior knowledge of the language, of course, allows the student to enrol at a higher level and attain the award more quickly. No single qualification in Italy is as dominant as the DELE or the DELF. Typical of Italian exams is CILS (*Certificato di Italiano come Lingua Straniera*), which was established by Siena University and is authorised by the Italian Ministry of Foreign Affairs.

Recreational language courses are offered by virtually every school and are preferred by many gap year students. Some programmes are much more structured than others, so students need to look for flexible courses that allow them to progress at their own rate. Many people agree that the fastest way to improve fluency is to have one-to-one lessons, though of course these are more expensive than group classes. Usually a combination of the two works best.

Another factor that can impede progress is if you are in the midst of your compatriots. A class in which many languages are represented is more likely to use the target language rather than slip into English. Even if you get to spend a lot of time in the company of locals, you may be expected to help them improve their English. One wily young woman studying French in Bordeaux during her gap year arrived at a solution to this problem:

> *The only real frustration of my time so far has to be coming across French people who wish to improve their English. They respond to your attempt in French with their own attempt in English. However, I have developed a cunning solution. I provide them with a quick explanation that I am in fact Icelandic or Russian, and we are soon back on track.*

Increasingly, major language schools are offering work experience placements to their 'graduates'. Many belong to WYSE Work Abroad mentioned in the chapter on *Work Experience*. Many language courses abroad combine language tuition with cultural and other studies. For instance, while learning Spanish, you can also take lessons in dance or cookery, or follow the course up with an unpaid internship; while studying Italian in Florence, you can also take drawing classes, and so on. The possibilities are endless. Living with a family is highly recommended, especially for beginners, since it usually forces you to speak the target language from the beginning. You might also consider learning a language in a country where it is a second language; for example, Projects Abroad offer French courses in Togo, normally in conjunction with a volunteer placement.

Andrew Cummings, who spent most of his gap year in South America, makes an interesting observation:

> *In terms of language development – and this is particularly pertinent with a language as variable and animated as Spanish – it would probably be a good idea to stay in the same place for as long as possible, especially if it's your first time really practising the language. When moving from Bolivia to Argentina, for example, I found that the spoken language differed immensely between the two countries; it took me a few weeks to really adapt to Argentinian Spanish, and for a while it felt as though if I'd stayed in Bolivia, I would have avoided that hiccup and improved more overall.*

CLIC (CENTRO DE LENGUAS E INTERCAMBIO CULTURAL)

Claire Potter taught English while living in Andalucia, Spain.

The first time I came to Andalucia, I was a 14-year-old school girl, and I spent two weeks in Almeria over Easter. I couldn't get over the colours, sights, and sounds of the Semana Santa processions, as well as the warm March sunshine, and I vowed to come back. It took me 12 years, but it's a decision I have never regretted. I did a CELTA teacher training course and packed my bags, coming to Spain after an enjoyable two-year period in Japan.

The first thing which struck me was how everybody seems to live life on the streets, chatting while enjoying tapas, beers, and wine until the early hours. Initially in Cordoba, the mixture of Arabic, Roman, and Catholic kings' architecture made it such a magical place, and the month of May, with a different festival every week, kept me there for five years. I also met my partner Miguel, with my Spanish quickly improving!

I loved my job, teaching English to students from five to 75 years of age, beginners' level to advanced. I moved from Cordoba to Seville for further job opportunities, where I became involved in teacher training. Seville may be bigger, but it also draws you like a magnet, with its elegance and feeling of *aqui estoy* ('here I am'). The April fair, flamenco, football, and the warm spring and autumn days are all here to be savoured. The coast is only an hour away, which can be a welcome escape in midsummer, and being here when Spain won the World Cup was an unforgettable experience.

I have met so many interesting people through my working and personal life over the years and have discovered so many hidden corners of Andalucia, I wouldn't swap living here and teaching English for anything.

In some cases, a preparatory course in teaching English as a foreign language (known as TEFL, pronounced 'teffle') is required by year-out placement agencies or individual language schools, whereas in others a willingness to communicate is sufficient.

If you are entertaining the idea of teaching English in your gap year, the best way to outrival the competition and make the job hunt (not to mention the job itself) easier is to do a TEFL training course, of which there are is enormous choice in the UK. Two standard recognised qualifications will improve your range of job options. The best known is the Cambridge Certificate in English Language Teaching to Adults (CELTA), administered and awarded by Cambridge Assessment (01223 553 355; www. cambridgeESOL.org/teaching). The other is the Certificate in TESOL (teaching English to speakers of other languages) offered by Trinity College London (020 7820 6100; www.trinitycollege.co.uk).

Both are very intensive and expensive, averaging £1,000. These courses involve at least 100 hours of rigorous training with a practical emphasis (full-time for four weeks, or part-time over several months). Most centres expect applicants to have the equivalent of university entrance qualifications, ie five GCSEs and two A levels, but some admit only university graduates.

For people confused by the number of TEFL training courses jostling for attention in the marketplace, Cactus TEFL (0845 130 4775; www.cactustefl.com) is the only international admissions and jobs service for TEFL. It delivers up-to-date information on hundreds of TEFL courses throughout the world, which can be used to compare prices. Cactus TEFL offers an impartial and informed advice service for anyone new to TEFL. The company advises over 1,000 trainees on courses all over the world every year.

A list of centres in the UK and abroad offering the Cambridge Certificate is available from Cambridge Assessment, which oversees the ESOL exams mentioned above; they are all linked from the company's website as well. CELTA courses are also offered at more than 250 overseas centres from the Middle East to Queensland, including 10 in the USA and 30 in Australia and New Zealand.

Centres that offer short introductory courses in TEFL or their own proprietary certificates vary enormously in quality and price. Although they are mainly intended to act as preparatory programmes for more serious courses, many people who hold just a short certificate go on to teach. Among the best known are:

i-to-i TEFL, Leeds (0113 205 4610; www.onlinetefl.com). Intensive TEFL weekend courses at venues in UK and Irish cities. Price for online course from £129.

Saxoncourt Teacher Training, London W1K 5SN, (020 7499 8533; www.saxoncourt.com). Offer a one-week Gap Year Teacher Training course four times over the winter months (fee: £190). Also offer a one-week introductory TEFL course (called FELT) monthly for £275, which can potentially lead to positions in China, Japan, and Taiwan.

TEFL Express (0800 0488861; www.teflexpress.co.uk). Online courses of various durations up to 120 hours (£369) and weekend courses (from £149) in London and Ireland. Affiliated to Language Link.

TEFL Time (01903 708178; www.tefltime.com). Weekend courses affiliated with the volunteer placement agency Travellers Worldwide. Course fee £199 (or £149 for Travellers Worldwide volunteers). Also offer an 80-hour distance learning course for £109.

TEFL Training, Witney, Oxfordshire (01993 891 121; www.tefltraining.co.uk). Twenty-hour practical and intensive weekend seminars in cities around the UK. £210.

Many advantages can be gained by signing up for a TEFL course in the place where you want to work, from Barcelona to Bangkok. Most TEFL training centres have excellent contacts with language schools and can assist with the job hunt. Among the best known providers of CELTA courses are the British Council and International House, offering the training in many cities from Madrid to Sydney. But scores of independent providers provide TEFL training courses of varying lengths; this small selection gives a flavour of the range available:

MY GAP YEAR:
STEFANIA AND PHOEBE

Stefania spent 24 weeks in Florence on an Italian Gap year programme:

I have an Italian background but I had little knowledge of the language. I was looking forward to the linguistic challenge, but was very nervous and excited. I definitely felt better prepared for the experience after talking to the CESA staff.

Having lessons solidly in Italian was the real challenge - but it made learning the language easier. I found the lessons fantastic; all the staff were lovely and helped as much as they could when you couldn't understand something. The school was really good and the location was so convenient, right in the centre of Florence.

Florence is a buzzing, small, safe town with an amazing culture and architecture. In free afternoons, I loved visiting the galleries and museums. I made some great friends, and it was brilliant to be able to travel around Italy and share the experiences with so many great people.

I found CESA Languages very reliable and helpful and recommend them to you! I just hope I get the chance to do it all again!

Phoebe spent 12 weeks in Cannes on a French gap year programme:

The important thing to come out of my gap year is my French. I have every confidence it has flourished under the instruction of my professor Katia, who was amazing and extremely patient. The teachers are brilliant, and with lessons taught solely in French, it is a steep learning curve. It is always challenging, but I made so much progress every month that you just await the next lesson with impatience as you know you're going to come up against something new.

The college atmosphere is unbelievable. Everyone becomes so close; living, eating, and learning together. The beach is so close and beautiful and there are so many things to see and to do. I now feel very well travelled, from meeting people from all over the globe.

There is so much to do at, and of course outside, college. Whether it was riding, scuba diving, or an excursion to a museum, the office was always packed with great ideas and helpful advice. The bar organised some great nights - karaoke, crêpe soirées, cheese and wine nights, icecream soirées - they were always brilliant and the best way to meet new people. All in all, it is impossible to be bored, and it was always more of a challenge to find free time as opposed to finding something to do. I think that the best testimonial of my time at the college is the fact that I'm actually extending my stay for a further six months and cannot wait to see what adventures the future has to hold.

If you're thinking about it - just pick up the phone and call CESA.

BridgeTEFL, Denver, Colorado, USA (+1 888 827 4757 toll-free in North America; 0808 120 7613 free phone in the UK; www.bridgetefl.com). BridgeTEFL is an accredited language training company which offers TEFL, IDELT (its own proprietary qualification), and CELTA teacher certification and job placement programmes in Asia, Europe, the Middle East, and Latin America. Also offers online TEFL course (www.TEFLOnline.com). TEFL training (2–4 weeks) available in many countries from Cambodia to Guatemala.

ibero School Argentina, Buenos Aires, Argentina (+54 5218 0240; www.iberotefl.com). TEFL/ TESOL Certification Programme. Four weeks with 95 hours of input classes and 6 hours of teaching practice with real students. $995. Can be taken in conjunction with Spanish course. Job placement assistance is given.

TEFL Corinth, c/o Anglo-Hellenic Teacher Recruitment, PO Box 263, 201 00 Corinth, Greece (www. teflcorinth.com). One-month training course for £1,300 including accommodation.

After finishing A levels, **Sam James** and **Sophie Ellison** from Yorkshire decided to spend their gap year in Barcelona if they could. They both signed up to do the Trinity Certificate in TESOL course at Oxford TEFL in their destination city, deciding that this would give them the introduction they needed, and it worked (see *Spain* chapter).

IT AND BUSINESS SKILLS COURSES

Colleges of further education and private colleges offer a wealth of courses that many gap year students might choose to pursue, possibly with a view to earning money quickly for a planned placement or expedition later in the year. IT and business skills courses can prove very useful for finding well-paid temporary work before and during university. Many vocational courses attract government grants for students, and the college should be able to tell you whether funding is available and how to apply.

The British Accreditation Council for Independent Further and Higher Education, or BAC (www.the-bac.org), accredits around 230 private colleges in the UK. Many of these offer business and IT courses, while others specialise in subjects such as hospitality management and cookery, which may be useful to those wishing to spend part of their gap year working for a tour company or in a ski resort. Note that many of BAC's accredited colleges specialise in tutoring students from abroad (eg for A levels), and not all of the colleges run short courses. The BAC website includes links to the colleges' own websites with details of the courses on offer.

OUTDOOR PURSUITS AND SPORTS COURSES

A recognised qualification in any sport will make it very easy to pick up work later in your gap year, and to find enjoyable holiday jobs throughout your university career. Skilled sportsmen and women can often find gainful employment in their area of expertise, whether instructing tennis locally, joining a scheme to coach soccer in the USA or South Africa, or making money teaching dinghy sailing in Sydney. Numerous multi-activity centres in Britain and Europe recruit staff to lead and instruct and offer their own pre-season training, sometimes free of charge.

A structured way of acquiring skills and qualifications during your sporting gap year is to participate in the Duke of Edinburgh's Award scheme (described in the *Expeditions* chapter). This can lead to a qualification in a variety of activity and sporting areas, including expedition skills.

A life-saving qualification allows you to work as a lifeguard, though there are different qualifications for pool and beach lifeguards. Further afield, diving instructors work at Red Sea resorts, mountain leaders are hired to guide groups in the Himalayas, trainee parachutists find work packing parachutes in the USA, and Competent Crew get positions on ocean-going yachts. The best starting place for acquiring the necessary training and certification is the governing body of the sport or pursuit that interests you, which will be able to point you towards instructors' courses in the UK and beyond; for example the Royal Yachting Association (www.rya.org.uk), British Canoe Union (www.bcu.org.uk), British Mountaineering Council (www.thebmc.co.uk), and British Horse Society (www.bhs.org.uk). Mountain Leader Training England (www.mlte.org) offers certificates at different levels, eg Walking Group Leader and the Single Pitch Award, some of which are offered by the Edale Youth Hostel (01433 670302; edaleactivities@yha.org.uk).

Many companies and youth training organisations run expeditions and related courses at varying levels. The Plas y Brenin National Mountain Centre in Snowdonia (www.pyb.co.uk) runs residential courses in a range of disciplines. The most ambitious courses are run by companies such as Jagged Globe, based in Sheffield (www.jagged-globe.com), which offers ice climbing and other courses in Scotland, Wales, and the Alps.

Surf-mad 18-year-old **Nick Braithwaite** spent part of his gap year in Australia doing a surf instructor/life-saving traineeship with Flying Fish before starting his geography degree at Swansea University (see the *Australia* chapter for more information and a case history from another Flying Fish 'graduate').

Exotic courses are available worldwide, from kitesurfing on the Pacific coast of Ecuador with the Academia de Español Surpacifico to polo training on an *estancia* in Argentina with The Leap.

MY GAP YEAR: ROSS FAIRGRIEVE

There are global shortages of qualified instructors in several sports including diving, watersports, and snow sports; Ross Fairgrieve chose a diving course for his gap year.

Over the course of my gap year, I went from a dive virgin to a PADI Divemaster on the Thai island of Koh Tao. Although I had wanted to learn to dive for a few years, it seemed destined to remain on the 'fifty things to forget to do before you die' list. But I decided on the Personal Overseas Development programme because I really liked the look of the experience that it offered, and I wanted to do something that could be helpful to me in the future (ie gaining a professional diving qualification) rather than 'just' travelling. I considered joining the organisations that offer marine conservation opportunities, but in the end I decided to concentrate on diving, knowing that I could always do something more conservation-based after university when I'm armed with an oceanography degree. I knew that I could just book the diving through a dive school and it would be cheaper that way. As this was my first time away from home for such a length of time, however, and because I had never been to Thailand before, I decided to pay a little bit of extra money for the support and peace of mind that having some guidance and support provided. It was also nice to have diving, accommodation, visas, full travel and dive insurance, and transport advice all arranged in one go.

SKI TRAINING

The past five years have seen a remarkable increase in the number of programmes specially tailored to avid or aspiring skiers and snowboarders taking a year out who want to improve their skiing or to train as instructors. A number specifically target gap year students, such as one offered in conjunction with the British Association of Snowsport Instructors (BASI), which lasts 10 weeks in Nendaz, Switzerland (gap@onthemountainpro.co.uk). The major focus of **Alice Mundy**'s year out was an 11-week course in the Canadian Rockies to become a snowboard instructor with NONSTOP Ski & Snowboard:

> *I decided on a course of this kind as I felt it combined one of my passions with a globally recognised qualification, which would open up the possibility of travelling around the world while being able to make a living. The course was expensive – just over £6,000 (covering flights and transfers, accommodation, weekday breakfast and evening meals, full season lift pass, 20 hours a week coaching, CASI Level 1 exam fee and selected weekend trips and activities) plus £200 dangerous sports insurance and £2,000–£3,000 spending money. So, it didn't come cheap for something that could be arranged on an individual basis (sorting out your own flights and accommodation and then entering for your instructor exams off your own bat). But by doing that, you would miss out on the high-level five-days-a-week coaching, which was the overwhelming advantage of this course for me. You receive invaluable preparation for the instructor examinations and the world of work as a snow sports instructor so, if it is your aim to use the qualification at some point in the future, the cost of the course is definitely justified. Also, it provided exactly the right balance that a lot of people my age were looking for – plenty of independence and the experience of living away from home, but enough aspects already taken care of and organised for you not to be totally terrified of having to make all the arrangements by yourself on your first big trip away.*

Many companies arrange these courses in a number of locations worldwide, mainly in Canada and more recently in New Zealand, but also in Europe and Patagonia. So far, instructor training has not been generally available in the USA to non-Americans. The providers usually claim that they can accommodate beginner skiers, though the majority of trainees have been on regular ski holidays for some years. There was no-one on Alice's course who had never skied before, and in her view it would defy logic for someone who had never even tried a sport to want to become an instructor in it. On the other hand, it is amazing how much you can improve. **Laurence Young** joined skivo2's gap year instructors' course in Courchevel, where he gained enough confidence to pass his Level 1 and 2 BASI exams, having had only three weeks' previous skiing experience. The pass rate for Level 1 in Alice's case was 100%, which indicates that it is an achievable goal even for those with minimal skiing experience.

Those who want to arrange to spend a whole season in a ski resort without joining one of these elite programmes can book accommodation through an operator that specialises in long-stay ski and snowboard holidays, such as Seasonaires (020 8123 7879; www.seasonaires.com). It has a large selection of shared accommodation for individual travellers, as well as seasonally let properties that are ideal for groups in a large number of resorts from Les Arcs in the French Alps to Whistler in Canada. You can then book your ski training course direct with the ski-snowboard governing body for that country such as the Canadian Association of Snowboard Instructors (CASI) or Professional Ski Instructors of America (PSIA).

Because **Adam Whale** had been skiing with Skivo2 since he had been knee-high to a grasshopper, it was not difficult for him to choose the school with which he wanted to train to become an instructor:

> *I had always wanted to do a ski season before going into work after university. I was really keen to spend a winter doing something I love, making new friends, experiencing a new culture and learning new skills. Having grown up skiing with Skivo2 in Courchevel, its gap course was the natural choice for*

me, as I already knew the quality it would provide. Becoming a ski instructor had been an ambition of mine since I started skiing aged 10. The package included training, 'shadowing hours', half-board accommodation, a lift pass, and mentoring. I feel the course was excellent value for money considering the quality provided.

After I passed, Skivo 2 helped with finding a job (in Italy) to get some teaching experience, and provided references for future job applications. Although I didn't plan it, my gap year changed my life, to the extent that I am now doing my fifth winter season, working for a top ski school in Verbier, and have found a job that I love. The time spent on my gap course prepared me for this and gave me an insight into the realities of the instructor's lifestyle. The training not only gave me the skills I needed to pass the initial course, but also the knowledge and discipline for how to train properly and get all the way to the top.

THE EDINBURGH SCHOOL OF FOOD & WINE (ESFW)

ESFW has been inspiring cooks in Scotland for 25 years.

The Edinburgh School of Food & Wine (ESFW) has built an enviable reputation since opening in 1986, with students aged 7–70 participating in a wide variety of leisure and professional courses. Based in an 18th-century coach house in the grounds of the Newliston Country Estate, 12 miles from the centre of Edinburgh and just 10 minutes from the airport, ESFW is registered as a learning provider with the British Accreditation Council – the only cookery school in Scotland to hold such a status.

ESFW is an inspiring place to study and develop cookery skills; its beautiful rural setting provides the perfect backdrop to immerse oneself in the craft of cookery. Single-day master classes allow participants to focus on a skill-set or cuisine of their choice, from Thai or Indian to Scotland's own seasonal larder. Both the enthusiastic novice and the budding professional delight in the creative recipes and professional tips to create faultless dishes.

For career-minded students, our professional courses provide an individual approach to student learning, coupled with practical hands-on learning. This ensures students leave with confidence in their core culinary skills, allowing them to build a platform for continuous professional development for life. ESFW has been a springboard for literally hundreds of culinary careers for the past 20 years, and has created a rich tradition of success among its graduates.

For your career:
- professional diploma and certificate courses
- chalet and gap year courses
- specialist masterclasses
- business courses – build your own business and explore your creativity.

For your enjoyment:
- one-day leisure classes
- Glenfiddich gourmet cookery

- school for men
- Veuve Clicquot champagne cookery
- school for women
- cocktail masterclasses
- wine tasting dinners.

For your business:
- corporate events
- team building
- food hygiene training
- wine and spirit education.

The Coach House, Newliston, Edinburgh EH3 6PD
(0131 333 5001; www.esfw.com info@esfw.com)

The days of the finishing school are over. However, a practical cookery course can prove immensely useful in finding temporary employment both at home and abroad. (It can also put you in a class of your own when you come to share a house with friends at university.) A catering certificate opens up many appealing employment options in ski resorts, private villas, or private yachts. A number are aimed specifically at young gappers who want to master enough impressive dishes to land a job in a ski chalet or for a yacht cruise company. In addition to the courses listed in the directory below, try the Well-Seasoned Chalet Cookery Course (www.well-seasoned.co.uk), offered in the off-season in Tignes, France.

The private courses are expensive, but some students (and their parents) decide to splash out in order to acquire an instantly recognised qualification such as Cordon Bleu or Tante Marie. A Food Safety in Catering Certificate can be acquired in half a day or even online (£35 via www.onlinefoodhygiene. com) and is useful for picking up casual work in restaurants to help fund your gap year.

Georgie Nightingall elected to learn to cook near the beginning of her gap year, even though she had no intention of working in a ski resort or on a yacht:

> *Going to The Avenue in Putney was one of the best choices I made in my gap year. I found that my confidence blossomed tremendously. I cooked well over 100 recipes in those four weeks and, naturally, I've had my fair share of disasters in the kitchen. But once the mistakes had been made, I found myself geared up and ready to prepare and cook a three-course meal at the end of the course. This was an absolute success, just as the course was. Not only do you learn a valuable skill, but it also teaches you to take risks, and to gain the confidence to try out something new, oblivious to the chances of failure. One week can ignite excitement and confidence; a month can bring about miracles!*

CREATIVE ARTS COURSES

YEAR OUT DRAMA, STRATFORD-UPON-AVON

Looking For drama?

Now approaching its 25th year, this course is designed for those wanting a year's intensive full-time practical drama training. It is open to all those who demonstrate the enthusiasm and commitment during interview and necessary performance potential in audition.

Run with a theatre-company feel, this unique course provides an exciting and challenging opportunity for all those wishing to acquire a wide range of practical theatre skills.

Every individual, whatever their background, theatre experience, or future plans, is given the confidence to take risks, make discoveries, and gain the rewards of stretching themselves physically, intellectually, and imaginatively.

With a reputation for excellence, this well-established and highly regarded course offers top-quality specialist teaching and directing in professionally equipped spaces.

The group work with a huge range of visiting theatre professionals on varying productions and performance projects. The year culminates with the group taking a production to Edinburgh and performing as part of the Edinburgh Fringe Festival.

It would be hard to express what my year in Stratford has meant to me in a few words, but I can tell you how lucky I feel to have met so many amazing people.
Katie, 2003-04

I would do it all again any time.
George, 2008-09

The year has helped past students attain places at the country's top drama schools and prestigious universities, including RADA, Drama Centre, LAMDA ,Central and Guildhall, and at universities such as Cambridge, Oxford, Bristol, Warwick, St Andrews, Manchester, and Harvard. We have enthusiastic and active alumni now established in a number of different areas in the theatre and wider arts.

For more information, call 01789 417 255 (or ask for Year Out Drama), email yearoutdrama@stratford.ac.uk or visit www.yearoutdrama.com

ART HISTORY ABROAD

R S came on the Art History Abroad (AHA) gap year course in 2002; his brother and sister also came on gap year courses with AHA in 2005.

As I'm a biology graduate and a solicitor, you may be forgiven for thinking that all I took from a trip to Italy in my gap year was a Coliseum fridge magnet and a headache. Perhaps that was all I expected too; but a few years down the line, I have realised how wrong that assessment was, and just how much Art History Abroad has shaped me.

AHA is not like any other course. Combining thorough scholarship, honed local knowledge, and infectious enthusiasm, the AHA tutors took us on our own 'Grand Tour' of Italy. We were led on a spell-binding journey through Italian history and culture, illuminated by some of the greatest art ever created. Papal indulgence, Medici politics and ancient Roman society were all covered as we travelled through Venice, Pisa, Florence, Siena, Rome, and Naples.

The course was so expertly pitched that you never felt that you were learning. There was no need to take notes, no final exam, and yet you could not fail to absorb everything you heard. Of course, the art was not the only memorable part of the experience. The food, wine, and unique nights out were all as good as it ever gets.

The legacy of an AHA course is more than the strong friendships and love of art that you obviously develop. The benefits for those who go on to study history of art are obvious, but for those like me who go on to other things, AHA is equally, if not more, rewarding. UK universities do not operate like they do in the USA, and students here do not get the chance to 'minor' in another subject. AHA gives you that chance.

On a personal level, AHA certainly helped build my confidence; and professionally, the graduate recruitment department at my law firm have told me that having 'Italian art' and 'entomology' listed as interests on my application form gave me a foot in the door that those with the more mundane 'reading' and 'travelling' never got.

While the vast majority of school leavers have no fixed idea what they want to pursue, a few may already have developed a leaning towards one of the creative arts or another vocation. Some do an art foundation course in their gap year purely for pleasure rather than as a springboard for applying to art college; further education courses like this are free of charge to those under 19. Some may want to pursue a creative interest in their gap year before heading to university, though more usually this kind of course is taken post-university.

The London College of Fashion runs summer courses in the capital. You might take the opportunity to build up a portfolio of photographs. Budding actors might consider auditioning for the National Youth Theatre in London (www.nyt.org.uk). Workshop auditions (both acting and technical) are held around the country during the spring half-term or at weekends, following the end of January deadline for applications. The boom in interest in media studies show no signs of abating, and many of those school leavers think of themselves as up-and-coming film makers. The idea of shooting a film while travelling abroad is very appealing, and many gappers add a clip to YouTube for their friends to enjoy, but even the most naïve 18-year-old will have worked out that it is next to impossible to make such a venture a commercial success. Although **Hannah Adcock** had graduated from university when she braved this field, and was already involved with a theatre company, her experiences are instructive. She and some university friends had set up a semi-professional production company with a strong theatrical background, specialising in Greek tragedy and Shakespeare. They then turned their hands to film-making and set up Outlook Productions to make a film in Greece. Plans for an adaptation of Shakespeare's *Twelfth Night* had been discussed over a long period, but it wasn't until the director and producer visited the Greek island of Patmos that they realised Patmos *was* the Illyria of their dreams (the magical land where the action in the play takes place). The island was so perfect that even one of the play's more inconsequential lines took on a deeper meaning, 'I prithee, foolish Greek, depart from me'!

The company felt confident that it could sell the film, either to digital TV channels or educational institutions, or perhaps to a distributor, because *Twelfth Night* is a well-known play, and school children have to study it. The company couldn't get funding from organisations such as the Arts Council, but it did attract private investors: people who had come to the company's theatrical shows, liked what they saw and believed in the venture. It is a good idea if you are a theatre/production company to keep a mailing list of people who appreciate your work. However, private investment only goes so far when you are making a digital feature film. Paying wages was out of the question, so cast and crew were invited to 'profit share'. This way, all rise or fall on the success or failure of the production, which is a huge risk but a good incentive to work hard! Hannah concludes: '*This is a great way to get into a tough sector – and not just by making the tea. You should get respect for initiative, but this is not a guaranteed money-spinner.*'

A handful of NGOs use film to publicise their causes. A newcomer to this edition is the Oregon-based Actuality Media, which puts together small groups of film-makers to make short documentaries in Central America (see entry in `Directory of Courses', p337).

DIRECTORIES OF COURSES

LANGUAGE COURSES

The following entries represent a tiny proportion of language schools worldwide. Of greatest interest are the first 13 entries, which are for companies, the majority in the UK, that represent a selection of language schools. Using an agency simplifies the selection process. Schools and agencies of interest to North Americans are listed in the chapter *A Year Off for North Americans*.

> **AMERISPAN STUDY ABROAD**
> PO Box 58129, Philadelphia, PA 19103, USA
> ☎ +1 800 879 6640
> ☎ +1 215 751 1100
> Skype: amerispan
> ✍ info@amerispan.com
> 🖳 www.amerispan.com

Specialist Spanish language travel organisation established in 1993, which has evolved to offering 15 languages in more than 45 countries in the Americas, Europe, Asia, the Middle East, Australia, and Africa.

COURSES OFFERED: Many worldwide study abroad options, including language programmes, volunteer/internship placements, college study abroad, and specialised programmes such as SALUD, an AMSA-inspired medical Spanish programme, professional and educator programmes, teenager and language and fun programmes.

ACCOMMODATION: Mostly homestays, but alternatives available in many locations.

> **BRIDGE-LINGUATEC LANGUAGE STUDY ABROAD**
> 915 S Colorado Boulevard, Denver, CO 80246, USA
> ☎ +1 866 574 8606 (toll-free in the USA and Canada)
> ☎ (0)808 120 7613 (free phone in the UK)
> ☎ +1 303 945 2234
> ✍ traveladviser@bridgeabroad.com
> 🖳 www.bridgeabroad.com

Bridge-Linguatec is a language training company, with language study and culture immersion programmes in Europe and Latin America.

COURSES OFFERED: Spanish, French, German, Italian, Portuguese, Russian, Mandarin/Cantonese, Japanese, and Arabic. Group, private, and combined group/private classes available. Courses include activities and excursions to help students get to know the local culture, as well as comfortable host family accommodation.

DESTINATIONS: Argentina, Brazil, Bolivia, Chile, China, Colombia, Costa Rica, Dominican Republic, Ecuador, Egypt, France, Germany, Guatemala, Honduras, Italy, Japan, Mexico, Morocco, Peru, Russia, Spain, Switzerland, Uruguay, and Venezuela, .

DURATION OF COURSES: Minimum 1 or 2 weeks. Classes start every Monday year-round in most locations; some have specific start dates.

ACCOMMODATION: Local host families, shared apartments, hostels, bed and breakfasts, and student residences.

OTHER SERVICES: Activities and excursions, special language and culture courses such as Business Spanish, French Cuisine, Roman Archaeology, and Brazilian Dance.

> **CACTUS LANGUAGE TRAINING**
> 4 Clarence House, 30–31 North Street, Brighton BN1 1EB
> ☎ (0)845 130 4775
> ☎ (0)1273 725 200
> ✍ info@cactuslanguagetraining.com
> 🖳 www.cactuslanguagetraining.com

Cactus is a specialist language travel agency. Learning options include language holidays abroad, evening courses in 41 locations and 24 languages across the UK, private and remote tuition, and in-company language and cultural training.

COST: Varies hugely from course to course (see website). One example: French and surfing in Biarritz - fortnight-long courses cost from £919 per person (course only).

OTHER SERVICES: Cactus co-operates with Global Vision International to arrange language courses in conjunction with GVI volunteer placements.

CALEDONIA – LANGUAGES, CULTURE, ADVENTURE
33 Sandport Street, Leith, Edinburgh EH6 6AP
☎ (0)131 621 7721/2
info@caledonialanguages.co.uk
www.caledonialanguages.com

Established in 1994, Caledonia's main focuses are arranging language, culture, and adventure travel abroad.

PROGRAMME DESCRIPTION: Caledonia offers short- and long-term language courses with accommodation (usually homestay, but other options are available) throughout Europe and Latin America. They also arrange volunteer work placements in Latin America, work experience programmes, language + activity courses (eg Spanish + dance in Spain, Cuba, Argentina, and the Dominican Republic; Spanish + trekking in Cuba; Portuguese + trekking in Brazil; French + sailing in Nice), and language + learning courses (eg Italian + history of art in San Giovanni; Spanish + cooking in Malaga; French + cooking in Aix-en-Provence). Volunteer community projects in Latin America for language clients include working with children in Lencois, Brazil, conservation in the cloud forests of Costa Rica, kindergarten in Peru, or teaching English in Ecuador. Work experience programmes are sometimes available working with partner language schools, companies and organisations according to the client's skills and experience.

DESTINATIONS: Caledonia's partner language schools are in France, Spain, Portugal, Italy, Germany, Austria, Russia, Argentina, Peru, Chile, Bolivia, Ecuador, Costa Rica, Brazil, Mexico, the Dominican Republic, and Cuba. Cuba is one of Caledonia's main destinations; tailor-made programmes can be taken year-round, to include dance, percussion, music, touring, and trekking, with or without language course.

PREREQUISITES: All levels are offered, from complete beginner to advanced. A higher level of Spanish or Portuguese is needed to work on volunteer and work experience programmes.

DURATION OF COURSES: Minimum 1 week (or 3–4 weeks if combined with volunteer placement), up to 12 months. Classes start year-round.

SELECTION PROCEDURES AND ORIENTATION: For volunteer and work experience programmes, a short language course is taken in the country for cultural and linguistic familiarisation before work can begin. Briefing meetings on the proposed work and occasional pre-placement site visits are arranged. Full support is given by the language school in-country.

COST: Volunteers and work experience applicants must pay an arrangement fee of £250 plus VAT, fees for the pre-placement language course in the overseas country (eg £1,355 for four weeks in Brazil, 20 lessons per week with half-board single-room accommodation). Accommodation is with local families.

CONTACT: Kath Bateman, Director.

CESA LANGUAGES ABROAD
CESA House, Pennance Road, Lanner, Cornwall TR16 5TQ
☎ (0)1209 211 800
info@cesalanguages.com
www.cesalanguages.com

Founding member of Year Out Group (yearoutgroup.org).

COURSES OFFERED: Beginner, intermediate, and advanced courses in French (Cannes, Nice, Montpellier, Rouen, Tours, Antibes, Bordeaux, Paris; or, for a more exotic option, Guadeloupe), Spanish (Seville, Nerja, Salamanca, Malaga, or Madrid in Spain; plus Argentina, Chile, Mexico, Costa Rica, Peru, or Ecuador), German (Berlin, Heidelberg, Lindau, Munich, or Cologne; and Kitzbühel or Vienna in Austria), Italian (Florence, Rome, Sorrento, Siena, and Viareggio), Portuguese, Mandarin/Cantonese, Russian, Dutch, Greek, and Arabic (in Morocco). Also combination courses, such as Italian/Spanish/French + cookery; German/Spanish + skiing; Spanish + diving/surfing; French + surfing/sailing.

DURATION OF COURSES: 1–48 weeks, with possibility of studying in more than one location during a year-out programme. At least one start date per month year-round. Set dates apply to language + activities.

QUALIFICATIONS OFFERED: DELE preparation offered in Spain; DELF, Alliance Française, and CCIP exams in France; TRKI exams in Russia. Full range of CEFR (European) exams offered in Germany and Austria.

COST: Languages for Life 8-week course in Seville or Madrid costs from £1,856, including shared apartment accommodation and 20 hours' tuition per week. A 4-week course with college residence accommodation and 20 lessons a week in Heidelberg costs from £724.

ACCOMMODATION: Options include student apartments or residences, on-campus accommodation, host families, sole-occupancy apartments, and hotels.

DON QUIJOTE
2–4 Stoneleigh Park Road, Epsom, Surrey KT19 0QT
☎ (0)20 8786 8081
uk@donquijote.org
www.donquijote.org

COURSES OFFERED: Intensive Spanish (20 lessons a week) and super-intensive (30 lessons a week) courses for all levels throughout Spain: Alicante, Barcelona, Cadiz, Granada, Madrid, Malaga, Marbella, Pamplona, Puerto de La Cruz (Tenerife), Salamanca, Seville, and Valencia, and Guanajuato, Mexico, plus many other destinations in Mexico and Latin America. Also available is Spanish for Life (12 weeks and longer) and a Spanish Study and Volunteer Programme at locations in Mexico and Latin America.

DURATION OF COURSES: 1–40 weeks.

QUALIFICATIONS OFFERED: Students will receive a certificate of attendance and level attained at the end of the course.

COST: From £431 for 2-week intensive course and shared twin-room lodging in a self-catering student flat. Spanish for Life courses start at £2,265 for 12 weeks, including student flat accommodation.

ACCOMMODATION: Homestay, residence, and flats.

FOLLOW-UP: Specialised courses available including a Spanish and Paid Jobs in Spain programme. Private tuition is available at all schools.

Language school association that inspects and accredits private language schools which teach the official language(s) of their country; currently over 100 schools in 90+ worldwide destinations.

COURSES OFFERED: French, German, Italian, Japanese, Mandarin/Cantonese, Portuguese, Russian, and Spanish courses worldwide, from short- to long-term and general to specialised, or in combination with local activities, cultural studies, cookery, dance, art, sport, etc. Some IALC schools arrange work experience, au pairing, and volunteering.

ACCOMMODATION: Normally a choice of family stay, hall of residence, guesthouse, or flat-share.

APPLICATION PROCEDURES: Contact IALC schools directly. The Canterbury office does not handle student enquiries. Contact details for member schools appear on the IALC website.

CONTACT: Jan Capper or Miguel Fenton at Head Office.

EIL UK
Elphick House, 287 Worcester Road, Malvern, Worcestershire WR14 1AB
☎ (0)1684 562577
✎ info@eiluk.org
🖥 www.eiluk.org

EIL is a registered charity specialising in developing understanding between cultures. Language learning programme with homestay offered in a range of countries. For example, one-to-one Spanish tuition in Ecuador with homestay starts from £465 for 2 weeks (travel not included).

EN FAMILLE OVERSEAS
58 Abbey Close, Peacehaven, East Sussex BN10 7SD
☎ (0)1273 588 636
✎ info@enfamilleoverseas.co.uk
🖥 www.enfamilleoverseas.co.uk

Arranges immersion language homestays in France with or without tuition. Also in Spain, Italy, and Germany.

CONTACT: Clare Cox.

IALC (INTERNATIONAL ASSOCIATION OF LANGUAGE CENTRES)
Lombard House, 12/17 Upper Bridge Street, Canterbury CT1 2NF
☎ (0)1227 769 007
✎ info@ialc.org
🖥 www.ialc.org

LANACOS
High Street, Wrotham, Sevenoaks, Kent TN15 7AH
☎ (0)1732 456 543
✎ languages@lanacos.com
🖥 www.lanacos.com

Language agency run by linguists.

COURSES OFFERED: Language courses in more than 200 locations: Spanish in many Spanish and Latin American cities; French in Paris, Côte d'Azur, Montpellier, Bordeaux, and Aix-en-Provence; German in Berlin, Cologne, Bavaria, Vienna and Salzburg; Italian in Rome, Florence, Milan, Venice, and Genoa; Portuguese in Lisbon, Algarve, and Brazil; Greek in Athens and Crete; Japanese in Tokyo; Mandarin in Shanghai; and Arabic in Cairo.

DURATION OF COURSES: 2+ weeks. Special 12-week gap year courses in France, Spain, Italy, Germany, China, and Latin America.

COST: £505 for a fortnight in Granada to £1,620 for 12-week course in Berlin or Cologne.

ACCOMMODATION: Homestays with full or half board, bed and breakfasts, single or shared apartments.

LANGUAGE COURSES ABROAD
67–71 Ashby Road, Loughborough, Leicestershire LE11 3AA
☎ (0)1509 211 612
✎ info@languagesabroad.co.uk
🖥 www.languagesabroad.co.uk

Language Courses Abroad Ltd is a UK-based language travel agency, offering in-country full immersion language courses at more than 100 schools. Trading name is Apple Languages (www.applelanguages.com). Member of WYSE (World Youth Student and Educational Travel Confederation) and ALTO (Association of Language Travel Organisations).

PROGRAMME DESCRIPTION: In-country language courses in Spanish, French, German, Italian, Portuguese, Greek, Russian, Japanese, Mandarin/Cantonese, and others, sometimes in preparation for work experience placements (see entry in 'Directory of Work Experience Abroad').

PREREQUISITES: Minimum age 16 for junior courses, otherwise 18, average age 18–26.

DURATION AND TIME OF PLACEMENTS: 1–40 weeks.

ACCOMMODATION: Shared self-catering student apartments, private studio apartments, host families, student residences or hotels.

CONTACT: Scott Cather, Language Travel Adviser.

TRAVELLERS WORLDWIDE
Caravelle House, 17/19 Goring Road, Worthing, West Sussex BN12 4AP
☎ (0)1903 502 595
info@travellersworldwide.com
www.travellersworldwide.com

Travellers is a Founder Member of the Year Out Group.

PROGRAMME DESCRIPTION: A huge range of cultural and language courses on offer in a wide range of countries.

DESTINATIONS: Argentina, Australia, Brazil, China, Ecuador, Guatemala, India, Kenya, Malaysia, South Africa, and Sri Lanka.

NUMBER OF PLACEMENTS PER YEAR: 1,000+.

PREREQUISITES: No qualifications or previous experience are necessary, just a good dose of enthusiasm. Minimum age 17. All welcome.

DURATION AND TIME OF PLACEMENTS: From 1 week to 1 year, subject to visa requirements, with flexible start and finish dates year-round.

COST: Prices start from £695 and include food, accommodation, airport pick-up, induction, orientation, 24/7 support on the ground and at home, but don't include international travel, visas, or insurance.

CONTACT: Jennifer Perkes, Managing Director.

VIS-À-VIS
2–4 Stoneleigh Park Road, Epsom KT19 0QT
☎ (0)20 8786 8021
info@visavis.org
www.visavis.org

COURSES OFFERED: Courses for all levels in French at schools in France (Paris, Annecy, Antibes, Montpellier, Nice, Royan, Montreux, and Vichy), Belgium (Brussels), and Canada (Montréal). Many activities and excursions available in all locations.

DURATION OF COURSES: Minimum 1 week.

COST: Prices start at about £976 (2011) for a 2-week course (20 lessons a week), including single-room half-board accommodation with a family in Annecy. Additional enrolment fee of £50 and accommodation booking fee of £44+.

QUALIFICATIONS OFFERED: Some courses prepare students for official language diplomas, such as the DELF and the more advanced level (DALF). These can be worked towards at the student's own pace.

ACCOMMODATION: Student flats and halls of residence are available at a higher cost for those wishing to mix with other students. Host families also accommodate students, which allows the student an insight into French culture.

LANGUAGE SCHOOLS ABROAD

FRENCH

ALLIANCE FRANÇAISE PARIS ILE-DE-FRANCE
101 Boulevard Raspail, 75270 Paris Cedex 06, France
☎ +33 1 42 84 90 00
info@alliancefr.org
www.alliancefr.org

Alliance Française has more than 1,000 language centres in 135 countries, including in the UK, where students can study French in their own country.

COURSES OFFERED IN PARIS: French language courses at 5 levels, with a choice of shared or individual classes at the school in Paris. Students have the chance to study general French or specialised French, eg French for tourism, medicine, or business.

DURATION OF COURSES: 20 hours a week intensive, or 9 hours a week extensive; minimum 2 weeks extensive.

QUALIFICATIONS OFFERED: Various French diplomas can be awarded, including those awarded by Paris Chamber of Commerce and Industry, and the Ministry of National Education. Normally, test can be sat after 128 hours.

COST: Varies, depending on the number of weeks: about €220 a week for intensive, €85 a week for 9 hours' instruction, plus annual enrolment fee of €58.

ACCOMMODATION: Provided on demand in student residence, studio flats or French families.

ELFCA – INSTITUT D' ENSEIGNEMENT DE LA LANGUE FRANÇAISE SUR LA CÔTE D'AZUR

66 avenue de Toulon, 83400 Hyères, Provence, France

☎ +33 04 94 65 03 31

🖰 elfca@elfca.com

🖳 www.elfca.com

COURSES OFFERED: Total immersion French language courses.

DURATION OF COURSES: 1–24 weeks.

QUALIFICATIONS OFFERED: Long-term courses lead to recognised qualifications; ELFCA is an exam centre for the TEF (Test d'Evaluation de Français de la Chambre de Commerce de Paris).

COST: From €200 per week for long-term courses lasting more than 22 weeks. Weekly charge for shorter stays is in the range of €230–€300; homestay accommodation with half-board costs €190 per week (shared) or €210 (single).

ACCOMMODATION: Homestay accommodation, apartment, or hotel.

CONTACT: Colette Samwells, Co-Director.

INTER-SEJOURS

179 rue de Courcelles, 75017 Paris, France

☎ +33 1 47 63 06 81

🖰 aideinfo.intersejours@wanadoo.fr

🖳 www.inter-sejours.fr

COURSES OFFERED: Language courses as part of a homestay in Paris (and French students placed abroad in England, Australia, New Zealand, USA, etc.). Language courses also arranged in Spain, Germany, Italy, Costa Rica, and Canada. European students are placed as au pairs in France, Spain, Italy, Germany, Austria (and French students in English-speaking countries including Canada, Australia, and New Zealand), or in hotel or restaurant jobs in the UK and Spain, internships in Ireland, etc. Volunteering opportunities in USA, Latin America, Asia, and Africa. Au pair stays organised in Europe, Australia, and Canada.

DURATION OF COURSES: Minimum 1 week up to 34 weeks, with Monday start dates throughout the year. Specified start dates for beginners or for courses leading to exams.

QUALIFICATIONS OFFERED: Opportunity to work towards the DELF examination and the *Certificat Pratique de Français*.

COST: Examples of price in Paris: 30 lessons in 2 weeks would cost €725. A standard course with 20 lessons over 2 weeks costs €545.

ACCOMMODATION: Accommodation and breakfast with a host family costs €189 per week in Paris or €210 half board in the suburbs.

CONTACT: Marie-Helene Pierrot, Director.

GERMAN

BWS GERMANLINGUA

Hackenstrasse 7c, D-80331 Munich, Germany

☎ +49 89 59 98 92 00

🖰 info@bws-germanlingua.de

🖳 www.bws-germanlingua.de

COURSES OFFERED: German language courses in Munich or Berlin, standard (20 lessons per week), intensive (25 lessons), or one-to-one.

DURATION OF COURSES: 2–48 weeks. Minimum 1 week for a tailor-made course. Can join on any Monday (unless total beginner).

COST: €370 for 2 weeks to €5,010 for 48 weeks. Prices higher for intensive courses (from €440), and one-to-one (€410 for 1 week with 10 lessons).

ACCOMMODATION: With a German family, in a flat shared with students, or in a studio apartment.

CONTACT: Florian Meierhofer, Proprietor.

CAMPUS AUSTRIA

c/o Cultura Wien, Bauernmarkt 18, 1010 Vienna

☎ +43 01 42 77 24 101

🖰 info@campus-austria.at

🖳 www.campus-austria.at

Source of information about German language courses at 16 different centres in Austria.

COURSES OFFERED: Some courses lead to Goethe Institut qualifications or the Austrian Diploma for German as a Foreign Language (OESD).

DURATION OF COURSES: Normally 2 or more weeks, year-round, with choice of holiday courses and youth programmes.

COST: Prices vary, but approximately €500 per fortnight excluding accommodation.

DEUTSCH-INSTITUT TIROL

Staudach 23, 6370 Kitzbühel, Austria

☎ +43 53 56 71 274

🖰 deutschinstitut@aon.at

🖳 www.gap-year.at

COURSES OFFERED: German language combined with ski and snowboard instruction, specially designed for gap year students. (See 'Directory of Specialist Gap Year Programmes'.)

DID DEUTSCH-INSTITUT
Gutleutstrasse 32, 60329 Frankfurt am Main, Germany
☎ +49 69 2400 4560
✆ office@did.de
🖥 www.did.de

COURSES OFFERED: Short- and long-term intensive German language courses year-round for adults (17+) in Berlin, Frankfurt, Hamburg, and Munich. Standard, intensive, premium courses. Summer programmes for juniors in many more cities throughout Germany. Group tuition in small classes or on individual basis.

DURATION OF COURSES: Short-term 1–7 weeks. Long-term courses last 8–48 weeks in Berlin, Frankfurt, Hamburg, and Munich.

QUALIFICATIONS OFFERED: Diploma examinations for long-term stays, at the end of each course level, B1, B2, C1, and C2 under supervision of GfdS, the German Language Society, Wiesbaden.

ACCOMMODATION: Choice of homestays with German families; shared flats, youth hostels, and apartments also available.

OTHER SERVICES: Internships are also offered, as well as university placement and university summer courses.

GLS CAMPUS BERLIN
Kastanienallee 82, 10435 Berlin, Germany
☎ +49 30 78 00 89 0
✆ german@gls-berlin.de
🖥 www.german-berlin.de

COURSES OFFERED: Language courses offered year-round at all levels, starting every Monday. GLS campus occupies 9,000m^2 in Berlin's trendy area of Prenzlauer Berg, with its own hotel and restaurant.

DURATION OF COURSES: 20, 30, or 40 lessons per week for any number of weeks. International mix in classes of about 8.

COST: Sample price for 2 weeks German language course with 20 weekly lessons, activity programme, and self-catered single room in a flat shared with Berliners is €464.

ACCOMMODATION: 50 studio apartments on campus (some mini-lots) and apartments near Brandenburg Gate.

Flat share with Berliners, bed and breakfast, host family, and other options.

OTHER SERVICES: Extended sight-seeing programme in and around Berlin. GLS runs an internship programme combining a language course of at least 4 weeks with a work experience placement in a Berlin-based company (see entry in 'Directory of Work Experience'.)

GOETHE INSTITUT
Headquarters in Munich, Germany
🖥 www.goethe.de
UK office: 50 Princes Gate, London SW7 2PH
☎ (0)20 7596 4000
✆ german@london.goethe.org
🖥 www.goethe.de/london

COURSES OFFERED: German language courses at all levels in 13 attractive locations in Germany and 136 institutes in 92 countries worldwide. All course details and institute addresses are on website (www.goethe.de/uun/adr/wwt/enindex.htm). Summer courses offered in several locations, including Heidelberg and Lake Constance.

DURATION OF COURSES: 2–12 weeks.

QUALIFICATIONS OFFERED: The Goethe Institut administers its own language exams, which correspond to the levels of the Common European Framework of Reference for Languages (CEFR) and range from A1 for beginners to C2 for language skills at the highest level.

ITALIAN

ACCADEMIA DEL GIGLIO
Via Ghibellina 116, 50122 Florence, Italy
☎ +39 055 230 2467
✆ info@adg.it
🖥 www.adg.it
🖥 www.italyhometuition.com

COURSES OFFERED: Italian courses for foreigners plus Art and Art History courses (see below). Intensive classes or one-to-one tuition.

DURATION OF COURSES: From 1 week to 6 months. Choice of 2–5 hours of classes a day.

QUALIFICATIONS OFFERED: Certificate attesting to the programme/level and the number of hours that the student has attended.

COST: 1-week intensive course costs €180 (4 hours a day); 8 weeks costs €1,140. Enrolment fee of €45.

ACCOMMODATION: All kinds of accommodation can be arranged, from single room in a family home from €32 a day half-board to €430 for 4 weeks in a single room in a flat, sharing kitchen and other facilities. School located in a peaceful area of the city centre.

OTHER SERVICES: Visits and social activities included in the price. Free wi-fi area for students, as well as a library and video library.

CONTACT: Lorenzo Capanni, Assistant Director.

THE BRITISH INSTITUTE OF FLORENCE
Piazza Strozzi 2, 50123 Florence, Italy
☎ +39 055 267781
info@britishinstitute.it
www.britishinstitute.it

Housed in two magnificent buildings on either side of the River Arno in the historic centre of Florence, and minutes from all the city's museums, galleries, and churches, the British Institute of Florence has a long tradition of excellence in its teaching, and is recognised as a centre for learning by the Tuscan Region.

COURSES OFFERED: The Institute offers students the opportunity of experiencing the life and culture of Florence within the framework of a structured programme of study. Courses are offered in Italian language, history of art, and life drawing.

DURATION OF COURSES: 1–12 weeks throughout the year.

COST: Fees vary according to the course chosen, eg a 4-week Italian language course €630 and a 4-week history of art course €615. 4-week combined Italian and history of art course is €1,150.

ACCOMMODATION: Can be arranged in local homes, *pensione* and hotels. Price for homestay accommodation starts at approximately €30 per night. There is a fee of €25 for arranging accommodation.

OTHER ACTIVITIES: A regular programme of events, including lectures, concerts, and films, is held in the Institute's Harold Acton Library overlooking the River Arno.

CENTRO CULTURALE GIACOMO PUCCINI
Via Vespucci 173, 55049 Viareggio (LU), Italy
☎ +39 058 443 0253
infopack@centropuccini.it
www.centropuccini.it

COURSES OFFERED: Italian language.

DESTINATION: Viagreggio is a seaside resort in Tuscany.

DURATION OF COURSES: Standard 2-week course includes 4 lessons per day; intensive course includes extra 10 or 20 hours of private tuition over the fortnight.

Courses offered year-round. 32-week courses suitable for a gap year (mid-January to mid-August, early May to December, or September to May).

QUALIFICATIONS OFFERED: Firenze Diploma Examination preparatory courses available (leading to DELI, DILI, DILC, DALI, and DALC; see www.acad.it).

COST: Courses lasting for 32–34 weeks cost €5,720. Standard course costs €300 for 2 weeks plus registration fee of €70. Family accommodation with breakfast from €260 per fortnight in a shared room, mid-season, or single room in an apartment for €507, high season.

OTHER ACTIVITIES: Sailing, riding, culinary courses, music courses, etc.

CONTACT: Elisa Campioni.

KOINE
Borgo Santa Croce 17, 50122 Florence, Italy
☎ +39 055 213 881
info@koinecenter.com
www.koinecenter.com

COURSES OFFERED: Italian language for foreigners offered year-round in Florence, Lucca and Bologna, and Elba Island.

DURATION OF COURSES: 1 week to 6 months.

QUALIFICATIONS OFFERED: Possible to study towards the Certificate CILS from Siena University.

COST: Sample cost in Florence: €1,620 for a month's tuition (20 hours a week), plus €310 for a month's basic shared accommodation without use of kitchen.

ACCOMMODATION: With an Italian family or in an independent apartment.

PICCOLA UNIVERSITÀ ITALIANA
Largo Antonio Pandullo 6, 89861 Tropea, Italy
☎ +39 0963 603 284
Skype: piccola.universita.italiana
info@piccolauniversitaitaliana.com
www.piccolauniversitaitaliana.com

Italian language school by the sea.

COURSES OFFERED: Italian language courses recognised by the Italian Ministry of Education, University, and Research, including individual crash courses in business Italian. Courses can be combined with activities and lessons in windsurfing, catamaran sailing, scuba diving, mountain biking, cooking, or painting. Courses are given to small groups of a maximum of 3–6 students.

DURATION OF COURSES: Any duration from 1 week. Courses begin every Monday, year-round (except during Christmas holidays).

QUALIFICATIONS OFFERED: Opportunity to work towards the CILS examination.

COST: 8-week conversation course costs €670; 8-week regular course costs €1,205; 8-week intensive course costs €2,387. Special rates for long stays. Registration fee of €100 includes transfer from and to the airport/train station at Lamezia Terme, or 2 excursions on the weekly cultural programme.

ACCOMMODATION: Accommodation is extra at €950 for 8 weeks in a single room (shared flat), or €1,365 in a single-room holiday flats in the centre of Tropea, with a sea or mountain view. Flats usually have 2 or 3 rooms, kitchen, and terrace or balcony.

OTHER ACTIVITIES: Cultural programme offers excursions in southern Italy.

SPANISH

ACADEMIA DE ESPANOL SURPACIFICO
Avenida 24 y Calle 15, Edificio Barre, 3er Piso, Manabi, Ecuador
☎ +593 5 2610 838
📧 surpacifico@easynet.net.ec
🖥 www.surpacifico.k12.ec
🖥 www.ecuadorspanishschools.com

COURSES OFFERED: Intensive Spanish programmes, with private or group lessons. Range of special courses and combinations with activities such as Spanish and surfing, Spanish and kitesurfing and medical Spanish. Also offer an ecological volunteer programme on an organic farm, volunteering with children, etc.

DURATION OF COURSES: Language courses last 2–24 weeks. Spanish and surfing: 1–8 weeks; Spanish and kitesurfing: 2–8 weeks. All courses can be started on any Monday of the year.

QUALIFICATIONS OFFERED: Courses are accredited by the Ecuadorian Ministry of Education and Culture.

COST: US$160 per week for 20 hours of private lessons; $120 for group lessons. Intensive Manta Activo programme (30–35 hours, combining Spanish classes with excursions on which students use the Spanish they have learned) costs $270–$310 per week. Spanish and surfing $400 a week, Spanish and kitesurfing $912 for 2 weeks. Ecological volunteer programme costs $1,152 for 6 weeks.

ACCOMMODATION: Homestay (private bedroom, all meals and laundry service) or shared student apartment (private bedroom in a furnished apartment).

CONTACT: Manuel Bucheli, Director.

AIL MADRID SPANISH LANGUAGE IMMERSION SCHOOL IN SPAIN
C/Nuñez de Balboa 17, 2°D, 28001
Madrid, Spain
☎ +34 91 725 63 50
📧 info@ailmadrid.com
🖥 www.ailmadrid.com

PROGRAMME DESCRIPTION: 12-week Spanish language course in Madrid and other cities in Spain with work placement options.

PREREQUISITES: Minimum age 17, average age 22.

DURATION AND TIME OF PLACEMENTS: 12–48 weeks with flexible start dates.

COST: 12-week programme from €3,500.

CONTACT: Maya Bychova.

CHILE INSIDE
Andrés de Fuenzalida 17, Oficina 51, Providencia, Santiago, Chile
☎ +56 2 335 9072
📧 info@chileinside.cl
🖥 www.chileinside.cl

PROGRAMME DESCRIPTION: Spanish language courses and accommodation throughout Chile.

NUMBER OF PLACEMENTS PER YEAR: 200–300.

DESTINATIONS: Chile.

PREREQUISITES: Minimum age 18.

COST: Programme fee depends on the Spanish course (group or intensive course, private classes), the location of the school, and the length of the programme. 1-week Spanish course in Santiago starts from $178 (without accommodation).

CONTACT: Marion Ruhland, Founder and Executive Director.

CIS – CENTRO DE INTERCAMBIO Y SOLIDARIDAD
El Salvador office: Mélida Anaya Montes
Language School, Ave. Aguilares y Ave.
Bolivar #103, Colonia Libertad, San Salvador, El Salvador
☎ +503 2235 1330
☎ +503 2226 5362
📧 info@cis-elsalvador.org
🖥 www.cis-elsalvador.org
US OFFICE: Los Olivos CIS, PO Box 76, Westmont, IL 60559–0076

COURSES OFFERED: Spanish classes and political-cultural programme. English teaching, and Fair Trade Crafts volunteer opportunities also available.

DURATION OF COURSES: Classes start every Monday. Any number of weeks can be booked. Volunteers must make a 10-week commitment for English teaching, with start dates specified on website.

QUALIFICATIONS OFFERED: Recreational courses.

COST: US$125 per week for the first 4 weeks of 4 hours of morning classes, plus a one-time $25 application fee. After 4 weeks, the weekly charge goes down to $115. $40 per week for afternoon political-cultural programme. Volunteers are eligible to receive a 50% discount on Spanish classes. Volunteers must also pay a one-time programme fee of $100.

ACCOMMODATION: Homestays with breakfast and dinner cost $80 a week. Alternatives in guesthouses or shared flats can be arranged.

CONTACT: Emily Salava.

ÍBERO SPANISH SCHOOL ARGENTINA
Uruguay 150, Capital Federal (1015), Argentina
☎ +54 11 5218 0240
✆ info@iberospanish.com
🖥 www.iberospanish.com

COURSES OFFERED: Spanish language immersion courses in Buenos Aires. 8 levels of Spanish classes from absolute beginner to superior. Course involves weekly activities that allow learners to practise Spanish in an informal environment. Students can choose themed course, eg on Che Guevara, Diego Maradona, or Jorge Louis Borges. Also offer TEFL training alone or in combination with Spanish course.

DESTINATIONS: Buenos Aires, Argentina.

DURATION OF COURSES: All courses last 3 weeks. Courses run Monday to Friday throughout the year. Students take a placement exam to establish the correct level, and a final exam upon the completion of each 3-week level. Standard course consists of 20 group lessons per week. 10, 20, or 40 hours per week of private lessons can also be arranged.

QUALIFICATIONS OFFERED: Courses can lead to CELU qualification (international examination from Argentina), or DELE from Spain.

COST: US$125 per week group Spanish lessons, including materials, application fee, and textbook. 4-week package including Spanish lessons, accommodation, airport pick-up, and Spanish textbook costs US$1,030. Accommodation can be arranged in shared apartments, homestays, or private apartments in downtown Buenos Aires.

CONTACT: Florencia Bozzano, Director.

JAKERA ADVENTURE VENEZUELA
Based in Mochima National Park but also a school in Merida, Venezuela
☎ +353 86 822 0333
✆ info@jakera.com
🖥 www.jakera.com
🖥 www.learn-spanish-in-latin-america.com

PROGRAMME DESCRIPTION: Adventure Travelling Classroom programme blends opportunity to learn Spanish with travel and expeditions, including a jeep safari to the Gran Sabana, hiking to the top of Roriama, sea kayaking among Caribbean islands and the Orinoco Delta Jungle, plus other adventure activities such as rafting and paragliding. Longer programmes include community volunteering in combination with intensive Spanish. 6-month programme also involves work experience in a Spanish-speaking environment, eg 1 month of teaching English, helping in a national park, farm or zoo, tour guiding, journalism, tourism, etc.

NUMBER OF PLACEMENTS PER YEAR: Around 400 (about two-thirds are from Europe).

DESTINATIONS: Venezuela. Jakera has two bases: beach resort of Playa Colorada and the university city of Merida.

DURATION AND TIME OF PLACEMENTS: 1 week to 6 months. Average duration is 8 weeks.

PREREQUISITES: Minimum age 18, average age 22–24. No need to be especially fit.

COST: Flagship 8-week Adventure Travelling Classroom programme costs £2,550, including accommodation (varies from shared dorm to hammock at base camp in Playa Colorada), meals, Spanish tuition, and expeditions.

CONTACT: Tim Poullain-Patterson, Director.

MALACA INSTITUTO
Calle Cortada 6, Cerrado de Calderón, 29018 Málaga, Spain
☎ +34 952 29 3242
✆ espanol@malacainstituto.com
🖥 www.MalacaInstituto.com

Students at Malaca Instituto from all over the world create a cosmopolitan environment and a culturally enriching experience. The Instituto is inspected by and meets the quality criteria of the Instituto Cervantes, CEELE, EAQUALS, and IALC.

COURSES OFFERED: A variety of Spanish language and culture classes are offered, from standard beginner to preparation for university entrance. Gappers usually take courses of between 16 and 36 weeks. Hispanic Studies programme is especially suitable. In addition, a range of courses short and long includes Spanish + dance, Spanish + cookery, Spanish + internships, as well as general intensive Spanish, summer courses, and one-to-one tuition.

DURATION OF COURSES: Hispanic Studies term I – 16 weeks; term II – 20 weeks.

QUALIFICATIONS OFFERED: Students can work towards the DELE examinations or Spanish university entrance if their level of language is suitably advanced.

ACCOMMODATION: All types with single and twin rooms.

MARIPOSA SPANISH SCHOOL & ECO HOTEL
San Juan de la Concepcion, Masaya, Nicaragua
☎ +505 4866 99455
📧 paulette.goudge@googlemail.com
💻 www.mariposaspanishschool.com

COURSES OFFERED: Intensive Spanish courses for all levels run year-round, 4 hours per day; extra classes available. Emphasis on Spanish as used in Nicaragua. 2 hours per day of grammar, 2 hours of conversation. Opportunities to integrate with the local community by volunteering in gardens, the Mariposa organic farms, local schools, building projects, etc. Income from school and hotel (owned by a British expat) supports a range of local projects, from solar power to childcare. Volunteers are placed individually and work alongside a local to help improve their Spanish. Wide range of afternoon and weekend activities and outings, and many discussions on Nicaraguan culture, history, or food.

COST: $225 per week or $750 per month to cover homestay, 20 hours of classes, volunteer work option, and 3 meals a day. Weekly charge of $350 for staying in the eco-hotel with classes and afternoon activities. Cabin accommodation can also be arranged.

CONTACT: Paulette Goudge.

MESTER SPANISH COURSES
Vázquez Coronado 5, 37002 Salamanca, Spain
☎ +34 923 21 38 35
📧 mester@mester.com
💻 www.mester.com

COURSES OFFERED: Spanish at all levels offered in Salamanca.

DURATION OF COURSES: 1–40 weeks starting every Monday. 40-week academic year course includes language classes (including business Spanish) and Spanish culture classes. Students do not need to know any Spanish before coming to the school.

QUALIFICATIONS OFFERED: Some courses are recreational; others lead to DELE and Certificate of Business Spanish (exam fees extra). All students who successfully complete their course are given a diploma or certificate of study on leaving.

COST: From €165 for a week-long course of twice-daily lessons of conversation and grammar to €4,000 for an academic year (865 lessons).

ACCOMMODATION: Full range, including homestays, student flats, university residences, and independent apartments.

CONTACT: Carolina Penacho, International Relations.

MONTANITA SPANISH SCHOOL
On the main street, on the hill, 50m before the bus stop, in Provincia de Santa Elena, Ecuador.
☎ +593 420 60166
📧 info@montanitaspanishschool.com
💻 www.montanitaspanishschool.com

COURSES OFFERED: Spanish language courses alongside lessons in Latin American history and culture. Most popular option is Spanish with surfing. Salsa, yoga and diving classes also available. Volunteer service can be arranged at local hospital, in a local nursery, or in primary schools.

DURATION OF COURSES: Average stay is 6 weeks, but can be shorter or up to 12 weeks (no visa requirements in Ecuador for stays of less than 3 months).

COST: $20 registration fee plus $140 per week for group classes, $205 for private lessons. Surf lessons cost $75 a week, salsa lessons $35 a week, and yoga lessons $25. Volunteering is free.

ACCOMMODATION: Accommodation is extra: student dormitory accommodation costs $36 a week, private cabanas $112.

CONTACT: Manuel Bucheli, Owner.

SPANISH IN THE MOUNTAINS
Isla Victoria s/n Bariloche, Patagonia, Argentina
☎ +54 2944 467597
📧 info@spanishinthemountains.com
💻 www.spanishinthemountains.com

COURSES OFFERED: Spanish as a second language. Lessons can be combined with outdoor activities in the mountains.

DURATION OF COURSES: Tailor-made.

QUALIFICATIONS OFFERED: Recreational only.

COST: $15 per hour for tuition.

ACCOMMODATION: Homestay at a cost of $17 per night.

CONTACT: Maria Eugenia Favret, Programme Co-ordinator.

LA UNION CENTRO LINGUISTICO
1A Avenida Sur No. 21, Antigua, Guatemala
☎ +502 7832 7337
✆ info@launion.edu.gt
🖥 www.launion.edu.gt

Organisation for sharing Spanish language and Guatemalan culture run by a group of experienced Guatemalan Spanish teachers. Also arrange volunteer placements (see 'Directory of Volunteering Abroad') and tours of Guatemala.

COURSES OFFERED: Spanish as a second language.

COST: $95-$125 for 4 hours of tuition over 5 days, depending on season and morning or afternoon.

ACCOMMODATION: Homestay at a cost of $95 per week.

CONTACT: Juan Carlos Martinez, General Director.

OTHER LANGUAGES

THE ATHENS CENTRE
48 Archimidous Street, 116 36 Athens, Greece
☎ +30 210 701 2268
✆ info@athenscentre.gr
✆ athenscr@ath.forthnet.gr
🖥 www.athenscentre.gr

COURSES OFFERED: Modern Greek.

DURATION OF COURSES: 3, 4, 5, 7, or 12 weeks throughout the year, and summer immersion course (3 weeks on the island of Spetses).

QUALIFICATIONS OFFERED: Serious courses with certificate given at end.

ACCOMMODATION: Hotels, pensions, apartment sublets, and studios, but no homestays.

COST: From €650 for 2-week course plus accommodation in apartment.

CIAL CENTRO DE LINGUAS
Lisbon office: **Av. da República, 41–8° E, 1050–187, Lisbon, Portugal**
☎ +351 21 794 04 48
✆ portuguese@cial.pt
🖥 www.cial.pt
Algarve office: **Rua Almeida Garrett, 44 r/c, 8000–206 Faro, Portugal**
☎ +351 289 807 611
✆ algarve@cial.pt

COURSES OFFERED: Full Portuguese language and culture course in six levels, with 60 lessons of language tuition for every level. Portuguese plus volunteering, professional internship, and surf courses available.

DURATION OF COURSES: 4 weeks for each course, with new courses every month.

QUALIFICATIONS OFFERED: Possibility of qualifying for the Diploma of Portuguese as a Foreign Language.

COST: 4-week course will cost €952 (2011), including textbook, audio CD, and social programme.

ACCOMMODATION: In individual rooms in private homes, with breakfast included.

CONTACT: Dr Alexandra Borges de Sousa, Director of Studies.

CRCC ASIA
106 Weston Street, London, SE1 3QB
☎ (0)20 7378 6220
✆ internships@crccasia.com
🖥 www.crccasia.com

A consulting company that runs China Internship Programme (see 'Directory of Work Experience Abroad') and finance, legal, and Mandarin courses in Beijing and Shanghai.

COURSES OFFERED: One-month intensive Mandarin study run by a well-known Chinese language school, located in either Beijing or Shanghai (price £1,495). 2-week intensive China finance course, run in association with experienced industry professionals from companies such as KPMG, Lehman Brown, and China BG Capital (price £1,795). 2-week intensive course introducing law in China, run in association with Chinese and international businesses, and taught by professionals and academics (also £1,795).

DURATION OF COURSES: 2 or 4 weeks.

COST: £1,495-£1,795, including visas, accommodation, Chinese business culture training, survival Mandarin lessons, welcome banquet, social and business networking events, and full support.

LIDEN & DENZ LANGUAGE CENTRES
St Petersburg office: **St Petersburg and Moscow, Central Booking Office, Inzhenernaya Str. 6, 191023 St Petersburg, Russia**
☎ +7 812 334 0788
Moscow office: **Gruzinski per. 3–181, Ground floor, 123056 Moscow, Russian Federation**
☎ +7 495 254 4991
✆ bookings@lidenz.ru
🖥 www.lidenz.ru
🖥 www.russiancourses.com

COURSES OFFERED: Russian language offered at all levels from leisure course to crash course, plus academic year courses and work experience and volunteer programmes. Starting from 2011, the school offers language plus mini-group modules on business Russian, music, and literature. These modules can be booked only in addition to any group or one-to-one course and consist of 5 lessons held in the afternoons. The maximum number of students in a class is 4.

DURATION OF COURSES: Minimum 2 weeks in a group with choice of 20 hours (standard), 25 (intensive), or 25 (combination course: 20 group plus 5 hours one-to-one). One-to-one lessons available with choice of frequency (15, 20, 30, or 40 hours a week; minimum duration 1 week). Fixed duration of academic year courses are 24, 36, or 48 weeks.

QUALIFICATIONS OFFERED: All students receive a graded certificate (in Russian) at the end of their stay, indicating course type, course dates, number of lessons, and level achieved. Liden and Denz in St Petersburg and Moscow are official preparation and testing centres for the state exam TRKI (Russian as a Foreign Language).

COST: Standard course costs €173–€270 per week, depending on overall duration. Surcharges apply in peak season.

ACCOMMODATION: Homestay in single room with half board is the most popular option, at a cost of €190 per week in St Petersburg and €220 in Moscow. Shared flats etc also offered.

CONTACT: Julia Patasheva, International Relations (julia. patasheva@lidenz.ru).

ART, DESIGN, DRAMA, FILM, AND MUSIC COURSES

ART AND DESIGN

ACCADEMIA DEL GIGLIO
Lingue Arte Cultura, Via Ghibellina 116, 50122 Florence, Italy
☎ +39 055 230 2467
✆ info@adg.it
🖥 www.adg.it

COURSES OFFERED: Drawing, painting, and art history courses, in addition to Italian language courses described above. Fresco workshop available over 4 weeks.

DURATION OF COURSES: 1 week to 9 months, with 14 hours of tuition per week.

COST: 1-week art course costs €180, 2 weeks costs €340, 12 weeks costs €1,710. Enrolment fee of €45.

ACCOMMODATION: All kinds of accommodation can be arranged, from single room in a family home from €32 a day half-board, to €430 for 4 weeks in a single room in a flat, sharing kitchen and other facilities.

OTHER SERVICES: Visits and social activities included in the price. Free wi-fi area for students. Library and video library.

ART HISTORY ABROAD
The Red House,
1 Lambseth Street, Eye, Suffolk IP23 7AG
☎ (0)1379 871 800
✆ info@arthistoryabroad.com
🖥 www.arthistoryabroad.com

Year Out Group founding member.

PROGRAMME DESCRIPTION: Art and cultural programme in various cities in Italy lasting 6 weeks. See 'Directory of Specialist Gap Year Programmes' for further information.

DUAL CITY SUMMER SESSIONS
From Central Saint Martins College of Art and Design and European partner schools
CSM Short Course Office, 10 Back Hill, Clerkenwell, London EC1Y5EN
☎ (0)20 7514 7015 (for public enquiries only)
✆ london@london-milan-courses
✆ london@london-barcelona-courses.com
✆ dualcity@csm.arts.ac.uk (for admin only)
🖥 www.london-milan-courses.com
🖥 www.london-barcelona-courses.com

PROGRAMME DESCRIPTION: Summer courses in art and design between London and Milan or Barcelona. Career-boosting creative short courses in desirable European cities.

DESTINATIONS: London, Milan, Barcelona.

DURATION AND TIME OF PLACEMENTS: 2–4 weeks.

PREREQUISITES: Minimum age 18.

SELECTION PROCEDURES AND ORIENTATION:
Schools help source hotels, hostels, residences, and apartments.

COST: From £1,975.

JOHN HALL VENICE COURSE
9 Smeaton Road, London SW18 5JJ
✆ info@johnhallvenice.com
🖥 www.johnhallvenice.co.uk

COURSES OFFERED: A pre-university course for students from across the academic spectrum. The course covers art, art history, architecture, music, opera, literature, global ecological and political issues, history, and world cinema. Introductory week in London is based at the National Gallery and includes visits to Tate Modern and an introduction to the commercial art world at Christie's. This is followed by 6 weeks in Venice, where daily lectures and visits (including a private visit to San Marco) are combined with practical classes in life-drawing and photography, with optional Italian and cookery classes, and visits to Padova, Ravenna, and Palladian villas in the Veneto. The extensions of a week in Florence and 6 days in Rome continue the study of history, art, music, and architecture on-site, and include private visits to the Uffizi, the Accademia, Settignano, the Keats Shelley Memorial House, the Villa Borghese Gallery, and the Vatican and Sistine Chapel.

DURATION OF COURSES: 1 week in London, 6 weeks in Venice. Extensions: 1 week in Florence, 6 days in Rome. Offered annually from late January to March.

QUALIFICATIONS OFFERED: Interest and enthusiasm.

COST: 1 week London and 6 weeks Venice: £8,970; extension to Florence £1,290, Rome £1,230. Travel to and from Italy, accommodation including breakfast and dinner in Italy, entrance fees and excursions, and a water bus pass in Venice are included in fees. Accommodation in London not included.

CONTACT: Victoria Gillions, Administrator.

LONDON COLLEGE OF FASHION
20 John Princes Street, London W1G 0BJ
☎ (0)20 7514 7552
shortcourses@fashion.arts.ac.uk
www.fashion.arts.ac.uk/shortcourses

Member of University of the Arts London.

COURSES OFFERED: Intensive evening, weekend, and daytime courses in make-up, beauty, and all fashion-related subjects, held at one of the University of the Arts' six central London sites. Some online courses are also available.

DURATION OF COURSES: 1–15 days intensive short courses or up to 10 weeks as evening classes. Evening classes are held during autumn, spring, and summer terms, and intensive courses are offered at Christmas, Easter, and during the summer.

QUALIFICATIONS OFFERED: Certificate of attendance.

COST: Prices range from £150.

OTHER SERVICES: Help can be given finding accommodation.

CONTACT: Short course office or courses can be booked online.

STUDIO ART CENTERS INTERNATIONAL (SACI)
Palazzo dei Cartelloni, Via Sant'Antonino 11, Florence 50123, Italy
☎ +39 212 248 7225
admissions@saci-florence.edu
www.saci-florence.edu

COURSES OFFERED: Accredited courses for university-level students (minimum age 18). Semester/Year Abroad, BGSU Master of Fine Art (MFA) programme, Post-Baccalaureate Certificate in Studio Art, Art History, or Art Conservation, late spring and summer studies; 2- and 4-week non-credit summer study. Studio art, art history, design, art conservation, and Italian cultural studies. Courses offered in 40 different studio and academic disciplines: drawing, painting, fresco, etching, lithography, serigraphy, sculpture, ceramics, black-and-white photography, colour photography, video, animation, digital multimedia, illustration, graphic design, interior design, contemporary furniture design, eco design studio, design futures seminar, Italian fashion design, batik, book arts, weaving, jewellery design, Italian late medieval and early Renaissance art history, Italian high Renaissance, Mannerist, and early Baroque art history, high Baroque and Rococo European and Italian art history, 19th-century European and Italian art history, modern European and Italian art, contemporary European and Italian art, history of photography, art history seminar, museology, art conservation, conservation of archaeological objects, history of Italian opera, history of Italian cinema, history of Italian theatre, Italian acting methods and techniques, creative writing, literature and visual art, and Italian language.

DURATION OF COURSES: Fall semester: 15 weeks (September to December); spring: 15 weeks (January to April); late spring: 5 weeks (May/June); summer: 4 weeks (June/July).

QUALIFICATIONS OFFERED: Post-Baccalaureate Certificate in Studio Art, Art History, or Art Conservation. Bowling Green State University MFA in Studio Art: First Year at SACI in Florence.

COST: Tuition from $4,500 for 4–5 weeks late spring or summer plus $1,550–$1,750 for housing. Semester tuition fees are $11,800–$12,050, plus $4,600 for housing.

ACCOMMODATION: Furnished apartments near the school in Florence's historic centre.

CONTACT: Marie-Louise Lodge, Director of Information Resources.

DANCE, DRAMA, FILM, AND JOURNALISM

ACTUALITY MEDIA
115 East Illinois Street, Newberg, Oregon 97132, USA
☎ +1 503 208 5042
✎ info@actualitymedia.com
💻 www.actualitymedia.com

COURSES OFFERED: 1-month outreaches, during which participants research, write, shoot, and edit a short documentary video for a non-profit organisation in a developing country. The participants work in crews of 4 as producer, director, cinematographer, and editor.

DESTINATIONS: Colombia, Nicaragua, Guatemala.

DURATION AND FREQUENCY OF COURSES: Each outreach is one month in duration, with 3 groups sent per month (more in summer).

PREREQUISITES: Minimum age 18, average age 22. Crew members should be excited by the idea of producing a short but compelling documentary for organisations working for a good cause. Candidates should have a sense of adventure and a love of learning, be creative, intelligent, and responsible.

COST: Around $2,500 for the outreach fee, including training, equipment, insurance, cell phone, and accommodation, but not including airfare or ground transport.

ACCOMMODATION: Participants live at a local secure travellers' hostel.

OTHER SERVICES: Language study can be arranged prior to programme, and also marketing internships with partner non-profit organisations may be available for alumni.

CONTACT: Aubrie Campbell, Production Manager.

ASAD – THE ACADEMY OF THE SCIENCE OF ACTING & DIRECTING
9–15 Elthorne Road, Archway, London N19 4AJ
☎ (0)20 7272 0027
✎ info@asad.org.uk
💻 www.asad.org.uk

COURSES OFFERED: Acting and directing courses. 1-year course is for the students to understand the basic laws of good acting and to become competent professionals. Students study the syllabus through lessons in theory and a series of assessed exercises. In addition, students have classes in the study of voice, movement, dance, and other subjects, including histories of art, music, psychology, and philosophy. Students take part in the directing students' exercises, exam days, and the Edinburgh Festival. This accumulated knowledge and experience leads to the presentation of 2 end-of-course plays. Intensive evening course covers the theory of acting (Tuesday and Friday evenings for 3 terms).

DURATION OF COURSES: 1 year comprising four 11-week terms.

QUALIFICATIONS OFFERED: Certificate of Merit issued by the school.

COST: From £3,770 first term, £2,450 subsequent terms. Evening courses, directing courses, etc. have varying fees.

ACCOMMODATION: Not provided, but help given with finding it.

DORA STRATOU GREEK DANCE THEATRE
8 Scholiou Street, Plaka, 105 58 Athens, Greece
☎ +30 210 324 4395
✎ mail@grdance.org
💻 www.grdance.org

COURSES OFFERED: Short courses for foreigners in Greek folk dance and folk culture, in conjunction with lectures and evening performances in outdoor theatre near the Acropolis.

DURATION OF COURSES: 1 week between May and September. 4 hours of instruction every afternoon.

COST: €120. Volunteers must fund their own stay in Athens.

CONTACT: Adamantia Angeli, Executive Director.

NEW YORK FILM ACADEMY
100 E 17th Street, New York, NY 10003, USA
☎ +1 212 674 4300
✎ film@nyfa.edu
💻 www.nyfa.edu

COURSES OFFERED: Film-making (write, shoot, direct, and edit), acting for film, screenwriting, producing, 3D animation, editing, and many others. Courses offered at other campuses (Universal Studios in LA and Abu Dhabi), with workshop locations in many other cities.

DURATION OF COURSES: 1- and 2-year programmes, 2-year MFA, as well as short-term workshops (1, 4, 6, and 8 weeks).

COST: $18,000 per semester for the film-making programmes. $3,650 for the short-term 4-week film-making workshops.

PRAGUE FILM SCHOOL
Pstrossova 19, Prague 110 00, Czech Republic
☎ +420 257 534 013
✆ info@filmstudies.cz
🖳 www.filmstudies.cz

COURSES OFFERED: Fast-track studies in practical film-making. Full-time programmes include directing, editing, screenwriting, and cinematography; acting for film; animation, and documentary production.
DURATION OF COURSES: Year programme, semester programme, and summer workshop (4 weeks).
PREREQUISITES: Minimum age 17.
QUALIFICATIONS OFFERED: Qualification accredited by the Czech Ministry of Education under the rubric of professional training.
COST: €2,460–€14,800.
ACCOMMODATION: Shared or private accommodation in school flats.

UP TO SPEED JOURNALISM TRAINING
c/o *Daily Echo*, Richmond Hill, Bournemouth BH2 6HH
☎ (0)1202 761 944
🖳 www.uptospeedjournalism.co.uk

COURSES OFFERED: 22-week fast-track course in journalism. The course is based in a newspaper building and accredited by the National Council for the Training of Journalists, the news industry's vocational training organisation. Students take the NCTJ's examinations in public affairs, media law, news writing, and shorthand. They also produce assessed coursework in both print and video journalism, learning to shoot and edit video and radio pieces. Feedback on all assignments is given by professional journalists.
DURATION OF COURSES: 22 weeks (September to February or February to July).
PREREQUISITES: Most are graduates, but anyone with three good A levels can enrol.
QUALIFICATIONS OFFERED: The 22-week course leads to the NCTJ Certificate in Journalism and gives people a chance of landing jobs in journalism during the remainder of their gap year, during their time at university, or when they graduate.
COST: £3,600. Advice given on local accommodation.
CONTACT: Tom Hill, Course Director.

WORLDWRITE
WORLDwrite Centre, Millfields Lodge, 201 Millfields Road, Hackney, London E5 0AL
☎ (0)20 8985 5435
✆ world.write@btconnect.com
🖳 www.worldwrite.org.uk

COURSES OFFERED: WORLDwrite is an education charity that uses documentary film-making as a medium for campaigning on global issues. The charity has broadcast-quality equipment, and offers a free training programme to volunteers with a passionate commitment to global equality. Courses are taught by TV and film professionals and tutors, and aim to give young people a fresh perspective through a first-hand, investigative film-making experience. Volunteers learn all aspects of production from camera to sound to compression, and their work features on the charity's news channel WORLDbytes.
DURATION OF COURSES: 2–3 days over long intensive weekends.
PREREQUISITES: Ages 16–25. Must feel strongly about global inequality and be familiar with the work of WORLDwrite (see website).
CONTACT: Ceri Dingle, Director, and Viv Regan, Assistant Director.

YEAR OUT DRAMA COMPANY
Stratford-upon-Avon College, Alcester Road, Stratford-upon-Avon, Warwickshire CV37 9QR
☎ (0)1789 417 255
✆ yearoutdrama@stratford.ac.uk

Founding member of Year Out Group.
COURSES OFFERED: Challenging, intensive, practical drama course specific to gap year students. Led by experts in professionally equipped performance spaces. Students benefit from working with theatre professionals on varying disciplines, including acting techniques, voice, movement, directing, text study, and performance. Students have the option to perform at the Edinburgh Fringe Festival.
DURATION OF COURSES: September to July, split into 3 terms.
COST: From £5,000 for the year, which includes production costs, travel, and tickets for frequent theatre trips. Accommodation costs are extra.
ACCOMMODATION: Students can live in halls of residence, with landladies or in shared houses.
FOLLOW-UP: Students are given help with auditions and UCAS applications. The Company has strong support from the Royal Shakespeare Company and other working professionals.

MUSIC

ROYAL COLLEGE OF MUSIC
Prince Consort Road, London SW7 2BS
☎ (0)20 591 4362
✆ admissions@rcm.ac.uk
🖳 www.rcm.ac.uk/Studying/Courses/
    Experience+Programmes

COURSES OFFERED: Gap year experience programme for talented young musicians who are accepted after audition. Course provides individual lessons on main instrument, opportunities for involvement in orchestras, ensembles, choral groups, etc, participation in core academic classes, concerts, masterclasses, and workshops.

DURATION OF COURSES: 1 academic year, September to July only.

QUALIFICATIONS OFFERED: Most students who enrol on the gap year programme decide to stay on and continue into year 2 of the BMus Programme (subject to passing exams).

COST: £8,170.

ACCOMMODATION: Possibility of residence in halls; not included in price.

CONTACT: David Harpham, Registry Officer.

BUSINESS SKILLS COURSES

KUDOS TRAINING LIMITED
Suite 10, The Sanctuary, 23 Oakhill Grove, Surbiton, Surrey KT6 6DU
☎ (0)20 8288 8766
✎ enquiry@kudostraining.org or jvev@kudostraining.org
🖥 www.kudostraining.org

COURSES AND QUALIFICATIONS OFFERED: Qualifications in business and management at differing levels, accredited by the awarding body the Association of Tourism and Hospitality Executives (www.atheuk.com). Courses on offer are the Higher Diploma for Management Assistants (HDMA; level 4), Advanced Diploma in Business Management (level 5), Postgraduate Diploma in Business Management (level 7). HDMA course is offered full-time, part-time, via distance learning, or blended (part distance, part attendance). Advanced courses offer progression routes to a degree, with certain universities linked with awarding body. Variety of short full-time courses also available, such as Graduate Diploma in Secretarial Skills, and Practical Office Skills for Managers. Secretarial Assistants course (level 3) will soon be available.

ACCOMMODATION: Can be arranged; accommodation always provided during weekend intensive courses and examination periods.

CONTACT: Elaine Howard, Principal.

OXFORD MEDIA & BUSINESS SCHOOL
5 Cambridge Terrace, Oxford OX1 1UP
☎ (0)1865 240 963
✎ courses@oxfordbusiness.co.uk
🖥 www.oxfordbusiness.co.uk

COURSES OFFERED: 12-week gap year 'life skills' course covering IT and business skills, to help students earn higher wages during their gap year and during university vacations. Intensive tuition in Microsoft IT and communication skills; essential project work to tight deadlines simulates a temping assignment in terms of prioritising, time management, working in teams, and production quality; all of these are part of the course assessment. The college also offers a 9-month executive PA Diploma course and 12-week graduate skills course.

DURATION OF COURSES: 12-week gap course starting September, January, and April; 9-month course also available.

QUALIFICATIONS OFFERED: OMBS College Certificate.

COST: 12 weeks is £2,450.

ACCOMMODATION: Shared houses within walking or cycling distance, or with host families in the locality.

FOLLOW-UP: Specialist in-house recruitment service, giving ongoing help with CV writing and interview technique as well as support in finding a job.

QUEST BUSINESS TRAINING
5 Grosvenor Gardens, London SW1W 0BD
☎ (0)20 7233 5957
✎ info@questcollege.co.uk
🖥 www.questcollege.co.uk

COURSES OFFERED: Professional programmes (24 and 36 weeks) and short courses lasting 2–10 weeks on offer. The latter focus on providing training in Microsoft Office skills, as well as other business-related topics. They offer a 10-week gap year course (starting September, January, and April) aimed at students who hope to use the rest of their gap year earning money by temping or working in an office. Course covers marketing, event and conference organising, as well as developing IT skills. Courses entitle students to make use of in-house recruitment team, providing guidance with CV development and job search.

COST: £3,292 for gap year course.

CONTACT: Nicola Feneley, Client Services Co-ordinator.

COOKERY COURSES

COURSES OFFERED: The 'Really Useful Course' is an intensive 1-week cooking course that includes practical day-to-day skills as well as first aid, car maintenance, and travel tips, ideal for gap year students and undergraduates. There is also the 2-week 'Basic to Brilliant Course' as well as the 2-week 'Chalet Cooking Course'. Also offered are 6-week courses of evening classes (1 basic and 1 more advanced).

DURATION OF COURSES: 1 week and 2 weeks, plus weekly evening classes over 2, 4, or 6 weeks.

QUALIFICATIONS OFFERED: Certificated first aid from the Really Useful Course; plus the Avenue Cookery School certificates for all courses.

COST: Really Useful Course: £620; Even More Useful/Advanced Course: £620; Basic to Brilliant Course: £1,200; Chalet Cooking Course: £1,200 (2 weeks); 6 evening classes: £330.

ACCOMMODATION: Can be organised locally. £120 per week (Monday–Friday), including dinner and breakfast.

PARTNERS: Mary Forde and Diana Horsford.

CONTACT: Sally Strahan (info@theavenuecookeryschool.com).

Situated on organic farm by the coast with access to excellent ingredients. Affiliated with www.jobsforcooks.com.

COURSES OFFERED: 12-week Certificate in Cookery course. Short courses also offered between April and September, including two, 1-week introductory courses in August.

DURATION OF COURSES: Certificate course starting January, April, and September lasting 12 weeks. Short courses given between April and July, including a 1-week introductory course in July or September.

QUALIFICATIONS OFFERED: Students who pass written and practical exams at end of course are awarded the Ballymaloe Cookery School Certificate of Food and Wine.

COST: €10,295 for 12-week Certificate course, excluding accommodation. 1-day courses cost €245, 2¹/₂-day course €575 and 5-day introductory course €895.

ACCOMMODATION: Self-catering student accommodation in converted farm cottages costs €105 per week in twin room and €145 in single. Nightly charges for short courses are €30 shared, €45 single, including continental breakfast.

CONTACT: Rosalie Dunne.

COURSES OFFERED: Short practical cookery courses. Full-day courses: back to basics and beginners. Full range of cookery courses on specialist topics such as pastry, chocolate, or bread-making, and basic first aid course.

DURATION AND FREQUENCY OF COURSES: Half-day, full-day, and evening.

COST: Full Day £110–£155. Half-day £55.

ACCOMMODATION: Bed and breakfast available.

CONTACT: Pippa Hackett, Operations Manager.

COURSES OFFERED: Cookery certificate courses.

DURATION OF COURSES: Certificate course lasts 4 weeks; chalet chef course lasts 1 week. Held in January, June, September, and October. For dates of future courses refer to website.

QUALIFICATIONS OFFERED: The certificate course is accredited by major ski chalet operators, yacht catering agencies, and by major companies offering retraining schemes. The chalet chef course is approved by major ski holiday operators.

COST: £1,600 for a 4-week course. Chalet chef course costs £400.

ACCOMMODATION: Local bed and breakfasts are available within 2 minutes' walk.

FOLLOW-UP: The courses are designed for people wanting to work in ski chalets or on yachts, and for those interested in catering to a high standard for small groups.

CONTACT: Kate Hughes.

EDINBURGH SCHOOL OF FOOD & WINE
The Coach House, Newliston, Edinburgh
EH29 9EB
☎ (0)131 333 5001
info@esfw.com
www.esfw.com

COURSES OFFERED: Practical hands-on cookery – from 1 day to 6-month diploma course.

COST: 4 week intensive course costs £2,450; 6-month (January to June) Diploma in Food and Wine course costs £9,500.

ACCOMMODATION: Assistance always offered.

FOLLOW-UP: The School works closely with ski companies, agencies, and restaurants offering opportunities in the UK and abroad.

FOOD OF COURSE COOKERY SCHOOL
Middle Farm House, Sutton, Shepton Mallet,
Somerset BA4 6QF
☎ (0)1749 860116
info@foodofcourse.co.uk
www.foodofcourse.co.uk

Principal Lou Hutton was the main teacher at the Grange, and has extensive experience running chalets as well as her own catering business.

COURSES OFFERED: 4-week foundation cookery course is suitable for gap year students who want to work in ski chalets, lodges, and galleys, or simply to broaden their culinary expertise. The school is based in a family home and offers individual attention while students gain confidence and develop their skills. This intensive hands-on course covers classic and modern methods of cookery, budgeting, and menu-planning. Students can take the basic food hygiene course and examination while studying. Wine tasting, guest cooks, and visits to local markets are organised throughout the course.

COST: 4-week foundation course £3,350.

ACCOMMODATION: In twin guest rooms with en-suite bathrooms and comfortable student sitting room with TV/DVD.

FOLLOW-UP: Graduates of the course can be put in touch with ski companies and employment agencies.

CONTACT: Lou Hutton, Principal.

THE GABLES SCHOOL OF COOKERY
Pipers Lodge, Bristol Road, Falfield, Gloucestershire GL12 8DF
☎ (0)1454 260 444
info@thegablesschoolofcookery.co.uk
www.thegablesschoolofcookery.co.uk

Specialists in training chalet hosts and yacht cooks.

COURSES OFFERED: 4-week cookery courses ideal for working in chalets or on yachts, as well as providing lifelong cookery skills.

DURATION OF COURSES: 4 weeks available year round.

PREREQUISITES: Minimum age 16; average age 18–50.

QUALIFICATIONS OFFERED: School certificate equivalent to NVQ 2/3.

COST: £3,450 inclusive.

ACCOMMODATION: 3-star accommodation in twin rooms with en-suite bathrooms.

FOLLOW-UP: School aims to find positions for all graduates.

CONTACT: Chris Winston, Partner.

LEITHS SCHOOL OF FOOD AND WINE
16–20 Wendell Road, London W12 9RT
info@leiths.com
www.leiths.com

Leiths School of Food and Wine is based in London and is non-residential.

COURSES OFFERED: The Leiths Essential Certificate in Practical Cookery is ideal for gap year students and anyone wishing to assist in chalets, villas, and lodges. Alternatively, the Foundation Certificate in Food and Wine is a longer course for those looking to work in private catering. On both courses, the day is divided between demonstrations and practical cooking sessions. Topics covered include meat, fish, and vegetable preparation and cooking, menu planning, costing, and time-planning. Each class is divided into suitable age groups and run by experienced, friendly, professional chefs.

DURATION OF COURSES: Leiths Essential Certificate lasts 4 weeks full-time, running in August/September each year. Leiths Foundation Certificate lasts 10 weeks full-time (September to December). 1-week introductory courses also available, suitable for students heading off to university.

QUALIFICATIONS OFFERED: Essential Certificate in Practical Cookery. Foundation Certificate in Food and Wine.

COST: 4-week Essential Certificate £2,720; 10-week Foundation Certificate £6,250. The fees cover teaching, equipment, and food (which can be eaten at the school or taken home). Extra items, including cookery books, uniforms, and chef knives, will need to be bought separately and will cost around £115. The school is non-residential but advice on accommodation can be given.

FOLLOW-UP: The company also runs Leiths List (www.leithslist.com), an agency for cooks, which helps to place students in suitable jobs, once qualified.

UK's leading recruitment website for finding jobs in ski and summer resorts.

COURSES OFFERED: Chalet cookery courses are run annually in England (at girls' schools in Surrey and Salisbury), and possible in Morzine, France (to be confirmed). New surf and cook course in Devon.

DURATION OF COURSES: 5 days in all cases, with starting dates between April and October.

PREREQUISITES: Minimum age 18 (unless Duke of Edinburgh's Award candidate, or not intending to work a season).

QUALIFICATIONS OFFERED: Natives cookery course is recognised throughout the industry, and candidates are guaranteed a job through natives.co.uk if they pass with a grade C or above. Chartered Institute of Environmental Health Level 2 award in food safety in catering.

COST: £489 for UK courses, £599 for courses in French Alps. £100 deposit is needed to secure a place.

FOLLOW-UP: 96% guaranteed job through natives.co.uk for those who pass.

OTHER SERVICES: Natives Jobs Fair in early July is the company's main seasonal recruitment event (www.natives.co.uk/skijobs/jobsfair/index.html). Check the website for upcoming dates. Season2season has a snow season (cookery course included), and a surf season (further details from www.natives.co.uk/season2season/index.htm).

COURSES OFFERED: Chalet Cooks (and recruitment), Off to University, Designer Dinners for Beginners.

DURATION OF COURSES: 5 days and 2 weeks, year-round.

QUALIFICATIONS OFFERED: Certificate on completion of the course, which is well recognised in the chalet industry. Access organisation for the Gold Duke of Edinburgh's Award, so participants can be awarded a certificate to show they have completed their residential project.

COST: Chalet Cooks: 5 days, £795–£845; 2 weeks, £1,590–£1,690. Off to University (5 days) £695–£745.

Designer Dinners (5 days) £845, including accommodation.

ACCOMMODATION: Students live on-site in cottages adjoining the family farmhouse.

CONTACT: Isabel Bomford, Director.

Ideal for aspiring chalet hosts and yacht cooks.

COURSES OFFERED: A cookery course beginning with essential skills and basic techniques, but moving on to more complex aspects. Part of the course will include the specialist skills needed to cook in a chalet or on board a yacht.

DURATION OF COURSES: 4 weeks.

QUALIFICATIONS OFFERED: Certificate of completion, and a food safety in catering certificate.

COST: £3,350, including shared accommodation.

ACCOMMODATION: Twin-bedded rooms with toilet/shower room and sitting area with TV/video and broadband internet.

COURSES OFFERED: Ultimate Chalet Host cookery course in the Alps is an authentic chalet course that teaches participants the practicalities of how to run a successful chalet with style and a minimum of fuss. Course teaches tasty recipes that are quick and easy to cook for large numbers, using ingredients that will be available in winter alpine resorts, using methods of cooking specific to altitude. It also covers how to deal with special dietary requirements, including 6-day vegetarian menu and wheat-free/dairy-free/vegan, etc. Tips are given on menu planning (useful if asked to present a weekly plan to your manager), managing a tight shopping budget, health and safety practices, tricks of the trade, and how to maximise your ski time.

DURATION OF COURSES: 1 week (6¹/₂ days) in summer and autumn (starting on every other Saturday between late May and late November).

QUALIFICATIONS OFFERED: Links with tour operators and independently run chalet operators. Almost all students who want to work a season after the course secure a job in a ski resort.

COST: £495, excluding flights, insurance, recreational activities, and drinks from honesty bar.

ACCOMMODATION: Rooms shared with one other at Chalet Chantelauze, with outdoor hot tub, included in course fee.

CONTACT: Laura Clarke, Director.

TANTE MARIE SCHOOL OF COOKERY
Woodham House, Carlton Road, Woking,
Surrey GU21 4HF
☎ (0)1483 726 957
✉ info@tantemarie.co.uk
🖥 www.tantemarie.co.uk

UK's oldest and largest independent cookery school, now owned by Gordon Ramsay and accredited by the BAC.

COURSES OFFERED: Variety of practical courses suitable for gap year students. Cordon Bleu Certificate course (11 weeks) offers a formal qualification useful for students who wish to work in ski chalets and on yachts, as well as gaining temporary employment during university vacations. The essential skills course (4 weeks) is a good foundation, though there is no formal qualification. Beginners course lasts 1 or 2 weeks and is a basic introduction to cookery.

DURATION OF COURSES: Essential skills course offered in July and September; Cordon Bleu Certificate course begins September. Beginners course offered in mid-July.

QUALIFICATIONS OFFERED: Internationally recognised qualifications, including Cordon Bleu Diploma and Certificate. Certificate of attendance for other courses.

COST: £2,825 for essential skills, £6,950 for certificate course, and £650 for 1-week beginners or £1,100 for 2-week beginners. Prices are inclusive of chef's whites (where applicable), knives, personalised recipe folder, all ingredients, and lunch each day.

ACCOMMODATION: Homestays arranged through the school

FOLLOW-UP: Certificate courses are excellent for short-term employment during vacations. Essential skills course recognised by many ski operators. Tante Marie offers employment advice and has good industry contacts.

CONTACT: Debbie Volans.

SKI TRAINING COURSES

ALLTRACKS ACADEMY
The Lawns, Goodworth Clatford, Hampshire
SP11 7RE
☎ (0)1794 388 034
✉ info@alltracksacademy.com
🖥 www.alltracksacademy.com

COURSES OFFERED: Ski and snowboard instructor courses, and improvement training camps in Whistler, Canada, and Val d'Isère, France.

DURATION OF COURSES: 3–11 weeks throughout winter from November to April. 11-week ski/snowboard instructor course, 11-week ski/snowboard improvement course, 8-week off-piste back-country ski/snowboard course, 4-week ski/snowboard instructor course; 3-week ski/snowboard improvement course.

QUALIFICATIONS OFFERED: Courses lead to instructor qualifications as well as recreational improvement camps.

COST: £2,950–£7,450. Fees include expert tuition from professional instructors and mountain guides, exam fees, return flights, central accommodation with hot tubs, wi-fi, etc, meals, official avalanche skills training and overnight back-country adventures.

ACCOMMODATION: Comfortable chalets.

CONTACT: Paul Beard, Director.

ALTITUDE FUTURES
Case Postale 55, 1936 Verbier, Switzerland
☎ +41 953 05 224
✉ info@altitude-futures.co.uk
🖥 www.altitude-futures.co.uk

COURSES OFFERED: Ski instructor and snowboard instructor gap course.

DESTINATIONS: Verbier, Switzerland; Tignes, France; Whistler, Canada.

PREREQUISITES: Minimum age 18.

DURATION OF COURSES: 10 weeks with 3 possible start dates, November, January, or February.

QUALIFICATIONS OFFERED: BASI qualifications and BASP (British Association of Ski Patrollers) first aid qualifications. Some successful participants stay on, working as instructors, or return in university holidays.

COST: £7,995 including half-board accommodation. Early bird booking price of £7,450.

CONTACT: Laura Turner, Office Manager.

BASECAMP GROUP
30 Baseline Business Studios, Whitchurch Road, London W11 4AT
☎ (0)20 7243 6222
✎ contact@basecampgroup.com
🖥 www.basecampgroup.com

PROGRAMME DESCRIPTION: Ski and snowboard instructor courses in the Alps, Rockies, and Andes, to improve all-round ability, and gain a recognised European and North American ski or snowboard instructor's qualification. Chance to improve skiing and riding (off-piste, freestyle, racing, etc). Courses include avalanche courses, first aid courses, ski/snowboard tuning clinics, French lessons, weekend trips, and social events. Assistance can be given in finding work after the course. As well as instructor courses, they offer 'Improvement Camps' which are courses specially designed to take students' all-round skiing ability to the next level, and 'Performance Camps', which concentrate on specific disciplines: freestyle and freeride. Also offer watersports and adrenaline sports programmes suitable for gappers, including kitesurfing, surfing, and mountain biking.
DESTINATIONS: For snow sports: Méribel and Val d'Isère, France; Whistler, Kicking Horse, and Banff, Canada; and Bariloche, Argentina. For watersports: Dahab, Egypt; Taghazout, Morocco; and the South African coast. For adrenaline sports: Whistler, Canada.
DURATION AND TIME OF PLACEMENTS: 2–11 weeks.
NUMBER OF PLACEMENTS PER YEAR: 300.
QUALIFICATIONS OFFERED: For snow sports: BASI in Europe, CSIA/CASI in North America. For watersports: BSA and IKO. For adrenaline sports: Professional Mountain Bike Instructors (PMBI).
PREREQUISITES: Beginners welcome on some courses, since many clients are spending their first winter in the mountains and are new to the industry. Several freestyle and freeskiing camps are run for more experienced skiers. Other requirements are course-specific (see website).
COST: £300–£800 per week, depending on length of programme and nature of sport. Usually includes all local requirements such as accommodation, food, coaching, exams, etc, but not flights.
CONTACT: Helen Nicholls and Fergie Miller, Course Advisers.

BRITISH ASSOCIATION OF SNOWSPORT INSTRUCTORS (BASI)
Morlich House, 17 The Square, Grantown-on-Spey Moray PH26 3HG
☎ (0)1479 861717
✎ basi@basi.org.uk
🖥 www.basi.org.uk or www.basigap.com

BASI runs training and grading courses throughout the year in five disciplines: Alpine skiing, snowboarding, Telemarking, Nordic, and adaptive. BASI also publishes the *BASI News*, in which job advertisements for ski and snowboard instructors appear.
COURSES OFFERED: BASI gap year course offered over 10 weeks leading to level 2 ski or snowboard instructor's qualification. Courses take place from January to March in Courchevel, Meribel, and Val d'Isère in France, and Nendaz in Switzerland.
PREREQUISITES: Minimum age 16. Students should be able to ski parallel or ride confidently on red runs, coping with a variety of snow conditions.
COST: £6,995–£7,995.
CONTACT: BASI Administration Department.

CORONET PEAK SNOWSPORTS SCHOOL
PO Box 359, Queenstown, New Zealand
☎ +64 3 442 4626/4163
✎ school@coronetpeak.co.nz
🖥 www.nzski.com/products/2010/coronetpeak/instructor.jsp

COURSES OFFERED: Queenstown Instructor Training Programme (QITP).
PREREQUISITES: Minimum age 17, average age 20.
DURATION OF COURSES: 10 weeks every winter from July to September.
QUALIFICATIONS OFFERED: Course prepares candidates for the NZSIA/SBINZ levels 1, 2, and 3 certification. With these qualifications, past graduates have gone on to teach in resorts in both the northern and southern hemispheres.
COST: From about NZ$3,500 to NZ$10,615, depending on what is included. Accommodation at a lodge can be provided, ie shared accommodation in a unit at the lodge complex.
CONTACT: Michel Marchand, Snowsports School Director.

DEUTSCH-INSTITUT TIROL
Am Sandhügel 2, 6370 Kitzbühel, Austria
☎ +43 53 56 712 74
✎ office@deutschinstitut.com
🖥 www.gap-year.at or www.deutschinstitut.com

COURSES OFFERED: German language combined with ski and snowboard instruction, specially designed for those on gap years.
DURATION OF COURSES: 12 weeks from end of September to just before Christmas. Course includes

8 weeks intensive German tuition at DIT in Kitzbühel, interspersed with 8 long (3-day) weekends skiing/snowboarding on the glacier at Kaprun. Also, 7-day trip to Vienna and Eastern Europe.

PREREQUISITES: Students can be complete beginners at German, but should already be good skiers or snowboarders.

QUALIFICATIONS OFFERED: Preparation for Austrian ski/snowboard instructor exams.

COST: €8,200 inclusive of everything except travel to Kitzbühel and insurance.

ACCOMMODATION: Half-board accommodation in Kitzbühel; full board in Kaprun.

GAPSKI SKI INSTRUCTOR TRAINING
85 The Crescent, Davenport, Stockport, Cheshire SK3 8SL, UK
☎ +33 6 03 31 43 21
info@gapski.com
www.gapski.com

COURSES OFFERED: Ski instructor training programme
DESTINATIONS: Tignes, France.
DURATION AND FREQUENCY OF COURSES: 10-week course once a year (from early January).
PREREQUISITES: Minimum age 18, average age early 20s.
QUALIFICATIONS OFFERED: Leads to a professional ski instructor qualification (BASI). All coaching is delivered by coaches from The Development Centre (www.tdcski.com).
COST: £7,695.
ACCOMMODATION: Alpaka Lodge Hotel for the full 10 weeks, including breakfast and dinner 7 days per week. Lunches are provided every day by the Loop Bar and Restaurant.
OTHER SERVICES: On successful completion of the course, opportunities to work as a ski instructor with a partner ski school may be available. All-inclusive package with free pair of Head skis and Gapski jacket, a season's pass for the Espace Killy (Tignes and Val d'Isère), and all BASI course fees.
CONTACT: Ben Harris, Course Manager.

ICE – INTERNATIONAL CENTRE OF EXCELLENCE
UK office: **3–4 Bath Place, Aberdovey, Gwynedd LL35 0LN**
☎ (0)870 760 7360
info@icesi.org
www.icesi.org
French office: 17, Le Cret 2, 73150, Val d'Isère

COURSES OFFERED: Official BASI gap courses for ski and snowboard instructors. Also BASI level 1 and level 2 Instructor courses, performance and preparation courses, and all-terrain 4 week courses.
DURATION OF COURSES: BASI instructor courses last 4, 6, or 10 weeks. 6-week summer course in Tignes also available.
QUALIFICATIONS OFFERED: Students can be placed in work following successful qualification and can gain work experience as part of the course. ICE uses BASI trainers exclusively for all ski instructor training, snowboard instructor training, and assessing.
PREREQUISITES: Minimum age 16 with parental consent; average age 19.
COST: 4-week residential course for £4,250, 6 weeks for £5,995, 10 weeks for £7,595. Course-only fees are level 1 (5 days) £395; level 2 (10 days) £545. Summer course costs £5,695.
ACCOMMODATION: Apartment accommodation, with evening restaurant meals provided throughout residential courses.
CONTACT: Rupert Tildesley, Director.

INTERNATIONAL ACADEMY
Sophia House, 28 Cathedral Road, Cardiff CF11 9LJ
☎ (0)29 2066 0200
info@international-academy.com
www.international-academy.com

Member of the Year Out Group.
COURSES OFFERED: Ski and snowboard instructor training courses run in partnership with the resident ski and snowboard schools in various resorts worldwide. Courses lead to recognised CSIA, CASI, BASI, NZSIA, or SBINZ qualifications. Professional programmes aimed at personal development and the improvement of technical/teaching skills.
DURATION OF COURSES: 5–12 weeks.
DESTINATIONS: Courses are run in Whistler Blackcomb, Banff/Lake Louise, and Castle Mountain in Canada, Val d'Isere/Tignes and Chatel in France, Verbier in Switzerland, and Cardrona Alpine Resort in New Zealand.
COST: £3,950–£8,450 depending on course duration and resort.
CONTACT: Alan Bates, General Manager.

NEW GENERATION SKI AND SNOWBOARD SCHOOL
Rue de la Chappelle, Le Praz, 73120 Courchevel, France
☎ +33 479 01 03 18
☎ (0)844 484 3663 (UK only)
instructorcourses@skinewgen.com
www.skinewgen.com

New Generation runs the official BASI (British Association of Snowsport Instructors) GAP courses. New Generation is a training centre for students wishing to pursue a career in ski or snowboard instruction.

COURSES OFFERED: 10-week Ski GAP courses in Meribel, Courchevel, and La Tania.

DURATION OF COURSES: Once a year, January to March, for 10 weeks.

QUALIFICATIONS OFFERED: All courses include instructor exams; successful candidates can teach in most countries, including on dry slopes and indoor slopes in the UK.

COST: £7,395, including fully catered chalet accommodation.

CONTACT: Euan Wright, New Generation Head Coach.

NONSTOP SKI & SNOWBOARD
Unit 3B, The Plough Brewery, 516 Wandsworth Road, London SW8 3JX
☎ (0)845 365 1525
✎ info@nonstopadventure.com
🖥 www.nonstopadventure.com
🖥 www.nonstopski.com
🖥 www.nonstopsnowboard.com

Member of the Year Out Group.

COURSES OFFERED: Ski and snowboard improvement and instructor courses.

NUMBER OF PARTICIPANTS: 500.

DURATION OF COURSES: 2–18 weeks.

DESTINATIONS: Fernie, Whistler, Banff, and Red Mountain in Canada, Porters and Club Fields in New Zealand, and Serre Chevalier in France.

PREREQUISITES: Minimum age 18; a good proportion of participants are gappers. Students should have at least 1 week's previous snow experience.

QUALIFICATIONS OFFERED: Internationally recognised CSIA (Canadian Ski Instructor Alliance), CASI (Canadian Association of Snowboard Instructors), NZSIA (New Zealand Snowsports Instructor Alliance) and the French 'Test Technique' and '*Préformacion*'. Also CAA (Canadian Avalanche Association) Recreational Avalanche 1 certificate, and St John's Ambulance basic first aid certificate. Freestyle and race coach qualifications can also be obtained.

COST: £2,300–£7,150, which includes flights, transfers, accommodation, weekday meals, lift pass, resort transport, professional coaching, weekend trips, and (depending on course booked) CSIA/CASI examination, first aid course, and avalanche course.

OTHER SERVICES: Work experience may be arranged with local ski school, and contacts for other ski schools can be provided for instructing jobs. Ski accommodation in twin rooms (some quad, triple, and single rooms available) in houses/lodges equipped with kitchens and living rooms with stereo and cable TV.

CONTACT: Adam Hillier, Course Adviser.

NOTHINBUTSNOW
309 Becket House, Brentwood, Essex, CM14 4GA
☎ (0)800 158 5248
✎ team@nothinbutsnow.com
🖥 www.nothinbutsnow.com

COURSES OFFERED: Ski instructor training courses, Snowboard instructor training courses, freestyle ski instructor training courses, freestyle snowboard instructor training courses, dual discipline ski and snowboard instructor training courses

DESTINATIONS: Big White Resort and Whistler-Blackcomb, British Columbia, Canada.

DURATION AND FREQUENCY OF COURSES: 4–11 weeks long. Courses run once or twice per winter season.

PREREQUISITES: Minimum age 18, average age 25.

QUALIFICATIONS OFFERED: Students have the option to complete exams, which are included in the course price, leading to recognised qualifications.

COST: £3,995-£7,245. Course packages are fully inclusive of return flights, transfer to resort, season pass, accommodation, expert tuition, exam fee, meals, and social events.

ACCOMMODATION: In Big White: luxury twin-occupancy condominiums. In Whistler Blackcomb: communal living based on 4 sharing a dorm-style room. In both resorts upgrades are available to private room with bathroom.

OTHER SERVICES: Option of undertaking work experience is included.

CONTACT: Leigh Mocock, Director.

PEAK LEADERS UK
Mansfield, Strathmiglo, Fife KY14 7QE, Scotland
☎ (0)1337 860 079
✎ info@peakleaders.com
🖥 www.peakleaders.com

COURSES OFFERED: Gap year ski and snowboard instructor courses in Canada, Switzerland, Argentina, and New Zealand. Snow sport courses involve coaching in powder, moguls, free skiing, freeriding, park and pipe, and ski tuning. Avalanche awareness, mountain first aid, team leading, back-country, freestyle, ski school shadowing, and off-piste skiing also available. Courses can be tailored to individual requirements.

DESTINATIONS: Courses are in Saas Fee and Verbier, Switzerland, Whistler and Banff, Canada, Bariloche in Patagonia, Argentina, and Queenstown, New Zealand.

DURATION OF COURSES: 4–12 weeks. Instructor training in Argentina and New Zealand finishes in September/October, the Saas Fee course finishes in November, and high-quality, well-organised candidates may be able to get jobs in Europe or Canada by Christmas.

COST: From £3,250 for short courses to £7,250, inclusive of instruction, flights (in some cases), hotel with half-board, lift tickets, and certification.

OTHER SERVICES: Optional extras are offered, such as skidoo driving, back-country training, Spanish and French language, and stopover in Buenos Aires. Job advice available.

PRO RIDE SNOWBOARD CAMPS
PO Box 1351, Whistler, British Columbia V0N 1B0, Canada
☎ +1 604 935 2115
☎ (0)800 404 6390 (UK free phone)
✍ snowboard@pro-ride.com
🖥 www.pro-ride.com

COURSES OFFERED: Freeride, freestyle, and snowboard instructor training. Opportunity to ride with sponsored pro riders and Olympic-level coaches. Courses cater for the intermediate to advanced rider.

DURATION OF COURSES: 2–12 weeks. Flexible start dates and length of training according to ability.

QUALIFICATIONS OFFERED: Both recreational courses and snowboard instructor training to work towards achieving Canadian Association of Snowboard Instructor certification.

COST: From C$3,495 for 2 weeks, to C$14,885 for 12 weeks.

ACCOMMODATION: Twin share in bright clean houses and condos in Whistler.

CONTACT: Karen Crute, Director.

ROOKIE ACADEMY
PO Box 402, Wanaka, New Zealand
☎ +64 3 443 5100
✍ info@rookieacademy.com
🖥 www.rookieacademy.com

COURSES OFFERED: Ski and snowboard instructor courses.

DESTINATIONS: Treble Cone in Wanaka, New Zealand, Copper Mountain in Colorado, USA, and Mont Sainte-Anne in Quebéc, Canada.

DURATION OF COURSES: 3, 7, 9, and 12 weeks for New Zealand courses; 3, 7, and 13 weeks for US courses; 6 and 11 weeks for Canada courses.

QUALIFICATIONS OFFERED: All courses include an internationally recognised ski or snowboard instructor exam. Only company in New Zealand to offer British and Canadian instructor qualifications in conjunction with the New Zealand qualifications.

COST: From NZ$19,700 for 12 weeks, NZ$12,000 for 7 weeks, etc. Prices for Canada are C$6,000 for 6 weeks, and C$12,500 for 11 weeks.

ACCOMMODATION: Shared apartment-style living, fully furnished; includes cleaning and linen service.

CONTACT: Garett Shore, Director.

SECTION 8 SNOWSPORT INSTITUTE
18–255 Anderton Ave, Courtenay BC, Canada V9N 2G9
☎ +1 250 702 7548
✍ info@section8ski.com
🖥 www.section8ski.com

COURSES OFFERED: 12-week signature Snowsport Leadership Training (SLT) programme. On this comprehensive, 3-month ski/snowboard instructor and mountain leadership training course, students learn from top CSIA/CASI-certified examiners, coaches, and mountain guides, while gaining a plethora of industry-recognised certifications themselves. Students receive a wide variety of technical ski or snowboard training with regards to: teaching demonstrations, performance carving, alpine racing, off-piste steeps, moguls, powder, trees, terrain park, etc. Also offer 4-week introductory instructor training and mountain safety course called Basic Training, which is essentially the first 4 weeks of the SLT programme.

DESTINATIONS: Mount Washington, Vancouver Island, British Columbia, Canada. Coastal Canadian experience in a resort that is off the beaten path. The mountains consistently receive one of the deepest snowfalls in North America, and Mount Washington Alpine Resort is one of the few places where you have a view of the ocean from the ski hill.

DURATION AND FREQUENCY OF COURSES: 12 weeks or 4 weeks from early January each year.

PREREQUISITES: Minimum age 18.

QUALIFICATIONS OFFERED: SLT course includes a number of certifications: CSIA/CASI level 1, CSIA/CASI level 2, CSIA/CASI Snow Park, Avalanche Safety Training level 1, Avalanche Safety Training level 2, CPR level C, and a 40-hour wilderness first aid certification. The 4-week Basic Training course includes CSIA/CASI level 1 and Avalanche Safety Training level 1.

COST: 12-week SLT: C$10,900, and 4-week Basic Training: C$5,600; both including standard shared room.

ACCOMMODATION: Ski-out chalets in the Mount Washington Village. Standard rooms are triple occupancy, with option of upgrading to single- or double-occupancy rooms. All chalets have full kitchens, laundry and wi-fi internet access. Evening meals are provided 5 nights per week.

OTHER SERVICES: All students are offered a voluntary practicum on free days throughout the course. Successful students are guaranteed a job interview with the local Snow School for the following season, with the possibility of becoming sponsored for a working visa. Back-country travel and alpine wilderness skills are also an integral part of this course, and will prepare participants for a wider range of experiences and professions. Weekly video analysis and performance evaluations speed up learning. Leadership and teaching skills are practised in the field and supplemented with evening workshops and theory sessions. Many extracurricular activities on offer, such as bonus surf week after the course, road trips to the mainland for an NHL hockey game, caving through karst systems, bungy jumping, sea kayaking, dodge ball, broom ball, ice hockey, indoor climbing, etc.

CONTACT: Tobin Leopkey, Programme Director.

SITCO – SKI & SNOWBOARD INSTRUCTOR TRAINING CO
PO Box 791, Queenstown, New Zealand
☎ +64 21 341 214/5
🖰 info@sitco.co.nz
🖳 www.sitco.co.nz
🖳 www.skiinstructortraining.co.nz
🖳 www.snowboardinstructortraining.co.nz

COURSES OFFERED: Keen skiers and boarders are trained to develop and achieve their ski and snowboard instructor qualifications in Queenstown, New Zealand. Courses also expose candidates to freestyle, freeride, and race influences, and include an avalanche awareness course, first aid course or off-piste awareness course, and a heli-ski/board day (covered in fee). SITCo also offers a level 3 course with different options.

DURATION OF COURSES: 5-, 8-, and 10-week courses, beginning July and ending September. Each course runs once per season. Training given on 3 days a week.

PREREQUISITES: Ski trainees should be able to ski a red/black run in control, with confidence so that there is

a realistic chance of achieving the NZSIA level 2. Snowboarders should be able to ride blue runs on and off trail, linking turns consistently and riding with confidence.

QUALIFICATIONS OFFERED: NZSIA level 1, level 2 and level 3.

COST: From NZ$8,100 for 5-week course, NZ$12,300 for 8 weeks, and NZ$14,500 for 10 weeks. Inclusive of accommodation, whole-season lift pass, transport between Queenstown and the mountain, and exam fees. Early booking prices available.

ACCOMMODATION: 5, 8, or 10 weeks of accommodation at Pinewood Lodge in central Queenstown; price based on 2 people sharing a quadruple room.

CONTACT: Gavin McAuliffe or Colin Tanner, Founding Partners.

SKI INSTRUCTOR ACADEMY
Marktstrasse 1 , 5660, Taxenbach, Austria
☎ +43 650 56 33 607
🖰 info@ski-instructor-academy.com
🖳 www.ski-instructor-academy.com

COURSES OFFERED: Ski instructor course, including 100% job guarantee (the only provider in Austria that offers a seasonal job after the course). Dual instructor course. Preparatory courses for BASI 2 and 3, preparatory courses for ISIA (international ski instructor qualification), powder clinics, race clinics, mogul clinics.

DURATION AND FREQUENCY OF COURSES: Instructor course is 6 weeks in November/December. Dual course lasts 8 weeks from October.

PREREQUISITES: Minimum age 16, average age 23. Applicants must already be able to ski basic parallel turns on red runs.

COST: €3,950.

ACCOMMODATION: Provided with half-board.

CONTACT: Wouter Kuit, Owner.

SKI LE GAP
220 Wheeler Street, Mont Tremblant, Québec J8E 1V3, Canada
☎ +1 819 429 6599
☎ (0)800 328 0345 (UK free phone)
🖰 info@skilegap.com
🖳 www.skilegap.com

PROGRAMME DESCRIPTION: Ski and snowboard instructor's programme operating since 1994, specifically designed for gap year students from Britain. The course combines ski/snowboard instruction with French conversation lessons, plus other activities such as igloo building, dogsledding, extreme snowshoeing, and trips to Montréal, Québec City, and Ottawa.

DESTINATIONS: Québec, Canada.

NUMBER OF PLACEMENTS PER YEAR: 200.

PREREQUISITES: All nationalities. Must be passionate about skiing, but all levels of ability accepted from beginners to expert.

DURATION AND TIME OF PLACEMENTS: 3 months from January, and 1 month intensive pre-season training course from late November for experienced skiers.

QUALIFICATIONS OFFERED: Up to 8 professional qualifications on offer. Ski le Gap candidates normally achieve 100% pass rate.

COST: £7,860 for 2012 for 3-month course. Price includes return airfare London–Montréal and full room and board, but not medical insurance or ski equipment. £3,700 for 1-month course excluding flights.

CONTACT: Amelia Puddifer, Programme Director.

SKIVO2 GAP YEAR PROGRAMME
UK office: 10 Bankhead Crescent, Arbroath, Angus, Scotland DD11 2DP
☎ (0)1635 37774
blake@skivo2.co.uki
www.skivo2.co.uk
France office:
☎ +33 681 53 77 15

COURSES OFFERED: 10-week ski instructor training course based in Courchevel, France. Course run by fully qualified BASI ski instructors.

DURATION OF COURSES: Early January to mid-March every year.

QUALIFICATIONS OFFERED: Successful candidates will achieve their BASI level 1 and 2 ski instructor qualification.

COST: £7,350. Luxury catered chalet accommodation is provided as part of the package. Full fitness programme, first aid course, and extras included in the price.

CONTACT: Dave Beattie and Blake Williams, Directors.

SNOWORKS
Tignes, France
☎ +33 6 84 44 07 48
☎ +33 6 8016 5348 (mobile)
☎ (0)8701 225 549 (UK booking)
info@snoworks.co.uk
www.snoworks.co.uk/gap.asp

COURSES OFFERED: 8-week fast-track ski instructors gap course leading to BASI qualifications in Tignes, France.

DURATION OF COURSES: 8 weeks starting around 24 October.

PREREQUISITES: Minimum age 18, average age 20.

QUALIFICATIONS OFFERED: Successful candidates will be qualified level 1 and 2 ski instructors by Christmas, allowing them to work a season in the Alps, America, or Canada; job advice is given.

COST: £6,955.

ACCOMMODATION: Half-board accommodation in Hotel Aguille Percee (Mark Warner hotel) in Tignes.

CONTACT: Phil Smith and Emma Carrick-Anderson, Directors.

SNOWSKOOL
Winchester, Hampshire, UK
☎ (0)1962 855 138
team@snowkool.co.uk
www.snowskool.co.uk

COURSES OFFERED: Ski and snowboard instructor training courses in the Canadian resorts of Sunshine Village, Banff, and Big White, British Columbia, as well as Treble Cone in New Zealand, and France's Three Valleys.

NUMBER OF PLACEMENTS PER YEAR: 150 for SnowSkool Canada, 40 for SnowSkool New Zealand, and 25 for SnowSkool France.

DURATION OF COURSES: Northern hemisphere courses run from January and southern hemisphere courses from July to September. Courses range in length from 2 to 13 weeks.

QUALIFICATIONS OFFERED: Internationally recognised CSIA, CASI, BASI, NZSIA, and SBINZ qualifications.

COST: Full season courses from £7,350 for 11 weeks in the Trois Vallées, to £8,450 for 10 weeks in New Zealand (including flights, accommodation, meals, tuition, and lift pass).

CONTACT: Philip Purdie, Director (phil@sportskool.co.uk)

SNOW TRAINERS
PO Box 846, Queenstown, New Zealand
☎ +64 21 258 6259
☎ +64 21 232 5708
info@snowtrainers.com
www.snowtrainers.com

COURSES OFFERED: Ski and snowboard instructor courses in Queenstown, New Zealand, Niseko in Hokkaido, Japan, and Colorado, USA. Trainers are NZSIA and PSIA examiners, trainers, and highly qualified coaches.

DURATION OF COURSES: New Zealand: 5-week (July–August) or 11-week (July–September) instructor courses. Japan: 8-week instructor course (January–

February), or 2-week improvement course in February. USA: 4, 8, and 12 weeks starting in January.

QUALIFICATIONS OFFERED: Participants train towards the internationally recognised New Zealand or USA level 1 teaching qualification on the short course, and towards levels 1 and 2 on the longer courses.

COST: Queenstown 5-week instructor course costs NZ$8,999; Japan 2-week improvement course costs NZ$4,950. 11-week instructor course in Queenstown and 8-week instructor course in Japan cost NZ$14,999. USA courses cost US$6,900 for 4 weeks, US$9,900 for 8, and US$13,900 for 12. Early booking discounts available.

ACCOMMODATION: Centrally located lodge-style accommodation.

CONTACT: Matt Phare and Tony Macri, Course Directors.

SUNSHINE WORLD
8 Brompton Place, Knightsbridge, London SW3 1QE
☎ (0)20 7581 4736
✍ alan@sunshineworld.co.uk
🖥 www.sunshineworld.co.uk
🖥 www.sunshineworldpoland.com

COURSES OFFERED: All-inclusive and customisable ski and snowboarding instructor training courses in resort of Zakopane in Poland. Ski and snowboard improvement courses also available.

DURATION OF COURSES: From 1 week to full 20-week season.

QUALIFICATIONS OFFERED: Option of taking official Canadian qualifications: CSIA for skiing, CASI for snowboarding.

COST: 4-week instructor training courses from £800, 8 weeks from £1,600, full season of 20 weeks from just £3,500. Fees include return flights from the UK, accommodation in Sunshine World's luxury chalet, equipment rental, lift passes, and instruction.

ACCOMMODATION: 34-person chalet with log fireplace, plasma TVs, games consoles, and DVD players, Jacuzzi room with heated stone floor, fully equipped kitchen with dishwasher, utility room with washing machine and dryer, ski and boot room, and large communal living area. Located just 5 minutes' walk from supermarket, bars, and clubs, and 10 minutes walk from the main high street.

CONTACT: Alan Garcia, Managing Director.

WARREN SMITH SKI ACADEMY
Switzerland: Chemin d'Amon 22, 1936 Verbier, Switzerland

☎ +41 79 359 6566
✍ theteam@warrensmith-skiacademy.com
🖥 www.warrensmith-skiacademy.com/
gap-year-ski-instructor-course.htm
UK:
☎ (0)1525 374 757

COURSES OFFERED: Gap year ski instructor courses and ski performance improvement courses.

DESTINATIONS: Verbier and Saas Fee, Switzerland.

DURATION OF COURSES: 9 weeks: early January to mid-March in Verbier; early July to early September in Saas Fee.

PREREQUISITES: Minimum age 16; average age 35.

QUALIFICATIONS OFFERED: BASI level 1 and level 2 qualifications. Academy has been known to achieve 100% pass rate.

COST: £7,499 with accommodation, £5,299 without accommodation.

ACCOMMODATION: Half-board, excellent food, en-suite, in centre of Verbier.

CONTACT: Warren Smith, Director of Coaching.

ZOOM CAMPS GMBH
Haus Waldrand, 3906 Saas Fee, Switzerland
☎ +41 79 607 29 46
✍ info@zoomcamps.com
🖥 www.zoomcamps.com

COURSES OFFERED: Alpine ski training, with options to do race training, freestyle ski training, performance ski and instructor training.

DESTINATIONS: Saas Fee, Switzerland.

DURATION AND FREQUENCY OF COURSES: 1 week between July and late November.

PREREQUISITES: Zoom Camps are mainly aimed at children, but instructor courses are for those aged 17 and over with a high level of skiing ability.

QUALIFICATIONS OFFERED: Candidates can begin ski racing training in order to pass entrance exams at different training centres, or to pass international tests such as the Eurotest or the Test Technique.

COST: From SFr470 for 6 days of training.

ACCOMMODATION: 3-star hotel with full board.

CONTACT: Liliana De Notaristefano, Communication & PR; David Prades, Head Coach.

SPORT AND ACTIVITY COURSES

BASECAMP GROUP
30 Baseline Business Studios, Whitchurch Road, London W11 4AT
☎ (0)20 7243 6222
✎ contact@basecampgroup.com
🖥 www.basecampgroup.com

PROGRAMME DESCRIPTION: As well as providing ski and snowboard instructor courses, Basecamp is now a partner of Ticket to Ride and offers watersports and adrenaline sports programmes suitable for gappers, including kitesurfing, surfing, and mountain biking.

DESTINATIONS: Watersports courses in Dahab, Egypt, in Taghazout, Morocco, and the South African coast. Adrenaline sports in Whistler, Canada.

DURATION AND TIME OF PLACEMENTS: 2–11 weeks.

QUALIFICATIONS OFFERED: For watersports: BSA (British Surfing Association) and IKO (International Kiteboarding Organization). For adrenaline sports: PMBI (Professional Mountain Bike Instructors).

PREREQUISITES: Requirements are course-specific.

COST: £300–£800 per week depending on length of programme and nature of sport. Usually includes all local requirements such as accommodation, food, coaching, exams, etc, but not flights.

CONTACT: Helen Nicholls and Fergie Miller, Course Advisers.

FLYING FISH
25 Union Road, Cowes, Isle of Wight PO31 7TW
☎ (0)871 250 2500
✎ mail@flyingfishonline.com
🖥 www.flyingfishonline.com

Flying Fish trains watersports and snow sports staff and arranges employment for sailors, divers, surfers, and windsurfers, skiers, and snowboarders (see programme details in 'Directory of Specialist Gap Year Programmes').

COURSES OFFERED: Professional dive training, international yacht training and sail and board sports instructor training programmes. There is a specially organised modular scheme for gap year students, offering training followed by work experience and a period of employment in Australia or Greece. Ski and snowboard instructor courses take place at Whistler in Canada.

DESTINATIONS: Training takes place at Cowes on the Isle of Wight, UK, at Sydney and the Whitsunday Islands in Australia, the Bay of Islands in New Zealand, Vassiliki in Greece, and Whistler Mountain in Canada. Jobs are worldwide with main employers located in Australia, the South Pacific, the Caribbean, and the Mediterranean.

DURATION OF COURSES: Courses last from 1 week to 4 months. Courses come with a 'professional' option, where trainees take part in a period of work experience as an instructor.

QUALIFICATIONS OFFERED: Flying Fish courses lead to qualifications from the Royal Yachting Association (RYA), Professional Association of Dive Instructors (PADI), the Yachting Australia Federation (YA), Surfing Australia (SA), Canadian Ski Instructors Alliance (CSIA), and the Canadian Association of Snowboard Instructors (CASI).

COST: Prices range from £460 for a 1-week learn to dinghy sail course in Greece to a 17-week yachtmaster professional traineeship in Sydney for £11,000.

ACCOMMODATION: Self-catering apartments. Varies according to course and destination, but always provided.

FOLLOW-UP: Possibility of employment following qualification. Placements in the Mediterranean, the Caribbean, and Australia. Qualifications gained can be used after the year out in holiday periods to gain extra cash.

GAP YEAR DIVER
Tyte Court, Farbury End, Great Rollright, Oxfordshire OX7 5RS
☎ (0)845 257 3292
✎ sales@gapyeardiver.com
🖥 www.gapyeardiver.com

PROGRAMME DESCRIPTION: Specialists in the field of recreational and PADI courses and marine conservation; also arranges language courses and adventure tours. Programmes are aimed at gap year students, graduates, and career breakers.

DESTINATIONS: Egypt, Gili Islands in Indonesia, Venezuela, Costa Rica, Thailand, Bahamas, Fiji, and Belize.

DURATION OF COURSES: 1 week to 7 months. Average trip duration is 10 weeks.

QUALIFICATIONS OFFERED: Full range of PADI courses up to instructor as well as marine science training.

COST: £545–£5,845 (depends on duration and destination). Trips tend to include transfers, accommodation, meals/catering facilities, rental of diving equipment, PADI materials, PADI certification costs (on some programmes), and range of specialised diving trips and local land-based activities. In some locations, language courses, marine conservation initiatives, videography courses, and community work are also included. All trips can be customised to individual requirements online.

ACCOMMODATION: Dorm rooms, self-catered houses or camp-style accommodation depending on location.

CONTACT: Ben Stillwell, Director.

NONSTOP ADVENTURE
Unit 3B, The Plough Brewery, 516 Wandsworth Road, London SW8 3JX
☎ (0)845 365 1525
✉ info@nonstopadventure.com
🖥 www.nonstopadventure.com

Member of the Year Out Group.

COURSES OFFERED: Surf instructor course in Morocco and mountain bike courses in Fernie in British Columbia, Canada.

DESTINATIONS: Taghazout, north of Agadir in the south west of Morocco.

DURATION OF COURSES: 12 weeks for surf course, offered twice a year, starting in January and September. 4-week bike experience is in August and includes a 1-week road trip.

QUALIFICATIONS OFFERED: BSA (British Surf Association) qualification.

COST: £4,500 for surf instructor course. Bike course is from C$3,640 (2011), rising to C$4,550 including shared accommodation.

OTHER SERVICES: Opportunity to speak French in Morocco.

CONTACT: Adam Hillier, Course Adviser.

PEAK LEADERS UK
Mansfield, Strathmiglo, Fife KY14 7QE, Scotland
☎ (0)1337 860 079
✉ info@peakleaders.com
🖥 www.peakleaders.com

Surf and mountain bike instructor courses and performance camps, with possible job offers on completion of some of the courses.

PROGRAMME DESCRIPTION: Range of sports instructor courses lasting 4–12 weeks in some resorts worldwide (see entry above for snow sport courses).

DESTINATIONS: Mountain bike rider camps in Whistler, Canada, and surf camps in south-west France.

DURATION OF COURSES: 4–12 weeks.

COST: From £3,250 for short courses to £7,250, inclusive of instruction, flights (in some cases) and accommodation.

PLAS MENAI
The National Watersports Centre, Caernarfon, Gwynedd LL55 1UE, Wales
☎ (0)1248 670 964
☎ (0)1284 673 943
✉ info@plasmenai.co.uk
🖥 www.plasmenai.co.uk

COURSES OFFERED: Multi-watersports instructor training (16 weeks, including a training module in Dahab, Egypt); professional yachtmaster training, windsurfing instructor (includes Dahab training module), and kayaking.

DURATION OF COURSES: 16 weeks. UK–Egypt course offered once a year January to April; UK only March–July and September–December.

QUALIFICATIONS OFFERED: Leads to 3 entry-level qualifications from national governing bodies: RYA Dinghy Instructor, RYA Windsurfing Instructor, and BCU-UKCC level 1 Kayak Coach.

COST: £5,795 with Egypt component; £4,995 for UK-only course. All prices include full board and accommodation for the duration of the course.

FOLLOW-UP: Graduates go on to teach at centres across the UK or abroad, or join a paid work experience programme.

CONTACT: Jane Parry.

SUBWAY WATERSPORTS
Turquoise Bay Resort and Palmetto Bay Plantation, Roatan, Bay Islands, Honduras, Central America
✉ internship@subwaywatersports.com
🖥 www.subwaywatersports.com/Courses/internship.htm

PROGRAMME DESCRIPTION: Internship working in a dive shop while training towards a PADI Divemaster qualification. Chance to learn about customer service and how to run a small business focusing on adventure in a resort atmosphere. Good introduction to life in the dive industry.

NUMBER OF PLACEMENTS PER YEAR: Average 30 per year (maximum 6 per month).

DESTINATIONS: Roatan, a tropical island in the Caribbean.

PREREQUISITES: Minimum age 20. Open water diving certification recommended. Must be friendly, fun, motivated, and a water-lover. Must be in good physical shape.

DURATION AND TIME OF PLACEMENTS: 4–8 weeks.

COST: $1,350 for 4 weeks; $1,950 for 6 weeks; $2,490

for 8 weeks. Prices include instruction, diving, equipment, accommodation, lunches, and airport pick-up. Prices do not include PADI certification cards, PADI books or insurance.

ACCOMMODATION: Room in apartments, shared with other interns.

CONTACT: Patrick Zingg, Owner (patrick@subway watersports.com).

THAILAND GAP INTERNSHIPS
GPO Mae Haad, Koh Tao, Suratthani 84360, Thailand
☎ +66 86 271 2212
☎ +66 86 059 1590
darius@gapinternshipsthailand.com
info@gapinternshipsthailand.com
💻 www.gapinternshipsthailand.com

PROGRAMME DESCRIPTION: Professional-level scuba training (divemaster or instructor), professional underwater videographer, freediver (master freediver/apnoea), Muay Thai boxing training, sailing, and trapeze performer courses on beautiful island of Koh Tao in the Gulf of Thailand. Many courses run as internships (see 'Directory of Work Experience').

NUMBER OF PLACEMENTS PER YEAR: 20+ per month.

PREREQUISITES: Most participants are age 18–25.

DURATION AND TIME OF PLACEMENTS: Variable, but 1–7 months is ideal, depending on programme. For example, trapeze performance course is 1 month.

COST: 7-month package that includes everything except food will cost about 45,000 Thai baht (£920) per month. 3-month Muay Thai internship can be done for less than 25,000 Thai baht per month (£500). Clean comfortable accommodation with a fan and private hot water bathroom is included in the price.

CONTACT: Darius Moazzami and Gary Bain, Co-owners.

UKSA THE MARITIME ACADEMY
West Cowes, Isle of Wight PO31 7PQ
☎ (0)1983 294 941
info@uksa.org
💻 www.uksa.org

COURSES OFFERED: UKSA offers a range of professional watersports and yachting programmes for those wishing to work in the marine industry during their gap year. Gap year programmes can be tailor made from any of UKSA's range of courses.

DURATION OF COURSES: 4–23 weeks.

QUALIFICATIONS OFFERED: RYA, BKSA (British Kite Surfing Association), and BCU watersports qualifications. MCA (Motor Cruising) and RYA yachting qualifications.

COST: From £3,380 to £14,980 for gap year programmes.

ACCOMMODATION: Range of options, included in the cost.

OTHER SERVICES: On-site gym, bar, and dining facilities. All professional courses include industry guidance for support with finding work after training.

WATER BY NATURE RAFTING JOURNEY
3 Wath Road, Elsecar, South Yorkshire S74 8HJ
☎ (0)1226 740 444
rivers@waterbynature.com
💻 www.waterbynature.com

COURSES OFFERED: White-water raft and kayak guide training in Turkey. Trainee raft guides will be taught to kayak on rivers up to grade 3, leading to a chance to guide in other destinations around the world or with Water by Nature.

PREREQUISITES: Very suitable for gap year. Affinity with white-water useful. Should have driving licence because may be expected to drive vehicles.

CONTACT: Hamish McMaster, Managing Director.

GAP YEAR SAFETY AND PREPARATION

OBJECTIVE GAP SAFETY
Bragborough Lodge Farm, Braunston, Daventry, Northants NN11 7HA
☎ (0)1788 899 029
office@objectiveteam.com
💻 www.objectivegapyear.com

COURSES OFFERED: 1-day pre-gap year preparation and safety awareness training. Course covers situation awareness, crime prevention, security advice, kit and equipment, safe food and water, dealing with corrupt officials, travel safety, legal and etiquette concerns, emergency first aid, and handling extreme situations such as kidnapping and environmental dangers.

DURATION OF COURSES: Course runs roughly every 3 weeks, usually on a Tuesday from 9.30am to 4.30pm in Earl's Court, London. Private courses and bespoke courses for schools are available.

COST: £160, including a simple lunch.

SPECIAL FEATURES: The company runs safety training courses for those ranging from gap year travellers to journalists covering conflict zones. At the end of the day's training, a separate briefing is held for female travellers.

SAFETREK
East Culme, Cullompton, Devon EX15 1NX
☎ (0)7971 811 414
✎ john@safetrek.co.uk
💻 www.safetrek.co.uk

COURSES OFFERED: Travel preparation and awareness for gap year and university students. Also skills for life.
DURATION OF COURSES: 1-day course run at above address or at different locations by appointment for groups of 5+.
COST: £150.
CONTACT: John Cummings, Director of Training.

ULTIMATE GAP YEAR
5 Beaumont Crescent, London W14 9LX
✎ info@ultimategapyear.co.uk
💻 www.ultimategapyear.co.uk

COURSES OFFERED: Gap year safety training: personalised individual 2-hour training suitable for anyone embarking on a gap year or independent travel. Training held at private homes in London or at above address in West Kensington.
COST: £200 per student (free place for second person).
CONTACT: Alex Cormack.

MISCELLANEOUS COURSES

HIMALAYAN GAP
1103 Radiant Lane, San Ramon, California 94583, USA
☎ +1 925 230 2070
✎ info@himalayangap.com
💻 himalayagap@gmail.com
💻 www.himalayangap.com

COURSES OFFERED: Himalayan Gap for participants aged 16+ offers five major areas of concentration: Hindi language, yoga, Thangka painting, Indian classical dance and music (sitar, santoor, Indian classical guitar, flute, tabla, or vocal music), and village volunteer work (stressing the strong link between community service and language study). Students are encouraged to choose an area of concentration (in which they can receive up to 150 hours of instruction), and can add on other activities.
DESTINATIONS: Uttarakhand state in the West Himalaya, India. Some programmes include trips to Bhutan, Everest Base Camp and Taj Mahal.
NUMBER OF PLACEMENTS PER YEAR: 10.

DURATION AND FREQUENCY OF COURSES: 10 weeks year-round, or 4 weeks in summer, which finishes with a 1-week trek to the Valley of Flowers.
COST: $8,960; includes all classes, shared accommodation in the home of the programme directors, food, laundry, housekeeping, and travel expenses between Mussoorie and Delhi. A 3-week trek in the Everest region is an add-on for $1,800 (£1,255 or €1,415).
CONTACT: Anchal Lochan, Founder.

JUBILEE SAILING TRUST YOUTH LEADERSHIP @ SEA SCHEME
JST, 12 Hazel Road, Woolston, Southampton SO19 7GA
☎ (0)23 8044 9108
✎ sales@jst.org.uk
💻 www.jst.org.uk

COURSES OFFERED: Course to develop communication, leadership, and team skills, while building a better understanding of disability. Skills will be built through tall ship sailing.
PREREQUISITES: Ages 16–25. Must be prepared to act as a full part of a tall ship voyage crew for the duration of the voyage.
SELECTION PROCEDURES AND ORIENTATION: By written application; mark form with 'Youth Leadership @ Sea', and enclose short personal statement of 200–400 words detailing why you think you should be chosen. Places are limited.
COST: Prices start from £425 for a 4-day voyage. This includes all accommodation, meals, and training. Subsidies of up to £300 are offered towards the cost of the Jubilee Sailing Trust Youth Leadership @ Sea Scheme.

VISITOZ
Australia: Springbrook Farm, 8921 Burnett Highway, Goomeri, 4601 Queensland, Australia
☎ +61 07 4168 6185
✎ joanna@visitoz.org
💻 www.visitoz.org
UK office
☎ (0)7966 528 644
✎ will@visitoz.org

COURSES OFFERED: Self-financing working holiday programme for young people who wish to live and work in outback and rural Australia for up to 1 year. Introductory package is 9 days: 4 days for meet and greet, paperwork, and jet lag recovery at the beach, followed by 5 days on the farm having an introduction to Australian agricultural techniques. VisitOz guarantees well-paid work, and participants go to their first job on the ninth day in Australia. Jobs are guaranteed for the duration of the working holiday visa as the participant travels around Australia, with holiday breaks in between. VisitOz has links with 1,800 employers Australia-wide. Jobs are in agriculture (with horses), in hospitality, construction, museums, childcare, and distance education teaching.

COST: A$2,090. Some places are available after arrival in Australia in the quieter months (March–June), but most people book direct from home at least 6 months in advance for the peak months (July–November and January–February).

CONTACT: Joanna and Dan Burnet in Australia; Will and Julia Taunton-Burnet in UK.

WEST ISLAND COLLEGE INTERNATIONAL – CLASS AFLOAT
159 25th Avenue, PO Box 37586, St-Eustache, Québec J7P 5M6, Canada
kwalsh@classafloat.com
www.classafloat.com

COURSES OFFERED: Gap year programme challenges youth academically, physically, and personally to become well-rounded, responsible global citizens. Students spend 4–8 months exploring up to 25 ports of call worldwide, while completing their first year of study at Acadia University, one of Canada's top liberal arts schools. Participants select from an inventory of courses that includes marine biology, anthropology, and political science.

DESTINATION: Destinations include Norway, Belgium, UK, Ireland, Portugal, Spain, Morocco, Senegal, Brazil, Grenada, St Barts, Dominican Republic, Bahamas, Bermuda, and more.

NUMBER OF PLACEMENTS: 20 gap year/university students.

DURATION OF COURSES: Full year programme from September to June, semester courses from September to December/January, or from December/January to May.

QUALIFICATIONS OFFERED: Gap year programme is designed to build leadership skills, foster personal development, and offer the opportunity to travel. Participants become global citizens as they embark on a college or university career.

COST: Full year fees (2012–13) C$48,400; single semester C$33,000.

CONTACT: Kirsty Walsh, Admissions Officer.

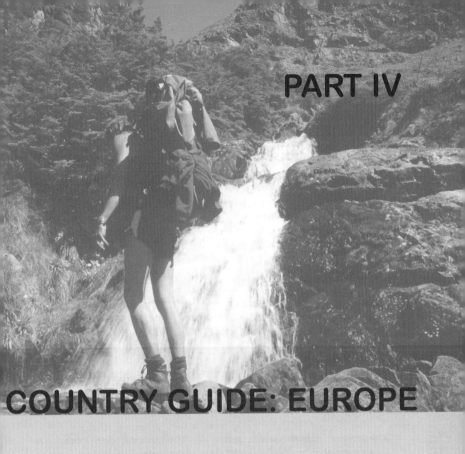

PART IV

COUNTRY GUIDE: EUROPE

BENELUX
FRANCE
GERMANY
GREECE
ITALY
RUSSIA AND EASTERN EUROPE
SCANDINAVIA
SPAIN AND PORTUGAL
SWITZERLAND AND AUSTRIA

BENELUX

Netherlands

The Dutch language is studied by so few students at university that the Netherlands does not attract very many gap year travellers. However, for those who want to experience the country's liberal traditions of tolerance, longer-term stays are better than just a brief sightseeing trip to Amsterdam.

Most Dutch people speak excellent English so a knowledge of Dutch is generally not essential for voluntary or seasonal work. The market for unskilled non-Dutch-speaking workers is far from saturated, since unemployment is the lowest in the EU at 4.2% (2011), with youth unemployment less than one-third of the Eurozone average. The Dutch have some of the most progressive laws in the world to minimise exploitation of workers.

AU PAIRING

Since Dutch is not a widely studied language, au pairing in the Netherlands is not well known; however, there is an established programme for those interested and able to stay at least six months. Working conditions are favourable, in that pocket money of €300–€340 is paid per month in addition to health insurance costs. The main agencies are reputed to offer solid back-up, guidance on contacting fellow au pairs, and advice on local courses. The agency with the largest incoming au pair programme is Travel Active in Venray (+31 478 551900; www.travelactive.nl), which places au pairs aged 18–25 as well as sending Dutch young people abroad on various work exchanges.

Jill Weseman was very pleased with her au pair placement in a village of just 500 people, 30km from Groningen:

> *After graduation, I accepted an au pairing position in the Netherlands, mainly because there is no prior language requirement here. I really lucked out and ended up with a family who has been great to me. Though the situation sounds difficult at best – four children aged 1½, 3, 5, and 7, one day off a week, and a rather remote location in the very north – I have benefited a great deal. The social life is surprisingly good for such a rural area.*

Two other agencies are located in the Hague: Au Pair Agency Mondial (+31 70 365 1401; www.aupair-agency.nl) and the House o Orange Au Pairs (+31 70 324 5903; www.house-o-orange.nl), which has families in Belgium as well. For others, see the website for the Dutch Au Pair Association NAPO (Nederlandse Au Pair Organisatie; www.napoweb.nl).

OPPORTUNITIES FOR PAID WORK

Neil Datta decided he wanted to spend part of his gap year in the Netherlands before applying to study medicine. He simply enquired at his local Jobcentre, which passed on details of a heavy labouring job registered through EURES, the Europe-wide employment service. Although the work itself was unexciting, he greatly enjoyed being based in small-town Holland, especially during the winter carnival in February (comparable to Mardi Gras). Furthermore, he was able to save enough money to fund a big trip to South East Asia afterwards.

The state employment service has been rechristened *UWV WERKbedrijf* and is a one-stop shop for jobseekers. However, both in cities and the country, many employers turn to private employment agencies (*uitzendbureaux* – pronounced 'outzend') for temporary workers. Therefore, they can be a very useful source of temporary work in the Netherlands. They proliferate in large towns – for example, there are nearly 350 in Amsterdam alone – though not all will accept non-Dutch-speaking applicants. *Uitzendbureaux* deal only with jobs lasting less than six months. Most of the work on their books will be unskilled labour such as stocking warehouse shelves, factory, or agricultural work, etc. Among the largest *uitzendbureaux* are Randstad, with up to 700 branches, Manpower, Creyf's, and Tempo Team, all of whose websites are only in Dutch. A good online recruiter is megajobs.nl.

The largest employer of seasonal work is the bulb industry, and Dutch agriculture generally employs thousands of short-term helpers. Young travellers continue to descend on the bulb-producing area between Leiden and Haarlem without a pre-arranged job; it is easier to find openings in the early spring and through the autumn than in high summer. Traditionally, itinerant workers congregate on big campsites, where the seasonal regulars will advise newcomers. Excellent earnings are possible with employers who offer a lot of overtime (paid at a premium rate). But the work is hard and boring and the area attracts hardened long-term travellers looking to save money for further travels.

In this richly agricultural land, other opportunities present themselves for students looking for outdoor work. The area around Roermond (about 50km south-east of Eindhoven and north of Maastricht in the province of Limburg) is populated by asparagus growers and other farmers, who need people to harvest their crops of strawberries, potatoes, and vegetables, especially in the spring. Elsewhere, the area of Westland between Rotterdam, the Hook of Holland, and Den Haag, is well known for tomato production; the whole region is a honeycomb of greenhouses.

Dutch hotels and other tourist establishments occasionally employ foreigners, especially those with a knowledge of more than one European language. A few tour operators such as Eurocamp employ young Britons as staff at their camps for the summer season. In **Adam Skuse**'s year off before university, he almost succeeded in finding hotel work but not quite:

> One very useful resource I found was the website holland.com, where I got a list of hotels and then systematically emailed them all asking for a job. Most had no vacancies, a couple told me to call them when I was in Amsterdam, and one actually arranged an interview with me. But even the knockbacks were pleasant. Quite a few offered to buy me a drink anyway. Alas, I never managed to find the hotel in time, ran out of funds and am now back in Blighty. I had plans for my gap year, but just ended up sitting around on the dole.

This kind of experience is exactly what this book is meant to help you prevent. Those setting their sights higher than work in hotels or campsites, fields or greenhouses, may find it difficult to find work without fluent Dutch. Urban Dutch people have such a high degree of competence in English after they finish their schooling that there is not much of a market for EFL teaching. A range of boating holidays for leisure and business is managed by Naupar, which employs 300 crew and a catering team of 100 for its fleet of 140 traditional sailing boats, such as platbodems. Applicants must have a knowledge of German as well as English.

OPPORTUNITIES IN AMSTERDAM

As throughout the world, hostels employ people to clean, cook, do maintenance, and for night porter duties. More usually, people work a few hours a day for a free bed and breakfast but no wage. **Saffery Ruddock** enjoyed this arrangement as a *whapper* (worker) at the Flying Pig hostel near the Vondelpark; she exchanged $3^1/_2$ hours of work a day cleaning, serving breakfast and doing odd jobs for a dorm bed and a '*brilliant atmosphere, busy, friendly, and relaxed*'. There are two other Flying Pig hostels, one downtown and one at the beach (www.flyingpig.nl), which were advertising jobs in 2011: '*The hostels always welcome passing travellers to help us out with tasks such as cleaning, breakfast, maintenance, and more.*' Most travellers work for food and accommodation, though EU passport holders and working holidaymakers do reception, bar, and maintenance work. Interested people should email headoffice@flyingpig.nl.

Justine Bakker recommends a place she worked in Amsterdam as a '*great place for travellers because it hires a lot of international people, especially for promotion*'. Boom Chicago (www.boomchicago.nl) on Leidseplein describes itself as a 'comedy institution' and employs nearly 100 people as cooks, waiters, bar staff, performers, and for promotion.

REGULATIONS

The Dutch have been tightening up regulations in an attempt to clamp down on squatters, drug abusers, and others perceived to be undesirable. This has been partly in response to the substantial influx of workers from the newly enlarged EU. For EU nationals who intend to stay for more than three months, all that is needed is an EU passport which can be taken to the local tax office (*Belastingdienst*) to apply for a Citizen Service Number (*Burger Servicenummer* or BSN). To apply for a BSN in Amsterdam, go to the big black building outside the train station in Sloterdijk (Kingsfordweg 1; +31 800 0543). You will have to have a BSN before being allowed to register with employment bureaux or take up a job.

Job agencies may not be willing to sign you up unless you have a Dutch bank account, and banks in areas frequented by short-stay workers have become reluctant to open accounts. Look for the Fortis Bank and PostBank, which allow you to open a giro account.

A worthwhile travel site is www.joho.nl '*the one-stop-organisation for travellers-backpackers, expats-entrepreneurs, international jobseekers, interns-language students, and volunteers-development workers*'.

Belgium

Belgium's proximity to Britain and its distinctive culture make it worth considering for a gap year experience. Its population of just over 10.5 million can be broadly divided between the French-speaking people of Wallonia in the south (about 40% of the total population), and those who speak Flemish (which is almost identical to Dutch) in the north.

WORK EXPERIENCE

The large number of multinational companies attracted by the headquarters of the European Union in Brussels have a constant and fluctuating demand for bilingual office workers. High-flyers who would like to work for the European Commission as administrators, translators, secretaries, etc must take part in open competitions; the Training Office of the EU can provide information (see entry in 'Directory of Work Experience Abroad'). The Commission does not offer any work placements or summer jobs other than the three- and five-month *stagiaire* positions in Brussels or Luxembourg for university graduates of all nationalities who are fluent in English and another EU language. Applications must be submitted online not later than the end of August for positions starting in March, and the end of January for positions starting in October.

The Brussels-based company M B Language arranges short work experience placements for students of French or German (+32 2 242 27 66; www.mblanguage.be). Linguistic and work experience exchanges last one or two weeks, though longer ones may be possible. The programme is designed for European students aged 16–18 heading into their final year at school. The placement fee is €300 for one week between October and May, and €375 in July and August, or €450/€475 for a fortnight.

A few years ago, sixth-former **Sarah Hajibagheri** from London sent a flurry of emails to European politicians requesting work experience. After an interview, she was hired by the MEP for London to carry out a six-month internship in which she helped deal with constituency correspondence, wrote parliamentary questions, and became a convert to the Conservative Party. Writing in the Education pages of the *Independent*, Sarah summed up her gap year:

I'm taking a degree in politics, philosophy, and economics at Durham University, and I wanted to pursue these fields on my gap year. Most MEPs reserve stagiaire positions for graduates; even then places are limited and highly sought after. Many stagiaires are unpaid; others gain a meagre allowance or anything up to €1,500 a month. Fortunately, my MEP was generous, giving me a comfortable salary and expenses, including Eurostar travel, language lessons, and a contribution to my rent. The young woman who disembarked from the train at Waterloo seven months later had grown up a lot from the nervous 18-year-old of last September. She'd worked in a graduate job, paid bills to her French landlady, thrown dinner parties without a microwave. So I would encourage anyone to take a gap year, and to spend that time pursuing their passions. In my case it was politics, for others it's baboons – but don't be intimidated. I always feel it's wishy-washy of people to say they took a gap year to find out who they were, but in Brussels I found out who I wanted to be. I worked alongside them every day, admiring their commitment, passion and drive. That's right: a politician.

Links to MEPs can be found at www.europarl.europa.eu. If you do pursue this idea, do plenty of research beforehand about which special interests the MEP has and which committees they sit on.

People who live in the south east of England can make use of the EURES Channel Network (www.eureschannel.org), which assists people looking for jobs in West Flanders and Hainaut in western Belgium, Nord-pas-de-Calais in northern France, and Kent, with bilingual Euro-Advisers in Mons, Lille, and Dover.

CASUAL JOBS

Odd jobs might be available at the popular hostel St Christophers at the Bauhaus at Langestraat 133–137 in Bruges (www.st-christophers.co.uk/bruges-hostels). Venture Abroad, based in Derby (01332 342 050; www.ventureabroad.co.uk), employs a few reps, including students with a background in scouting or guiding, for its programme in Belgium. Ski-Ten International takes on French-speaking tennis instructors and monitors to work at summer camps (+32 81 21 30 51; martine@ski-ten.be).

For more casual opportunities, the best way to find out about short-term general work is to visit a branch of the Belgian employment service in any town. A special division called T-Interim in Brussels (www.tbrussels.be) specialises in placing people in temporary jobs. Most jobs will require a good knowledge of at least one foreign language. As the capital of the European Union, Belgium has a high demand for au pairs. The government stipulates that au pairs be paid €450 a month for 20 hours of work a week. While many British and North Americans make their arrangements over the internet, Stufam in Wemmel (+32 2 460 33 95; aupair.stufam@scarlet.be; www.aupair-stufam.be) makes a few placements in Belgium.

VOLUNTEERING

The Flemish association of young environmentalists called Natuur 2000 in Antwerp (www.natuur2000.be) organises short summer conservation workcamps open to all nationalities. The fee of €60 for five days covers accommodation, food, insurance, and local transport. Young people interested in participating in residential archaeological digs in Namur lasting one to three weeks in the summer should contact Archeolo-j (www.skene.be/cultura/archeoloj/index.html). Residential archaeological digs accept paying volunteers, some for teenagers, some for adults. The fee is €349 for 8 days, €629 for 15 days and €770 for 22 days (2011).

COURSES AND INFORMATION

A few UK-based language course agencies send candidates to Belgium to learn French, including Vis-à-Vis. A number of language schools advertise in the English language monthly magazine *The Bulletin*, on sale at newsstands in Brussels.

The Federation Infor Jeunes Wallonie-Bruxelles is a non-profit organisation that co-ordinates youth information offices in French-speaking Belgium (www.inforjeunes.be). These can give advice on work as well as leisure, youth rights, accommodation, etc. The website of the Brussels branch has links to useful job info at www.inforjeunes-bxl.be/jobs-etudiants for those who are French speakers.

Luxembourg

If Belgium is sometimes neglected, Luxembourg is often completely bypassed. Yet it is an independent country with a low rate of unemployment, and a number of useful facilities for foreign students. The national employment service (Administration de l'Emploi) or ADEM at 10 rue Bender, L-1229 Luxembourg (+352 2478 53 00) operates a Student Employment Service for those looking for summer jobs in warehouses, restaurants, etc. To find out about possibilities, you must visit this office in person, although EU nationals looking for long-term jobs may receive some assistance from EURES counsellors. The Centre Information Jeunes (CIJ) in Luxembourg City (+352 26 29 32 00; www.cij.lu) also runs a holiday job service between January and August for students from the EU. Wages in Luxembourg are very high; the minimum for those over 18 is €1,758 per month.

Opportunities for gap year work experience may be available for linguists since many multinational companies are based in Luxembourg. Addresses of potential employers can be obtained from the membership list of the British Chamber of Commerce in Luxembourg (www.bcc.lu).

FRANCE

Near destinations have been somewhat eclipsed in recent years by the more exotic far-flung gap year destinations such as Peru and Ghana, but there is still plenty of glamour to be found in good old France. Your ambition may be to get to know Paris, to spend the winter in a French ski resort, to live with a provincial family as an au pair or a paying guest, or simply to improve your schoolboy/girl French by conversing with the natives. All are worthy aims for occupying part of your gap year.

SOURCES OF INFORMATION

The former state employment service Agence National pour l'Emploi or ANPE is now known as Pôle Emploi (www.pole-emploi.fr), with dozens of offices in Paris and hundreds throughout the country. The website lists all the branches by region, providing addresses and telephone and fax numbers. For example, the ANPE in Narbonne (ANPE, BP 802, 29 rue Mazzini, 11108 Narbonne Cedex) has seasonal hotel vacancies from May to September, and others can provide details of when agricultural work is available. Although EU nationals should have equal access to the employment facilities in other member states, this is not always the case unless the jobseeker speaks good French and has a stable local address.

One of the 27 regional offices of the Centres d'Information Jeunesse (CIJ) may be of use to the newly arrived gap year traveller. They can advise on cheap accommodation, local jobs, the legal rights of temporary workers, etc. The main Paris branch is CIDJ (Centre d'Information et de Documentation Jeunesse), whose foyer noticeboard is a useful starting place for the job- or accommodation-seeker in Paris. It can also provide booklets and leaflets for various fees on such subjects as seasonal agricultural work, possibilities for work in the summer or winter, and the regulations that affect foreign students in France. Check the website www.cidj-librairie.com for a complete list, which includes Etrangers en France: Vos Droits for €22. CIDJ may be visited at 101 Quai Branly, 75740 Paris Cedex 15 (+33 1 44 49 12 00; www.cidj.com). In order to find out about actual vacancies, you must visit the CIDJ offices in person, preferably first thing in the morning. CIDJ Paris annually registers about 10,000 summer jobs.

COURSES AND HOMESTAYS

A good transition between the A level classroom and a holiday or job in France is an intensive French language course in Britain (see entry for Alliance Française in the 'Directories of Courses', or try the Institut Français attached to the French Embassy at 14 Cromwell Place, London SW7; www.institut-francais.org.uk/courses). An even better one would be a French course abroad (again, see listings in the 'Directories of Courses').

The British Council manages several student exchanges with France including the Charles de Gaulle Bursary Trust, which has annually given £1,000 to 17–19-year-olds who submit an impressive proposal for a project they want to pursue or study for up to a month. Unfortunately, at the time of writing the bursary was under review; check with the Council's Belfast office on 028 9024 8220. Past bursary holders have completed projects on scouting in France, *L'influence arabe et égyptienne sur la culture française*, and *Les écrivains irlandais en France*. Hundreds of British students do an exchange term or year in France. For example, more than 1,000 British students participate in the Erasmus European student exchange, though this scheme is open to undergraduates rather than school leavers. Several hundred more attach themselves to the British Institute in Paris (part of the University of London), and of course the Sorbonne is a magnet for students wanting to take language and civilisation courses.

During her gap year, **Jennifer** from England was as pleased with the extracurricular activities on her eight-week course in Cannes fixed up through CESA as she was with the lessons:

Cannes was definitely the best part of my overseas gap year. The college was perfect for me, and being able to see the festival was just amazing. A Norwegian friend from college and I actually walked the red carpet and saw a film due to some unbelievably good luck in being at the right place at the right time. Just crossing the road on the way home from a bar, a car stopped us and offered us two tickets to see the film Blindness. We initially thought they were fakes, and politely declined. However, the driver insisted we take them, and left us with two tickets to the balcony. Lots of photos and laughs later, we were possibly the luckiest people in Cannes! That was just one of the many fun experiences I had in Cannes, and now I only wish I could go back.

A rough estimate of how much a 20-hour course will cost outside Paris per week would be €300 plus a further €200–€250 for accommodation with a host family. Obviously, prices are higher in Paris. Some language schools double as au pair agencies such as Inter-Séjours (aideinfo.intersejours@ wanadoo.fr) and Institut Euro'Provence in Marseille; which makes a language course much more affordable. A cheap way to have a base in France from which to improve your knowledge of the language is to participate in a work exchange, for example the one offered by the Centre International d'Antibes, a French language school on the Côte d'Azur. Volunteers with the right to work in Europe do administrative or domestic work for at least three months, in exchange for free accommodation and/ or French tuition (v.farris@cia-france.com; www.learn-french.fr/work_exchange_program.htm).

As elsewhere, language studies can be combined with other activities. One of the most interesting is a gap year course offered near Biarritz on the Basque cost of France, where you can learn to surf while improving your French, with the option of also doing classes in French cookery. The four-week course with the Ecole de Surf de Guéthary Jorly SARL will cost a cool €3,125 (www.gap.surf.france.free.fr).

WORK EXPERIENCE

Work experience placements are referred to as *stages* in France, and are widely available through a number of organisations. The major language school France Langue, with centres in Paris and Nice, arranges for its trainees to work in hotels, and if desired to obtain the Paris Chamber of Commerce and Industries Hotel and Tourism Industry French certificate; see www.france-langue.fr/en/specialized_ programs/hotel_and_tourism_industry_french.php.

Eurolingua offers hotel work experience in the south of France, lasting three to six months, to people who are already connected to the hospitality sector. The work is paid and comes with free staff accommodation and meals in the hotel. The programme is preceded by an appropriate French for Tourism course in Montpellier; details at www.eurolingua.com. The programme fee is €1,595. An identical programme is offered by the London-based agency WAVA (www.workandvolunteer.com).

A small company run by a French woman called Boost your French, based in Aberystwyth (01970 626 884; www.boostyourfrench.co.uk), sends Britons on both paid and unpaid work placements in France, mainly for the summer but sometimes longer. Most participants are studying French at university or are Erasmus students, though the occasional gap year student joins the programme, as one recounts here:

I had just passed my A levels and wanted to earn some money during the summer, but I also wanted to have an interesting time and learn more French. So I decided to look for a job in France. I was not successful in my search until I came across Catherine's website. She offered me a job as a shop assistant on the coast near Bordeaux. I had a fantastic time, making lots of friends, and I earned money and definitely learned more French. Now, I am in my first year at university and I intend to go back to work in France next summer.

The long-established Club des 4 Vents (www.cei4vents.com) has a variety of workplace openings for young people over 18 who have an intermediate standard of French (see entry for CEI in 'Directory of Work Experience Abroad').

As a student studying French and Spanish at university, **Andrew Cummings** was lucky (or unlucky) enough to have access to what he and his fellow students refer to, and not all that affectionately, as 'modern languages spam', ie emails, mostly of dubious relevance, that are circulated indiscriminately to everyone in the department. Andrew chanced to read one of the many from companies requiring an intern and haphazardly applied:

A world music and culture magazine in Paris advertised in July saying they wanted an intern for five months from November. I wrote to them in December saying I would be available for three months but not until February. They ended up giving me an internship, so it seems that it doesn't hurt to approach companies of interest with a CV and a cover letter.

My duties included translation, writing short artist biographies in English and in French, adding English subtitles to French videos on the website, finding videos and images to accompany articles, and uploading music. At times, there was very little to do, which meant I could be given dull tasks to fill up the time. But I liked working to a given timetable because it added structure and direction to my life. At university, I can't seem to get anything done until the last minute so work hangs over me until the deadline arrives. When you're working, you leave the office and that's it: no more work until the next day. After working as a journalist at the Bolivian Express earlier in my year out [see Latin America chapter], it was interesting to see how a similar magazine functioned, and from a different angle. Obviously Paris is very expensive, but it's also very big. If you take the time to discover less central or obviously 'cool' areas of the city, you'll always be able to find food, drink, or accommodation that's not extortionate (at least by Parisian standards).

PAID OPPORTUNITIES FOR YEAR OUT STUDENTS

The best areas to look for work in the tourist industry of France are the Alps for the winter season, December to April, and the Côte d'Azur for the summer season, June to September, though jobs exist throughout the country. The least stressful course of action is to fix up work ahead of time with a UK campsite or holiday company in summer or a ski company in winter.

One important feature of working for a French employer in France is that you should be paid at least the *SMIC* (*salaire minimum interprofessionel de croissance*) or national minimum wage. There are slightly different rates for seasonal agricultural work and full-time employees; at present the basic SMIC is €9 per hour gross with a maximum working week of 35 hours. The rate is adjusted every year to take account of inflation.

With a deferred place to read French and Spanish at university, **Frances Pountain** knew that she wanted to spend part of her gap year in a French-speaking environment. Based on previous trips to France, she and a friend decided to head for Montpellier, not least because they were able to get a dirt-cheap flight with Ryanair in February (but spent nearly 10 times that on an eight-month insurance policy with Endsleigh). They arrived cold, with nothing pre-arranged:

At first, we worked solely on improving our French and having some fun. But after a few months we found jobs with a newspaper and leaflet distributing agency called Adrexo (www.adrexo.fr). We found this job by looking in local publications especially Top Hebdo (www.topannonces.fr). The job of distributing publicity was fairly easy and still allowed time to enjoy being in Montpellier.

Going to France was exciting yet had lots of very trying times at the beginning since we hadn't arranged anything before going. With hindsight I would have probably tried to set up either a work placement/ job or a language course ahead of time, as sometimes we didn't feel we had much direction there. Yet I feel my gap year has been very rewarding. Going to live in France has helped my French no end.

CAMPSITES AND HOLIDAY CENTRES

British camping tour operators hire an army of language students to staff their network of campsites throughout France. These companies offer holidaymakers a complete package, providing pre-assembled tents and a campsite courier to look after any problems that arise. Since this kind of holiday appeals to families, people who can organise children's activities are especially in demand. In addition to Europe-wide companies such as Eurocamp and Canvas (mentioned in 'Paid Seasonal Jobs'), the following all take on campsite reps/couriers and other seasonal staff for France:

Carisma Holidays (01923 287 344; www.carismaholidayjobs.co.uk). 2011 wage range £135–£180 per week.

In2Camping, Blackpool FY2 0HJ (01253 593 333; www.in2camping.com). Wage £130 per week.

Matthew's Holidays, Surrey KT24 6RP (01483 284 044; www.matthewsfrance.co.uk/jobswithus. html). £200 per week, less £50 for mobile home accommodation provided.

Venue Holidays, Kent TN23 1QU (01233 629 950; jobs@venueholidays.co.uk; www.venueholidays. co.uk).

The best time to start looking for summer season jobs from England is between September and February. In most cases candidates are expected to have at least A level standard French, though some companies claim that a knowledge of French is merely 'preferred'. It is amazing how far a good dictionary and a knack for making polite noises in French can get you. Many impose a minimum age of 21.

The massive camping holiday industry generates winter work as well. Brad Europe has depots in Nantes and Beaucaire near Avignon that clean and repair tents and bedding on behalf of many of the major companies. Staff (who need not speak French, though it is an advantage) are needed for the laundry and distribution for four to six months in winter and summer. *Gite* accommodation is provided free of charge in addition to the UK minimum wage. A driving licence is essential for the delivery drivers but not for the laundry operatives. Brad Europe's UK office is in Wigan (01942 829 747; info@ bradeurope.com; www.bradeurope.com/vacancies.html).

Outdoor activity centres are another major employer of summer staff, both general domestic staff and sports instructors. Try the major tour operators such as Acorn Adventure (www.jobs-acorn.co.uk) and PGL (www.pgl.co.uk/recruitment). Manor Adventure, based in Shropshire (01584 861 333; www. manoradventurejobs.com), hires sports instructors and other staff for its adventure centre Le Chateau du Broutel along the coast from Boulogne.

For work in an unusual activity holiday, contact either Bombard Balloon Adventures, in Beaune (+33 3 80 26 63 30; www.bombardsociety.org/jobs) or France Montgolfières based in Montrichard (+33 2 54 32 20 48; jane@franceballoons.com). Ground crew are hired by these hot-air balloon companies for the summer season May to October. The job requires excellent physical fitness and strength, a cheerful personality, clean-cut appearance, and a clean driving licence. Montgolfières requires its staff to speak French.

SKI RESORTS

France is the best of all countries in Europe for finding jobs in ski resorts, mainly because it is the number one country for British skiers, 200,000 of whom go there every year. The main problem is the shortage of worker accommodation; unless you find a live-in job you will have to pay nearly holiday prices or find a friend willing to rent out his or her sofa. If trying to fix up a job from Britain, Jobs in the Alps (www.jobs-in-the-alps.co.uk) recruits young people of EU nationality and a very good knowledge of French to work in ski resorts.

Another agency is UK Overseas Handling (UKOH) in Hove (0845 862 1479; ukoh@ukoh.co.uk), which provides seasonal and annual staff to the French tour operator Eurogroup. Eurogroup owns hotels, restaurants and chalets in ski and beach resorts in France (and the rest of Europe). Applicants must hold an EU passport and have a UK National Insurance number. Excellent ski recruitment websites include www.natives.co.uk and www.seasonworkers.com, which provide databases of alpine and other vacancies.

If you attempt to find work in a ski resort on your own, success is far from guaranteed, and competition for work is increasing. Val d'Isère attracts as many as 500 ski bums every November/December, many of whom hang around bars or the Jobcentre for days in the hope that work will come their way.

Several companies can arrange for you to train as a ski or snowboard instructor in the French Alps; see entries in the 'Directory of Ski Training Courses' for Basecamp Group, which runs courses in Val d'Isère and Méribel, New Generation, SkiVo2 (in Courchevel), Gapski, Snoworks, and several others in Tignes.

YACHTS

A few months on the Riviera would be hard for someone taking a gap year to fund unless some means of earning money could be found. Yachts may provide the answer. It is not impossible to penetrate the world of yacht owners and skippers in glamorous resorts such as Antibes and St Tropez. It is essential to start looking early, however, preferably the beginning of March, since by late April most of the jobs have been filled. Boats frequently take on people as day workers first and then employ them as crew for the charter season if they like them. Deckhands on charter yachts are paid a weekly wage, usually around £100, which can sometimes be doubled with tips from big-rollers. The charter season ends in late September (convenient if you're returning to university) when many yachts begin organising their crew for the trip to the West Indies.

Kevin Gorringe headed for the south of France in June with the intention of finding work on a private yacht. His destination was Antibes, where so many British congregate, and he began frequenting likely meeting places such as La Gaffe English Pub and the Irish bars. The main crewing agencies in Antibes are housed in the same building, La Galerie du Port on Boulevard d'Aguillon, and include Blue Water Yacht Crew Agency.

GAPPERS' TIP

Competition will be fierce, so doggedness together with charm and a good measure of luck will be needed for success. Look tidy and neat, be polite, and when you get a job work hard. The first job is the hardest to get, but once you get in with the community of yachties, people will help you move on to other boats.

GRAPE-PICKING

Although the French tourist industry offers many seasonal jobs, there are even more in agriculture, especially the grape harvest. Farmers almost always provide some sort of accommodation, but this can vary from a rough and ready dormitory to a comfortable room in their own house. Food is usually provided, but again this can vary from the barely adequate to the sublime: one picker can write that '*the food was better than that in a five-star hotel, so we bought flowers for the cook at the end of the harvest*', while another may complain of instant mashed potatoes or of having to depend on whatever he or she can manage to buy and prepare. When both food and accommodation are provided there is usually a deduction of one or two hours' pay from each day's wage.

The work itself will consist either of picking or portering. Picking involves bending to get the grapes from a vine that may be only $3^1/_2$ ft tall, and filling a pannier which you drag along behind you. The panniers full of grapes are emptied into an *hotte*, a large basket weighing up to 100lb, which the porters carry to a trailer.

After visiting the French equivalent of a Jobcentre and also a private agency in Epernay at the beginning of September, 19-year-old **Anna Ling** and her boyfriend were given a list of phone numbers for potential farm employers. Preparing for a marathon of ringing round, they bought a local phone card but struck lucky on their very first call. They visited the vineyard in Champagne, were interviewed in the home of the wine-grower, and told to come back when the harvest started, which was 20 September.

A Dutch agency called Appellation Controllée (+31 50 549 2434; info@apcon.nl; www.apcon.nl) mediates between grape-growers in Beaujolais north of Lyon, Burgundy, Chablis, and Champagne and up to 500 Europeans looking for jobs in the *vendange*. Work lasts between one and three weeks in September. In exchange for working eight hours a day, seven days a week you will earn net wages of about €50 a day, plus get full board and lodging. The ApCon agency fee is €99 and it also provides a message board. After signing up with ApCon, **Danielle Thomas** from the Netherlands was set up with a grape-picking job in Beaune at the beginning of her gap year. In 11 days, she earned about €650 gross, €550 after deductions were made for tax and food costs. At her farm in Meloisey, accommodation was provided for grape-pickers who had worked with the farming family before, but first-timers were asked to bring their own tents and sleep in the garden. Danielle had no trouble identifying the good and bad aspects of her experience:

> *The work was very hard, though very enjoyable because of the team. Back pain was experienced often and at the end I had a lot of cuts in my hand, 22 to be exact. I would not advise sleeping in a tent, since at that time of year, I woke up cold every day and not in the right mood for the day's work. Breakfast was limited, though both lunch and dinner were very large and impressive, five-course meals, including soup and bread, salad and vegetables, meat or fish, a variety of cheeses, and finally a dessert. With each lunch and dinner, local wine or the farm's own was also provided. Dinners were very social and fun. This was my first* vendange *, and I must say, even though the work was hard, it was a very pleasant experience. The family was very welcoming and the food was exceptional! I met a lot of really nice people and I hope to go back some time. I'd advise anyone thinking of doing* vendange *in the future that it would certainly be a good idea – as long as you have an open mind and are ready for hard work!*

DANIELLE'S TIPS FOR GRAPE PICKING

- *Bring waterproof clothing and wellingtons, as the weather may change at any moment.*
- *Bring rubber washing-up gloves (not cloth gloves), since in the mornings the grapes are wet and your hands get very wet.*
- *Handcream is also a good idea.*
- *And most importantly, do not expect the French to be able to speak English, so bring a phrase book.*

The demand for pickers in all regions is highly unpredictable. Whereas there is usually a glut of pickers looking for work at the beginning of the harvest (early to mid-September), there is sometimes a shortage later on in the month. Harvests differ dramatically from year to year; a late spring frost can wreak havoc. The element of uncertainty means it is very difficult for farmers to make any definite commitment in advance.

ENGLISH TEACHING

A more realistic possibility than finding employment with a language school is to offset the high cost of living in Paris or the other cities by doing some tutoring, which sometimes shades into au pairing. Language exchanges for room and board are commonplace in Paris and are usually arranged through advertisements (in the places described below in the section on Paris) or by word of mouth. Many long-stayers in Paris have used the noticeboard at the American Church (65 Quai d'Orsay, Invalides metro station) to good effect. Sometimes, families post notices offering accommodation in exchange for English conversation with their children.

The British Council sends hundreds of undergraduates studying French at British universities and recent graduates aged 20–30 to spend an academic year in primary or secondary schools throughout France as assistants (assistants@britishcouncil.org). Assistants give conversation classes for 12 hours a week and are paid €940 (gross) a month. Occasionally pre-university students are accepted in this capacity. For example, a local education authority in the Vendée offers a 'Gap Year for Francophiles' in French primary schools or acting as an assistant in the local lycée. The only requirements are that you be aged 18–25, have an A level in French and have some experience of living in France. In exchange for 20 hours of teaching a week between the end of September and the end of May, you receive free board and lodging with a local family and a monthly allowance of €170 (after national insurance contributions); further details at www.gapyear-france.com.

AU PAIRING

Au pairing has always been a favoured way for young women in their gap year to improve their French and, increasingly, young men too. The pocket money for au pairs in France is linked to the minimum wage (*SMIC*) and is currently about €80 in Paris per 30-hour week plus a city transport pass. The most established au pair agencies in France are members of UFAAP, the Union Francaise des Associations Au Pair, an umbrella group set up in 1999. Member agencies have links from their website www.ufaap.org. While some agencies charge nothing, others charge a registration fee, which can be steep (€160+). Here are some agencies to contact:

Association Familles & Jeunesse, Nice (+33 4 93 82 28 22; info@afj-aupair.org; www.afj-aupair.org). Places more than 300 au pair girls and boys, mainly in the South of France, plus the French Riviera and Corsica.

Butterfly et Papillon, Annecy (+33 4 50 67 01 33; www.butterfly-papillon.com). Member of IAPA.

Europair Services, Paris (+33 1 43 29 80 01; europairservices@wanadoo.fr; www.europairservices.com). Member of IAPA.

France Au Pair – Eurojob, Royan (+33 5 46 23 99 88; contact@eurojob.fr; www.eurojob.fr).

Inter-Séjours, Paris (+33 1 47 63 06 81; www.inter-sejours.fr). Registration fee of €240.

Mon-agence-au-pair.com, Landivisiau, Britanny (+33 6 04 46 20 47; monagenceaupair@gmail.com, www.mon-agence-au-pair.com). Regstration fee of €50, plus a further charge of €190 when contract with family is accepted.

Oliver Twist Work & Study, Pessac (+33 5 57 26 93 26; www.oliver-twist.fr).

Quite a few foreigners are too hasty in arranging what seems at the outset a cushy number, and only gradually realise how little they enjoy the company of children and how isolated they are if their family lives in the suburbs (as most do). Unless you genuinely enjoy small children, it might be better to look for a free room in exchange for minimal babysitting (eg 12 hours a week). **Matt Tomlinson** went into his au pair job with his eyes open:

> *I'd heard too many horror stories from overworked and underpaid au pair friends to be careless, so chose quite carefully from the people who replied to my notice on the upstairs noticeboard of the British Church (just off the rue de Faubourg St Honoré). My employers were really laid back, in their mid-20s, so it was more like living with an older brother and sister. The little boy was just over two, while the little girl was three months old, and they were both completely adorable. On the whole it was great fun. Baking chocolate brownies, playing football, and finger-painting may not be everybody's idea of a good time but there are certainly worse ways to earn a living (and learn French at the same time).*

VOLUNTEERING

Anyone who is prepared to exchange work for subsidised board and lodging should consider joining one of France's many volunteering associations. The majority of short-term projects last two or three weeks during the summer, and cost between €8 and €18 a day. Many gap students join one of these to learn basic French and make French contacts, as well as to have fun.

ARCHAEOLOGY

A great many archaeological digs and building restoration projects are carried out each year. Every May the Ministry of Culture (Direction de l'Architecture et du Patrimoine, Sous-Direction de l'Archéologie) publishes a national list of summer excavations throughout France requiring up to 5,000 volunteers, which can be consulted on its website (www.culture.gouv.fr/fouilles). Without relevant experience, you will probably be given only menial jobs, but many like to share in the satisfaction of seeing progress made.

Anthony Blake describes the dig he joined, run by the History Department of the University of Le Mans: '*Archaeology is hard work. Applicants must be aware of what working 8.30am–noon and 2–6.30pm in baking heat means! That said, I thoroughly enjoyed the working holiday: excellent company (75% French, so fine opportunity to practise the language), weekends free after noon on Saturday, good lunches in SNCF canteen, evening meals more haphazard as prepared by fellow diggers. Accommodation simple but adequate.*'

CONSERVATION

France takes the preservation of its heritage (*patrimoine*) very seriously, and there are numerous groups both local and national engaged in restoring churches, windmills, forts, and other historic monuments. Many are set up to accept foreign volunteers, though they tend to charge more than archaeological digs:

Association pour la Participation et l'Action Régionale (APARE/GEC), L'Isle sur la Sorgue (+33 4 90 85 51 15; www.apare-gec.org). An umbrella organisation that runs volunteer work-camps at historic sites in Provence (plus a few in North Africa). Cost of €100 for 2 weeks, €136 for 3 weeks.

Chantier Histoire et Architecture Médiévale (CHAM), Paris 75014 (+33 1 43 35 15 51; www.cham.asso.fr). Volunteer projects to protect historic buildings, not just in mainland France but in far-flung places including Réunion Island (a *département* of France in the Indian Ocean near Mauritius), and in Africa. See the CHAM website (which is in English) for details. Camps cost €10 a day, plus €30 registration fee.

REMPART, Paris (+33 1 42 71 96 55; www.rempart.com). Similar to the National Trust in Britain, in charge of endangered monuments throughout France. Most projects charge €5–8 per day plus €38 for membership plus insurance.

UNAREC (Etudes et Chantiers), Délégué International, Clermont-Ferrand (+33 4 73 31 98 04; unarec.di@wanadoo.fr; www.unarec.org). Hundreds of international volunteers for short-term conservation projects and longer-term professional training, accepted via partner agencies.

Try to be patient if the project you choose turns out to have its drawbacks, since these organisations depend on voluntary leaders as well as participants. **Judy Greene** volunteered to work with a conservation organisation and felt herself to be '*personally victimised by the lack of organisation and leadership*', more specifically by one unpleasantly racist individual on her project. Tolerance may be called for, especially if your fellow volunteers lack it.

Paris

Like all major cities in the developed world, Paris presents thousands of ways to earn your keep, while being difficult to afford from day to day. Unless you are very lucky, you will have to arrive with some money with which to support yourself while you look around.

Expatriate grapevines all over Paris should prove helpful for finding work and accommodation. Many people find their jobs as well as accommodation through one of the city's many noticeboards (*panneaux*). The one in the foyer of the CIDJ near the metro stop Bir-Hakeim has already been mentioned as being good for student-type jobs such as extras in movies, but sometimes there are adverts for full-time jobs or *soutien scolaire en Anglais* (English tutor). It is worth arriving early to check for new notices.

The other mecca for job and flat-hunters is the American Church at 65 Quai d'Orsay (Invalides metro stop). Official notices are posted on various boards inside and out; the cork board in the basement is a free board where anybody can stick up a notice. Obviously it is necessary to consult the notices in person; they are not available by phoning the church or on the internet.

Arguably the most eccentric bookshop in Europe is Shakespeare and Company at 37 rue de la Bûcherie in the fifth *arrondissement* (on the south side of the Seine). It has a noticeboard and is also useful as a place to chat to other expats about work and accommodation. The shop operates as a writer's guesthouse. If you are prepared to write a short account of yourself and pitch in with doing chores for a couple of hours a day, you may be allowed to stay free for a limited period, assuming there is space. **Hannah Adcock** describes herself as a 'rather solemn' 18-year-old when she read *Work Your Way Around the World* and found out about this opportunity:

> Soon after, I found myself living at this hippy Parisien bookstore with a view of Notre Dame, a treat of inedible pancakes to look forward to and orders to clean the floor using newspaper and cold water. Kids staying at Shakespeare's do most of the jobs for free. You'll only get a paid job if (a) the owner really likes you, (b) you went to a university like Cambridge or Harvard, and (c) you're really cute. The room overlooking Notre Dame is lovely, but when I was there it smelt foul and a highly evolved species of bedbug lurked, as big as rats (ok – exaggeration). Shakespeare's is brilliant, but working there has its 'interesting' aspects!

Since that time, Shakespeare & Co has been brought into the 21st century by the daughter of the elderly owner. Most expat locations such as Shakespeare & Co, the WH Smith Bookshop on the rue de Rivoli and dozens of others distribute the free bilingual newsletter *France-USA Contacts* or *FUSAC* (www.fusac.org), which comes out on the first Tuesday of the month. It comprises mainly classified adverts which are best followed up on the day the paper appears. An advert under the heading 'Work Wanted in France' starts at €36.

DISNEYLAND PARIS

The enormous complex of Disneyland Paris, 30km east of Paris at Marne-la-Vallée, employs about 12,000 people in high season, both on long-term and seasonal contracts. Seasonal positions from March or May to September are open to EU nationals. The minimum period covers the high season from the end of June to the end of August.

'Cast members' (Disneyspeak for employees) must all be over 18, have a conversational level of French and preferably a third European language. The majority of jobs are in food and beverage, housekeeping, merchandising, and custodial departments, though one of the best jobs is as a Disney character. Further details are available from Service du Recrutement-Casting, Disneyland Paris, BP 110, 77777 Marne-la-Vallée Cedex 4 (http://disneylandparis-casting.com). Casting tours are conducted around Europe in February for the start of the season in March. For all jobs, the well-scrubbed look is required (though they do now tolerate neatly trimmed facial hair), and of course they are looking for the usual friendly, cheerful, and outgoing personalities. The monthly gross starting wage is €1,216 from which deductions are made for social security (from €170). Staff accommodation costs €250 per month and a contribution is made to travel expenses on completion of a contract.

MY GAP YEAR: KEITH LEISHMAN

Keith Leishman, from Dundee, was a cast member several summers ago before taking a law degree (with French).

Getting the job was initially quite frustrating. I first sent a letter to the company around November. After another couple of letters and emails without reply, I was just about giving up hope. Finally, around March, I received notification of an interview in Edinburgh and was offered the job. After that you are pretty much left to your own devices and simply expected to turn up at Disney the day before your contract begins. (This was rather a shock to me after working for Eurocamp the year before, who provided transport to France and some preparatory material beforehand.)

I was employed on the ticketing side of operations. I had to wear a Prince Charming costume and supervise the entrance of guests to the park, stamping their hands for readmission. This meant standing for the whole shift in what were often scorching conditions. This was very beneficial for my French as people would ask a whole range of weird and wonderful questions.

The staff apartments were comfortable enough and equipped with kitchens, though I did not cook much due to the cheapness and accessibility of Disney canteens. I could eat well for a few euros a day. Another of the main advantages of working at Disneyland is the mixture of nationalities. The sheer number of young people from all over the world means there are always lots of parties and barbecues in the residences. On days off, I usually went into Paris which is only 40 minutes away on the train. I stayed for two months of the peak summer season and found it quite hard to keep up the Disney smile when I was hot and tired. The job is demanding because you are creating an illusion. All the same, I would urge anybody with an interest in people and a desire to improve their French to try the experience.

GERMANY

Students who have studied German at school and may intend to pursue those studies in higher education should consider spending at least part of their gap year in Germany, doing either a language course or a work experience placement, as an au pair or a volunteer. Even if you are not planning to specialise in modern languages, German can be combined with many commercial and other subjects to make you ultimately very employable. The economic powerhouse of Europe absorbs a great many foreign students in various capacities. With one of the lowest unemployment rates in Europe, work experience placements, some even paid, are available. These can sometimes be found independently, though it is of course easier with the help of a mediating organisation, teacher or contact.

The stereotype of the obsessively efficient and hard-working German is found by many gap year students to have a basis in truth but is not the whole picture. Germany can be inflexible and rule-bound, but on an individual level, many Germans are helpful and humorous.

PLACEMENT ORGANISATIONS

The Zentrale Auslands- und Fachvermittlung (International Placement Services), or ZAV, part of the German Federal Employment Agency, has an international department (Auslandsvermittlung) for dealing with applications from German-speaking students abroad. Details and application forms are available from ZAV (Villemombler Strasse 76, 53123 Bonn; +49 228 713 1330; ZAV-Bonn.Ferienbeschaeftigung @arbeitsagentur.de). All applications from abroad are handled by this office. Although people of any nationality can apply through the ZAV, only citizens of old EU countries (who have German language skills) are entitled to expect the same treatment as a German. This special department of the ZAV finds summer jobs for students of any nationality (Team 327 – Ferienbeschäftigung). Students must be at least 18 years old, be available to work for at least two months, and apply by March. ZAV places students in all kinds of jobs, but mainly in hotels and restaurants, in industry, cleaning, and agriculture.

The IJAB (International Youth Exchange) in Bonn has a EuroDesk which administers European student exchanges (info@jugendhilfeportal.de; www.eurodesk.de).

The Working Holidays in Germany scheme places language and gap year students from the UK and the old EU countries in the field of rural tourism. Participants are given weekly pocket money of €51, and full board and lodging with families on farms or in country hotels. In return, they look after children and/or horses and farm animals, or take up serving and kitchen duties. The preferred stay is three to six months, though a six-week commitment is also allowed; details available from Terre des Langues e.V. in Regensburg (+49 941 565 602; terre-des-langues@t-online.de; www.workingholidays.de). A fee of €200 (2011) is payable after the placement is agreed, at least four weeks before the start date.

Internships for American students and graduates up to the age of 30 who can function in German are available in business, finance, engineering, or technical fields through CDS International in New York (+1 212 497 3502; www.cdsintl.org). If needed, the first month can be spent at an intensive language course, after which participants undertake a paid or unpaid internship, which they have secured previously with the help of CDS's partner agency GIZ (Deutsche Gesellschaft für Internationale Zusammenarbeit). The average monthly remuneration will cover living expenses. The CDS programme fee is $700.

WORK EXPERIENCE

Work placements can be organised in a wide range of sectors including tourism, trade, telecommunications, marketing, and banking, depending on timing and availability. Most internships are organised in conjunction with an intensive language course. Usually an upper intermediate level of language ability is required for work experience to be successful. Most are unpaid or are rewarded only with a subsistence wage. Board and lodging will generally be provided only in the tourism sector. The websites www.prabo.de and www.praktika.de (in German only) are free internship databases for companies, students, and anyone else who is offering or searching for internships in Germany. (The word for internship in German is *praktikum*.)

DID-Deutsch-Institut is a major language course provider (see 'Directory of Courses'), which can also arrange two- to six-month internships following on from their four-week language courses in Berlin, Frankfurt, and Munich; the processing fee for an internship is €450, in addition to the preceding language course lasting a minimum of six weeks (costing eg €1,100). Similarly GLS (Global Language Services) combines a minimum 4-week language course with an internship in a Berlin-based company of six, eight, or 12 weeks. Host companies want their trainees to speak German to at least an intermediate (B1) level.

Astur GmbH (+49 661 92802 0; info@astur-gmbh.de; www.astur-gmbh.de) organises linguistic stays in about 50 cities and towns around Germany with unpaid work experience placements lasting four to 12 weeks. Applicants must be students from the old EU aged 18–25 with an excellent standard of German to work in a German company, normally in industry, sales, marketing, administration, accountancy, tourism, law, translation, or computers. Astur also arranges hotel experience placements for which candidates need an intermediate level of German after a compulsory pre-placement language course. The Astur fee (2010) includes homestay accommodation starting at €1,320 for four weeks, €2,390 for 10 weeks.

WAVA tries to match a student's area of interest with an internship in companies in Berlin or Bremen. Unless they are fluent in German, participants must do a four-week German course on arrival (from £550 plus internship fee of £700). Accommodation and food can also be arranged. Graduates with a background in economics or business and who can speak German have a reasonable chance of finding teaching work in a German city, since most of the demand comes from companies. A TEFL certificate has less clout than relevant experience when looking for freelance English teaching work. University students and recent graduates who would like to spend a year as an English language assistant in a German secondary school should contact the British Council at assistants@britishcouncil. org or www.britishcouncil.org/languageassistants. They send students with at least an AS level in German and recent graduates aged 20–30 to spend an academic year in schools, mainly secondary schools, throughout Germany. Altogether, they place 350–400 assistants who work 12 hours a week and are paid €800 a month (net).

School leavers with a particular field of interest can try to pursue it in their gap year in Germany. For example, **Robin Lloyd** from Hampshire had always been interested in car design. With an A level in German and a place at Bristol University to do German and Engineering, he made contact with a number of motor car manufacturers in Germany, only to be told that he was too young and that they just accepted students already embarked on a university-level engineering degree. The one exception was BMW in Munich, which offers many internships, and who provided Robin with a pleasant flat on his own and enough wages to support himself in Munich for nine months. Although he found the formal protocol of German industry a little hard to swallow, he greatly enjoyed Munich, and quickly developed a social life based on the city's Irish pubs. If you intend to look for a placement with a company, take evidence of any qualifications and some good references (*zeugnisse*), which are essential in Germany.

AU PAIRING

Among the longest-established agencies is the non-profit Roman Catholic agency IN VIA with 40 branches throughout Germany (+49 761 200 206; aupair.invia@caritas.de; www.aupair-invia.de). Its Protestant counterpart is affiliated to the YWCA: Verein für Internationale Jugendarbeit, headquartered in Frankfurt (+49 69 469 39 701; au-pair-vij.org). VIJ has 13 offices in Germany and places both male and female au pairs for a preferred minimum stay of one year, though six-month stays are also common. Scores of private agents operate all over Germany, many of them members of the German Au Pair-Society (www.au-pair-society.org), which has contact details for its 45 members. Commercial au pair agencies do not charge a placement fee to incoming au pairs.

Abroad Connection, Landsberg (+49 8191 941378) and Munich (www.abroadconnection.de).
Au Pair 4 You, Berlin (www.aupair4u.de).
Au-Pair Vermittlung AMS, c/o Anna-Maria Schlegel, Freiburg (+49 761 70 76 917; info@aupair-ams. de; aupair-ams.de). Information in English on website.

The minimum monthly pocket money for an au pair in Germany is fixed by the government at €260. Some families offer to pay for a monthly travel pass, a contribution of up to €100 per semester to your language course, and even your fare home if you have stayed for the promised period of nine months, typically up to €150. In return they will expect hard work, which may involve more housework than au pairs usually do.

VOLUNTEERING

Countless opportunities exist throughout the vast nation of Germany for undertaking voluntary work, whether in environmental protection or in community service. The green movement in Germany is very strong, and many organisations concentrate their efforts on arranging projects to protect the environment, or preserve old buildings, such as the restoration charity Open Houses Network (www. openhouses.de); it charges volunteers less than €40 per week for food and accommodation.

IJGD, Bonn (+49 228 22 80 00; www.ijgd.de). Scores of camps in Germany. British applications accepted by Concordia, VAP, and UNA Exchange.
Internationale Begegnung in Gemeinschaftsdiensten (IBG), Stuttgart (+49 711 649 02 63; www.ibg-workcamps.org). Projects in both eastern and western Germany. Applications in UK as above, plus via VFP (vfp@vfp.org) in the USA.
Mountain Forest Project (Bergwald Projekt e.V.), Würzburg (+49 931 452 6261; www. bergwaldprojekt.de). One-week education and conservation projects in the alpine forests of southern Germany. Basic knowledge of German is essential, since the foresters conduct the camps in German only. Hut accommodation, food, and insurance are provided free, though participants must pay an annual membership fee of SFr60/€40.

COURSES AND HOMESTAYS

The Goethe Institut is the long-established provider of German language tuition, whether as preparation for university studies or simply to speak it for leisure purposes. A list of addresses in Germany with full course details offered by each one is available from the website (www.goethe.de), or from the Goethe Institut in London. The Goethe Institut administers language exams at all levels, leading to internationally recognised certificates in line with the Common European Framework of Reference for Languages (CEFR), ranging from A1 for beginners to C2 for language skills at the highest level.
Alastair Holt decided to spend 12 weeks of his gap year learning German in Berlin arranged through CESA:

I met people from all corners of the world and had the opportunity to explore the underschön city that is Berlin. Due to the length of my programme and the full immersion technique, I was very happy with my progress. I felt that staying with a host family was invaluable; meal times in particular offered an opportunity to listen and speak German. I also conducted my social life exclusively in German. My main memories from the course are: strolling around Berlin by night with friends from the language school, going to an excellent jazz bar, watching Hertha Berlin at the Olympia Stadium, drinking German beer in a scenic beer garden, playing ultimate frisbee in the Tiergarten, and having lots of fun and laughs in class! If you have a gap year it is worth taking an extended course to make significant progress.

In addition to CESA, all the major language course agencies run extensive programmes in Germany. Among the most popular destinations for year-out language students are Munich, Heidelberg, and Freiberg, though less picturesque places will be cheaper. It might be worth noting that the purest German is spoken in the north, but even if you are living in Bavaria where there is a pronounced accent, the teaching will be of standard German.

As mentioned, language courses can sometimes be followed by *stages* (internships) for those who achieve a satisfactory level of German. One of the great educational institutions of Germany is the Volkshochschulen (VHS) or folk high schools, which can be found in nearly every town of the republic. In addition to offering German for foreigners, they run a range of evening classes in drama, handicrafts, sport, and so on, all at subsidised rates. Most bookshops sell the prospectus of courses available for terms beginning in September and January.

GREECE

Once the darling of backpackers, Greece has lost some of its lustre over the past two decades. Some consider Greece old hat, and mass tourism has been moving away, as more long-haul beach paradises such as Thailand have come into vogue. Some gappers are still attracted by the party scenes in Corfu and Rhodes, while others might be put off that it has been spoiled. Although many young people may want to spend time relaxing on a Greek island, few consider longer-term possibilities in Greece during their gap year. Anyone planning to read classics or archaeology at university will be attracted to the great sites of Greek antiquity as well as to the beautiful scenery and climate, friendly and carefree people, and memorable wine and food.

AU PAIRING AND TEACHING

Living with a Greek family is one of the best ways of organising an extended stay. Yet au pairing hours tend to be longer in Greece than elsewhere, partly because there is no expectation that a gap year student will need time off to study the language. The Nine Muses Agency accepts applications from young European and American women for au pair positions, including for summer-only roles, and can also place candidates after arrival in Athens. Hotel positions are also sometimes available. Contact the Athens agency on +30 210 931 6588; www.ninemuses.gr. The owner Kalliope (Popy) Raekou prides herself on her after-placement service, meeting au pairs regularly at coffee afternoons. There is no fee to au pairs. **Riitta Koivula** from Finland moved with Popy's help from an unsatisfactory situation on Kos to a much better one in Athens:

> I started my work as an au pair on Kos when I was 19. At first I was so excited about my new family and the new place, since I had never been to Greece before and I loved the sun and the beach. I lived in a small village called Pili, where almost no-one spoke English. But soon I got tired of the village because winter came, tourists left, and it wasn't so warm to spend time on the beach any more. I also got tired of the family. The three little girls didn't speak English and they were very lively. The working hours were also terrible: 8 to 12 in the morning and then 4 to 10 in the evening every day except Sundays. I was very homesick on Kos, and decided I wanted things to change. So I went to Athens in November and was soon given a new family. I fell in love with Athens and its people right away. My new family was the best and we are still very close. I met other au pairs and one Finnish au pair became my best friend. I learned so many things, even to read, write, and speak Greek, because we took Greek lessons during the spring with Popy. I have many happy memories of Athens and friends who are still dear to me.

Another au pair agency in Greece is In-Globe in Thessaloniki (www.inglobe.com.gr) mentioned in the next section.

Thousands of private language schools called *frontisteria* are scattered throughout Greece, creating a huge demand for native English speaker teachers. Unfortunately for gap year students, all but the dodgiest schools will expect to see a university degree (which is a government requirement for a teacher's licence). The basic hourly wage is currently just less than €9 gross (€7.41 after compulsory deductions).

University graduates who fancy the idea of taking a gap year teaching English in Greece should be aware that agencies exist to match graduates with 10-month vacancies. Interviews are carried out in Greece and the UK during the summer for contracts starting in September. These agencies are looking for people with at least a BA and usually a TEFL certificate (depending on the client *frontisterion*'s requirements). The following undertake to match EU nationals with *frontisteria* and do not charge teachers a fee:

Anglo-Hellenic Teacher Recruitment, PO Box 263, 201 00 Corinth (+30 27410 53511; jobs@anglo-hellenic.com/www.anglo-hellenic.com). Scores of posts in wide choice of locations for university graduates from the UK, with a recognised 120-hour TEFL Certificate. Anglo-Hellenic offers a one-month training course from TEFL Corinth (www.teflcorinth.com) for £1,300, including accommodation.

Cambridge Teachers Recruitment, 17 Metron Street, New Philadelphia, 143 42 Athens (+30 210 258 5155). Interviews conducted in UK in summer by Andrew MacLeod-Smith (macleod_smith_andrew@hotmail.com). One of the largest agencies, placing up to 60 teachers per year in vetted schools. Applicants must have a degree and a TEFL certificate, a friendly personality, and conscientious attitude.

OTHER GAP YEAR OPPORTUNITIES

SEASONAL WORK

Seasonal jobs can be arranged from the UK, preferably by contacting relevant tour operators in February or March. Mark Warner (020 7795 8375; www.markwarner.co.uk/recruitment) runs several resort hotels in Greece requiring British staff who are paid a weekly wage starting at £50, on top of free travel, accommodation, meals, use of facilities, medical insurance, and so on. Other possibilities exist with Olympic Holidays (overseas-jobs@olympicholidays.com; www.olympicholidays.com) who are always on the lookout for outgoing EU nationals to work a season as resort reps (minimum requirement: decent GCSE grades in maths and English; customer service experience preferred). Yachting holiday companies are a possible source of jobs, which can either be fixed up ahead of time or on the spot. Sailing holiday operator Sunsail (02392 334 600; www.sunsail.co.uk/hr), now part of the giant TUI group, uses an online recruitment process to hire a large number of sailors, watersports instructors, flotilla hosts, qualified nannies, etc for its Sunsail Club Vounaki, three other bases in Greece, and several flotilla holidays. Sailing Holidays in London (www.sailingholidays.com) hire flotilla skippers and hostesses, boat builders, and marine engineers for their upmarket holiday programme in the Greek and Dalmatian islands; most of their recruitment takes place at the London Boat Show in January. The specialist tour operator Setsail Holidays in Suffolk (01787 310 445; boats@setsail.co.uk) recruits a similar range of staff for the May to September season in the eastern Med, promising pocket money of £125–£160 per week.

In-Globe Agency is a recruitment agency based in Thessaloniki and registered with the Ministry of Labour. It aims to find staff from all over Europe to fill positions in holiday resorts in Greece and Cyprus, and recruits up to 2,000 Europeans aged 18–55 for summer jobs in tourist hotels on the islands, and also in its internship programme for trainees. Summer jobs and internships are open to students (primarily students of hospitality and tourism) and last only four months (June to September), whereas professional work experience placements can be for up to 18 months. Basic monthly salaries start at €500 in addition to free accommodation, meals, social insurance, and the possibility of paid flights. For details contact Maria Tsilempi Kaltsidou (+30 2310 588200; maria@inglobe.com.gr).

The internet is bound to turn up further possibilities. The monthly electronic jobs listing *Jobs Abroad Bulletin* (www.jobsabroadbulletin.co.uk) carries a sprinkling of vacancies in Greece in the spring. For example, before the 2011 summer season got under way, it carried adverts for a solo guitarist for a surfers' bar on Rhodes (www.surfersparadise.gr), kids' club staff for Crete, and a night receptionist for an Athens hostel (www.hostelaphrodite.com). Be aware that some ask applicants to submit a photo, and they are clearly interested in hiring fit and attractive staff. Patient surfing will lead you to the websites of individual bars and restaurants that have a 'jobs' icon.

While hunting on the net for a suitable summer vacancy, **Annelies van der Plas** made use of www. wereldwijzer.nl, the largest online travel community in her native Netherlands. After spending days searching online and placing adverts, she finally received a reply from a Dutch man who asked her if she would like to work behind the bar at the Camel Bar on Kos (www.camel.gr/jobs.php). She was asked to send a picture to the Greek boss and was soon offered a job, but no contract (which is typical):

It was a kind of gamble to go alone as a blonde girl of 19, and my parents were a little bit worried, but they did not object to it, especially because many Dutch people worked on Kos. My plan was to work about two months at the Camel Bar. The boss had an apartment ready for me, for €200 per month or €100 if I shared. The apartment itself was nothing special, but the beautiful view of the harbour from the balcony made it worth the money. When I was working at the Camel Bar, I saw that it was not hard to find another job on the island. Mostly jobs behind the bar were already taken, so those available consisted of getting people in. I noticed that the salary was most of the time the same, about €30 a night, paid daily, weekly, or monthly. I luckily received my money every week, although I did not get my salary for my last week, which meant I worked a whole week for nothing. There was nothing I could do; the police were very corrupt.

A good feature of the job was the free drinking and the contact with the people. I met a lot of people, and every evening seemed like a night out. Sometimes people say that you have to smile or act more happy, which is hard when you are tired, and irritating, because tourists don't understand that you work seven nights a week. The boss was happy with me because there were people who only wanted to be served by me. Also, the tips were much better on the terrace and I could talk more to the people. Be careful when you are working in Greece. Most bosses don't care about you. A good colleague of mine got very sick for many days. She did not get her money that week. In two months, I saw that most Greek people regard the tourists as idiots. Most bosses think only of money, and they don't care if the customer is not happy with their drink because they will never see them again. My last piece of advice: if you are a (blonde) girl, be careful of the Greek men.

Undoubtedly, the motives of some employers in hiring women are less than honourable. If you get bad vibes, move on. Some women find the legendary attention paid by prowling male Greeks intolerable; others have said this unwanted admiration is not unduly difficult to handle. Once you have established your reputation (one way or the other), you will be treated accordingly, at least by the regulars. On her gap year, **Emma Hoare** lasted precisely 20 days in a job as receptionist in a hotel on Mykonos before realising that she was being totally ripped off and her boss was a big, fat, disgusting, immoral bully, whom another disgruntled ex-employee described as 'feral'.

It is also possible to show up and shop around for a job, but don't expect anything to happen quickly. Young women are far more likely to be hired by a bar or restaurant than men. Many gap year travellers stop a while in one place and swap some labour for free hostel accommodation. They enjoy the hostel atmosphere and the camaraderie among its workers, and regard the job as a useful stop-gap while travel plans are formulated, often based on the advice of fellow travellers. Those who stick at it for any length of time may find themselves 'promoted' to reception; in this business, a fortnight might qualify you for the honour of being a long-term employee. The work is easy-come, easy-go, and is seldom secure even when you want it to be.

It is sometimes worth checking the classified advertisements on the website of the English language daily *Athens News* (www.athensnews.gr/classifieds). Another interesting possibility for people over 18 is at the holistic holiday centre on the island of Skyros in the northern Aegean. A number of 'work scholars' help with cleaning, bar work, and domestic and maintenance duties in exchange for pocket money of £50 a week and the opportunity to join one of the 250 courses on offer, from yoga to windsurfing (www.skyros.com).

CONSERVATION

Elix-Conservation Volunteers Greece in Athens (+30 210 382 5506; www.elix.org.gr) is a non-profit organisation promoting intercultural exchanges and nature and heritage conservation. Projects include work in protected landscapes, conservation of traditional buildings, and work on archaeological sites. Applications can be sent directly or through a partner organisation in your country (e.g. UNA Exchange and Concordia in the UK).

Earth, Sea and Sky (www.earthseasky.org), a private UK-based NGO which grew out of a travel agency, recruits volunteers to carry out island-based wildlife research, conservation and tourist awareness work on the Ionian island of Zakynthos. Their planned SOS Sea Turtle rescue station will require volunteers with a range of skills, for short- or long-term placements. On the same island, a project to protect sea turtles actively uses volunteer helpers. Archelon is the sea turtle protection society of Greece (+30 210 523 1342; www.archelon.gr), and it carries out research and conservation on the loggerhead turtle on Zakynthos, Crete, and the Peloponnese. A free campsite is provided for those who stay at least a month; volunteers will need at least €15 a day for food plus pay a registration fee of €200 or €300 (the lower fee is for the periods on either side of the high season mid-June to 21 August).

Another turtle conservation organisation is MEDASSET (Mediterranean Association to Save the Sea Turtles; +30 210 361 3572; www.medasset.org), which offers volunteers free accommodation at the head office in Athens in exchange for working for a minimum of three weeks. Volunteer work is office-based only, and includes assisting staff with projects, letter writing, computer-orientated and archiving tasks, database updating, internet research, etc. No prior knowledge in sea turtle conservation is required, just a passion and interest in the environment.

Bears are even more threatened than marine turtles. Arcturos accepts short-term volunteers at its environmental centre in the Prefecture of Florina in northern Greece, which serves as a bear protection centre (+30 23860 41500; mstyliadou@arcturos.gr; www.arcturos.gr).

COURSES

Enjoyable as it is to master the Greek alphabet and learn simple greetings with which to befriend the locals, not many gap year students want to make a formal study of modern Greek. Any who do should enquire about courses in Athens, Thessaloniki, and Crete, or summer courses on islands as is offered in Evia by Nine Muses (mentioned above; www.ninemuses.gr/school.htm). CELT Athens (www.celt.edu.gr) puts on modern Greek summer schools in Athens and Paros.

Emily Reardon decided she would like to spend the month of February in Greece, since she had been studying Greek in New York. She contacted a couple of language agencies and did her own research on the internet (checking past clients' feedback online) and chose the Athens Centre. Emily loved everything about Athens and Greece. She adored the Athens Centre, her coursework, classmates, the staff, the set-up, and the accommodation offered (small, clean, Ikea-furnished studio/efficiency apartments shared between two). The group planned things like eating out and travelling to one of the islands together, yet Emily felt safe and explored on her own as well.

An alternative to the Athens Centre is the Aegean Center for the Fine Arts (+30 22840 23 287; studyart@aegeancenter.org), which has been offering fine arts courses to individuals in small groups for 45 years at its centre on the Cycladic island of Paros. Students can create their individual curriculum with the help of artists in residence, choosing from among the visual arts (photography, print-making, painting, and drawing) and literary arts (creative writing, literature, voice). One student said that she felt as though she had spent a whole semester on a film set rather than real life. The 13-week session from early March costs €8,500 (2011); tuition fees can be reduced on the work-study programme.

Anyone interested in Greek folk culture might wish to contact the Dora Stratou Greek Dance Theatre in Athens (www.grdance.org), which runs short courses and workshops on traditional dance and theatre over the summer, as well as daily classes during the winter. The organisation presents daily summer performances at the outdoor theatre on Philopappou Hill in Athens and takes on about 10 unpaid foreign student volunteers to help look after the large costume collection and assist at performances.

ITALY

Italy has always been a favourite destination for young people wanting to expand their cultural horizons. In the 18th century, the Grand Tour of Europe was considered to be an essential part of the education of young men of good breeding or fortune, and was centred on Italy. Generations of educated people journeyed between the great artistic centres of Venice, Florence, and Rome. Although their modern-day equivalents are more likely to be young women, seldom accompanied by a private tutor, some gappers do enrol in courses that will help them to appreciate the art and civilisation of ancient Rome and Renaissance Italy.

Italy is still a remarkably welcoming country and Italians are capable of breathtaking generosity and hospitality, with no expectation of anything in return.

SPECIALIST GAP YEAR PROGRAMMES

Two exclusive cultural programmes in Italy maintain the tradition of the Grand Tour and are still aimed at young people of fortune since they are expensive. Art History Abroad and the John Hall Venice Course both provide a superb introduction to European art and culture. Both are aimed at school leavers who may be planning to go on to university to study art history, or who may just have an independent interest in western history and civilisation. For an account of the benefits that **Ella Hickson** reaped from the AHA course, see her case study on p14.

John Hall offers courses in Italy for non-specialists on European civilisation, especially the visual arts and music, including architecture, conservation, opera, design, literature, and world cinema. Practical options include Italian language, drawing, painting, and photography. The spring course consists of an introductory week in London followed by five weeks in Venice, where accommodation, meals, lectures, visits, and classes are included in the price of £6,990, with optional extra periods in Florence and Rome.

MY GAP YEAR:
GEORGINA NIGHTINGALL

Georgina Nightingall found that the John Hall course she took in Venice opened her eyes to the beauty of art, not just in painting, sculpture, and architecture, but also in opera, music, literature, world cinema, photography, and in the Italian landscape. What she most appreciated was the experience of being in one place long enough to begin to feel like a local.

We're on the second to last day and I've just spent the last half hour looking through all the pictures I've accumulated over the last seven weeks. So many good times to reminisce about, so many lectures to reflect on, instances to laugh about, and many nights never to forget. And to think: I might never have been here, on this fabulous course, if I had made a different decision! I'd always hoped that I would be able to persuade my parents that paying the equivalent of a school term's fees to send me off to Italy to learn about art was a good investment; and I managed.

I will leave not only with a fresh knowledge of art history in Italy, but, with a desire to download the Mozart symphony he composed at the ripe age of eight, to see the opera La Bohème on stage, to read all of Keats's Odes, to watch the billion international non-Hollywood films that Ryan [the course's film critic] has recommended, to photograph every aspect of each city I come across (even if it's London and it makes me look like a complete tourist), even perhaps to learn a bit of Italian (beyond the restaurant version), despite my terrible language skills. John Hall Venice may have a lot to do with looking at paintings in churches but only a third of the lectures are on art history. Some cover modern and contemporary art that is hidden away in Peggy Guggenheim's house (four minutes' walk from 'our home' at Hotel Messner), or in the large and controversial Pinault collection (two minutes' walk from 'home'). Other lectures deal with a wide curriculum of arty or cultural subjects and they all have a link: Venice.

At first, I was unsure about the idea of living in just one city for five weeks. I now realise that it was the most marvellous idea. Not only do you get that 'pre-university feeling' but I learnt to truly appreciate living and studying in a foreign city. Venice is an amazing city to live in: in no other city have I had to wade through knee-high puddles in wellington boots; its **aqua alta** is one of its many original qualities. Whenever I enter a new, unfamiliar place I experience a rush of adrenaline; I still get those feelings just wandering around each day. Venice's windy street layout surpasses the busy souks of Marrakech (or any other city for that matter); all you have to do is listen and you will hear nothing. Literally nothing. It's a silent city; the absence of any industrial form of road traffic is absolutely noticeable, there aren't even any bicycles. Even the **vaporetto** is peacefully quiet.

Venice has played home for over a month now, and we still never run out of things to do. The tourists head straight for St Mark's, but we know that Dorsoduro has many hidden treasures. We've had the chance to try out the local specialities - eating fish and ice cream (though not together), where all the locals, plus John Hall, hang out. The idea of a cold city in early February never sounds that appetising but it produces some quite extraordinary settings – the fog gives Venice that mysterious feeling it's known for. The rain highlighted the incredible reflections of the Gothic and Eastern architecture in the streets. It's like walking through history; no other city remains so untouched, almost like a museum. But Venice is a mystery and beauty that cannot be encapsulated in mere mortal words; it demands a physical reaction. All five senses must be used to appreciate it properly; you must be there to appreciate it. As a city of textures, light, water, and reflections, it is a haven for photographers and artists. As you sit patiently on the vaporetto waiting, a cool breeze across your face, the gentle rocking of the boat to and fro, like a cot, relaxes you entirely and sends you off into a dream state until you realise you're not dreaming, it's just Venice, man's most impressive accomplishment, and you're living in the middle of it.

I would love to have visited many other important cities in Italy but then we'd be tourists in all of them; wandering around with maps trying to cover the main big attractions before rushing off on a coach to the next place. The John Hall course opened my eyes to art in the world, and I'm not talking about paintings hanging on walls. So much more than that. I lived, smelt, and breathed the world in a new and fresher way after this course. Suddenly, it helped me to see. I can't believe I'd missed out on all of this before.

Art History Abroad offers four six-week programmes in the autumn, spring, early summer, and late summer, plus two-week courses in July and August. Its six-week programme involves travel throughout Italy, with all tuition on-site and not in classrooms, so that students are introduced to a broad spectrum of Italian life; the inclusive fee is £6,990 from summer 2010.

Based in Greece, the Aegean Center for the Fine Arts (www.aegeancenter.org) offers a 14-week semester course every autumn, which is divided between Italy and Greece. The first three weeks are spent in the Tuscan hill town of Pistoia visiting museums and studying art, then proceeding to Venice and Rome, before Athens and Paros; the inclusive fee is €9,500.

COURSES AND HOMESTAYS

Italian is one of the easiest and most satisfying languages to learn, especially if you already have some knowledge of a Latin-based language. Many courses combine Italian language lessons with art history, cuisine, etc. The British Institute of Florence runs year-round courses in Italian language, history of art, and life drawing, with other courses in opera, etc. Summer courses relocate to Massa Marittima near the Tuscan coast, though **Fiona Roberts** was happy to spend her summer in 'the inescapably Italian' city of Florence, where she recommends folding up your map and just wandering around the tiny winding streets (avoiding the crocodiles of American tourists plugged into their headphones):

When my friend and I first arrived in Florence, our Italian extended no further than 'Si', 'Grazie', and not-so-useful pizza and pasta names. Although having languages at GCSE and especially A level was for me an advantage in learning Italian, the course would be perfectly approachable and manageable without it. The classes were often extremely funny, sped by and, to cap the lot, the vending machines sold chocolate croissants. Easily pleased, perhaps? Probably the most atmospheric evening was the first Sunday where, fresh from a week of classes, we watched Italy win the World Cup. The atmosphere was incredible, as everyone seemed to dash back home, grab a vespa, an Italian flag, and a small child and race round the city, beeping their horns, until dawn. Sleep may have been difficult but I think we all fell in love with their good-natured enthusiasm.

MY GAP YEAR: CHARLOTTE SNELL

Charlotte Snell, from Aberdeenshire, had been desperate to travel ever since she could remember, but had missed out on taking a year away after school because her parents were moving house that year. She couldn't face going straight from finals at Durham to a law conversion course in London, so investigated gap year alternatives.

Deferring the start date of the conversion course was easy, and the law firms that I asked all said that they encouraged prospective applicants to take time out and gain some wider experience of the world. So my decision was made. With regards to financing my gap year I was very lucky. My parents were very supportive of my plans and agreed to pay for the course at the British Institute in Italy, on the basis that it furthered my education. My three months in Florence were without doubt the highlight of my gap year (even though the travelling I did afterwards was amazing!), and I would recommend it to anyone without hesitation. I was in the intermediate group for Italian, having done it for GCSE several years previously. The lessons were very conversation-orientated, but backed up with a thorough teaching of the grammar. This made a pleasant change from learning languages at school in England and consequently I feel I have a much more useful vocabulary. My teacher was first-class, and taught us a lot about Italian culture, the way of life, and modern issues as well as just the language. Also, the staff made living abroad as easy as it possibly could be, and it was this that made the price of the Institute (which is quite high) worthwhile.

I also took History of Art at the Institute. Having previously had no interest in art history, I decided after a month of wandering around Florence and feeling ignorant that I had better learn. As my budget was quite tight, the Institute kindly allowed me to do a selection of the lectures. The lecturers were excellent - and after three years at university I've seen some bad ones! - dynamic and interesting. There was also a good balance between lectures and tours, the tours being very important as they brought the many wonders of Florence to life. The Institute also runs a number of other courses, such as cookery, which I didn't attend, and organises all sorts of cultural programmes. For example, when I was there they were running a film series, showing the films of Elizabeth Taylor and Richard Burton on a Wednesday night. I went to several and had a lot of fun debating the films afterwards with the random mix of people who turned up to watch. One of the highlights was waking up at 5am and climbing up to the Piazza Michelangelo to watch the sun rise over one of the most beautiful cities in the world.

Other institutes to consider include the Accademia Italiana in Florence (www.accademiaitaliana.com), which offers courses in Italian plus design (fashion, furniture, graphic, textile, etc), while Linguaviva (www.linguaviva.it) offers a range of courses on Italian culture and language, plus organising internships in Florence and Milan. After a compulsory four weeks of Italian language classes (€700), the internship placement fee for 8 weeks is €840, 12 weeks for €1,050, and 16 weeks for €1,260 (2011). The Accademia del Giglio in Florence (www.adg.it) offers Italian courses for foreigners, plus drawing, painting, and art history courses.

An excellent source of Italian language, art, and cookery school listings is the website www.it-schools.com. Serious courses often work towards one of the six levels of the *Certificazione di Italiano come Lingua Straniera* (*CILS*) exam, which now mesh with the Common European Framework of Reference. Some language schools are in lovely settings like the Piccola Università Italiana in Tropea (see 'Directories of Courses'). **Isobel Pyrke** spent 11 enjoyable weeks studying Italian in beautiful Sorrento on the Bay of Naples, arranged by CESA:

As I had never heard or spoken to anyone who had taken a language course in their gap year and I had never studied Italian before, I didn't know what to expect. Linguistically I felt I improved much more than I expected. The teachers were fantastic and I feel I formed some good relationships with them during my time there. The lessons were good, although two hours of solid language learning followed by another two solid hours is quite hard going. I liked the way it left my afternoons free, however. The school was in a good position, easily accessible from the main square. Sorrento is a small town, so it is easy to meet and socialise with people. By the time I left I couldn't walk down the street without bumping into someone I knew. It is also very safe, much more so than London. I'm going back in the summer so I suppose that speaks for itself.

An average starting price for one week's intensive study of Italian would be €180–€240, and €700 for four weeks. Accommodation in one of the major cities would cost a further €15–€30 a night or €500+ a month bed and breakfast with a host family. Needless to say, courses in central Florence or Venice will be more costly than ones in more obscure towns.

Matteo Symonds, a 19-year-old client of CESA, put to the test the maxim that the longer you stay, the more fluent you become:

The 32-week academic year in Italy was fantastic. I divided my time between Rome, Milan, and Florence, three months in each. On the course, I met people from all four corners of the planet, including Serbia, Holland, China, Brazil, and many from Japan. Only 6% of the students were British, which was to our advantage because we spoke Italian to each other. It was about three months into studying that I could start to put coherent sentences together. The extracurricular activities in Milan were diverse, including trips to San Siro to watch prestigious teams in Serie A like AC Milan and Internazionale; and weekly outings to the Casablanca Bar, with its happy hour deal of €6 for a drink and all you could eat. I ended up in Florence, where the clubs are fantastic and the city is small enough to get around on foot.

Milan is the fashion capital of the world, and many students go there to study fashion and design. Some centres offer courses taught in English, for example the Istituto Europeo di Design (www.ied. edu), which attracts a lot of Americans – including **Lauren McHale** from California. Not only did she have a long-held interest in fashion design but, while pursuing her passion for snowboarding in the Rockies two years earlier, she had fallen in love with an Italian snowboarder, and was determined to move to Italy: '*I have always wanted to do fashion design, so Max showed me round the schools in Milan while I was visiting in the summer. I found IED, went back home for a month, convinced my parents that it was a good idea, and within a few months, I was going to fashion school in Milan, and living my dream in Italy.*'

The Spannocchia Foundation offers an intriguing internship opportunity, mainly to young Americans, to spend time on an *agriturismo* farm in Tuscany while studying the language (see entry in 'Directory of Work Experience Abroad'). **Katie White** from Massachusetts loved her spring-time experience there before college:

I was one of eight interns at the Tenuta di Spannocchia, a 1,200-acre farm, agriturismo , and educational facility. The internship programme included daily farm work, Italian lessons, field trips to surrounding areas of interest, and educational presentations on food issues and Italian culture. The interns worked 30+ hours a week for three months. The conditions were excellent; our intern group lived together in a house on the property which was cleaned regularly, we received meals from the farm, and the work was never too taxing. My gap year included so many exquisite moments that I really don't think I can pick one out. I remember distinctly one moment this spring while I was harvesting leeks on a sunny morning overlooking the Tuscan landscape and thinking that I was the luckiest, happiest, healthiest girl alive (or at least that I knew of).

PAID OPPORTUNITIES FOR GAP STUDENTS

TEACHING

Hundreds of English language schools around Italy employ native English speakers, though the majority are not suitable for gap year students unless they have acquired a TEFL qualification. But some do manage to find openings, despite their lack of a certificate. **Natalia de Cuba** could not persuade any of the language schools in the northern town of Rovereto where she was based to hire her without qualifications. So she decided to enrol in the Cambridge Certificate course run by International House in Rome. She found the month-long course strenuous but not terribly difficult, and worth the fee (which now stands at €1,775 plus accommodation; www.ihromamz.it). Good training centres will have links with potential employers throughout Italy.

Several Italian-based chains of language schools account for a large number of teaching jobs, though most operate as independent franchises so must be applied to individually. Chains include the British Schools Group (www.britishschool.com) with more than 60 member schools. Other chains include British Institutes with 175 associated schools (www.britishinstitutes.it) and Oxford Schools based in Venice (www.oxforditalia.it) with 13 schools in north-eastern Italy.

A useful starting place for information on training and teaching English in Italy is www.teaching englishinitaly.com, a site maintained by Sheila Corwin, an American resident in Florence who has been working and living as an English language teacher and teacher trainer in Italy (on and off) since 2002. Her website includes affordable online options in basic TEFL certification, and allows registration for on-site courses in TEFL, TESOL, and CELTA, and a Teaching Practice (TP) programme is also available in Florence and other cities in Italy (sheila@teachingenglishinitaly.com).

As in other European countries, summer camps for unaccompanied young people usually offer English as well as a range of sports. ACLE Summer & City Camps in San Remo, Liguria (+39 0184 506070; www.acle.org) advertises heavily for more than 400 young people with a genuine interest in children who must be '*fun-loving, energetic, and have high moral standards*' to teach English and organise activities including drama for two, four, or more weeks. The promised wage is €225–€275 per week plus board, lodging, insurance, and travel between camps within Italy. However, summer staff must enrol in a compulsory five- or six-day introductory TEFL course, for which a deduction of €150 will be made from earned wages.

A less well-known organisation also based in San Remo might be worth comparing: Lingue Senza Frontiere (+39 0184 533661; www.linguesenzafrontiere.org). It promises to pay tutors €450 net plus board and lodging every two weeks at its English immersion summer camps. It also takes on English-speaking actors for the academic year. A smaller outfit to try is the English Camp Company (info@ theenglishcampcompany.com) based in Assisi.

AU PAIRING

Summer-only positions are readily available. Most Italian families that can afford live-in childcare go to holiday homes by the sea or in the mountains during the summer and at other holiday times.

The average weekly pocket money for au pairs is in the range of €70–€90, and for mother's helps €500–€800 a month. Wages are slightly higher in the north of Italy than in central and southern parts of the country because the cost of living is higher. The demand for nannies and mother's helps able to work 40+ hours is especially strong, since a high percentage of families in Italy have two working parents. The London-based agency Totalnannies.com (020 8542 3067) specialises in Italy and has up to 100 vacancies in Italy at any given moment. Most staff at Italian agencies speak English and welcome applications from British au pairs. Make sure first that you won't be liable to pay a hefty registration fee. Try the following:

ARCE (Attivita Relazioni Culturali con l'Estero), Genoa (www.arceaupair.it). Long-established agency, makes placements throughout the country.
Celtic Childcare, Turin (+39 011 533 606; www.celticchildcare.com).
Euroma, Rome (+39 06 806 92130; www.euroma.info). Placements not just in Rome.
Intermediate SNC, Via Bramante 13, 00153 Rome (+39 06 57 300 683; www.aupairinrome.com; www.intermediateonline.com). Intermediate has its own language school in the Aventino district of Rome. It can also fix up work experience placements for candidates who know enough Italian.
Roma Au Pair, Rome (+39 06 863 21519; www.romaaupair.com). No placement fee for au pairs.

Working in Italy is something of a hit and miss situation, and if you can't speak a word of Italian, you will be at a distinct disadvantage. Contacts are even more important in Italy than in other countries. **Louise Rollett**, for example, first went out as a paying guest to a town near Bologna, and then extended her stay on a work-for-keep basis as an English tutor. **Dustie Hickey**, meanwhile, went for treatment to a doctor in Milan who immediately offered to pay her to tutor his children in English.

You are not expected to speak Italian if you work for a British tour operator; in fact, German is probably more sought after than Italian because of the high number of German tourists in Italy. Try any of the major campsite tour companies such as Canvas, Eurocamp, or Keycamp, which are looking primarily for people over 18 with customer service skills. The smaller Venue Holidays (www.venueholidays. co.uk) employs summer season reps at campsites on the Venetian Riviera, Lake Garda, and in Tuscany.

WINTER RESORTS

Crystal Holidays, part of the TUI Travel Group (020 8541 2223; www.jobsinwinter.co.uk) hires resort reps and chalet staff for work in the Italian Alps as well as staff for summer holidays. Another major summer and winter seasonal employer is Collett's Mountain Holidays (www.colletts.co.uk/ recruitment), which in addition to the usual run of resort jobs also looks for artists and walks organisers. The ski department of PGL Travel (www.pgl.co.uk/recruitment) offers some jobs as ski reps, leaders, and ski/snowboard instructors (to BASI-qualified skiers), especially for short periods during half-term and Easter holidays. If you haven't fixed up a job with a UK tour operator, job openings can be found (with difficulty) on the spot in the winter resorts of the Alps, Dolomites, and Apennines. Many are part-time and not very well paid.

OTHER JOBS IN TOURISM

As throughout the world, backpackers' haunts such as hostels and campsites often employ travellers for short periods. While planning her escape route from a less-than-satisfactory summer au-pairing position in Naples, **Jacqueline Edwards** asked in the Sorrento youth hostel about job possibilities, and a few weeks later moved in to take over breakfast duties in exchange for free bed and breakfast.

By making use of www.hostels.com **Stephanie Fuccio** from the USA had little difficulty prearranging a hostel job:

> *Never in a million years did I think that watching MTV would be part of my daily life in Rome. The hostel I was working at was Hostel Casanova [Via Ottorino Lazzarini, 12, 00136 Rome; +39 06 397 45228; hostelcasanova@yahoo.com]. I was working 7 days a week (I was a bit scared about running out of money since this was the first leg of the trip). The shifts would alternate from evening to morning every day: one day doing the morning shift when the hostel was cleaned, and the next day the evening shift. As well as getting to stay there for free, they paid me and my co-worker €20 per day in cash, which was really nice. Rome was so cheap (from a San Franciscan's point of view) and with great weather, it was easy to save. I came to Italy with $700 cash and a plane ticket, I left with about $600 and a plane ticket to England and Ireland, having been there about five weeks total.*

VOLUNTEERING

Many Italian organisations arrange summer work projects that are as disparate as selling recyclable materials to finance projects in the developing world, to restoring old convents or preventing forest fires. An intercultural exchange organisation with a website in English and a far-reaching long-term incoming programme is AFSAI (Viale dei Colli Portuensi 345, 00151 Rome; +39 06 537 0332; www. afsai.it).

Here is a selection of voluntary organisations that run working holidays. In some cases, it will be necessary to apply through a partner organisation in your home country:

Abruzzo, Lazio and Molise National Park, Centro Operativo Servizio Educazione, Via Roma, 67030 Villetta Barrea (+39 0864 89102; centroservizi.villetta@parcoabruzzo.it; www.parcoabruzzo.it). Volunteers carry out research and protection of flora and fauna in remote locations, eg in Pescasseroli and Villetta Barrea. Volunteers must cover their insurance and registration fees: €80 for 7 days, €140 for 14 days.

Emmaus Italia, Boves (+39 0171 387834; www.emmauscuneo.it). Workcamps to collect, sort and sell second-hand equipment to raise funds for social and community projects worldwide.

LIPU (Lega Italiana Protezione Uccelli), Trento (+39 0521 273043; www.lipu.it). Long-established environmental and bird conservation association, which publishes a catalogue of summer projects at its bird reserves (*gasi*) throughout Italy.

La Sabranenque, Centre International, rue de la Tour de l'Oume, 30290 Saint Victor la Coste, France (+33 04 66 50 05 05; sabranenque.com). French-based organisation uses voluntary labour to restore village and monuments in Altamura (inland from Bari in Southern Italy). The cost of participation is £180 for three weeks in July/August.

Volunteers can also join archaeological camps. The national organisation Gruppi Archeologici d'Italia in Rome is the umbrella group for regional archaeological units that co-ordinate two-week digs (+39 06 3937 6711; segreteria@gruppiarcheologici.org; www.gruppiarcheologici.org). Paying volunteers may join these digs (eg €220+ for 1 week; €330 for 2 weeks).

Malta

Although small in area (30km by 15km), Malta has much of interest and is an independent nation state within the European Union. The student and youth travel organisation NSTS in Valletta (www.nsts.org) markets English courses in conjunction with sports holidays for young tourists to Malta. NSTS runs a work and study programme, which arranges work experience placements in the hospitality industry in Malta for young English-speaking travellers.

RUSSIA AND EASTERN EUROPE

With the accession of Bulgaria and Romania to the EU in 2007, the divide between Eastern and Western Europe has been further eroded. Together with Hungary, Poland, the Czech Republic, Slovakia, Slovenia, Lithuania, Latvia, and Estonia, the former Soviet bloc countries are looking to the west and to the future, where the English language dominates. The demand for native speakers to teach English continues to be strong in both the cities and more far-flung corners of this vast region.

During the heady days immediately after the various Communist governments fell (before many of today's gap year travellers were born), thousands of young westerners flocked to Prague, Budapest, and Kraków. Many of them supported themselves for short and longer periods by teaching English to a population which clamoured for access to English-language media and culture. Naturally, the clamour has subsided and pay for English teachers has dropped, but there is still a demand for native speaker teachers of English at summer camps and in institutes.

Russia, the Baltic States, and other states of the former Soviet Union

ENGLISH TEACHING

Several English-teaching schemes are described in this chapter suitable for pre- or post-university experiences. Opportunities tend to be in small provincial towns and industrial cities rather than the glamorous capitals. In Russia, the Baltic states (Latvia, Lithuania, and Estonia) and the other states of the old Soviet Union, the English teaching situation is more fluid. Native speakers can still arrange some kind of teaching, often on a private basis, but with no guarantee of earning a living wage from it.

PLACEMENT ORGANISATIONS

The major chains have multiple franchise schools in the region, particularly Russia, including International House, EF English First, and Language Link. Volunteers are placed by the non-profit organisation Sharing One Language or SOL (www.sol.org.uk) in state schools in a number of eastern and Central European countries, especially Hungary, Slovakia, Romania, and Serbia. Candidates must be graduates, preferably with a recognised TEFL certificate. Contracts with individual schools are mostly for a complete academic year September to June. All posts include a local salary and free housing.

The youth exchange company CCUSA runs a Summer Camp Russia programme, whereby teacher-counsellors from the UK and USA are placed in youth camps in Russia for four or eight weeks between mid-June and mid-August. Participants must be between the ages of 18 and 35, have experience working with children and/or abroad, and have an interest in learning about Russian language and culture. Camps are widely scattered from Lake Baikal in Siberia to the shores of the Black Sea. The programme fee of £995 includes round-trip travel from London to Moscow, visa, travel, insurance, orientation on arrival and room and board.

Australian **Paul Jones** spent the summer in Russia as a gap within a gap, since he was already on a working holiday in the UK to fund trips to Europe and beyond:

I worked as a counsellor in a summer camp near the city of Perm. When I first arrived, my heart sank because it looked like a gulag (for which the area around Perm is famous!) but you soon forget the physical conditions . . . mostly, anyway. If I didn't like the food at the start, I definitely learnt to like it by the end and now reminisce about the worst of it! My job, as with American summer camps for kids, was to help lead a group of up to 30 children for their three weeks' stay at the camp. Because I did not speak the language, I was placed with two other leaders, so my services weren't really necessary. However, this region of Russia doesn't exactly get many international visitors, so the role I played at camp sometimes felt more like being a rock star! The types of activities the kids did ranged from football, basketball, and swimming (the colour of the pool was scary) to singing, dancing, and crafts. But while I tried as best I could to lead my group of kids in their daily activities, every single kid in the camp wants a piece of you because you're the foreigner! So a lot of the job is to just be there and share a different culture with the kids (and their parents sometimes), other Russian counsellors, and the Camp Director. In return, they also shared their culture. I've actually stayed in contact with a number of the local counsellors. The ones that don't speak English very well make up for it with sign language and friendliness. I found that a few words in Russian go a long way towards bridging the culture gap. And if possible take some souvenirs for the kids. Even a pack of cards with the British flag on them provides 52 little gifts.

A Russian youth organisation called SFERA runs short voluntary teaching projects in the Russian Federation (http://dobrovolets.ru/eng.php). CCUSA also runs a summer camp in Croatia, where English-speaking counsellors are needed; details from www.campcalifornia.com.

A new company called Angloville (www.angloville.com) is offering a true working holiday, whereby native English speakers agree to chat for a solid week in their mother tongue to Polish businesspeople, in exchange for free on-site accommodation and food in a spa hotel in a remote country location in Poland.

COURSES AND HOMESTAYS

Ironically, the study of Russian has been in sharp decline since Russia abandoned communism and decided to throw in its lot with western capitalism. Compared to the heady 1960s, few schools and universities now offer Russian. The big language agencies such as Caledonia, CESA, and IALC offer Russian courses in Russia, particularly St Petersburg. Liden & Denz Language Centres (see entry in 'Directory of Language Courses') run Russian language courses from casual beginners to advanced academic, and can all arrange a follow-up work experience or volunteering placement.

One of the most surprising (and cheapest) destinations for gappers who want to qualify as ski or snowboard instructors is Zakopane in Poland with Sunshine World (see entry in 'Directory of Ski Training Courses').

VOLUNTEERING

The vast region of eastern Europe is a hive of volunteering activity during the summer, so if a short-term group voluntary project appeals to you at all, contact the main UK workcamp organisations listed in the chapter *Volunteering*, all of which have partners in Eastern Europe. Projects vary from excavating the ancient capital of Bulgaria to organising sport for gypsy children in Slovenia. There is also a high proportion of much-needed environmental workcamps.

Many international voluntary schemes are particularly active in the region including the fully funded European Voluntary Service (EVS) Programme (see entry in 'Directory of Specialist Gap Year Programmes'). Volunteers aged 18–30 are given free travel, food, accommodation, and an allowance for the duration of two to 12 months. Kitezh Children's Community for orphans in Kaluga, 300km south of Moscow, has close links with the Ecologia Youth Trust in Scotland (see entry in 'Directory of

Volunteering Abroad'). The trust specifically recruits students in their gap year to spend two to three months at Kitezh and provides extensive preparatory information, down to profiles of the resident children. The joining fee is £1,320 for two months, including visa support, but not visa fees or airfares to Moscow.

MY GAP YEAR: NATALYA KENNEDY

Natalya Kennedy is among the many volunteers who have found Kitezh a friendly, welcoming and inspiring place to spend some time.

I came to Kitezh because the three-hour delay of a BA flight from Moscow to London led me to start a conversation with my neighbour, who succeeded in instilling in me a curiosity to see the place that obviously meant so much to her. So six months later, just out of school and eager to take on the world, I packed my bag, told my friends they wouldn't hear from me for a while, and set off from Moscow's slushy Tyopli Stan bus station. I didn't have any aims beyond a vague hope that my Russian would improve and that I'd meet some interesting people who lived a different way of life. The driving force behind daily life in the village is a group of extremely intelligent, dynamic, and enthusiastic young teachers who keep the place buzzing.

Living in what is as near as possible the middle of nowhere has its advantages. The beauty of the surrounding countryside is breathtaking. Experiencing the beauty and loneliness of the Russian landscape at first hand is truly awe-inspiring. Of course, life here certainly isn't all sweetness and light. The language barrier is undoubtedly my biggest problem. It makes it difficult for relationships with anyone to progress beyond basic friendliness and curiosity, and I have days when I feel really upset about it. On the positive side, having a limited ability to speak has forced me to explore other means of communication; it's surprising how far you can get with a combination of practical jokes, a limited vocabulary, hugs, and smiles. I think that of all the great memories I'll have of this place, the one that stands out is when one of the small children said as we looked out over the frozen lake: 'It's as if we've fallen into a magical world.' I don't think I've ever felt happier than I did as I walked back through the snow towards the twinkling lights and smoking chimneys with a child clinging on to each hand. It's the sort of humbling moment which makes you want to do something meaningful with your life.

Romania

The children's homes and special schools of Romania continue to accept voluntary input, though not on the scale of a decade ago. Inspire Volunteer (www.inspirevolunteer.co.uk) has programmes in Transylvania, where volunteers teach and look after orphans and disadvantaged women and children. Oyster Worldwide sends volunteers for one- to three-month placements to orphanages in Brasov (as well as to a nearby bear sanctuary).

A few British charities have recruited volunteers for summer language camps in the past. DAD International UK-Romania (+40 788 473523; www.dad.ro) sends volunteer teachers to several language camps in central Romania.

Bulgaria

Teaching opportunities in the private sector are still very scarce. A Bulgarian agency of long standing appoints 60–80 native speakers to teach in specialist English language secondary schools for one academic year, for which the deadline is the end of May. Details are available from Teachers for Central and Eastern Europe (21 V 5 Rakovski Boulevard, Dimitrovgrad 6400; +359 391 24787; tfcee@usa.net; www.tfcee.8m.com). Students, preferably with a TEFL background, are accepted from the USA, UK, Canada, and Australia, to spend an academic year teaching. The weekly teaching load is 19 40-minute classes per four-day week. The salary in Bulgarian levs is equivalent to $200. Benefits include free furnished accommodation, 60 days of paid holiday, paid sick leave, and work permit. A summer programme is also available at Black Sea resorts for which the application deadline is 20 June. TfCEE charges an application fee of €60.

SCANDINAVIA

Not every gap year traveller wants to hit the trail to the tropics. The Scandinavian countries of Denmark, Sweden, Finland, Norway, and Iceland exercise their own fascination and can be visited as part of an InterRail tour of Europe, or separately. One way of getting away from the notoriously high cost of living and of travel in this region is to join one of the organised schemes described in this chapter, for example working on a Norwegian farm or teaching at a Finnish summer school.

The demand for English-speaking au pairs is very small, and in fact has one of the long-established agencies in Denmark has closed. One possibility is the Scandinavian Au-Pair Center (scandinavian@aupair.se; www.aupair.se) in Helsingborg, Sweden, whose website lists a certain number of family vacancies in Norway and Denmark as well.

Denmark

Work is available on farms and in factories, offices and hotels; the main problem is persuading an employer to take you on in preference to a Danish speaker. Copenhagen, the commercial and industrial centre of the country, is by far the best place to look for work. It is also the centre of the tourist industry, so in summer it is worth looking for jobs door to door in hotels, restaurants, and the Tivoli Amusement Park. Among the largest employers of casual staff in Denmark are newspaper distribution companies. To get a job as an *omdeler* or 'paper boy/girl', contact A/S Bladkompagniet's office in Rødovre (+45 70 20 72 25; bladkompagniet@bladkompagniet.dk) or in Copenhagen (+45 35 27 73 20). Another big hiring company is the morning paper *Morgenavisen Jyllands-Posten* (+45 80 81 80 82; avisbud@jp.dk/cni@daoas.dk). It employs 4,000 people on weekdays and 5,000 on Sundays to deliver all its papers before 6.30am on weekdays and 8am on weekends.

The long-established WWOOF Denmark (VHH) distributes a list of around 50 member farmers, most of whom speak English. In return for four or more hours of work per day, you get free food and lodging. Always phone, email, or write before arriving. The list of farmers can be obtained only after joining WWOOF in Denmark for €15 (www.wwoof.dk). Many young Europeans end up picking strawberries in Denmark in the summer, although earnings are not as attractive as they once were. The EURES website (www.seasonalwork.dk) provides a wealth of information about harvest work and invites EU passport holders to apply online. EURES estimates that 2,000 foreigners are offered jobs on seasonal harvests in Denmark each summer. Pickers get paid between Kr 5.25 and Kr 6.50 per kilo, and can expect to pick not more than 5kg an hour when they start out. The season lasts from early June to near the end of July, and applications are processed between April and mid-May. Most employers expect you to bring your own tent and cooking equipment and may charge Kr 20–25 for camping. The island of Fyn has been recommended for fruit-picking work, especially the area around Faaborg. But Samsø is where most pickers head in June. The website www.samsobaer.dk/summerjob.html is a central resource for three Samsø farms.

Finland

At one time, the Centre for International Mobility (CIMO) in Helsinki arranged short-term paid training opportunities for foreign students. However, the Erasmus practical training programme has virtually replaced that, and CIMO no longer offers placements to students from EU countries. British students and graduates who want an on-the-job training placement in Finland lasting between one and 18 months in technical subjects should apply to IAESTE (www.iaeste.org.uk).

The Nordic School in Russia (+7 812 303 86 96; www.nordicschool.ru) mounts an ambitious series of summer schools at eight different colleges in Finland for Russian children aged 7–17 learning English (age range varies among camps). Native English speakers – from the USA, Canada, Australia, and New Zealand as well as the EU – are recruited to implement an intensive programme of conversation lessons, for one to five fortnight-long camps. Teachers are given accommodation and meals plus a wage of €400–€500 at the end of each camp, and also offered transport to another location for those working at consecutive camps.

The University of Helsinki Language Centre offers Finnish courses for foreigners who are not enrolled as students; for details of summer and termly courses, contact Language Services (www.helsinki.fi/kksc/language.services/eng). Finnish courses for foreigners are also available from the Open University (www.avoin.helsinki.fi) and the Helsinki Summer University (www.kesayliopistohki.fi).

Norway

Atlantis Youth Exchange in Oslo (+47 22 47 71 70; www.atlantis.no) runs the excellent Working Guest Programme, which allows people aged between 18 and 30 of any nationality to spend two to six months in rural Norway (Americans and other non-Europeans may stay for no more than three months). The only requirement is that they speak English. In addition to the farming programme open to all volunteers, placements in family-run tourist accommodation are available to European nationals. Farm guests receive full board and lodging, plus pocket money of at least NOK 1,000 a week (£110+) for a maximum of 35 hours of work. The idea is that you participate in the daily life, both work and leisure, of the family: haymaking, weeding, milking, animal-tending, berry-picking, painting, house-cleaning, babysitting, etc. A wardrobe of old, rugged clothes and wellington boots is recommended. Application should be made through partner organisations where available; all are listed on the Atlantis website. British participants can apply through WAVA in London (0800 80 483 80; www.workand volunteer.com). Atlantis distributes submitted applications with photos, references, medical certificate, etc. to Norwegian farm families participating in the scheme, and then host families that want to offer a placement contact applicants directly to conduct a telephone interview. The registration fees charged by WAVA are £580 for two months to £870 for six months.

Robert Olsen enjoyed his farm stay so much that he went back to the same family for another summer:

> The work consisted of picking fruit and weeds (the fruit tasted better). The working day started at 8am and continued till 4pm, when we stopped for the main meal of the day. After that we were free to swim in the sea, borrow a bike to go into town or whatever. I was made to feel very much at home in somebody else's home. The farmer and his daughter were members of a folk dance music band, which was great to listen to. Now and then they entrusted me to look after the house while they went off to play at festivals. Such holidays as these are perhaps the most economical and most memorable possible.

Atlantis also runs a programme for 200 incoming au pairs who must be aged 18–30 and willing to stay at least six months, but preferably between eight and 12 months. The programme has become so popular that applications are accepted only through partner agencies, and at the moment there is none in the UK. Interested Britons should seek advice from Atlantis, since it may be possible to apply through an agency in another country. The pocket money for au pairs in Norway is NOK 4,000 per month, which sounds generous until you realise that it could be taxed at 25%–35% depending on the region. Atlantis can advise on possibilities for minimising tax by obtaining a *frikort*, which entitles you to a personal allowance. Anyone interested in learning Norwegian should find out about the International Summer School offered at the University of Oslo (www.summerschool.uio.no).

Sweden

With the amazing success of Stieg Larsson's trilogy of novels and the televising of Henning Menkel's detective Wallander, awareness of Sweden has been raised in the popular consciousness. Unfortunately, there aren't many ways of arranging an extended stay there without breaking the bank. There is no youth agency equivalent to Atlantis, and few casual work opportunities.

WWOOF is now represented in Sweden (www.wwoof.se). In order to obtain the list of 100 WWOOF farms in Sweden, as well as contact details of organic farms in many other countries, you must pay the membership fee of €25 online. Stiftelsen Stjärnsund (www.frid.nu) is located amongst the forests, lakes, and hills of central Sweden. Founded in 1984, the community aims to encourage personal, social, and spiritual development in an ecologically sustainable environment. It operates an international working guest programme lasting from one week to three months starting throughout the year, but is at its busiest between May and September when most of the community's courses are offered. First-time working guests pay SEK 500 for their first week of work, and if the arrangement suits both sides it can be continued with a negotiable contribution according to hours worked and length of stay. Enquiries should be made well in advance of a proposed summer visit.

Swedish language courses are available at the Uppsala International Summer School (www.uiss.org).

Iceland

The private employment agency Ninukot (PO Box 12015, 132-Reykjavik; +354 561 2700; ninukot@ninukot.is; ninukot.is) originally specialised in agricultural and horticultural jobs throughout Iceland, but has branched out to offer roles in babysitting, gardening, horse training, and tourism as well. Its welcoming website is in English, and holds out the prospect of an easy-to-arrange working holiday in Iceland for EEA nationals.

The majority of vacancies are on farms, looking after animals, working the farm equipment, and helping with the household chores, but can involve harvesting and packing produce, training horses, or looking after guests on holiday farms. During the summer months from May to September, Ninukot offers jobs in small family-owned hotels and restaurants all over Iceland. In other sectors, it is possible to apply year-round. Jobs are open to EEA citizens aged 18–30 with a driver's licence and good English (other languages are a plus). Experience is not essential but makes placement easier. Pay starts at €1,077 a month with a deduction of €10 a day for board and lodging, and terms for flight reimbursement are the same as for au pairs: after completing six months, the family or employer pays for a one-way airfare to Iceland, and return fare after 12 months.

A voluntary organisation called Worldwide Friends (WF, or 'Veraldarvinir' in Icelandic; Einarsnes 56, 101 Reykjavík; +354 55 25 214; wf@wf.is; www.wf.is) offers an interesting range of two-week projects (workcamps) that international volunteers can join. Many are concerned with the environment. The participation fee is normally €150 depending on the project and the duration.

SPAIN AND PORTUGAL

Spain

At the beginning of the 21st century, the popularity of Spanish studies continues to escalate. It is possible to take short intensive language courses in all the major Spanish cities. Spain has never lost its pre-eminent position as a favourite destination for British holidaymakers, and gap year travellers are no exception. Many book themselves on cheap packages to the Canaries, Ibiza, and the Balearic Islands or any of the Costas, as a good place to unwind after exams or after rigorous travels in developing countries. With an explosion in cheap and flexible flights from various UK airports with no-frills airlines, it is now possible to fly very easily to one of many Spanish cities. However, the cost of living is relatively high, and opportunities for picking up a job to fund further travels are not as numerous as they were before Spain succumbed to the recession.

The demand for native speakers of English to teach remains strong, but unqualified and inexperienced 18-year-olds will have difficulty finding a position during the academic year (with exceptions; see below). They might have more luck at summer language camps. It is always worth checking the English language press in Spanish resorts and cities for the 'situations vacant' columns, which sometimes carry adverts for live-in babysitters, bar staff, etc. If you can arrange to visit the Spanish coast in March before most of the budget travellers arrive, you should have a chance of fixing up a job for the season. The resorts then go quiet until late May when the season gets properly under way and there may be jobs available.

COURSES AND HOMESTAYS

All the major agencies such as CESA, Caledonia, Languages Abroad and Lanacos have links with many institutes in Spain, or you can investigate Spanish-only companies such as Don Quijote (www. donquijote.org) and Mester (www.mester.com). It usually saves money (but not time) to book directly with the school in Spain, as **Annabel Iglehart** from Castle Douglas in Scotland did with Mester (see 'Directory of Language Courses'):

> *I completed my university degree last July and am taking a year (or two) out to gain new skills and participate in interesting activities around the world. I didn't take a year out before I went to university, and because of this I think that I am making the most of my opportunities now. As soon as my exams finished, I got straight down to organising my year out. I worked for two months in a variety of jobs in Edinburgh and then went to Salamanca, Spain to do a three-month intensive Spanish language course with Mester. The course was fantastic. The classes were fast-paced and the teachers excellent. I met loads of people who I am still in touch with now, the social events organised by the school being a lot of fun, and there was something for everyone. I lived with a Spanish family for a while and then moved to a flat with other students, something I had arranged before I headed out there. Mester is a company in Spain that provides excellent courses in Spanish, for any number of weeks, and in a variety of cities in Spain. I'm afraid I cannot remember exactly how much it cost, but it was roughly £1,300 for three months. I had an intensive course (five hours of tuition a day), stayed for three weeks with a Spanish family and the rest in a self-catering flat. The costs are calculated according to the type of course (there are many to choose from) and the class of accommodation. The schools seem to be a lot less busy in winter time (when I was there, September to December), and so this can mean that classes are smaller, but not always. Classes are never more than 10 people I am told.*

Living with a family usually forces you to speak more Spanish from the beginning. Homestays can often lead to longer-lasting friendships and subsequent exchanges arranged on a private basis.

The youth exchange organisation Relaciones Culturales Internacionales (Calle Ferraz 82, 28008 Madrid; +34 91 541 71 03; spain@clubrci.es) places native English speakers with families who want to practise their English, in exchange for room and board; the placement fee is €150 for stays of up to three months, €350 for a year.

The non-profit Instituto Cervantes (www.cervantes.es) is the largest worldwide Spanish teaching organisation, with headquarters in Madrid and a network of centres around the world (comparable to the Alliance Française for French). It also has centres in London and Manchester.

Of course, many other things can be studied in Spain apart from language. Learning some of the traditional dances, such as Sevillanas, Malagueras, the Pasadoble, or even the very difficult Flamenco, is the aim of some gap year travellers.

OPPORTUNITIES FOR PAID WORK

Year out students have successfully found (or created) their own jobs in highly imaginative ways. One of the most striking examples is a 19-year-old student who wrote to the address on a Spanish wine label and was astonished to be invited to act as a guide around their winery for the summer. **Tommy Karske** returned home 'knowing a lot about wine, and believing that anything is possible'.

Many yachts are moored along the Costa del Sol and all along the south coast. It might be possible to get work cleaning, painting or even guarding these luxury craft. There are also crewing possibilities for those with no time constraints and outgoing personalities.

Year-round resorts such as Tenerife, Gran Canaria, Lanzarote, and Ibiza afford a range of casual work as bar staff, DJs, beach party ticket sellers, timeshare salesmen, etc. A good starting point for finding out about seasonal job vacancies in Ibiza, Mallorca, and Minorca is www.balearic-jobs.com.

RYA-qualified windsurfing and sailing instructors, BCU-qualified kayak instructors, and SPSA-qualified climbing instructors are in demand for the season April/May to September. The largest sailing and windsurfing centre in the Mediterranean hires staff for the season (beginning of May to end of October). Minorca Sailing Holidays (Richmond; recruitment@minorcasailing.co.uk) recruits qualified sailing and windsurfing instructors as well as nannies, reps, maintenance staff, and others for their sailing centre in the Bay of Fornells on the north coast of Minorca. After doing a sailing and windsurfing instructor's course in Sydney, Australia with Flying Fish, **Nina Fitton** worked for Minorca Sailing over the summer season before university:

> *It's long hours, low pay, and hard work, but the kit available to all us instructors was vast, the social life was good, and it was great fun. I worked about 10 hours a day, six days a week, teaching windsurfing and dinghy sailing to all age groups, but generally kids. On my day off and during my free time, I could use any of the boats or boards, so my personal sailing improved loads. Like on the Flying Fish course, all us instructors were about the same age (gap year or students), and all enjoyed the same wind-related sports, so I had a blast.*

Jobs with British tour companies such as Canvas and Eurocamp can be fixed up months in advance from home. TJM Travel (www.tjmtravel.co.uk) need reps and children's staff to work at a watersports holiday centre in Tossa de Mar on the Costa Brava from early May to the end of September. Agencies in the major Spanish cities may be able to assist, for example the Easy Way Association (+91 548 86 79; www.easywayspain.com/ingles/employment.htm) in Madrid charges a fee starting at €370 for placing Spanish-speaking or hospitality-trained people in restaurant jobs for a minimum of two months.

Some language schools can arrange work experience placements (mostly unwaged) in Spanish firms. Check out ONECO Training Agency in Seville (www.oneco.org) for internships and training.

ENGLISH TEACHING

The great cities of Madrid and Barcelona act as magnets to thousands of hopeful teachers. Opportunities for untrained native speakers of English have all but disappeared in respectable language academies. However, some determined students have obtained a TEFL certificate at the beginning of their gap year and gone on to teach.

MY GAP YEAR: SAM JAMES

Sam James and his girlfriend Sophie Ellison headed off to Barcelona after A levels to do the four-week Trinity Certificate course, which they found demanding but passed. Then they did the rounds of the language schools.

'Though tedious, this did work, and we doubt we would have found work any other way. Job availability didn't seem that high in Barcelona when we were looking in October, and we both accepted our only job offers. (Our age may have put off some employers.) Most schools seem to have recruited in September, so October was a bit of a lean month. I got my job by covering a class at two hours' notice for a teacher who had called in sick. When this teacher decided to leave Barcelona, I was interviewed, and offered her classes on a permanent basis. I got the job permanently about a fortnight after handing out CVs. Sophie was asked to her first interview after about three weeks of job-hunting. She was selected, but then had to wait for several more weeks while her contract was finalised.'

Conventional wisdom says that the beginning of summer is the worst time to travel out to Spain to look for work since schools will be closed and their owners unobtainable. However, Sam handed round his CV again in May (when his hours were cut) and was given some encouragement. He thinks that because so few teachers look for work just six weeks before the end of the academic year, employers are sometimes in need of replacements. With so many no-frills cheap flights on the market, it might be worth a gamble. Sam had to teach a variety of age groups in Barcelona during his gap year and, despite the problems, ended up enjoying it:

'The children I taught were fairly unruly and noisy. The teenagers were, as ever, pretty uninterested in learning, though if one struck on something they enjoyed they would work much better. Activities based on the lyrics of songs seemed to be good. They had a tendency to select answers at random in multiple choice exercises. On the other hand, they were only ever loud rather than very rude or disobedient. The young children (8-12) were harder work. They tended to understand selectively, acting confused if they didn't like an instruction. Part of the problem was that the class was far too long (three hours) for children of that age, and their concentration and behaviour tended to tail off as the time passed.'

Sam blamed his lack of job security and bitty hours on Barcelona's popularity, 'the result of the great supply of willing teachers here keeping working conditions down, and making it hard to exert any leverage on an employer when one is so easily replaced'. For this reason, other towns may answer your requirements better. There are language academies all along the north coast and a door-to-door job hunt in September might pay off. This is the time when tourists are departing, so accommodation may be available at a reasonable rent on a nine-month lease.

Without a TEFL qualification, the best chance of a teaching job in Spain would be on a summer language camp for children. Some pay a reasonable wage; others provide little more than free board and accommodation. Try for example TECS Summer Camps in El Puerto de Santa María, Cádiz (+34 902 350 356; http://recruit.tecs.es), which recruit camp support staff and monitors for at least a month, plus assistant camp monitors and activity teachers for two months. It is also possible to arrange an informal exchange of English conversation for a free week in Spain. At least two companies, Vaughan Town and Pueblo Ingles, offer programmes whereby holiday resorts in Spain are 'stocked' with native English speakers and Spanish clients who want to improve their English. In the case of the former, 17 English native-speaking volunteers participate alongside about the same number of Spanish adults in an intensive six-day 'talk-a-thon' on a one-to-one basis. In exchange for making English conversation, participants receive free room and board, and transport from Madrid. The Pueblo Ingles programme lasts eight days, and the average age of participants from all over the world is 40.

More information is available from:

Pueblo Ingles, Madrid (+34 91 391 3400; anglos@puebloingles.com; www.morethanenglish.com).
Vaughan Systems, Madrid (+34 91 748 5950 ext 126; www.vaughantown.com). Company also offers free training to people willing to spend a year being paid to teach in various parts of Spain (http://volunteers.grupovaughan.com).

Catharine Carfoot went on what amounts to a classic working holiday at the Vaughan Village several summers ago:

Back in June of that year, I took part in an English language immersion programme in Spain. It wants native English speakers (any flavour, although in practice North Americans predominate) to go and talk a lot of English to Spaniards. All people have to do is get themselves to Madrid in time for the pick-up (by the way, the cheapest option for getting to Madrid is to fly with Ryanair to Valladolid and then take a bus from there). At the end of the week, you will be delivered back to Madrid, unless you have extraordinary stamina and can manage two (or more) continuous weeks in the programme. It isn't a way to make money, but of course people can and do make friends and contacts both with the other 'Anglos' and with the Spaniards. It's also a week off worrying about food, drink, and where to sleep.

AU PAIRING AND WORK EXPERIENCE

Au pair links between Spanish agencies and those in the rest of Europe have been increasing, partly because Spanish is gaining popularity as a modern foreign language. Young people can often arrange to stay with Spanish families without having to do much in the way of domestic or childcare duties, by agreeing to help with English tuition. The pocket money for au pairs at present is €55–€75 a week, plus €25 per month for transport.

If you deal directly with a Spanish agency, you may have to pay a sizeable placement fee. Here are some of them:

BEST Programs, Pozuelo de Alarcón, Madrid (www.bestprograms.org). Au pair placements for Americans and Europeans; fee $1,050 for three months. BEST also organises internships lasting from two weeks to six months in Madrid, Seville, Barcelona, and Marbella mainly for North Americans. Paid and unpaid internships are arranged for a fee of €1,680 for 3+ months. All programmes include language course, insurance and a lodging search on request.

Costa del Sol Au Pair Agency, Manilva, 29692 (+34 95 289 0484; info@costadelsolaupair.com). Located between Marbella and Gibraltar, agency places au pairs in Malaga area, Granada, Estepona, Sotogrande, and Gibraltar.

Easy Way Association, Madrid (+34 91 548 8679; www.easywayspain.com). Also makes hotel and restaurant placements.

Globus Idiomas, C/Gómez Cortina 5, 2°B, 30005 Murcia (globus@ono.com; www.globusidiomas.com). Member of IAPA. Registration fee €100.

Instituto Hemingway de Español, Bilbao (+34 94 416 7901; www.institutohemingway.com). Accepts most nationalities. Also places interns in local companies, as volunteers and English teachers.

International Au-Pair & Language Abroad Group, Marbella (+34 952 90 15 76; www.languageabroad.info).

Planet Au Pair,Valencia (+34 96 320 6491; www.planetaupair.com). Registration fee of €295 for stays of three months or less and €324.50 for longer stays.

VOLUNTEERING

The Sunseed Trust (+34 950 525770; www.sunseed.org.uk), an arid land recovery trust, has a remote research centre in south-east Spain, near the village of Sorbas in Almeria, which explores ways of reclaiming deserts. The centre is run by both full-time volunteers, who stay a minimum of five weeks, and working visitors, who stay two to five weeks and spend half the day working. Weekly charges for part-time volunteers are £74–£84 according to season and for full-time volunteers £64–£74 (2011). Typical work for volunteers might involve germination procedures, forestry trials, hydroponic growing, organic gardening, designing and building solar ovens and stills, and building and maintenance. Living conditions are basic and the cooking is vegetarian. Occasionally, workers with a relevant qualification in appropriate technology, etc are needed, who are paid a small stipend.

The Atlantic Whale Foundation (www.whalenation.org) is working to protect whales and dolphins in the Canary Islands. Volunteers who join the project for four or more weeks contribute €110 per week.

Portugal

Portugal is seen by gap year students mainly as a place in which to relax and have fun rather than spend a large part of their gap year. There is a long and vigorous tradition of British people settling in Portugal, and the links between the two countries are strong so, with luck, you might be able to chase up a contact to provide initial accommodation and orientation. If you want to extend your stay, ask members of the expatriate community for help and advice. A good idea is to scan the advertisements in the English language press or place an ad yourself.

If your chosen language is Portuguese, one of the best-known language schools is CIAL Centro de Linguas in Lisbon, which offers a well-structured series of courses, normally 15 lessons a week for four weeks. Students are billeted in private homes both in Lisbon and Faro.

According to some British backpackers, all you need for a working holiday is to fly to Faro with a tent and hitch a lift to Albufeira, where any number of bars and restaurants might hire you for the season. Wages are not high, but accommodation is cheap. If you are aiming a little higher and know some Portuguese, it would be worth contacting the British-Portuguese Chamber of Commerce (Camara de Comércio Luso-Britanica) in Lisbon (www.bpcc.pt).

Two summers ago, **Richard Ferguson** was astonished at the ease with which he started earning. On the recommendation of someone at home in New Zealand, he looked up a contact in Lisbon who helped him to get his first job in a pizzeria:

> *I've been working in Lisbon for almost two months now. My new Portuguese friend and I simply asked the owner of a pizzeria where we were eating, and I was told to start to work the next day. I was working six days 11.30am to 4pm then 7pm to closing time for €750 per month, plus tips of about €80 a month. All the workers were immigrants and these wages were below average, so after a while I moved on to a rival pizzeria with better pay and conditions. It's an awesome environment – like a family, and I'm living for next to nothing with colleagues in an apartment owned by the pizzeria's owner. I'm loving it, and as long as I can resist the temptation to drink every night in the Bairro Alto (upper town), I'll make enough to cover the return ticket to Brazil I've already bought (and then some) by the time I leave in December.*

SWITZERLAND AND AUSTRIA

Switzerland

Every winter, a small army of gap year travellers migrates to the Alps to spend the winter season working and skiing at a Swiss or Austrian ski resort. One of the disadvantages of spending any time in Switzerland is the very high cost of living. But of course, this goes along with the high wages that can be earned by people willing to work hard in hotels in the summer season as well as the winter. All legal workers should earn a minimum of SFr 3,300/€2,175 a month (gross).

Switzerland is not a member of the European Union. However, a bilateral agreement with the EU has removed the main obstacles to the free movement of labour. The immigration system is now more in line with the rest of Europe so that EU jobseekers can enter Switzerland for up to three months (extendable) to look for work. If they succeed, they must show a contract of employment to the authorities and are then eligible for a short-term residence permit (valid for up to one year and renewable) or a long-term permit (up to five years) depending on the contract.

The Swiss are very *korrect* in regulating employment, and foreign workers (including au pairs) will have many deductions made from their earnings. Students staying longer than four weeks must obtain Swiss medical insurance unless they can prove that their cover is as extensive as the Swiss. Few students head for Switzerland to study French or German, although it is possible. While it is true that many Swiss and Austrian people speak a dialect of German, language schools teach *Hoch Deutsch*.

OPPORTUNITIES FOR PAID WORK

TOURIST INDUSTRY

Provided you have a reasonable CV and a knowledge of languages (preferably German), a speculative job hunt in advance is worthwhile. The Swiss Hotel Association's online recruitment site http://jobs. htr.ch is unlikely to be much use to school leavers; for example, a random check revealed that there were hundreds of vacancies being advertised, but most were for German speakers with professional hospitality experience.

Quite a few British travel companies and camping holiday operators are active in Switzerland, such as Canvas and Eurocamp. The Jobs in the Alps Agency (www.jobs-in-the-alps.com) places waiters, waitresses, chamber staff, kitchen porters, and hall and night porters in hotels, cafés, and restaurants in Swiss resorts, in both winter and summer. Most ski tour operators mount big operations in Switzerland, such as Crystal Holidays (www.jobsinwinter.co.uk) and Ski Total (www.workaseason.com). A Swiss company that advertises for resort staff and ski instructors is Viamonde in Anzère (www.viamonde.com).

GAPPERS' TIP

The main disadvantage of being hired by a UK company is that the wages will be on a British scale rather than on the much more lucrative Swiss one.

Swiss hotels are very efficient and tend to be impersonal, since you will be one in an endless stream of seasonal workers from many countries. The very intense attitude towards work among the Swiss means that hours are long: a typical working week would consist of at least five nine-hour days working split shifts. Whether humble or palatial, the Swiss hotel or restaurant in which you find a job will probably insist on very high standards of cleanliness and productivity.

A number of ski and snowboard instructor courses are run in Verbier, Saas Fee, and Gstaad, by Altitude Futures, International Academy, Peak Leaders, the Ski Academy Switzerland, and Warren Smith (see 'Directory of Ski Training Courses').

Sometimes it is necessary to escape the competition from all the other gap year travellers and other jobseekers by moving away from the large ski stations. **Joseph Tame**'s surprising tip is to go up as high as possible in the mountains. After being told by virtually every hotel in Grindelwald in mid-September that they had already hired their winter season staff, he despaired, and decided to waste his last SFr 40 on a trip up the rack railway. At the top, he approached the only hotel – and couldn't believe it when they asked him when he could start. Although at 18 he had never worked in a hotel before, they were willing to take him on as a trainee waiter, give him full bed and board, plus a decent monthly wage.

SUMMER CAMPS

The Swiss organisation Village Camps advertises widely to recruit staff over 21 in its multi-activity language summer camp for children in Leysin. It also hires up to 100 ski counsellors and other staff for the winter season. Jobs are available for EFL teachers, sports and activity instructors, nurses, and general domestic staff. For jobs with Village Camps, room and board are provided as well as accident and liability insurance, and a weekly allowance from €175. Recruitment starts just after the new year; an application pack is available from Village Camps, Recruitment Office, 14 rue de la Morache, 1260 Nyon (+41 22 990 9405; personnel@villagecamps.ch; www.villagecamps.com/personnel).

ESL (www.esl-languages.com) is a Swiss language school that organises holiday language courses in Switzerland as well as France and Germany. It hires tutors and activity leaders for the summer season (jobs@esl.ch) at centres in Leysin, Zug, and Ascona.

Another camp operator looking for seasonal summer or winter staff is Les Elfes in Verbier (www.leselfes.com). Most of its staff are over 20, and its policy is to accept a limited number of gap year travellers (18–20) for work experience only. The Haut-Lac International Centre (1669 Les Sciernes; +41 26 928 4200; jobs@haut-lac.com) employs teachers and monitors of any nationality for both their summer and winter camps for teenagers.

WORK ON FARMS

Young Europeans who are interested in experiencing rural Switzerland may wish to do a stint on a Swiss farm. Agriviva in Winterthur (+41 52 264 00 30; www.agriviva.ch) places young people aged 16–25 on farms throughout Switzerland for short stays. Young volunteers must be nationals of the old EU countries and know some German or French. One programme is called 'Work and Learn', which combines a two-week language course through frilingue.ch with a farm placement of equal length. The other option is a farm *stage* which can last longer and involves no language learning; For both programmes, the Agriviva registration fee is SFr 40.

In addition to the good farm food and comfortable bed, farm volunteers will be paid SFr 20 per day worked. On these small Swiss farms, English is rarely spoken and many farmers speak a dialect that some find incomprehensible. The hours are long (typically 48 per week), the work is hard, and much depends on the volunteer's relationship with the family. Most people who have worked on a Swiss farm report that they are treated like one of the family, which means both that they are up by 6 or 7am and working till 9pm alongside the farmer, and are invited to accompany the family on any excursions, such as the weekly visit to the market to sell the farm-produced cheeses.

WWOOF Switzerland (wwoof@gmx.ch; http://zapfig.com/wwoof) keeps a constantly updated list of farmers around the country, currently 45. To obtain the list, you must join WWOOF at a cost of SFr 20/€15 in cash. Volunteers must apply with a photocopy of their passport and an accompanying letter stating why they want to become unpaid volunteers.

Joseph Tame made use of the WWOOF website to fix up a place on a farm in the spring:

I can honestly say that it has been an absolutely fantastic experience. The hours could be thought fairly long by some (perhaps 35 per week), considering there is no money involved, but I absolutely love the chance to work outside in this land that reminds me so much of the final setting in The Hobbit *. From our farm, your eyes take you down the hillside, over the meadows covered in flowers, down to the vast Lake Luzern below, and over to the huge snowcapped mountain Pilatus. It really is paradise here. The family have been so kind, and as I put my heart into learning all that I can about the farm they are only too happy to treat me with generosity. I really feel a part of the family.*

AU PAIRS

For those interested in a domestic position with a Swiss family, there are rules laid down by each Swiss canton, which principally apply to non-EU nationals as Europeans can work in Switzerland in any capacity. The regulations were relaxed a couple of years ago, and au pairs and nannies from any country of the world are now able to work in Switzerland, provided they come through one of the handful of authorised agencies (contact details below). Non-EU candidates must be under 26 and can stay as an au pair for one year only. They are required to spend at least three hours a week studying the language. Families usually pay the language school fees or at least make a substantial contribution. The agencies are at pains to remind potential au pairs that Swiss German is very different from the German learned in school, which often causes disappointment and difficulties.

Au pairs in Switzerland work for a maximum of 30 hours per week, plus babysitting once or twice a week. The monthly salary is normally SFr 700–800. Rates may be slightly higher for older girls and are generally higher in Geneva than Zürich. In addition, the au pair gets a four- or five-week paid holiday plus SFr 18–20 for days off (to cover the cost of food). Au pairs are liable to pay tax and contributions, which can mean a deduction of up to a fifth of their wages, unless the family is willing to pay or subsidise these costs.

Pro Filia (+41 44 361 5331; www.profilia.ch) is a long-established Catholic au pair agency with branches throughout the country. The agency registration fee is SFr 40, plus a fee of SFr 290 is to be paid on taking up the placement.

Independent au pair placement agencies include Perfect Way in Brugg (+41 56 281 39 12; www.perfectway.ch), which vets all families and distributes a list of other au pairs and their contact details. The agency Au Pair Link (part of Wind Connections), in Erlenbach near Zurich (+41 44 915 4104; www.aupairlink.ch), accepts au pairs mainly from Australia and Canada, where it has in-country interviewers.

VOLUNTEERING

The Mountain Forest Project (www.bergwaldprojekt.ch) runs one-week forest conservation projects in the alpine regions of Switzerland and southern Germany. MFP welcomes foreign volunteers who know some German. It provides hut accommodation, food, and accident insurance during one-week education and conservation projects.

Austria

Like its alpine neighbour, Austria offers seasonal employment to gap year travellers hoping to save some money and do some skiing. Some knowledge of German will be necessary for most jobs apart from those with UK tour operators. There is no shortage of hotels to which you can apply, however, either for the summer or the winter season. The largest concentration is in the Tyrol, though there are also many in the Vorarlberg region in western Austria. The main winter resorts to try are St Anton, Kitzbühel, Mayrhofen, and St Johann-im-Pongau, which is a popular destination for British holiday-makers thus creating a demand for English-speaking staff. Wages in hotels and restaurants are lower than in Switzerland, although still reasonable.

The Deutsch-Institut Tirol in Kitzbühel (www.gap-year.at) offers a 12-week German language course combined with a ski and snowboard instructors' course specially designed for gappers (see entry in 'Directory of Specialist Gap Year Programmes'). This takes place in the autumn, and the ski instruction is on the glacier at Kaprun. The Ski Instructor Academy guarantees winter employment in the Austrian Alps to anyone who completes its instructor course in Taxenbach.

After spending the first part of her gap year doing a German language course in Dresden, **Rosie Curling** decided she needed to consolidate her new skills by working in a German-speaking environment. She headed for Lech in Austria, where she had a friend, and within 24 hours of arriving she had a job as a *commis* waitress:

It would be fair to say that my five months in Austria were a rollercoaster ride of emotions. For the first three weeks I was lonely and homesick, finding the work tough, relations with my colleagues a strain and communication difficult. However, after the Christmas period, I began to make friends, enjoy the wonderful skiing, and realise that the work was a means to an end, namely to have some serious fun. Again, I was experiencing a new lifestyle, which was incredibly relaxed as the major responsibility of the day was deciding where to ski and then where to après ski. Life assumed an idyllic routine: get up at 8.50am, be the first on the slopes, ski till 11am, work the lunch shift, a couple more hours skiing, a bit more work in the evening, then hit the night scene. Despite (or possibly because of) all this, it was also an incredibly constructive period. For a start, I saved £2,500 (to fund a Trans-Siberian railway trip). My German is now almost fluent, although I speak an Austrian dialect; my skiing has improved from a grade 4/5 to 3a, but most importantly I have made some lifelong friends, mainly Austrians and Swedes.

Because Austria is a very popular destination for British skiers, jobs abound with UK tour operators, though most are looking for staff over 21. The various brands within TUI Holidays such as First Choice Holidays (www.tuitraveljobsco.uk) hire hundreds of people for the summer and winter season.

OPPORTUNITIES FOR PAID WORK

SUMMER WORK

Two Vienna-based organisations that run summer language camps are the similarly named: English for Children (+41 01 958 1972-0; www.englishforchildren.com) and English for Kids (+41 01 667 45 79; www.e4kids.at), both of which are looking for young monitors and English teachers with experience of working with children, and preferably some TEFL background. English for Kids promises a salary from €1,000 net for four weeks, plus full board and accommodation.

WWOOF Austria is in Puch/Weiz (+43 676 505 1639 evenings only; office@wwoof.at; www.wwoof. at). Membership costs €25 per year, which entitles you to the list of around 220 Austrian organic farmers looking for work-for-keep volunteer helpers.

AU PAIRS

Austria has a well-developed tradition of au pair placement. According to new regulations that came in to force in 2009, all au pairs must receive €450 per month for working 20 hours per week. Placement agencies include Au Pair Austria, Vermittlungs-agentur in Vienna (+43 1 405 405 0) and Asten (+43 7224 68359; www.aupairaustria.com), and Friends Au Pair Vermittlung (www.aupairvermittlung.at), which charges a registration fee of €50.

LANGUAGE COURSES AND HOMESTAYS

Deutsch in Graz (+43 316 833 900; www.dig.co.at) can arrange homestays from €165 per week, with language courses in Graz and suburbs. The Austrian Education Ministry's organisation Campus Austria at the University of Vienna comprises 16 language schools, all providing German language training to a high standard. Some courses lead to Goethe Institut qualifications, while others lead to the OSD (Austrian diploma for German as a foreign language). Campus Austria's website (www.campus-austria.at) has clear links to the courses and prices. One of the schools, the Alpha Sprachinstitut in Vienna (www.alpha.at), offers some interesting courses, including German and music (in co-operation with the Konservatorium). A company that offers unpaid work experience in settings such as a travel agency, import business, ski school, or hotel is Apple Languages (www.applelanguages.com); an eight-week placement without accommodation costs €418 following on from a minimum four-week language course.

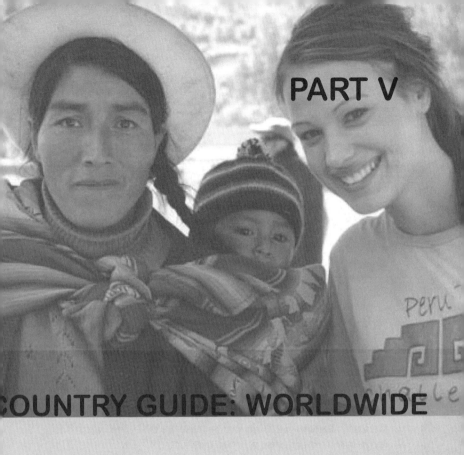

PART V

COUNTRY GUIDE: WORLDWIDE

AFRICA
ASIA
AUSTRALIA AND NEW ZEALAND
NORTH AMERICA
LATIN AMERICA

CHANGING WORLDS

Helen Thomson went on the Changing Worlds Medical Placement in January 2010.

The medical placement in Kenya with Changing Worlds was enjoyable, while very educational and eye-opening! Every day, we went into the local public hospital, first to ward six, which is for children aged less than two years old. Here, we spent an hour or so washing, weighing, dressing, and feeding the abandoned babies. The work done here is much appreciated, as the nurses on this ward are so busy that often the babies go 24 hours without being changed or fed. Unfortunately this work can be tough, though, as these abandoned babies have had their medical needs neglected, and consequently come in to hospital very ill. Sadly, we had two babies that died within the first six weeks. However, this was not a deterrent to working on these wards – it motivated us to get up early every morning just so we could care for them.

Then after ward six, we rotated to different parts of the hospital. The first week we spent in the nursery, where there were about 30 babies crammed into a tiny (and really hot) room. These babies all needed to be washed, weighed, and fed which can be very time-consuming! One of these babies was the son of a woman on the psychiatric ward, so this placement also gave us the opportunity to visit there, which was like nothing I had ever experienced before.

The second week, we spent in the maternity unit watching live births. We then spent a week in theatre, where we saw a range of operations such as a gall bladder removal, hip replacements, caesarean sections, bone reconstructions, appendix removals etc . . . The surgeons were all very accommodating, and even let us assist with minor things such as cleaning the area to be operated on.

Other weeks, we spent in orthopaedics, paediatrics (for children over two years old), and the voluntary counselling centre for people with HIV and AIDS. For the remainder of our placement, we continued our rotations to other wards such as ICU, gynaecology, the laboratory, the pharmacy, female/male wards, and so on.

The medical placement was a truly pleasurable experience that taught us all about life in the caring profession. There was a good mix of practical work and observation time, while still allowing us the option to try other placements such as teaching and orphanage work. I speak for the three of us who were doing the medical placement when I say that it is a rewarding and challenging experience in the hospital, and definitely not one to be missed!

Kenya provided so many amazing memories. On the placement side, it is impossible not to have a good and successful time if you are willing to work and you have a good attitude. You can also climb Mount Kenya; we visited the Maasai Mara, swam in a lake with crocodiles and hippos, and kissed a giraffe. I made some amazing friends and I can't wait to go back. If I had the opportunity to restart my gap year tomorrow, I would snap it up with both hands!

WORLDWIDE EXPERIENCE

Conserve . . . Develop . . . Teach

We are the gap year specialist in conservation and community projects. We strive to help conserve what man is fast destroying – our very own environment – and with the help of our volunteers we aim to make a difference. All of our projects have been formulated with the assistance of the Worldwide Experience team, to give you the best possible journey, wherever you choose to go. All our projects are run by specialists in their field, who are specifically trained to impart their skills and knowledge.

As well as offering programmes for conservation and community work, we also offer tailor-made specialist programmes for schools and colleges that enable them to get hands on with conservation and community work. We also run a programme for veterinary students at university helping contribute towards their EMS, called Vets Go Wild.

Conservation is our main focus, as wild animals will cease to exist if man continues to eradicate the environment. Our volunteers help play a part in helping to make sure that for generations to come, the things they have witnessed on our programmes are still around for others to see. We concentrate on marine conservation, and have identified several front-running placements where you can assist with ongoing efforts, including research and educating the local community.

Most projects have an element of community to them. However, we do have programmes that are solely based around community work. The aim is to help support the development of independent and sustainable projects that respond to the identified needs of underprivileged communities.

Our projects last from two weeks all the way up to three months, and run year-round, allowing you the flexibility to travel when it is convenient for you. Our experienced team will be happy to assist with any questions you may have, and are on hand to ensure your placement is a truly life-changing experience.

Together we can make a difference.

Like so many gappers, **Angela Clegg** fell in love with Africa (and since she had got married just a month before setting off, she must know a thing or two about falling in love):

> *Africa has something about it, something you instantly fall in love with. The one thing that struck me the most about Tanzania was the local people and their way of life. They are never too busy for you; in fact they had a saying 'poleh poleh in Africa' which means 'slowly slowly in Africa'. To them, there is no excuse for a short meet and greet! I honestly thought seeing their lack of resources would devastate me, when instead I came back feeling why can't England be like Africa? Why does everyone have so much hostility and no time for each other? I never in a million years thought I would be thinking England should be like Africa.*

Many organisations large and small can assist in setting up a placement in Africa in a Ghanaian orphanage, coaching kids' football in a South African township, assisting a lion project at a Zimbabwean game park, or teaching village children in Tanzania.

Conditions can be quite tough, and many gap students teaching or working in rural Africa find themselves struggling to cope, whether with the loneliness of life in a rural West African village or being confronted with the devastation wrought by HIV/AIDS. A certain amount of deprivation is almost inevitable; for example, volunteers can seldom afford to shop in the pricy expatriate stores and so will have to be content with the local diet, typically a staple cereal such as millet usually made into a kind of stodgy porridge, plus some cooked greens, tinned fish or meat and fruit. Typically, the housing will not have running water or electricity, which means that showers consist of a bucket and cup, and toilets are just a hole in the ground. Local customs can come as a shock, for example, being treated with something akin to reverence, even though you may feel yourself to be just a naïve school leaver. But the rewards can also be tremendous, and any efforts you put in are bound to be appreciated. When **Amelia Cook** started out teaching in a Ghanaian primary school, she was bowled over (not just figuratively) by the curiosity of her class:

> *Even our first shaky classes using ideas from our own schools were met with great enthusiasm. Once my class of 45 teenage boys (plus many others who had sneaked in at the back) literally knocked me over in their enthusiasm to see what was in my bag of props for that day's lesson.*

Regional crises also flare up, and in recent years conflicts in Kenya, Zimbabwe, and Madagascar have resulted in the last-minute cancellation of volunteer programmes. Try to research in advance any local issues that may be causing concern. Often the news will report on a crisis which is confined to a single area, leaving the rest of the country welcoming, safe, and friendly. The Foreign and

Commonwealth Office regularly updates its travel advice for every country in the world (www.fco.gov.uk/travel), and includes risk assessments of current trouble spots. The warnings need not be taken as gospel (see introductory section on 'Travel Warnings', taking Sudan as an example, p32). Often the most useful preparation is to talk to someone who has survived and enjoyed a similar placement in the recent past.

MY GAP YEAR: MATT RIDDELL

Matt Riddell was coming to the end of his BTEC National Diploma in Public Services when he decided he needed a challenge, and fixed up a placement through Travellers.

I was motivated to take a gap year for a number of reasons, first, so that I could do a bit of travelling and see other parts of the world. I had never been further than France before, and I wanted to see other cultures and how they are different to ours. Second, and more importantly, I wanted to help others who are in need. There were other issues - for example, I am not the most outgoing person, and I had hardly been away from home before, so I wanted to put myself out of my comfort zone to see how I would react and whether or not I could achieve something that later on in life I would be proud to say that I had done.

My placement in Zambia was teaching conversational English at the Nalituwe Basic School. The school is in a dire state - the ceilings and walls are literally falling down, the majority of the windows are broken, as are most of the doors. Their light switches were simply a death trap. They just consist of two bare wires hanging out of the wall, and the kids twist them together to turn the lights on. There are not enough desks for the pupils, they sit three to each. Some of the desks are broken, and if there are not enough, the pupils who are not sat at a desk either stand throughout the lesson or sit on the windowsill. When I first saw the school, I just felt like breaking down into tears - I was certainly not expecting to see it like this.

During college and the build-up to Zambia, I was fully set on joining the police force when I returned. Now, I have realised that there is more to life than just being wrapped up in our own culture, and the feeling of satisfaction that I got from teaching is something that I want to have with me. I am planning on returning to Zambia later on in the year to carry on teaching at the same school, and I am going to look into living out in Zambia as a full-time teacher.

Action against the spread of HIV/AIDS in sub-Saharan Africa is a matter of the utmost urgency, and a number of agencies are tackling the issue head-on. **Emily Kidson** describes her HIV project in South Africa as tough, since she was thrown in at the deep end, and on occasion felt overwhelmed by the magnitude of the task:

> *With South Africa as my dream destination, the search for a programme was narrowed somewhat and concluded with the aptly named Gap Year South Africa Limited. HIV/AIDS awareness was something I was interested in through studying geography at A level. I attended an HIV conference in my local area in order to get to grips with the basics.*
>
> *The five-week programme in South Africa incorporated accommodation, some food, airport pick-up, a few activities, and daily transportation to the HIV/AIDS awareness programme at Kwa-ford inner city township school. The work proved tougher and less organised than expected, there was poor communication with teachers, and the condition of the school left unmentioned for a good reason. Many times, we had to think on our feet and just try our best. The children's faces were so expectant, but the teachers we were supposed to work with were often absent, so it was difficult to know where to start.*
>
> *I do regret not applying for a year's working visa. The opportunities for employment were far greater than expected, and a small income would have perhaps prolonged my travels. The highlight has to be doing the highest bungee jump in the world at Bloukrans Bridge.*

SENDING AGENCIES

The main year-out agencies, such as Lattitude Global Volunteering and Projects Abroad send volunteers to a range of African countries, primarily South Africa, Ghana, Kenya, and Tanzania. The following organisations also recruit gap year volunteers for Africa, mostly for work in schools and community projects. Most have entries in the 'Directory of Specialist Gap Year Programmes' in the first part of this book.

Adventure Alternative (www.adventurealternative.com). One- to three-month programmes for gap year students (among others) in Kenya, combining teaching/community work with climbing, trekking, rafting, safaris, and independent travel. Participants teach and work in rural or slum schools.

Africa, Asia & Americas Venture (www.aventure.co.uk). Places 18–24-year-old volunteers in teaching, sports coaching, community, and conservation work experience placements in Kenya, Uganda, Tanzania, Malawi, and South Africa, usually for one term. The 2011 participation fee is £3,500 for 4 months plus airfares.

AfricaTrust Networks (www.africatrust.org.uk). Three- or six-month residential programmes in Ghana (Cape Coast and Kumasi), Morocco, and Cameroon for gap year students and others, to work with needy children and adults.

Amanzi Travel (www.amanzitravel.co.uk). Agency in Bristol, set up by someone inspired by her own gap year in Africa, offering range of mainly short-term volunteering and expedition opportunities in nine countries.

Azafady (www.madagascar.co.uk). Lemur Research and Conservation Programme and 10-week Pioneer programmes allow volunteers to work on primate conservation and humanitarian projects at grassroots level in Madagascar.

Blue Ventures, London (www.blueventures.org). Volunteers are needed for on average six weeks to carry out marine research, coral reef conservation, and day-to-day management of award-winning marine research programme in south-western Madagascar. Fee for six weeks is £2,200 for non-divers; £2,000 for PADI divers.

MY GAP YEAR: KATIE YEWDALL

Katie Yewdall left Madagascar several years ago, but she says that she still thinks about her time with Blue Ventures on a nearly daily basis.

I was expecting the beautiful seas, stunning aquatic life, long beaches, quaint huts, and friendly, smiling locals (all of which were very much present), but I wasn't expecting quite how much I would learn about myself, what it was like to live another life and, of course, the true meaning of conservation. I thought of myself as someone who was pretty knowledgeable about the natural world and developing countries, but the project in Madagascar was something different altogether. Andavadoaka, where the site is located, is a very typical small African fishing village, with the usual juxtaposition of wooden huts and a couple of 20-inch televisions (the village 'cinema', where they all loved to gather to watch old kung fu movies!) Being right on the beach, it is obvious how reliant the cash-poor locals are on the marine resources; not only is it an essential food source, but marine products are their only source of income. Tragically, the much-needed lucrative foreign market may be encouraging the villagers to overexploit their precious resources. They need the ocean for many generations to come, but they equally need the money now. I learnt that there is no simple resolution to the problem of conservation.

The experience was not free of difficulties; early mornings, boat breakdowns, mundane but necessary cleaning tasks and a lack of chocolate reminded me that I wasn't on a beach holiday, but feeling part of a research team that was doing valuable work always made up for it. One of the greatest things about the project was opportunity to get as involved as you wanted to be. If you wanted to spend your free time soaking up the sun, you could, but the chance to get further involved with the many research areas was there. The volunteers who threw themselves into the project and didn't wait for the staff to motivate them were the ones who had the most rewarding experience. Chatting to the locals, meeting people in the village 'bars', and exploring the surroundings made for a very refreshing experience. On the whole, I feel I am a less selfish, more open-minded, motivated, and confident person since my return, and I would recommend Blue Ventures to anyone.

BUNAC (www.bunac.org). Runs various volunteering programmes in South Africa (from three weeks of wildlife conservation to 33 weeks in a caring role). Also, Volunteer Ghana (two to six months for £880–£1,600).

Camps International (www.campsinternational.com). Gap year placements in rural villages in Kenya and Tanzania (including Zanzibar). Community and wildlife projects followed by trek up Mount Kenya or Kilimanjaro or a scuba diving course.

Cross-Cultural Solutions (www.crossculturalsolutions.org). Volunteers work side-by-side with local people in the areas of care-giving, teaching, healthcare, and community development, to help realise community-led initiatives. Volunteer opportunities are available in Ghana, Tanzania, South Africa, and Morocco.

Dodwell Trust (www.dodwell-trust.org). Arranges for about 60 volunteers a year to spend three weeks to eight months volunteering in Madagascar.

Global Vision International (GVI) (www.gvi.co.uk). Placements from one to 12 months in many countries in Africa, including Namibia and Madagascar.

The Leap Overseas (www.theleap.co.uk). Has a variety of volunteering programmes through Eastern Africa, which combine working on safari with community and conservation projects. Six- or 10-week options available based in the Maasai Mara, Okavango Delta, private game reserves, at the beach, or on Mount Kilimanjaro. £1,700–£2,400 excluding travel.

Madventurer (www.madventurer.com). Madventurer programmes combine overland travel with group projects in rural areas in Uganda, Ghana, Kenya, Tanzania, and South Africa. Most are short-term, lasting typically six weeks.

Operation Wallacea (www.opwall.com). Marine and forest research projects in Egypt, Madagascar, Mozambique, and South Africa from £975.

Quest Overseas (www.questoverseas.com). Thirteen-week Africa programme, with departures from January to April. Voluntary project in Tanzania, Kenya, Rwanda, or Malawi, followed by expedition through southern Africa, scuba diving course in Mozambique, etc. £4,400 excluding flights, plus £850 suggested project donation.

Reefdoctor.org (www.reefdoctor.org). Hands-on conservation programme for enthusiastic volunteers to become research assistants for four, six, eight, or 12 weeks in Madagascar, starting monthly. Based in Ifaty fishing village, volunteers help to survey the coral reef in the Bay of Ranobe.

Sudan Volunteer Programme (www.svp-uk.com). Needs volunteers (undergraduates or graduates) to teach English in Sudan for eight months, starting in early September or early January. TEFL certificate and knowledge of Arabic are not required. Volunteers pay for their airfare (from £425) plus initial insurance (£60). Local host institutions pay for living expenses in Sudan; most are in the Khartoum area or in smaller towns in northern Sudan (see first-hand account by Chris Milner on p47).

Ticket to Ride (www.ttride.co.uk). Arranges gap year surfing adventures combined with some community volunteering. Some courses lead to qualifications as surf instructor and beach lifeguard (no previous surfing experience necessary). The longest trips include the little-known coastline of Mozambique. Cost is £5,295 for 13-week Africa gap year programme.

Travellers Worldwide (www.travellersworldwide.com). Teaching (English, maths, drama, etc) and sports coaching placements in Ghana, Kenya, South Africa, and Zambia. Conservation placements with elephants, lions, whales, dolphins, sharks, and the other 'big five' game animals in South Africa, Zimbabwe, and Kenya. Professional work experience internships in law, web design, journalism, TV, veterinary, medicine, etc. Placements start from £675 and are available year-round, with flexible start and finish dates.

VAE Teachers Kenya, contact addresses in Herefordshire and Gilgil in Kenya (see entry in 'Directory of Specialist Programmes'; www.vaekenya.co.uk). Three- or six-month gap year placements from January, May, or September, teaching in rural schools in the central highlands of Kenya.

Venture Co (www.thebookbus.org). Recruit volunteers to join the Book Bus crews to work with children in Malawi and Zambia.

MY GAP YEAR:
STEPHANIE McCULLOUGH

Stephanie McCullough remembers her time volunteering in Zambia with Venture Co.

I'd never been to Africa, and prior to the trip I was filled with nervous anticipation. I was worried what the people of Meheba Refugee Settlement would think of our group of western do-gooders. Entering Zambia, I watched the country roll by, children running and waving, colourful clothing, and the dusty shades of orange and yellow. Meheba defied all my expectations. A vast scrubland, dotted with towering termite hills, it was divided into spacious plots for the refugee families. Although we felt every bit the white strangers, everyone was incredibly friendly, curious, and welcoming. They came from all over Africa, and though they possessed little, they did not complain. Each had a story to tell. One man, who taught himself English from a dictionary he carried under his arm, had lived in the camp for 25 years, and hoped to write a book about his experiences. A 13-year-old girl shared her story of pain and violence with me, but ended with her eyes glistening with hope.

During the day, we worked with groups of children in classroom corners or outside in the sun. We shared our favourite childhood books and created hats, masks, stories, and drawings. I've never met children more eager to learn. Together, we chased the Gingerbread Man, invited the Tiger to tea, and bounced my inflatable globe. Even the teenage boys gathered around to hear the children's stories.

Camp life took some adjustment, with its tents, long-drop toilet, and bucket shower in the trees. We spent the evenings playing games, star-gazing on top of termite hills, watching the local football match, and occasionally battling vast armies of ants. In our spare time, we helped build a school kitchen as most of the locals stood by watching.

Travelling with VentureCo and the Book Bus proved an incredibly emotional experience. It hurt to leave, and some day I hope to return. Not for the sunsets or the landscapes, but for the people. Meheba was different to anything I've ever experienced, but it strengthened my feeling that we are all essentially the same. I recommend the experience to everyone.

Village-To-Village (www.village-to-village.org.uk). Charity working to reduce poverty in Tanzania, which sends volunteers to the Kilimanjaro region to assist on various projects including teaching English in primary schools and orphanages, teacher training, as well as construction and sustainable agriculture projects.

Volunteer Africa (www.volunteerafrica.org). A UK charity active in Tanzania, working with village projects in the Singida Region of Tanzania. Volunteers may join the project for two to 12 weeks.

Volunteer Uganda (www.volunteeruganda.org). Gap year travellers needed for three-month placements starting February and July to live in an enclave in Kirima, Uganda, overlooking the Bwindi Impenetrable Forest, home to 300 mountain gorillas. Gappers will assist in local primary schools and do outreach work.

Zanzigap (www.zanzigap.com). Gap agency sends young people to teach English and other subjects in secondary schools in Zanzibar. £2,500 fee for nine months.

MY GAP YEAR:
SAMANTHA FULLER

Samantha Fuller found the perfect way to end her year out that ticked all the boxes.

Although I was having an amazing time on my year abroad studying in Bordeaux, the itch started again around March and the travelling bug struck. I was due to work in England over the summer before returning to university in Brighton, but I was worried what three months of not speaking any French would do to my level. I had already had a fantastic five months with Projects Abroad in Bolivia during my gap year, and a plan started germinating: August, one month, where could I go? And more importantly where could I have an absolutely amazing time while speaking French and getting some teaching experience? Morocco!

Projects Abroad is based in Rabat, the capital, which is on the coast about a third of the way down. Although Morocco in the summer is very hot, Rabat was a good place to acclimatise as it benefits from the sea breezes and is a little bit cooler (although it was still around 35 degrees Celsius). Rabat itself is a large city, but the majority of volunteers are housed with families who live in the medina at its heart. The medina is the centre of the old town, and is essentially a walled part of the city with meandering (and at first confusing) side streets and alleys.

I was on a teaching placement in Rabat as I'm considering doing a PGCE after I graduate, so I decided this would be the best way to get some actual teaching practice. I was a little worried about how this would go as I literally had no teaching experience, and I won't lie – I did do quite a lot of preparation to start with, but I soon settled into it. I shared classes with another girl, and we all worked at Centre Amal Shabab Takaddoum, which provides internet access, day care for disabled children, as well as free language classes in English, German, and Spanish. As an English teacher, I taught a beginners' class for 1.5 hours in the morning and then a class of upper intermediates from 4pm to 5.30pm. Games such as hangman, alphabet races, and memory games were always well received.

Overall, I had an amazing time in Morocco. The teaching was at times challenging, but the students who turned up to the classes learnt and practised English with native English speakers, which will undoubtedly help them with future studies and job prospects. The Moroccan family I lived with were experienced with volunteers and welcomed me into their family. I learnt a lot about Moroccan culture and practices through them. Travelling to different cities at the weekends meant I had a chance to see other parts of Morocco while having a safe base in Rabat.

COURSES AND WORK EXPERIENCE

A few of the main language course organisers can arrange Arabic courses in Morocco, Egypt, and the Middle East, for example Amerispan (http://study-arabic.amerispan.com). CESA offers beginner and more advanced courses in Fez, Morocco, for three or six weeks. **Jill Cavanagh** was very happy with the Arabic course that CESA arranged for her in Fez:

> My aim was to gain a basic grounding in Arabic, and to learn about Morocco and Islam from being exposed to the culture. I left feeling I had a strong beginning in conversational Arabic. The family I stayed with were very welcoming and supportive. I was invited to join in many family activities, and was always offered help with homework, etc. Plus I was fed wonderfully. The down sides are far outweighed by the good aspects of life here. The men aren't that big a deal. Yeah, they hassle you a bit, but you quickly learn how to deal with this, and even though it doesn't go away, you get used to it.

Other courses of possible interest to year-out students revolve around music and dance. For example, it is possible to study drumming at the Academy of Music & Art in Kokrobite not far from Accra in Ghana or on the Senegalese island of Ile de Goree.

WorkTravelSA.org in Cape Town (www.worktravelsa.org) arranges unpaid work placements in hotels, safari lodges, and in a provincial hospital in South Africa for at least six weeks. Opportunities to do paid work are very limited in Africa, although Ghana has a long tradition of welcoming foreign students to participate in its educational and commercial life. Anyone with a diver's certificate might be able to find work at Red Sea resorts like Sharm el Sheikh and Hurghada. If you aren't sufficiently qualified but want to gain the appropriate certificates, the Red Sea is a good place to train. Specialist companies like Gap Year Diver (see entry in 'Directory of Sport & Activity Courses,') send gappers to Egypt. At local dive centres, you can sometimes get free lessons in exchange for filling air tanks for a sub-aqua club. The Basecamp Group has started to offer kitesurfing courses in Dahab, Egypt, and Taghazout, Morocco.

Vocational placements for aspiring medics and other professionals are arranged by Global Volunteer Projects (www.globalmedicalprojects.org) in Ghana and Tanzania.

GRASSROOTS AND VOLUNTARY ORGANISATIONS

The large majority of volunteers in Africa are trained teachers, doctors, nurses, agricultural, and technical specialists who have committed themselves to work with mainstream aid organisations such as VSO and Skillshare Africa for at least two years. However, openings for unskilled volunteers do exist through smaller charities and indigenous NGOs. It may be possible to offer your services on a voluntary basis to any hospital, school or mission you come across in your travels, though success is not guaranteed. If you have a useful skill and a letter of introduction from a church or family friend, your way will be made smoother.

Till Bruckner is a veteran world traveller who has developed a strong preference for fixing up teaching and voluntary placements independently after arrival rather than with the help of an agency:

> *My advice to anyone who wants to volunteer in Africa (or anywhere else) is to go first and volunteer second. That way, you can travel until you've found a place you genuinely like and where you think you might be able to make a difference. You can also check out the work and accommodation for yourself before you settle down. If you're willing to work for free, you don't need a nanny to tell you where to go. Just go.*

However, for those who find this prospect daunting (and unless you are a mature and seasoned traveller you probably will), you might like to pursue the middle way, that is to make contact with smaller or local organisations in Africa that actively welcome volunteers from abroad. An impressive database of grassroots non-profit volunteer organisations across Africa can be accessed by joining British-based Volunteer4Africa.org. A modest membership fee of £5 is charged. A Cape Town-based agency that offers pricier 'travel work experiences' in a range of countries is You2Africa (www.you2africa.com).

The following is a smattering of African NGOs and companies out of thousands of other possibilities:

- **ICEYOM (International Centre for Education Youth Orientation and Mobilization)**, www.world pulse.com. Placements in many charities in different countries for all types of voluntary service including hospitality, conservation, teaching, water and sanitation, community and fundraising throughout Africa, including Liberia, Cameroon and Nigeria. Placement fee from £350.
- **Ikando** (www.ikando.org). A volunteer and intern recruitment agency based in Accra which deals with education positions lasting up to eight weeks, as well as many others. Volunteers stay in the Ikando house in the centre of Accra and cover their living expenses (£92 per week after their initial fortnight at £531).
- **Kenya Voluntary & Community Development Project**, PO Box 554, Bondo, Kenya (with office in Nairobi International Youth Hostel; www.kvcdp.org). Accepts everyone over 18 to work with children, teaching in sustainable agriculture, conservation, etc. in Wagusu/Abimbo village in Bondo District, Nyanza province, western Kenya. Placement fees from $527 for two weeks to $1,169 for two months.
- **RIPPLE Africa**, 18 Eden Way, Pages Industrial Park, Leighton Buzzard, Bedfordshire LU7 4TZ (www.rippleafrica.org). A charity working in Malawi, started in 2003 by a British couple, based at Mwaya Beach on the northern shores of Lake Malawi. The charity recruits volunteers to assist in the local nursery, schools, health centre, etc. Variable start dates and lengths of stay. Sample price is £1,200 for 12 weeks, which includes accommodation but not local transport, food, or placement fee of £300.
- **RUSO (Rural Upgrade Support Organisation)**, Ghana (www.interconnection.org/rap/volunteer_info. html). International volunteers join tree planting, AIDS awareness education, fish farming, and other projects, especially in the Kome area of Ghana. The cost to volunteers is a $300 registration fee plus $25 per week for stays of one to three months, or $15 a week if staying three to six months.

- **RVO (Robbooker Voluntary Organization)**, Kumasi, Ghana (www.robborg.org). Service/volunteer projects in Ghana lasting two to 24 weeks. Prices from $800 for one month to $2,780 for six months include homestay accommodation with meals.
- **Soft Power Education**, Jinja, Uganda (www.softpowereducation.com). British-registered charity and Ugandan NGO refurbishing government primary schools in Uganda, among other projects. Self-funding volunteers stay for one day to 12 months (paying £75 per week).
- **STAESA** (Students Travel and Exposure South Africa; www.staesa.org). Provides volunteers with work placements in a range of community projects and small-scale industries throughout sub-Saharan Africa. Costs are from $395 for two weeks in Benin including host family accommodation to $5,000+ for one year in any of the 17 African countries in which STAESA has partners.

Some people are apprehensive about living and working close to people who must endure such poverty. But the experience is not always negative, as **Simon Preddy** discovered on his gap year:

> *Initially, when we first hit our village in Uganda, the kids would come running out of their houses shouting 'Mzungo mzungo, how are you?' which means 'white man'. By the end of the trip, the kids were running out shouting at white people 'Simon Kate, how are you?' Myself and another volunteer called Kate had replaced the word 'mzungo', which really made me feel as though we had truly become a part of the community in those three months.*
>
> *When I think of Africa now, I don't imagine deserts with thin children and no water; I see poverty, but I see immense happiness in that poverty. Ugandans may not have much money, but they have got something much more there than we have here – they have smiles. The bonds of community and family are so much stronger, and it made me wonder what we were missing. In this sense, the best reward from Africa for me was the inspiration to try and find or create those bonds here in the UK. In this sense, Uganda changed my life – I now have a passion for travel, but still have a love for Britain.*

South Africa

Undaunted by the frightening levels of violent urban crime, many year out and volunteer agencies have programmes in South Africa, the majority of which involve placing volunteers in orphanages or special schools. One of the advantages of being attached to a school is that most gap year volunteers are free to travel during school holidays. Many in South Africa choose to do the Garden Route or explore the Cedarberg mountain range, the Drakensberg, or Kruger National Park.

- **African Conservation Experience** (www.ConservationAfrica.net). Sends people to game and nature reserves in southern Africa where they do conservation work with rangers and conservationists, and get first-hand experience of animal and plant conservation. The total cost is £5,220 for 12 weeks, including airfares from London (see 'Directory of Specialist Gap Year Programmes' and account in section on 'Expeditions' below).
- **All Out Africa** (www.alloutafrica.com/volunteer). With offices in Swaziland, Mozambique, and South Africa, All Out Africa offers a broad range of volunteer programmes in those countries.
- **Edge of Africa** (www.edgeofafrica.com). Offers volunteer experiences in wildlife, environmental, sports, medical, and community projects along South Africa's famous Garden Route for up to eight weeks. (See p207 for Lynn Munro's description of her gap year placements here.)
- **Willing Workers in South Africa (WWISA)** (www.wwisa.co.za). A community service volunteer organisation based in the Crags, near Plettenberg Bay. Whatever their age and skills, volunteers work on projects alongside local villagers according to their interests, options, and available dates, in the areas for example of schooling and education, youth development, business development, healthcare, and environmental research. Programmes are geared to the social and economic enhancement of the local rural community of Kurland Village. Prices from £700 for a fortnight to £2,600 for 3 months.

Worldwide Experience (www.WorldwideExperience.com). Strives to conserve what humans are fast destroying by supporting conservation and community projects through the recruitment of volunteers. Placements in South Africa, as well as Kenya and Malawi, might include anything from cheetah tracking to teaching a class of children about conservation.

TOURISM

Britons are no longer able to obtain a working holiday visa for South Africa, in a reciprocal move after the UK withdrew that privilege from South Africans. However, Australians and Canadians can obtain 12-month visas that allow them to pick up casual work to supplement their travels. Cape Town is the tourist capital of South Africa, including backpackers, though jobs are harder to find here than elsewhere.

Roger Blake made extensive use of South Africa's youth hostels and several times was able to extend his stay by working for his keep:

> There are more than 100 hostels in South Africa, many of which 'employ' backpackers on a casual basis. Within two weeks of arrival, I was at a hostel in George on a work-for-keep basis. Through contacts made here, I also sold T-shirts at the beach for a small profit and did a few days at a pizza place for tips only. Then I was offered a job at a hostel in Oudtshoorn (Backpackers Oasis). They gave me free accommodation and 150 rand a week to run the bar and help prepare the ostrich braai (barbecue) that they have every evening. Also, I did breakfasts for fellow travellers, which was like being self-employed, as I bought all the ingredients and kept all the profit. It was a small but worthwhile fortune after six weeks here.

Although Johannesburg is often maligned as a big bad city, it is the earning capital of South Africa with better job possibilities than many other places. The areas to head for restaurant and pub work are Sandton, Rosebank, and Dunkeld West.

CONSERVATION AND WILDLIFE

An increasing number of companies and eco-tourism operations are marketing the South African wilderness to gap year students (and others) as a place to learn skills and see big game, for big prices. One recent volunteer has noticed an exact correlation between price and number of big cats: '*lions, leopards, and cheetah attract tourists like bees to honey*,' according to **Kirsten Shaw**, who spent part of 2011 volunteering at Daktari (see entry in 'Directory of Volunteering Abroad').

The African Conservation Trust (www.projectafrica.com) is a South Africa-based trust that recruits self-funding volunteers to staff environmental research projects in South African national parks, Malawi, and others.

The Tembe Elephant Park in Maputaland in north-east KwaZulu-Natal, near the Mozambique border, is home to more than 200 African elephants plus some black rhino, white rhino, buffalo, hippo, lion, leopard, and various antelope species. Tembe welcomes gap year volunteers, who pay £175 per week. They can participate in lion and leopard monitoring, teaching in local schools and other projects (www.gap-year-south-africa.org).

The South African National Foundation for the Conservation of Coastal Birds (SANCCOB) requires volunteers to help with the cleaning and rehabilitation of oil-soaked birds, since oil pollution is a major problem in the coastal waters of South Africa. Volunteers must pay a joining fee of 1,000 rand and fund their own living expenses for at least six weeks (www.sanccob.co.za).

Another volunteer placement company is AVIVA (Africa Volunteering & Ventures Abroad) in Cape Town (www.aviva-sa.com). Its range of placements includes working with AIDS orphans, helping out at an alternative tourist lodge, and working in Kruger National Park.

MY GAP YEAR:
RISETTE DE HAAS

Risette de Haas, from the Netherlands, is a little older than gap year age, so she ended up going as a volunteer co-ordinator at a wildlife centre in South Africa that accepts paying volunteers (including many gappers), and her account sent from there in spring 2011 gives a good flavour of the place.

I wanted to work with wildlife or children, and I wanted to do something 'good'. First, I looked for jobs with big organisations, so maybe I could get a paid job. But those are very hard to find, and they ask for experience or specific subjects I didn't have or hadn't studied. So I changed my online search to 'free' job, as a non-paying volunteer. After searching for about two months, I found Daktari Wildlife Orphanage and Bush School [see entry in 'Directory of Volunteering Abroad'] So my two passions could be realised in one place, working with animals and with children. Daktari offers a few placements for volunteers over 18 who can speak English to stay for six months or longer. The placements are free, and you get housing and food during the week. I made contact with the owner Michele and, after a few emails, and reading some blogs by previous volunteers, I decided that this was my opportunity. The only things Michele asked were whether my English was sufficient to do my job, and of course whether I was truly enthusiastic.

Because I am staying at Daktari for more than six months, I don't have to pay for my stay, as the other volunteers do. But you get more responsibilities, and for me that meant taking on the job of volunteer co-ordinator/camp manager. I make sure that the volunteers and the children are happy at Daktari, and that the animals are taken care of. My weekends are officially off, but when we get a new volunteer I show them around and have an introduction meeting with them. It is hard work and quite long hours, but I love it ,and the thing I do here gives me so much energy that it is easy to keep up. The smiles of the kids, the attention to the animals and the 'family' of volunteers, perfect! Even when you work in the office at Daktari, you still have dogs, squirrels, and warthogs running around.

We get volunteers from all over the world, so as a co-ordinator you have to be open-minded and adaptable to work with all these different nationalities; the same with the staff and the local children who come to us for a week at a time. We are in the bush here. There is no electricity and things are very basic, we have power and light via solar, but that sometimes runs out. We also have hot running water for showers fuelled by gas. For me, coming to the bush was what I needed and put everything in perspective. I'm happy here. But again that doesn't count for everybody. Some volunteers come with an idea about South Africa which turns out to be very different, so my job is to talk to them and try to keep them happy.

I'm still working at Daktari (at the time of writing). I have another four months of my year here to go). I love it here and love the job I'm doing. Some kids just steal your heart, and you want to know if they get all the best opportunities they deserve. I love the bush, I love Africa, and I also love working for a charity. I know now that I made the best decision in my life by coming here. It changed everything.

EXPEDITIONS

The African continent hosts a huge variety of scientific and conservation expeditions, and most interests can be accommodated, from measuring the height of waterfalls in Lesotho to tracking warthogs in a Ghanaian national park. If by any chance you know someone doing a PhD on a relevant African subject, you might be able to persuade him or her of your usefulness. But most gap year students will join a more formal expedition, either one organised through a university, a regional expedition society or with BSES, which counts Namibia among its current destinations.

When exploring the African bush, always take the necessary precautions proffered by locals, rangers, and other old hands, to avoid what happened to a round-the-world Australian cyclist (nicknamed Locky), whom **Mark Nash** from Cambridge met on his travels:

The story goes that in the middle of the night, near Archers Post, a town in Kenya surrounded by national reserves, Locky was woken up by movement outside his tent. Thinking it was someone messing with his bike, he unzipped his tent in a sleepy haze and shouted out to scare away the intruder. I've heard you can scare a lion away if you act fierce enough; well, I'm guessing Locky must not have been that fierce, because the lion, startled, immediately jumped on the tent with Locky inside. After a few frantic moments for Locky at the bottom, and a few frustrating claws and bites on the part of the lion, it was confused by the tent 'prey', jumped off, grabbed one of Locky's panniers and disappeared into the bush. Locky decided he should put his tent back together as best he could, glad that it had proved itself lion-proof(ish). He was just crawling in again when he heard a noise behind him. Finding no food in the bag, the still-hungry lion had been attracted by noises coming from the tent it thought it had vanquished earlier. In Locky's words: 'I was inside the entrance of the tent facing out shitting myself. The lion was about 5m away, approaching slowly this time. As it walked towards me, I aimed the small can of pepper spray I carried, which I had got out after the first attack and, not having used it before, managed to spray the first lot just above my right eye! About 2m away now, my second spray got the lion right in the face. It stopped, shook its head a couple of times, sneezed or something, turned around and left.'

Even more frightening and potentially lethal was the experience of 18-year-old **Grace Forster**, whose diving group on Tanzania's Pemba Island near Zanzibar was attacked by machete-wielding bandits who robbed the group of thousands of dollars and put Grace in hospital, although she made a full recovery.

But most trips and expeditions are safe and peaceable, including those venturing into the deserts of North Africa. Just after A levels, **Anna Ling** spent the summer in Morocco living on a daily budget of €4. While she was staying in Marrakesh and Essaouira, she came across a true working holiday opportunity. Tour companies that organise trips into the Sahara ask long-stayers to round up a group of at least eight people, and then take you along for free. Anna felt this would have been perfectly possible, since up to half of backpackers join one of these four- to five-day tours (which cost upwards of £100) and include a camel ride, food, and accommodation. Unfortunately, she had to leave to meet a friend in Spain.

ASIA

Lumping together places as different as Java and Japan, or Hong Kong and Ho Chi Minh City, is a dangerous business. The gap year experiences of the student who spends six months in Singapore because her uncle can arrange a job for her in his export business may have almost nothing in common with those of the gap year volunteer who teaches at a village school in Nepal. Different corners of the vast continent of Asia beguile individuals for personal and possibly inexplicable reasons. Perhaps a childhood book, acquaintance, or memory has bequeathed a longing to visit a faraway and mysterious place. This may not be the kind of reason that cuts much ice with college admissions tutors, but it can be what sparks incredible and memorable experiences.

There are dangers in spending time at a young age in a seriously alien country. This is true of Bolivia, Zambia, or even Romania, but somehow the culture shock which gap year travellers experience in the Indian subcontinent or in a small industrial Chinese town is especially acute. A novelty-seeking foreigner is not really what a struggling village in Bengal or Borneo most needs. Preconceptions about what benefits you will be able to bring are often proved misguided in the first week. **Andy Green** spent a couple of weeks with a long-established voluntary organisation in India: '*I feel that I was of no help to Indian society whatsoever. Due to differences in climate, food, and culture, it is difficult to be productive. I could have paid an Indian a few pounds to do what I did in two weeks. It was, however, an experience I'll never forget.*' In other words, the experience is bound to benefit you, the gap year traveller, but its value to local people may be questionable. That is not to say that a six-month attachment to a school or orphanage will not be valuable for the local community, but its value might lie in unexpected places.

The climate is not a trivial concern. Although **Robert Abblett** had carefully planned his trip to India and had the addresses of organic farms where he intended to work, he had not counted on the debilitating heat, and decided to enjoy a holiday instead. This is an alternative worth considering, ie to make your fortune at home or in a western country, whether as an accountancy trainee in England, chambermaid in Switzerland, or tomato picker in Australia, in order to finance months of leisurely travel in the developing countries of Asia.

Culture shock and disorientation will be an inevitable part of the process. **Christina Hall** was more amused than frustrated by her first bewildering few weeks in India: '*The main problem lies in the auto-rickshaw drivers; you tell them "I want to go to xyz," and they wobble their heads like dashboard buddies and I assumed this means yes. Often it does, but sometimes it means "Well, I vaguely know that this place is in Chennai. Let's go on an adventure and see if we can find it, I'll try to overcharge you for the privilege of getting lost with me, and then I'll drop you off at the street next to where you started."*'

Of course, the kinds of adjustment you will need to make will be quite different in the countries of Asia with developed or rapidly developing economies, principally Japan, Taiwan, Korea, China, the Hong Kong Special Administrative Region, and Singapore. Special schemes permit pre- and post-university students to work in some of these countries, mainly as teachers of the English language.

GAP AGENCIES

Almost all the key gap year organisations make placements in a number of Asian countries. India and Thailand are probably the most popular destinations, though opportunities exist throughout the continent. To give a taste of the range of choices, Travellers Worldwide (www.travellersworldwide.com) organises teaching placements (IT, music, maths, arts and crafts, drama) in Brunei, Cambodia, China, India, Malaysia, Sri Lanka and Thailand; hands-on conservation placements working with orang-utans, elephants, pandas, monkeys, marine life, etc in Cambodia, Malaysia, and Sri Lanka; professional work experience internships in law, medicine, care, media, and journalism in China, India, Malaysia, and Sri Lanka; and sports coaching placements in India, Malaysia, and Sri Lanka. Some gap-sending organisations specialise in one destination such as Starfish Ventures for Thailand and Gap Guru for India (though the latter has been expanding its range of countries). Gap Guru offers an interesting range of projects in India, such as working at a software company and helping at a crocodile sanctuary.

MY GAP YEAR: IMMA RAMOS

Imma Ramos was delighted to win first prize in a gap year essay-writing contest sponsored by Gap Guru a few years back, which funded six months of voluntary work in India plus a 10-day travel option.

I chose to stay in Delhi for a month because I was attracted to the city and also the chance to intern at a charitable children's publishing company, which also runs a school for disadvantaged children. Later, I spent over a month in Kochi (Kerala) because I wanted to work as a reporter and trainee editor for a national newspaper, and also three months at a school in Chennai, attended by many children from fisher-folk families who were affected by the tsunami.

I love writing about art, so I soon took on the role of art critic on the newspaper placement. It was a very exciting internship, as I had to be proactive and go to the latest exhibition openings where I interviewed the artists and wrote about the shows. I accompanied the senior photographer on some of his projects too, which was fantastic - we travelled around on his motorbike! I stayed with lovely Indian families who were incredibly welcoming and generous. Whereas in Delhi we usually ate dal, alu gobi, vegetable curry, rice, and naan bread, in Kochi the food was very different - dosas and coconut chutneys. I loved it!

A few days after arriving in India I went on the Gap Guru Himalayan trip with a fellow volunteer, from Manali to Keylong to Leh. Visiting Buddhist monasteries and passing through awe-inspiring mountainous landscapes was a magical experience. It was such an incredible trip, and a great way to start my gap year. After my placement finished I spent a month travelling around Rajasthan with a group, and just before taking my flight home from Mumbai, I fulfilled my ambition of seeing the Ajanta and Ellora caves. Travelling and absorbing such diverse cultures was enormously stimulating, both visually and intellectually. In my first week I missed home but after a month I didn't want to come back!

If you want to spend time in a less well-travelled country of Asia, it will be necessary to sift through the literature of all the relevant organisations to find which ones (if any) offer what you are looking for; for example, Coral Cay Conservation has projects in the Philippines, Travellers Worldwide in Mauritius, Raleigh in Sabah-Borneo, Lattitude in Vanuatu, and Travel to Teach sends people to Laos to teach English, computing, etc.

EXPEDITIONS AND CONSERVATION

The mainstream London-based conservation expedition organisers all run projects in Asia. These expeditions are usually open to anyone reasonably fit who can raise the cost of joining (typically £3,000; see 'Directory of Specialist Gap Year Programmes' for further details):

Coral Cay Conservation (www.coralcay.org). Recruits volunteers to assist with reef and tropical forest surveys in the Philippines and Cambodia, to help protect some of the world's most diverse tropical environments. Full training in marine and terrestrial ecology is provided.

Gapforce (www.gapforce.org). Volunteers are sent to assist on both land- and sea-based conservation projects, and to undertake sport volunteering, teaching, and community work in range of countries including India, Nepal, Fiji, and China.

Global Vision International (GVI) (www.gvi.co.uk). Placements from three weeks to one year. Wildlife and community work in Thailand, Nepal, Sri Lanka, etc, and conservation work including work with orang-utans in Sumatra and turtles in Vanuatu.

MY GAP YEAR: SADIE BROWN

Sadie Brown wanted to see the world before proceeding to Chichester University to study Performing Arts. She was impressed with the credentials of the Orangutan Foundation, which is a registered charity.

The project in Borneo was part of a long-term conservation effort for maintaining the forest, which is currently being destroyed for palm oil plantations, logging, and mining, taking with it a lot of the wildlife. We worked with a local NGO that concentrated on educating communities about maintaining their forest, as it would benefit them as well as the wildlife. We worked in a village where, apart from one other person, we were the first westerners to go there! There, we built a dam in the forest to get the villagers fresh water to drink; we then built them two cesspit toilets in an effort to make their washing more hygienic. From our efforts, we hope that if loggers who want to take over their land approach them they will decline the offer.

The highlight has to be working with the locals in the village in Borneo - population about 50. It was a one-street village. Their enthusiasm for work and gratitude were so enlightening. Volunteering abroad is such a great experience, which I recommend to travellers, especially if you are looking to do something different with your gap year and gain valuable experience. It is totally unique, and you will not forget your time out there; it is so fulfilling as well, to do something that is making a difference in a developing country, even if it is a very small difference. My experiences on these projects make me want to return to the places I worked in and see all the villagers again.

I was also so glad to have the opportunities to see orang-utans in Borneo as they are amazing animals, and it was truly heartbreaking to see the ones in the care centre, which were injured from having their habitat torn down by humans. I found it hard to deal with emotionally, as they have 97% the same genes as humans, yet some people believe they just do not deserve any rights. It is a good and bad thing about volunteering; you see the harsh reality, and it's a real eye-opener, but drives you to help fight against it all.

Operation Wallacea (www.opwall.com). Volunteer students, divers, and naturalists assist with surveys of marine and rainforest habitats on remote islands of south-east Sulawesi in Indonesia. Dive training can be given, and land surveys for studying birds and mammals also organised.

Orangutan Foundation (www.orangutan.org.uk). Volunteers are based in Kalimantan, Indonesian Borneo, and participate in hands-on conservation fieldwork for six weeks. Volunteers must note that there is no direct work with orang-utans, although wild and/or rehabilitated orang-utans will be in the vicinity where volunteers work.

Raleigh (www.raleighinternational.org) is an established youth and education charity that arranges for 17–24-year-olds to take on challenging environmental, community, and adventure projects as part of five- or 10-week programmes. Raleigh runs expeditions in Borneo and in India, based in Karnataka in the Western Ghats region, one of the world's most biodiverse hot spots. **Olivia Hayward** describes the community projects she worked on, building 10 composting toilets in the remote village of Hosekerasunda:

I hate being a tourist, and this definitely wasn't for tourists. It was a wonderful introduction to Indian culture; we lived in their school, ate the food they cooked for us, swam in the reservoir every day, learned some Kannada (the local language), and had a fantastic time.

CAUTION

So many gap year travellers and other backpackers are wandering around India, Nepal, and Thailand that it can be a challenge to get away from them (assuming that is your ambition). Although it is a good idea to try to step off the well-worn path between Goa, Kathmandu, and Ko Samui, it may be unwise to stray too far from the beaten track. During his year out, **Joel Emond** from Bristol was travelling alone in north-east China. Unwittingly, he wandered out of a national park mentioned in his guidebook and into North Korea where he was instantly arrested and put in jail. The Korean authorities contacted the

British Embassy in Beijing to confirm that Joel was not a spy. Unfortunately, they got his name wrong and requested information about Joe Lemond. After several weeks, someone in Beijing twigged, and the problem was resolved – but not before Joel had gone on hunger strike in protest at the vile diet of rotten cabbages.

One way of exploring Asia in a protected environment is to join an overland tour such as those offered by Exodus (www.exodus.co.uk) or Intrepid Travel (www.intrepidtravel.com), which runs shorter and longer adventure trips in Asia. After volunteering for an orang-utan project in Borneo (see above), **Sadie Brown** joined a 30-day tour with GAP Adventures through Cambodia, Vietnam, and Laos: '*Prior to that, I travelled on my own from Singapore to Bangkok; for that, I had advice from friends. I think the lowest point of my gap year was the frustration of travelling alone, which is why I was happy to be on the 30-day tour! It took away all those worries. The cost of the tour at first seemed quite steep [currently £1,500], but I feel it was worth it as the transportation, accommodation, and tour leader were all brilliant.*'

TEACHING

Throughout Asia, thousands of people of all ages are eager for tuition in English. Native English speakers, whatever their background, are wanted to meet that demand, and school leavers can find voluntary placements in a range of countries. It can be a daunting prospect standing in front of a class of eager learners when you are just 18. Most teaching will be of conversational English rather than grammar. Several of the sending agencies insist that you do a short TEFL training course beforehand.

Paid teaching work is available primarily to people who have a university degree. Most commercial language school directors are looking for teachers who are older than 18 and who have finished university. In the case of Korea and Japan, a BA or BSc is virtually essential for obtaining the appropriate visa. Teaching English in Japan is one of the classic jobs for people filling a gap in their lives (see next section).

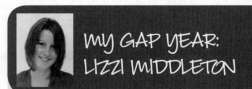

MY GAP YEAR:
LIZZI MIDDLETON

Lizzi Middleton's placement in India involved teaching English in a rather unexpected setting.

Not quite believing that I was embarking on what was to be the biggest adventure of my life so far, I arrived in Delhi, and a few days later caught a 15-hour overnight bus to McLeodganj in north-west India, seat of the Tibetan government in exile and home of His Holiness the Dalai Lama. It was a further hour's hair-raising bus journey down into the valley to my placement at the Jamyang Choeling Himalayan Institute for Buddhist women. The nunnery is in a very secluded area of the countryside, set in front of the stunning backdrop of the snow-capped foothills of the Himalayas. It was unbelievably picturesque and was a welcome relief after the madness of Delhi!

Finding out what we were meant to be doing, and where we were meant to be, was our first major challenge. Tibetans are notoriously vague - we had been warned about this but it was vague on a level that I've never experienced vague before! This was one of the real cultural differences that I had to adapt to. Having just completed my A levels, with the careful structuring of time that they had required, and coming from a family where we always let each other know where we are, life at Jamyang Choeling was quite a change. I had to learn to be very easygoing, to not mind when a class just didn't turn up, or when there was only half a class there.

My classes were loosely organised according to ability, but to be honest that didn't mean much. Lessons were fun - I realised soon after I arrived that these women needed their hour with me to be educational but light-hearted. They get up at 5am every day, and apart from an hour for lunch and an hour for dinner, they don't stop until 10 or 11pm - they're studying Buddhism all day. My first few lessons were pretty diabolical, as I tried to find my feet in a completely alien situation. I had no idea of how I was going to learn the names of 90 women, none of whom had any hair and who all wore exactly the same clothes!

The teaching was the reason that I was there, but there were lots of other things to be done at the nunnery too. Cooking for 90+ three times a day is no mean feat, and so every day from 10am to noon I cut up vegetables with a small team of nuns. I found that it was a great time for the nuns to practise the English that they were sometimes too shy to use in front of each other in the classroom, and it was also an opportunity for me to learn some Tibetan and to listen to their stories - often of escape over the Himalayas from Tibet itself. I made some amazing friends. Together we had a huge amount of fun - riding on the roofs of local buses, swimming in the river, shopping for food for our leaving party, teaching each other national dances (I'm afraid we ended up opting to teach the Macarena), blowing up balloons, and a lot of the time just sitting and chatting about the similarities and most of all the differences between our lives, religions, and cultures. It's just amazing to have the opportunity for a first-hand insight into such different perspectives, on both everyday things and on moral issues. That's definitely something that I'll take from this experience. I've gone from having one pen pal from a Year 9 French lesson, who has written to me once in four years, to having 90 on the other side of the world, who've all desperate to practise their newly learnt language skills!

The situation is different on the Indian subcontinent, where very few private English language schools exist. Many gap students find themselves attached to schools, and sometimes with a rather indeterminate role – as **Lizzi Middleton**'s story above illustrates, it can be just as enriching an experience as teaching English or anything concrete.

Many other gap year students have found their placements thoroughly rewarding and worthwhile. But some have found themselves attached to schools for privileged children and wonder why they are there. **Rachel Sedley**'s main complaint about her placement in Nepal arranged by a commercial gap year agency (now defunct) was that she was teaching in a private school for privileged children, when she had been led to believe that she would be contributing her time and labour to more needy pupils. She suspected that she was there partly to boost the prestige of the school and its head. So anyone with strong views about the kind of school in which they want to work should find out as many details as possible beforehand.

There follow brief descriptions of the language teaching situation in the main countries of Asia, together with contact addresses. More detailed information on paid teaching in the countries of Asia is contained in the 2012 edition of *Teaching English Abroad*, also by me (Vacation Work/Crimson Publishing, £14.99).

JAPAN

Japan is not quite as ideal a destination for a post-university gap year or two as it used to be. After stagnating for some years, the Japanese economy was dealt a grievous blow by the earthquake and tsunami of 2011. The marketplace in which English language academies are now competing is more desperate than it once was, and it seems that the glory days for English teachers are over. Of the five largest chains of language schools, three have filed for bankruptcy over the past few three years.

Yet groups of *eikaiwa* (conversation schools) do remain in business, alongside thousands of English schools in Tokyo, Osaka, and many other Japanese cities who hire *gaijins* (foreigners) to teach. A great many of these are willing to take on native speakers of English with no teaching qualification, as long as they have a university degree and preferably some teaching experience.

Britons, Canadians, Australians, and New Zealanders are eligible for a working holiday visa for Japan. The annual quota of working holiday visas for Britons aged 18–30 is 1,000. Visa holders may accept paid work in Japan for up to 12 months, provided it is incidental to their travels. Applicants must show that they have sufficient financial backing, ie savings of £2,500 or £1,500 and a return ticket. Note that applications are accepted from April, and once the allocation has been filled, no more visas will be granted until April of the following year. Further details are available by ringing the Japanese Embassy on 020 7465 6565 or on the embassy webpage (www.uk.emb-japan.go.jp/en/visa/work_hol.html).

Most participants make use of the services of the non-profit Japan Association for Working Holiday Makers (JAWHM; www.jawhm.or.jp), whose principal offices are in Tokyo, Osaka, and Fukuoka. Note that there is a membership charge, and you must show your working holiday visa stamp to be eligible for its assistance.

Graduates should investigate the government's competitive JET (Japan Exchange & Teaching) Programme. Anyone with a bachelor's degree in any discipline who is under 39 and from the UK, USA, Ireland, Canada, Australia, or New Zealand (plus a number of other countries) is eligible to apply. For British applicants, details may be obtained from the JET Desk at the Japanese Embassy (020 7465 6668; www.jet-uk.org). About 200 Britons join the programme each year. Applications in Britain are due by the last Friday in November for one-year contracts beginning late July. The annual salary is 3,600,000 yen (currently equivalent to £26,500).

MY GAP YEAR:
MARCUS STARLING

Marcus Starling spent two fantastic years with JET in Kagoshima, a city in the far south of Japan, which is known as the 'Naples of the East' because of its smoking volcano.

I had applied unsuccessfully for my ideal job on the civil service fast stream, and wanted to gain some more post-university experience and independence before applying again. Having done a very varied gap year before university, I wanted to spend sufficient time in one place to learn a language and make it feel like a second home. I applied for two jobs abroad - one teaching English in a school in China, the other on the JET programme. JET paid far better, was well organised, internationally recognised, and looked to be a good opportunity to learn about Japan's culture and language. I taught at four junior high schools (ages 12-15) on a rota basis, with occasional day visits to primary schools and leading kids' summer activity programmes. My travel experiences in Japan were unforgettable, particularly visiting some of the small sub-tropical islands off the coast.

JET pays for your flight to Japan (and the return flights at the end), so the initial cost is limited to your first month's rent and the money you need to equip your new home and settle in. I found I spent £1,000 of my parents' money in the first month, but was able to pay them back within a couple of months by living a modest lifestyle on what seemed a very generous first salary. I should say that Japan isn't actually that expensive a place to live, providing you adapt your tastes (although it is an expensive place to travel). There's something special about Japan, hot spring baths, smoke from the volcano drifting over the bay, politeness and curiosity from people living down the street, and small shrines hidden away in forests. Sometimes, the curiosity and questions that were so welcome when I was a new visitor became a bit predictable when I had lived there for over a year and knew more of the language and culture - but this was far outweighed by the kindness behind these approaches.

A number of the largest language training organisations recruit graduates abroad as well as in Japan. Among the main employers are:

AEON Corp, Recruitment office in El Segundo, California (+1 310 662 4706; www.aeonet.com). As of May 2011, AEON is still actively recruiting teachers, and all of its 300 branch schools have re-opened after closure following the earthquake. Interviews in several American and Canadian cities, plus Sydney and London between February and April.

Berlitz (http://careers.berlitz.com). Must be already residing in Japan with a work visa to be considered, so vacancies seldom listed on the main Berlitz careers site.

ECC Foreign Language Institute, with regional offices in Osaka, Tokyo, and Nagoya. Recruitment website for job applicants is http://recruiting.ecc.co.jp/index.html. Recruitment sessions for 150 schools throughout Japan take place in San Francisco, Toronto, and London (see website for details).

Interac, Tokyo (www.interacnetwork.com/recruit). 1,500 full-time assistant language teachers (ALTs). Overseas recruitment schedule can be found online.

The most common means of recruitment is online (eg via websites such as www.jobseekjapan.com), by word of mouth among expat teachers, and by advertising your services. The free weekly English language magazine *Metropolis* (www.metropolis.co.jp) has a classified advertisements section, which could be worth checking for jobs. Another useful free publication is *Tokyo Notice Board* (www.tokyonoticeboard.co.jp). The twice-monthly free electronic newsletter *O-Hayo-Sensei* (which means 'Good Morning Teacher') has pages of teaching positions across Japan at www.ohayosensei.com. Many of these are open only to candidates who are already in Japan. To find private students, try www.findateacher.net, which according to **Joseph Tame** really works. Simply enter your details (what you teach, what area of Japan you teach in, how much you charge, etc), and the students will make contact. Joseph was also impressed with gaijinpot.com when he was looking for bits and pieces of teaching work.

CHINA

Recruitment of teachers for the People's Republic of China is absolutely booming in the private sector. The internet is a prolific source of possibilities and is expanding all the time. Any web search or a trawl of the major ELT job websites is bound to turn up plenty of contacts, such as www.jobchina.net, which has long lists of jobs, all dated and described in detail. With an invitation letter or fax from an official Chinese employer, you will be able to obtain a Z visa (valid in the first instance for three months), or an F visa (business or cultural exchange visa).

MY GAP YEAR: PAULA WEALE

Paula Weale was 18 when she went to rural China to teach English in the small town of Li Li with the help of Projects Abroad.

The countryside was not as green as I imagined, and the towns larger yet still distinctively Chinese. Out here, you must contend with the constant stares of curiosity that convince you after a while that you have grown a tail and antlers. You soon get used to these though. The first problem to overcome is the language. The next is the food, which is nothing like the Chinese you find at the local takeaway. The third is the cold in winter: out here, the thermal vest is my best friend, and I have to wear three pairs of socks. My host family were always willing to help with haggling. In Li Li, you could buy most modern comforts in one of the many local supermarkets (except deodorant), and western brands are available, but at a price. It can be difficult to decide which bottle is conditioner and which is shampoo, but it's all a trial-and-error experience in China!

The day of my first lesson was really nerve-racking. I had the first week to watch classes and prepare my own, but I'm not a qualified teacher so all I had was my native language. I was amazed at where inspiration would appear from, and after initial hiccups the lessons were great. I found enthusiasm I never knew I had. The students were very keen to speak with me and improve their English, since this was the first time they had seen a western person in the flesh. They'd bring in cameras and books for me to sign between classes so it was like being a celebrity in rural China. Make sure to bring pictures from home, as these are immensely popular. There are many weekend opportunities to take a class out to the park or skating in the town.

To anyone coming to China, I'd say that living in the country is a real adventure. The experience taught me to survive through tough times and how to get on with life when resources were limited. By being a teacher, I was able to see life from another culture's perspective, which I'd never have managed as a backpacker passing through. I was accepted by the community and looked after by everyone I met, really. When in the cities I felt safer than I do in London.

IST Plus in the UK (www.istplus.com) runs Teach in China for graduates from the UK, while BUNAC runs a teach and travel programme including a four-week TEFL course, lessons in Mandarin, and placement as an intern teacher for five months. BUNAC's six-month programme costs £2,095.

TAIWAN
The country remains a magnet for English teachers of all backgrounds. Hundreds of private language institutes or *buhsibans* continue to teach young children, cram high school students for university entrance examinations, and generally service the seemingly insatiable demand for English conversation and English tuition.

Many well-established language schools are prepared to sponsor foreign teachers for a resident visa, provided the teacher has a university degree and is willing to work for at least a year. On arrival, check the 'positions vacant' column of the English language *China Post*, although work tends to result from personal referrals more than from advertising.

The following language schools hire on a large scale:

Hess Educational Organization, Taipei City (www.hess.com.tw). Specialises in teaching children including kindergarten age; 500 native speaking teachers (NSTs) are hired for more than 150 branches. Very structured teaching programme and curriculum.

International Avenue Consulting Company, Taichung City (www.iacc.com.tw).

Kidscamp/ALV, Tao-Yuan City (www.kidscamp.com.tw). Hires native speakers for summer and winter language camps. Interviews via Skype are acceptable.

Kojen ELS, Taipei (www.kojenenglish.com). Employs 200–300 teachers at 21 schools, mostly in Taipei, but also Kaohsiung and Taichung. Must have a degree, but experience not needed.

SOUTH KOREA

Although Korea does not immediately come to mind as a likely destination for British EFL teachers, it has been long known in North America as a country that can absorb an enormous number of native speaker teachers, including fresh graduates with no TEFL training or experience. Hundreds of language institutes (*hogwons*) in Seoul, the capital, Pusan (Korea's second city, five hours south of Seoul), and in smaller cities employ native speaker teachers of English. The majority of these are run as businesses, so that making a profit seems to be what motivates many bosses rather than educating people. Certificates and even degrees are in many cases superfluous, though a university degree will be needed in order to obtain the right visa, unless you are an undergraduate willing to undertake a paid teaching internship, for example via TeachAway (www.teachaway.com).

EPIK, the English Program in Korea, is a scheme run by the Ministry of Education, and administered through Korean embassies in the west, mainly in the USA and UK, to place about 2,000 foreign graduates in schools and education offices throughout the country. The annual salary offered is 1.8 to 2.5 million won per month (depending on qualifications) plus accommodation, round-trip airfare, visa sponsorship, and medical insurance. Current information should be obtained from the EPIK website (www.epik.go.kr), or by contacting the local Korea government representative via edu@koreanembassy.org.uk.

In the UK, jobs in Korea can be fixed up in advance through www.huntesl.com, and also through Flying Cows in Nottingham (www.flying-cows.com), which is willing to consider anyone with a degree. After doing a two-week evening course on TESL in her final term of university, **Jessie Cox** from Canada scoured the job forums at www.eslcafe.com to find some decent recruiters who would not renege on their agreements. Before long she was on her way to provincial Korea:

> *I taught at the only middle school in a small farming town, and the biggest problem I encountered was the extremely low level of English among most of the students. Even simple directions were hard for me to give, so we had to spend some time learning simple instructions such as 'Open your book to page 22', or 'Repeat after me'. The language barrier also made discipline more of a challenge for me. If the Korean teacher wasn't in the room at the time, I was pretty much limited to 'Stop that!', 'No!', and 'Be quiet please'. I was mostly responsible for leading pronunciation and speaking exercises, along with conducting memory tests in which the students had to recite a passage from the textbook. The teaching was mostly textbook-based. The best feature of working in a state school as the only non-Korean teacher was the chance to be completely immersed in Korean culture in a way that would never be possible as a tourist. The wages at public schools in Korea are quite good, and the pay of 1.8 million won per month was more than enough to cover expenses. Although I travelled quite a bit, including to Thailand and Mongolia, I still managed to save about C$10,000 over the year. The biggest reward of my experience in Korea was seeing the world from a different perspective. I was able to climb mountains, visit Buddhist temples, visit the border between North and South Korea, explore ancient palaces, and even eat a live octopus!*

GAP YEAR THAILAND

'I am interested in volunteering to help teach English in a school, but I'm not a qualified teacher. Will I be of any help?'

Certainly the situation may be different in different countries, but people who go to Thailand quickly find that they are much more helpful – and welcomed – than they had anticipated.

As Andrew Hynd said: 'I originally had my reservations about how useful I would be as a volunteer English teacher. But the children loved having a British teacher in the school. I cannot describe the warmth and generosity of not only the teachers and students, but of the people of the town too. I will remember this experience and the people I have met for the rest of my life.'

Andrew's mentor at school, Chon, said: 'He is very helpful. He comes here and helps us with the students a lot. The school will greatly welcome more volunteers.'

If someone is looking for a paid job in a school in Thailand that would usually not be possible without teaching qualifications. On a volunteer programme it is not necessary for people to be qualified/experienced teachers. The schools have Thai national teachers of English, who teach grammar and other basics. What they are looking for from volunteers is first-language English speakers to help students to improve their spoken English.

Stephanie Morrison was at a school in Surin, in rural Thailand. After two weeks she said: 'I am based in kindergarten, primary and secondary school. I've also got two university students who want some tutoring which they pay me for; and two teachers have asked me to help them in learning conversational English.' As Stephanie's experience confirms, the opportunity to earn a bit of pocket money, if volunteers wish, is easily available.

Scott Tyler was at a school in Bangkok. His only previous experience of teaching was the briefing and orientation programmes provided by Gap Year Thailand. His mentor at school, Hasnee, said: 'He helps in the English class. He has really achieved a fantastic result in helping them. The result is quite amazing. They speak better English this year.'

Dilys Ewart said 'I went to Thailand as an unqualified volunteer teacher of English, and within two months had three job offers for paid employment as a teacher. I had thought I would go to Thailand and get some teaching experience but I never thought I would get three job offers – and one of the best memories of my life.'

There's more detail on each of these case studies at www.gapyearthailand. org.uk.

MY GAP YEAR: ALISON WHITE

Alison White lived in a small temple in a small Thai town teaching English to monks, a placement arranged by Real Gap. Here, she sums up the good and the bad bits.

I am delighted by:

- the friendliness of everyone - the smiles and courtesy
- the beauty of the temple area - set in woods, with buffalo, loads of dogs, and golden Buddha images everywhere
- the young monks who are so friendly and helpful
- the old women who can't speak a word of English, but who always laugh and offer words of wisdom in Thai
- the children at the school who are so respectful and well behaved.

My challenges are:

- sleeping on a cold hard floor where I get bitten regularly by ants, fleas, and mosquitoes
- seeing my favourite stray dog and her five young puppies scrounge around for food and affection, which is never offered by the locals but warmly received
- remaining non-judgmental about the Rayban-wearing chief monk with the mobile phone permanently attached to his ear.

Thailand is famously welcoming, and one of the most popular destinations for gap year travellers. Many of the general and specialist placement agencies send volunteers to this country, such as Volunthai, Travel to Teach in Chiang Mai and Gap Year Thailand (see directory entries), and also Teach-to-Travel in Lopburi Thailand (www.teach-to-travel.com).

Independent-minded gap year travellers can occasionally pick up casual teaching work in Bangkok, but most respectable schools now want their native speaker teachers to have a university degree. The noisy Khao San Road is lined with expat pubs and budget accommodation, many with noticeboards offering teaching work and populated with other foreigners (known as *farangs*) well acquainted with the possibilities. They will also be able to warn you of the dubious schools that are known to exploit their teachers and other scams. One of the best all-round sources of information about teaching in Thailand is the website www.ajarn.com, with stories and tips as well as many job vacancies.

The Thai authorities keep changing the visa goalposts, and the situation is hard to fathom. The relevant pages on www.ajarn.com provide the current picture. For those staying for an extended period on a tourist visa, they must leave the country every 15 days to renew it. Some schools will help their teachers to obtain the Thai teacher's licence (for which you need a university degree), work permit, and non-immigrant B visa, for which you will need multiple documents (including a police clearance from the country of origin).

MY GAP YEAR: JULIA BOWLER

Julia Bowler reflected on the hospitality she had encountered during her three-month teaching stint at Wattharoe School in Rayong Province, arranged by Gap Year Thailand.

I took sooooo many photos of the children in lessons, around school, playing, and with me teaching them. My last lessons were spent singing, playing games, and generally getting the kids to recall everything I'd taught them since arriving. Starting to teach feels like a lifetime ago, and saying goodbye was a lot harder than I had anticipated.

On the last weekend with my Thai family, they decided to take me to stay in a resort up in Nakhon Nayok, another Thai province. When we got back to their home, I made gaeng fang and pla tord for my Thai family (a curry dish and a large fried fish). I think my cooking is getting rather good now, and I am confident with a lot of things, but I am nervous about making it for people at home in England in case it's too spicy.

I was careful not to expect too much on my birthday, as it was after term had ended. However, when they told me that the school was going to hold a party meal for me, I was so surprised, and touched at how much effort had gone into it. They had cooked all my favourite Thai dishes; presented me with a gorgeous hand-made lamp with shells from our local beach, and then a van arrived and started unpacking a karaoke system they had hired for the evening. The headmaster made a speech and presented me with a gift of a gold-engraved pendant with the King of Thailand on. I even had a hand-made cake which said 'HAPY, BIRTH DAY JULIA' in all different colours, and all the teachers sung a very odd version of 'Happy Birthday'. I couldn't stop smiling the whole evening. The teachers have said I am welcome to come back and visit whenever I want. So have my Thai family. I know I will be returning to Thailand – I have fallen in love with it.

Ashleigh Davey on the same programme was equally touched by the treatment she received, and proud of what confidence her Thai gap year had given her: '*I left Ireland a little girl from a rural area who had never been farther than a holiday in Spain with my family. And there I was, standing in front of 100 people in traditional Thai dress dancing and saying goodbye. Amazing.*'

VIETNAM AND CAMBODIA

The largest growth area in English teaching has been in those countries that were cut off from the west for many years, namely Vietnam, Cambodia, and Laos, where a number of joint venture language schools have been opened employing native speaker teachers. The specialist organisation Teachers for Vietnam (see entry in 'Directory of Volunteering Abroad') places graduates from all English-speaking countries, though its headquarters are in the USA.

Outreach International (www.outreachinternational.co.uk) has a long-established programme in Cambodia, a country that tends to be under-represented in the brochures of the main agencies, although BUNAC also runs a programme there. Outreach sends volunteers aged 18–22 to work for three or more months with local NGOs, for instance to teach English (which can open a range of employment opportunities for local people), computing or art to land mine victims, or to work in a small orphanage or art and craft centre. These placements are suitable for volunteers wishing to pursue a career in overseas development or aid work, or those who want genuinely to help a damaged and vulnerable section of society. Physiotherapists and older volunteers are needed for some of the projects, but others are ideal for younger people.

MY GAP YEAR: LAURA PARKER

Laura Parker described her Outreach International placement in the provincial town of Kratie as an 'absolutely superlative experience'.

The work that Veterans International does is admirable, and working with the staff there was both entertaining and enlightening. The staff are really eager to improve their language skills, and I spent about four hours a day teaching. This focused on report writing, yet I also found using the English language Cambodia Daily newspaper for general language work particularly interesting. It was far more relevant to them than any Euro-centric textbook, and invariably sparked interesting discussions about Cambodian politics, history, and scandals.

Apart from teaching duties, simply chatting and getting to know the patients, and having them help me practise my Khmer, was a rewarding activity. One patient, a 16-year-old girl with polio, had applied for a grant to set up the first beauty parlour in her village. She came back to the centre with all the equipment she'd bought from the market and, within no time, we'd kicked the boys out of the office, and all the girls, patients and staff alike, spent the afternoon . . . um . . . 'testing' the merchandise! I think the biggest contrast to a

UK working environment was the pace that everything moves at in Cambodia. SLOWLY! It is easy to get used to this, as it's the most sensible way of coping with the heat and humidity, but far less easy to snap out of once back in stressy, constantly-on-the-go Europe.

Compared to Phnom Penh, Kratie town is, in my opinion, an infinitely nicer place to spend three to six months (or more!), and I think that if anyone has reservations about being based in the provinces for fear of being too remote or lonely or far from creature comforts, they couldn't be more wrong. Once you've been in town for a week, people realise you're not a passing tourist, and will start to recognise you and take an interest. They just generally want to chat and befriend you. Prices will start dropping for you in the market, and you will soon find it hard to get to and from work without bumping into people you know. I was invited along to all the celebrations and parties, and it really angered me how the guidebooks give barely two pages to the entire province. Not only is it a base for exploring the exciting north east of Cambodia (think elephant trekking, minority villages, swimming in stunning waterfalls, and a giant crater lake), there are also a multitude of diversions in town itself - from the trivial, such as getting regular professional manicures costing 125 pence, to the active such as going swimming in the Mekong every day at sunset. I even made the 20-minute swim across one day, fully clothed of course - Khmer style! The river in Kratie is gorgeous, gorgeous, gorgeous, and is very clean. Little beats snacking on fresh fruit shakes or sugarcane juice at one of the riverside stalls, watching the sun set (in technicolour) over the Mekong, on your cycle home from work.

I certainly had some of the funniest times of my life there. Everything in Kratie is a little bit off the wall (in a very charming way), and 'bizarre' was a word I used daily. From having friends give me Khmer hip hop dance lessons (not dissimilar to the Macarena), to the endless amusement of observing the Khmer can-do attitude towards transportation (four piggies on a moto? five people on a push-bike? No problem!), life in Kratie never ceased to amuse, and I can guarantee that volunteering there would be both ridiculously fun, and ultimately rewarding, a combination that makes leaving the hardest part of the placement.

NEPAL

After a decade-long campaign against Nepal's constitutional monarchy, the Maoist rebels have secured its abolition and form the government. Nepal's political problems are not over, but foreigners should no longer be fearful of getting waylaid while trekking and forced to hand over money.

So once again Nepal is a destination to consider for short-term volunteers and casual English teachers. However, people who find voluntary openings in Nepal will be faced with a visa problem. Tourist visas (which can be purchased on arrival for $100 cash) are valid for 90 days (shorter stays are also available for less), and can be extended for $2 a day thereafter, up to a maximum of five months normally. Note that a hefty fine or even prison sentence can be imposed on foreigners found overstaying their visas. A range of organisations make it possible for self-funding volunteers to teach. Of course, living expenses are very low by Western standards, although the fees charged by mediating or gap year organisations such as i-to-i and Africa & Asia Venture, as well as by Nepali agencies (some listed below) can increase the cost significantly. If you want to avoid an agency fee you can make direct contact with schools on arrival. Relevant organisations include:

Alliance Nepal (www.volunteerworkinnepal.org). Opportunities to teach English, help in an orphanage, etc in the Pokhara Valley and Chitwan area for two weeks to three months. Prices from €200 for two weeks to €600 for 12 weeks.

Cultural Destination Nepal, Kathmandu (www.volunteernepal.org.np). Volunteer Nepal, a service work programme. Fee of €650 includes two-week pre-service orientation and homestay throughout. Placements last two to four months, starting February, April, June, August, and October.

HELP (Himalayan Education Lifeline Programme), Kent (www.help-education.org). Volunteer teachers, nurses, and child-carers work in needy schools in Himalayan India (Sikkim, West Bengal, Ladakh, and Himachal Pradesh) and Nepal (Kathmandu Valley, Pokhara, and Chitwan). Fee from £390 to include admin fee and donation. £75 per month needed in addition, for accommodation with host families or in school hostel.

Hope and Home Volunteer Program, Kathmandu (www.hopenhome.org). Volunteer opportunities in the fields of teaching English as well as community, health, and environmental programmes in the Kathmandu Valley, Pokhara, Chitwan, and Nawalparasi. Programme fees cover homestay accommodation and food: from $400 for two weeks, to $1,000 for three months.

Insight Nepal, Pokhara (insight@fewanet.com.np; www.insightnepal.org.np). Seven-week and three-month placements for all post-A level and high school graduate native speakers of English. Participation fee of $690 for seven weeks or $950 for three months.

KEEP (Kathmandu Environmental Education Project), Thamel, Kathmandu (www.keepnepal.org). Opportunities for volunteers to teach English in trekking villages, government schools, etc. Volunteers stay with a host family and must be self-funding.

After **Melissa Evans**'s placement in Kenya was cancelled at the last moment, due to the mass violence that followed the rigged elections, her gap year agency Adventure Alternative had to live up to its name and quickly find her an alternative adventure. It arranged for Melissa to fly a month later to Nepal where she taught in a school:

> It was very very rewarding, as the children really thrived on being taught by a foreign teacher. I found the teaching a challenge as the children struggled with English pronunciation. Sometimes, I found myself unable to understand the children and vice versa. However, familiarity over the three months allowed the language barrier to break down, and conversing with the children was easier by the end of my placement, as I had learned a little Nepali and they had grown used to my pronunciation. Before my gap year, I had the ambition of being a teacher. However, after travelling for the first time my ambition changed, and now I aim to found an orphanage.

INDIA

Volunteering in India sometimes takes the form of teaching, but more often it involves social projects. A wide range of organisations in the UK, in addition to India specialists such as Gap Guru, Learn Overseas, and Development in Action, send volunteers to teach English or undertake other voluntary work in India. For example, Cross-Cultural Solutions, with offices in the USA, UK, Canada, and Australia (www.crossculturalsolutions.org), places volunteers in local organisations in the Himalayas and New

Delhi (as well as Thailand and China). Among the many projects supported by the UK-based Development in Action (entry in 'Directory of Volunteering Abroad'), teaching assignments and social welfare placements are most common. These last for a summer, or five months from September.

MY GAP YEAR: CLAIRE MULLINEAUX

Claire Mullineaux returned from India after a successful pair of placements through Changing Worlds.

After a 10-hour flight with British Airways spent watching Sex and the City, we arrived at the smelly, hot, and humid Chennai airport. Even at 4:30am, there was a sea of excited brown faces awaiting our arrival at the gate. We had a few days to acclimatise and see the sights. We found this very interesting, and were enthralled by the huge platters of food we were given, ranging from bland chutney to 'stupidly spicy orange stuff' (yes, that's the technical name!). We drank from coconuts. On the Friday of that week, we were all taken to our individual placements.

In our orphanage there were 15 houses. Each family had a mother figure and between seven and 11 children. Some children were blood relatives, but every child in the family was treated with the same love and loyalty as each other. I am told a lot of the children were brought there after the tsunami. We taught lower kindergarten on three days a week and upper kindergarten on the other two. We preferred the older ones as they had some idea what we were talking about. The language barrier was quite large, so we took to making exotic sounds and shaking our heads in a bobbing manner like the rest of the Indian population. It is a general response meaning 'yes', 'no', 'maybe', and 'I don't know'. It works!

We ate dinner in the family homes, which was a good time to get to know them and the Indian style of living. The water only came on for 30 minutes at 6am, and sometimes it was late or stopped early (just when we'd shampooed our hair normally). Sometimes it didn't come on at all, which was very frustrating. We were filthy by the end of the day, and although we had to wash under a cold tap it was very refreshing.

After three months, I went to the medical placement at Gremaltes Hospital. I will never forget what I learnt in and out of the classroom. I worked mainly in schools, hostels, slums, and jails teaching nutrition and personal hygiene. I was involved in CAP programmes (Children's Action for Progress), and activity days at Gremaltes. I helped in several fields: leprosy, HIV/AIDS, TB, diabetes, nutrition, skin infections/diseases, joint diseases including arthritis, eye diseases, and fungal infections. I taught post-med students and nurses from all over India and America, which was both horrific and hugely rewarding at the same time. I cannot begin to tell you how amazing this experience was. Nobody really understands what it means when they're told a gap year changes you. Now I understand.

MondoChallenge offers rural placements mainly in the district of Darjeeling in the Himalayan foothills, and has programmes in six of the main cities across India.

SRI LANKA

Volunteers for Educational Support & Learning or VESL (www.vesl.org; see entry in 'Directory of Specialist Gap Year Programmes') is a British charity largely run by volunteers which provides rural Sri Lankan and other Asian communities with exposure to enthusiastic and creative native English speakers.

MY GAP YEAR: RICHARD NEW

Richard New was placed by VESL in a school in Nelliady on the Jaffna Peninsula (in the Tamil north of the country) before communal unrest made the area too dangerous for volunteers. He appreciated the insights he gained that mere travellers never could.

The north of Sri Lanka is probably the most fascinating place I have ever visited. Having emerged from 20 years of civil war, there is much evidence of the scars of battle. Yet the people were some of the most hospitable and positive that I have ever met. Their welcome was as warm as their climate. From the first day, Dan and I were made to feel part of the community.

Our school was well equipped compared to others on the island, yet resources were still scarce. Regardless of problems, the students were enthusiastic and keen to learn. If I could stop them talking about cricket, developing their spoken

English was both challenging and rewarding. I think we made good headway in improving their listening skills especially, and even the younger students became better at understanding complex instructions. On the last day, I was genuinely moved to see my pupils recite poetry by William Wordsworth at a full school assembly. They were also keen to tell me about their lives and country, so I think that overall they taught me as much as I taught them.

Our home life was equally interesting. Dan and I lived with a family who welcomed us into their lives. Due to the lack of electricity, our nightlife tended to end promptly at 8.30. Yet life was not tedious. Dan and I went to a Hindu temple for their annual festival where we were welcomed, fed, and blessed. We were special guests at a local football match, and experienced the thrill of a Karavedy local derby. Most interesting was a tour around an Arrack factory (distillery of the local tipple). It showed us the harsh working environment many Sri Lankan labourers must face. Such experiences would be impossible for most travellers to the area. VESL gave me a unique opportunity to understand the culture and people of northern Sri Lanka.

VOLUNTEERING

Many young people who have travelled in Asia are dissatisfied with the role of tourist, and would like to find a way of making a contribution. It must be stressed that westerners almost invariably have to make a financial contribution to cover food and accommodation as well as their travel and insurance.

If you have never travelled widely in the developing world, you may not be prepared for the scruffiness and level of disorganisation to be found in some places. Not many 18-year-olds would be capable of contributing or benefiting much from a long attachment to a grassroots charity in developing regions. A further difficulty with participating in local voluntary projects (of which there are many) is in fixing anything up ahead of time. Occasionally Asian charities have a representative abroad (usually a committed former volunteer) who can send information about voluntary possibilities, but this is unusual.

INDIAN SUBCONTINENT

Here is a selection of indigenous organisations that can sometimes use paying volunteers:

Bangladesh Work Camps Association, Dhaka (www.mybwca.org). Places volunteers in two-week community development camps between October and March for a fee equivalent to $300. Detailed camp information is available in English. BWCA can also accommodate foreign volunteers on a medium-term basis (one to three months) and longer term.

Dakshinayan (www.dakshinayan.org). Works with tribal peoples in the hills of Rajmahal and nearby plains. Volunteers join grassroots development projects every month and contribute $300 per month.

First Light (www.firstlightindia.org). An NGO running a school in a remote tribal village in West Bengal. A team of international volunteers teaches basic English and sport to the children. The all-in fee to cover living costs is $150 per month.

Mother Teresa's Home for Dying Destitutes, Kolkata. This and other homes run by the Missionaries of Charity in other Indian cities accept committed volunteers, but can offer no accommodation.

Rural Organization on Social Elevation, Kanda (www.rosekanda.org). A community organisation in the Himalayan foothills with the charming acronym 'ROSE', in the state of Uttarakhand. It places volunteers in poor villagers, to teach children and carry out environmental work and organic farming. Volunteers pay Rs 600 a day for board and lodging and a Rs 6,000 registration fee.

Samaseveya Sri Lanka, Anuradhapura. An established NGO that has been doing useful work following the January 2011 floods in Batticaloa. The National Secretariat in Talawa (samasev@sltnet.lk) invites volunteers to help in rural locations.

SMILE Society (www.smilengo.org). Kolkata-based organisation that arranges workcamps and internships in teaching, health, rural development, etc for students from abroad. Volunteers pay no fee but only cover their basic living costs of €100 per week for stays of up to three weeks, and €80 for stays of four to 24 weeks.

Volunteers for Rural India, Harrow (www.vri-online.org.uk). Operates the Explore Rural India scheme for anyone over 18. Volunteers start with three weeks at Amarpurkashi Polytechnic in Uttar Pradesh learning about development, and then join a hands-on project in the region between September and February. The placement fee, which includes orientation and training, is only £265, while living expenses are £2–£3 a day.

Youthreach, New Delhi (www.youthreachindia.org). Matches volunteers with NGOs working to assist disadvantaged children, women, and the environment. Tasks for volunteers include reading to children, teaching academic subjects and art and craft, as well as subjects that require special skills or professional training. Volunteers must be self-supporting but pay no fee to participate.

SOUTH EAST ASIA AND THE FAR EAST

Starfish Ventures (www.starfishvolunteers.co.uk) is a British company that places volunteers of all nationalities in development projects in Thailand, mainly in Surin province, including teaching, dog rescue, school garden construction, and turtle conservation.

Volunteers including gappers are sent out to northern Thailand each year to work in communities of Karen tribespeople. Details of the programme are available from the Karen Hill Tribes Trust (see entry in 'Directory of Specialist Gap Year Programmes').

If signing up for a wildlife project locally, make sure you will feel comfortable. Long-time animal lover **Pascale Hunter** visited an elephant sanctuary in Chiang Mai, but felt that the animals were not treated well. Her friend was very shocked when the *mahout* (elephant handler) took out his slingshot, shot a squirrel, and stuffed it into his pouch for dinner.

Japan is a famously expensive country in which to travel. One way around it is to join a workcamp. More and more workcamp organisations are being established; links to all of them can be found at www.nvda-asiapacific.org, the Network for Voluntary Development in Asia. Joining a short-term volunteer project can be a good way to visit an exotic place such as Mongolia. For example, an NGO in Ulaanbaatar that places international volunteers is the New Choice Mongolian Volunteer Organization (www.volunteer.org.mn). It arranges short- and long-term placements for volunteers to teach English, renovate buildings, etc. for a fee of $945 for a month to $2,045 for up to three months.

Japan and Korea have WWOOF organisations, both of them web-based. It costs 5,500 yen (or A$73) to join WWOOF Japan (Sapporo; www.wwoofjapan.com), whose list of member farms has expanded to 350; and 50,000 won ($53) for the Korean list from WWOOF Korea (www.koreawwoof.com).

While doing his year abroad of a degree in Japanese at Sheffield University and on previous trips, **Joseph Tame** has had a wonderful time WWOOFing:

I spent a few weeks in a beautiful little seaside village on the southern island of Shikoku, working as a volunteer for an organic tangerine co-operative. We would be picked up by local farmers at about 6am, and work with them on the tangerine terraces until 11am when the heat got to be too much to bear. One particularly memorable day was when an Australian WWOOFer and I were given the job of picking caterpillars off the leaves of a huge field of organic Japanese potatoes. Over the course of three hours, we collected two huge sacks of creepy crawlies, but at the end of the day forgot to tie the sacks up – when we returned to the field the following day we found the caterpillars had all escaped and returned to their former homes!

PAID WORK AND WORK EXPERIENCE

Few paid jobs are available to gap year travellers unless they have a contact in Beijing or Singapore, for example, who is able to arrange a business internship. The booming Chinese economy and seeming whole-hearted embracing of western business means that increasing numbers of Chinese companies do take on American and European staff. London-based CRCC Asia (see entry in 'Directory of Work Experience Abroad') is a consulting company that runs internship programmes in Beijing and Shanghai. Placements in legal firms, finance offices, etc don't come cheap: the fee for finding an unpaid position in Beijing is £2,000 for two months, which includes accommodation and visa costs.

A couple of other work experience agencies and a sprinkling of Asian companies focus on matching foreign young people with professional internships, for example Next Step Connections in China and Junior Expat in Indonesia (see entries in 'Directory of Work Experience Abroad').

MY GAP YEAR: JON MCLEOD

During his gap year journalism placement in Shanghai, Jon Mcleod arranged through Projects Abroad, he had a few bizarre experiences. At one point, he was seconded to work as photographer when Daniel Craig came to town to promote a film. Some of the questions being asked by local journalists made Jon wince, for example about Craig's sightseeing itinerary and wardrobe and, bizarrely, who his 'ideal man' might be (a classic example of Chinglish).

Infamous for its absence of press freedom, and until recently relatively shy on the global stage, China is admittedly a curious setting to seek experience and insight into the exposing world of journalism. Sterile, though, it is not. Underpinned by dramatic economic growth, there is a buzz and expectancy surrounding the communist country formerly cloaked in privacy – especially in its most international city Shanghai.

447

A three-month internship with 'That's Shanghai' magazine proved a thrilling, frustrating, and ultimately very valuable experience. The most important aspect was the opportunity to write. Writing short round-ups on the month's happenings, writing restaurant and bar reviews on a heavy stomach and light head, writing about upcoming music, theatre and opera events, and a sporting feature. The role booted me beyond comfort zones of sport and news into the unknown and perturbing territories of books (an uneasy admission given my placement) and opera (yet to convert). But there is nothing more satisfying than to see your piece in print, nor more sobering (but beneficial) when it's edited copy.

Two months of Chinese lessons had armed me with only the basics; as the novelty wore off, the motivation began to haemorrhage and the simplest of phrases were still left hanging awkwardly in the air. Beyond work and the intoxicating lifestyle of Shanghai (I will recover but my bank account won't), trips to Hangzhou, Beijing, and Tibet afforded a wonderful insight into more traditional and historical elements of Chinese and Tibetan culture. From the imposing and communist feel of Tiananmen Square, to the distinctive colour and vibrancy of Lhasa; all were a powerful contrast to the intensely unique and fruitful setting of Shanghai.

HOMESTAYS AND COURSES

With China becoming a global power to be reckoned with, many people with an eye to the future or just an interest in the language are deciding to study Mandarin/Cantonese. Through CESA, **Lucy Millett** signed up for a four-week course in Beijing, in preparation for studying Chinese/Mandarin/Cantonese at university:

Beijing was great, safe, and cheap, with loads of things to do and see. There were lots of bars and clubs on Sanlitun (the bar street) and plenty of shopping streets, touristy sites, quieter and less-visited temples and museums. It was horribly dry, though, grey and sometimes quite smelly, and always noisy, which added to vibrancy. The people are friendly and the place is exciting, I came home craving peace. I loved learning the characters, being able to impress people with simple sentences, looking at the way bits of language linked and clicked together. I found the pinyin [Chinese phonetic alphabet] difficult to pronounce at times, though, and some of the grammar very tricky.

The Japan Homestay Service in Chiba-city (http://home.att.ne.jp/orange/star/homestay) places foreigners with Japanese families for varying charges; the only requirement is 'not to hate Japanese food'. The Hokkaido International Foundation (www.hif.or.jp/en) arranges two-week homestays, mainly for foreign students living in Japan and also an intensive eight-week Japanese Language and Culture Programme in the summer that costs $4,750.

MY GAP YEAR: LORNA DAVIDSON

Lorna Davidson's choice of gap year activity was different from most, although she achieved her goal of getting fit. Through Real Gap, she spent three months at a Martial Arts Academy in China and experienced why 'kung fu' is Chinese for 'hard work'.

I hadn't done much exercise before arriving at the academy, and after hearing about the extensive training I was worried I wouldn't be able to cope. When I first began my training, I didn't know the difference between internal and external martial arts, or even what Shaolin was – it was just something out of Crouching Tiger, Hidden Dragon that looked cool! The training is pretty much suited to you and your skill levels. This made it a lot easier to be around people who had been there up to eight months and were practically flying when I could barely kick above my hip. It's very intense. I stuck it out, and ended up loving the training so much I stayed for an extra month. Sanda classes were hard work, as they involved constantly moving, kicking, spinning, and ducking. In other classes, we learnt different styles of jumping, flipping, cartwheeling, butterfly kicks, and other fancy-named twists. Power training involves weightlifting and other physically challenging tasks, while power stretching involves your master putting you through excruciating pain for 30 seconds in every body part to make you more flexible. It was my favourite, as I always felt very relaxed afterwards, and after two months I could quite easily do the splits, which was one of my goals when going there. Every Friday we had to do the mountain. The mountain was the culmination of the week's training, when everyone had to run half-way up the mountain to some steps, which then had to be run up and down four times before we were allowed to go to the bottom to have a shower. When I first arrived, I could barely even get up to the steps, but by the end I managed to get up and down four times.

I will never forget my last night, when a whole load of my friends (whom I had only known for two months) took me out to dinner. We spent the rest of the night roasting marshmallows in my room using chopsticks and candles, and laughing about the great times we had spent together. Even the translators and the dog joined in.

Dive training is a popular choice for gappers and is offered by (among others) Thailand Gap Internships on a small island near Koh Samui. **Ross Fairgrieve** enjoyed the course on Koh Tao so much that he found himself getting out of bed early in the mornings for the first time since he was seven. He really enjoyed hopping on a moped, sometimes with a local dog on the back, knowing that he had a day of scuba diving and meeting new people from all over the world ahead of him.

MY GAP YEAR: LAUREN SMITH

Lauren Smith is another gap year student who fell in love with Koh Tao. She had booked the usual round-the-world itinerary, but her plans changed completely when she got to Thailand. She stayed on Koh Tao for an extra month, and decided to return later in her gap year after she had gone back home to Shropshire to save more money.

I wanted to use my gap year before going to Cardiff University to study Journalism, Film and Media to further my work experience in the film industry, as it's a hard industry to break. I researched independently to see if there were any videography courses, and found Oceans Below (www.oceansbelow.net) on Koh Tao. I got in contact directly with the company. It was very helpful, but suggested as I had not dived before to look into the opportunities available at Thailand Gap Internships, which offers internships up to and including PADI Divemaster, before I went on to do training and an internship in underwater videography. TGI seemed very personal, adapting the internship to suit the individual and finding the cheapest cost possible.

Completing your Divemaster qualification is done in your own time, although you are expected to help with customers, loading and offloading bags and tanks from the boats. Interning in underwater videography is harder work. You're expected to meet the morning boat between 6am and 7am, depending on the company. You film open water divers till about 11am, then you have the afternoon to capture and edit all the footage from the morning and burn the completed film to CD. After an hour's break, you meet the customers from the morning, show them the movie, and offer to sell it to them. Your day usually finishes at about 7pm.

I felt that the costs of the course were justified. It was an experience of a lifetime, spending five months on one of the most beautiful islands in the world. Not only that, but I've gained valuable work experience that will help me later in life. I hope that my training in videography will make finding a job in the industry easier.

Alternative dive internships can be investigated, such as Mermaid Dive Centre's Learn in Asia instructor training programme in Pattaya, Thailand (www.mermaiddive.com).

TURKEY

Turkey is a wonderful country to travel in, with a wealth of important historic sites, such as Troy and Ephesus, which you will certainly have heard of. Its economy has strengthened considerably since the Turkish lira lost six zeros against the dollar a few years ago. Turkey is a good choice of destination for fledgling English teachers, though few opportunities are available to pre-university gappers with no TEFL training or experience. Although Istanbul is not the capital, it is the commercial, financial, and cultural centre of Turkey, so this is where most of the EFL teaching goes on.

For short-term opportunities, the education department of the youth travel and exchange organisation Genctur in Galatasaray, Istanbul (www.genctur.com), organises summer camps for children where English, German, and French are taught by native speakers who work for seven hours a day in exchange for free board and lodging. Pocket money may also be given according to experience and skills. Applicants must have some experience of working with children.

A WWOOF exchange is operated by the Bugday Association in Istanbul (www.bugday.org/eng). At present, there are about 70 member farms.

Au pair jobs in Turkey usually involve more tutoring of English than domestic chores. The following agencies make placements in Turkey:

Anglo Pair Agency, 40 Wavertree Road, Streatham Hill, London SW2 3SP (020 8674 3605; anglo. pair@btinternet.com). Nannies and au pairs (around 100) for summer or academic year. Au pairs earn £50–£65 a week. Agency has office in Istanbul.

ICEP (International Cultural Exchange Programs) (icep@icep.org.tr). Au pair in Turkey programme for three to 12 months (www.icep.org.tr/english/aupairturkey.asp). Minimum pocket money $200 a month. Interns with Turkish companies receive accommodation, meals, and $150 a month. ICEP also places qualified English teachers who earn from $450 a month.

One persistent problem is that it is generally not acceptable for young women to go out alone in the evenings. But Turkish families are usually very generous and allow their live-in child-carers to share in family life on equal terms, even in their free time and on holidays.

The main Aegean resorts of Marmaris, Kusadasi, and Bodrum absorb a large number of foreign travellers as workers. Other places firmly on the travellers' trail, such as Antalya on the south coast and Goreme in Cappadocia, are also promising. The best time to look is March or early April. Major Turkish yachting resorts are excellent places to look for work, not just related to boats but in hotels, bars, shops, and excursions. A good time to check harbourside noticeboards and to ask captains whether they need anyone to clean or repair their boats is in the lead-up to the summer season and the Marmaris Boat Show in May.

THE MIDDLE EAST

Few gap year students are likely to be seriously considering the Middle East at a time when the region is so troubled. With mass unrest and brutal retaliations in Syria, and alarming reports of government repression in Bahrain and Yemen, this is probably not the best year to tell your family you are off to those countries. Ongoing tensions between Israelis and Palestinians and an escalation of anti-western sentiment throughout the region have dampened enthusiasm for travel and employment in the Middle East. The Iraq and Afghanistan wars have undoubtedly destabilised the area and fanned the flames of Islamic distrust of the west.

Yet many parts of the Middle East remain reasonably calm and untroubled. For example, Jordan has wonderful sights and possibilities for studying Arabic. Perhaps intrepid young travellers can play a small part in diminishing the distrust and tension between the two cultures.

ISRAEL

In the past, Israel was a magnet to young travellers, both Jewish and non-Jewish, who flocked to this tiny complex nation to volunteer on Kibbutizim, earn money on moshavim (co-op farm communities) and pick up bar jobs in Tel Aviv and Eilat. Nowadays, young travellers have barely heard of kibbutzim let alone moshavim, and a recent change in visa regulations mean that paid casual work has pretty much vanished. However, a number of kibbutzim and archaeological digs do take on foreign volunteers (see the entry for the Kibbutz Program Center and the section of Archaeology, both in the 'Volunteering' chapter).

In response to the rise in tuition fees from 2012 and the resulting interest in compressed gap year experiences, a company called Minigap Israel (www.minigap.co.uk) offers a three-month summer trip which includes a short stay on a kibbutz, a hiking expedition and exposure to Jewish culture; the cost is £2,450–£3,950.

AUSTRALIA AND NEW ZEALAND

Australia

Australia has developed a magnificent industry to cater specifically for backpackers and working holi-daymakers. Most hostels both in the cities and the countryside are well informed about local jobs avail-able to travellers; some act as informal employment agencies. Bus companies have routes that shuttle between fruit-picking regions for the benefit of working travellers. Outback properties offer training in the skills necessary to work on a station and then double as a placement agency. Recruitment agencies and employers with seasonal requirements target the backpacking community by advertising in the places they frequent. Free newspapers, magazines and websites carry employment advertisements specifically addressing an audience of backpackers. Employers even co-operate with regional tourist offices to find seasonal staff, as in the South Australian fruit-growing region of the Riverina. There is no shortage of information and assistance available for the newly arrived working holidaymaker.

However, optimism needs to be tempered with realism. Picking up casual work to cover all your travelling expenses is not nearly as achievable in the Australia of 2011–12 as it was 10 years ago. Partly because of the overwhelming numbers of young foreigners on working holiday visas – many of them new graduates fleeing a dire employment situation at home – it is an employer's rather than a jobseeker's market, and the job hunt can be a struggle. In the areas that backpackers have colonised, such as certain suburbs of Sydney and some Queensland islands, travellers on working holiday visas are not at all popular since they have a reputation for Ibiza-type behaviour.

Roger Blake is someone who is willing to turn his hand to anything and has successfully 'blagged' (ie talked) his way into all manner of jobs around the world. Yet he found Australia an uphill struggle, certainly compared to New Zealand. Although he managed to survive on his occasional earnings, he warns to expect a 'rough ride': '*I have met SO many travellers who are leaving Australia after just three months or less of their working holiday visa, thoroughly disgusted with the attitude of employers towards backpackers and the associated struggles of finding an (often lousy) job in the first place . . . But it is not all doom and gloom, and I've had fun between troublesome times.*'

On a more positive note, the economic situation in Australia is relatively robust (partly due to its raw materials, which it can sell to China) and there are still plenty of easy-come, easy-go jobs. For example, of the three newly graduated friends Seb, Alan, and Ali who arrived in Melbourne at the beginning of 2011 with their shiny new working holiday visas, one quickly found work in a smart city restaurant, another in a call centre (a job redeemed by the good wages and camaraderie among the staff, many of them Britons on the same visa), and the third found part-time work at a garden centre, helped by his Diploma in Horticulture. These jobs funded a brilliant lifestyle in Melbourne, but none found it very easy to save for travelling further or even for surf weekends on the nearby resorts along the Great Ocean Road.

RED TAPE

The number of working holiday visas keeps steadily rising, and went from 114,000 in 2006 to 175,000 in 2010. The visa is for people intending to use any money they earn in Australia to supple-ment their holiday funds. Applicants must be between the ages of 18 and 30 and without children. The rules have been relaxed to encourage more working holidaymakers to do jobs in rural areas. You used to be eligible for a working holiday visa only once, but now you can apply for a 12-month extension provided you can prove that you have spent at least 88 days working in regional Australia, for example fruit-picking, pearling, sheep-shearing, or volunteering to help with cleaning up and rebuilding after the devastating floods in Queensland.

Most people apply for a Working Holiday Maker (WHM) visa online, though you can also submit a paper application to any Australian representative outside Australia. When you apply online for an e-WHM visa, there is no need to provide proof of funds, nor do you send in your passport. Applying online via the Australian Department of Immigration website (www.immi.gov.au) is normally straightforward and hassle-free, and should result in an emailed confirmation inside the promised 48 hours that is sufficient to get you into the country. Your passport isn't physically inspected, but your eligibility to work is registered online, which prospective employers can check. The fee for the WHM visa is A$235 (currently £155).

All visa information can be checked at www.immi.gov.au or by ringing the Australian Immigration and Citizenship Information line 09065 508 900 (charged at £1.02 per minute).

PLACEMENT AGENCIES AND SPECIAL SCHEMES

Naturally, Australia is not included as a destination by those gap year organisations that focus on developing countries. However, the following do make placements down under, often in boarding schools, doing conservation work, or working on outback properties: Lattitude Global Volunteering and Changing Worlds are two that have quite large programmes in Australia.

BUNAC, London EC1 (020 7251 3472; downunder@bunac.org.uk). Offers a Work Australia package.

Changing Worlds (01883 340 960; www.changingworlds.co.uk). Paid placements in hotels in tourist hot spots, and on farms throughout Queensland, including some with riding opportunities. Voluntary placements in a zoo and on conservation projects. Teaching placement in Melbourne (mainly outdoor education). Pocket money placements last from three to six months. Most groups go out in September, March, and July; other departure times available on enquiry.

Involvement Volunteers Association, Victoria, Australia (+61 3 9438 6007; ivworld wide@ volunteering.org.au). Volunteers are placed in a network of voluntary projects around Australia (and worldwide) for up to a year. Package costs A$1,200.

IST Plus, Teddington, Middlesex (www. istplus.com/wataus). Work and Travel Australia programme for £320.

Lattitude Global Volunteering, Reading (0118 959 4914; volunteer@lattitude.org.uk; www. lattitude.org.uk). Five- or 11-month programmes as school assistants, in outdoor education, or conservation.

TravellersWorldwide (01903 502 595; www.travellersworldwide.com). Hands-on conservation placements working with kangaroos and dolphins, among others, in wildlife sanctuaries and rehabilitation centres. Challenging volunteer teaching placements with refugees (Australia) or underprivileged children (New Zealand). Professional work experience internships also available in journalism, law, medicine, care, TV, physiotherapy, architecture, etc. Placements start from £995 and are available year-round with flexible start and finish dates.

VisitOz, Queensland (www.visitoz.org). Provides a year-round programme for young people with a working holiday visa who wish to live and work in outback and rural Australia for one year (see entry in 'Directories of Courses').

In addition to the gap year specialists, an increasing number of backpacker travel and youth exchange agencies are offering packages that may be of special interest to first-time travellers in their gap year. Some are all-inclusive; others simply give back-up on arrival. Typically, the fee will include airport pick-up, hostel accommodation for the first few nights, and a post-arrival orientation that advises on how to obtain a tax-file card, suggests employers, and so on. Some even guarantee a job. Various perks are thrown in, such as a telephone calling card and maps.

Downunder Jobs, Hotel Discovery, 167 Franklin Street, Melbourne (www.downunderjobs.com). Helps people with a working holiday visa to set up work, as well as providing first four nights of accommodation and a range of other back-up services for a fee starting at A$245.

Travellers Contact Point. Sells Ultimate Oz arrival package (www.ultimateoz.com.au) for A$599, which includes seven days of accommodation and activities in Sydney, plus airport transfer, access to Job Search service, 12-month mail-holding service, etc.

Workstay Australia (www.workstay.com.au). Source of working holiday and general travel information for backpackers travelling in Australia.

When **Matt Applewhite** chose Australia through a gap year agency, he was not bothered by the fact that the country was considered a soft option by some of his contemporaries. It didn't always feel like a soft option when he looked at his very full timetable of teaching and supervising, but he ended up having not only a fascinating but a fulfilling year in the Northern Territory:

> *As I walked around Kormilda College for the last time, it seemed that every room, every corner had a memory associated with it. A glimpse of the college canoes awakened the vivid memories of Year 8 outback camps, when by day under the blazing sun we noisily splashed around the leafy billabongs and bushwalked through Crocodile Dundee's backyard. A traditional Aboriginal drawing in the library allowed me to reminisce about my trip to the remote community of Peppimenarti, and the way in which the welcoming community allowed me to observe the elders silently weaving traditional baskets, watch the village children learn English in the community school, and appreciate their cultural traditions, dignity and warmth. I reflected on all the experiences I'd relished, and how lucky I'd been to spend time in this place.*

WORK EXPERIENCE

Private employment agencies are very widespread and can be a good potential source of jobs for travellers, especially those with office skills, computer, data processing, or financial experience. A surprising number positively encourage UK travellers on working holidays, often by circulating their details to hostel managers. The offered wages are good too: from A$17.50-$20 an hour for clerical work, up to A$25 for computing. This might be an ideal route for a student who has done a secretarial or business skills course at the beginning of their year out. Note that in some cases lower youth wages may apply to those under 20.

Two companies that mediate unpaid work experience placements in Australia are Australian Internships and Intern Options (see entries in 'Directory of Work Experience Abroad'). The latter operates out of a London office and has an impressive range of unpaid work experience placements available in Australia and New Zealand; its fixing fee is £800 for unpaid internships in Sydney.

Australian Internships is based in Brisbane and offers internships in many fields of employment. Obviously, the hospitality industry is one with a multitude of openings, one of which was filled by **Ane du Preez** from South Africa. She is currently completing a food and beverage internship in a four-star resort in the lovely Western Australian town of Broome:

> *I've been working at a fantastic resort, and I am grateful to be part of something so wonderful. I did an RSA [Responsible Service of Alcohol] course, worked in different restaurants at the resort, and can't wait to get more experience and learn more about weddings and wine. There is no better place to learn about wine than Australia! I have only been here for a few months, but I have already got memories for a lifetime. I went kayaking at the port and on a camel ride on the beach, had kangaroo steak, and visited the pearl farm at Willie Creek. There is so much more to experience in Broome. I can't wait for*

more – I will stay focused and try to make the most of my experience here. Life is progress and not a station.

Anyone with experience of the horse industry should contact the agency IEP-UK in the UK (www.iepuk. com), whose Australian partner is IRE (International Rural Exchange) in rural Western Australia (www. ire.org.au).

Interesting research projects take place throughout Australia, and some may be willing to include unpaid staff looking for work experience. For example, a research station in northern Queensland operated by the Australian Tropical Research Foundation in Cape Tribulation (www.austrop.org.au) welcomes paying volunteers who usually stay two or three weeks, though extensions are possible. Volunteers assist in research and station activities such as radio-tracking bats, counting figs, stomping grass for forest regeneration, constructing buildings, digging holes, and running the Bat House visitor centre. Volunteers are asked to pay US$35 a day to cover food and accommodation.

MY GAP YEAR: HOLLY TATE

Holly Tate hugely enjoyed a 10-week work experience placement in Sydney with Pedestrian TV (www.pedestrian.tv). Her internship was in the area of film, with duties including video production, online publishing, interview research, and conducting interviews.

When I contacted Intern Options they replied quickly, seemed really helpful, and dedicated themselves to finding me an internship that suited me. They gave me a couple of job profiles, but with the third I found something that really interested me. I arrived in Sydney at the beginning of January and started straightaway. My internship has been brilliant, and I've really been able to get stuck into the office workload. I generally work a full week, but my bosses are really easygoing and if I want to take an afternoon or day off every now and again to go and do stuff in the city they're more than OK with it. The office is really small, everyone gets on well, and it's a pretty fun place to work. Since I arrived, I've learnt a lot of things, such as editing, which I'd never done before. They've included me in lots of production meetings and creative brainstorming sessions for new projects, which has been invaluable experience for when I apply for jobs back home.

The Australian Institute of Marine Science (AIMS) at Cape Ferguson near Townsville (+61 7 4753 4240; www.aims.gov.au) maintains a register of applicants interested in temporary or casual work, and also has some places for graduates and undergraduates looking for work experience in marine research; it would be most unusual for a school leaver to be accepted, although anyone with a scuba diving certificate and a keen interest should make contact with relevant members of permanent staff who might be willing to support an application.

THE JOB HUNT

The glut of travelling workers is especially bad in Sydney and on the Queensland 'Route' between Sydney and Cairns, whereas Melbourne and Adelaide may offer better prospects. In addition to asking potential employers directly (which is the method used by most successful jobseekers in Australia), the main ways of finding work are online recruitment sites such as jobaroo.com or www.bestjobs au.com, online job adverts on sites such as craigslist, and noticeboards, especially at backpackers (ie hostels).

Some charities are perennial advertisers for paid fundraisers. The most amusing account of earning money this way comes from **Chris Miksovsky**, who was paid an hourly wage (but only a few hours a week) as a street collector in Brisbane:

> *My year in Australia ended with a rather fitting and hilarious job – collecting for the Wilderness Society, a sort of Australian Greenpeace, wearing a koala costume. After a brief interview with the Koala co-ordinator ('So, Chris, do you have any experience walking around as a big furry animal?'), I found myself in a busy square wearing a full-body fluffy grey koala suit complete with fake felt claws and droopy oversize ears. Actually, it works. Takings per hour were about A$25 on average. For me, probably the best thing was that you learned to not take yourself so seriously.*

The Wilderness Society runs a national face-to-face membership campaign called 'Wilderness Defenders', which aims to sign up people to donate by standing order. The charity has so far succeeded in protecting millions of hectares of Australian wilderness. It is always hiring new people for its teams, with some chances of travelling around the country (www.wilderness.org.au). Commission is paid on top of a basic wage. In his post-university gap year(s), **Richard Griffiths** worked in Sydney as a charity fundraiser/campaigner for the Wilderness Society, an experience which eventually fed into him becoming a UK policy adviser on climate change.

As mentioned, the dense network of hostels is a goldmine of information. Gappers find employment in the hostels themselves too. **Stephen Psallidas** describes the proliferation of work:

> *I've met loads of people working in backpackers' hostels. Typically, you work two hours a day in exchange for your bed and a meal. Work may involve cleaning, driving the minibus, staffing reception, etc. and is always on an informal basis. I will be jumping on the bandwagon myself soon. I'll be completely shattered from picking tomatoes so I'm going to 'work' in a hostel in Mission Beach, where the owners invited me to take on a job when I stayed there earlier. I'm going to rest up in a beautiful place before continuing my travels, and not spend any of my hard-earned dollars.*

THE OUTBACK

Most of Australia's area is scorched, sparsely populated land that is known loosely as the outback. Beyond the rich farming and grazing land surrounding the largest cities, there are immense properties supporting thousands of animals and acres of crops. Many of these stations (farms) are so remote that flying is the only practical means of access, though having a vehicle can be a great help in an outback job search.

Your chances of getting a job as a station assistant (a jackaroo or jillaroo) will be improved if you have had experience with sheep, riding, or any farming or mechanical experience. Several farmers are in the business of giving you that experience before helping you to find outback work, like the one mentioned on p354 in the VisitOz scheme.

JJ Oz (+61 0428 617 097; ww.jjoz.com.au) offers a choice of five- and 14-day courses at Bingara north of Tamworth, New South Wales (NSW); the costs are A$670 and A$1,580 respectively, including transport from Sydney. In the same area, the Leconfield Jackaroo and Jillaroo School (Kootingal, NSW 2352; +64 02 6769 4230; www.leconfieldjackaroo.com) runs an 11-day outback training course costing A$950; on completion, successful participants will be guided in the direction of paying jobs.

CONSERVATION VOLUNTEERING

Several organisations give visitors a chance to experience the Australian countryside or bush. The main non-profit conservation organisation in Australia is called, predictably enough, Conservation Volunteers Australia (www.conservationvolunteers.com.au), and it places volunteers from overseas in its Conservation Experience projects, though the charges are quite steep. Sample projects include tree planting, erosion and salinity control, seed collection from indigenous plants, building, and maintaining bush walking tracks, etc. Overseas volunteers are welcome to become involved in a two- to six-week package, which will include food and accommodation and all project-related transport; bookings must be made via an approved agent, which in the UK includes Oyster Worldwide and WAVA.

Nicky Stead was forced to take a gap year at the last minute and hurriedly started researching. The project that caught her eye was doing conservation work in Australia, and soon she was saving money for the placement and the flight. She had done a few conservation projects in the Lake District so she knew what she was letting herself in for, and this appealed to her more than teaching. So she signed up for eight weeks based in Adelaide and had a marvellous time:

> *Going to Australia was the best thing I ever did. Everything worked out as it was meant to, I had no problems at all. We lived in Adelaide, but travelled all over South Australia on different projects. We planted trees by a flooded mineshaft, built a fence on the coast of the Great Australian Bight, and weeded on the banks of the huge River Murray. We worked from 8am to 4pm, which was not unreasonable, and with a break mid-morning and an hour for lunch it wasn't too strenuous. The fee I'd paid covered food, accommodation (which was often very very basic), transport, and training. At the end the estate manager wrote me a great reference.*

More ad hoc opportunities may present themselves and cost considerably less. **Daniele Arena** from Italy stumbled across a project on the coast of Queensland that appealed to him:

> *One of the most amazing experiences I had in Oz was the time I was volunteering at the Turtle Rookery in Mon Repos Beach. We could pitch our tent for free, and gave a small contribution of A$5 a day for food. The work was to patrol the beach waiting for nesting turtles and, when they came in, to tag and measure them and the nest. This goes on between November and March. I was fortunate enough to get this by chance, but normally there's quite a few people who want to do it.*

For further information, contact the Mon Repos Conservation Park on +61 07 4159 1652.

WWOOF is very active in Australia, and has a huge supply of unpaid work opportunities on organic farms, etc. WWOOF Australia's headquarters are near Buchan in Victoria (+61 03 5155 0218; www. wwoof.com.au), and their publicity is widely distributed through backpacker haunts. The *Australian WWOOF Book* contains about 2,200 addresses throughout the country for organic farmers and hosts looking for short- or long-term voluntary help or to promote cultural exchange. The list comes with membership, which is sold with accident insurance at a cost of A$60 within Australia (A$30 extra to cover overseas postage, or A$5 within Australia).

An internet-based exchange for work-for-keep volunteers can be found at www.helpx.net, where more than 600 Australian hosts are listed. To register for the premier service of this excellent online community, it is now necessary to pay €20 for two years' membership.

FRUIT PICKING

Many gap year students fund their travels around Australia by migrating between fruit and vegetable harvests. A short surf of the internet will soon take you to harvesting information since the need is so acute. The National Harvest Labour Information Service, based in Mildura, Victoria (+61 1800 062 332; www.jobsearch.gov.au/harvesttrail), is funded by the federal government, and therefore free to users. Alternative sources of vacancies are www.harvesthotlineaustralia.com.au and www.goharvest. com (for around Darwin, Bundaberg, and Stanthorpe Queensland only).

Although harvesting work is often not hard to *get*, some find it hard to make any money. The apple/ pear/grape crates may look quite small at the outset but will soon seem unfillable, with mysterious false bottoms. Many eager first-timers do not realise how hard the work will be physically, and give up before their bodies acclimatise. But you should have faith that your speed will increase fairly rapidly, and with it your earnings.

THE TOURIST INDUSTRY

Casual catering wages, both in the cities and in remote areas, are reasonably good; for example, the award rate for casual waiting staff in New South Wales starts at A$19 an hour, with weekend loadings. Although tipping was traditionally not practised in Australia, it is gradually becoming more common, and waiting staff in trendy city establishments can expect to augment their basic wage to some extent.

Standards tend to be fairly high, especially in popular tourist haunts, so inexperienced gap year students have little chance of being hired to work in a restaurant or pub. A common practice among restaurant bosses in popular places from Bondi Beach to the Sunshine Coast is to give a jobseeker an hour's trial or a trial shift and decide at the end whether or not to employ them.

MY GAP YEAR: LAURA PANTRY

Laura Pantry's reasons for heading down under for a gap year, instead of doing a PhD as she had intended, were different from most. After six months of chemotherapy she decided she wanted to take a year out rather than return to studying. After doing a basic online search she came across one that strongly appealed, a three-month voluntary placement in a Queensland zoo arranged by Changing Worlds.

I was determined to incorporate some voluntary work into my gap year, even though I knew my chosen destination of Australia wasn't usually a location where voluntary work was offered. The zoo placement was obviously perfect. I then worked various hospitality jobs to fund my travels around the rest of the country. Finding work was never a problem. I had some bar/waitressing experience (the most important factor seemed to be experience) and I wasn't fussy. This led me to jobs from luxury hotels to outback pubs.

Working in the zoo was a dream come true. Every day, I was genuinely thanked for my help and made to feel valued. The work wasn't all menial. We were entrusted to carry enclosure keys and allowed to work independently once we had proven our reliability. Hospitality jobs varied. Pay was generally good; some agency jobs were dependent on available shifts, other positions like the outback pub jobs were full-time and included food and board on top of a weekly wage.

My money was saved until I could afford to go out on another adventure. By working hard, I was able to visit Stradbroke Island, the Gold Coast, Sunshine Coast, rainforests, and wildlife parks. I was also able to buy a car with friends and drive across the country, stopping at Uluru and Kings Canyon, then driving across the Nullarbor to Perth. I stopped to earn more funds, then flew to Melbourne to explore the markets and Phillip Island before getting to Sydney for Christmas and New Year. I climbed the Harbour Bridge and sunbathed on Bondi Beach. All in all, I did as much as I could, time and money permitting.

My advice is go out with a list of 10 things you have to do before you come home. If you can do more it'll be a bonus. Incidentally, since coming back off my gap year I've decided to retrain as a nurse and am in the final stages of the course. I have been offered a job on the Gold Coast of Australia, and am due to move back there in October. So I guess you could say my gap year really did change my life!

One tourist area which is not normally inundated with backpacking jobseekers is the stretch of Victoria's coast between Dromana and Portsea on the Mornington Peninsula near Melbourne. Although most jobs don't start until after Christmas, the best time to look is late November or early December.

If exploring Australia is your target rather than earning high wages, it is worth trying to exchange your labour for the chance to join an otherwise unaffordable tour. Camping tour operators in Kakadu and Litchfield Park have been known to take people on this way; try for example Intrepid Connections (www.connections.travel).

DIVING AND WATERSPORTS

The dive industry is a substantial employer. Non-divers (almost exclusively female) can try to find work as 'hosties' (hostesses) who make beds, clean cabins, and generally tidy up. Culinary skills and an ability to speak Japanese would be definite pluses. A non-diver would almost certainly be able to fix up some free dive lessons and thus obtain their basic Open Water Diver qualification while being paid to do so.

Year-out travellers who have a sailing qualification might find temporary work instructing. To take just one example, Northside Sailing School at Spit Bridge in the Sydney suburb of Mosman (www. northsidesailing.com.au/employment.html) offers casual instructing of kids during school holidays to travellers who have experience in teaching dinghy sailing.

MY GAP YEAR: NINA FITTON

Nina Fitton spent the beginning of her gap year with Flying Fish in Australia.

Having been on a number of sailing/windsurfing family holidays, I thought it would be good to improve my personal skills and get the instructor qualifications so that I could work at a holiday centre during the summer of my gap year, and in future uni holidays. So I signed up for the 12-week sail/windsurf instructor traineeship with Flying Fish in Sydney. Living in Manly was amazing - wonderful weather, fantastic shops, a great beach, relaxed lifestyle, and excellent nightlife. The first six weeks were spent sailing in Topaz Magnos. We were worked hard, but it was intense and successful training, which improved my sailing loads. One day we went out in 30 knots of wind, and caned it up and down, kite up, crew on the wire, flat out - great fun. I passed my sailing instructor moderation with flying colours - I obviously perform well under pressure!

Moving on to the windsurfing ... it's now my favourite hobby. One day, I could hardly balance on the board with a 3.5m sail, the next I was planing across the bay, in the harness and footstraps. So much fun! Again, I passed the instructor moderation, so I'm now qualified to teach both sports.

The people on my course, and on all the other Fish courses in Sydney (yachting, diving, surfing), were awesome - a great group who provided endless entertainment. We tended to all go out as one big group, having warmed up for the evening at home playing 'Beer Pong', building human pyramids, having cake fights. The socials were also always amusing - with Bond or Hawaiian themes, cocktails, barbecues, a real mixture. There were evenings spent singing karaoke, trolley racing, midnight swimming on Manly Beach or in a hotel fountain, at the Sydney Opera House Bar, or at a mask party.

My gap year's been awesome, I can't imagine not having taken a year out. It's changed me as a person, making me so much more confident and giving me skills and hobbies that I wouldn't have if I'd gone straight to uni. I've met loads of great people, and done loads of cool stuff.

Flying Fish runs a structured watersports training and recruitment programme in Australia. After yacht, dive, surfing, and windsurfing training, graduates can take advantage of the free careers advice and a recruitment service to help find work in the industry for the rest of their gap year. Many trainees who have completed Professional Dive Training with Flying Fish at the Pro Dive Academy in Sydney go on to work at Pro Dive's network of resorts in Australia and the South Pacific. (See entry for Flying Fish in 'Directory of Specialist Gap Year Programmes'.)

SKI RESORTS

Another holiday area to consider is the Australian Alps, where ski resorts are expanding and gaining in popularity. Jindabyne (NSW), on the edge of Kosciuszko National Park, and Thredbo are the ski job capitals, though Mount Buller, Falls Creek, Baw Baw, and Hotham in the state of Victoria are relatively well-developed ski centres too. The big companies do their hiring between January and Easter, though you might be lucky if you show up in the resorts couple of weeks before the season opens in June. Check out sites such as www.fallscreekemployment.com and www.thredbo.com.au (search 'Snow Jobs').

TRAVELLING FAIRS

Although it is partly a case of being in the right place at the right time, you might find a job at a travelling fair such as the Melbourne Show. To get a place, you need to go to the site and walk around asking for work. Some jobs are paid hourly, while others pay a percentage of takings; the latter should be accepted only by those with very outgoing personalities who can draw in the punters. Even if you don't land a job before the show opens, it is worth hanging in there in case of last-minute cancellations. You can also get a job dismantling the rides at the end, which is very physically demanding work.

Geertje Korf, on a gap year between studying archaeology and taking up a career, was at first thrilled to land a job with a travelling fair, but it wasn't all as exciting as she had hoped:

> *The work itself was good enough, helping to build up the stalls and working on the 'laughing clowns' game. But the family I got to work for were not extremely sociable company. As a result, when we left one place and headed for the next, I would spend time (about a week) until the next show day lonely, wandering around incredibly hot and dusty little country towns where there was absolutely nothing to do, while the showmen sat in a little circle drinking beer and not even talking to me.*

Loneliness was not a problem for **Sam Martell** from the Orkneys when he spent a year going round the world after university – and he earned a fair whack for a short burst:

> *A girl I met on a tour at Byron Bay got me a job in Brisbane at the Queensland State Fair in the second week of August. I was paid cash in hand working on a bouncy castle, rescuing scared kids from the slide and chatting to the mums – it was great. In seven days, I clocked up $73^{1}/_{2}$ hours and took home A$735, which meant I could afford the Whitsundays sailing trip.*

AU PAIRING

The demand for live-in and live-out childcare is enormous in Australia. Applicants are often interviewed a day or two after registering with an agency and start work immediately, provided they have a couple of checkable references. A number of au pair agencies place European and Asian women with working holiday visas in live-in positions, usually for a minimum of three months. Not all placements require childcare experience. As in America, a driving licence is a valuable asset. As well as long-term posts, holiday positions for the summer (December to February) and for the ski season (July to September) are available. Try any of the following:

Australian Nanny & Au Pair Connection, Kooyong, Victoria (+61 3 9824 8857; www.australian-nannies.info).

Dial-an-Angel (+61 1300 721111; www.dial-an-angel.com.au). Long-established agency with franchised branches throughout Australia.

Family Match Au Pairs & Nannies (+61 2 4363 2500; www.familymatch.com.au). Agency places many working holidaymakers; 25–35 hours per week, for pocket money of A\$180–\$250, plus all live-in expenses.

People for People, Brookvale, NSW (+61 2 9971 1393; www.peopleforpeople.com.au). Welcomes working holidaymakers for three-month summer positions. Starting wage of \$210 per week (live-in) for 30 hours per week.

New Zealand

All those nervous mothers of prospective gap year students who used to believe that New Zealand was the safest destination on earth have had to think again since the devastating earthquake of February 2011 destroyed much of Christchurch; several backpackers were among the 172 confirmed dead. One of the worst aspects of the disaster is that recurring aftershocks have damaged early attempts at repairing buildings and sewerage systems. It will be a long time before Christchurch regains its former status as a safe and welcoming haven for backpackers.

Most year-out travellers simply travel around New Zealand rather than work or study. Typically, students earn money in Australia to fund a holiday in New Zealand, which includes the obligatory bungee jump or other adrenaline sport in Queenstown. Other enterprising gappers get a working holiday visa for New Zealand (see below) and hunt out their own jobs.

PLACEMENT ORGANISATIONS

Lattitude Global Volunteering has been sending year-out travellers to boarding schools for many years. Because New Zealanders are so fanatical about sport, schools place a strong emphasis on outdoor activities, and gappers make ideal helpers. Most of these placements last for a whole year from the end of August, though a few seven-month placements start in February.

Specialist agency Tutors Worldwide (www.tutorsworldwide.org) has offices in Wales and Auckland, and recruits school leavers to spend an academic year at prep schools and high schools around New Zealand. Many posts involve a lot of coaching and supervision of sporting activities. The placement fee is £500.

BUNAC in London (020 7251 3472; downunder@bunac.org.uk) has a Work New Zealand programme that provides a Work Exchange Holiday Visa (unique to BUNAC) or an ordinary working holiday visa, job assistance from BUNAC's partner organisation IEP, and other benefits, for a programme fee of £349. You can also buy a package directly from IEP (www.worknewzealand.org.nz).

Another gap year placement company to operate in New Zealand is Changing Worlds (www.changingworlds.co.uk), which offers three or six-month job placements on the ski slopes or in hotels in Queenstown, or the chance to volunteer on farms or in a school. Opportunities exist to do unpaid work in a boatyard with dinghies and yachts. The programme fee, including flights, is £2,630.

RED TAPE

Visitors from the UK need no visa to stay for up to six months. Young travellers entering the country might be asked to show an onward ticket and have about NZ\$1,000 per month of their proposed stay (unless they have pre-paid accommodation or a New Zealand backer who has pledged support in a crisis). In practice, respectable-looking travellers are unlikely to be quizzed at entry.

The UK Working Holiday Scheme was considered so successful in addressing severe labour shortages in seasonal work that the maximum duration has been extended from one year to 23 months, and the quota removed. The scheme allows any eligible Briton aged 18–30 to obtain a working holiday visa, allowing them to take temporary or full-time work in New Zealand. Applicants must have the equivalent of NZ$350 for each month they intend to stay, as well as enough to cover a return airfare. Participants are permitted to work for up to 12 months of the two-year visa validity, either consecutively or cumulatively. Anyone who has worked for at least three months in horticulture or viticulture can apply to extend their working holiday permit by three months. Information can be obtained from the New Zealand Immigration Service at New Zealand House, Haymarket, London in person, by phone on 09069 100 100 (charged at £1 per minute), or online at www.immigration.govt.nz, an admirably comprehensive and up-to-date site.

Applications for all working holiday schemes can be made online from anywhere in the world. The fee (currently NZ$140/£70) will be payable by credit card at the time of application. Other working holiday schemes (maximum duration one year) are open to Irish, American, Canadian, Dutch, Japanese, and many other nationalities, mostly on a reciprocal basis.

CASUAL WORK

New Zealand is a country where it may be better to take enough money to enjoy travelling, and perhaps supplement your travel fund with some cash-in-hand work, odd jobs, or work-for-keep arrangements. Because New Zealand has a limited industrial base, most temporary work is in agriculture and tourism. As in Australia, hostels and campsites are the best sources of information on harvesting jobs (and there is a wealth of budget accommodation throughout New Zealand). Often, local farmers co-operate with hostel wardens, who collate information about job vacancies or may circulate notices around youth hostels – for example 'Orchard Work Available January to March; apply Tauranga Hostel' – so always check the hostel noticeboard (bearing in mind that some hostels entice jobseekers with a vague promise of local work simply to fill beds). **Ian Fleming** soon realised how valuable hostels could be in his job hunt:

> *During our travels around the North and South Islands, the opportunity to work presented itself on several occasions. While staying in the Kerikeri Youth Hostel, we discovered that the local farmers would regularly come into the hostel to seek employees for the day or longer. (This was in July, which is out-of-season.) My advice to any person looking for farm work would be to get up early, as the farmers are often in the hostel by 8.30am.*

Backpackerboard.co.nz has lots of useful job information and tips on budget travel for backpackers in New Zealand. Two recent adverts offered free accommodation in exchange for gardening, and another urgently needed helpers on a llama farm park on the South Island. Similarly, the Travellers' Billboard part of the Budget Backpackers Hostels group website (www.bbh.co.nz) includes job information; at the time of writing, there were 45 hostel vacancies listed, among others.

Private agencies are also involved in the working holiday market. New Zealand Job Search (www.stayatbase.com/work) is a specialist job search centre for travellers attached to BASE Auckland ACB backpacker hostel (Level 3, 229 Queen Street; +64 0800 462 396; jobs@nzjs.co.nz). Work starter packs starting from NZ$345 include a 12-month registration with NZ Job Search, job placement service and various perks (one-way airport transfer, orientation session, sim card, etc.).

Gap Year NZ, based in Leeds (www.gapyear-newzealand.co.uk), is a commercial website dedicated to helping people take a gap year in New Zealand. The website offers live job listings in various work fields, including fruit picking, hospitality, clerical and adventure tourism, plus general information to help plan a trip. The affiliated Indie Travel Company (www.indietravelcompany.com) sells starter packs to New Zealand (and Australia) from £75.

A good resource is Seasonal Jobs NZ (www.seasonaljobs.co.nz), which provides details on current job vacancies. The fact that there are two other sites offering a similar service indicates how much seasonal work is available in this agricultural little country (www.seasonalwork.co.nz and the Hawkes Bay-based www.pickapicker.co.nz).

RURAL AND CONSERVATION VOLUNTEERING

WWOOF NZ (www.wwoof.co.nz) is popular and active, with 830 farms and smallholdings on its fix-it-yourself list that welcome volunteers in exchange for food and accommodation. The list costs NZ$40 for online access only, NZ$50 for a printed booklet.

Another organisation matches working visitors with about 350 farmers throughout New Zealand. Farmstays can last from three days to several months. Farm Helpers in New Zealand in Palmerston North (www.fhinz.co.nz) charges NZ$25 for its membership booklet, containing all the addresses. No experience is necessary, and between four and six hours of work a day are requested. The co-ordinator advises that hosts in the Auckland area tend to be oversubscribed, so that it is best to head into the countryside.

Another possibility is the free internet-based exchange of work-for-keep volunteers that can be found at helpx.net, where an impressive 725+ hosts in New Zealand are listed. Originally set up by a British backpacker in New Zealand, the scheme is flourishing and expanding and now offers an upgrade to premium membership for €20 for two years.

The New Zealand Department of Conservation (DOC) carries out habitat and wildlife management projects throughout New Zealand, and publishes a detailed *Calendar of Volunteer Opportunities* (see www.doc.govt.nz) that lists all sorts of interesting-sounding projects, from counting bats to maintaining historic buildings and cleaning up remote beaches. Most require a good level of fitness and a contribution to expenses, though not always. The DOC also needs volunteer hut wardens at a variety of locations. Details are available from any office of the Department of Conservation.

Paul Bagshaw from Kent spent a thoroughly enjoyable week on an uninhabited island in Marlborough Sound, monitoring kiwis, the flightless birds whose numbers have been seriously depleted. An ongoing programme removes them from the mainland to small islands where there are no predators:

> *The object of the exercise was to estimate the number of kiwis on Long Island north of Picton. As the kiwi is nocturnal, we had to work in the small hours. Because it's dark, it's impossible to count them, so we had to spread out and walk up a long slope listening for their high-pitched whistling call. During the day, they hide in burrows and foliage, so it is very rare to see one. One night, when we heard one rustling around our camp, my girlfriend went outside with a torch and actually managed to see it. She was so excited that she couldn't speak, and resorted to wild gesticulations to describe its big feet and long beak. The island has no water source except rainwater which collects in tanks, all very basic. We lived in tents and prepared our own meals from supplies brought over from the mainland. Our one luxury was a portaloo.*

Conservation Volunteers New Zealand, with an office in Auckland (+64 09 376 7030; www.conservation volunteers.co.nz), is a non-profit organisation operating on both islands, which it accepts overseas volunteers to monitor wildlife, plant trees, maintain tracks, and so on. Overseas volunteers can book a four-week or six-week package through CVA's office in Victoria, through agents abroad (see website), or on arrival in Auckland.

Easily confused with this is the New Zealand Trust for Conservation Volunteers (NZTCV), which matches both local and international volunteers with conservation projects of all kinds to counteract the loss of native bush and wildlife. Details are available on its website (www.conservationvolunteers.org.nz). NZTCV has created a central database on which individuals can register to be put in touch with organisations running conservation projects.

SKI RESORTS

The last couple of years have seen several New Zealand ski schools beginning to offer instructor training to people from the northern hemisphere. Skiers and riders from all over the world congregate in New Zealand during the northern summer (ie from the beginning of July to October). The New Zealand ski schools listed in the 'Directory of Ski Training Courses' operate in several ski centres in the South Island: Queenstown, Cardrona, Treble Cone at Wanaka, and other locations. Many of New Zealand's ski fields are wonderfully uncrowded compared to their European counterparts. Most courses lead to the NZSIA (New Zealand Ski Instructors Alliance) levels 1 and 2 exams, qualifications that are recognised around the world; every year, graduates from New Zealand's ski schools go on to work in resorts worldwide.

MOTHERS' TIP

All the ski schools in New Zealand profess to be ideally suited to gap year travellers, since they provide a safe and friendly English-speaking environment, while being on the other side of the world.

A confirmed skier since adolescence, **Pete Thompson** was delighted to discover that the three-month ski season in the New Zealand Alps fitted neatly into the summer vacation from Exeter University:

Using a mixture of money left over from my gap year before uni, work from the previous summer, and some parental loans, I did a season with SnowTrainers in New Zealand during the summer between my second and third years of university. I was recommended SnowTrainers by a friend whom I met in Exeter, who had done it on his gap year. At the time, I thought all the companies based in Queenstown would be pretty much the same, so I just took his advice. It turned out for the best and I'm glad I went with SnowTrainers. The group was much more international than those taking the other courses, with participants from Poland, the US, and Canada, as well as England, Scotland, Ireland, Australia, and of course New Zealand. Once the various companies had crossed paths, it made for great friendly rivalries on the slopes and in the bars. The course in NZ was brilliant because everyone was there for the same reason, and we lived together, skied together, and partied together.

LATIN AMERICA

Two or three decades ago, when everybody was flocking east, few adventurous young travellers from Britain considered South or Central America. Possibly because Britain has few colonial ties with that part of the world, it was less well known than India, South East Asia, or Africa. With the recent decline in airfares to the Americas, the situation has changed, and thousands of gappers now head to that great Spanish-speaking continent (including Portuguese-speaking Brazil). They travel independently, mostly sticking to the gringo trail (see chapter on travel in Latin America), going on adventure tours, joining a grassroots voluntary organisation, or signing up with one of the specialist gap year programmes that combine volunteering in community service or scientific research, language study, and active travel.

PLACEMENT AGENCIES

The project and expedition organisation Quest Overseas (www.questoverseas.com) operates a 13-week package from January to April, split into three phases: an intensive Spanish language course

MY GAP YEAR: ANNA FRAYLING-CORK

Anna Frayling-Cork chose to go to South America in her gap year with the Christian organisation Latin Link, partly because she thought the chances of doing worthwhile work would be better.

Anna welcomed the fact that the organisation has a residential orientation week in England, where she could learn about what was in store for her in the four months ahead, meet her fellow volunteers, and generally calm her nerves. The two seven-week projects that comprised her gap year were in Argentina, one in a distant suburb of Buenos Aires, the other near the centre of Salta, which is an attractive historic city, though security at their lodgings was an issue. In both cases, the team was assigned the task of helping to build a church or pastor's house. At times they had to question how useful their contribution was, especially in the first project where the official building supervisor never showed up, and so work was directed by the pastor himself.

One of the great advantages of joining a project is that inevitably you meet potential travelling companions. After their stint as volunteers was over, Anna and three friends took a marvellous trip by bus and train to Arequipa (where a bus strike stranded them for a while), to Machu Picchu (of course), on to Lake Titicaca and La Paz, and back to Argentina, which involved a scary change of train in Oruro in the middle of Bolivia, in the middle of the night.

in Quito or Sucre or Portuguese course in Brazil, followed by a month-long attachment to a voluntary project such as working with deprived children in Peru, conserving Peru's rainforests, or working in animal rehabilitation in Bolivia. Finally, the longest stint is a six-week expedition in the Andes, which is also available on its own if preferred. The current average cost, excluding flights but including insurance is £4,400, plus a suggested project donation of £700.

Gap year specialist Venture Co (www.ventureco-worldwide.com) combines a language course, local aid projects, and expeditions on a range of programmes lasting from 49 to 105 days in Latin America. Programmes start with a two-week intensive Spanish course given in Quito, Ecuador, in Cusco, Peru, or in Pucón in Chile. Participants then spend four weeks on a local aid project before embarking on an eight- or nine-week expedition through the Andes.

MY GAP YEAR: LAURA BROWN

Laura Brown remembers her time in Mexico at a special needs school and disabled children's centre.

It is difficult to find the words to describe life in Mexico volunteering with Outreach International. Every day was like a new adventure full of amazing sights, sounds, and feelings. Small cobbled streets unsuitable for cars, stray dogs everywhere, pick-up trucks full to the brim with Mexican men on their way to work, children playing in the streets, and restaurants selling the most amazing food.

We were picked up from the airport and taken to stay at a Mexican family's home. Our first week was an experience; we washed outside under the stars and eating tortillas! The family spent time teaching us Spanish and taking us to the river to swim. Then in the evenings we would listen to Mexican music, dance, and drink the family's home-brewed tequila. You can't really get more Mexican than that!

I worked at the disabled children's centre. The children receive food, drink, physiotherapy treatment, and lots of love. It really is an amazing place run by volunteers and completely reliant on donations. While I was there, I helped to set up a new project at a local special needs school. This involved running PE classes for all of the children. They have never had any form of physiotherapy or PE at the school, so the staff and children were very grateful for our input. We were usually greeted at the gate with beautiful flowers for our hair and lots of kisses! Resources were so limited that myself and another volunteer went out to buy new equipment ourselves. In England, parachutes are used a lot in schools for PE activities, so we made one. The children absolutely loved it, and we are so proud to have been able to give them something they can keep and continue to use in the future.

Working life was good, but it was difficult to accept the conditions that the children live in, and the poor access to services they have. It is very challenging, but the rewards gained from making the children laugh, building relationships with them and seeing them improve, far outweighs the negatives. In addition, I could pass my knowledge on to the members of staff that work at the centres. It made me feel like we were building a better future for these children. It really doesn't take a lot to make a small difference, and hopefully enough small differences can make a big change in the future.

Outreach International has been sending volunteers overseas since 1997, and offers gap year programmes in Ecuador (including the Galápagos), Costa Rica, and Mexico. All the projects encourage volunteers to learn the local language and offer good language training. The placements include helping in orphanages, running a Feed the Children programme, organising sea turtle and whale conservation, arts and crafts projects, and English teaching in coastal primary schools. There are also projects working with dolphins and volunteering at the premier dance school in Mexico. In Ecuador, compassionate volunteers are needed to help run a project for street children and to work at an orphanage. Opportunities are also available to work in the Amazon rainforest. Volunteers live together in an Outreach International house but work in pairs on their project. **Charlotte Kane** was lucky enough to be sent to the Galápagos by Outreach International to teach English:

> I have just got back to Quito from Galápagos. I had the time of my life out there and was absolutely devastated to leave. The family that I stayed with were the nicest people that I have ever met. Teaching at Ingala was great – I had never taught adults before and I really enjoyed it. I think that everyone going to Galápagos will want to see more of San Cristobal than the beaches close to the town, and also some of the other islands as well, because being in Galápagos for that length of time is a once-in-a-lifetime experience. Sometimes we were taken out on boats and did some incredible exploring with the fishermen and other boat owners. This was the best way of seeing the wildlife (and free). On other occasions we paid for a trip. A four-day tour of the islands cost $400, a day's snorkelling at Kicker Rock is $60, and diving $100. I really didn't mind spending the money, because I wanted to make the very most of my time there.

Travellers Worldwide offers teaching and many other placements and courses in Argentina, Brazil, Ecuador, Peru, and Guatemala, while The Leap also has a variety of programmes that combine volunteering in eco-lodges with community and conservation projects in South America. Options are available in Argentina (including riding and polo tuition), Costa Rica, Ecuador, and Venezuela.

NON-SPECIALIST PLACEMENT ORGANISATIONS IN THE UK

The following accept gap year travellers for Latin American projects if they fulfil their criteria (which in several cases include strong Christian commitment), but they do not specialise in placing those on years out:

Caledonia Languages Abroad (www.caledonialanguages.co.uk). Language courses for all levels and voluntary work projects starting throughout the year, mostly for at least four weeks in Costa Rica, Argentina, Bolivia, Brazil, Ecuador, Peru, and Venezuela. Language course cost (eg £1,355 for four weeks in Brazil) plus a £295 arrangement fee.

EIL (www.eiluk.org) provides volunteering opportunities lasting from four to 24 weeks in Argentina, Brazil, Chile, Ecuador, Guatemala, etc, with an average fee of $3,000 for 12 weeks.

ICYE-UK: Inter-Cultural Youth Exchange (www.icye.org.uk). International exchange organisation that sends volunteers to spend a year abroad and undertake voluntary work placements, for example in drug rehabilitation, protection of street children, and ecological projects. Placements available in Bolivia, Brazil, Costa Rica, Ecuador, Honduras, Colombia, and Mexico.

Latin Link STEP Programme (www.latinlink.org.uk). Self-funded team-based building projects in Argentina, Bolivia, Brazil, Ecuador, Chile, Peru, Costa Rica, Honduras, and others, for committed Christians only. Spring programme runs March to July; summer programme for three or seven weeks.

MondoChallenge (www.mondochallenge.co.uk). Makes volunteer placements in several small mountain village schools in the Monte Grande region of Chile north of Santiago, close to La Serena.

EXPEDITIONS

Raleigh International (www.raleighinternational.org) has been running projects in Costa Rica and Nicaragua for more than a decade. Volunteers on community projects live and work alongside local families in remote regions to improve the infrastructure. **Lucy Cavoizy** describes the rewarding time she had on expedition to Costa Rica and Nicaragua with Raleigh International:

> *In a small village in Nicaragua, we built a system of pipes and filtering tanks to bring drinkable water directly to the families' homes. Seeing the excitement on the family's face when they finally had a tap in their kitchen was one of the highlights. The host country participants helped us know more about the Costa Rican and Nicaraguan community, and to interact better with the locals on the projects. Raleigh is definitely a unique experience you shouldn't miss. You get to meet some really good people and have amazing experiences.*

Operation Wallacea (www.opwall.com). Volunteer students, divers, and naturalists assist with surveys of marine and forest habitats in Honduras, Guyana, Mexico, and Peru, and carry out turtle and manatee monitoring in Cuba's Guanahacabibes Biosphere Reserve at the extreme western tip of the island.

Trekforce Worldwide (www.trekforce.org.uk/expeditions/belize-expedition). Expedition and conservation programmes that suit gap year students (among others) in the rainforests of Central America, concentrating on rainforest conservation, scientific, and community projects. Extended programmes of up to five months offer a combination of jungle survival training, conservation project work, teaching in rural communities in Belize, trekking, diving, and language course in Guatemala.

COURSES

As mentioned earlier in this book, trends show that increasing numbers of people are learning Spanish. Whereas most prospective learners think of developing their language skills in Spain, more and more are looking to the many Spanish-speaking countries of South and Central America, particularly Ecuador, Chile, Argentina, Mexico, Guatemala and Costa Rica. A number of schools have been working very hard to bring their courses, whether in travellers' survival Spanish or at a more advanced level, to the attention of potential clients in Europe and North America. Not only are the prices very competitive when compared to courses in Spanish cities, but you are likely to receive a warmer welcome if staying with a family.

Many cultural exchange organisations and Spanish language course providers can advise or even place their 'graduates' in voluntary positions and internships, where they will have a chance to immerse themselves in the Spanish language. Chile Inside (www.chileinside.cl) in Santiago is an agency that can fix up internships, volunteer placements, and working holidays in the tourist industry, the latter for a registration fee of $540 for up to two months.

Keri Craig's successful time in Costa Rica, arranged by Caledonia, makes it clear why the country is another favourite destination for people who want to learn Spanish:

> *Everyone at the school was friendly and so helpful, whether it was organising extra classes or booking hotels at the weekend. My teacher Gaby was wonderful, and my Spanish improved no end having endless gossips with Gaby each afternoon. Considering my Spanish was very basic, I was very pleased with the way it developed so quickly. It was certainly an advantage being so immersed in the culture. The dance classes after school were my particular favourite. Frank and Victor were amazing teachers, and soon had us salsaing like the locals. My only complaint would be the Thursday night dance class outing – European boys just can't dance like the Latin men!*

Individual language schools often have links with local projects, and can arrange for students of Spanish to attach themselves to projects that interest them. As is typical among gappers, **Carisa Fey** started her big trip round South America with a short language course in Quito, which led to some voluntary work afterwards teaching knitting to street kids. APF Languages in Quito (www.apf-languages.com) is one school, for example, that combines a programme of Spanish tuition with homestays and ecological or humanitarian volunteering. Jakera is a youth-oriented company located on the Caribbean coast of Venezuela that offers Spanish language programmes in conjunction with adventure travel and volunteer work experience (www.jakera.com), mostly through UK agencies such as The Leap.

Almost any Spanish language school in Guatemala, especially the city of Quetzaltenango, can help arrange a volunteer position. Antigua is another very popular destination, as evidenced by the number of tour buses arriving daily. To find links to many of these language schools, visit www.xelapages.com/schools.htm, which also has a link to volunteering opportunities. Casa Xelaju in Quetzaltenango (+502 7761 5954; www.casaxelaju.com) runs Spanish courses and refers clients to internships and voluntary work in Guatemala.

WORK EXPERIENCE

It will not be easy for a school leaver to find paid work or work experience opportunities in South or Central America. Although demand for English teachers is ubiquitous, from dusty towns on the Yucatan Peninsula of Mexico to Punta Arenas at the southern extremity of the continent, south of the Falkland Islands, most of the customers are businesspeople looking for something more professional than most gap year students can offer in the way of conversation practice. Furthermore, in a land where baseball is a passion and US television enormously popular, American (and also Canadian) jobseekers have an advantage. More detailed information about teaching in Latin America can be found in the 11th edition of *Teaching English Abroad* (2011–12, £14.99, available from bookshops and Crimson Publishing).

English is of course not the only thing that can be taught. The flourishing skiing industry of Chile and Argentina creates some openings for ski instructors. The Scotland-based firm Peak Leaders UK (see entry in 'Directory of Specialist Gap Year Programmes') runs snowboard and ski instructor courses in the resort of Bariloche in Argentine Patagonia specifically for gap year and time-out students. The nine-week course (from the end of July to the beginning of October) costs £7,100.

Travellers (www.travellersworldwide.com) offers internships in law, medicine, care, business, and photography in Argentina, Brazil, and Guatemala. Teaching, care, and orphanage volunteer placements can be made in Argentina, Brazil, Guatemala, and Peru, while sports coaching placements are also available in Brazil. In addition, the company offers a range of language and cultural courses, eg music and dance (tango, salsa, samba, and ballet).

Work experience placements in a number of fields can be arranged by several agencies in Ecuador; see the entry for ELEP in the 'Directory of Work Experience Abroad', or try EcuEVP in Quito (www. ecuevp.com). Argentina is among the most Europeanised countries in Latin America. A cultural exchange organisation, Grupo de Intercambio Cultural Argentino (www.gicarg.org), invites paying volunteers and prospective interns from abroad to work in various sectors in Buenos Aires. Assignments last between one and six months, although internships are limited to eight to 12 weeks. A four-week Spanish language course with GIC is compulsory on the internship programme, starting at $1,200, including accommodation in a student residence.

MY GAP YEAR:
ANDREW CUMMINGS

As a student of modern languages, Andrew Cummings was keen to spend his year out in South America. He chose two very different destinations – the first an English language magazine in La Paz, Bolivia, where he got journalistic work experience. The second was as a waiter at an upmarket restaurant in Buenos Aires, which he found very tough. The three months he spent at *Bolivia Express* afforded a wonderful glimpse into a rich culture, and he loved getting acquainted with the fascinating capital city, which he describes vividly.

La Paz itself is unique. High-rise apartment blocks and offices stand next to tiny restaurants and quaint squares, and the snow-capped mountains tower in the distance, always there to remind you of the stunning location (and the altitude!) There are some elements that might feel really familiar to a European visitor, and some completely alien: businessmen and cholitas (women in traditional dress) walk side-by-side on the pavements, while teenagers in high-tops and Ray-Bans twiddle with their iPods during a festival celebrating an Aymara god. For me, the city had a lot more character than Paris or even Buenos Aires; it's one of the most amazing, stimulating places I've ever seen.

The internship at the cultural publication Bolivian Express provided a very hands-on approach to journalism. It's very easy to get in contact with talented, influential people in La Paz, both because of the links the Bolivian members of the team already have and because of the accommodating nature of the people there. You'll find that you're given the tools to put together a fairly well-informed, interesting article very quickly. The first day we arrived, we were asked if we had any article ideas for the first issue of the magazine. Still mildly jet-lagged and vaguely suffering from altitude sickness, it's hardly surprising that we weren't feeling too creative. But if you walk down the street in La Paz, there's a wealth of things that stick out, things that you might be able to write about; needless to say, at the next meeting, we had plenty of ideas up our sleeves. The cost of living in Bolivia is incredibly low, so it probably works out that even with the flight to South America, you spend no more than you would if you had to pay for accommodation, food, and luxuries in Europe.

MY GAP YEAR: KELLEN BRANDEL

Fresh out of high school in Arizona, Kellen Brandel chose to attach himself to an NGO in San Salvador, partly because it was one way he could afford to have a gap year in a Spanish-speaking environment. El Salvador is not the first destination to come to mind when 18-year-olds head off, so he was not too surprised that some relatives and friends felt uncomfortable with his decision.

I began my gap year by heading down to San Salvador in Central America. I mainly researched options using the internet and, after finding a few legitimate programmes, was most impressed with the one I chose (CIS - the Center for Exchange and Solidarity) because of its communication and quality of information, not to mention costs. I spent the first three months as a volunteer English teacher for CIS, a grassroots NGO founded by an American woman in the 1990s. I spent the next month backpacking through the countryside of El Salvador, Honduras, Guatemala, and Belize before returning to San Salvador and spending an additional three months teaching again. While I volunteered abroad, I also studied the native language, Spanish, in a sister school at this particular NGO.

The costs were quite reasonable. The average week consisted of spending about $80 for host family, including meals and utilities, and $57 for Spanish school, provided you were an English volunteer ($100 for passers-by), as well as a few additional expenses.

My volunteer position was that of an English teacher for adults, mainly in the evenings. The working conditions were great, and the co-ordinators were very helpful in providing us with material, ideas, and support. At first I was wary about teaching adults, as most of my students were in their late 20s and 30s. But I think I gained their respect and was laid-back enough that the age difference didn't seem to matter. After that, we were able to relax and eventually make jokes about my young age. It was professional, but the atmosphere at CIS is also really laid-back.

CIS has a number of programmes that reach out across the country's borders, and I was able to participate in some trips to different communities that receive assistance from CIS. We were able to meet local organisations, including an anti-mining group from the north and a women's group against domestic violence. I really loved getting to know the people, making a connection that is so much more than you could do in just a week or so of volunteering or working. Over the course of seven months, I got to know my students on a much more personal level than many teachers get to, and that to me was really special. The low point would probably be the amount of English spoken. For many the balance is good, but since I already had a strong foundation for the Spanish language, at times I found only English speakers at CIS, and I wanted to focus on the acquisition of the foreign language. But once I became more involved with locals outside CIS, that too improved.

My gap year was amazing, the highlight beginning when I boarded the flight in LA and ending when I touched back down in the States.

VOLUNTEERING

Short-term voluntary work projects are scattered over this vast continent, though many of the opportunities are confined to Spanish-speakers. The internet has made it much easier to unearth opportunities for volunteering, whether from one of the mainstream databases such as www.idealist.org, www.traveltree.co.uk, or www.wwv.org.uk. One specialist website is www.volunteersouthamerica.net, founded by Steve McElhinney after he had been looking himself for 'grassroots, zero-cost volunteer work' in Argentina. Finding volunteering opportunities that did not involve paying a large amount of cash to a third party was more difficult than he anticipated, and he spent dozens of hours trying to track them down. He then posted his findings on the website and now keeps it updated.

MY GAP YEAR:
AFTON BLIGHT

Afton Blight, from Michigan, signed up with SKIP Peru (www. skipper.org) to volunteer with children in a poor district of Trujillo, which gave her plenty of opportunities to get to know the culture.

Throughout high school, I investigated various pre-university options. I come from a farming background, which I enjoyed, but I didn't want to limit myself to a career simply because it was within my comfort zone. I also have other interests such as Spanish, carpentry, music, and serving others. I was really undecided about what I wanted to do, and I liked volunteering, so I worked with Peruvian kids and families for nine months. Living in Peru allowed me time apart from everything I knew. The population of Trujillo is over a million people, who walk or ride in taxis everywhere; I come from a small town that has no public transport. Trujillo is on the coast of the Pacific Ocean yet it is very dry with little vegetation, in huge contrast to my home in the States which is surrounded by crop fields and large coniferous trees.

Every morning I worked as an English teacher in two schools in the poor district of Trujillo called El Porvenir. After a good home-cooked lunch and a quick siesta, the other volunteers and I would walk back to the SKIP office to aid kids with their math, history, reading, etc, until around 5pm. El Porvenir is a very dry and sandy area with limited electricity and other luxuries, but SKIP provides necessary amenities for the volunteers and Peruvian families whom it supports. As an English teacher, there was not a lot of supervision. I was able to teach classes at my own pace with my own material, which allowed me to be very creative with my lesson plans and subjects covered. It is a great job for people who are self-motivated, and if I needed materials or help with anything there was always someone willing to step in.

Meanwhile, I became close to a native family during my stay in Peru, which allowed me to see Peruvian culture from an authentic point of view. Not only did they help me to improve my Spanish speaking skills, but they allowed me to travel, cook, and spend holidays with them. I really enjoyed their companionship during my stay in Peru, and we are still in frequent contact. Not only did I learn a ton about Peruvian culture, but I lived with foreigners from around the world who taught me about their beliefs, countries, and lifestyles. The other volunteers also made it apparent to me how much I did not know about my own country and the world.

COUNTRY GUIDE: WORLDWIDE

LATIN AMERICA

475

A good source of opportunities is on www.volunteeringecuador.org, whose listed projects charge $18 a day ($480 a month) to cover living expenses plus a one-off registration fee of $190. In some cases, a centralised placement service makes choosing a project much easier, though you will have to pay for the service, as in the case of Volunteer Bolivia (www.volunteerbolivia.org) located in Cochabamba. It encourages its clients to sign up for a month of Spanish tuition while staying with a local family before becoming a volunteer; a combined language course, homestay, and volunteer placement programme costs $1,670 for one month, $2,450 for 12 weeks.

For animal lovers, the Inti Wara Yassi wildlife reserve in Bolivia accepts volunteers to help care for injured animals (www.intiwarayassi.org). On **Rob Harris**'s gap year, he was placed here by Quest Overseas, and divided his time between working in monkey quarantine (feeding, cleaning, and looking after newly arrived capuchin monkeys before they were deemed adjusted enough to join the main group in the monkey park) and building the infrastructure of the new park to receive more animals in very remote and basic jungle living conditions.

Staying in Amazonia can be arranged by many conservation NGOs such as the Fundación Fauna de la Amazonia (www.amazoniarescue.org) in Ecuador. Through the UK charity You Volunteer (see entry in 'Directory of Work Experience Abroad'), you can volunteer to teach and care for children as part of the Arajuno Road Project in Amazonian Ecuador. Both schemes start at an affordable $500 a month.

According to **Anna Ling**, who spent some months chilling on Lake Atitlán in Guatemala, anyone wanting to find bar work in the lakeside towns like San Pedro will be able to do so without too much effort, needing only to wait a week or so, as bar staff are always moving on. In general, the pay is $6 for an eight-hour shift, though tips can easily double that. Over half the bars are American or English-run, the others French or Spanish, so Spanish is not a necessity, though obviously a knowledge of the language will work in your favour. Anna also did something that contributed to local development rather than just backpackers' jollity:

> The local village of Santa Cruz on Lake Atitlán is a wonderful place and home to the Amigos (www.amigosdesantacruz.org), a charity that has brought a clinic to the village, along with a paediatrician, dentist, resident doctor, and many volunteers, who also work in outreach programmes, bringing medical care to the more remote villages. They have also built a library and a school offering free education to all children under 12, and scholarship programmes for older children. They are in the process of building a large new centre for vocational education. They give families water filters and generally help the health and happiness of the village in any way they can. I went up to the village to see Pam, the current brains behind the operation, and within the hour I was teaching an English class. I was soon given a classroom and started an enrichment afternoon with the local kids, doing arts, craft, and music projects. The organisation is so well run that anyone willing to give some time will be put to good use, whether in construction, medicine, or teaching, or any other interests.
>
> Visas are not a problem at all, neither for work nor volunteering. No one even asks to see a passport. Language is no problem either. Personally I'm trying to live very much on a tight budget, and paid language lessons ($3–$6 per hour) would push me way over my daily price watch. But volunteering at the school has been the best opportunity for learning Spanish I could imagine. I take up a dictionary and the kids speak really slowly and clearly and it has helped so very much.

GRASSROOTS VOLUNTARY ORGANISATIONS

Hundreds of small NGOs and charities, some run by expats, can be found throughout Latin America. As you travel throughout the region, you are bound to come across orphanages, environmental projects, and so on, some of which may be able to make temporary use of a willing volunteer. The Quaker-run peace and service centre in Mexico City, Casa de los Amigos, has information on a variety of volunteering opportunities throughout the country. The Casa also has its own volunteer programme for those who speak Spanish and are able to commit for at least six months to a year, working for peace and social justice. The Casa is at Ignacio Mariscal 132, 06030 Mexico, DF, Mexico (+52 55 5705 0521; amigos@casadelosamigos.org), and provides simple accommodation from about $10 per night.

One of the most acute problems in many South American cities is the number of street children. Working with one of the many charities that are tackling this problem can be both discouraging and rewarding by turns; for example, CENIT (Spanish acronym for 'Centre for the Working Girl') in Quito has an entry in the 'Directory of Volunteering Abroad'. A typical project was recently described on a post-university gapper's blog:

> *Casa Hatunsonqo in the interior of Peru is a home for children between the ages of four and 18 who are either orphaned or whose parents are unable to take care of them. Many parents cannot afford to care for them, often because the fathers are dead or in prison and their mothers cannot manage alone, and many others are unable to due to alcoholism. At the home they have a bed, meals, (limited) books, help with homework, and their clothes are washed, but more generally they have adult care and affection.*
>
> *When I got off the bus in Pomacanchi, I met the other volunteers, four Spanish women (two were nurses) and the cook, who is the only constantly resident adult there. Daily routine was helping prepare food and wash clothes while the children were at school, and while they were at home to see to the basic tasks of getting the children fed, washing their faces, brushing their teeth, putting on cream against the cold and harsh sunlight at altitude, helping with homework, etc. Many of the children needed better nourishment, medical and dental care, books, clothing – it was frustrating to see the extent of what they lack, when these things would be so easily provided in the UK. Despite all this, the children were affectionate, cheerful, and generous with each other. From the first day they called me 'tia'. The smaller children throw their arms around you and are so trusting you have to hold them very securely, as they lean back from you with no fear.*

A less stressful opportunity exists in the Nicaraguan countryside at an eco-centre that has been created by British expat Paulette Goudge (see 'Directories of Courses' entry for Mariposa Spanish School & Eco Hotel, p333). One returning visitor was very impressed with this unique place, and thinks that '*Three to 12 months working with Paulette would offer a unique and very special experience for gappers, both to understand about Nicaragua and the poverty there, learn Spanish, and make a very real difference in an exciting, new, and growing project*'.

The Galápagos islands have people as well as animals, and a charity that works to improve education and health facilities for the local populace is Galápagos ICE (www.galapagosice.org).

Two volunteer agencies in Argentina are Insight Argentina (insight@helpargentina.org) and Buenos Aires Volunteer (bavolunteer.org.ar).

TEACHING PLACEMENTS

ARGENTINA

Colonias de Inmersión al Idioma (CII), Buenos Aires (+54 11 4831 8152; www.ecolonias. com). Offers TEFL internships to university students or recent graduates, combining a 60-hour TEFL course (from Bridge), plus placement in English immersion camps or schools throughout Argentina. Programme lasts three to 12 months and costs from $1,750 for early applicants. CII also recruits language facilitators to work in schools. Participants must have a university degree, speaking knowledge of Spanish, and TEFL certificate.

Connecting Schools To The World, Buenos Aires (www.connectingschools.com.ar). Places college graduates in towns in Argentina where teachers are hard to come by. Participants receive ESL training in Buenos Aires, four hours of Spanish classes a week, and homestay in an Argentine home. Teachers must be lively, be passionate about teaching, be willing to become part of the community, and wish to make a difference. Minimum stay is one semester, starting 15 January or 9 July. Interested volunteers should send resumé and three references to connectingschools@gmail.com.

La Montana Spanish School, San Carlos de Bariloche, Patagonia (+54 2944 524 212; volunteer-work@lamontana.com; www.lamontana.com/volunteer-work). Students who complete a Spanish course, usually lasting four weeks, can be placed in rural schools around Patagonia for at least a month, but typically two. Modest placement fee is charged.

Pasantias Argentinas, Córdoba (+54 351 474 5947; www.pasantias-argentinas.com). Arranges professional internships in Córdoba, including English teaching placements. Open to all native English speakers who have achieved a speaking knowledge of Spanish via a Pasantias language course; intensive course price from €120 per week. Donation to voluntary project €100.

Road2Argentina, Buenos Aires (+54 11 4821 3271; www.road2argentina.com). Places ESL interns for one to four months between March and November, as part of a cultural exchange and language immersion programme. International interns are accepted without relevant training or experience to help in private or public school classrooms. Programme fees start at $1,190 for one month, and include accommodation in a student residence.

CHILE

Programa Inglés Abre Puertas (English Open Doors), Ministerio de Educación Santiago (+56 2 487 5464; voluntarios@mineduc.cl; www.puntonorte.cl/voluntarios). English immersion courses taught in state schools in small towns and villages throughout Chile. Volunteers receive a small monthly stipend of 85,000 pesos ($175) in addition to free room and board. Participants must be university graduates (minimum age 21) and stay for five months; compulsory insurance charge of $500.

Voluntarios de la Esperanza, Carabineros de Chile 33, Santiago de Chile (+56 2 717 99 37; or in the USA +1 617 674 2649; info@ve-global.org). Works with partner institutions to place volunteers to work with at-risk children, including teaching English. Application process is competitive and no registration fee is charged.

ECUADOR

Teach English, Volunteer (http://Ecuador.teach-english-volunteer.com). Programme overseen by the Direccion Provincial de Educacion in one of the poorest regions of Ecuador, the Andean province of Hispana de Chimborazo. Volunteers teach in primary schools for at least four months and in exchange are given food and accommodation by a local family. Basic knowledge of Spanish needed. No fee charged.

CONSERVATION

An increasing number of organisations, both indigenous and foreign-sponsored, are involved in environmental projects throughout the continent. For opportunities in Ecuador, investigate www.my-quito.com/eco-tourism.html.

The Fundacion Charles Darwin operates an International Volunteer and Scholarship Program (Charles Darwin Research Station, Casilla Postal 17–01–3891, Quito, Ecuador; vol@fcdarwin.org.ec; www.darwinfoundation.org). Volunteers must be at least third-year undergraduates, preferably studying environmental science, and willing to stay for a minimum of six months. Without relevant scientific skills, international volunteers have to cover all their expenses, including airfares to and from the islands, food, and accommodation.

The highest concentration of projects is probably in Costa Rica where the National Parks and Communities Authority runs a voluntary programme Asociacion de Voluntarios para el Servicio en las Areas

Protegidas (ASVO). To be eligible, you must be willing to work for at least 30 days, be able to speak at least minimal Spanish, and provide a copy of your passport and a photo. The work may consist of trail maintenance and construction, greeting and informing visitors, beach cleaning, research, or generally assisting rangers. There is also a possibility of joining a sea turtle conservation project. Details are available from the San José office (+506 258 4430/223 4260; info@asvocr.org or evargas@asvocr.org; www.asvocr.org). Food and accommodation cost $20 a day, in addition to a $30 registration fee.

> **GAPPERS' TIP**
> *One British volunteer has warned that security at the national parks can be lax, allowing the odd confidence trickster to pose as a volunteer and rob money and valuables from the volunteers' dorms.*

BUNAC has conservation volunteering programmes (among others) in Peru under the auspices of a partner student organisation that provides back-up during the two- or three-month placements. Students (including gap year students) and recent graduates can participate if they have basic conversational Spanish. The programme fee is currently £1,400/£1,900 for two/three months in Lima, but more in Cusco.

The organisation Rainforest Concern (020 7229 2093; www.rainforestconcern.org) has rainforest conservation projects in Central and South America (as well as Asia). Volunteers and students who are prepared to work for part of the day can stay at a cloud forest lodge in Ecuador or help with turtle protection projects in Panama and Costa Rica; some are arranged through a partner travel agency. Africa, Asia & Americas Venture and Quest Overseas work with Rainforest Concern by sending volunteers to conservation projects in Ecuador and Costa Rica.

The Caribbean

The islands of the Caribbean are far too expensive to explore unless you do more than sip rum punch by the beach. Few agencies make placements in the Caribbean. Greenforce (part of Gapforce) is one that does, in recruiting fee-paying volunteers for marine projects in the Bahamas. Yet a number of gap year travellers have managed to spend time in this exotic part of the world by working for their keep, mostly on yachts.

Research opportunities exist as well; see for example the entry for the Bimini Biological Field Station in the 'Directory of Volunteering Abroad'. The Bermuda Institute of Ocean Sciences (St George's GE01, Bermuda; +441 297 1880 ext 115; www.bios.edu) accepts volunteer science interns to help scientists conduct research for three to six months. Applicants (who are usually upper-level undergraduates or recent graduates in relevant subjects) should make personal contact with the faculty member(s) for whom they wish to work (see website). Note that immigration restrictions mean that the station cannot hire foreigners to carry out work other than research.

Cuba's economy is suffering badly, but its music and vibrant culture attract some prospective year-out travellers. Several years ago, **Nick Mulvey** from Cambridge arranged to spend several months studying guitar with a Cuban musician before starting his university course in World Music at SOAS. Caledonia Languages Abroad arranges Spanish courses in Santiago and Havana, and you can add salsa and drumming classes, diving, and trekking. But the infrastructure continues to disintegrate, and almost no gap year placement organisations include Cuba on their list of destinations.

The Cuba Solidarity Campaign (London N4; 020 8800 0155; finance@cuba-solidarity.org.uk) still runs its work/study 'brigade' twice a year, in which volunteers undertake agricultural and construction work for 15 days in July and December/January. No specific skills or qualifications are required, but applicants must be able to demonstrate a commitment to solidarity work. The cost of the brigade is £1,035 (summer 2011), which covers the full cost of flights, visas, transfers, accommodation, and food.

St Eustatius National Parks Foundation in the Netherlands Antilles has a volunteer programme to maintain park trails and a botanical garden, plus participate in a marine turtle monitoring programme organised by the STENAPA Foundation. Volunteers from overseas available for one to three months should apply through the British-based www.workingabroad.com. The cost for two months is £1,230.

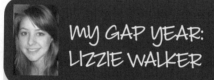

MY GAP YEAR:
LIZZIE WALKER

Lizzie Walker burnt herself out during A levels, and taking a gap year before proceeding to UCL seemed a very good idea.

When I was eight, I had decided I wanted to be a marine biologist, so a marine expedition really would be like living a childhood dream. I soon found a number of organisations that arrange for people to work abroad, study the reefs, and learn to scuba dive. It hadn't ever occurred to me that I could do something along those lines until it appeared on my Google search, and goes to show that there really is so much out there to suit anyone. Initially, I booked myself on an expedition to go to Madagascar, conducting coral reef surveys and working with the local people. When this fell through due to the political situation in the country, I was absolutely gutted. But after searching around a little more, I came across Coral Cay, a conservation group that offers marine expeditions to the Philippines and Tobago. Tobago really appealed to me, and I signed up straightaway. Tobago is English-speaking, and really easy to get to, which reassured me as I hadn't felt too confident about travelling for the first time through Madagascar as a single British female. The fact that I was able to fit in a six-night stay in a New York hostel on my way here was just the icing on the cake.

I'm writing this from Tobago. The expedition site is right on the beach, and every night I fall asleep to the sound of the sea. I'm surrounded by people from totally different backgrounds, but who share a love for the ocean and scuba diving. It can be hard at times - we're living in close quarters and work long, hard days, but we also have a fantastic team - and great Saturday night parties! I'll be gaining qualifications in scuba diving, marine science, and first aid that are going to be much more use to me than my GCSEs ever were. I have another 11 weeks left in Tobago, and I know I'm going to love every second of it. I can't say I ever thought living on a beach in paradise was a realistic dream, but here I am living it - and it doesn't get much better than this.

NORTH AMERICA

USA

The spirit of Jack Kerouac is far from dead, even though not many gap year travellers are familiar with his *On the Road* these days. Dubious foreign policy notwithstanding, the lure of America continues to be strong among young Britons and Europeans. The home of so many heroes and of ideas that have shaped the thinking of most people in the west, the USA attracts a wide range of people, including school leavers, who want to experience the reality for themselves. Extended travel around the United States is expensive, but various schemes and travel bargains can bring this vast country within reach. It is possible for students to qualify for an Exchange Visitor Programme visa, which permits them to enter the USA and work legally. For information about the formalities needed for visiting the USA as a tourist, see the Part II chapter on North America.

RED TAPE

The non-immigrant visa of most interest is the J-1, which is available to participants in government-authorised schemes known as Exchange Visitor Programmes, who are permitted to take legal paid employment. Note that some key programmes, such as BUNAC's Work America, are open only to students already in higher education, and therefore those taking a gap year immediately after school are not eligible.

The J-1 visa entitles the holder to take legal paid employment in the USA. You cannot apply for the J-1 without going through a recognised Exchange Visitor Programme such as BUNAC, IST Plus, or Camp America. Only they can issue the document DS-2019 necessary for obtaining a J-1 visa. Participants on an Exchange Visitor Programme can work on a J-1 visa in any job for up to four months between May and October, or for the winter season between 21 November and 30 April. After the work period finishes, they are permitted a further 30 days for pure travel in the USA. Applicants for non-immigrant visas for work or study or anyone planning a trip that will last more than 90 days must schedule a face-to-face interview at the US Embassy for a non-refundable fee of $140.

Numerous opportunities are available on summer camps and as au pairs (both jobs described below). Some are open only to full-time students, while others accept those between school and university as long as they have a confirmed place at a tertiary education institution. Other summer camp programmes are open to non-students over 18 with specific skills.

Apart from the J-1 visa available to people on approved Exchange Visitor Programmes, the other main visa category of interest is the H category, which covers non-immigrant work visas in special circumstances. The H2-B is for temporary or seasonal vacancies that employers have trouble filling with US citizens. For example, the chronic shortage of workers on the ski fields of Colorado means that a certain number of employers can obtain the necessary Labor Certification confirming that there are no qualified US workers available to do the jobs. A petition must be submitted by the employer to the US Citizenship and Immigration Services (USCIS), and there is a strict quota. The maximum duration of the H2-B visa is one year. It remains difficult to get a visa, and applicants have to jump through more and more hoops. For example, despite a thriving American ski industry, very few ski or snowboard instructor courses are held in the US, largely because of visa impediments.

By law, all employers must physically examine the documents of employees within three working days and complete an I-9 form that verifies the employee's right to work. Employers who are discovered by USCIS to be hiring illegal aliens are subject to huge fines, and those caught working illegally run the risk of being deported and – prohibited from travelling to the USA for five years – or in some cases for good.

WORK AND TRAVEL PROGRAMMES

A number of exchange organisations help candidates from around the world to obtain a J-1 visa.

BUNAC (16 Bowling Green Lane, London EC1R 0QH; 020 7251 3472; www.bunac.org.uk) administers three summer programmes in the USA. The only one open to gap year students is Summer Camp USA, since the other two are restricted to students registered in full-time tertiary education, including final-year students. The Work America Programme allows participants to do any summer job they are able to find; Summer Camp USA is the second, open to anyone over 18 interested in working on a summer camp as a counsellor; the third is KAMP (Kitchen and Maintenance Programme), which is open to students who want to work at a summer camp in a catering and maintenance capacity. All participants must join the BUNAC Club (cost £5), travel between June and the beginning of October (either independently or on a BUNAC flight for £525), pay the varying programme fees, and purchase compulsory insurance (£143).

BUNAC's Work America student participants must find their own summer job in the USA, either by using BUNAC's job listings or by waiting to pound the pavements job-hunting on arrival. In addition to the registration fee of £320 for first-time applicants, you must submit a letter from your principal, registrar, or tutor on college headed paper showing that you are a full-time degree-level student. You are also required to take at least $600 in support funds, or $1,000 if you haven't pre-arranged a job.

In addition to BUNAC, the principal work and travel programmes (as distinct from career-oriented internship programmes described below) are broadly comparable. UK programmes that provide full-time university students with the opportunity to live and work in the USA for a maximum of four months, include CCUSA (www.ccusa.com), IST Plus (www.istplus.com), Real Gap Company (www.realgap.co.uk), Outbreak Adventure Recruitment (www.outbreak-adventure.co.uk/recruitment), Global Choices (www.globalchoices.co.uk), and WAVA (www.workandvolunteer.com). An agency in Wales called Ancer Recruitment offers a work and study programme, H2-B programmes for seasonal jobs, and hospitality internships for varying fees (www.ancerimmigration.com). Many companies with a high Google ranking such as www.jobofer.org, based in Kalingrad, specialise in the placement of non-English-speaking candidates in these same programmes.

SUMMER CAMPS

Summer camps are uniquely American in atmosphere, even if the idea has spread to Europe. An estimated eight million American children are sent to 10,000 summer camps each year for a week or more to participate in outdoor activities and sports, arts and crafts, and generally have a wholesome experience. The type of camp varies from plush sports camps for the very rich to more or less charitable camps for disabled or underprivileged children, which often tend to be short-staffed. British young people are especially in demand as soccer coaches on summer camps.

It is estimated that summer camps employ nearly a third of a million people. Thousands of 'counsellors' are needed each summer to be in charge of a cabinful of youngsters and to instruct or supervise some activity, from the ordinary (swimming and boating) to the esoteric (puppet-making and ham radio). Several summer camp organisations are authorised to issue J-1 visas, primarily Camp America and BUNAC, but a few smaller ones are also mentioned below.

After camp finishes, counsellors have up to six weeks' free time and usually return on organised flights between late August and the end of September. Some camps are staffed almost entirely by young people from overseas, which can be useful if you are looking for a post-camp travelling companion.

With its Summer Camp USA programme, BUNAC is one of the two biggest counsellor-placement organisations in the field, sending several thousand people over 19 (or 18, if expert in something in demand) as counsellors at children's camps. The registration fee of £429 includes camp placement, return flight, insurance, land transport to camp, and pocket money of $790–$1,215 (depending on age) for the whole nine-week period. Obtaining a police background check will incur an extra expense of £45 in England (free in Scotland), as will the compulsory fee to register with SEVIS, the US government system for monitoring international exchange students. The fact that you do not have to raise the money for the flight is a great attraction for many; the camp that decides to hire you advances the amount from your wages to BUNAC, which in turn puts it towards your flight. Interviews, which are compulsory, are held in university towns throughout Britain from November; the programme fills up early, and in 2011 was closed from mid-March.

The other major camp recruitment organisation is Camp America (020 7581 7373; www.campamerica.co.uk), which each summer arranges for up to 9,000 people aged 18 or over, from around the world, to work on children's camps in the USA. Camp America provides a free return flight from London to New York and guidance on applying for a J-1 visa. The camp offers free board and lodging plus pocket money. At the end of your contract, you will be given a lump sum of pocket money, which will range from $600 to $950 depending on experience and qualifications. Upfront charges include the registration fee of £601, which includes £200 to cover insurance but excludes the US visa fee of $140 and the compulsory police check.

One way to secure a placement early and avoid last-minute uncertainty is to attend one of Camp America's recruitment fairs, held in various British cities between January and March, which is what **Colin Rothwell** did: '*At the recruitment fair, you could actually meet the camp directors from all over the States and find out more about particular camps. If you are lucky, like me and a thousand others, you can sign a contract on the spot.*'

Summer camps provide more scope for employment than just looking after the kids. BUNAC's Kitchen and Maintenance Programme, otherwise known as KAMP USA, and Camp America's Campower are open only to degree-level students (including final-year students) who are given ancillary jobs in the kitchen, laundry, or maintenance department, for which they will be advanced their airfare and in some cases paid more than the counsellors.

Other summer camp agencies include Camp Counselors USA (www.ccusa.com) and Camp Leaders in America (CLIA; www.campleaders.com).

INTERNSHIPS AND WORK EXPERIENCE

Internship is the American term for traineeship, providing a chance to get some work experience in your area of career interest as part of your academic course. These are typically available to undergraduates, recent graduates, and young professionals, and are almost always unpaid. Several organisations in the UK are authorised to help candidates find work placements in the USA and obtain a J-1 visa valid for up to 18 months. Among others, IST Plus, Real Gap, WAVA, and Global Choices in the UK (see web addresses above) help full-time students and recent graduates to arrange course-related placements in the USA lasting from three to 18 months. The placement can take place at any time during your studies – during the summer, as a sandwich year, or up to 12 months after graduating. Although you are responsible for finding your own course-related position, the programme organisers supply practical advice on applying for work and a searchable database of internships/work placements. Those who qualify get a J-1 visa. Programme fees differ, but may start at £400 for students who can fix up their own training position, rising to more than £2,000 for non-students who want a placement arranged for them.

The UK/US Career Development Programme is administered by the Association for International Practical Training (AIPT) in Maryland (www.aipt.org). This programme is for people aged 18–35 with relevant qualifications and/or at least one year of work experience in their career field. A separate section of the programme is for full-time students in hospitality and tourism or equine studies. InterExchange (www.interexchange.org) and the Alliance Abroad Group (http://allianceabroad.com) are both accredited to grant J-1 and H2-B visas to European candidates.

After a consultation with Taking Off, a consultancy in Boston, **Elisabeth Weiskittel** fixed up a short internship at the Ocean Mammal Institute (www.oceanmammalinst.com) on the island of Maui in

Hawaii in the middle of her gap year. Every January, the woman in charge of the institute takes some of her students and a few interns (often people taking a year off) to Hawaii for 19 days for a fee of $2,500 (2012):

The purpose of the institute was to study humpbacked whales and the effects of nearby boats on their behaviour. Our data was intended to support a pending law restricting the use of speedboats and other craft in these small bays where the whales and their calves were swimming. One group watched and recorded the whales' behaviour in the morning and had the afternoon off, and the other group watched in the afternoon and had the morning off. I had no problem adjusting to life in Hawaii. Most people were there to get a tan and go to bars, but even if that's not your scene it's still lots of fun. During our last week, there was a large conference on environmental issues, which all the interns were invited to attend. Some of the speakers were well-known, and one or two spoke to our group, such as the founder of Greenpeace. When the internship ended, I flew back home to New York for a few days to do my laundry and repack, and then continued my gap year in Italy.

CHILDCARE

The au pair placement programme allows thousands of young Europeans with childcare references to work for American families for exactly one year on a J-1 visa. They apply through a small number of sponsoring organisations, which must follow the guidelines that govern the programme, so there is not much difference between them. The arrangement differs from au pairing in Europe since the hours are much longer and, if the au pair comes from the UK, there is no language to learn.

The basic requirements are that you be between 18 and 26, speak English, can show at least 200 hours of recent childcare experience, have a clean driving licence and provide a criminal record check. The childcare experience can consist of regular babysitting, helping at a local crèche or school, etc. Anyone wanting to care for a child under two must have 200 hours of experience looking after children of that age, and must expect the programme interviewers to delve into the experience you claim to have. The majority of candidates are young women, though men with relevant experience (eg sole care of children under five) may be placed. (It is still not unusual to have just a handful of blokes among hundreds of au pairs.)

The job entails working up to 45 hours a week (including babysitting), with at least one and a half days off per week plus one complete weekend off a month. Successful applicants receive free return flights from one of many European cities, four-day orientation in New York that covers child safety and development, and support from a community counsellor. The counsellor's role is to advise on any problems and organise meetings with other au pairs in your area. Applicants are required to pay a good faith deposit of $400, which is returned to them at the end of 12 months but which is forfeited if the terms of the programme are broken.

The fixed amount of pocket money for au pairs is $195.75 a week, which is a reasonable wage on top of room, board, and perks, plus a completion bonus of $200. An additional $500 is paid by the host family to cover the cost of educational courses (three hours a week during term-time), which must be attended as a condition of the visa. Au pairs are at liberty to travel for a month after their contract is over, but no visa extension is available beyond that.

As in all au pair–host family relationships, problems do occur, and it is not unusual for au pairs to chafe against rules, curfews, and expectations on housework, etc. When speaking to your host family on the telephone during the application period, ask as many day-to-day questions as possible, and try to establish exactly what will be expected of you, how many nights babysitting at weekends, restrictions on social life, use of the car, how private living arrangements are, etc. The counsellors and advisers provided by the sending organisations should be able to sort out problems, and in extreme cases can find alternative families. Consider carefully the pros and cons of the city you will be going to. **Emma Purcell** was not altogether happy to be sent to Memphis, Tennessee, which she describes as the '*most backward and redneck city in the USA*':

I was a very naïve 18-year-old, applying to be an au pair for a deferred year before university. During my first eight months, I experienced both highs and lows. I was very lucky with my host family, who have made me feel like one of them. I travelled the USA and Mexico frequently, staying in suites and being treated as royalty since my host dad is president of Holiday Inn. On the down side, I lost numerous friends who did not have such good luck. One was working 60 hours a week (for no extra pay) with the brattiest children, so she left. Another girl from Australia lasted six months with her neurotic family, who yelled at her for not cleaning the toaster daily and for folding the socks wrong. She finally plucked up the courage to talk to her host parents, and their immediate response was to throw her out. A very strong personality is required to be an au pair for a year in the States.

About half a dozen agencies in the UK send au pairs to the USA, and it is worth comparing their literature. The Au Pair in America programme (see 'Directory of Specialist Gap Year Programmes') is the largest organisation, placing thousands of young people from countries around the world in au pair and nanny positions throughout the country. It has representatives in Europe, South Africa, Australia, etc, and agent/interviewers throughout the UK and worldwide. The programme operates under the auspices of the American Institute for Foreign Study (AIFS), though some of the selection has been devolved to independent au pair agencies such as Childcare International in London (www.childint. co.uk).

Other active au pair Exchange Visitor Programmes are smaller but may be able to offer a more personal service and more choice in the destination and family you work for. Try for example Au Pair Care Inc in San Francisco (www.aupaircare.eu; 0203 286 2042 for info in the UK); EurAupair (www. euraupair.com), whose UK partner is EurAupair UK in Shropshire (01952 460 733; maureen_asseuk@ yahoo.co.uk). You can also make direct contact with the US offices of GoAUPAIR (www.goaupair.com), and Interexchange's Au Pair USA in New York (+1 800 AU PAIRS (287 2477) or +1 212 926 0446; www.aupairusa.org).

SEASONAL JOBS

Labour demands in summer resorts sometimes reach crisis proportions, especially along the eastern seaboard. Dozens of sites may prove useful, though www.coolworks.com and www.jobmonkey.com are especially recommended for seasonal jobs in the tourist industry.

The majority of seasonal jobs will pay the minimum wage of $7.25 (2011), though some states have legislated a higher wage, eg California and Massachusetts ($8), but five southern states have no minimum. People in jobs that rely on tips earn a pittance since the minimum hourly wage for tipped employees in the US starts at an appalling $2.13 (Georgia) and rises to $5.69 (Connecticut). Live-in jobs are probably preferable and are often available to British students, whose terms allow them to stay beyond Labor Day, the first Monday in September, when most American students go back to 'school' (ie university). After working a season at a large resort in Wisconsin, **Timothy Payne** concluded:

Without doubt the best jobs in the USA are to be found in the resorts, simply because they pay a reasonable wage as well as providing free food and accommodation. Since many resorts are located in remote spots, it is possible to save most of your wages and tips, and also enjoy free use of the resort's facilities. Whatever job you end up with you should have a good time due to the large number of students working there.

Popular resorts are often a sure bet, especially if you arrive in April or May (before US students do). **Katherine Smith**, who got her J-1 visa through BUNAC, describes the range of jobs she found in Ocean City, a popular seaside resort in Maryland that absorbs a large number of Britons:

I decided to spend my summer in Ocean Beach because I knew the job scene would be favourable. I found a job as a waitress in a steak restaurant and another full-time job as a reservations clerk in a hotel by approaching employers on an informal basis and enquiring about possible job vacancies. In my case this was very fruitful, and I found two relatively well-paid jobs, which I enjoyed very much. Other jobs available included fairground attendant, fast food sales assistant, lifeguard, kitchen assistant, chambermaid, and every other possible type of work associated with a busy coastal town. Ocean City was packed with foreign workers. As far as I know, none had any trouble finding work; anyone could have obtained half a dozen jobs. Obviously the employers are used to a high turnover of workers, especially if the job is boring. So it's not difficult to walk out of a job on a day's notice and into another one. It really was a great place to spend the summer. I would recommend a holiday resort to anyone wishing to work hard and have a really wild time.

The Disney International Programs at the Walt Disney World Resort near Orlando in Florida are made up of two programmes: the Disney International College Program (five to 12 months for students and recent graduates), and the one-year Cultural Representative Program. Participants in both programmes work in front-line roles at Disney's theme parks and resorts (www.disney internationalprograms.com). People from the UK and about a dozen other countries are hired to represent the culture, heritage, and customs of their countries in a themed pavilion. In the UK, the annual recruiting presentations usually take place in March and October; for details in the UK and Ireland contact Yummy Jobs in London (enquiries@yummyjobs.com). Any job that involves tips is usually more lucrative than others; wages can be swelled by more than $100 in a five-hour shift. The gated staff apartments have lots of facilities and a buzzing social life.

After checking out the feedback on an unofficial website for International College Program alumni, most of it enthusiastic, **Catherine Howard** from Cork, Ireland, decided to apply to work in Florida. Unfortunately, there is no separate Irish pavilion, but she sent an application off to Yummy Jobs anyway for the J-1 Cultural Resort Program. After she had paid processing charges of about US$2,000, the company found her a front-desk position at the Walt Disney World Swan and Dolphin Hotel next to Epcot, but not owned by Disney. Interestingly, the literature from the sponsoring organisation in the USA made the training and visa scheme sound far more rigorous a process than it actually was, and in the end her interview at the US embassy in Dublin lasted all of 60 seconds.

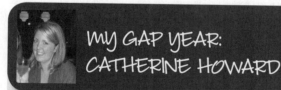

MY GAP YEAR: CATHERINE HOWARD

Catherine Howard had a wonderful 18 months, in spite of sometimes balking at American business culture.

I loved my job. Everyone was really nice and helpful, and I did actually enjoy chatting with guests. You are in Disney World after all, so for the most part, guests are usually happy to be there. Sometimes it was difficult to stomach the touchy-feely parts of corporate America. At pre-shift meetings, we would talk about 'core values' and making our guests feel special, and no pre-shift was complete without each of us reciting an example from our own lives where we were made to feel special as well. The Americans did this willingly without irony or self-consciousness, but it wrecked my head. The way I saw it, our time would be better spent fixing the actual problems the hotel had, instead of feeling special, but this attitude got me into trouble with the manager, so my advice would be to smile and suck it up instead! (This was the same manager, mind you, that introduced a directive whereby, if a guest asked us how we were today, we had to reply with a word of three syllables or more, eg 'good' was not allowed, but 'wonderful' or 'fantastic' was OK. My favourite was 'homicidal'.)

I loved my time in Florida and going there is one of the best decisions I ever made. But my first three months or so were one of the lowest points in my entire life, because I made one crucial mistake: I never learned to drive. I couldn't quite fathom what people meant when they said that in Orlando you couldn't walk anywhere. Not only was I a freak - the only person over the age of 16 in the entire state of Florida who couldn't drive a car - but when it came to finding an apartment, my options were severely limited. Four months in, I learned to drive, bought a car, and moved into a much nicer apartment with one of my new best friends.

During my 18 months in Orlando, I got to:

- see a space shuttle launch from Cape Canaveral - one of my top three dreams
- spot celebrities: the best one was seeing Steven Tyler in the queue for Pirates of the Caribbean!
- attend a Hallowe'en screening of The Rocky Horror Picture Show, in costume
- watch fireworks every night on my way home from work (and the Seaworld fireworks from my patio every night in the summer)
- go to Mickey's Very Merry Christmas Party at the Magic Kingdom - twice
- drink and eat my way around Epcot's Food and Wine Festival
- go to Washington DC, Miami, Mardi Gras in New Orleans, New York at Christmastime, etc
- wake up to sunshine almost every single morning.

Subsequently, Catherine wrote a hilarious book about her experiences called *Mousetrapped: A Year and a Bit in Orlando*, which is highly recommended.

SOCCER COACHING

Soccer is growing hugely in popularity in North America, including among girls, and demand is strong for young British coaches (now referred to as 'professional trainers') to work on summer coaching schemes. A number of companies, some of which work with BUNAC, recruit players to work regionally or throughout the country.

Most companies prefer to hire candidates with a National Coaching Licence, eg FA level 1 coaching, which can be acquired after doing a course lasting 24–40 hours (see www.1st4sportqualifications. com). You are likely also to need an enhanced Criminal Records Bureau check and emergency first aid certificate. There are also ancillary job openings for general counsellors with some companies. Organisations hiring soccer coaches include:

Goal-Line Soccer Inc, Corvallis, Oregon (+1 541 753 5833; info@goal-line.com; www.goal-line. com). Minimum age 21. Mostly in Oregon and Washington. Recruits through BUNAC for July and early August only.

Soccer Academy Inc, Manassas, Virginia (www.soccer-academy.com). European-based coaches should apply to Mark Jennings in Derbyshire (07814 390 740; mmarkjenco@aol.com). Interviews for the summer take place in November, and chosen candidates attend a training weekend in Manchester in April.

UK Elite Soccer, Cedar Knolls, New Jersey (+1 973 631 9802; www.ukelite.com). Offers soccer camps, coaching, and programmes in 18 states, mainly on the east coast. Seasonal coaches needed March to November, and 70 summer coaches in July to August.

United Soccer Academy, US Sports Institute, Bound Brook, New Jersey (+1 732 563 2525; www. unitedsocceracademy.com/employment-home.html). Five- to nine-month contracts starting in March and June. The sister company US Sports Institute hires European coaches in a wide range of sports from golf to hockey, with many openings for sportsmen and women who can coach in several sports (see www.ussportsinstitute.com/employment-home.html).

MY GAP YEAR: DOM SAMUELS

Dom Samuels was in the last year of his undergraduate programme when he decided to apply for a summer/fall coaching role in the USA.

After an initial assessment of applicants in Leeds (among other locations), I attended an intensive four-day course at Lilleshall, the National Sports Centre north of Telford, which encompassed various teaching/coaching techniques and forms of assessment. I was told to expect an email, and I remember well the subject line of that email. It read 'Welcome to LA . . .'. Unbelievable!

Coaching children from the ages of three to 19 meant work was varied every day, and I had the opportunity to really get to know some of the children. During the fall, coaching wouldn't commence until after school on weekdays, and lasted from 4pm till 9 or 10pm. Summer camp hours were different, with coaching in the morning or all day. One of the most notable days was when, along with a handful of other coaches, I was sent to coach Hispanic children in downtown LA. Unbeknown to us, there was a heat wave that weekend and we were scheduled to coach from 8am till 3pm. It was 'extra work', but saw us paid for the extra hours, which is always nice in the next paycheque. However, not only did the children feel the heat wave, so did we. We were coaching them on astroturf, and the rubber base of it was melting so our feet were literally burning as we coached. When we got back to our host's house, we were greeted with two words: 'Beer, pool'. If you're not a people person, this job isn't for you.

I think the job is glamorised by some: coach in the sunshine, party every weekend, meet great and like-minded lads and ladies, get put up in plush mansions . . . I bonded with many families I stayed with and struggled emotionally to say goodbye. But that's the job. You go into a place, provide a service, get out, and do it all again somewhere else. Although many aspects of the job are appealing, the emotional connection that I made with many people is somewhat ignored. I have met and made friends and family for life. Utah and California are homes from home for me.

The time off we got was rare, so I indulged whenever possible, usually taking a road trip. En route from Vegas to Arizona we saw a sign which said, 'Grand Canyon, 49 miles west ridge', which we assumed would be no more than a couple of hours out of our way, including time for a few Kodak moments. Not quite. We drove and drove until the road actually ended. We were at the Colorado river. Seven lads, one with a geography degree and a map of the entire US, and we couldn't navigate our way to the biggest hole in the planet. Hilarious!

VOLUNTEERING

Volunteers for Peace (www.vfp.org) places hundreds of foreign volunteers on about 35 projects in the USA, ranging from accompanying a group of disabled people on holiday to joining a peace camp in New England; the fee for joining is $300. BUNAC has a Volunteer USA programme in association with American Conservation Experience (ACE), based in Flagstaff, Arizona, in which volunteers are deployed on environmental projects, often in areas of outstanding beauty such as the Grand Canyon or Yosemite National Park, for eight to 12 weeks. Cost is £295, plus flights and insurance.

Voluntary opportunities in the USA range from the intensely urban to the decidedly rural. In the former category, you can build houses in deprived areas throughout the USA with Habitat for Humanity (www.habitat.org), or work with inner city youth, the homeless, etc. in New York City through the Winant Clayton Volunteers (www.winantclayton.org.uk).

The American Hiking Society (AHS) collates volunteer opportunities from around the USA to build, maintain, and restore foot trails in America's back-country. No prior trail work experience is necessary, but volunteers should be able to hike at least five miles a day, supply their own backpacking equipment (including tent), pay a $275 registration fee, and arrange transport to and from the work site.

Food is provided on some projects. For a schedule of projects, go to www.americanhiking.org, or ring the Volunteer Vacations department of the AHS on +1 301 565 6704, ext 206.

The ever-growing Student Conservation Association (+1 603 543 1700; www.thesca.org) places anyone 18 or older in conservation and environmental internships in national parks and forests across the USA. If accepted, interns are placed with a land-management agency (such as the National Park Service or US Forest Service) anywhere in the country for three to six months. Positions range widely, from wildlife management to native plant restoration to wilderness rangering to trail work to fisheries. During the internship, participants work alongside agency employees, basically doing the same work as they do, and gain an insight into normally impenetrable organisations. Travel expenses within the USA, housing, training, and a weekly stipend are provided.

At a loose end after university, **Emily Sloane** decided to spend some time in the great outdoors:

I did a six-month internship in the glacier-covered North Cascades National Park in Washington State. I was a member of the native plant propagation team, and spent my season taking care of nursery plants, gathering seeds and swinging pick-mattocks to loosen up restoration sites so that we could revegetate them. I had ample time to explore the mountains, picking up some mountaineering equipment and skills, and as an intern was given occasional special privileges, like a spot on an elite botanical expedition for a nearby university or a ride over the mountains in my boss's friend's ultralight glider. My supervisors were lovably insane, leading us in Pilates sessions at the beginning of every workday, screaming out classic rock songs as we planted in the November snow and (per my request) donning wigs for an entire workday as a birthday gift to me. One of my best summers EVER.

The Appalachian Mountain Club (AMC) in Gorham, New Hampshire (www.outdoors.org) is one of the oldest outdoor recreation organisations in the country. It operates a system of back-country hiker huts in the White Mountains of New Hampshire, maintains hundreds of miles of trails, and offers environmental education and conservation activities. The AMC hires plenty of Europeans to work at its base lodge at Pinkham Notch at the foot of Mount Washington, New England's tallest peak (notorious for its horrendous weather). The work there might not itself be terribly exciting – kitchen or housekeeping duties, most likely – but it provides access to a very beautiful area and a community of rugged, outdoorsy folks. It might be possible for a foreigner to score a back-country job although, as these positions are much more competitive, it would be prudent to plan ahead (apply by December for the following summer). The busiest season at the AMC's facilities runs from late May to late August.

Canada

Canada is one of those countries your mum probably won't mind you visiting for part of your gap year (New Zealand is another, as you may have read). It has what mums like in abundance: low crime rate, prosperity, orderliness, polite and friendly inhabitants, and an excellent communication system. On the down side, it is expensive (especially compared with Laos and Bolivia and all the other countries of which she probably doesn't approve) and bureaucratic (as you will soon discover when you look into obtaining a student Employment Authorization). It is also the country that inspired the writer Saki to say '*Canada is all right, really, but not for the whole weekend*'. However, most gappers who choose to work or travel in Canada end up disagreeing strenuously with him.

SPECIAL SCHEMES

The Canadian government has just made it easier to go on a working holiday to the country: as of 2011, the new International Experience Canada (IEC) working holiday programme is open to all Britons aged 18–35 (and to nationals from 25 other countries). Participants no longer need to be students nor to fix up a job in advance. A further liberalisation of the rules is that it is possible to reapply for a second year. BUNAC used to have the exclusive right to dispense these open visas, but now it simply packages the arrangement for those who want agency back-up. To facilitate a smooth transition, the Canadian Embassy will continue to reserve places on the scheme for BUNAC until 2013.

The main requirement for applicants is that they must have proof of funds, currently C$1,000 per month for the first three months. Additional outlays will be a participation/visa fee paid to the government of C$150, plus police clearance and suitable insurance cover, which are both required. The website of the Canadian High Commission in London (www.canadainternational.gc.ca) carries the relevant information. If successful, the IEC visa is valid for any job or internship within the life of the visa.

The majority of jobs that gap year students get are in ski resorts such as Banff and Whistler and other hotels and restaurants in remote but scenic locations. Finding work in the big cities is more difficult. Although there are plenty of jobs in the resorts, accommodation can be a major headache.

Oyster Worldwide arranges paid hotel or crèche jobs for students in the Canadian ski resorts of Banff and Whistler, as well as Mont Tremblant in Québec. The five- or six-month jobs start in November or late February and cost from £1,645 (or £2,245 with flights). Hotel staff are paid on average C$9 an hour and some will have about C$12 a day deducted for room and board. Gap Year Canada is a company run by an English expat who pre-organises chalet accommodation and seasonal jobs in and around Banff; the all-in fee of C$5,500 includes accommodation (see entry in 'Directory of Specialist Gap Year Programmes').

Several schemes designed for gap year travellers who want to ski or train to be ski instructors in Canada are described below under the heading 'Ski Resorts'.

THE JOB HUNT

On average, working holidaymakers who start the job hunt on arrival take at least a week to find a position. Even Canadian students sometimes find it hard to get summer jobs in the cities. It will be necessary to look presentable, eager to please, positive and cheerful, even if the responses are negative or the employers unhelpful.

Almost all waitressing and shop jobs pay the statutory minimum wage. This varies by province, mostly in the range C$8.80–$10.25, the latter being the rate for Ontario (2011). This usually results in an average weekly wage of C$320, while average accommodation costs C$500 a month in a shared house (although more in Toronto and Vancouver).

Although most famous for its skiing and snowboarding, Whistler should not be overlooked in summer by gappers on a working holiday visa. Short-term housing rents drop dramatically, jobs are just as easy to find if you get there before the season starts and temperatures regularly exceed 30 degrees Celsius. **Pete Thompson** was so smitten by Whistler after spending the winter season of 2010 there as a ski instructor that he couldn't resist staying on:

Whistler is one of a few resorts worldwide that is big and exciting enough to entertain visitors year-round. The atmosphere changes with the disappearance of the snow. Very early ski mornings are replaced by late night partying in the forests, at full moon parties, or at casual evening barbecues, watching the sun set at around 10 or 11pm. Wildlife is everywhere, black bears being particularly easy to spot on walks or camping trips. So after you've enjoyed a Whistler winter, trade in your skis for a mountain bike, your board for board shorts, and stay for the summer.

SKI RESORTS

The past few years have seen an explosion in companies offering programmes to young skiers and snowboarders from the UK, who are taking a year out partly to improve their form or even to train as instructors.

MY GAP YEAR:
ROB ASHPOLE

Rob Ashpole had always wanted to take a year out between school and university, with the main ambition of becoming a ski instructor. He started looking at different companies that offered the training while he was in his lower sixth, as a target to aim for at the end of the two years.

After results day, I went on holiday with my family to western Canada, and this was vital in helping me to choose a ski instructor training course. We flew into Calgary at the beginning of September and drove to Banff; this allowed me to have a look around the town site of Banff and the different accommodation options available with the different courses. Hotels in Banff were willing to show us around rooms used for the courses, and the Best Western Siding 29 Lodge, used by the International Academy, stood out as the best of the accommodation I saw. I visited Whistler too - it is an awesome place, but it's a much larger pedestrianised town and didn't have the same intimacy as Banff.

My travels in western Canada confirmed that Banff/Lake Louise was where I wanted to go, with International Academy, which offered a five week November-December course. I arranged my own insurance for the trip with the British Mountaineering Council (www.thebmc.co.uk), around £250 for a year's snow sports insurance, although the IA offers its own insurance with a winter sports insurer. There were only five of us on the early winter course, three skiers and two snowboarders. Everyone got on really well.

It was right at the beginning of the ski season, so the area had a limited number of lifts open at the beginning, though this was not a problem as the pistes at Lake Louise are fairly long, and gradually more runs opened. On the positive side, you benefit from quieter slopes, shorter lift and cafeteria queues. Unfortunately, on our very first run down, one of the snowboarders fell and broke his arm, which meant that he missed almost all of the training, but he did pass his level 1 Canadian Association of Snowboard Instructors (CASI) qualification.

Training provided by the staff at Lake Louise was exceptional; they use a variety of training methods, as well as video analysis, so your overall skiing technique improves rapidly. The training also helps you to discover the vast amount of land covered by the ski area. The mountain offers awesome views over to Chateau Lake Louise Hotel, Lake Louise, Temple Mountain, Valley of the Ten Peaks, Mount Whitehorn … the list is endless! There are so many different parts to the mountain and a great variation in terrain, from awesome powder in Boomerang Bowl to the bumps on Lynx. There is the opportunity to shadow some ski school lessons at Lake Louise, which proved to be great help.

The test for the level 1 CSIA qualification takes place over four days, focusing for two days on ski improvement and two on ski teaching. Everyone in our group passed, despite that week being incredibly cold, down to -42 degrees Celsius, making the area the coldest inhabited place on earth for that week! Unfortunately the last day of the test was the last full day of the course and the next day, 19 December, we were on the way back to the UK, except for one of our group who had a work visa and managed to get a job at the Lake Louise ski school.

The experience inspired me to return to get my level 2 CSIA that same winter. I returned from Canada at the end of March 2009, which proved a sad experience as I had had such a great time and made many new friends. I am so glad that I took the opportunity to take a gap year; I had always wanted to be a ski instructor and I achieved what I wanted. I hope I'll be able to return to Lake Louise some time so I will be able to take the Canadian Ski Coaches Federation (CSCF) level 1 qualification, as well as see some of the friends that I made there.

UK-based gap year companies such as International Academy and NONSTOP Ski & Snowboard tend to run programmes in the well-known resorts of Whistler, Banff, and Fernie (see entries in the 'Directory of Ski Training Courses'). Other possibilities include Alltracks Academy, which offers its instructor courses and improvement training camps at Whistler, Revelstoke, and Red Mountain. Ski Le Gap is active in Québec, where it runs one- and three-month programmes during the ski season in the resort of Mont Tremblant. The course combines ski and snowboard instruction with French conversation lessons, plus other activities such as igloo-building, dogsledding, and extreme snowshoeing. The programme is geared to British students and prices are £7,260+ (2012), which includes London–Montréal airfares.

Other companies providing instructor courses include PowderTrip, with an office in London (08454 900 480; www.powder-trip.com), and which operates in Fernie and Kicking Horse, British Columbia. It is possible to qualify as an instructor in little-known resorts such as Mount Washington on Vancouver Island; check out Section 8 Snowsport Institute (+1 250 702 7548 (SKI8); www.section8ski.com), which offers a four-week basic training course for C$5,040 and the full 12-week Snow Leadership course for C$11,445 from January. The Canadian Rockies Academy (www.canadianrockie sacademy.com) offers 11-week winter sports programmes in the Marmot Basin near Jasper (north of Banff) for an all-in price of £6,300+, including return flights from London to Calgary; ring 01656 890 156 (in south Wales) for more information.

For those who do not want to embark on the expensive and demanding instructors' courses but still experience a season on the slopes, it is possible to pick up work in Whistler/Blackcomb and the other main resorts such as Banff/Lake Louise, provided you have an IEC visa, Banff is always in desperate need of cheap labour; there are literally thousands of young travellers, mainly Canadian students, Australians, Kiwis, and Brits in town. No-one seems to struggle to find employment, and as a result many employers are very flexible with hours. Many offer staff accommodation at a heavily subsidised rate, which is incredibly useful since rents in Banff are a killer. It's not unheard of for five people to share a two-bedroom flat to save money.

For Banff, consider Sunshine Village Resort, which employs about 400 seasonal staff, with limited basic accommodation provided depending on the position. Its website (www.skibanff.com) has lots of useful information for prospective staff, including dates of their annual hiring clinic held at Banff International Hostel in mid-October. You can contact the human resources department for more information (on a toll-free number in North America +1 877 WORK SKI (877 967 5754) or +1 403 762 6546 from abroad; jobs@skibanff.com).

Moving west to the Pacific, the Whistler Chamber of Commerce posts employment information at www.whistlerchamber.com. Intrawest is the company that runs the ski operations at Whistler (as well as many other North American ski resorts). The employment link on the site www.whistlerblackcomb. com gives dates of the annual recruiting fair and allows you to apply online; alternatively, you can ring the jobline on +1 604 938 7367. Often, there is an exodus of workers after the Christmas rush, so it is possible to get a job once the season begins even if you haven't lined anything up at the main hiring time of October/November.

MY GAP YEAR: PETE THOMPSON

Pete Thompson had spent three months training to be a ski instructor in Queenstown, New Zealand, and countless weekends riding as a teenager, so he thought he knew just what to expect of a season working in Whistler.

I got more than a few surprises during my time in Whistler. I didn't expect to find over a thousand instructors from all over the world working with me in the ski school. I didn't expect to be there for the second snowiest season in the resort's history. Despite the region earning the nickname 'the Pacific North-wet', I didn't expect it to rain as much as it did down in the village (it was, at least, snowing on the slopes). I didn't expect to ski over 130 days and still feel like I hadn't seen all of the runs on the mountain, because of the sheer amount of skiable terrain. More than anything, however, I didn't expect to stay for the summer.

My job as a ski instructor teaching all ages and abilities meant every day was different. I got to spend almost every day on the mountain, and on my skis. Because of a lack of work in other departments in the ski school, I started work on the adaptive programme. At times when the resort isn't as busy, it's not uncommon to be given no work for a whole week. One such week I was lucky enough to be asked to help out WASP (Whistler Adaptive Sports Programme), which was particularly busy. While I'm not qualified to teach handicapped skiers, it was great to help out, mainly with sit-skiers who needed help getting on and off the chair and getting up when they fell. I loved the experience, and hope to get qualified to do more in the future. It was great to see beginners in the sit-ski determined to get the hang of it, and also seasoned skiers who flew down any run they could on the sit-ski. Many were eager to show that their chair wasn't a life-support machine, and that they are perfectly capable of removing themselves for whatever reason, especially to ski. It was particularly eye-opening during après ski, when I learnt that hundreds of dance moves are possible while in a wheelchair, as the rowdy group from the UK regularly dominated the bars and pubs where they went to celebrate.

On my days off, I did some of the most exhilarating skiing I've ever done. The snow was deeper, softer and falling on a more regular basis than anywhere I had been in Europe, the USA, or New Zealand. The number of professional and generally incredible skiers on the slopes was unbelievable, if somewhat intimidating, and I spent more time than ever before trying to compete with them at the top of fairly terrifying lines, cliffs, and jumps, failing more than a few times. I had been right to think that Whistler would offer me amazing skiing and an unforgettable six months.

SUMMER CAMPS

As in the USA, children's summer camps are very widespread, and employ a huge number of camp counsellors and ancillary staff. Unfortunately, the big recruitment drives conducted worldwide by Camp America and BUNAC are for American camps only. However, CCUSA co-operates with a Canadian company called NYQUEST to supply camp staff for Canadian camps (see entry in the 'Directory of Work Experience Abroad').

VOLUNTEERING

Some interesting practical community projects are organised by Frontiers Foundation (+1 604 585 6646; www.frontiersfoundation.ca) in low-income communities in Canada, including First Nations communities in isolated northern areas. Volunteers of many nationalities, who must be at least 18 and energetic, may join the Operation Beaver programme as tutors (eg of maths, science, English, music, drama), teaching assistants, or recreation workers, along with assisting in First Nations offices. Some projects take place on wilderness camps for native children or in schools in the three northern territories (Yukon, the Northwest Territories, and Nunavut). Placements last 10 months from September. Some volunteers, preferably with relevant experience, are taken on for at least three months over the summer to help build and renovate housing. All expenses are paid within Canada, including domestic travel and medical insurance, plus pocket money of C$50 a week.

According to **Emily Sloane**, watching the rivers break up in the spring was one of the most spectacular things she has ever seen, and her five months with Frontiers Foundation turned out to be one of the best experiences of her life:

> *From February to June, I worked as an education volunteer in a Gwich'in village in the Northwest Territories through Frontiers Foundation. The school I worked in desperately needed help and positive energy. I became the teaching assistant in the grade 4–6 classroom, and I think that my presence allowed the overly stressed teacher to relax a bit. And of course, being in the Arctic had its perks. I was able to attend a caribou hunting field trip in the Yukon in March, during which I got up in the middle of the night to use the outhouse in temperatures of 60 below. I'd go cross-country skiing after school every day, sometimes with several husky puppies at my heels, and as the days grew longer, my skis were sometimes prolonged until 10 or 11 at night. All in all, a thoroughly satisfying experience.*

If you are interested in working your way from farm to farm and want to meet Canadians, you might consider volunteering for WWOOF Canada (World Wide Opportunities on Organic Farms). You can access all the 900 host farms at the WWOOF Canada website (www.wwoof.ca) after becoming a member. Membership costs C$50 or C$62 per couple. All volunteers must have valid tourist visas. The Canadian authorities permit volunteer work in exchange for accommodation and meals, provided it is not the main object of the trip.

COURSES

Although culturally hard to distinguish from the USA in some respects, Canada has its French language and culture to guarantee its distinctiveness. Few gap year travellers think of Canada when considering places to improve their French, but the French-speaking province of Québec has lots of language schools (mostly for English-speaking North Americans). For example, the Point3 Language Centre (www.point-3.com) and College Platon (www.platocollege.com), both in the buzzing bilingual city of Montréal, offer short intensive courses with homestays. The UK-based language agency Vis-à-Vis can place students of French in Canada as well as in France and Belgium. But bear in mind that the Québecois accent is very different from Parisian French and incorporates many more loan words from English.

The three-month semester programme offered by Yamnuska Mountain Adventures (www.yamnuska.com) is ideal for a gap year (apart from the price, which is a cool C$13,000), and indeed the company belongs to the British-based Year Out Group. The Mountain Skills and Outdoor Leadership Semester starts in March or September, and is based in Canmore near Banff, Alberta. The course includes mountaineering, rock climbing, ice climbing, ski touring, trekking, and avalanche education.

INDEX OF ADVERTISERS

YOUR GAP YEAR

INDEX OF ADVERTISERS